# PSYCHOLOGICAL FOUNDATIONS OF LEARNING AND TEACHING

# PSYCHOLOGICAL FOUNDATIONS OF LEARNING AND TEACHING

## Second Edition

### John A. R. Wilson
University of California
Santa Barbara

### Mildred C. Robeck
University of Oregon
Eugene

### William B. Michael
University of Southern California
Los Angeles

**McGraw-Hill Book Company**
New York   St. Louis   San Francisco   Düsseldorf
Johannesburg   Kuala Lumpur   London   Mexico
Montreal   New Delhi   Panama
Paris   São Paulo   Singapore
Sydney   Tokyo   Toronto

# PSYCHOLOGICAL FOUNDATIONS OF LEARNING AND TEACHING

1234567890MUMU7987654

This book was set in Times Roman by Black Dot, Inc. The editors were Robert C. Morgan, Nancy L. Marcus, and James R. Belser; the designer was Jo Jones; the production supervisor was Thomas J. LoPinto. New drawings were done by ANCO Technical Services.
The Murray Printing Company was printer and binder.

**Library of Congress Cataloging in Publication Data**

Wilson, John Abraham Ross.
    Psychological foundations of learning and teaching.

    Bibliography: p.
    1.  Educational psychology.  I.  Robeck, Mildred
(Coen) date  joint author.  II.  Michael, William
Burton, joint author.  III.  Title.  DNLM: 1.  Psychol-
ogy, Educational.  LB1051 W749p 1974
LB1051.W59  1974        370.15       73-21533
ISBN 0-07-070855-X
ISBN 0-07-070856-8 (pbk.)

## ACKNOWLEDGMENTS

We wish to thank the authors and publishers who permitted us to use tables, quotations, and illustrations from their published copyrighted works. Recognition for the use of tables and illustrations is given in the text where the material appears. Quoted segments are keyed to the reference section, but formal acknowledgement of the privilege of using the material is cited below.

Dorothy Baruch, *New Ways to Discipline: You and Your Child Today.* Copyright © 1949, McGraw-Hill Book Company. By permission of the publishers.
Benjamin S. Bloom, M. D. Engelhart, E. J. Furst, W. H. Hill, and D. R. Krathwohl, *Taxonomy of Educational Objectives: Handbook I, The Cognitive Domain.* Copyright © 1956. By permission of David McKay Company, Inc., and Longmans, Green & Co., Ltd.
Jerome S. Bruner, *The Process of Education* p. 56–57, 58. Copyright © 1960 by the President and Fellows of Harvard College. By permission of Harvard University Press.
L. E. Cole, *Human Behavior: Psychology as a Biological Science.* Copyright © 1953, Harcourt Brace Jovanovich. By permission of the publishers.
Dominique G. Cote, S. R. Levy, and P. O'Conner. *Le Francais: Ecouter et Parler.* Copyright © 1962, Holt, Rinehart and Winston. By permission of the publishers.
H. J. Eysenck, "Learning Theory and Behavior Therapy." Copyright © 1959, *Journal of Mental Science*, 105. Reprinted by permission of the publishers.
A. Gesell, *The First Five Years of Life.* Copyright © 1940, Harper and Row, Publishers, Inc. By permission of the publishers.

To Nora,
Martin, and Joan,
who postponed many things they would like to have done while the
writing of this book was accomplished

# CONTENTS

# PREFACE

Based on the latest research findings, the second edition provides the tools to aid teachers in using learning and human development theory to help the learner become a free, self-directing, creative individual.

The student and teacher are dynamic individuals who create their private worlds through living and learning. Behavioral objectives that handle routine learning are constructed and the teacher learns to use these same procedures to define affective goals, complex conceptual goals, and independent creative goals. We have drawn on our various personal experiences in writing multilevel complex goals to illustrate how classroom teachers can use this knowledge to sharpen learning and to advance it beyond the humdrum rote level at which behavioral objectives are often implemented. This humanistic extension of behavioral objectives removes much of the threat and the frustration that have surrounded the use of clearly stated goals.

Central to this book is a learning-motivation model which enables teachers to plan lesson sequences that supply necessary underpinnings, build motivations systematically, help students see relationships for themselves, and move them to creative self-direction in applying their learning. The model is simple enough so that its main outline can be grasped in a single college-class period and complex enough so that new dimensions continue to emerge as the teacher uses it. This model also provides a thread that runs through this book and ties together the diverse subject matter contained in educational psychology.

The affective dimensions of the model have been expanded to include a chapter on affective associations and another on affective conceptualizations. Studies on encounter groups, alienation, the search for identity, and behavior modification are included under associations. Discipline control is treated as an example of the application of affective learning by the teacher.

Helping the child to understand his own motivations and to build new ones forms the core of the work on affective conceptualizations. Teachers can help the students see the emotional dynamics of their lives in a new framework. Different therapy systems are reviewed as examples of building conceptualizations. Self-discipline, as contrasted with discipline control, is treated as the conceptual result of students organizing their affective associations into meaningful patterns. Stress is placed on the kinds of activities that teachers can use to help students know and manage themselves better.

The explanation of the psychological process is undergirded by a neurological description of the interaction between learning and motivation, perception and memory, the influence of dominant and nondominant hemispheres on the reactions of children with learning difficulties, and the processes that move thought to action. Understanding how the brain functions during learning makes it possible for teachers to capitalize on natural tendencies and to avoid useless confrontations, particularly with children who have learning difficulties.

The human development section of the book views development as an interaction of learning and maturational processes. Personality development is treated as the habitual response the individual makes to societal pressures in order to maintain his individuality. One concern here involves ways that a teacher can use this knowledge to promote healthy personality development. Similarly, understanding physical growth enables the teacher to utilize any evidence of change to enhance the child's potential. In addition, learning experiences that maximize perceptual strengths and minimize perceptual deficiencies can be planned when the teacher has a broader knowledge of the way perceptual systems operate.

Material on emotional developmental sequences is designed to help teachers minimize stress which sometimes comes from working at cross purposes to the emotional needs of students. Many students find the information about emotional development useful as a means of understanding their own developmental changes. Stress is not as threatening to an individual when it is understood to be normal and is recognized as something that will pass in time.

Piaget's theory of cognitive growth is discussed in order to help the teacher apply Piaget's ideas. Many ways in which these ideas can be practiced and tested in the classroom are included in the chapter on cognitive development.

The chapters on intelligence steer a middle course in the controversy about the importance of nature or nurture in the development of intellectual ability. As with all other kinds of development, native propensities and learning experience interact to generate intellectual performance. Considerable attention is paid to the evidence that intelligence is a multiple, rather than a single, capacity and that individuals are likely to strengthen facets that they use and stunt those not used. Teachers can find ways to help young people capitalize on their strengths.

We have provided systems through which teachers can evaluate the outcomes of their instruction, for appraisal of teaching success is an indispensable part of the teacher's skill. Mastery learning, as well as programs less directly committed to complete mastery, all require understanding of the way to evaluate how well a student has learned given material and to determine which students have mastered specific parts of the instructional sequence.

Various kinds of tests and scales convey information to teachers about the progress of their pupils. Several measurement instruments are discussed and guidelines for selecting and using them are provided. Particular emphasis is given to the measurement of affective outcomes—a more difficult task than measurement of cognitive learning. New ways of demonstrating the effectiveness of behavior modification in particular learning situations are explained.

A solid introduction to elementary statistics is provided. This foundation is all that many teachers need in order to read the literature with understanding. It is sufficiently detailed to enable the teacher to handle the statistical computations needed in most classroom experimentation. Illustrations are clear and explicit so that the teacher can learn skills by working out their own problems with the models provided.

Each chapter of this book begins with a statement of its objectives by which you can gauge your learning simply by checking yourself after studying the chapter to determine if you have accomplished them. We have suggested a number of creative activities that can be used to apply the chapter material in teaching situations.

For learning purposes, we suggest that you proceed from a careful reading of the objectives and introductory paragraphs to a survey of the topic headings and of the summary before reading the text of the chapter. This orientation should make the study of each chapter more fruitful. A glossary has been provided at the end of the book as an additional learning aid. While we have not given exhaustive references, numerous leads are provided for the student who wishes to explore any topic further.

We are indebted to the many students in educational psychology and early childhood education who have given us feedback to make this material comprehensible. Our appreciation goes to the teachers and parents who provided much of the illustrative material. We extend our thanks to those who worked on the manuscript, showing an interest and a dedication that were reinforcing to us and made the task manageable. Particular thanks go to Robert C. Morgan, our editor at McGraw-Hill, and Nancy L. Marcus, who have been outstanding in their support. We also want to thank the authors and publishers who gave permission to use illustrations and quoted materials which were cited throughout the book.

John A. R. Wilson
Mildred C. Robeck
William B. Michael

# Chapter 1

(Courtesy of the United Nations)

# MOTIVATION FOR BETTER TEACHING

As a result of studying this chapter, you should be able to:

( Explain the function of learning theory in classroom teaching

( Illustrate, using concrete examples, decision making based on knowledge of learning principles

( Illustrate decision making based on intuitional interaction with concrete examples

( Contrast decisions made on the basis of intuition with those based on knowledge of levels of learning

( Evaluate the use of clearly stated objectives

( Read the following terms with comprehension:

IQ
mean
standard deviation
reliability
validity
correlation

Prospective teachers are raising the same questions with reference to educational psychology that they raise with reference to their own lives. What is real? How do we know? How do we become? How do we attain freedom? Teachers struggle with these questions in formulating learning goals for their students. How do I help Sarah find herself? What knowledge is worth learning? How does learning take place? Can I, as a teacher, make learning happen, or is it caught rather than taught? How can I motivate Tom to want to read? How do I free students to become creative?

These questions are conceived differently by individual teachers according to their own systems of valuing people and their own beliefs about how others learn. Some of the methodologies used in classrooms reflect these differences in philosophical approach. Behavior modification, inquiry training, programmed reading, sensitivity training, and creative dramatics are all based on different and particular views about learning and teaching. A teacher is effective as an educator only to the extent that he can selectively vary his methodology to utilize the strengths of each student and transform the content so the student can make it his own. The themes of this chapter will be expanded in subsequent chapters of this book.

## DECISION MAKING IN THE CLASSROOM

No one decision fits all students; herein lies the challenge for the classroom teacher. Schools are organized so that a teacher is responsible for a *group* of students, but the fallacy in this organization is that groups do not learn, only individuals learn, and they each learn differently. A book that is exciting to Marvin may be abstruse to Joe. A lesson that is critical in Ellen's skill sequence may be obfuscating for Elaine and boring for Jim.

Similarly students of educational psychology differ in their experience and knowledge of the real world and their technical orientation to psychology. Decisions about teaching strategy necessarily have an element of compromise because each individual functions within particular constraints. These constraints may be imposed by the teaching system, the needs of the student body, or the individual teacher himself. Decision making is further complicated by aspirations of the community.

### Freedom through Competence

The classroom teacher who has shown he can reach the goals of the school earns for himself a great deal of freedom about how he achieves these goals. When children are happy in school, parents tend to evaluate the teacher favorably. When children are learning academic skills, the principal usually attends to other problems and leaves the curricular decisions to the teacher. The neophyte teacher who wants freedom needs to demonstrate effectiveness in meeting the goals of the system first. In order to do this, the goals must be clearly and correctly defined.

In a time of educational change the goals of the school may be seen differently by new and experienced teachers, by poor and affluent parents, and by individual students. Even where many conflicting expectations are present, the teacher who gets constructive results is respected for his professional competence. Hugh, who believed in an open classroom, succeeded in a traditional school because his pupils learned to read well, while Stewart thought the principal was punishing him for his open-classroom philosophy when he was reassigned at midterm to the room next to the office. Any teacher who values freedom to work in his own way must be prepared to demonstrate his professional competence.

## Building toward Positive Motivation

Teachers who understand emotional associations and are sensitive to the pleasure or punishment students feel are able to build positive motivation toward particular content and activities. Motivation to achieve in school reflects the student's positive interaction between learning *cognitive*, or knowledge, content, and *affective*, or emotional, components. The lack of attention to affective goals is one of the major omissions in most school planning. Although parents and principals rarely talk about affective learning, they are highly sensitive to signs of children's motivation. When pupils come home with long faces and make excuses in the morning to avoid going to school, adults should be concerned about the affective learning that is accumulating. Most parents are tuned to happy enthusiasm about school and give considerable effort to overcoming problems that occur in a teacher-pupil relationship that is otherwise positive. The feelings of the students are valid, and the observations of the parents are an important part of the appraisal system. Affective learning may be defined as the feelings of pleasure and punishment that are a facet of experience and determine motivation. Prospective teachers need to learn to read affects and to plan the objectives for teaching them in the same way they write objectives for cognitive goals.

## Developing Self-Discipline in Students

Another essential skill of teaching is the ability to control the class sufficiently to allow learning to flourish. Many student teachers are repelled by the idea of imposing their will on younger people and therefore resist learning the techniques or the theory of discipline. They assume that in a climate of love students will be good. When instead they find students competing for attention and power, they slip into using authoritarian techniques that were once used on themselves and that they resented.

Learning theory provides the guidelines for social interaction that eventually develops self-discipline in the students. Techniques in behavior modification are an effective means of changing the disruptive patterns in certain students. However, it is necessary to go beyond behavior modification to help the problem student understand his relations with others. The teacher who knows the laws of social interaction has an advantage over one who reacts on an incident-by-incident basis. The novice who functions from a learning structure can quickly become a pro, whereas the teacher who reacts instinctively to disruptive or hostile behavior is not likely to help the child make the needed behavior changes. Any use of such techniques, however, first requires effective observation of the students both as a group and as individuals.

## Observing the Student

Observations of students can be obtained by using precise and sophisticated testing instruments or by simply watching students. Observation data also include the children's papers, their art work, the questions they ask, the number of errors they make per hundred running words of oral reading, and their athletic prowess.

Student teachers differ markedly in what they are able to grasp from observing more experienced teachers. The most important observations involve what a student learns from day to day, what a particular student does not know, and what the next step in his sequence should be. The validity of one's own observation of what a student learns needs to be checked against his achievement on standardized tests. The most difficult kind of observation involves the simultaneous reaction of several students to a significant idea, such as the cause of a war or the meaning of a set. The higher levels of intellectual functioning are more likely to be achieved when teachers are able to observe and recognize what is happening within individual students.

### Defining Objectives Clearly

Only when the teacher determines what the student knows can meaningful or useful objectives be defined. Defining objectives in behavioral terms implies that the instruction will result in the students' doing something that can be seen and verified. The level of complexity varies as the objectives deal with higher intellectual processes, and analyzing successful performance becomes increasingly difficult. This way of planning objectives is a departure from the traditional way, which puts the instructor at the center of the process by outlining the content to be covered or the teaching activities to be performed. Chapter 3 enlarges on how to write objectives in terms of the varying levels of student behavior to be achieved, and Chapter 17 describes ways of evaluating these changes.

### Analyzing and Selecting Materials

There is an increasing tendency on the part of school administrators and consultants to make available a variety of programs from which the teacher can select the materials that best implement his objectives. Although it is important to know how to prepare materials for particular situations, it is a waste of teacher effort to write or make materials that are already available at small cost. Nearly all published material is based on particular assumptions about the nature of the learning process. Teachers who are predisposed to stimulus-response techniques can find programs in almost every subject which teach skills by discrete steps. Other materials focus on the concepts or generalizations that students are expected to evolve. Some materials emphasize the self-actualization of the learner and build understandings that lead to self-direction. The teacher must be confident of his ability to determine the kind of learning implicit in a program and to choose one that fits his value system.

Analysis and selection of materials are one way that teachers who are highly disposed to particular approaches can build in flexibility for learners who need a different structure than the teacher is predisposed to provide. This selection assumes the ability on the teacher's part to analyze and project student behavior that is consistent with the objectives determined for his learning. It also assumes a willingness on the teacher's part to let the student be his own person with his own cognitive style and his own value system. In this way the child who does well in programmed learning is free to pursue Buchanan and Sullivan's *Programmed Readings* (1965) or Crowder's tutor text.

### Communicating and Accounting for Goals

The partners in the learning enterprise (students, teachers, parents, and administrators) must each know what the objectives are if the objectives are to be achieved. When a student knows what he is trying to learn, described in terms of his own levels of performance, he is in a position to know when he has arrived and to experience the inner satisfaction of achievement. Parents are more likely to make reinforcement explicit when they are included in the definition of progress. Competition between students loses its impact when students no longer need comparative status in their natural and necessary struggle for recognition. They gain self-esteem as they attain the specified increments leading to a larger goal. To talk with parents and students about progress the teacher must first be clear with himself on what the objectives are and how learning will be demonstrated. It is important to realize, however, that the objectives and their demonstration may vary from student to student.

At all levels of government those who provide the resources for schools are demanding increasing evidence of the effect of particular programs, especially experimental projects, on the learners. In the same way that feedback to the student can be reinforcing to him for his efforts, an evaluation in terms of the learning achieved can be reinforcing and self-enhancing to the teacher. It is easy to be so close to the program and so involved in the day-to-day interactions with students that their progress over a period of weeks or months becomes obscured. Evaluation through measurement (testing) goes beyond the bits and pieces of learning to capture the integrative effect of learning on the student group. A constructive approach to accountability can help the teacher balance the competing parts of the curriculum and help him revise his priorities in planning new ways to reach his goals. School at any level can seem so discouraging and unfinished at times that knowledge of progress is needed by teachers as well as students. Test results that provide knowledge of student progress confirm to the teacher that he is competent or indicate that he should reevaluate his interaction with students. On the long-term basis the motivation of students to achieve in school will be reflected, to some extent, in their achievement on school tests.

## IMPROVING LEARNING IN SCHOOLS

Two movements are operating on a nationwide scale which could change education. The advocates of one of these trends would shift most teacher education to the classroom, where training would be practical and teaching would be learned by apprenticeship. The appeal of this movement is that the experience is relevant and the cost of internship is less than regular training. The prospective teacher learns by doing and avoids the theoretical abstractions that seem to some to postpone the real preparation for teaching.

The other movement grew out of major discontents with classroom practice at all levels and is taking opposite directions in demanding change. At one extreme are those who think the schools are too free, as evidenced by the elimination of dress codes, self-selected curricula, unstructured reading programs, and pass–no-pass grading criteria. Contrariwise are those who call the school lockstep because of grading standards, lack of individualization, insensitivity to the feelings of students, frozen curricula, and structured sequences for teaching. These feelings of discontent reflect the imperfection of the schools in a time of rapid change. Schools can and should do a better job of educating children. The challenge is to make the best possible use of the experience of master teachers, implementing the psychological research which makes improvement possible. A combination of knowing and doing is needed to help young teachers develop themselves as artist teachers.

## Teacher as a Significant Variable

A recent example of massive and well-financed educational research is the integrated studies of approaches to beginning reading financed by the United States Office of Education for a period of three years (Dykstra, 1968). More than 30 separate investigations tested various methods and materials in an integrated effort which allowed cross comparisons of many variables on the achievement of children in learning to read. Most of the projects were under the direction of experts in the methods being tested. National-level conferences were held to increase the sophistication of the design and the evaluation of results. The most significant finding was that variation in the children's achievement from teacher to teacher was greater than variation due to methods or materials, including language experience, basal readers, Initial Teaching Alphabet (i/t/a), linguistic programs, phonics programs, and combinations of these. Although the in-service training of teachers was controlled, the differences between teachers persisted even in projects where teachers chose the approach they would use. The studies were considered successful since most observers agreed that the teachers involved in the experiments increased their efficiency.

Following closely on these experiments was the President's survey on literacy in the United States (America, 1969). The survey showed that approximately 15 percent of the adults in the United States were functionally illiterate. Most of the individuals who could not read such forms as job applications, drivers tests, and social security forms were native Americans who had attended school for the required number of years. They represented a visible failure on the part of the schools. This evidence from objective evaluation supports the subjective impressions that improvement in education is needed.

## Implementing Change

Many of the proposals for changing the schools are frustration outbursts that assume almost anything must be better than the present situation. Basic to this attitude is a naive implication that present teachers and administrators refuse to implement obvious improvements. In the real world of the school, substantial improvements in performance are difficult even though immense effort goes into corrective education. Careful analysis of the learning theory upon which proposed changes rest can save everyone involved the expense and disappointment that too often result from enthusiastic adoption of proposals that have been inadequately conceived. In the long run, new programs produce their own failures as well as their successes.

An analysis of the theoretical substructure of a proposal for change suggests the relationship of the expected performance of students and the teaching strategy designed to bring about the improvement. Psychological theory is invaluable in comparing proposals that compete for the teacher's attention. Analysis often makes it possible to select the one new approach that has the greatest potential for making a difference in a particular classroom. Even when an innovation seems likely to be highly beneficial, it makes sense to try out a proposal in a single classroom where the teacher is convinced it will work well. Records need to be kept of difficulties encountered so that other teachers can avoid the same pitfalls. If a new approach produces the improvements that have been promised, it can be expanded to include half a dozen other teachers. During this period, a formal evaluation should be conducted to compare the effectiveness of the new procedures with others that are still being used. If objectives have been clearly specified for the first year and redefined after the first year of a new program, it should be possible to determine how well the goals of the school are being met during the course of the academic year.

To many teachers and administrators a slow and deliberate introduction of an innovation is frustrating, but the imposed introduction of change without allowing time for other staff members to accept the new ideas is almost always disappointing. A policy of gradual change allows an individual teacher to experiment with a good idea before having to convince other teachers that the idea is good.

Time allows the teacher who is reluctant to change (1) to pick up the affective loading from enthusiastic teachers who are trying the new program and (2) to learn about the theoretical basis for the innovation. Evidence from careful evaluation is convincing to other teachers if an experiment indeed produces more effective learning than that which prevails.

### Evaluation of Student Change

The most important evaluation that a teacher makes is his ongoing judgment of what a student has learned as the basis for deciding what he will be taught next. Bloom (1971) described *formative evaluation* as determining the degree of mastery of a given learning task and pinpointing the part of the task not yet mastered (p. 61). Formative evaluation is not used to grade the student, but to help the student and the teacher plan the instructional steps and study strategies for mastery of the task. *Summative evaluation* is a general assessment of the outcome of an entire course or a unit of work. It is used to grade students and to report to parents or administrators. Summative evaluations provide the data for comparing programs, teaching strategies, and pupil performance.

If the teacher defines his objectives in terms of the behavior of students, both formative and summative evaluations are possible in the classroom. However, the more complex the intellectual function, the more difficult to observe and measure the student's behavior. Affective objectives are particularly difficult to describe in behavioral terms, but the struggle is necessary if the teacher intends to influence motivation through affective learning. A goal such as "increases liking for poetry" can be evaluated by measures such as number of poems read without coercion, questions asked about a poem or poet, or

sophistication of interpretations on a written test.

The emphasis in formative evaluation is on individual learning. Even students who are having trouble in a course know a certain percentage of the associations basic to his success. A fourth-grade pupil who is having difficulty in addition may know over 90 of the 100 addition facts quite well. Only a few of the combinations are giving him trouble. Unfortunately each student usually has a somewhat different list of difficulties, and therefore group instruction tends to improve the facility of students with the facts they know but to do very little to clarify the facts that trouble them. In individualized instruction the efforts of both teacher and student are focused on the items to be learned, with assurance that the use of time will be profitable. Even after competencies are defined, each individual's strengths and weaknesses must be diagnosed and the teacher must develop ways of having different students work constructively at different things at the same time. These requirements are more formidable than they appear at first glance, but if each student is to achieve mastery of an area of study, he must be seen and treated as a unique person with unique needs.

### SELF-DIRECTED LEARNING

The goal of educational psychology, as conceived by the authors, is that the reader will become self-directed in pursuing the theories of learning even though this search may lead him to conclusions which differ from the learning-motivation model presented in this book. Self-direction is conceptualized here as a fusion of knowledge and the motivation emerging from an understanding of oneself. To function at a high level in applied psychology the ideas of many theorists must be thoroughly understood so that they can be weighed for possible use in the classroom. The theoretical structures must be conceptualized in order to broaden the decision-making base from which the teacher functions. Understanding does not necessarily mean acceptance, but it requires evaluation on a rational basis. To illustrate the need for technical knowledge, two widely discussed interpretations of the same data follow.

Rosenthal and Jacobsen (1968) reported their study on self-fulfilling prophecy in *Pygmalion in the Classroom* as indicative of the importance of the teachers' expectations for children based on their reported IQ's.

> To anticipate briefly the nature of this new evidence it is enough to say that 20 percent of the children in a certain elementary school were reported to their teachers as showing unusual potential for intellectual growth. The names of these 20 percent of the children were drawn by means of a table of random numbers, which is to say that the names were drawn out of a hat. Eight months later these unusual or "magic" children showed significantly greater gains in IQ than did the remaining children who had not been singled out for the teachers' attention. The change in the teachers' expectations regarding the intellectual performance of these allegedly "special" children had led to an actual change in the intellectual performance of these randomly selected children. [pp. vi–vii]

R. L. Thorndike (1968) reviewed their book, including the published data on which the Pygmalion conclusions were based (Table 1-1). His critique did not deny their thesis but negated the evidence for their findings.

> On the Reasoning Test, one class of 19 pupils is reported to have a mean "IQ" of 31! They just barely appear to make the grade as imbeciles! And yet these pretest data were used blithely by the authors without even a reference to these fantastic results! What kind of a

test or what kind of testing is it that gives a mean "IQ" of 58 for the total entering first grade of a rather run-of-the-mill school? [pp. 709–710]

In order to make one's own judgment about the relative validity of these two very different interpretations of the same data, an understanding of a few terms that are widely used in educational psychology is necessary.

## Terms Used in the Literature

Most students and indeed most experts do not need a mastery of all the intricacies of statistics. A few concepts are presented here to help the student read the rest of this book and related studies of his own choosing.

*IQ* is an abbreviation for intelligence quotient. It was originally calculated by dividing the mental age (as determined by a standardized test) of a subject by his chronological age and multiplying by 100 to get rid of decimals. If Tommy had a mental age (MA) on a test of 10 years and a chronological age (CA) of the same 10 years, his IQ would be $10(MA)/10(CA) \times 100 = 100$. If his mental age were 9.0, the result would be $9.0/10.0 \times 100 = 90$, or less than the norm of 100 IQ. If he tested at 11.5 MA, the same formula would show $11.5/10.0 \times 100 = 115$ IQ, indicating above-average intelligence as measured by this test. The obvious question is whether 115 is high enough or 90 low enough to make a real difference as far as curriculum is concerned. In statistics, individual differences are calculated as distance from the average of all the scores.

*Mean* may be defined as the arithmetic average of an array of scores for a class or a school population. The mean indicates the central tendency of a group of scores and is used to compare the achievement of two or more groups on the same measure. In Table 1-1, the first-grade subjects reportedly showed

**Table 1-1   Means and Standard Deviations Selected from Rosenthal and Jacobson Data**

| Class | N | Experimental | | N | Control | |
| | | Mean verbal "IQ" | Mean reasoning "IQ" | | Mean verbal "IQ" | Mean reasoning "IQ" |
|---|---|---|---|---|---|---|
| 1A | 3 | 102.00 | 84.67 | 19 | 119.47 | 91.32 |
| 1B | 4 | 116.25 | 54.00 | 16 | 104.25 | 47.19 |
| 1C | 2 | 67.50 | 53.50 | 19 | 95.68 | 30.79 |
| 2A | 6 | 114.33 | 112.50 | 19 | 111.53 | 100.95 |
| 2B | 3 | 103.67 | 102.33 | 16 | 96.50 | 80.56 |
| 2C | 5 | 90.20 | 77.40 | 14 | 82.21 | 73.93 |

From Robert L. Thorndike in Book Review: Rosenthal, R., and Jacobson, L. Pygmalion in the classroom, *American Educational Research Journal*, Nov. 1968, 5(4), p. 709. By permission of AERA.

an average verbal IQ score of 105.7 and the second graders an average verbal IQ of 99.4. From these data the two groups were close to the normal mean IQ of 100. These averages do not tell us, however, anything about the individual scores used to calculate the mean. An indication of the spread of the scores is needed.

*Standard deviation* is a measure of the amount of variability or dispersion in a group of scores. How it is derived is explained in Chapter 19. For the reader it is important to know that standard deviation is based on the normal probability curve (Figure 19-7). This bell-shaped curve approximates the distribution of chance scores such as those arising from tossing a hundred pennies. A tabulation of the number of heads (or tails) showing on each of many tosses is made to form the distribution of possible outcomes. Most of the time this number will be somewhere near 50, although on exceedingly rare occasions there may be as many as or more than 65 heads or tails. Probability theory states that in 68 percent of the tosses the number of heads (or tails) will be within one standard deviation of

the expected value of 50 heads (or 50 tails). In this example the standard deviation can be calculated to be 5, which is interpreted as indicating that in 100 sets of tosses of 100 coins, the number of heads (or tails) would vary between 45 and 55 in 68 out of 100 sets. In Table 1-2 the standard deviation is indicated in the column headed "S.D."

In the first-grade data 68 percent of the verbal IQ scores could be expected to be within 84.5 and 126.9, or 105.7 ± 21.2. On inspection, these data do not look unreasonable. But consider the comparable data re-

**Table 1-2   Verbal and Reasoning IQs Extrapolation from Rosenthal and Jacobson Data**

| | First grade | | Second grade | |
| | Mean | S.D. | Mean | S.D. |
|---|---|---|---|---|
| Verbal | 105.7 | 21.2 | 99.4 | 16.1 |
| Reasoning | 58.0 | 36.8 | 89.1 | 21.6 |

From Robert L. Thorndike in "Book Review: Rosenthal, R., and Jacobson, L. Pygmalion in the classroom, *American Educational Research Journal*, Nov. 1968, 5 (4), p. 710. By permission of AERA.

ported for the test of reasoning where an average IQ is 58. This is analogous to a point on the curve where 99 heads are turning up and only 1 tail is showing. The standard deviation of 36.8 indicates that *many* of the scores were in a probability range of *one in a million* in the general population. Clinical experience indicates that children with an IQ of 58 have great trouble learning to read under very careful teaching. Those below this "mean" would be almost certain to find it impossible. The likelihood of finding a population with such a low mean in a typical school is infinitesimal. Small wonder that Thorndike concluded that the data reminded him of a clock which struck 14 and should be thrown out.

*Reliability* is a term frequently encountered in judging the confidence one puts in a test score. Reliability means the regularity or consistency of getting the same answer on a measurement of behavior. To compensate for human error, reliability should be high. When the reliability coefficient is low, either the instrument is poor (as when a rubber tape measure is used) or the testing conditions are inappropriate (as when a child is given a test that is outside his experience). Reliability of scores should be approximately .90 (on a scale from 0.0 to 1.00) for teachers to put much faith in the test results of individual students.

*Validity* is the extent to which a test actually measures what it purports to measure, or represents a relevant indicator of the characteristic under consideration. Using a fisherman's rule it may be possible to get reliable measures of 18 inches for a fish that is only 6 inches long on a more standard or valid scale. An example of poor validity is a test of problem solving that requires the person examined to read difficult vocabulary, thus making it a reading comprehension test rather than one of quantitative intelligence. Validity is difficult to establish because it is difficult to

find a criterion against which to check scores that is not in some way contingent on artifacts of the testing situation. Individually administered intelligence tests such as the Stanford-Binet and the Wechsler correlate with each other in the .80s, indicating relatively high validity.

*Correlation* is the extent to which one set of measures is associated with another. If the person who gets the highest score on measure X also gets the highest score on measure Y, and this perfect rank-order relationship continues throughout the range to the lowest score, the correlation is perfect and is shown as 1.00. If, however, the orders are completely reversed so that the person who gets the highest score on measure X gets the lowest on measure Y, and the person who gets the second highest score on X gets the second lowest on Y, etc., the relationship is perfect-negative and is shown as −1.00. In the real life of the school, correlations somewhere between these extremes are usually found. A trend in which most students who get high scores on a vocabulary test also get high scores on a reading comprehension test is shown in Chapter 19 along with the way a coefficient is calculated. In the example shown, the positive rank-difference correlation is .676. Readers in the field of educational psychology need to be aware that correlation does not imply causation but merely that a statistical relationship exists. However, a high positive or negative correlation permits the relatively accurate prediction of the standing of an individual on one variable (measure) from knowledge of his placement on the other variable.

## Self-Selection of Content

The field of educational psychology is so extensive that experts spend their whole professional career in pursuing one part as a specialization. This book is an overview of learning theory, human development, and educational measurement and evaluation. While an acquaintance with each of these areas is important, students should feel free to delve into one or more areas in depth. The references cited in the text are major sources within areas of specialization. These references often provide bibliographies that permit expanding the horizons of study to an almost unlimited degree, and names of authors that reappear in the literature can be checked for new findings. Knowing that some students gain great satisfaction from studying a topic of their choice in depth, the authors have attempted to present the major themes of educational psychology with the expectation that individual students would be motivated to pursue an area of particular interest while knowing its relationship to the field as a whole.

### Keeping Up with New Knowledge

The student who gets satisfaction from understanding and applying the principles of learning and development is likely to keep up with new knowledge after he gets his credentials. The payoff for his work will come in the form of classroom results and the satisfaction of knowing why his pupils are achieving the objectives he conceived for them. Such a teacher is not likely to jump on an old bandwagon because it comes under a new name or to apply educational research in an irrelevant setting. In short, such a person is freed to use new knowledge selectively and to have energy left over to do his own thing.

### STRUCTURE OF THE BOOK

**Psychological Bases for Teaching** In addition to this chapter, the first section pre-sents an overview of the learning-motivation model and a discussion of objectives and how teachers write them. The exploratory work of stating detailed objectives in specific terms has come primarily from educational psychologists involved in testing and from programmed instruction. A committee of test experts set out to supply a common set of definitions that would make their own work easier and facilitate communication between them. They hoped that their definitions would be useful to teachers as well.

Programmed instruction has required very careful definition of the objectives being sought so that the small, precise steps would eventually lead to a clearly defined goal. The increased clarity of the educational goals that has come from testing and programming makes the psychological structuring of classroom teaching more manageable for the teacher.

**Nature of Learning** Theories of learning, both historical and contemporary, have been integrated into a three-level model for learning and teaching. The implication is that level 1 learning, forming associations, is basic to level 2 learning, conceptualization of the relationship between and within associations. Level 3 learning, creative self-direction, is a fusion of cognitive and emotional production. In this part, the emphasis is on the essential interaction between affective and cognitive learning. Particular attention is paid to the emotional components that lead to reinforcement of an activity, thus increasing the probability of its repetition.

No hierarchy of value is implied in this learning-motivation model, but a hierarchy of complexity is inherent. Although a teacher frequently starts a new term with his mind set for a fresh beginning, the students never come with a *tabula rasa* ("blank tablet") mind. They bring associations and conceptualizations which differ from student to student but which relate to the curriculum in unique ways. The teacher's first task is to discover what the students already know about the subject and whether or not their past learning represents those bits and pieces (associations) which are needed for meaningful discovery of major ideas. Some pieces of information and some conceptualizations will be hazy or totally inaccurate. Some students will need to begin almost from scratch to build basic associations before they can discover relationships between them.

In creative self-direction, the student uses his knowledge to express ideas in new ways or to extend his ideas to new areas of his environment. The most urgent necessity for the child or youth is for his teacher to help him work at successively higher levels. Only then can his full potential be reached.

Learning is a by-product of the organism's attempts to meet its needs. Learning consists of changes in the neurological system that occur because the organism did certain things that produced certain results. On the association level, neural chains are linked together because they occur together in time (classical conditioning) and because linkages also occur to the pleasure and punishment centers of the brain, which reinforce the action positively or negatively (operant conditioning). From these groups of associations, cognitive structures are formed, which are the conceptualizations of the learner. Education is effective to the extent that affective and cognitive conceptualizations combine to produce a creative, self-directed individual. Learning is neurological change that occurs because the organism is going about the acts of living, rather than because it is attempting to learn something. Intention is part of the living process of human beings.

**Human Development** The ability to interpret each student's behavior within his group sets the superior teacher apart from the one who merely conducts classes. Groups do not learn; individuals perceive, conceptualize, or generate ideas intellectually. However, the accumulated efforts of many people are essential for the achievements of a society. Individuals are stimulated by interaction with others, but the learning that results is an accretion of individual growth. People become individuals as a result of their patterns of growth, their interaction with others, and their responses to the demands of the physical environment.

Although each student is different from all others, he is like his peers in an infinite number of ways. Knowing the normal sequence of human development provides a standard against which growth in individuals can be appraised. The more complete the teacher's knowledge of the major phases of development, the sharper his ability to discriminate between significant and temporary aberrations in the growth of young persons. Teachers need to be aware of commonalities in order to be sensitive to variations within student groups.

A dynamic interaction of four personality structures, based on learning, is described in Chapter 10. Other dimensions of human development include physical, perceptual, and emotional growth. Both nature and nurture are important if intelligence is to develop in optimal ways.

**Measurement and Evaluation** A distinction is made between measurement (which provides a numerical base for appraisal) and evaluation (which is the teacher's interpretation of the numerical results). Without a knowledge of evaluation techniques, teachers are unable to plan lesson sequences that are appropriate either for groups of learners or for individuals. Unless teachers are able to measure what has been taught, they cannot get the feedback necessary to determine whether the students have reached the goals that have been set for them.

The function of testing is to provide both the teacher and the student with feedback concerning what has been learned so that future study and instruction can be arranged. Even the most sophisticated tests are not perfect, and the teacher must make constant judgments on the significance of the scores. Techniques are available to help the teacher make these judgments. The authors intend the final part of this book to meet the basic requirements of most classroom teachers in the measurement and interpretation of student performance.

## SELF-DIRECTED ACTIVITIES

1 Read three journal articles on learning or teaching that are relevant to your field. Analyze them for the decision-making responsibilities that are assumed for the teacher, and decide whether the conclusions are intuitive- or theory-based.
2 Read one journal article in your field that is data-based. Note the technical terms, and check your understanding in the context of the article.
3 Recall examples of affective learning in your own school experience. Evaluate the effect these affective loadings had on your motivation.

# Chapter 2

Interaction on a field trip. (Courtesy of SCIS)

# PERSPECTIVES ON LEARNING AND MOTIVATION

In this chapter, the individual is conceptualized as a unique person who learns through the interaction of cognitive and motivational levels. After studying the chapter, you should be able to:

◖ Develop different orientations to learning problems

◖ Establish communication with diverse kinds of learners

◖ Utilize the contributions of theoretical psychology

◖ Define a model for interaction of affective and cognitive learning at the following levels:

    association
    conceptualization
    creative self-direction

◖ Use and define the following terms correctly:

    intervening variable
    hypothetical constructs
    imprinting
    conditioned response
    reinforcement

Educational psychology is the study of the individual's growth and learning as a consequence of his interaction with the environment. Particular emphasis is focused on cognitive and emotional development, processes of learning during maturation, and measurement and evaluation of the effectiveness of teachers in promoting learning. As an individual interacts with the people and things around him, he evolves a unique emotional and cognitive makeup. In so doing he alters his ways of dealing with the social and physical environment and his ability to expand his private world. Repeated failure to deal with problems in a satisfying way constricts the individual so that he becomes less able to undertake the challenges of life. Interaction with the environment may be either ability-producing or ability-destroying for the individual.

An understanding of educational psychology provides insights and skills that enable a teacher to work with others in ways that enhance, rather than diminish, their abilities. For example, it is known that positive reinforcement is generally better than negative reinforcement in modifying behavior. However, continuous reward unrelieved by challenge eventually ceases to be reinforcing. A balance must be established for each individual. Challenges which are successfully dealt with by a person are more growth-producing than success without effort. Human motivation in the classroom is complex, but feedback from evaluation data can keep teachers informed about the need for modification in the instruction of individuals.

## PRESENT VARIETY IN THEORIES OF LEARNING

The study of how individuals grow and learn can be approached from many points of view. Writers of educational psychology all work from some personal orientation, with the hope of providing prospective teachers with strategies they can use in their classrooms. Students interested in mastering the psychological theory basic to teaching may experience a sense of shock at the many discrepancies that exist among theories of learning (Figure 2-1). One of the major differences among educational psychologists is an emphasis upon central, or neurological, intermediaries in learning, as opposed to an emphasis upon peripheral, or muscular, intermediaries (Hilgard & Bower, 1966). This distinction between neural and muscular changes during learning is important because this book is based on neurological control of peripheral functions. In teaching language skills, for example, this orientation emphasizes connections in the central nervous system between a word symbol and its related meanings. However, reading may be conceived as an extension from speech, to oral reading, to subvocalized silent reading. As a teacher, your concept of the nature of learning influences the procedures you use to teach reading.

A second difference among educational psychologists concerns theories that emphasize the learning of habits as contrasted with theories in which cognitive structures are considered the essential element. A teacher who is oriented to habit formation, for example, is likely to achieve class control by having pupils practice the proper ways of going to assembly, entering the classroom, or sharpening pencils. On the other hand, a teacher who is predisposed to cognitive structures for learning would seek to make the students conceptualize their mutual need for a system of class behavior.

A third major dichotomy exists between theorists who propose intervening variables as a way of explaining what happens between a stimulus and a response and those who propose hypothetical constructs for the same purpose. An *intervening variable* is a derived

Overview

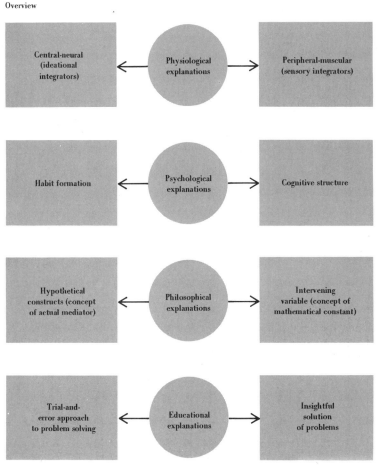

**Figure 2-1** Dichotomies that separate learning theorists (rectangles) and different orientations to theory (circles).

constant which is usable in different situations that measure responses. An example of an intervening variable is the mathematical *g* (gravity) for the acceleration of a free-falling body. On the other hand, a *hypothetical construct* is a logically derived explanation of the relationship between real processes that go on within the organism. For example, in this book we postulate that there is a neurological linkage mechanism that produces conceptualizations from related associations. This is a hypothetical construct that is subject to testing.

A fourth dichotomy separates the theorists who emphasize trial and error as the means of solving problems as contrasted with those who emphasize insight. Trial-and-error learning was conceived by E. L. Thorndike (1913) to explain the gradual increase in the efficiency of a cat finding its way out of a puzzle box. Insight is considered to be something more than the mere joining together or slight modification of old habits; *insight* involves the sudden grasping of relationship within an experienced context. The theorists from each theoretical orientation are able to provide convincing interpretations of different learning experiences. In order to avoid confusion, it is necessary to understand that different theorists are working from different assumptions. For instance, B. F. Skinner in his experiments with pigeons was concerned with overt peripheral-muscular responses, habit formation, intervening variables, and trial-and-error approaches to problem solving. Piaget, by contrast, described learning in terms of central-neural activity, cognitive structures, hypothetical constructs, and insightful solution to problems.

The theoretical position held in this book is explained in a learning-motivation model, which is an extrapolation from, and an integration of, the contrasting themes outlined above. These dichotomies are opposite ways of looking at learning processes which in real life are continuous. Inputs such as vision and hearing or muscular responses such as speech and writing are peripheral functions. These inputs from various senses are integrated within the central nervous system where responses are initiated. This continuous activity of stimulation, integration, and generation is real, and understanding what is happening within the learner tends to make teaching a rational act rather than trial-and-error behavior. When problems are too difficult for a person to understand, but when something must be done about them, the probability is that he will operate on a trial-error basis. But if an individual is able to conceptualize the problem in a rational context, he is more likely to find insightful solutions.

Habits are stereotyped responses to repeated experiences. When a number of associations are related in some way, the learner structures them into conceptualizations. It has become possible to put different points of view into a construct which is complementary and universal rather than dichotomous and divisive.

Hypothetical constructs sometimes turn out to be physical realities when investigated. When experimental studies are systematically organized to test theory, numerical constructs emerge which can be interpreted as intervening variables. The teacher need not choose between theories, but can select the aspect of the learning paradigm that is most relevant to a particular classroom problem.

## PRIVATE WORLD OF THE INDIVIDUAL

Psychology made its first important contributions to knowledge at a time when the nature of human interaction was assumed to be mechanical, measurable, and observable. As the contributions of behavioral psychology accumulated, it became increasingly difficult to question the premises on which the impressive progress of this discipline was based. Evidence is accumulating that the conflict of the last century between mechanistic and humanistic views of the world may be resolved through a synthesis that preserves and enhances the contributions of both material and immaterial systems of philosophic thought. The world of science has come to be viewed as a hierarchy of complexity that runs from atoms through molecules, cells, tissue, organs, individuals, specific populations, communities, and ecological systems (Simpson, 1967). This book seeks to provide the teacher with an orientation to human behavior that synthesizes aspects of educational psychology that formerly were considered dichotomous.

Freedom of choice is the *rational* consequence of the increasing complexity of man's nervous system, compared with the nervous systems of lower animals. The *potential* for this freedom has been an evolutionary development that has at the same time increased individuality and the complexity of inner experience. Complexity and individuality increase according to a species' position in the animal hierarchy and as a result of learned experiences. Both inherited and learned patterns of behavior can be observed in man. Increased complexity can be traced in the expanding flexibility of action reflected in the following sequence: (1) inherited response patterns, which have no flexibility; (2) imprinting, which has a small potential for alternative response patterns; (3) conditioned responses, which have varying weights of environmental determination; and (4) self-directed learning.

The choices that an individual makes as a result of his freedom and the pressures and possibilities that exist in his environment develop his private world. Each person's world is unique; since no two people are under precisely the same pressures, they do not make the same choices. The central thesis of the private-world concept is the essential aloneness of each person as he encounters forces that insistently compel him to assert his individuality, even when such a course is destructive to his well-being. The separation of the individual from the external world leads to a sense of uniqueness, but also to a sense of loneliness. Although differences exist among the private worlds of students, there is a substantial overlap in the private worlds of students who have had similar experiences, thus making group teaching possible. Each person has the potential to expand his private world to encompass parts of the world of another. This overlap is accomplished through communication, which is effective even though imperfect and distorted.

### Imperfection in Communication

A person's awareness of the dichotomy between self and the world outside of self is critical in learning. This inner world of feelings, understandings, and insights cannot be measured or observed easily, but the individual establishes his own identity through this separation. The process of learning to distinguish between the self and the rest of the universe is basic to mental health and seems to be causally related to some of the motivations that determine what people will learn (Hamachek, 1971).

The unconscious assumption that the world outside of self is the same for a student as for the teacher often leads to confusion and lack of communication between them. One of the difficult tasks that the teacher faces as he seeks to understand students is to develop an appreciation of the nature of their private worlds. Few would deny that the world of the blind or the deaf is different from the world of people whose sensory acuity is normal. Even the world of the color-deficient person can be understood as different from one's own in subtle or pronounced ways. However, this understanding has an intellectual rather than an emotional base and may develop as an abstract concept of the nature of a private world in which color discrimination is different. Continuous attention is required if teachers are to keep in focus the idea of a world that is different for *each* student.

The concept of a world apart from oneself is not within the functioning awareness of most people, although each normal adult has learned to distinguish between himself and the rest of the universe. The *out-there*—all that is not self—may include in a detached way the activity of one's own body and one's own thoughts when perceived in objective terms. In most contexts, however, the idea of *self* incorporates one's own body and mind and sets them in counterdistinction to all else. In this book, the out-there is defined as the universe outside oneself, which is translated uniquely by each person and becomes part of his private world.

Fortunately, people have many similar experiences, so that certain commonalities exist in their worlds. Most people see light waves of 550 millimicrons as yellow-green. Most people feel water of 125°F as hot. The vocabulary used within a culture tends to reflect similar experiences. Lack of communication between ethnic groups often springs from an unawareness of the differences between their perceptions of the social rather than the physical world.

**Individual Bases of Experience** Some differences between the world of the adult and the world of the child or the adolescent are obvious. A second-grade class was asked to draw portraits of community helpers. The teacher's curiosity was aroused when most of the children drew adults whose noses were upturned, with large nostrils. No instruction had been given on how to draw a face, and so the teacher wondered whether they were imitating the work of one pupil whose drawing they admired. The teacher understood the phenomenon later, when she was sitting on her heels to talk with a child and looked up to see the principal at the doorway. From this level, his nose looked like those in the children's drawings. Another teacher took a group of three- and four-year-olds to the bird refuge to feed the ducks and geese. The geese in particular were aggressive and threatening. The teacher understood the children's nervousness better when he realized that they were seeing geese face-to-face. By imagining the geese to be the size of a horse, he was able to gain some insight into the children's viewpoint. The sizes of objects, their colors, and the sounds they make differ according to the background and sensory apparatus of the individual observing them.

The science of semantics is based on the concept of imperfect communication. The educated American uses the word "democracy" with a spectrum of meanings that overlap in many particulars. The typical Russian who uses the same word also covers a spectrum of meanings, but there are crucial differences. The young woman or man who becomes a VISTA volunteer goes to live with Americans whose experiences, including emotions, are far removed from their own; these people may coin new words, use forbidden words, or attach meanings to words that are apart from the volunteer's own definition of them. The teacher is sometimes surprised to find differences in the meanings he and the students attach to words used in the classroom. Many discipline problems are rooted in honest misunderstandings between the student and the teacher—misunderstandings that are based on the different experience backgrounds that constitute a culture or a subculture.

**Translation of the Sense Organ Input** The teacher may understand the uniqueness of each child's experiences, at least intellectually, when he realizes that the data on which a person's information is based are screened, sorted, and translated during perception. Both input and interpretation are subject to error, so that there are differences in the data that are fed into the brain and the nervous system. Data are coded and interpreted within a frame of reference that includes the particular individual's previous experiences. A person who reads these pages interprets them automatically as part of the reading process and is unaware that the meanings come primarily from himself. Teachers and other responsible adults cannot all be trained in the folkways of all pupils, but each can know the significance of individuality in learners, and each can be taught to extend himself empathically and to broaden his base of communication.

**Genetically Transmitted Behavior**

Human beings, like other forms of life, inherit many mechanisms—particularly those for survival—that permit no flexibility of action. Complex animals also inherit the potentiality for indeterminate modes of action, which makes learning by experience possible. Subsequent sections discuss these increasingly indeterminate and increasingly free modes of action, which include imprinting, conditioned learning, conceptual learning, and creative learning. The logical establishment of a human potential for freedom is critical to the rationality of much of a teacher's work.

**Inheritance of Explicit Behavior** Teachers are concerned primarily with that facet of student development which is unique to human beings—the use of language for storing and transmitting knowledge. However, there is a large substructure of genetically inherited behavioral functions that human beings have in common with other living organisms, some of which are basic to motivation.

Control of most of the functions that keep the organism alive—such as heartbeat, body temperature, balance, breathing, and swallowing—is involuntary. Individual differences that exist are primarily due to gene structure. Many of these life processes are very complex, requiring serial adjustments and timed intrusions into other activities. Swallowing is an example of a complex activity that is involuntary. The muscles of the tongue and diaphragm must perform a synchronized series of responses, the soft palate must cover the entrance to the nose cavity, the larynx must close the windpipe (interrupting the breathing process), and the epiglottis must open the trachea. This control mechanism is coded in the DNA (deoxyribonucleic acid) molecules, which carry the genetic codes that determine physical and mental characteristics. These molecules act very much like a computer program, having subroutines available at critical points. Neurological control of swallowing apparently develops before birth. Almost always these DNA-controlled activities take place outside consciousness, although they can be brought into partial voluntary control with effort. A child may hold his breath until he lapses into unconsciousness, but in that condition his normal breating resumes. Variations in the effectiveness with which the inherited process operates contribute to the differences in the life spaces that individuals inhabit.

**Instinctive Behavior in Lower Animals** Some instinctive activities are very complex. The honeybee returns to the hive and by a series of movements commonly called dances informs other worker bees about honey sources at an indicated distance and in a specific direction. This system of communication seemed, when first observed, to require a high-level thought process. However, further experimentation has shown that if the bee's antennae are stimulated, she will perform the whole complex rite whether or not there are bee onlookers. The inherited nature of this communication ability was confirmed when experimenters found that bees raised in isolation were able to give this kind of report as well as those having grown up in contact with other bees. The mechanisms for instinctive behavior are inherited, rather than developed through learning.

Wooldridge (1963), in *The Machinery of the Brain*, described the activity of a solitary wasp, "Spex," as she prepared her eggs, comparing it to a set of subroutines stored in a computer. The wasp dug a burrow, found a cricket (which she paralyzed but did not kill), dragged the cricket to the entrance of the burrow, left it to go inside for an inspection, came out again, and finally took the cricket into the burrow. When the sequence was interrupted, the wasp dragged the cricket back to the mouth of the burrow, again went inside for the inspection, and returned for the cricket. Wooldridge reported that one investigator moved the cricket 40 times, but the wasp always followed the same routine. If she did not find the cricket at the edge of the burrow when she returned from her inspection, the whole routine had to be run again. These actions parallel those of a computer, where a recirculating instruction will cause an operation to be repeated until precise and specified conditions are met, enabling it to go forward.

**Inherited Mechanisms for Response** In behavior the random firing of the neurons often obscures the essential rigidity of some highly stylized patterns of response. When the number of neurons involved in a response mechanism is small, one spontaneous firing tends to make the pattern of action seem more subject to control by the individual than it actually is. The sea urchin is a good illustration of this point. When danger approaches, signaled by a change in the chemical composition of the water, the urchin opens its jaws at the base of the needles and points them in the direction of the approaching danger. This same pointing activity can be observed in a small piece of the sea urchin's exterior having only one needle. All that is required to make the needle point is water that contains the chemical signal. No reference back to a central nervous system is possible. A sort of restlessness of the sea urchin's needles due to random firing of the neurons distracts the observer, who tends to confuse the danger response with more of the same random restless activity.

Many activities, both in humans and in other species, are under the control of genetically inherited mechanisms. Generally these processes are basic to elemental survival; evolution has not entrusted them with any degree of freedom.

### Degrees of Freedom in Behavior

Within the phylogenic hierarchy an expanding flexibility of action can be observed. These increments of freedom allow an individual person increasing control over various functions from inherited response patterns, having no flexibility; through imprinting, with a small potential for alternative response patterns; to more complex interaction with the environment.

**Minimal Freedom: Imprinted Responses** Imprinting is behavior acquired during a brief, predetermined time in the life of the individual which, once acquired, is irreversible and resembles instinctive behavior. It is controlled by less rigid neural patterns than those which control instincts. Imprinting, although it results in highly predictable behavior, contains some flexibility about the object of imprinting. The young duck has been carefully studied (Hess, 1964) as a prototype of imprinting activity, although the same phenomenon is observable in many other species, including human babies. In the case of the duck, one form of "learning" is imprinted between the thirteenth and seventeenth hours of life, as it follows the first moving object that comes into its field of vision. Ordinarily this will be the mother duck (which has survival value), but the attachment is effective for other objects or large creatures. A duckling may follow a little red wagon or a person and become attached to it. This tendency to follow and become attached is very closely ingrained and cannot be avoided, but the nature of the object to be followed is not precisely specified in the DNA code. The inherited coding required for following indeterminate objects is much simpler than that required for selecting a specific object for attachment. The limited freedom or flexibility represented by imprinting was apparently sufficient for the survival of the species even though some individuals failed to survive.

Sluckin (1965) noted that the tendency of a baby to smile at those who are caring for him may be an imprinted type of learning, although some research seems to suggest that the smile reflex in infants may be selected, from among many facial reflexes, for reinforcement as social behavior by adoring adults. Almost certainly the nursing of a baby by its mother involves primitive protective responses that are nearly always reinforcing. When this feeding activity is painful to the mother, as it sometimes is, her responses can be more rejecting than reinforcing. Negative patterns of behavior in a child can begin with this primitive rejection.

A number of reflex patterns, similar to subroutines on a computer, are inherited through the molecular structure of the genes and are physiologically developed through mother-child intimacies. Even if one of the normal, wholesome relationships fails, there are still many other protective responses that support the infant emotionally. Those who have watched a mother bristle at any threat to her child have seen a response that is supportive and developmentally beneficial to the child. Many of the basic interactions that occur between the child and his parents also occur among other mammals. Controlled imprinting is being attempted in monkeys by giving the newborn their first visual experience and supportive contact with human caretakers rather than with monkey mothers. After the relationship has been established through imprinting, conditioning is attempted by the substitute mothers to teach the young monkeys novel behavior. The results of the ongoing research will be interesting in terms of the potential influence of the caretaker (mother) as a teacher.

It would be difficult to overemphasize the importance of parents' responses to their offspring with feelings of awe, wonderment, and protection. The result of these systems for responding is the probability that the reinforcements required to stabilize learning experiences will occur. These genetically inherited tendencies could explain why children all over the world, regardless of the culture into which they are born, tend to learn in much the same way, even though the content of their learning may be different.

**Limited Freedom: Conditioned Responses** Imprinting was shown to contain an element of flexibility not present in the genetically inherited patterns. However, even primitive forms of conditioned learning involve more flexibility than imprinting. Pavlov (1927) conditioned his dogs to salivate in response to light, sound, or touch as a substitute for meat powder. Children learn to speak different languages, to be quiet or noisy, and to be happy or sad by conditioning. Often the learning process is so much a part of the ongoing social environment that it seems automatic. Pavlov's dogs learned to respond to many different kinds of stimuli under many different conditions, as compared with the imprinted "learning" of the ducklings. Children learn to respond to a wide range of stimuli and to produce a variety of responses as a result of their learning. Greater freedom to respond in alternative ways is more evident in *conditioned* than in *imprinted* behavior.

**Human Freedom: Conceptual and Creative Learning** The tendency of an individual to behave in genetically determined ways declines with his ability to react selectively to his environment. As each moment passes, decisions are made to use this word rather than that, to study rather than go to the movies, to snarl a reply rather than try to reason diplomatically. Each person is sure that for him, at least, these choices are real and important. Arguing from objective evidence, thus excluding all self-knowledge, it is possible to build an impressive case that none of these decisions is real—that decisions are predetermined by subtle chains of conditioning contingencies.

The evolving complexities of organisms seem to have assured some flexibility as desirable for survival in the natural world. The lesson to be learned from imprinting is the possibility of intervention in a predetermined sequence of behavior—the thin edge of chance or unpredictability. When some flexibility, as opposed to complete rigidity, is present in an activity as crucial to survival as the duckling's natural tendency to follow its mother, variability of response has been established as a fact of life. Many people find the implications of learning as conditioning extremely distasteful, because it smacks of outer control, of otherdirectedness, of human beings who are automatons pushed by the waves of chance or, worse still, pushed by some other equally nonresponsible person. However, when the element of freedom in conditioning is compared with the rigidity of instinctive behavior or with the nearly inflexible patterns of imprinting, the trend toward choice becomes apparent.

**Choice as the Builder of Private Worlds**

Following this line of analysis, the freedom to choose from among a multitude of alternatives, so apparent to the individual in his own inner life, is based on a real need to choose. The freedom that is involved is an extension of the freedom that is evident in imprinting and conditioning. The biological purpose that this freedom serves is probably some simplification of the coding in the ultracomplex DNA molecule of human beings. This degree of freedom has enabled the individual to meet and solve complex needs without the neurological apparatus becoming impossibly cumbersome.

The conflict between the materialists and the humanists (Adler, 1968) is resolved in the following synthesis. The human being is a part and a product of the evolutionary process. The problem of dealing with increasingly complex situations has led to the rise of species with increasingly flexible ways of meeting situations—in other words, with increasing increments of freedom. Human organisms have become so complex that survival as Homo sapiens requires an individual to function at a level of freedom that characterizes him as human, in the meaning of the immaterialists. In spite of humanness, man is still part of the continuation of animal evolution, and large areas of his life are organized and controlled to function within a context of rigid prescription.

The teacher who understands the nature and possibility of individual freedom will function differently from one who sees human action as merely the result of complex, externally controlled, conditioned contingencies. Freedom and acceptance of external control are both learned. Freedom grows as the individual successfully encounters opportunities to express himself creatively. Perhaps the most significant goal of the school is to make more individuals more fully human.

**Choice and Excluded Choice** Each choice excludes the unchosen as an effective ingredient of experience. One of the difficulties of research into a learning process is the impossibility of having a child live through one set of experiences and then live through a different set without his having the impact of the original experience. Past input has an effect that can never be erased, although it may be repressed if it is too painful. The irreversibility of experience remains a fact, whether based on genetically inherited activities, on imprinting, or on more complex types of learning. The boy who stays home and studies French vocabulary, rather than going to see a movie, has increased his knowledge of vocabulary at the expense of what he would have learned at the movie. If he is reinforced, the probability that he will meet his responsibility as a student rather than indulge in what he views as a pleasure is also strengthened.

The girl who becomes pregnant must live with the result of her choice and become a mother or seek an abortion. The future holds other choices, but to eliminate stored experience is impossible.

The teacher must accept the reality of the student's past experience. The student cannot escape from the effects of past choices, and thus both he and the teacher must build upon the accumulated past, rather than upon what might have been if different choices had been made. Telling a reluctant student that he should change his behavior cannot erase his past learning, nor does this show him which choices he should make in order to effect the change. The undisciplined child who moves toward cooperation needs encouragement for his improvement rather than punishment for his lapses or the discrepancy between his behavior and that of another student with a different accumulation of experience. One purpose of education is to help the student identify alternatives before he makes limiting choices.

In the private world that each person builds from his life experience, each choice makes a difference. Most choices are of no apparent consequence, but each shapes the future in important ways—in terms of both the accretion of positive choices and the exclusion of other possible choices with their attendant effects. People who respond to their environment in independent and innovative ways continue to become more individual in their selection and interpretation of experiences. The geology major who takes his date for a ride sees a world of talus slopes, igneous dykes, and glacial deposits, while she, an art major, sees the action of clouds, the sharpness of shadows on soft grass, and the bleached purple of an unpainted barn. Individual sensitivities such as heat-cold perception, pressure awareness, and auditory stimulation are determined in part by the sensory apparatus, but

to a large extent they are perceived within a context of stated experiences that have become increasingly selective. Connected to almost all these input mechanisms is the impossibility of really knowing, except by analogy, whether the impressions that another person receives are the same as one's own or different. A person's subtle responses to other individuals shape his interpretations of human relationships as warm, threatening, fearful, or pleasant, and thus his decision to seek, avoid, challenge, or ignore them.

**Unknowable Private Worlds** An emphatic or sensitive person tries to approximate an understanding of the world of the people close to him. Writing or reading literature is largely a struggle to find a base line for dialogue about sensory perceptions and social impressions. How can you tell another person that the colors you see are different from those which he sees? When the poet William Carlos Williams (1951) expresses his pleasure at the sight of a red wheelbarrow, a reader may experience pleasure also, without knowing why this stimulus of a mundane wheelbarrow arouses him aesthetically. The ways in which people interact can be interpreted from only one position at a time.

Professional people who probe the obscure inner world of the individual see the same client differently. Psychiatrists look for past experiences and try to decide which should be relived and experienced differently by the client. Sociologists try to identify the combinations of stress that cause people to riot, move, murder, desert, vote, bribe, prostitute, or congregate. Political scientists try to learn how people who say they are undecided will finally vote or to discover whether people vote for the reasons they say they do. Advertisers collect data on the appeal of colors, sounds, smells, and textures to individual persons, but their campaigns are based on the percentage of people that they hope to reach, rather than on the individual persons to be persuaded. Teachers know that motivation for school learning is an individual matter and that expressed goals are, at best, a limited extension of the private self.

### Reality of "Out-There"

The potential for misunderstanding others, as each person builds his own private world from the interactions of internal and external experience, is always present. Physicists know that a table is made up of particles of negative electricity spinning around particles of positive electricity with spacing between them that is comparable to the spacing between the planets orbiting the sun. Biologists know that living things are made up of molecules also—complex molecules such as DNA—which interrelate to form living cells. Scientific evidence confirms this world of molecules as the real world, although it is not the world of human perception. A frog apparently inhabits a world of light and dark, angular moving objects, changes in light intensity, and variations in water temperature. A frog will die of starvation in a field of dead flies because he has no way of knowing they are available as food unless they move. The real world of the frog is different from the real world of the human being, and both are different from the conceptual world of the physicist, whose world varies from that of the biologist.

Although the individual can never fully know how the world outside himself differs from the world of sensory experience, this world outside does exist. His evidence of a real, existent world is the constant input of sensory data from outside himself. A newborn infant begins visually to explore the world outside himself and thus begins the long process of identifying self from all else that is not self. This constant interplay between himself and the universe beyond him is important to his continued existence because this interaction builds the conception of nonself as well as self.

**Need for Interaction** An experiment in isolation of human adults pointed up this necessity for interaction with the world outside the individual (Zuckerman, 1969). College students were paid $20 a day for just relaxing quietly. They lay on soft beds with shades over their eyes in a dimly lit room from which all noise except a soft hum was shut out. What better situation for thinking could be imagined? The student subjects found this isolation unbearable. After only two to seven days, they suffered from hallucinations—little green men, for example, were seen wandering over a plain with enormous sacks on their backs. These isolated subjects became highly suggestible. In order to prolong contact with a human technician outside, they would agree to such inaccuracies as "2 and 2 are 7." Their motor coordination failed. The walls and floor seemed to weave back and forth, and this feeling of imbalance lasted for several days after they were removed from confinement. None of the men would return to continue the experiment even though double the pay was offered. This experiment indicated the reality and the importance of contact with the world beyond the individual, and it also has implications for brainwashing and thought control. Without having been subjected to brutality or starvation—except of the sensory apparatus—the subjects became anxious to accept new ideas, simply in order to maintain contact with the world outside themselves.

**Need for Novelty** Besides the need for interaction, human beings appear to require novelty in the messages they receive from the world outside themselves. Platt (1962) in *Excitement of Science* outlined the need throughout our waking life for a continuous novelty and variety of external stimulation of our eyes, ears, sense organs and all our nervous network. Platt quotes Warren Weaver on the relationship between the freedom of choice of the sender of information and the certainty of the receiver that he is interpreting the message correctly. The greater the freedom enjoyed by the sender, the more information he sends, but at the risk of greater uncertainty on the part of the receiver that the message is being translated as intended. Conversely, as the uncertainty decreases, the amount of information becomes less and the freedom of the sender diminishes. Thus greater freedom of choice, greater uncertainty, greater information go hand in hand. Platt says that novelty needs to be interpretable; novelty must fit within some parameters of background, or it ceases to be information-bearing and becomes only noise—which is still preferable to no contact. In planning lessons, the teacher should bear in mind that variety and novelty are stimulating to the learner—variety of materials, pacing, noise level, student involvement, and movement. For this stimulation to be communication, rather than noise, novel experience must be related to past meanings.

**Need for Verification** Objective measurements of objects provide further evidence of the reality of the world outside the individual. Precise measurements of the elements of the environment are the cornerstone on which the physical sciences have been built. The gravitational effect of the moon has been measured, and calculations about the return of space explorers from the moon were made on the basis of these measurements. Chemists measure precisely the ways in which molecules are put together, and this knowledge enables them to change a deadly poison into a wonder drug. Other scientists replicate the research with the same results, confirming the previous outcomes and the reality of the world in which they work. In the social sciences, the measurements have been of a different order but of similar importance in verification and prediction.

## SCIENTIFIC BEHAVORISM IN PSYCHOLOGY

When systematic psychology was in its infancy, introspection was an integral component of research. The psychological experiments of Wilhelm Wundt (1874), in the first psychological laboratory, consisted of three parts: (1) a known and preferably measurable stimulus, (2) an introspective report, and (3) a known and preferably measurable response. As part of the step involving introspection, subjects were asked to describe inner feelings such as anger or fear. It was this part of the experiment that caused the difficulties, for even the reports of trained subjects tended to be unreliable. Reports made by untrained subjects tended to be contradictory.

As time passed, and with some enthusiastic prodding by Watson (1913) and other psychologists who shared his views, it became increasingly the practice to drop the introspective part of the experiment and to rely on the measurable stimulus ending in a measurable response, which meant that experiments could be repeated by other researchers and the results confirmed or rejected. In one experiment, Watson and Rayner (1920) used an infant subject, Albert, to condition a fear of loud noises to white, furry objects. The child was presented with a white rat (stimulus). As he reached for it, a hammer was struck on an iron bar behind him. The loud noise, which was naturally frightening, caused the child to withdraw his hand and to cry (response). After several like experiences, the child withdrew and cried when the rat was shown. During such experiments the subject's behavior was observed without the need for interpretation. Watson was interested primarily in experiments involving animals, and the fact that animals are notoriously poor reporters of introspection may have had some bearing on the enthusiasm displayed for eliminating this part of the psychological experiment.

In any case, the discipline of psychology made its greatest advances in the context of rigorously designed experiments which could be replicated by others and which generated results that could be treated statistically. The statistical analysis indicated whether the observed differences in the responses being measured were due to chance or were large enough to make it probable that they were actually being produced by different stimulus situations. Within this frame of reference, a vast amount of information has been accumulated. It is now possible to select from a given population the best potential Army officers, the persons most likely to succeed as corporation executives, the men most likely to do well as streetcar conductors, and the high school seniors most likely to pass introductory biology. These methods of study have led to some understanding of the conditions under which complicated kinds of learning are likely to take place, at least for a predictable percentage of the groups selected. In most of this research, the emphasis has been on scientific rigor, which has paid off in man's ability to control new areas of his environment.

Much of the basic research on learning has been done with rats or other laboratory animals—in which case the feelings or opinions of the subjects, by experimental design, have been irrelevant to the findings. In the context of the behavioral approach, the importance of the outer world—the ways in which the stimulus situation can be varied to produce predetermined response patterns in an organism—assumes a dominant role. The success of the rigorous scientific approach has led some psy-chologists to the conclusion that belief in individual freedom merely indicates a lack of knowledge of the control mechanisms actually in force; as these control mechanisms are discovered, the areas of the indeterminate will gradually disappear. B. F. Skinner (1971) in *Beyond Freedom and Dignity* states this position clearly and succinctly. "The direction of the controlling relation is reversed: a person does not act upon the world, the world acts upon him" (p. 211).

### Security in the Measurable

Scientists, including psychologists, find security in the observable and the measurable. Quantitative research is respectable, can be replicated by others, and provides probability data for prediction and control of behavior. Kendler (1963) in *Basic Psychology* points out areas in which the rigor of stimulus-response (S-R) psychology has contributed to success in understanding the processes of interaction in learning. He asks a rhetorical question: "Why do the people who are critical of S-R psychology spend so much time criticizing results and so little time producing any substantial body of empirical results that can be critically studied?" Students of learning processes should be aware of the necessity for explaining and implementing certain areas of behavior within the S-R framework for learning.

### Seduction of Successful Measurement

The temptation to assume that what is not measurable or controllable is not real stems in part from the monumental discoveries made by scientists after they broke with pseudo-sciences to conduct rigidly objective studies of the universe. Some scholars of biological and behavioral science have adopted this sequence: observation of repeatable phenomena, hypothesis by induction (prediction), and testing by repeated observations. This ability to predict growth and behavior has led to the idea that living as well as nonliving matter operates or functions in accordance with mechanistic, invariable laws. Hardin (1961) in *Biology* explains "cause" in a scientific sense using the example of an automobile with a driver. Rather than the motion of the car resulting from the will of the driver, Hardin prefers an alternative description in terms of what happens to the car. Compressed gasoline ignites and explodes, this force moves the pistons up and down, and energy is transmitted by the drive shaft to the rear axle and wheels, causing the car to move. He points out that this mechanistic description represents the kind of attention to detail and control of conditions that accounts for progress in science. Details of cause and effect in both men and cars are important. However, teachers—whose work requires them to be observers of human behavior—should note that the car does not move unless someone turns the key. They need to consider the extent to which such an act is one of choice or decision.

Simpson (1967), another biologist, cited three major differences between the physical and the biological sciences, which cause him to question the application of typological investigation and deterministic philosophy to living things. First, nonliving objects are extremely simple compared with living organisms. A hierarchy of complexity runs from atoms through molecules, cells, tissues, organs, individuals, specific populations, communities, and ecological systems. The cell is lowest in the hierarchy of organisms—that is, those having the basic properties of life. Simpson's second point is that the physical sciences deal with objects within a type of specifying commonality, but are not generally concerned with the variability of individual things. Physicists recognize the variant states

of molecules within a type of material when subjected to specified conditions. Although they work with statistical procedures that cancel variations and determine the properties and activities of the mass, the atoms and molecules described are assumed to be alike. By contrast, organisms as small as viruses or as complex as identical twins are individuals; no two are exactly alike. Organisms must vary to exist through many generations. Simpson's third reason for going beyond typological premises to study living things is that most physical science content is nonhistorical, while the study of living things inevitably involves development, change, growth, and evolution. Physical forces and chemical reactions occur in predictable ways and continue to operate in accordance with the same formulas without regard to time. Biological research requires the asking of teleological questions about the function and purpose of an organisms's use of his environment. Of a similar cleavage among psychologists, Simpson says:

On one hand are behaviorists, brass instrument or physiological psychologists, descriptive and objective but in a typological and idealistic way, intentionally ignoring individuality, personality, historical factors, purpose, and teleological aspects of psychology. They virtually exclude the psyche from psychology, and their understanding and explanation of what they observe, being limited to the physical level, are grossly incomplete. Yet for a time and in some quarters, this necessary but insufficient approach was considered the only adequately scientific one, just as extremists among biophysicists and biochemists have claimed a monopoly on scientific biology. In psychology as in biology, the limitations of such an approach are transcended by an organismal science (although the psychologists do not call it that), including clinical, individual and introspective methods, with attention to personality, histories, variation and teleology. [pp. 371–372]

In the light of the success of the statistical approach to psychology, it may seem presumptuous to claim significance for such behavior as that of the duckling who follows the little red wagon, the cat who curls up and goes to sleep rather than struggling to escape from people, and the child who draws pictures of spaceships when he should be studying his spelling, all of which have important meanings for teachers. The inherited genetic patterns of responses, the limited possibilities for choice that characterize imprinting, and the organism's susceptibility to conditioning obviously control major sectors of human performance where responses are predictable. However, the really important things about human beings are not the ways in which they are the same but the ways in which they are unique.

The end result of a long evolutionary and development sequence seems to be the emergence of individuals who have some freedom to be creative or destructive, productive or sedentary, in a variety of life situations. In this civilization, no one is always free, and few have no freedom of action or mobility. Many are chained to comformity. The chief purpose of the school is to free each individual student from inhibitions on thought and initiative by giving him as many choices as he can control, as early as he can learn to understand the results of his choices. Much of the evidence concerning freedom is private and individual. To the extent that this evidence is not subject to verification or replication, it has been suspect. Both the inner private world and the outer substantive world are real.

## Reality of the Private World

The cumulative potentiality of successive choices, even when a large number of them are predetermined by conditioning contingencies, means that no two people can ever have the same experiences. Insofar as exper-

ience determines what learning will take place, no two people are going to learn exactly the same things. Insofar as what is learned determines the nature of the world in which a person lives, no two people are going to live in the same world.

Perhaps a digression will illustrate the significance of choice in the structuring of different personal worlds. Some years ago at the University of Cambridge, a six-week summer session was given to prove the statement, "I am bigger than I was when I was born." On the face of it, this seems like a silly occupation for grownups, but buried in this statement is a crucial question: What or who am "I"? What is the essence of "me" that sets me off from my fellows and makes me unique, different, and a thing apart?

As a person grows from a baby to an adult, nothing measurable remains the same. Skin cells perish in a few weeks, muscle cells last a little longer, and even bone cells are replaced approximately every seven years. A baby has not learned attitudes. If the adult—physically, mentally, and emotionally—is no longer the same as he was when he was a baby, in what way may he be thought of as being the same person and hence bigger than he was when he was born? This topic, stated in different terms over the years, has been argued since before the time of the Greeks. Philosophical questions arise concerning the soul, the personality, or the essential "me." These are intangibles that periodically are thought to be nonexistent because they cannot be located in the body. Is man really nothing more than a body with its hormone balances?

Quite possibly, "me" is the unique result of the choices I have made, choices from which I have created my world and by which I have separated myself from the world I have created. If this description is accurate, "I" becomes a constantly changing entity in a world of flux. The continuity in growth is uniqueness; the constant separating and differentiating the self is experience.

Mention has been made of the impossibility of knowing, except by analogy, the world of others. In our schools, many children come from backgrounds that are foreign to the world of most teachers. The words used in discussions may be the same, but the meanings are different. One penalty of individuality is a measure of distortion in the messages that they communicate to each other.

## LEARNING-MOTIVATION THEORY

The focus of this book is a learning-motivation model, which integrates research findings about conditioned response learning, conceptual insight, and motivational dimensions of behavior. This structure enables the teacher to approach all learning situations with professional intention. Since this model leads students to self-directing, creative activity, part of the suggested teaching method involves encouraging the student to escape from the control of others, including the teacher. The idea of teaching students to become independent of the teacher is a frightening concept for some individuals.

### Definition of Learning

*Learning* is a by-product of an organism's attempts to meet its needs. Each response to a need involves integrated neural activity, which is recorded as a pattern, thus modifying the neural system to some extent. These changes in the central nervous system alter the subsequent responses of the individual. As an illustration of learning, consider the effect on a student of his first attempt to dive. One of his needs is to maintain prestige in his group by diving when his turn comes. An opposing need is to give in to his fear and retreat. Still another need is to satisfy the expectation of

the instructor. Whether the potential diver withdraws, dives successfully, hurts himself when he hits the water, or breathes water into his lungs, a changed person—one who has learned—will line up next time at the pool.

Personal introspection indicates that moment-by-moment choices between needs must be made. Some choices are so easy the selection is almost automatic, while others are difficult. In some psychotic states the necessity to choose is so agonizing that the individual slips out of the real world into fantasy, where choices are suspended. Essentially, the choices an individual makes involve a decision concerning which of a multitude of needs will be satisfied at any particular time. If one need is attended to, others may remain unsatisfied, at least temporarily. Learning is the concomitant of this process of attempting to meet different needs. When the result of a choice is satisfying, a connection is made to the neural centers of the brain where pleasure affects are generated. This extra circuit through the pleasure centers seems to ensure that the response pattern will operate again when the same stimulus situation occurs. In other words, the person has learned to respond in a particular way under certain conditions. When a lack of success attends a particular attempt to meet a need, no pleasure circuit is established and in some cases a punishment circuit is connected instead. When the stimulus situation is again presented, the original response does not normally come into play, and what has been learned is not to respond. In a stimulus situation that once called forth a response that was punished, a completely new need may be chosen for gratification. The student who succeeds in solving an algebra problem, and finds pleasure in his success, has learned a method of approaching an algebra problem that he will probably try again when a similar problem is presented. He has also learned to try to solve algebra problems. The student who does *not* succeed in solving the problem, and finds his failure punishing—either because he is dissatisfied with himself or because he is censured by the teacher—has learned to avoid the approach he used or even to avoid algebra.

Motivation, like other patterns of behavior, is learned. If students can be motivated, they can be taught. If not, schoolwork is a burden to them and to the teacher as well. The motivated learner becomes self-directing. Motivation is related to attitudes, incentives, and the developing personality. The learning-motivation model shows the interaction between cognitive and affective learning, outlines the steps that will eventuate in a motivated student, and explains the relationship of pleasure to motivation and to future cognitive learning.

### Processes of Learning

Learning changes the individual as a person and thus changes the world in which he lives. At the same time, the changes in the person make further learning of the same kind more likely. Man learns to learn. The process takes place at different levels, depending on the presentation of the material, on the prior experiences of the learner, and on his intellectual ability.

**Level 1 Learning: Association**   All initial learning consists in the formation of associations, including the classical conditioning investigated by Pavlov and others as well as the operant conditioning described by Skinner. Most of the S-R learning, which represents nearly all the experimental evidence, comes under the rubric of *association learning*. Probably most teaching is on an association basis. Spelling, rules of grammar, historical chronology, and multiplication tables are usually presented as associations to be learned. This kind of learning is more easily tested and graded than more complex types. The factual material presented in lectures is often absorbed as association learning. Most attitudes are learned by association.

**Level 2 Learning: Conceptualization**
The process of conceptualization is built on a base of associations which are necessary but do not ensure emergence of a conceptual structure. *Conceptualization* is the process of grasping the commonalities or the relationships within material when these are seen as a pattern. Helping students to generate conceptualization is more difficult than teaching for associations. When the concepts are presented fully structured—for example, someone else's conceptualization of a law in chemistry—they are usually absorbed as associations by the learner. The units are larger than in most other incidences of association learning, but the process of acceptance and storage seems to be very similar to stimulus-response learning of simpler materials. Some students may transform and bring to life the already-formed conceptualizations presented by the teacher, but a student is more likely to grasp relationships when the teacher provides a setting in which he is able to develop, derive, or discover the inherent structure for himself.

Many teachers find it difficult to allow a student time to build his own conceptualizations. It seems a long time compared with that needed to short-circuit the process by giving the student the answer. Teachers who understand the difference between the transfer value of association and conceptual learning are more ready to concede the need for planning ways to help the individual develop his own cognitive structure. Conceptualizations as well as associations are formed in the realm of attitudes and emotions, just as they are formed in the factual or cognitive areas of knowledge.

**Level 3 Learning: Creative Self-Direction** Like other levels of learning, *creative self-direction* can be explained logically and can be taught. Under favorable circumstances, people are able to progress from association formation, through a process of conceptualization, to the kind of learning that characterizes the creative artist. The motive power comes from the emotional, or affective, dimension of learning, and the unique elements come from varying the cognitive conceptualizations that have been learned. When the student has reached this third level of functioning in a particular sphere of activity, he will have found the strength and ability to function as a free agent. Until he has the understanding and independence to initiate his activities on this basis, he is confined to working at the conceptualization or association level. The teaching for level 3 learning requires willingness on the part of the teacher to allow the student freedom to become his own master in certain spheres (Figure 2-2).

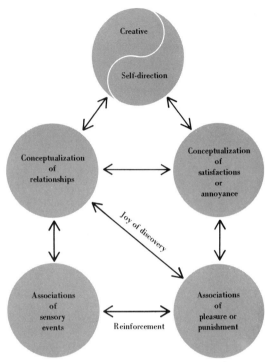

**Figure 2-2** Learning-motivation model

### Cognitive Associations

*Association* learning (level 1 learning) is conceived as the addition of bits of experience, knowledge, or awareness to an existing chain of information or sensitivities. When two sensory events occur together in time, they tend to become associated by a linkage that occurs within the brain (Kendler & Kendler, 1962). When one of the events is remembered, the associated experience will probably be recalled also. Hearing the same music that one heard at a party is likely to bring back memories of the people there. The joining of the two incidents seems to require nothing more than that they occur together in time, although several such associations may be necessary before recall occurs easily.

*Contiguity* is the psychologists' term for associations formed because events occur together in time or space. The work of Pavlov (1927) on classical conditioning emphasized this point of view. Guthrie (1952), a stimulus-response psychologist, and Tolman (1932), who was primarily a cognitive psychologist, both considered contiguity to be the most important element in learning. When a teacher has a child look at a word and say it, he expects learning by contiguity to take place.

### Affective Associations

Not all theorists have differentiated between cognitive and affective learning, although a substantial number of the stimulus-response psychologists consider the most pertinent cause of learning to be the *effect* that follows behavior. B. F. Skinner (1953), in his operant conditioning, emphasizes the importance of effect in learning. E. L. Thorndike (1913) was an early exponent of the value of effect in explaining learning. On the contemporary scene, one group of psychologists is involved in training for sensitivity toward other people, which is directed almost entirely toward affective learning (Perls, 1969). Another group uses the theory of effect to modify behavior (Patterson, 1965b). When the child answers correctly, the teacher's smile can generate an effect that stabilizes learning.

The physiological basis for pleasure and punishment effects has been located in the brain and explored by neurosurgeons using electronic probes. (Pribram 1971). Normal activities that are linked to the pleasure centers are continued and resumed by the organism. But activities are avoided, even at considerable effort, when the linkage is to centers that are punishment-evocative. Although the neurology of learning is a complex and difficult subject, mastery of it gives the teacher a power and a control over learning that make the effort important and worthwhile.

The brain is composed of some 10 billion neurons, some of which become linked as learning takes place. Researchers, particularly neurologists, have discovered the manner in which some of these linkages occur, the location of the storage in the brain, and the conditions that make storage efficient. Many of these findings were made as a result of exploration of human brains prior to and during surgery for tumors, head accidents, or epilepsy so that essential functions would not be destroyed. Penfield (1969), of the Montreal Neurological Institute, used a very fine electrode to stimulate various parts of the brain while talking to his conscious patient to make certain that critically important areas for speech would not be removed by surgery. During one of these exploratory excursions, the patient started reliving an experience he had not recalled in 20 years. His memory of it

was sharp, as though he were replaying a video tape of this segment of his life. Further explorations by Penfield and others seem to indicate that everything attended to by an individual is stored, although much of this stored experience is not subject to retrieval under normal conditions.

**Reinforcement through Pleasure** Olds (1956) was exploring the brain of a rat with electrodes when he discovered what he later called the *pleasure centers*. This was a serendipitous discovery that occurred because he had inserted the electrode in a place he had not intended. He noticed that the rat seemed stimulated when the current was turned on and would repeat, over and over again, whatever it had been doing at the time of the stimulation of these groups of neurons. In order to test his subjective analysis, Olds devised an apparatus that would enable the rat to demonstrate its desire to receive the stimulation. The cage was rigged with a bar that could be connected to a source of current, so that by pressing the bar the rat would be able to stimulate its own pleasure center through a surgically implanted electrode. In other to establish a basis for comparison, Olds first allowed the rat to run in the cage when the apparatus was not connected. Under these conditions, the rat pressed the bar from 20 to 25 times an hour. After the current had been turned on and the rat was able to self-stimulate the arca of the implant, the bar pressing increased to levels of 2,000 to 5,000 times an hour, which was a statistically significant change. This experiment was replicated with other rats. Whatever the effect of the current, the rats acted as though they wanted it to continue. The implication seems clear that *reinforcement*—which elsewhere has been described as likely to produce repetition of an act—very probably is a behavior manifestation of connections to the pleasure centers.

The effects of pleasure and punishment associations on learning and the affective or emotional components of learning can be summarized as follows:

**1** Connections to the pleasure centers—*reinforcement*—lead to repetition of the activities involved in the learning. The learning tends to be stable and available.

**2** No affective or emotional component—*no reinforcement*—tends toward extinction of behavior learned previously, which can be restored to performance strength by relatively small amounts of reinforcement, or connections to the pleasure centers. The learning is not forgotten, but is not used.

**3** Connections to the punishment centers—*punishment*—lead to avoidance of the learning or activity. Usually, punished behavior is replaced by an activity that is pleasure-producing or reinforcing, although what that activity will be is indeterminate.

Punishment centers have also been located in rats and other animals. Laboratory stimulation of these centers in the brain has caused animals' hair to stand on end and has made them shriek, quiver, and bite objects hard enough to break their own teeth. In some cases, animals have died when the punishing stimulation was continued. Brady (1958), whose monkey subjects would operate a lever for hours to minimize punishment stimulation, concluded that punishment-center stimulation was distinctly unpleasant.

**Self-Stimulation** Heath (1963) implanted electrodes in human patients who had been suffering from narcolepsy, a disease in which the patient falls asleep after each few minutes awake. Self-stimulation was controlled by the patient pushing a button. The sensation was reported to be distinctly pleasant and the stimulation kept the patient awake.

Observation of the effects of pleasure and punishment on children suggests that they also have connections to both the pleasure and punishment centers that normally function through regular neural circuits in the brain. These internal connections can be effective in much the same way that the external electrode connections used in laboratory experiments are, although the cause-and-effect relationship cannot be determined with the same assurance.

Suppose that the teacher has been trying to teach the child to associate the word "ballerina" with the toy ballerina, as one step in building vocabulary. When the child indicates the establishment of the association by saying the word, the teacher is likely to reward him in some way for his success. She may smile, pat him on the head, relax, or in any one of many ways indicate acceptance of his response. Even the removal of a frown may constitute reinforcement.

As a result of the teacher's reinforcing activity, connections take place within the child's neural system that link the word and the object in their association to the pleasure centers in the brain. This linkage seems to constitute the true reinforcement of the learner. Now the child has associated the word, the object, and the pleasure. The effect of this affective association should be remembered in relation to the effect that linkage to the pleasure centers had on the bar pressing of the rats—they tended to repeat the action that caused the stimulation. If a pleasure association has been formed, the child is more likely to make the response "ballerina" when the object is shown than would be the case if no such association had occurred.

The connection of an association formed by contiguity to a pleasure center seems to be the essence of operant conditioning. In other words, classical conditioning is association due to contiguity, while operant conditioning has the added element of reinforcement. The difficulty in distinguishing between operant and classical conditioning under complex circumstances thus becomes understandable, although the theoretical distinction is extremely useful in planning learning events. In the case of the child learning vocabulary, not only does he repeat the word "ballerina" when the object is shown, but because of the pleasure stimulation of the teacher's reinforcing activity, he also visualizes the object and says the word to himself, thus renewing his pleasure stimulation without having the object or the teacher present.

Pleasure stimulation is present by intention in most classrooms. Attractive books, word games, music, snacks, playtime, and a feeling of success at having accomplished a difficult task are examples. Sometimes the teacher rewards the children—for example, by awarding gold stars or A's, by giving them candy, or simply by praising them. What is pleasure-producing, and therefore reinforcing, to one child may leave another uninterested. The teacher who expects to be successful in building positive motivation toward school will need to discover the reinforcements that are effective with different children.

## Cognitive Conceptualizations

If a person discovers a structure within a group of related associations, he is conceptualizing. This kind of learning seems to be different from the process of forming associations. If the process of association learning can be considered a linking of neurons into chains, the conceptualization process might be thought of as a grid which short-circuits some of the association chains. Conceptualization is the process of abstracting the commonality in associations, meaning that the relevant relationship is grasped. The teacher, who has structured the learning situation to facilitate this conceptualization, will want to reinforce,

or reward, the child for his discovery. This reinforcement probably links the experience of discovery to a pleasure center, thus increasing the probability of similar attempts to grasp relationships in the future. The pleasure that accompanies discovery learning has been described by Suchman (1962). The gestalt school of psychology emphasized *insight* as the important ingredient in learning. The saying "The whole is more than the sum of its parts" points up the importance of insight into the relationships that underlie what is to be learned. Tolman (1932) spoke of his rats' developing "cognitive maps," which were products of insight. When a student conceptualizes the consistent relationship of the radius of a circle to its circumference, he is experiencing insightful learning. Piaget (1970) described his psychological theory in a book called *Structuralism*, where he distinguished between additive and conceptual learning in various disciplines including biology, mathematics, and social science. One critical point in teaching for discovery of relationships is that some of the children in a group do not make the conceptualization on their own, but learn the correct answer by listening, thus forming another association. The child's thinking process, rather than the content of the learned material, determines the level on which he is functioning. Different children can learn the same content in different ways and will have it available for different uses, depending on the process they followed. A child who originally learned a relationship by being told it as a bit of information by the teacher or by a classmate may later mentally manipulate the bits of information he has stored and come to his own conceptualization. The student who made no conceptualization may still remember the material as associations that he can repeat at appropriate times—such as examinations—without any understanding of the relationship, in this case the common element that is involved. The child can learn by association that "ballerina," "bicycle," "bat," and "ball," for example, all begin with 'b' without understanding that one way to group or classify words is by their initial sounds.

### Affective Conceptualizations

If a person is successful in conceptualizing the relationships within a group of experiences and has a store of associations that include pleasure components, he may conceptualize the relationship of his pleasure to his accomplishment in this area of activity. He comes to see himself as one who derives satisfaction from certain kinds of experience. Fortunately, affective conceptualization is nearly always self-reinforcing, but the teacher should nevertheless support the student in his search for a positive self-image.

**Patterns of Punishment** The effect of punishment in the classroom is to make a connection to the punishment centers rather than to the pleasure centers of the central nervous system. This association of disapproval tends to be disruptive to the learner and to cause avoidance of whatever brought about the punishment. Earlier in this chapter, it was mentioned that animals have been known to bite objects hard enough to break their own teeth in an attempt to escape from punishment stimulation, which is an extreme manifestation of this phenomenon. The student who is persistently confused by a course of study will learn to avoid this kind of punishment in the future.

Not only is there a lack of cognitive success in such situations, but a conceptualization can also develop that school itself is distasteful—that it causes failure and should be evaded, if possible. When such a conceptualization is present—and with it the determination to avoid this kind of experience—the student has developed a well-established learning difficulty. In many cases, his conceptualization of himself as a failure turns out to be satisfying. The whole process can now be terminated, and any further failures are positively reinforcing evidence that confirms his self-accepted inability to do the required work.

Remediation under these circumstances is very difficult. Careful structuring and patient work are required to build new association pathways to skirt the old and painful habits of thought. New approaches to the subject, such as i/t/a in reading or Cuisenaire in arithmetic, are often effective in remedial situations because they provide different beginning experiences. The old associations connected with the subject can be avoided.

Children probably never have completely bad experiences with a subject area; however, many pupils do develop concepts of school and of themselves that are so painful that they learn very little. Case histories of school dropouts indicate that they learned to dislike school early in their careers. Too often the attempts at remediation are so loaded with familiar punishment and failure associations that successful learning is impossible.

**Mixed Patterns of Pleasure and Punishment** Neither wholly negative nor wholly positive patterns are common. In most cases, parts of the experience are satisfying, punishing, or perhaps neutral. One of the results of research on the punishment centers of laboratory monkeys was the finding that the effects of stimulation to the punishment centers could be reversed by making a comparatively brief series of stimulations to the pleasure centers a part of the sequence (Wooldridge, 1963). The effectiveness of this reversal seems most likely to be realized when the learning is still on the association level. Once conceptualizations have taken place, reversal seems likely to be much more difficult.

When the cognitive content is unorganized, so that inherent relationships are obscured, the conceptualization becomes difficult. If the emotional toning from the pleasure and punishment centers is mixed, conceptualizations about learning being pleasure-producing are likely to be difficult to make. Under circumstances of mixed patterns of information, learners are neither self-motivated nor completely turned off. They tend to grope while looking for clarifications that are difficult to find.

As a practical matter in teaching, particularly in a new field of study, lessons should be structured so that the students can get positive reinforcement, even for very limited or partial success. The point is to see that no doors to later success are needlessly closed. It is important for each learning experience to be sufficiently satisfying so that the student will come back and try again where he left off. As the nature of motivation becomes better understood, the schools will be able to increase pupil learning.

### Creative Self-Direction

When the student has been able to conceptualize the nature of a relationship within the material and also to conceptualize the pleasure he enjoys from working in a particular area, he will probably want to continue the activity on his own. He is ready to move to the level of creative self-direction. The characteristics of this kind of learning include the independence of the student and his purposefulness. The creative activity reflects the human need for novelty, combined with familiarity with the particular content that he has been using. The self-direction is an outgrowth of the satisfaction or pleasure he has derived from working with the material.

Psychologists from otherwise different orientations have implied *purpose* as an im-

portant ingredient in learning. Hull (1943) spoke of "drive reduction" as the basis of learning. From one point of view, this can be conceived as reinforcement or effect, but from the point of view of the rats in Hull's study, it probably involved purpose. Tolman (1932) emphasized purpose as the basis for developing cognitive maps. The gestaltists described the behavior of apes as a series of purposefully organized trials that focused on obtaining food, which was a reinforcing agent. Lewin (1935) spoke of goals, barriers, and threats—all of which imply purpose. The student who prepares an original and outstanding science exhibit is demonstrating purposeful learning that is both creative and self-directing.

### APPLICATION OF THE LEARNING-MOTIVATION MODEL

An instructor at Palmgrove Community College used the learning-motivation sequence to launch his course on problems in engineering. His purpose was to create, on the part of the students, a mental set for self-direction in which they would see themselves as flexible professionals who were able to cope with a changing technological world. He had found that the self-image of students influenced the way they approached the content of his courses. As a stimulus problem he asked them to discuss the implications of contracting Howard Missile Corporation to design and develop a rapid transit system for Cairo, Egypt.

### Foundational Associations

The engineering instructor launched a discussion to elicit the information his students already had about the local armament factory. Some of the bits of knowledge he saw as basic to the larger problem were the particular skills of engineers, accountants, and supporting personnel; the array of buildings and equipment presently used to assemble missiles; and available sources of financial support.

On the affective side, the associations he elicited were attitudinal habits of dependence on weekly paychecks, fear of unemployment, fear of changing work routines, and a mental set toward national defense.

### Planned Conceptualizations

At the second level of discussion, the instructor used inquiry techniques to help students arrive at the conceptualizations that would generalize to radical changes in their goals. First, they conceived the present human and material components as a pool of multiple resources available for production. Next they classified the interlocking needs for a producer for a rapid transit system. Then they took up the problems of the local engineers in transferring their skills to a new line of production. Most of the *students arrived at the conceptualization* that the more an engineer's training had *focused on principles* of physical stress, electrical transformations, aerodynamics, propulsion and suspension systems, and computer guidance systems, the greater the transfer value to new problems. This line of thinking was in contrast to their former mental set toward *learning the specific techniques* of missile production. As the students began to see themselves as engineers who could manage the theory, they were freed of hangups and fears that tended to confine them to immediate job preparation at the local plant.

### Goals of Self-Directing

These discussions of professionalism in engineering consumed several class periods, but by that time the students had formulated their own goals for the course. Many of the students were thinking up ways in which engineering science could be applied to other priorities that were their own. They could see the principles of engineering as basic to many different problems. Their intellectual energy increased when they became emotionally open to consider what they wanted to do with their lives. They were freed to approach their theoretical courses as potentially useful to themselves, rather than as preconceived hurdles to a certificate to practice engineering.

### SUMMARY

Psychology interprets man's interaction with his environment. The individual's separate kinds of experience create a private world, in which he lives and from which he cannot escape. This private world can be known and shared by another only on the basis of analogy. One facet of the development of this world is the need to establish an identity that separates the self from the external world. The effect of this separation is to create problems of communication.

The success of psychology as a science, based on the predictability of human action, led some scholars to assume that what was not measurable was not real. The increase in complexity of living organisms is reflected in the following sequence, which is a significant one in learning theory: (1) completely controlled, genetically inherited response patterns; (2) imprinting, which has some potential for alternative response patterns; (3) conditioned responses, which are more flexible; and (4) self-directed learning, which involves choice. Learning is a by-product of the individual's attempts to satisfy his needs. This idea has implications about the reality of the selection process that determines what will be learned. Success aids learning, but failure hinders it.

This chapter also dealt with the reality of

the private world, the nature of self, and the problems of increasing dissimilarity which contribute to decreasing empathy. The teacher who tries to communicate with different students needs to be aware that their private worlds constitute the reality with which he continually copes.

A learning-motivation theory was outlined which shows the interaction between cognitive learning and emotions at three levels: (1) association learning, in which facts and details presented by others are accepted and stored; (2) conceptualization, in which material is organized and inherent meanings and structures are discovered; and (3) creative self-direction, in which the student uses ideas and knowledge to create something new, at least to him, and on his own volition. The student's thinking process, rather than the content of the subject matter, determines his level of learning.

The way in which the pleasure centers and the punishment centers of the brain function to control repetition or avoidance of certain activities forms the determining link in learning. Events that occur together in time come to be associated by linkages in the nervous system. According to the theoretical function of the pleasure and punishment centers, associations that are linked also to the pleasure centers can be repeated imaginatively, as well as in a setting like that in which the original association was made. If, however, the association is linked to the punishment centers, the association will tend to be avoided, and alternative responses will be sought.

As students learn, patterns of association are formed from which they can extract conceptualizations about relationships within the material. The more clearly and unambiguously the learner experiences these patterns, the more likely he is to discover the relationships within the bits of associated information. At the same time that cognitive learning is progressing, affective or attitudinal learning is also being structured. Just as conceptualizations about the relationships within the content are formed, so also conceptualizations are developed within the pleasure or punishment dimensions of this learning. When a student has been able to understand the relationships within a particular area of knowledge and at the same time has also discovered that he enjoys this particular kind of activity, he is in a position to proceed on his own to explore and create new knowledge for his own pleasure. This kind of creative, self-directed learning is limited in area and scope when it first occurs.

When the associations are punishing in nature—because of failure to learn the material and disapproval of the teacher or other significant adults—the student may conceptualize the content as meaningless and conceptualize his involvement as undesirable or inadequate. Under these conditions, some students get a reverse kind of satisfaction from accepting themselves as failures, unable to learn particular kinds of content. When this kind of conceptualization of self as a nonlearner takes place, the learning disability that has been established is very difficult to correct. Subsequent chapters elaborate the rationale and present the research which undergirds the learning-motivation model.

## SELF-DIRECTED ACTIVITIES

1 Visit a psychological laboratory on your campus and ask to observe the learning experiments in progress.
2 Explore a child's way of looking at the world by probing what he means by what he says.
3 Analyze a number of your own classes to see what levels of learning are expected of you.
4 Analyze a novel or a play to determine how the motivations of the protagonists evolved.

# Chapter 3

Building behavioral objectives based on outcomes. (Courtesy of the United Nations)

# APPRAISAL AND OBJECTIVES IN EDUCATION

This chapter is designed to help teachers translate their goals into behavioral objectives. When you have finished studying it, you should be able to:

◖ Distinguish between objectives that express broad purposes and those that describe behavior

◖ Formulate objectives that reflect your personal teaching goals

◖ Write objectives that indicate the sequence of learning from associations, to conceptualization, to self-direction

◖ Outline a number of ways to organize objectives based on goals

◖ Describe the relationship of objectives and evaluation

◖ Develop objectives for a given task-oriented learning experience

◖ Read the literature on behavioral objectives with comprehension of the following terms:

    programmed instruction
    inferred process objectives
    criterion-referenced items
    cognitive domain
    affective domain
    psychomotor domain

The learning-motivation model stresses the way in which learning is multifaceted (Chapter 2). Affective loadings in a learning situation determine whether or not a stimulus will lead to a response. Bits and pieces of experience or learning are essential if conceptualizations are to take place. When the conceptualizations are about affects, self-images change. When conceptualizations about the cognitive structure are fused with conceptualizations about the affective loadings of a learning situation, creative self-directing activity is likely to take place. These small bits of creative self-directing activity in life situations are the foundations of the humanist's self-actualization. In life everything has beginnings, but often the end result would be difficult if only the beginnings were known. The more human types of learning, those that set individuals apart as free souls, have many, many earlier experiences that are satisfying. The freedom to be, and how it is used, depends on the nature of these early satisfying experiences.

Conditioning has been found to lead to other types of learning, whether this effect was intended or not. By using small steps that are carefully controlled and immediately reinforced, autistic children have been brought from nonspeaking self-stimulation to effective interaction with their environment. This is a major accomplishment, but eventually the children have to move from responding to a trainer with words that have been programmed for them to using words and sentences for their own purposes. They must be able to function away from teachers and parents and make decisions for themselves. The step from programmed response to free response is an important one that has required the psychologists who work with these children to rethink some of their basic premises about the nature of learning.

## PERSONALIZED OBJECTIVES

Successful teaching requires a clear idea of the nature of the goal being sought for the student. Different tactics are needed to teach ballet dancing than to teach computer programming; however, there are general principles that cut across many different kinds of learning. The ultimate goal of teaching, assumed in the learning-motivation model, is to free the student to make his own decisions about his learning. If the student is to be free in any area of endeavor, the basic associations for productive thinking need to be available. This assumption increases the teacher's responsibility for defining objectives in ways that allow the student to go beyond learning associations to generating ideas of his own. The *Kindergarten Evaluation of Learning Potential (KELP)* (Wilson & Robeck, 1967) illustrates how objectives can be stated and measured over many facets of a curriculum. These objectives, in each area, move from forming associations to generating conceptualizations and include creative self-directing activities as a final goal of a particular learning sequence.

During the last few years a great deal of interest has been focused on writing objectives that are specific and that can be clearly observed in the behavior of the learner. Specifying outcomes in this way leads to *behavioral objectives*. Initially, the objectives stressed were behaviors that could be easily seen and obviously measured. The behaviorally oriented practitioners have begun to find that it is important to plan learning that the student can expand when the teacher or conditioner is no longer present. For instance, in speech correction the learner must use the new speech after he has left the clinic and pieces of candy are no longer dispensed for correct usage. It is easier to write objectives that involve obvious behaviors than to conceive learning sequences that open new worlds to the student and can at the same time be evaluated for success. It is possible—but difficult—to organize objectives that allow each student to be an individual with his own purposes.

One of the problems for teachers is the need to know the student's present level of competence in relation to the goals that are being defined. Ways of appraising present status should become part of the whole evaluation of goal achievement. At first glance it would seem that an appraisal of each student should be made and the goals defined in terms of his needs. At the present state of the art, schools are not designed to provide growth experiences in many areas that are important to students. Almost nothing is taught about child rearing, and little expertise is available about money management, even though both these areas of life are highly important to most young adults. Even when the goals of the school are kept within traditional areas, working out appraisal systems can best be done in terms of the ultimate goals being attempted. When the student is seen as a dynamic individual—one possessing his own goals which must be harmonized in conscious terms if the potential for learning at school is to be achieved—the formulation of objectives becomes a challenging task. If the challenges are to be successfullly met, ways of appraising the base line of present knowledge and skill must be included as an essential element in the teaching-learning process.

### Entering Behaviors

Information relevant to entering behaviors will be found in some later chapters which describe typical behavior at different ages in physical, cognitive, and affective development. For example, intellectual potentialities of the individual in relation to learning are set forth in the framework of Piaget's sequence of cognitive development. Principles of physical growth (Chapter 11) emphasize the need for certain neural and muscular structures to form before the child is able to learn such things as skipping or batting a ball. Emotional development (Chapter 13) explains how surmounting crises of growing up within a culture constitutes the possibility for forming new attitudes about solving problems in a social context.

Although teachers, in terms of their experience, often make fairly accurate judgments concerning the entering behaviors of many students, more dependable and correct decisions are possible with the addition of objective measures provided by tests and scales. A variety of different instruments and approaches to the assessment of student behaviors is described in Chapter 18.

### OBJECTIVES THAT DESCRIBE BEHAVIOR

This chapter defines behavioral objectives and explains the historical and philosophical precedents from which they evolved. Examples of learning-motivation sequences at elementary, secondary, and college levels differentiate between the teacher's long-term goals for students and the day-to-day objectives that are observed or inferred from their behavior. At the self-directing level the prospective teacher can involve himself in formulating personal objectives by pursuing some of the open-ended activities at the end of each chapter of the book. Determining one's own base line of competence will help appraise the present status of future students.

Behavioral objectives describe, according to certain specifications, what students will do as a result of a particular block of instruction (Kibler, Barker, & Miles, 1970). Precise descriptions of desired behaviors have been evolved by three groups of researchers: program writers for teaching machines, test writers, and researchers in behavioristic psychology, working with three different goals.

*Programmed instruction* is designed to carry the whole weight of teaching without the interaction of an instructor. Learning is achieved by following a carefully designed series of frames that reflect an analysis of the components of the task to be learned. Precisely defined steps and goals which anticipate the learner's probable responses are needed. Program objectives are for students with preestablished needs and are pursued on an individual basis. Appraisal of the student's present level of knowledge as well as the speed with which he masters new ideas is important in selecting programs that will have sufficient challenge to keep the student working but will not be so difficult that he gives up in despair.

Over a period of time, sequences have been developed that program the teacher in his interaction with students. Blocks of material are broken down into units, and ways of presenting the material and of reinforcing the student are prescribed. Questions to be asked under different circumstances are specified, and alternative ways of handling correct and incorrect answers are stated. Teachers trained to interact according to this plan are thought to be more effective than mere programmed materials (Engelmann, 1969).

In a different approach, also evolved from programmed learning, teachers define their own instructional objectives with the same precision as professional programmers do (Popham & Baker, 1969). Most teachers have not had the time necessary to define their objectives in detail, but they are able to tailor their approximations to the needs of the students being taught. An exercise in writing objectives usually clarifies the goals that motivate their teaching.

*Test writers* took another route to behav-ioral objectives, a route based on their need to recast psychological processes into observable behaviors. They had been concerned for some time with complex problem-solving objectives such as those set forth by Bloom et al. (1956) in the *Taxonomy of Educational Objectives.* To achieve a parsimonious system for writing test items and to minimize duplication of effort, Bloom and a number of other test writers met several times to work out a classification which incorporated a hierarchy: knowledge, comprehension, application, analysis, synthesis, and evaluation. Within this framework, achievement test items could be written and standardized. The process objectives that eventually resulted from Bloom's *Taxonomy* tended to be more broadly conceived than those developed by programmers who assumed that long-range goals had already been determined. For example, one of the measured objectives, classified as synthesis, is for the student to produce the plans for a senior high school which satisfy a specified population, function, and location. By contrast, an example of a goal for programming was to cast B. F. Skinner's *A Science of Human Behavior* into programmed form (1953). The programmers often started with a book or a well-defined course, and their task was to break down the content into small, interlocking steps which proceeded from the beginning to the end of the material. Such a group of steps was called a task analysis.

The test makers were interested in developing evaluation materials that would satisfy a wide range of educational consumers. When preparing a test for wide usage, they found it necessary to analyze curriculum guides in order to develop a battery of items. While curriculum guidelines with a philosophical statement of goals were acceptable to many people because their own individual interpretations could be read into them, test makers found them difficult to evaluate. Statements of purpose such as "prepare the pupils to function mathematically as citizens in a technical society" were found too indefinite to test.

Although the efforts of Bloom and his coworkers represented a significant step in clarification of educational goals, the definitions did not describe observable behaviors. To translate these process objectives into behavioral terms, Metfessel, Michael, and Krisner (1969) devised action verbs such as "to identify" or "to differentiate" for specifying the intended behavior. These verbs were matched with direct objects, such as terms or categories, so that the combination resulted in a description of observable behavior. This instrumentation of the *Taxonomy* improved the speed and clarity with which teachers and others can state curricular objectives. These writers also operationalized the principal dimensions of the *Taxonomy of Objectives: Affective Domain* (Krathwohl et al., 1964). For instance, conceptualization of a value includes "Forms judgments as to the responsibility of society for conserving human and material resources."

Teachers traditionally have planned objectives for their daily lessons, but these objectives have tended to be stated in terms of what they themselves would do or in terms of content to be presented. Some curriculum writers prescribed the activities in which children would participate, rather than the changes that would result in their behavior as a consequence of an educational experience.

*Researchers in behaviorist psychology* can be credited with placing the focus of learning on observable behavior. To them, the acceptable research design included a stimulus situation of some kind with an observable behavior to follow (Watson, 1913). The mental processes between the stimulus and the response were not considered knowable, therefore not germane, to the experiments' descrip-

tion of the conditioning process. Their insistence on obtaining behavior in observable, objective forms made testing much easier. This focus has tended, however, to limit objectives and instruction to learning that can be observed. Not all the objectives of the *Taxonomies* can be incorporated easily into a framework of externally observable responses.

## Goals and Objectives

Students who plan to become teachers already have some well-defined ideas of the purpose or broad goals of education in the lives of children. They expect that children will learn to read well and enjoy reading, to be interested in social problems and participate in public issues, to have some kind of skill for earning a living, and to develop some personal activities that enrich their lives. These purposes, stated in abstract terms, are embraced by most of the groups and individuals who are concerned with education.

The teacher, who is responsible for translating these purposes into the objectives of an instructional unit, may find himself in disagreement with colleagues, parents, or administrators about the means needed to achieve these ends. The ability to articulate instructional objectives can be extremely helpful in ensuring that the dialogue between the teacher and other responsible adults is constructive and defines the relationship of this unit to the overall purposes of the school. For example, the goal of a particular skill for earning a living might be defined differently by two teachers of vocational education. Instructors in electricity might state their course objectives in either of the following ways: (1) The student can explain the flow of electricity on the basis of electron movement, can describe the changes in flow due to moving through a transformer, and can diagram the function of a circuit breaker, or (2) the student can make a union of conduit and BX-cable, can solder a wiring connection, and can trace the hot and cold wires in a circuit. In the first set of objectives the teaching emphasis is on theory, and in the second set the focus is on skills. Both statements reflect a teacher's view about the relative efficiency of different steps in educating a student to become an electrician. The first teacher's objectives are to elicit evidence of conceptualizations about the principles of electricity, whereas the objectives of the second are to observe techniques based on associations.

Objectives are a translation of purposes into the specific performances that represent the terminal behaviors of students in a unit or a course (Krathwohl, 1965). Mager (1962) specifies three necessary elements in a behavioral objective: (1) a statement of the *observable behavior* which will be expected of the student in demonstrating mastery, (2) a description of the *conditions* or the learning task with its constraints under which the student demonstrates his competence, and (3) a specification of a *criterion* level of performance. The more concrete course goals are, the easier they are to break down into behavioral objectives. Kibler et al. (1970) added two elements to the behavioral objectives: (4) the *product* or result of behavior and (5) a *description of the learner*. An electronics teacher might define a behavioral objective for a single lesson: The student will make two T joints in a junction box (behavior). He will join the hot wires and the cold wires using a pocket knife, electrician's pliers, a soldering iron and solder, and insulating tape (conditions). Both joints will pass inspection for solidarity of contact at the twisting stage, the soldering stage, and the final stage (criterion). The union will conduct current safely (product). The student is an adolescent or an adult in a class in electricity (description of the learner). The specificity of the statement implies evaluation as part of performance.

## Inferred and Observable Behavior

A distinction is sometimes made between inferred and observable behavior. For each response seen there is always an internal process which may be the most important result of instruction. The more complex the intellectual functioning, the more obscure the process that precedes an observable behavior. The more mature the student, the more complex his internal processing is likely to be. Some writers prefer to state course or teaching objectives in terms of the intellectual process which is anticipated and inferred. Behavioral objectives, in terms of student performance within a given lesson, are objectives that can be conveyed to the student. This distinction is used in the examples in this chapter and it represents a level of objective writing that beginning teachers can be *expected* to achieve.

## Precautions in Using Behavioral Objectives

Behavioral objectives constitute the teacher's expectations about the observable effect his teaching will have on students. However, preformulated objectives have the disadvantage of leaving the student out, treating him as an object, unless these objectives themselves specifically incorporate student planning. The student's motivation, attitudes, and appreciations influence his behavior and result in outcomes which are vitally important but which are not easily described in criterion terms.

## Affective Objectives

The difficulty in describing affective goals does not warrant bypassing them, even though much of the behavior resulting from the affective domain is internal. These affects are nonetheless real and are significant on both a short- and long-term basis to the student and to the teacher. Perceptive teachers have learned to interpret the affective responses of a pupil although they may be hard put to define these responses for other observers since the cues they use are subtle and nonverbal. Overly rigid or preconceived objectives may distract both teachers and learners from discovering creative directions and imaginative goals for individuals.

In the subsequent section on formulating objectives for learning, guidelines are developed for writing objectives in the affective as well as the cognitive domain. These sequences go beyond predictable and structured behavior and build in the expectation of self-selection and self-direction for the student. As teachers become adept at thinking of student learning as observable behavior, they will want to supplement their own written objectives with others that have been developed as learning packages. Although most of the programs commercially available at present are limited to association learning, the teacher can expand these limited objectives to anticipate conceptualization and creative production.

### Goals, Process Objectives, and Behavioral Objectives

In summary, statements need to be differentiated among (1) *goals* that are broadly philosophical, global, nonmeasurable, almost timeless in their applicability, and directional in their intent (Swanson, Freedman, & Knight, 1972); (2) *inferred process objectives* that reflect *nonobservable*, hypothesized psychological activities of the learner (Bloom et al., 1956; Krathwohl et al., 1964); and (3) directly *observable process objectives*, or *behavioral objectives* manifesting themselves in learner activities that are operational, measurable, relatively time-bound, highly specific, and discretely quantifiable (Mager, 1962). Both *inferred process objectives* and the *observable process objectives* are behaviors that can result from the teacher's intentions and actions. Often teacher *behavior* in the form of instructional activities portrays an intention to bring

about certain inferred process objectives within the learner, and student *behavior* in terms of attainment of performance objectives furnishes inferential evidence of the manifestation of the desired, nonobservable, hypothesized psychological processes set forth in the inferred process objectives.

**Requirements for Behavioral Objectives** The carefully stated behavioral objective not only provides benefits for planning instruction and for constructing test items for evaluation purposes, but also furnishes a means for illustrating the interplay of three widely discussed educational concepts of *content*, *process*, and *product*. To summarize, the five requirements for a well-formulated behavioral objective include:

1 Statement of *conditions* or *stipulations*, in essence describing the learning task and its constraints (*content*).

2 Designation of the *learner* (such as a fourth-grade pupil or a student in a ninth-grade mathematics class).

3 Use of *action verbs* (such as to construct, to define, to describe, to differentiate, to identify, to match, to name, or to order) that indicate observable activities, although sometimes more complex objectives stated as inferred processes (such as to solve, to analyze, to synthesize, or to apply) may be used.

4 Specification of an outcome (product).

5 Specification of the *standard* or *criterion* of an expected or acceptable level of performance with a possible time limitation.

An example which reflects cognitive association learning may be helpful in illustrating the realization of the five requirements for behavioral objectives as well as in interpreting the interaction of content, process, and product.

*Objective:* Given 20 addition problems consisting of 5 two-digit numbers arranged vertically (condition or content), a pupil in the fourth grade (learner) can write (action verb-observable process) the answer (the written answer being the product) to 18 out of 20 problems in not more than 5 minutes (standard or criterion, quantity, and time specified).

It is apparent in this objective that the learner *processes content* (test items or stimulus material embodying given information) to obtain *products* (outcomes or new information in the form of written or orally presented responses). The process is both nonobservable (thinking activities following exposure to stimulus material) and observable (the actual writing down of an answer). The moment after the content has been processed and the answer has been recorded, a product results. There are circumstances when the process itself, as in acting on a stage or giving a lecture in college, if observed by another may be considered a product and certainly could be recorded by video tape to become a product. Even in simple but especially in complex problem-solving activities, teachers often show as much (or more) interest in the process (steps leading to the solution of the problem) as in the final answer (product) itself. Instructors interpret the feedback gained from observing student processes and examining student products to form decisions for individualizing and modifying instructional strategies, for revising their objectives, and for selecting and devising new instructional materials. Such decisions, as will be seen in Chapter 17, arise from ongoing process evaluation and product evaluation.

**Criterion-referenced Items**   As can be seen, the illustrative behavioral objective can easily be translated into test items that operationalize it. The criterion or standard is often modified to specify that a certain percentage of students in a given group will answer one item correctly. Such a circumstance arises when there are several behavioral objectives and a given test item corresponds to each one. Thus it is not uncommon to specify a standard or criterion that 80, 85, or 90 percent of the students will answer a given item correctly. Such a test item that parallels an objective is said to be a *criterion-referenced item* in that a criterion or standard has been established for what will be considered an adequate response level by a group or class. Tests which consist of several criterion-referenced items are known as criterion-referenced tests. Scores on these tests indicate not only the level of student performance, but also the degree to which teachers are considered accountable for having their students meet a standard of performance that may have been set either by the teacher or by administrators.

## WORKING FROM GOALS TO OBJECTIVES

When behavioral objectives are written by teachers for students prior to a period of instruction, the teacher needs to remind himself that his objectives do not automatically become those of the student. In the objectives for the Kindergarten Evaluation of Learning Potential (KELP), Robeck and Wilson (1969) made a distinction between pupil behavior and teacher behavior. The difference was between what the teacher saw the children learning and what he could help the children see as their own learning. Writing objectives is easier if the teacher first thinks about what students will be able to do as a result of a block of lessons and then decides how much of this can be communicated to pupils as behavioral objectives on a short-term basis. To accomplish this second step, the teacher anticipates the ability of the children, when guided, to understand and express their own goals and judge their own products. At least in the cognitive domain children are more likely to accomplish the teacher's objectives if they themselves are aware of what they are trying to learn. The learning-motivation model presents an interlocking relationship between cognitive and affective learning and implies that all instruction has self-direction for the learner as the ultimate goal. This sequence, beginning with associations that are basic to complex learning, serves as a model for writing objectives. The difficult task of analyzing what a student needs to know to achieve an objective is made manageable when objectives are based on the levels of associative, conceptual, and self-directed learning. The KELP bead design sequence which follows is an example of how the teacher can build in the observation of affective learning when writing objectives. Creative self-direction results in behavior that is observable and can be criterion-referenced in terms of the product.

The need to write behavioral objectives can be threatening to experienced teachers who confront this requirement for the first time. Specifying the emergent learning in behavioral terms for non-present students appears at first sight to be an impossible task. Actually, of course, teachers have been approximating behavioral objectives as long as schools have been organized. In the following pages the steps in working from goals to objectives will be outlined for slices of content in kindergarten, junior high school, and college. In thinking about the evolution of objectives for these three situations, the reader will, it is hoped, be able to generalize how to write objectives for his own subject area at his own level of responsibility.

Goals arise out of questions such as: What am I trying to do? What sort of learning is possible at this time? Why are the students here? How well does the traditional sequence accomplish these purposes?

In the instance of complex behaviors involving conceptualizations within either the cognitive or the affective domain, it is exceedingly difficult, if not virtually impossible, to state a single behavioral objective to describe nonobservable or inferred psychological processes as simple behaviors. The 20 or 30 such objectives that might be required to describe the numerous observable behaviors manifesting the conceptualization process would constitute, in effect, a detailed sequence of numerous performances to be expected in an instructional unit such as a lesson plan or a teacher's manual. To effect an economy of space and yet to realize a fair degree of comparability in the communication of intended outcomes in student behavior, inferred process objectives may be used as a compromise even though, admittedly, verbs such as to comprehend, to analyze, and to synthesize are not so uniformly interpretable as verbs such as to list, to identify, or to match. Thus the objectives that illustrate cognitive and affective behaviors at the association, conceptual, and creative self-direction levels are not entirely "pure" in the sense that the verbs describe only observable behavior, but they do represent, at the higher process levels, approximations to precise statements of planned teacher behavior and expected student behaviors or outcomes. Many of the teacher's goals for kindergarten children represent input and stimulation that are important to long-term learning, but are not reflected in the immediate responses of the children.

### Kindergarten Sequence

The kindergarten teacher may see his role in various ways, such as helping young children become oriented to school by helping them make the transition from family to peer group activities, building readiness skills for reading or music education, and encouraging the spontaneity and creativity of childhood. As the beginning teacher moves from these rather generalized ideas to the specific things students will learn to do, the statements become less stereotyped and more original if they are done well. Typically, young children learn many things while doing one activity. Integrating more than one purpose into each activity complicates writing objectives but meets the reality of learning strategies. In the following sequence the learner is specified as a kindergarten child and the process, one of the five factors of learning, is specified in the heading.

**Cognitive Associations**   When the question becomes, What is important in reading readiness? the teacher's objectives will include the development of many abilities, including visual discrimination, sensorimotor integration, and left-to-right sequencing. The problem becomes even more specific as materials and activities are considered for helping children to reach these objectives. Selecting materials does not define objectives but does limit the kind of objectives that can be

reached. The KELP bead design item reflects the teacher's readiness objective for children to learn left-to-right sequencing, eye-hand coordination, and color and shape discrimination (Table 3-1). To formulate the next step, behavior in students, a three-part statement of the objective is needed. The first part indicates what the child will do—match, manipulate, or complete. The second part limits the conditions under which the learning will be demonstrated. In the example, the KELP bead design item readily defines the conditions because the materials are organized as a feasible task for a child of this age during one kindergarten activity period. The third part of the objective specifies the criterion level required to reach successful performance; in this case all five design cards are matched correctly.

**Affective Associations**   When the objectives of association learning shift from the cognitive to the affective, describing and observing the behavior become more difficult because the affects tend to be subjective,

**Table 3-1   Kindergarten Bead Design: Level 1—Cognitive Associations**

| Teacher goals |
| --- |
| 1 To help children develop left-to-right progression |
| 2 To stimulate the integration of sensorimotor systems: visual, tactile, and kinesthetic |
| 3 To encourage children to associate labels and forms: spheres, cylinders, and cubes |

**Behavioral objectives (observed by teacher, read across)**

| Pupil behavior | ⟶ Conditions | ⟶ Criterion |
| --- | --- | --- |
| To match | KELP bead design cards (1/2 inch wooden beads, 3 shapes, 6 colors) | 5 out of 5 designs strung correctly in one activity period |
| To manipulate | beads by stringing in left-to-right sequence according to the models | 5 out of 5 design sequences |
| To undertake and complete | a defined activity | 5 out of 5 designs completed in one work period |

**Table 3-2   Kindergarten Bead Design: Level 1—Affective Associations**

| Teacher goals |
| --- |
| 1 To help children increase their work attention span |
| 2 To reinforce children for finishing a task |
| 3 To help children associate pleasure feelings with independent activity |
| 4 To encourage children to express their feeling about kindergarten activities |

| Behavioral objectives (observed by teacher) | | |
| --- | --- | --- |
| **Pupil behavior** ——→ | **Conditions** ——→ | **Criterion** |
| To attend to | bead design construction | shown by persistence in stringing more cards than previously recorded; lack of diversion |
| To have fun | matching bead designs | shown by verbal or non-verbal expressions of pleasure during task |

restrained, or thoroughly internalized. However, the pleasure or punishment a student experiences during learning determines, in a large part, whether he will use the learning, and hence these objectives are crucially important even though they are difficult to behavioralize. The decisive question is, Is the student enjoying or disliking this activity? In either case these feelings are being associated with the cognitive task, and neural structures are being established. Prospective teachers, in the course of their own socialization, learned long ago to discern these effects even though they might find it difficult to describe in words the behaviors that convey the unspoken messages of affect (Table 3-2).

**Cognitive Conceptualizations**   When a teacher's purpose is to stimulate intellectual functioning that goes beyond memory responses, the objectives will focus on building relationships. The questions might be, How can I get students to relate the different parts of their learning? How can I get students to think inductively? How can I get students to

synthesize and generalize from their isolated experiences? Writing behavioral objectives for conceptualizations usually should start with a specific understanding to be achieved by the student. It is then necessary to provide associations and to arrange integration of them so that an observable response is likely which indicates that the conceptualization has been achieved. The bead design item was designed to help teachers observe when a conceptualization of repeated pattern was achieved by setting a memory task that research had shown was possible for five-year-olds only after the child had discovered and used the principle of pattern rather than mere memory recall (Table 3-3).

**Affective Conceptualizations**   The most difficult objectives to conceive and to verify are the learner's own conceptualization about his feelings. The teacher not only must identify the moment of conceptualization but must help the student see the relationship between an insight or a grasp of relationships and his own "becoming" as a learner. Two kinds of

**Table 3-3   Kindergarten Bead Design: Level 2—Cognitive Conceptualization**

| Teacher goals |
| --- |
| 1 To encourage the discovery that bead designs are made of repeated *patterns* |
| 2 To test for conceptualization of design elements by checking memory for *structured* sequences |

**Behavioral objectives**

| Pupil behavior | ⟶ Conditions | ⟶ Criterion |
| --- | --- | --- |
| To analyze | a KELP bead design into its pattern parts | by explaining or demonstrating the repeated element in an eight- or nine-bead sequence |
| To conceptualize | bead design as repeated patterns | by stringing an eight- or nine-bead sequence from memory |

affective conceptualization are shown in the bead design (Table 3-4). First, there is the interaction between pleasure associations and the source of the pleasure that is exemplified in the objective. To identify himself with the pleasure feelings that come from learning.

Second, there is the interaction between affective and cognitive learning at level 2 as exemplified in the objective To discover, I like doing hard things, thus expressing the tie between pleasure feelings and conceptual functioning.

**Table 3-4   Kindergarten Bead Design: Level 2—Affective Conceptualization**

| Teacher goals |
| --- |
| 1 To reinforce conceptualization in children by responding to their exclamations of insight, level 2 functioning in KELP, expressions of Aha! excitement |
| 2 To select activities that contain *inherent* relationships, thus helping the child experience the *pleasure* of making discoveries |

**Behavioral objectives**

| Pupil behavior | ⟶ Conditions | ⟶ Criterion |
| --- | --- | --- |
| To identify | in a learning context of bead designing (at which he has been successful) | feelings of pleasure or power expressed verbally or non-verbally |
| To discover | during successful achievement with bead designs | "I like doing the hard things," expressed spontaneously in an accepting atmosphere |

**Creative Self-Direction** The teacher's purpose—to have children develop creative production and maintain their spontaneity—can be built into the objective. Although it is difficult to teach children the conventions of school behavior while preserving their individual integrity as a person, level 3 behavior is easier to observe, in many ways, than is conceptualization. It is difficult to write this kind of behavioral objectives because they must be left open to permit the learner freedom of response; therefore the nature of the production is left unspecified in absolute terms. Part of this openness comes from the need for the child to express himself, that is, from the affective or motivational drive. Another channel to creative self-direction is the transmutation of cognitive conceptualizations to new forms of expression or new forms of knowledge. The teacher's recognition of level 3 functioning depends on his being able to permit both affective and cognitive independence. In the bead design a very small creative act is sought in the objective, To create a design of his own. The child may approach this cognitively by changing the color or shape of one of the designs he has practiced, or he may show his initiative and self-direction by using the idea of design in making paper chains or large bead construction or parquetry blocks (Table 3-5).

The feasibility of writing objectives for conceptual and creative learning has been demonstrated in field tests of KELP since 1964 (Wilson & Robeck). Kindergarten teachers are able to observe and record criterion behaviors at the levels defined and to adapt the curriculum to individual learners.

**Table 3-5  Kindergarten Bead Design: Level 3—Creative Self-direction**

Teacher goals

1 To stimulate the child's desire to use newly acquired ideas of design in self-directed ways

2 To encourage the child to try his own ideas in new situations

3 To start the child building an image of self as one who can initiate and create new things

Behavioral objectives

| Pupil behavior | ⟶ Conditions | ⟶ Criteria |
|---|---|---|
| To create | a bead design or a design sequence (given freedom to select his own materials) | which is different from the bead patterns he has practiced or which incorporates different materials |
| To use | his discoveries from previous experiences involving structure | for his own purposes, e.g., using the concept of design sequence to make a chain for the Christmas tree |
| To begin to feel safe | in going beyond the teacher's specific instructions | by producing extensions of classroom projects and activities that reflect himself |

## Secondary-School Sequence

Writing objectives for students in junior and senior high schools requires particular attention to the conceptualizations students form in each area of study. The example outlined for hypothesis formation in secondary science can be a prototype for complex learning in almost any area of study (Tables 3-6 to 3-10). A primary purpose of science education is to induce students to use the scientific method in their approach to life's problems. One of the goals within this purpose is to have students construct hypotheses about the cause of an effect. A hypothesis is a cognitive conceptualization which is stated so that it can be tested and confirmed or rejected.

In elementary and secondary science, teaching objectives have been developed which reflect the thinking of both scientists and educators. With the shock of Sputnik I in 1957, a reordering of national priorities oc-curred that gave high-level attention to science education. Money was made available to support study groups such as the one sponsored by the American Association for the Advancement of Science (AAAS, 1966), the Biological Sciences Curriculum Study (BSCS, 1965), and the Chemical Education Material Study (CHEMS, 1963). These programs have tended to focus on conceptualization of the major ideas and processes of scientific method. Their objectives were specific and specifically stated, although not always in the terminology of the programmer.

## College Sequence

There is a temptation for college instructors and authors to tell students how to write behavioral objectives when they go out to classrooms, but the instructors often do not manage the time to write them for their own

**Table 3-6  Junior High Science:  Formulating Hypotheses by Studying the Effect of Temperature on Dissolving Time—Cognitive Associations***

| Teacher goals |
|---|
| 1  To familiarize students with relevant vocabulary: dissolve, reactions, mean, median, Celsius, Saccharin tablets, linear, range |
| 2  To arrange experiences in dissolving selected solids in water of varying temperatures |

| Behavioral objectives | | |
|---|---|---|
| Student behavior ⟶ | Conditions ⟶ | Criteria |
| To record | dissolving time—in seconds—of sugar placed in warm (40°–50°C) and cold (15°–20°C) $H_2O$ | by observing within 2 seconds of mean time |
| To repeat | dissolving seltzer tablets under similar conditions; 2 trials | by observing to 1 second accuracy |
| To use | relevant vocabulary (reaction, dissolve, etc.) | in discussing obser-vation experiences |

*Adapted from AAAS, *Science—A process approach*, Part F, Formulating Hypothesis 3—The Effect of Temperature on Dissolving Time, Rev. ed., American Association for the Advancement of Science, 1970.

**Table 3-7  Junior High Science:  Formulating Hypotheses by Studying the Effect of Temperature on Dissolving Time—Affective Associations**

| Teacher goals |
| --- |
| 1 To assure students' feelings of success during observation of reaction time |
| 2 To promote generalized satisfaction in scientific observation by creating a responsive and supporting environment |

| Behavioral objectives | | |
| --- | --- | --- |
| **Student behavior** | ⟶ **Conditions** | ⟶ **Criteria** |
| To begin | setting up experimental conditions (materials and apparatus) | with enthusiasm and without delay as noted by the teacher |
| To cooperate | with other group members in the experimental situation | by taking turns and by assuming responsibility as judged by group members |

courses. Chapter 1 outlined eight professional skills that teachers use to make the necessary decisions in the classroom. This list represents a selected group of characteristics in teachers who are likely to free their students to become independent learners. These competencies of teachers are restated as the instructor's goals for a course in learning and human develop-

**Table 3-8  Junior High Science:  Formulating Hypotheses by Studying the Effects of Temperature on Dissolving Time—Cognitive Conceptualization**

| Teacher goals |
| --- |
| 1 To stimulate students to conceptualize the relationship between the temperature of the water and the dissolving time of selected compounds |
| 2 To structure the recording procedures for graphic data so that students may discover the linear and predictive relationships |

| Behavioral objectives | | |
| --- | --- | --- |
| **Student behavior** | ⟶ **Conditions** | ⟶ **Criteria** |
| To discover | the linear relationship of water temperature and solubility through inspection of a linear graph | by stating orally the relationship in the form of a hypothesis |
| To demonstrate | the difference between dependent and independent variables in experimentation | by identifying each manipulated condition from all other factors |
| To formulate | a hypothesis as a generalization from preliminary observations | by stating and formal testing in an experimental setting |

**Table 3-9  Junior High Science:  Formulating Hypotheses by Studying the Effects of Temperature on Dissolving Time—Affective Conceptualization**

| Teacher goals |
| --- |

1 To build in students a concept of self as competent in making observations

2 To develop in students awareness of satisfaction in discovering relationships within data

| Behavioral objectives | | |
| --- | --- | --- |
| **Student behavior** | ⟶ **Conditions** | ⟶ **Criteria** |
| To communicate | pleasure at being able to develop and test hypotheses | by revealing verbal and nonverbal expressions of feelings which are judged consistent by the teacher |
| To help classmates | with laboratory routines and interpretations of observations | thus demonstrating self-confidence in his own ability and knowledge of the scientific method |

ment. One of these skills will be restated and analyzed here into behavioral objectives according to the same format that has been proposed for writing kindergarten and junior high school objectives.

The example requires that the college stu-dent, as part of his practicum, identify a pupil who is unmotivated for a particular activity and build motivation into this situation. In this sequence the instructor refers to the college teacher, the student refers to the prospective teacher in training, and the pupil is the child or

**Table 3-10  Junior High Science:  Formulating Hypotheses by Studying the Effects of Temperature on Dissolving Time—Creative Self-Direction**

| Teacher goals |
| --- |

1 To motivate students to use the scientific method to attack new problems and to help them develop the appropriate skills

2 To convey approval when independent self-initiated projects are undertaken

| Behavioral objectives | | |
| --- | --- | --- |
| **Student behavior** | ⟶ **Conditions** | ⟶ **Criteria** |
| To use | graphing skills (given no required assignments) | on his own initiative to explore relationships within new data |
| To analyze | variables that must be held constant while others are manipulated (given free laboratory time) | to generate a hypothesis on his own initiative |

**Table 3-11  College Teaching of Ways to Motivate Pupils—Cognitive Associations**

| Instructor goals |
| --- |
| 1 To teach students how to identify behavior characteristics that reflect motivation in learners |
| 2 To assist students in the identification of affective responses of pupils as pleasurable or punishing |
| 3 To provide opportunities for students to acquire basic facts about pleasure and punishment connections in the limbic system |
| 4 To help students apply Skinner's reinforcement theory in behavior modification of pupils |

| Behavioral objectives | | |
| --- | --- | --- |
| Student teacher behavior | ⟶ Conditions | ⟶ Criteria |
| To observe and discriminate | pupil expressions that reflect motivation or lack of motivation in group activity | by listing pupils who are or are not "with it" |
| To interact | with pupils while looking for the positive, neutral, or negative potential effects of reinforcers | keeping a tally of responses to praise, candy tokens, frowns, and reprimands |
| To explain | motivation in terms of pleasure and punishment connections | when questioned can report probable neural connections |
| To select | reinforcement schedules for situations involving operant conditioning | 4 out of 4 graphs showing time and performance |

youth who is being motivated. The instructional program is focused on cognitive learning by the student as he studies motivational principles while applying them in an attempt to achieve affective learning in a pupil. The instructor's purpose is to have the student become self-directing through this experience of successfully changing the motivation pattern of a pupil. In writing objectives the instructor begins by identifying the basic information a student will need to understand how motivation is learned. Along with these cognitive goals, the relevant affective learnings are anticipated and plans for getting feedback from the student are formulated (Tables 3-11 to 3-15). The instructor expects that the student who derives pleasure from his interactions with children, and comes to see himself

as one who is good at interpreting and modifying behavior in desirable ways, is likely to continue to use his skills when he becomes a teacher.

The interrelatedness of learning and the possibility of defining behavioral objectives across a spectrum that includes creative self-direction can be seen in the use of Figure 3-1, which was developed for use in a teacher education program. It is possible to start with the kind of creative self-directing activity that is desired and work down from there. The authors often start with a cognitive conceptualization and then analyze the kinds of associations that would have to be learned if the conceptualization were to be possible. Need for evidence that the affective learning is substantially positive is built into the figure. A

### Table 3-12    College Teaching of Ways to Motivate Pupils—Affective Associations

| Instructor goals |
| --- |
| 1 To stimulate a student teacher's feelings of pleasure as he learns to manipulate reinforcement schedules |
| 2 To analyze affective responses of students to their assignments, thus influencing instruction and subsequent assignments |

| Behavioral objectives | | |
| --- | --- | --- |
| Student teacher behavior | ⟶ Conditions | ⟶ Criteria |
| To reveal | affective responses during discussion groups or office interviews | with relative enthusiasm which results from attempts to change motivation in pupils, as judged by the college teacher |

### Table 3-13    College Teaching of Ways to Motivate Pupils—Cognitive Conceptualizations

| Instructor goals |
| --- |
| 1 To help the student grasp the relationships of *response* characteristics and motivation |
| 2 To teach the student to categorize affective responses as indicative of classes of pleasure or punishment feelings in pupils |

| Behavioral objectives | | |
| --- | --- | --- |
| Student teacher behavior | ⟶ Conditions | ⟶ Criteria |
| To synthesize | a pattern of affective responses that characterize lack of motivation to engage in school activities, versus presence of motivation to participate enthusiastically | by writing three descriptive paragraphs of positive, neutral, and negative syndromes, using behavioral terms |
| To conceptualize | the durability of neurological connections between affective loadings and cognitive experience | by using neurological explanations for behavior observed in the learning environment |
| To demonstrate an understanding | of the role of reinforcement in modifying the motivation pattern of a pupil | by designing and implementing a reinforcement system to achieve change |

### Table 3-14   College Teaching of Ways to Motivate Pupils—Affective Conceptualization

#### Instructor goals

1 To help the student see himself as one who is good at (a) observing the affective loading of pupil motivation, (b) selecting effective reinforcments for individual pupils, and (c) utilizing strategies to achieve change

#### Behavioral objectives

| Student teacher behavior | ⟶ Conditions | ⟶ Criteria |
|---|---|---|
| To incorporate | accounts of success in modifying unmotivated to motivated pupil behavior | in open-ended reports or discussion groups |

### Table 3-15   College Teaching of Ways to Motivate Pupils—Self-Direction

#### Instructor goals

1 To provide opportunities for students to go beyond the requirements of the course to apply their skill in teaching motivation voluntarily

2 To encourage students to apply learning-motivation principles to their own study practices

3 To allow students to create complex strategies for helping pupils conceptualize the cause-effect of their own motivation to achieve in school

#### Behavioral objectives

| Student teacher behavior | ⟶ Conditions | ⟶ Criteria |
|---|---|---|
| To seek out | other pupils who lack motivation for school learning | by designing and implementing a reinforcement schedule on his own initiative that results in improved motivation for the pupil, in the judgment of the supervisor |
| To organize | his own study schedule to maximize the pleasure and satisfaction feelings from courses | as reflected by an improved grade point average or related self-initiated activities |
| To create | a counseling strategy to change the self-concept of a pupil | as inferred from an improved gradepoint average in line with the pupil's goals |

| Area of study | | | | |
|---|---|---|---|---|
| **Level 3** | | **CREATIVE SELF-DIRECTION** | | |
| Activity | | Conditions | | Criterion |
| | | | | |
| **Level 2** | **COGNITIVE CONCEPTUALIZATION** | | **AFFECTIVE CONCEPTUALIZATION** | |
| Activity | Conditions | Criterion | Reinforcement indicator | Criterion |
| | | | | |
| **Level 1** | **COGNITIVE ASSOCIATIONS** | | **AFFECTIVE ASSOCIATIONS** | |
| Activity | Conditions | Criterion | Reinforcement | Criterion |
| | | | | |

**Figure 3-1**   Form: Summary of Teaching Objectives

check is made to see that the teachers-to-be understand their own emotional responses. Finally the kinds of creative self-directing activities that might be expected are outlined. The free and creative objectives cannot be specified in detail, but it is possible to define them in such a way that they can be recognized when they occur. The expectation that they will occur gives a different flavor to the whole process of defining behavioral objectives than would be the case if people were not thought of as free and self-directing.

## TAXONOMIES OF EDUCATIONAL OBJECTIVES

In evaluating or judging the effectiveness of the teaching-learning process, instructors typically prepare tests, the items of which correspond to the objectives of a curriculum unit.

The degree of congruence between the number of objectives that a student has mastered, as reflected by his answers to test questions, and the number of objectives sampled by the test affords the teacher and student an indication of how successful they have been. Teachers are becoming aware of the importance of the affective, or motivational, component of the learning hierarchy as comparable to the cognitive objectives of the school (Figure 3-2). Ways to organize objectives and evaluate the progress of pupils in the affective and psychomotor domains are outlined in subsequent sections.

### Cognitive Domain

*The Taxonomy of Educational Objectives: Cognitive Domain Handbook I* (Bloom et al., 1956) furnishes a basis for generating objectives that sample different levels of intellectual functioning and a framework around which test items can be written to parallel *inferred process objectives*. Within the cognitive domain, objectives are broadly divided into (1) knowledge and (2) intellectual abilities and skills. *Knowledge* can be considered the ability to recall or remember ideas or phenomena, when required, in much the same form in which they were stored. Some reorganization or regrouping is always necessary in the recovery of stored material, but in the general classification of knowledge, this transformation is minimal. The other subdivision incorporates a hierarchy of five *intellectual abilities and skills*. The items in both classifications are arranged from simple to complex and from concrete to abstract. Each of the subclasses of educational objectives defines a category in three ways: (1) by giving a description of the class, (2) by providing a list of educational objectives from the published literature, and (3) by including some illustrative test questions that represent the category.

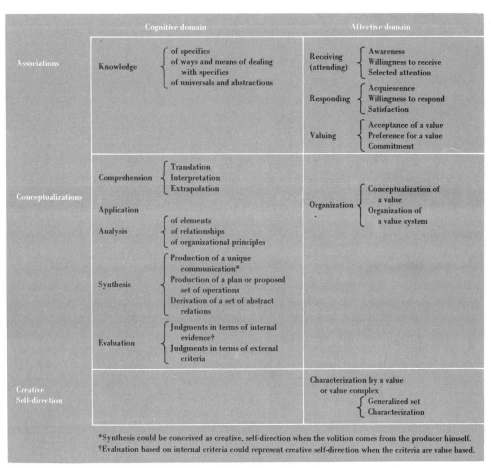

**Figure 3-2** Relationship of the learning-motivation model and Bloom's cognitive and Krathwohl's affective *taxonomies*.

**Knowledge** In the knowledge division, the range is from knowledge of specifics, such as the fact that Salem is the capital of Oregon, to knowledge of theories and structures, such as that relating to the changes that take place in the electron orbits of atoms under specific energy conditions. The reader is referred to the handbooks (Bloom et al., 1956; Krathwohl et al., 1964) for a complete treatment of any one of the topics.

**Knowledge of specifics** This category is defined as "the recall of specific and isolable bits of information" and is made up of two subdivisions, knowledge of terminology and knowledge of specific facts (Bloom et al., 1956, p. 63):

*Knowledge of terminology* includes the basic vocabulary items that must be mastered in any new field before much progress can be made in understanding it. An example of an educational objective would be "knowledge of the vocabulary of the fine arts sufficient to be able to read and converse intelligently." A sample question might be the multiple choice item (Bloom et al., p. 65):

*Directions:* In each group below select the numbered phrase that most nearly corresponds in meaning to the word at the head of that group. Put the number in the parentheses at the right.

**a.** Impressionism                                ( )
**1** The use of shadowy forms in painting to create an illusion
**2** The use of colors next to one another such that the eye sees them differently from the way they are actually placed on the canvas
**3** The placing of sharply lined objects close to one another
**4** The photographic reproduction of a scene to create a true impression of it

(Refer to the Summary of this chapter for answers to test items.)

*Knowledge of ways and means of dealing with specifics* includes the use of information such as conventions, trends and sequences, classifications and categories, criteria, and methodology. A knowledge of ways and means, within the Bloom hierarchy, implies that the particular system for dealing with information has been conceived by someone else and that the knowledge is acquired in its original form. A knowledge of a teaching method, read and reported accurately, would fall into this category.

**Knowledge of universals and abstractions** This is defined as "knowledge of the major ideas, schemata, and patterns by which phenomena and ideas are organized" (Bloom et al., 1956, p. 75). It is the most complex ordering of knowledge, and takes many of the specifics and methodological approaches and joins them into complex structures. The two subdivisions of this category are (1) knowledge of principles and generalizations and (2) knowledge of theories and structures. This latter subdivision is defined as "knowledge of the body of principles and generalizations, together with their interrelations, which present a clear, rounded, and systematic view of a complex phenomenon, problem, or field." The structure itself is the important element. An objective within this realm might be "knowledge of a relatively complete formulation of the theory of evolution." A test question for evaluating such knowledge might be (Bloom et al., 1956, pp. 76, 77):

*Directions:* Items a, b, and c, are concerned with possible evidence in support of the theory of biological evolution. Select from the key list the category to which the evidence mentioned in the item belongs.

**1** Comparative anatomy
**2** Comparative physiology
**3** Classification
**4** Embryology
**5** Paleontology
  **a** Intergrading forms of plants and animals differing from earlier species indicate that

evolutionary change is probably taking place today in all living organisms.  ( )

**b** Hematin crystals from the hemoglobin of various vertebrates have the same chemical composition.  ( )

**c** The human heart has two chambers at a very early developmental stage. (Bloom et al., 1956, p. 88)  ( )

### Intellectual Abilities and Skills

The second broad division of the cognitive domain consists of intellectual abilities and skills, which, in the *Taxonomy*, are ways of handling knowledge which may already be part of the background of the individual or which may have to be acquired prior to the various manipulations described in the following section. The emphasis in this area is on mentally organizing or reorganizing the knowledge basic to the thought processes involved, and normally represents conceptualization.

**Comprehension** The first of the abilities in the *Taxonomy* is *comprehension*, which, involves somewhat more than memory for knowledge. The comprehension may be of oral, written, pictured, or concrete presentations. In Bloom's definition, comprehension does not imply complete understanding of the material since higher levels of skills are involved in higher-order processing of intellectual materials. Three kinds of comprehension are subsumed under the general term: *translation, interpretation*, and *extrapolation*.

**Translation** requires the possession of adequate knowledge about the topic and knowledge of the transmuted form. One aspect of translation is the student's ability to interpret the subsections accurately, since if he lacks this ability, he is unlikely to be able to handle the larger message correctly when it hinges on the less complex part. Translations may be from abstract to concrete form, from abstract to more abstract form, or any number of similar transformations. Translation is a

foundation stone for the more complex skills of application, analysis, and synthesis.

An educational objective for translating from one symbolic form to another might be "the ability to translate an algebraic concept in mathematical form into visual or geometric form." An examination question illustrating this ability would be:

> **1** Newton's law of gravitation is expressed algebraically as $F = Mm/G_d z$, where $F$ represents force, $M$ and $m$ are two massses, $G$ is a constant, and $d$ represents the distance between the masses. Assuming that $M$ and $m$, as well as $G$, remain the same, or constant, which of the following graphs [Figure 3-3] shows how the force changes as the distance between the masses varies? (Bloom, p. 102)

**Interpretation** involves the student's ability to identify and comprehend the major ideas in a communication and to understand the relationships between them. This process goes beyond translation, but is less complex than analysis or evaluation, although it resembles these in many respects. A requirement is the understanding of the relationships between the parts and the ability to relate them to the already-stored material in the mind.

**Extrapolation** requires the student to take given information and build upon it. In a sense, this is the way a reader fills in the gaps in any written presentation. The assurance with which these extensions can be made depends on both the skills of the interpreter and the clarity of the communication that is being extended. Before an individual can carry out the extrapolation, he must first translate and interpret the document. Many errors of comprehension are due to the fact that the process of extrapolation is carried on without adequate regard for the limits to which the communication can be extended with assurance.

**Application** The next higher level of cognitive processing is *application.* In the *Taxon-*

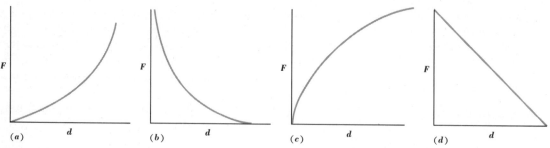

**Figure 3-3** Graphs for test questions involving the relation of force and distance. (*From Bloom et al., 1956, p. 102.*)

*omy*, application implies more than the ability to apply knowledge under direction. It also involves the probability that the student will apply the skills and abilities he developed in the solution of problems. One of the most important purposes in any field of study is that the knowledge become transferable, or operative in other contexts. In comprehension, the student is able to use the material if he is specifically asked to; in application, however, he demonstrates that he will actually do so under varying circumstances. An objective in this area would be "the ability to apply the learning-motivation model in a classroom situation." Testing for this principle is not easily carried out on a paper-and-pencil basis, but would be possible through extended observation of the teacher in his own classroom. The appraisal of application is a critical part of the whole evaluation process and one that should be developed and used to restructure curricular practice.

**Analysis** The process of comprehension is sharpened and formalized in analysis, which deals with form as well as content. When analysis functions at a high level of sophistication, it forms the basis of evaluation. In literary criticism, careful analysis and evaluation are fused into one matrix. Although there is a great deal of overlap between comprehension, analysis, and evaluation, there are differences in the processes, as evidenced by the fact that a person may comprehend the meaning of a

communication without being able to analyze it very effectively. Another person may be able to do the analysis but may make unsatisfactory evaluations on the basis of it. Analysis is subdivided in the *Taxonomy* into three parts: *analysis of elements, analysis of relationships,* and *analysis of organizational principles.*

**Analysis of elements** may reveal that although a well-written communication contains many parts that fit well together, the material contains unfounded assumptions. The identification of critical elements may be fundamental in determining the meaning of a communication. Some of the objectives of teaching for analysis include "skill in distinguishing facts from hypotheses" (p. 146) and "the ability to distinguish a conclusion from the statements that support it." (p. 146) The following test question would probe the ability to analyze literature (Bloom et al., 1956, p. 152):

1 "For what men say is that, if I am really just and
2 am not also thought just, profit there is none, but
3 the pain and loss on the other hand is unmistakable.
4 But if, though unjust, I acquire the reputation of
5 justice, a heavenly life is promised to me. Since then
6 appearance tyrannizes over truth and is lord of happi-
7 ness, to appearance I must devote myself. I will
8 describe around me a picture and shadow of virtue
9 to be the vestibule and exterior of my house; be-
10 hind I will trail the subtle and crafty fox."

Which of the following best states the conclusion of the argument?

1 "For what men say is" (line 1)
2 "if I am really just" (line 1)
3 "profit there is none" (line 2)
4 "appearance tyrannizes over truth and is lord of happiness" (lines 6 and 7)
5 "to appearance I must devote myself" (line 7)

**Analysis of relationships** reveals the way in which the elements in a communication fit together. Frequently material is unclear because the writer has related parts that are not equivalent. Arguments are used that are essentially non sequiturs, and while not necessarily obvious, the breaks serve to make communication misleading. When an editor checks to see that the headings in a piece of writing are parallel in construction, he is analyzing relationships. The statement "As teachers' salaries rise, the consumption of alcohol increases" contains another relationship that is subject to analysis. Extrapolation of this statement would imply a cause-and-effect relationship between the amount of money teachers earn and the amount they drink, but analysis shows that the two parts of the statement are independent and not necessarily related in any way. The ability to perform this kind of analysis is highly important in determining the validity of advertising claims that may be true as written but misleading as commonly extrapolated.

**Analysis of organizational principles** involves investigation of the structure and organization of the message. The way in which arguments are marshaled and presented has an influence on the meaning of the message. Often the intent is conveyed as much by the juxtaposition of the materials as by what is actually said. In countering an argument, analysis of the forces of these relationships is often necessary. Skill in cross-examination depends largely on the ability to analyze the presentation of the evidence for the more subtle nuances it contains and then on the ability to bring questions to bear on the points involved, making explicit—and often thereby destroying—certain implications that derive their importance from the structure of the argument. Among the objectives Bloom et al. (1956, p. 148) cite in this area are "the ability to infer the author's purpose, point of view, or traits of thought and feeling as exhibited in his work" and "ability to see the techniques used in persuasive materials, such as advertising, propaganda, etc."

**Synthesis** The fifth major category in the *Taxonomy* is synthesis. Whereas analysis consists in taking a communication apart to see its structure, synthesis is the opposite process—taking parts and putting them together into a new whole. Much of synthesis is creative, although some restructuring is by command and is done without much volition on the part of the student and so would not qualify as self-directed learning. In the *Taxonomy*, the process of synthesis is evaluated in terms of the student's product from which the process is inferred. There are three subdivisions of synthesis.

**Production of a unique communication** means conveying experience or a message to others. Suggested educational objectives include "the ability to tell a personal experience effectively" or "the ability to make an extemporaneous speech." Tests to evaluate this objective ordinarily require the writing of an essay, a poem, or a musical composition or the production of some other unique message (Bloom et al., 1956, p. 169).

**Production of a plan or proposed set of operations,** is the second subdivision. Whether the plan is carried out or not is not germane to the task of synthesis at this level. Quite regularly the plan needs to meet a set of specifications that have been determined beforehand. An objective peculiarly important to a teacher would be "the ability to plan a set of lessons." A test for this objective would involve a request to see the lesson plan, which would then be analyzed for the completeness with which it covers the lesson topic; the thoroughness with which probable contingencies have been anticipated, such as the need for audio-visual aids; and the provisions it makes for meeting the needs of deviant students in the class.

***Derivation of a set of abstract relations*** is a kind of synthesis in which the student may be building a classification system or may be generating new propositions or relations from given data or theories. The intellectual act in this synthesis consists in the production of a logically consistent and data-consistent schema. Guilford's model of intellect represents such a synthesis at a very high level (Chapter 15).

The following item would test the derivation of theory (Bloom et al., 1956, p. 184):

A housing concern has made some experiments on methods of heating houses. A room was constructed with walls that could be heated or refrigerated at the same time that air of any temperature was being circulated through the room. Several individuals were asked to record their sensations as the conditions were varied as follows:

| Trial | Wall temperature | Air temperature | Sensation |
|-------|------------------|-----------------|-----------|
| 1 | 85 | 85 | Uncomfortably hot |
| 2 | 85 | 50 | Uncomfortably hot |
| 3 | 70 | 85 | Comfortable |
| 4 | 70 | 70 | Comfortable |
| 5 | 70 | 50 | Comfortable |
| 6 | 50 | 50 | Very cold |
| 7 | 50 | 70 | Uncomfortably cold |
| 8 | 50 | 85 | Cold |

How can you explain the sensation of "coldness" by a person in a room where the air temperature is 85 and the wall temperature is 50 (all temperature Fahrenheit)? Consider the following questions and organize your thinking under the outline given below:

a Make all the suggestions you can which you believe will explain why a person is cold in a room where the air temperature is 85 and the wall temperature is 50. Give your reasons why you believe each of these suggestions will explain the phenomenon.

b What kinds of evidence would you want to collect which would enable you to decide among your suggested hypotheses?

c Now go over the suggestions which you have made above and select the one which you believe to be the "best" explanation and give your reasons for your selection.

**Evaluation** The last major category in the *Taxonomy* is evaluation. In this context, evaluation involves the use of standards either of internal consistency or of some external criteria. The emphasis is on a judgment, after careful analysis, and involves all the previous categories to some extent. Evaluation is differentiated from opinions, which may be snap judgments based on undifferentiated values that may or may not be applicable. Evaluation is not necessarily the last step in the process in problem solving since it may initiate new analysis, comprehension, or even the obtaining of new knowledge before proceeding with the problem solving. In this regard the evaluation is a recurring function similar to that conceived by Guilford (Chapter 15). Evaluation has some overtones of value judgments in the kinds of external criteria against which it is set. Schools have been careful about the way in which they have taught for evaluation of social relations because of the danger of special pleading, and in these areas the emphasis has usually been on internal consistency, although a document may be consistent and quite damnable on other grounds.

***Judgments in terms of internal evidence*** may be made "from such evidence as logical accuracy, consistency, and other internal criteria" (p. 188). The steps in this process are varied, but generally follow a process of analysis and then decision based on analysis. An objective cited is "judging by internal standards, the ability to assess general probability of accuracy in reporting facts from the care given to exactness of statement, documentation, proof, etc." (Bloom et al., 1956, pp. 188, 189).

**Judgments in terms of external criteria** is "evaluation of material with reference to selected or remembered criteria." Under this heading come comparisons with standard works, judgments about how well the material will fulfill certain roles, and judgments about how well the work satisfies the specifications, as in evaluating a set of building plans prepared from a set of specifications. Evaluation by categories means that a product or action may be judged excellent under some conditions but quite unsuitable in others. A formal evening gown is considered unsuitable classroom attire for either teacher or student, but the same dress may be entirely appropriate at a New Year's Eve ball (Bloom et al., 1956, p. 190).

An objective cited for the development of this level of thinking is "the ability to identify and appraise judgments and values that are involved in the choice of a course of action" (p. 192). This ability could be appraised by means of the following test item (Bloom et al., 1956, p. 200):

Jane is faced with the problem of selecting material for a school dress. The dress will receive lots of wear and will be laundered frequently. Which of the fabrics would be her best choice? [Samples of fabrics given as part of the test item.]

Check the qualities the fabric you choose possesses which make it supeior for Jane's purpose.

\_\_\_\_\_ **(a)** Material is colorfast to washing.
\_\_\_\_\_ **(b)** Material is crease-resistant.
\_\_\_\_\_ **(c)** There is little or no sizing in the material.
\_\_\_\_\_ **(d)** Material is easily cared for.
\_\_\_\_\_ **(e)** Material is soft and will drape easily.
\_\_\_\_\_ **(f)** Weave is firm, close and smooth.
\_\_\_\_\_ **(g)** Material is colorfast to sunlight.
\_\_\_\_\_ **(h)** Material will not show soil easily.
\_\_\_\_\_ **(i)** Design is *printed* with the grain.

This treatment of *Handbook I: Cognitive Domain* (Bloom et al.) has been extensive in the hope that the reader will gain a substantial understanding of some of the ways in which the more complex objectives of the schools can be delineated and means devised for testing to see whether these goals are being achieved. Young teachers would increase their effectiveness by using the *Handbook* in its complete form as a standard reference, with a regular review of their lesson plans, to analyze the number and level of goals being achieved. Decisions about ways of increasing the range of the goals would then be made more intelligently.

### Relation of the Cognitive Domain to Guilford's *Intellectual Operations*

Guilford (1967) in *Nature of Human Intelligence* approached the problem of classifying and describing cognitive functions by factorial analysis of the responses of many subjects to intelligence test items. He distinguished between the *content* (e.g., figural or semantic), the *process* (e.g., memory or evaluation), and the *product* (e.g., classes or implications). This framework is also useful as the basis for developing behavioral objectives in which the nature of the learner's thinking process is important and must be inferred (Figure 3-4). The products are arranged in a hierarchy from simple "units" to complex extrapolation. In Guilford, each intellectual operation involves all three dimensions: content, process, and product. Before attempting to write objectives in this format, the teacher should study Guilford's construct of intelligence (Chapter 15).

### AFFECTIVE DOMAIN

Perhaps the most intensive and systematic attempt to include teaching for affective learning took place in what has come to be called the Eight-Year Study (Chamberlin, Chamberlin, Drought, & Scott, 1942). In this project a number of private and public schools persuaded a number of universities and colleges to accept their graduates even though their pattern of studies had been different from the entrance requirements published by the institution. Thus freed of the domination of the colleges to which the students might go, the high schools were able to undertake radical experiments in curricular development that reversed some of the hallowed concepts of the proper way to organize a school. In some schools, curricula were built in which the emphasis was on affective learning, with an implicit assumption that knowledge of content would follow when beliefs and attitudes were made the primary focus. The follow-up of the students as they attended college vindicated the hypothesis. Academically the students did as well as other students who had had more formal preparation. In cocurricular activities such as campus politics, campus journalism, and social action, the experimental students were substantially more successful than the controls. Many of the questions in the handbook on the affective domain (Krathwohl,

Bloom, and Masia, 1964) came from the Eight-Year Study.

The committee that developed the *Taxonomy of Educational Objectives, Handbook II: Affective Domain* adopted a principle of increasing intensity of the affect as the base on which the ordering of objectives would take place. In general, the most elemental objective would be to make the student dimly aware that a phenomenon existed. Increasingly complex objectives would involve the student's being willing to attend to the material, responding positively, going out of his way to respond, systematizing the responding, and finally having a value system that dominated his life outlook. The trend here is from simple attention to dominance of the affect in the person's life. This ordering made it possible to define and classify emotionally toned objectives. The locus of the affective learning is thus the individual. The way in which the affects are internalized became a crucial concept in the structuring of the *Taxonomy* (Figure 3-2).

Krathwohl et al. (1964) subdivided the objectives in the affective domain into five major categories with thirteen subcategories. These will be listed with a brief explanation of the major categories only. The reader is referred

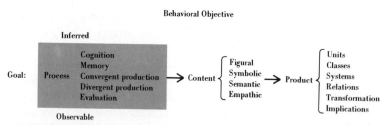

**Figure 3-4** The teacher's goals for a course or a student are expanded to describe inferred or process objectives according to Guilford's intellectual operations. Content, representing given information or stimulus material, is a more complex concept than Mager's "conditions." Product represents a hierarchy of observable outcomes or responses reflecting newly generated information which could be extended to specify criterion levels of behavior.

to the handbook for a more complete treatment.

## Receiving (Attending)

Awareness
Willingness to receive
Selective attention

In this level of the *Taxonomy*, the student becomes increasingly willing to attend to the material being presented, although all parts of the receiving are at an uncritical level. At the level of selective attention, discrimination takes place. Keeping a list of books to read on a topic would indicate that a student is attending to the common topic of the books.

## Responding

Acquiescence
Willingness to respond
Satisfaction

There is more active participation by the student at this level of the *Taxonomy* than at the "receiving" level. Acquiescing represents sufficient involvement to move out of oneself. Much of the affective response envisioned by Krathwohl at this level is similar to what many teachers call "interest," but the term "interest" covers a wide range of activities and is less precise in its meaning. Responding at the satisfaction level probably assures continued participation.

## Valuing

Acceptance of a value
Preference for a value
Commitment

Valuing is a process of internalization in which the individual personalizes the worth of certain beliefs, objects, or attitudes. At the first level the valuing is fairly passive. The student accepts the value, but without going out of his way to practice it. In the succeeding stages the valuing becomes more active. Testing for valuing seeks evidence of some considerable intensity. At the stage of commitment, the duration of the valuing is significant. Perhaps one of the most important aspects of valuing is the significance the individual places on the object of value. At the level of commitment, valuing is not forced from the outside—the student accepts it as part of himself.

## Organization

Conceptualization of a value
Organization of a value system

At the organization level in the *Taxonomy*, the relationships between different values are brought to the forefront of the individual's thinking. Krathwohl expressed some doubt about whether this organization takes place at the level designated or whether it may not have already started to form at a considerably lower level of involvement. The difference between the stages is primarily in the complexity of the organization. As the organization takes place, the possibility of change of attitude or value either by addition or by replacement becomes less likely. At the same time, the certainty with which the person is able to act on the values involved increases. He is more sure because he has analyzed and conceptualized what it is he believes and why he has arrived at this particular method of dealing with his problems. Under these circumstances, he is able to withstand considerable buffeting and still persist in the beliefs he has established. Testing for the organization of an individual's value system is difficult, but as Krathwohl shows in his examples, it is by no means impossible.

## Characterization by a Value or Value Complex

Generalized set
Characterization

At this highest level of the *Taxonomy*, the person has developed a philosophy of life—he knows who he is. Krathwohl pointed out that arrival at this stage of development seldom takes place before the individual has been out of school for a considerable period of time. There is an interaction between the affective and the cognitive spheres, and the goal is one of personal integrity. As Krathwohl conceives characterization, few people achieve a status in which their life-style is completely dominated by a value complex. Krathwohl said: "The great humanitarian figures of history—Socrates, Christ, Lincoln, Gandhi, Einstein—have achieved the characterization we refer to at this level. Each is universally held in high esteem precisely because his philosophy of life characterizes and pervades all of his behavior." Many students move toward becoming characterized by a value complex as they commit themselves to become scientists, doctors, historians, or humanitarians. As their dedication and role identification increase, the externalization of their role concept becomes increasingly obvious (Krathwohl et al., 1964, p. 171).

**Relation of Affective Domain to Learning-Motivation Model** The relationship between the steps in the hierarchy of the affective domain and the motivation sequence of the learning-motivation model is striking. The first three major categories—receiving, responding, and valuing—are stages of increasing complexity that can be achieved on an association basis. Most of the description in the *Taxonomy* is of the ways in which the associations are formed. The organization level is one of conceptualization of various kinds. In the *Taxonomy*, the term conceptual-

ization is used in much the same way it is in the learning-motivation model and with reference to precisely the same kinds of affects. Finally at the highest stage, characterization by a value or value complex, the same interaction of the cognitive and affective aspects of the person's life comes to the fore. In the *Taxonomy* there is more emphasis on the integration of the values into a complete whole, while in the learning-motivation model considerable emphasis is placed on the possibility of the young person's exemplification of self-directing activity being piecemeal and imperfect. A student may show these characteristics very clearly in certain rather narrow phases of his life, while operating at a much lower level of sophistication at other levels that involve different affects. The more completely unified and self-directing the individual becomes, the closer he will come to the unity anticipated in the *Taxonomy* (Figure 3-2).

### Psychomotor Domain

In the original analysis of objectives, the *Taxonomy* study group delineated a collection of objectives in an area that they designated as the *psychomotor domain*. The committee had very little call to prepare examination questions for this field and found few questions that fit comfortably within this area of learning. These objectives related to handwriting, physical education, trade training, and physical manipulation of materials and objects. Many important aspects of this kind of learning take place before the child comes to school. The early learning of bodily control, which has permanent effects on the self-concept that the individual eventually develops, is nearly completed before the child enters school. Psychomotor functions that develop during the school years are often outside the curriculum that is evaluated through a testing program. As the importance of early childhood education became known, an interest in the psychomotor domain was revived.

Kibler, Barker, and Miles (1970, pp. 66–75) defined a hierarchy of psychomotor objectives that focused on early childhood and physical education. Their classification included gross bodily movements, finely coordinated movements, nonverbal communication behaviors, and speech behaviors. Teaching objectives that cover the psychomotor domain will very likely be extended and tested by these or other researchers.

## SUMMARY

The ultimate goal of teaching is to enable the student to set goals for learning and to accomplish them on his own. Teachers can help students reach long-range goals by defining objectives in terms that can be measured. Highly defined goals have evolved from the work of people in the programmed learning field, from test makers, and from researchers in behavioral psychology. The work of these groups in stating behavioral objectives for the learner, rather than focusing on the aims of the instructor, has developed a requirement for teacher expertise in writing objectives. As learning processes become complex, interpretation of the changes in students moves from observing overt behavior to interpreting inferred reactions.

When writing behavioral objectives, five elements are needed: (1) the learner is designated, (2) action verbs specify the observable behaviors or the inferred processes, (3) conditions or stipulations describe the learning task, (4) standard or criterion of acceptable or expected performance is stated, and (5) the nature of the product is indicated. This level of specificity when stating objectives makes possible the construction of test items that indicate success or failure in meeting the intended criterion.

The learning-motivation model provides a format from which to develop behavioral objectives that extend teaching goals from associations to conceptualizations and creative self-direction for both teachers and students. Objectives should be directed to affective as well as cognitive outcomes.

Bloom et al. developed a hierarchy of cognitive educational objectives that included (1) knowledge and (2) intellectual abilities and skills which were arranged in a hierarchy of inferred processes: comprehension, application, analysis, synthesis, and evaluation. In the same way, Krathwohl et al. developed a hierarchy for the affective domain that included receiving or attending, responding, valuing, organization, and characterization by a value or value complex. Kibler et al. published an outline of psychomotor skills which form a basis for objectives in physical education, early childhood education, and vocational training. Guilford's *intellectual operations* form still another construct from which the teacher can write objectives that are comprehensive, meaningful, and practical.

To the student whose curiosity was piqued by the sample test items, the key:

### Answers to Test Questions

| | |
|---|---|
| Impressionism | (2) |
| Biological evolution | a (5) |
| | b (2) |
| | c (4) |
| Newton's G | (b) |
| Literature | (5) |
| Home economics | (a–h inclusive). |

## SELF-DIRECTING ACTIVITIES

1 Write goals for yourself in one of the courses you are taking.
2 Using these goals, write a five-part statement of objectives.
3 Analyze a curriculum resource guide in a specific grade and content area. Classify the objectives as (a) behavioral, (b) inferred, and (c) nonobservable.

# Chapter 4

(*Courtesy of the United Nations*)

# FORMING COGNITIVE ASSOCIATIONS

The learning-motivation model, which deals with associations, is expanded in this chapter so that you can:

€   Trace the historical sequence in the development of conditioning theory

€   Design reinforcement schedules for teaching situations

€   Establish distinct models of classical and operant conditioning

€   Identify and assess the value of associative learning in school curricula

€   Utilize cognitive associative functions in developing conceptualization and encouraging creative self-direction in students

€   Use and define the following terms:
    contiguity
    reinforcement schedule
    superstitious learning
    biofeedback
    alpha waves
    noxious stimuli

Association learning is primarily additive in nature. When bits of information are linked together because they occur together in time, this linkage involves the pleasure and/or punishment centers in the brain. It includes classical and operant conditioning, under which paired associate learning, serial learning, and rote learning can usually be subsumed. Many kinds of behavior—including much schoolwork, most attitudes, most emotional habits, and many personality structures—are learned as conditioned responses. Graphs that illustrate association learning tend to show slow and steady increases in efficiency, although irregular countours, due to regressions and short spurts, are common (Figure 4-1). The slope of the performance line is quite smooth in contrast to that of conceptualization, which seems to progress by sharp rises to new plateaus (Figure 4-2). Each learning experience can move a student a finite distance toward creative self-direction when the teacher has this purpose in mind.

As individuals react to their environments, the multisensory inputs are woven together to form the ongoing present. Sights, sounds, smells, and tactile pressures, along with sensations of heat and cold, are interwoven to create ongoing experience. Part of that experi-

ence is an affective loading that makes repetition or avoidance of the task probable in the future.

Conceptual memory is constructed, or abstracted, from this flow of the present into the past. Past ideas and present experiences overlap and interweave to give an individual a present intellectual content that is manageable. An example of how separate associations are abstracted into a single concept can be understood in how we think about "dog." We know about dogs from many, many sight-sound-smell experiences with particular dogs, but when we think "dog," it is usually a composite of many sensory experiences rather than a single unique experience at a single point in time.

Much of the sorting of sensory input is almost mechanical and results in association learning. This chapter discusses the historical backgrounds of association learning; operant conditioning, with particular attention to the work of B. F. Skinner; classical conditioning; and finally the application of association learning in particular subject-matter areas.

## HISTORICAL BACKGROUND OF ASSOCIATION LEARNING

Much of the early research on school learning concerned ways in which children memorize most easily, the effects of massed and spaced practice, and other easily measured aspects of learning. The early laboratory experiments were quickly seen as having importance for the classroom. Some of the important background work, such as that of Pavlov, is basic to an understanding of the processes of learning.

### Thorndike: Contiguity and Effect

Edward L. Thorndike (1913), the father of educational psychology, was one of the first to study association learning and apply his find-

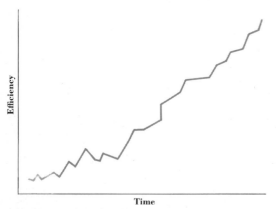

**Figure 4-1**  A cat in a difficult puzzle box—association learning.

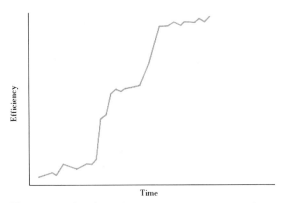

**Figure 4-2** Ape in a simple structural situation. Concept formed at sharp rise.

ings to the classroom. He conceived of learning as having two elements: *contiguity* and *effect*. According to the theory of contiguity, associations are formed between events because they occur together in time. Learning also occurs as the result of effect. According to the theory of effect, associations are formed because of the pleasantness or unpleasantness that results from the activity.

Thorndike thought of learning as a process of forming bonds between neurons. The principal problem was to find ways of forming bridges across the synapses (Chapter 9). To depict the increasing ease with which the bonds can be formed, he used the illustration of several people making a pathway through a hedge. The first person who pushes through has difficulty, but each time the same opening is used, the passage becomes smoother and more effortless. In the same way, the original bonds are difficult to build, but as time goes on and the same connections are made, the process becomes more and more effortless.

Thorndike's theory of intelligence suggested that the more bonds formed in the brain, the more intelligent a person becomes. He believed that the school should help learners systematically increase the number of bonds that are formed, should see that bonds are formed in areas that are going to be needed, and should see that the learning situations are pleasant. To put his ideas into concrete form, he developed arithmetic texts, dictionaries, spellers and materials for reading instruction—all based on a selection of material that the students would need in their immediate lives or in the reasonably near future. Jonçich (1968) writes, "Thorndike's . . . goal . . . [was] the establishment of an experimental science of man, a science of human nature describable in the terms of matter and energy" (p. 7). For many years Thorndike was used as a point of departure when exploring theories of learning. During his most important years Teachers College, Columbia University, was the preeminent school for advanced teacher education in America. Many school superintendents and more professors of education studied under him; therefore his influence on American education has been enormous.

### Pavlov and Bechterev: Classical Conditioning

Two Russian scientists, Pavlov (1910), a physiologist, and von Bechterev (1913), a neurologist, conducted experiments for half a century on the nature of classical conditioning. Their work established the relation of learning to the closeness of events in time. Almost all readers are familiar with Pavlov's studies of dogs. In the typical classical conditioning experiment, a dog was operated on so that the researcher could collect the saliva it secreted and measure the number of drops. Meat powder was blown into the dog's mouth, and a base level of salivation was established. At the next step, a bell was rung just prior to the insertion of the meat powder, and the saliva was again collected. After this process had been repeated several times, the bell was rung without the insertion of meat powder. Pavlov found that the conditioned dog salivated at about the same rate when the bell was rung without the insertion of the meat powder as when meat powder was used.

The training process can be diagramed as shown in Figure 4-3. The meat powder was called an unconditioned stimulus (UCS)— which was an unfortunate translation from the Russian word meaning "unconditional." The salivation was called an unconditioned response (UCR). The bell was called a conditioned stimulus (CS), and the salivation then became a conditioned response (CR).

Certain characteristics of this kind of conditioning should be noted. (1) The relationship between the UCS and the UCR is normally an automatic connection formed early in life. The conditioned response is built from strong primitive connections although secondary conditioning is possible—for example, by connecting a colored light to the bell. (2) The proximity of the CS and the UCS in time is important, with best results being obtained when the CS precedes the UCS by about one-half second. Given these conditions of primacy and contiguity, conditioning can be established in very simple organisms as well as in Homo sapiens. The basic associative potential, the possibility of substituting one stimulus for another in the nervous system, seems to be a fundamental characteristic of the nervous system. Neural patterns become linked because events occur at the same time.

Often it is difficult to separate the effects of classical conditioning from those of operant conditioning. With the rise in popularity of behavior modification, which is usually considered operant conditioning, a renewed interest in the work of Pavlov has developed. Franks (1969) entitled the first chapter of *Behavior Therapy: Appraisal and Status* "Behavior Therapy and Its Pavlovian Origins." Much of Pavlov's later work explored learning situations that now would be classed as operant in nature although he did not bifurcate conditioning along the lines of classical and operant stages. Pavlov, who had won a Nobel Prize in physiology before he began his research on learning, was interested in the neurological foundations that made learning possible. Pavlov's influence on Soviet psychology can be gauged by the sixty-page references to his work in Cole and Maltzman (1969) *A Handbook of Contemporary Soviet Psychology.* This is twice the number of references to Luria or Vygotskii, who have become the most cited contemporary authorities.

## Guthrie: Learning, a Factor of Contiguity

Guthrie (1952), who was for many years the dean of the graduate school at the University of Washington in Seattle, developed an interesting theory of learning that is closely related to research on classical conditioning. Guthrie claimed that we learn movements by contiguity in time. He believed that thought is dependent on slight movements, particularly movements of the vocal cords but those involving other muscles as well. Learning, according to this theory, is completed in one operation. Repetition does nothing to strengthen the process, and reinforcement or affect has nothing to do with learning either. The apparent benefits of practice in learning to shoot baskets in basketball, for example, are due not to any additional learning the practice brings, but to the necessity of learning the various movements involved in such a complex activity and to the complex patterns that arise when what was learned on the last trial is

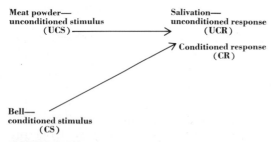

**Figure 4-3** Classical conditioning. A bell is rung, and meat powder is given to the dog, who salivates. After repeated associations, the bell alone produces salivation—the conditioned response.

replaced with new learning. Some examples of Guthrie's reasoning may be helpful.

A mother went to him after a public lecture to ask his advice about training her son to hang up his coat when he came into the house. A conversation followed:

*Guthrie:* Your son comes into the house and throws his coat on the floor? Do you tell him to come and pick up his coat and hang it in his room?

*Mother:* Yes, I do.

*Guthrie:* You see, there's a sequence of cues your son has learned as he comes in: the sight of the doorknob, the pull of the door on his arm, the smell of dinner cooking. He throws down his coat, goes to his room, is scolded, and then picks up his coat and hangs it up. I suggest that next time he put the coat back on, go outside, and come back in again. If he's thinking about hanging up his coat, these same cues become linked with his going to his room to do it. If he doesn't learn the new pattern at once, have him go back to the street and establish a longer sequence of cues.

According to the account, the new regime worked exactly as Guthrie had predicted. The new pattern persisted for several weeks.

Using this technique, Guthrie developed three patterns for changing undesirable behavior. Each of these requires finding ways to ensure the establishment of new behavior—in the presence of old stimuli—to replace the unwanted patterns. The first scheme involved wearing down the trainee so that more desirable behavior took over and became operative in the presence of old stimuli. An example of this would be the breaking of a horse. The wrangler gets on and the colt bucks at the unaccustomed weight on its back, but if the wrangler persists, the horse gets tired and finds itself with the weight still on its back. Fatigue finally forces the horse to walk normally, so that the next time it has a weight on its back it will walk or run as it did at the *end* of the training session. The same technique

has been used with children who cry because they are afraid of the dark. If they are allowed to cry until they give up and find themselves in the dark without crying, they will have established a new pattern—being in the dark without crying.

Guthrie's second technique involved keeping the new stimulus within the tolerance of the old pattern. In breaking a horse, this would consist of first gentling him by putting a hand on his back, eventually adding a light blanket, then a heavier load. Finally the horse is saddled, and a rider can mount him. Each addition of weight must not be large enough to cause the horse to buck or toss. Using this technique with the child who fears the dark would involve diminishing the light gradually until finally he finds himself in the dark without crying.

The third pattern involved presenting the stimulus when a competing response was in progress so that the stimulus became associated with the new response rather than the old. The child who cries at the sight of a furry animal—a conditioned response—can be trained to accept the same animal if it is presented to him when he is eating a favorite food. The association is established between the animal and the desirable food stimulus situation. Care must be taken with this technique, since the animal could become the dominant stimulus and condition distaste for the food. The learning that results from these patterns requires repetition in order not to become extinct.

While Franks (1969) looks to the work of Pavlov as basic to behavior modification, Paul (1969) finds certain phases of behavior therapy, particularly systematic desensitization, to be direct application to Guthrie's principles for changing behavior. Homme, de Baca, Cottingham, and Homme (1971) also find the training programs developed by Guthrie fundamental to successful behavior modification programs (Chapter 5).

Guthrie's theory may not be as universal as he thought, but it explains many learning situations that might otherwise be baffling to teachers. The child who has excellent work habits in Miss Smith's room becomes sloppy and careless in Miss Jones's room. The two stimulus situations are different, and the child responds to each according to the associations he has learned. Unfortunately, no cues have been developed that would make transfer to other settings possible.

## OPERANT CONDITIONING

At the beginning of the historical discussion of association learning, mention was made of E. L. Thorndike's (1913) hypothesis that learning occurs as a result of contiguity or effect. He stated: "When a modifiable connection between a situation and a response is made and is accompanied or followed by a satisfying state of affairs, that connection's strength is increased; when made and accompanied or followed by an annoying state of affairs, its strength is decreased" (p.4).

In terms of the learning-motivational model, Thorndike's law of effect is the linkage of the associations formed to the pleasure or punishment centers. The association is probably strengthened by repetition in the imagination, with the consequent pleasure stimulation, as well as the result of practice when the association can be made again in actuality. A decrease in strength of the connection seems to be due to the tendency to avoid those connections that are tied to the punishment centers. Some forgetting is avoidance response.

### Skinner: Operant Conditioning

The most notable exponent of the use of effect in learning has been B. F. Skinner (1953), of Harvard University. He gave the name "operant conditioning" to the process of learning which he studied and distinguished

from classical conditioning. In classical conditioning, the stimulus leading to a well-defined result is replaced with a substitute conditioned stimulus. In operant conditioning, a response is selected and reinforced. The essence of operant conditioning is to ensure one response over a number of other possible responses in the same general stimulus situation. The model may be illustrated by putting an earth worm into a T maze in which one arm leads to soft, moist earth and the other to sandpaper (Figure 4-4). The earthworm is positively reinforced by the moist-earth side, and negatively reinforced by the rough, scratchy environment when it enters the sandpaper side. Soon it learns to make the turn that leads to the moist earth. As many stimulus cues as possible are removed, so that the learning is made to depend on the reinforcing effect of the choice.

In most of Skinner's operant conditioning experiments, the negative reinforcement is eliminated and learning is based on positive reinforcement alone. In the experiment with the earthworm, there is no well-defined stimulus that would make the worm's movement along the main corridor of the maze predictable, and certainly no stimulus is apparent that leads to a right rather than a left turn. Worms tend to wander, and given this slight cause can

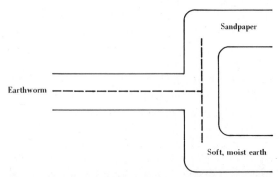

**Figure 4-4** Operant conditioning. The earthworm soon learns to make the turn leading to the moist earth.

be conditioned to wander in specific ways. The characteristics of operant conditioning, then, are (1) a moving organism, (2) a point at which various alternatives are possible, and (3) one alternative that is in some way more beneficial to the organism than the other. Although Skinner would not use these terms to explain reinforcement, the organism learns to choose the reinforced or more pleasure-producing response with great regularity.

Experimental work has been done using many kinds of animals, as well as children, with operant conditioning as the modus vivendi. In much of Skinner's research, pigeons or rats were used, in what has come to be called a Skinner box (Figure 4-5). When used with pigeons, this experimental device consists of an enclosed space; three sides are made of glass or other material, and in the fourth is set a disc or other apparatus that is connected to a food tray, a light, a buzzer, and a mechanism for recording the number of times the pigeon pecks in a given period. The apparatus can be run automatically around the clock, and generates vast quantities of data.

**Building a Response Pattern** Most of Skinner's research explored ways in which the response pattern varies when different schedules of reinforcement are applied. The initial stages of getting response patterns started are very important, both to teachers who are eager to apply the model in the classroom and to the research worker who wants to replicate the experimental studies. The principal problem in starting the training of pigeons is to shape their behavior so that they will peck at a disc—a response that is not native to pigeons. The shaping may be initiated by reinforcing the pigeon each time he moves toward the desired goal. The steps are usually small, the first being to have the pigeon locate the feeding tray. Skinner demonstrated that this learning can be accomplished by a gradual process that requires close observation of the bird and

**Figure 4-5** The key-pecking apparatus for pigeons. In the typical experiment, the pigeon is reinforced for pecking the key when it is illuminated. Placing filters or a monochromator between the light source and the key makes it possible to vary the intensity and hue of the light falling upon the translucent. key. (*From Guttman, N., and Kalish, H. I., "Experiments in discrimination." P. 78.* © *1958 by Scientific American, Inc. All rights reserved.*)

provision of food at critical times. Some of Skinner's associates found that this first bit of learning could be expedited by making a trail of food leading directly to the food tray. Once the location of the food tray has been learned, the experimenter can shape the bird's behavior, so that it will peck at the disc, by reinforcing it with food each time it comes closer to the desired response. In the early training period, every correct response is rewarded with food. After a connection between pecking at the disc and a food reinforcement has been thoroughly established, many different kinds of schedules can be set up.

In teacher-student relationships, the importance of establishing thoroughly the connection between the reinforcement and some phase of desired behavior cannot be over-emphasized. The establishment of the reinforcement is more complex than in the case of the pigeons, for whom food is sufficient as a reward. The classroom contains many students who have diverse needs and for whom there are many potential modes of reinforcement or reward. The efficacy of food as a reinforcer for the pigeons is assured by keeping them at 75 percent of their normal body weight. Teachers are not able to use starvation as a motivating device. They must be both careful and skillful as they analyze the needs of the individual child in order to determine what will be reinforcing to him.

One technique that has been used with success is to establish a token economy in which the children can exchange tokens for things they want. One grade 4 teacher organized a store in the classroom which he stocked with yo-yo strings, candy, gum, pencils, hair clips, and other articles attractive to fourth graders. The children could exchange their tokens for the articles in the store. This ensured that the reinforcer was of their own choosing. Montgomery and McBurney (1971) used a token economy in working with severely mentally retarded children at Camarillo State Hospital, California. The investigators were able to control meals, ground privileges, and room conditions, as well as treats, so that real needs would be found that could be reinforced. While some items or behaviors such as teacher praise are reinforcing to most children, they will not work with all children. To be a reinforcer, an activity or an article must be wanted by the particular student.

After Skinner's pigeons had been conditioned to the connection between disc pecking and food, reinforcement schedules were arranged that gradually changed from a reward on every successful trial to reinforcement on an intermittent basis. Two variations were used: one based on the work ratio (number of pecks) and the other based on the time interval. Activities built under schedules of intermittent reinforcement are much harder to extinguish—to stop—than activities developed on schedules of regular reinforcement. An illustration of regular versus intermittent results might clarify this piont. If a car starts every time the starter is activated, the driver is less likely to keep on trying the starter to the point of running down the battery than is the person whose starter catches on an indefinite basis—sometimes it starts on the first try, and other times not until perhaps the tenth try.

**Fixed Interval Reinforcement** Students in secondary school and college often act as though they were operating on a fixed interval schedule of reinforcement. Just before an examination they study very hard, then relax until another test looms on the horizon, when the intense activity starts all over again. In *intermittent reinforcement* at fixed intervals, the pigeon is gradually conditioned to a schedule in which it is rewarded for the first peck after an interval, e.g., two minutes (Figure 4-6). The long period during which few pecks at the disc are made is shown on the graph as the flat part of the stairs. This is followed by a period of intense pecking where the activity curve is very steep, terminating in the reinforcement, after which the cycle repeats. Apes and rats, as well as pigeons, show this same staircase work graph when they are reinforced on a fixed time schedule. In establishing these intermittent schedules, it is necessary to move gradually from reinforcement after every response to reinforcement after very short intervals, and eventually to reinforcements after long intervals.

**Variable Interval Reinforcement** One way to avoid the tendency of students to slack off after a test and also to cut down on their excessive studying just before another test is to give quizzes in a random fashion throughout the term. Students are advised that the

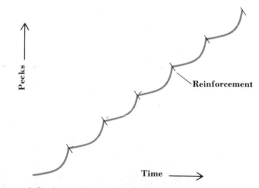

**Figure 4-6** Intermittent reinforcement—fixed interval.

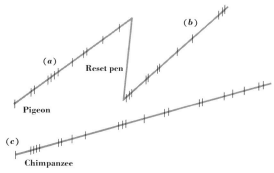

**Figure 4-7** Variable interval reinforcement. a, b, c (*From Skinner, B. F., The experimental analysis of behavior, © 1957, American Scientist, vol. XLV. P. 347. By permission of the author and publisher.*)

tests will be coming, but they are not told when. In work with animals, scattering the reinforcements in this way leads to work output patterns that are quite different from that which results from fixed interval reinforcement. An average time interval is selected during which a certain number of reinforcements are given, but these are dispersed over the time interval in such a way that one reinforcement might follow right after another, or there might be quite a long period between reinforcements.

Work output that is reinforced on a variable interval basis averaging three minutes is shown in Figure 4-7. Graphs *a* and *b* show the effect of reinforcement on the output of a pigeon who is as likely to be reinforced on the next peck as on any other. Graph *c* shows the output of a chimpanzee who works more slowly than the pigeon. The output in both cases shows no sudden spurts of work and also no slacking off. Steady, continuous work is the result of this kind of reinforcement schedule in pigeons, chimpanzees, and children.

**Fixed Ratio Reinforcement**   On the theory that they would improve performance, teaching machines were designed that reinforce students after *each bit of work* by assuring the student of the correctness of his

response. When working with animals, researchers have found it possible to schedule reinforcements with a counter rather than a timer. In this way, a pigeon can be reinforced after it has made a specified number of pecks. This schedule is known as a *fixed ratio schedule.* The more work the pigeon does, the more food it receives. Work output was increased when a pigeon was reinforced after every 200 pecks (Figure 4-8). The steepness of the graph shows a very high work output. There is a small rest period immediately after each reinforcement, but the work is accomplished at a high level of speed. Huston (1968), who used intracranial stimulation as the method of reinforcement, reported success in building a fixed ratio schedule by gradually decreasing the size of all reinforcements but the last, rather than by gradually lengthening the interval between reinforcements.

Teaching schedules have been devised that have the advantages of piecework—that is, ratios that enable a student to increase his performance and his reinforcement on an intermittent basis determined by the number of bits produced. Students work very hard if they can move through school purely on the·basis of attainment. Under such circumstances, the goals of education need to be completely specified, and very precise measures of attainment have to be developed. Mastery learning as developed by Bloom (1971) is a step in this

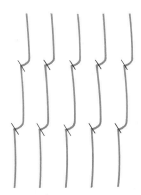

**Figure 4-8**   Fixed ratio reinforcement.

direction. The interest in performance objectives with highly specified criteria is a similar move.

**Variable Ratios** These schedules give payoff for production averaged around a predetermined rate. Gambling operators in Reno and Las Vegas run their machines on a variable ratio schedule which is advantageous from their point of view. The *variable ratio schedule* accounts for the element of uncertainty to the patron—the next pull may always be the lucky one. By making the schedule on a ratio rather than an interval basis, it is possible to ensure that the house will receive the intended proportion of the money entering the machine. With a time interval machine, a period of disuse could be to the player's advantage. Schools have not made use of this kind of schedule to increase learning efficiency. The slopes of performance are very similar to those achieved with fixed ratio scheduling, although the small steps at the point of reinforcement are often missing.

**Mixed Schedules of Reinforcement** Skinner (1957) wrote:

> Interval and ratio schedules have different effects for several reasons. When a reinforcement is scheduled by a timer, the probability of reinforcement increases during any pause, and the first reponse after a pause is especially likely to be reinforced [because the pause uses part of the time interval]. On ratio schedules, responses which are part of short runs are likely to be reinforced. Moreover, when a given schedule of reinforcement has had a first effect, the performance which develops becomes itself an important part of the experimental situation. This performance, in combination with the schedule, arranges certain probable conditions at the moment of reinforcement. Sometimes a schedule produces a performance which maintains just those conditions which perpetuate the performance. Some schedules generate a progressive change. Under

still other schedules the combination of schedule and performance yields conditions at reinforcement which generate a different performance, which in turn produces conditions at reinforcement which restore the earlier performance [p. 349].

An experimenter can decide to reinforce only responses that are preceded by a short pause, e.g., three seconds. Under these conditions, the slope of the work curve immediately falls off. In another schedule, only responses that are parts of short runs will be reinforced, in which case the work curve immediately speeds up. Both these sequences can be combined into a self-regulatory sequence with a start in a low output reinforced after a pause of three seconds, followed by a burst that is reinforced as part of a short, fast run, which in turn leads back to the need for a pause. The effect is a bit like a roller coaster and is an accentuation of the steps characteristic of the fixed interval schedule. Figure 4-9 shows a portion of such a double sequence. Pigeons can learn such schedules without any external cues. Schedules can also be combined and the performance triggered by association with specific cues. Figure 4-10 shows a performance graph of a pigeon that had been reinforced on a three-minute fixed interval schedule cued by a red light on the key, a variable interval schedule with a one-minute average

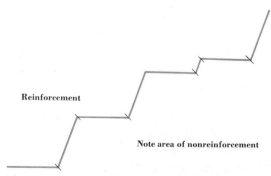

**Reinforcement**

**Note area of nonreinforcement**

**Figure 4-9**   Pause, run reinforcement sequence.

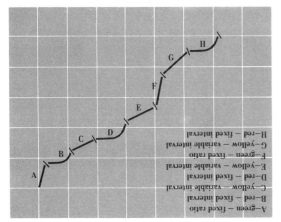

**Figure 4-10** Mixed schedules cued by colors. (*From Skinner, B. F., The experimental analysis of behavior. © 1957, American Scientist, vol. XLV. P. 351. By permission of the author and publisher.*)

time cued by a yellow light, and a fixed ratio schedule with reinforcement after 15 pecks cued by a green light. Which light is showing at points A, B, C, D, E, F, G, and H? The pigeon knows!

It is possible for a single organism to react selectively to different kinds of reinforcement schedules at the same time. Figure 4-11 *a* and *b* shows the results of reinforcing a chimpanzee on a fixed ratio basis for operating a toggle switch with his right hand, while at the same time reinforcing him on a variable interval basis for operating a switch with his left hand. The characteristic work patterns are evident in the two graphs; the chimpanzee seems to have separated the different schedules and to be reacting selectively to them, as he would if they had been presented separately rather than simultaneously. Some interaction between the two parts of this operation is apparent. Pauses, larger than usual, in the fixed ratio schedule coincide with reinforcements on the variable interval (Skinner, 1957). Perhaps the chimpanzee lets go of the levers and eats at these points.

**Superstitious Learning** One of Skinner's experiments involved reinforcing pigeons every 30 seconds for whatever they were doing at that precise time. This schedule of reinforcement led to some odd kinds of activity on the part of the pigeons. One of them learned to hop on one foot, another went around with a drooping wing, and still another spent quite a lot of time and effort stretching its neck. According to Skinner, these are manifestations of superstitious activity, learned as follows: Mechanisms that are within the pigeon's repertoire are reinforced by chance when the pigeon happens to be performing in a specific way at the time it is rewarded. The reinforcement increases the probability that this particular activity will be repeated, thus making it more likely that when the next reinforcement comes along, after 30 seconds, the same activity will be in progress and, as a consequence, will again be reinforced. As time passes, a well-defined habit of behavior is developed.

Skinner implies that our own superstitions develop in this way. In most cases, superstitions can be supported by well-documented evidence of an empirical relationship and, by implication, the probability of a causal relationship. A man who is reinforced when he has a rabbit's foot in his pocket tends to carry

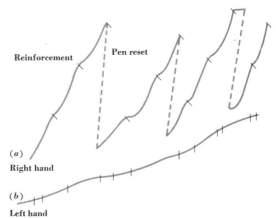

**Figure 4-11** (a) Fixed ratio; (b) variable interval. (*From Skinner, B. F., The experimental analysis of behavior. © 1957, American Scientist, vol. XLV. P. 353. By permission of the author and publisher.*)

a rabbit's foot around with him more often. Because he has the rabbit's foot with him more often, he is more likely to be reinforced in some way while it is on his person. The process is cumulative. In time, because of the number of times the rabbit's foot has been associated with reinforcement—or, in other words, good luck—the man tends to attribute to the rabbit's foot the magical power of bringing good luck with it.

**Social Learning by Operant Conditioning** Much learning in children is conditioning. When a little girl is seen playing house, playing with dolls, smoothing her skirt, or looking in the mirror and admiring herself, the observer is likely to smile or say something to indicate approval. It is not long before the little girl devotes most of her time to such activities. Of all the things she does, these are the ones selected for reinforcement and thus for repetition. Similarly, a little boy is reinforced for playing with tools, playing with soldiers, or engaging in other activities considered appropriate to his sex. In other cultures, different activities are considered appropriate for boys or for girls, and these are selected for reinforcement and become the dominant activity patterns. Operant conditioning tends to ensure that the same kinds of activities will continue to be held in esteem by the group. The automatic, unthinking reinforcement sequences by which appropriate responses are selected and strengthened constitute a tremendous force toward conservation in any culture. The language that is learned and the accents that are characteristic of it in any particular region seem to be acquired by this mechanism.

**Emotional Learning by Operant Conditioning** Skinner demonstrated that pigeons can be conditioned to become actively aggressive warriors, a reversal of their normal peaceful roles. His method of developing

these tendencies was to provide a light cue and to reinforce each indication of aggression, such as moving the head toward another bird, and thus gradually increase the aggression until battling, more reminiscent of fighting cocks than of pigeons, took place. In the early stages of the shaping, no emotional signs were apparent, but as time went on they ruffled their feathers and displayed all the symbols of aggressive bird action as part of their fighting stance.

Skinner's pigeons acted as though noradrenaline had been fed into their systems. This training of the pigeons, in which the emotions developed after the aggressive acts had been learned, lends credence to the James-Lange theory of emotions, current during the early part of this century, according to which we do not fear the bear and then run away, but rather we run away and then come to fear the bear. The implications in terms of the learning of aggression by young delinquents is obvious. Basically, these young people become criminally inclined because they are reinforced, gradually, for acting more and more hostile. It is always easy, after the fact, to find the causes of a person's misbehavior. The trick is to be aware of them beforehand and to find ways to avoid setting them in motion. Society has a large stake in finding ways to forestall the development of criminals. Teachers will be called upon increasingly to help in the solution of these problems. An understanding of the significance of Skinner's work on operantly conditioning aggression is basic to the development of countermeasures.

Much of the psychology taught to young parents during the last 30 years has been inclined toward negativism more than toward the development of positive kinds of interaction with children. Parents have been told not to strike their children because this leads to a sense of inferiority on the part of the child. They have been told not to restrain, not to overprotect, and not to do this, that, or the other thing. Many parents have found these rules frustrating and immobilizing. Skinner's operant conditioning puts the accent on the positive by looking for what is desirable and reinforcing all tendencies in these directions.

Students preparing to be teachers often ask how they can survive while waiting for the desirable behavior to occur, particularly in pupils who already have fixed aversive attitudes and habit patterns. In general, the problem is the same as that faced by the experimenter working with the naïve pigeons: How does one get started before the pigeon knows there is a food tray? Basically, the answer involves making sure that the pigeon locates the food tray quickly, even if this necessitates a trail of corn leading to the tray. With younger children, the teacher sets up an attractive plan that assures an instance of the desired behavior. With secondary school students, initial structuring, or obvious ties to reinforcement, are imperative.

In Skinner's studies, when the aggressive actions of the pigeon stopped being reinforced, the actions also stopped. In retraining obstreperous students, removing reinforcement for aggression and implementing reinforcement for socially desirable activity will reshape the patterns of behavior. An understanding of operant conditioning enables the teacher to stress positive approaches even though operant conditioning has the disadvantage of being incomplete.

## CLASSICAL CONDITIONING

Since most of the association learning that takes place in schools is tied to pleasure or punishment in some way, the conditioning is probably operant rather than classical. This section will help to make the distinction clear between the two kinds of conditioning. In avoidance learning, careful analysis is necessary to understand the mechanism at work in classical conditioning. Some experiments have been concerned with responses that are not normally under the control of the subject. These are mentioned here to help the reader realize the unconscious nature of much learning. Other research has shown a lack of conditioning when the response was under the control of an aware subject.

### Research on Conditioning People

In his experiments on human subjects, Razran (1939) used pictures of foods as unconditioned stimuli. The subjects placed a measured and weighted roll of cotton in their mouths to collect the saliva that they generated during a specified period of time while viewing the pictures. After training, the conditioned stimulus—the ringing of a bell—called forth salivation but none of the other activities that accompany eating such as reaching, chewing, and swallowing were observed. Perhaps these responses are too easily controlled by the conscious life of the individual for them to be subject to conditioning in this way. These results suggest that some forms of human behavior are more amenable to conditioning than others.

Hudgins (1933) worked on conditioning inaccessible responses in human subjects. In one of his experiments, he shined a light into the eye of his subject and at the same time said "contract." The pupil of the eye did contract because of the effect of the light. After he had paired the light with the word "contract" some 200 times, he found that a reliable conditioned response had been established between the word "contract" and the contraction of the pupil of the eye. The experiment was carried forward to the point where his subjects could achieve pupillary contraction merely by thinking the word "contract."

Menzies (1941) carried out a similar experiment in which he was able to get people to change their body temperature by saying a code word to themselves. He built his experiment on the knowledge that when one hand is immersed in ice water, the other hand becomes chilled, at least slightly, because of bilateral reflex action. Menzies was able to condition the word "chill" into this sequence so that a measurable drop in the subject's body temperature occurred when the subject merely thought the word "chill."

Such responses seem to be independent of the will of the subjects. When asked what they had done to bring about a response, they answered, "nothing." The pupil of the eye contracted and the temperature of the hand dropped, not because a subject willed these events to take place, but because of a linkage in the neural system. These experiments show something of the malleability of the nervous system and its potentiality for making associations between unlikely activities.

Popular interest has focused on *biofeedback* mechanisms which enable people to control their life processes by controlling their internal reaction to stimuli. In biofeedback experiments the mechanical apparatus used electroencephalograms (EEG), galvanic skin responses (GSR), or measures of muscle tension to inform the subject of his success in controlling normally automatic life processes. For instance, the muscles across the forehead become tense when a person becomes anxious or disturbed. A connection to this muscle can be circuited so that a bell rings or a light goes on whenever the tension in the muscle exceeds a specified limit. The individual quickly learns to relax the muscle and also to lower his state of tension when the biofeedback gives a warning. At first the relaxation requires external information which the subject is able to interpret and as a result control his internal state, using previously unnoticed biological information. *Alpha waves*, the brain waves characteristic of a relaxed state, can be generated for increasing periods of time when a person is kept informed through the EEG of when he is generating alpha waves and when he is not.

### Direct Stimulation of the Brain

At the University of Michigan, Doty and Giurgea (1961) experimented with direct stimulation of the brain of a cat by means of implanted electrodes. They inserted a fine wire into various locations in the motor control area of the brain; stimulation led to a response such as lifting a paw, turning the head, scratching, or curling the tail, depending on the precise site in which the electrode was placed. They inserted another electrode into a different area of the brain, the visual cortex, and after a current had been run into the two electrodes from 150 to 200 times, the motor activity occurred with stimulation to the visual cortex only. The stimulus to this area had become a CS for the motor activity. No awareness of the stimuli or of the effects was involved. The unaware nature of such conditioning is clear; when a human being has similar electrodes inserted into his head, he is astonished that his hand or foot moves because it does so without volition on his part and without his awareness that the current has been turned on.

### Conditioning Noxious Stimuli

Pavlov (1927), in working with dogs, was the first to investigate the possibility of conditioning a noxious stimulus to produce a happy response. He started with a mild shock, associated with feeding and the responses feeding produces, such as tail wagging, salivation, and related activities. As the experiment progressed, the strength of the shock was increased to the point where it was sufficiently powerful to produce pain in most dogs, but it continued to be the signal for food and pleasurable activities for his conditioned animals.

The pulse rate did not go up, the breathing did not quicken, and none of the pain or fear symptoms normal to shock were observed. In other experiments, he conditioned dogs to identify pinpricks of the skin—deep enough to draw blood—as signals for pleasant activities.

Segundo, Galeano, Sommer-Smith, and Roig (1961), working in Montevideo, conducted some experiments related to Pavlov's work on noxious stimuli. In these experiments, cats were given a subcutaneous shock, and an audible tone was conditioned to the cessation of the electric current. After the connection had been thoroughly established by repetition, the tone alerted the cats to the fact that the electric shock was about to stop and it became a signal for them to relax. In the latter stages of the experiment, the current was not turned off when the tone was sounded. The cats, however, continued to act as though the current had been turned off. The conclusions drawn from their external appearance were substantiated by EEG records, which indicated a lowering of tension. All the other responses normally associated with pain, such as rapid breathing, higher pulse rate, hair standing on end, and other signs of discomfort, became less intense or ceased to occur. There is some reason to believe that hypnosis, when used as an anesthetic, turns off the pain centers in a somewhat similar manner.

These studies indicate that conditioning of processes far removed from normal voluntary control is possible. When in battle or caught in fires, for example, people seem to be able to turn off very painful stimuli from physical injury until a more convenient time. In the meantime, they may have done physical damage to themselves, as they have continued to walk on a fractured leg or to act in ways that, for their long-range good, would ordinarily have been halted by pain. Probably this same

mechanism enables a trapped animal to amputate its own paw in order to escape.

Experiments on noxious stimuli may involve classical substitution or may be examples of positive operant learning. Brogden, Lipman, and Culler (1938) put groups of guinea pigs into a squirrel cage that could be rotated by running. For one of the groups, running shut off an electric current; for the other group running did not stop the shock. In the cage where running turned off the current, running became an important activity for the guinea pigs. In the other cage, they learned to sit tight, hold their breath, and cringe in fear. The animals that ran may have been responding to operant conditioning by reinforcement for running rather than to classical conditioning.

**Generalization of Conditioning** The process of generalization in conditioning—carrying forward responses learned in one context to another situation—is an important facet of learning. Pavlov (1927) did rather thorough studies of *spatial generalization*, using food as the UCS. After he had conditioned a dog to a vibration frequency applied to the shoulder, he found that the same vibration applied to the front paw and the side near the shoulder was nearly as effective in producing salivation. Vibrations applied to the side near the thigh lost a good deal of power, and the hind paw and thigh were both outside the area to which the stimulus spread. Other similar experiments, some of them involving students as subjects, showed similar generalization patterns. The closer the stimulus was applied to the original location of the CS, the more intense was the response to it.

**Discrimination Conditioning** Guttman (1956) demonstrated the sharpness with which discriminations can be conditioned. Pigeons learned to respond to 550 millimicrons of light.

After the response was well established, the food mechanism was turned off, and no further reinforcement was given. Then a random pattern of light sources with wavelengths varying in increments of ten around 550 millimicrons was presented to the pigeons (Figure 4-12). A high degree of specificity was obvious for each of the pigeon groups. They only responded within a color range too small for many human beings to distinguish.

Pavlov experimented with dogs to discover their breaking point as they were required to make discriminations. He trained dogs to distinguish a circle from an ellipse by feeding them on a circle and not feeding them on various ellipses. In time, the dogs became very well able to distinguish between these different forms. After the discrimination was well established, the ellipses were gradually brought nearer and nearer to the shape of a circle. The dogs lost their appetites and became snappish, irritable, and morose, presumably because they were unable to cope with this demand for a decision.

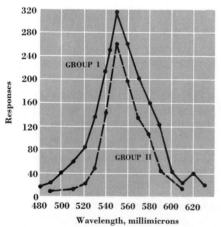

**Figure 4-12**  Specificity of response to monochromatic light. Pigeons were acquisition-trained to a light of 550 millimicrons. Then they were subjected to nonreinforced training under different wavelengths. The clear stimulus generalization gradients shown resulted. (*From Guttman, N., "The pigeon and the spectrum and other perplexities." Psychological Reports, 1956, 2, 451.*)

## APPLICATION OF ASSOCIATION LEARNING

Traditionally most school experiences have been designed to form associations of a cognitive nature. While there has always been some emphasis on understanding and interpretation in school subjects, the principal effort of the teacher has been on developing skill in reading and mathematics, learning historical details, and learning the symbols and valences of chemical elements. Although the courses included generalizations and concepts, many of the tests and examinations were primarily fact-oriented, reflecting the preoccupation of the teacher with factual content. One result of the better understanding of the nature of conditioning by school personnel has been the sharpening of instructional strategies, particularly in programmed learning schedules, computer-assisted instructional materials, behavioral objectives in learning, and mastery learning paradigms. All these strategies can be used for teaching conceptualization and creative self-direction, but most of the developmental work has been focused on the simpler learning tasks.

### Mastery Learning

Related to the work on behavioral objectives has been a movement to establish the validity of mastery learning. Bruner (1966) stated that any subject could be taught in an intellectually honest manner to any age group if the increments in the sequence were made small enough. Carroll (1963) defined aptitude as the amount of time needed to master a learning task. He defined the quality of instruction as the degree of efficiency in presentation, explanation, and ordering of the task, compared with the optimal for a given learner.

Bloom et al. (1971) described a teaching procedure in which classes of students in test theory changed from approximately 20 percent A's in 1965 to 90 percent A's in 1967 on comparable examinations. The essence of the change to mastery learning was (1) the establishment of a success criterion, rather than a normal curve for grades, thus reducing competition and encouraging cooperation; (2) analysis of the content into hierarchies from simple to complex, using some of Gagné's (1965) ideas; (3) diagnostic tests of progress; (4) prescriptive work to assure mastery of elements not already learned; (5) the organization of groups of three or four students who help each other understand the materials; and (6) production of supplementary written or audio-visual materials. An important element in the improvement of learning is the establishment of standards that constitute mastery. Bloom used the standard of the A level achieved by previous classes for the base line of mastery.

While mastery learning can be structured at any level, one way of helping students raise their level of functioning is to base their grade on the learning-motivation model. Grade C represents factual accuracy in retrieval of the content gained through reading, lectures, and films. A B grade indicates conceptualization of the important relationships, and generalizations to synthesize or to interpret the material in his own language. An A represents innovative use of major ideas to conduct miniresearch, design a learning sequence, or in some way go beyond the material as presented. When high proportions of students achieve mastery levels, adjustments are required in the grading policies of the institutions.

Block (1972) described unusual success in preparing Korean students for entry into advanced physics courses where the numbers, after the mastery learning instruction, swamped the available resources of the school. These techniques can be used for all levels of learning, although it is easier to specify the terminal objectives and to develop the hierarchies when the material to be learned is clearly defined. Mastery learning will become increasingly important in school operations during the years ahead.

## Language Development

Rheingold, Gewirtz, and Ross (1959) demonstrated the effectiveness of operant conditioning in increasing speech vocalization. They used 22 three-month-old babies as subjects. First, they established a base line of vocalization over two days using 9 three-minute sessions each day, during which they leaned over the crib without reinforcing vocalization. Reinforcement for each vocalization was then started on the same schedule and consisted of a smile, three "tsk" sounds, and a light touch to the abdomen with finger and thumb extended. This reinforcement was continued for two days, followed by two days of extinction, during which the experimenters leaned over the crib—as they had done in the base-line studies and in the conditioning—but used the expressionless face of the base-line period. The effect of the conditioning was to nearly double the output of vocalization from the base line to day 2 of the conditioning (Figure 4-13). The implications of this study in terms

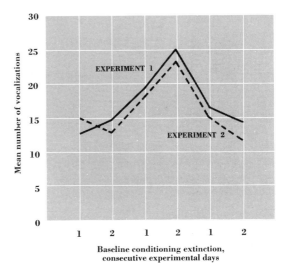

**Figure 4-13** Mean number of vocalizations on consecutive experimental days. (*From Rheingold, H. L., Gewitz, J. L., and Ross, H. W. Social conditioning of vocalizations in the infant. Journal of Comparative and Physiological Psychology, 1959, 52, 68–73. Copyright © 1959 by The American Psychological Association and reproduced by permission.*)

double the output of vocalization from the base line to day 2 of the conditioning (Figure 4-13). The implications of this study in terms of language development are clear. Children whose parents reinforce them for vocalization from a very young age almost certainly will show more speech output than children from homes lacking this reinforcement.

Hewitt (1971) described a process used to teach Peter, a nonspeaking, autistic child, $4^1/_2$ years old, at the Neuropsychiatric Institute, University of California, Los Angeles. A booth was constructed so that the therapist could open a shutter and let light, food, and sight of herself become available to Peter. Opening the shutter was contingent on his dropping a ball into a container that rang a bell.

During the second phase, Peter was trained to imitate the therapist as she clapped hands and performed series of operations. Reinforcements consisted of recorded music, rotation on swivel chair, or sequences of a color cartoon, etc. This training took a month.

During the third phase, with candy as a reinforcer, Peter learned to imitate speech sounds and words. After he had learned to say "go," he suddenly stopped responding for a week and would not cooperate. Hewett returned to training for production of vowel sounds which had already been established. During a six-month training period Peter learned 32 words by careful conditioning on the part of his teacher.

In the fourth phase of the training Peter was conditioned to use the words he knew in situations in the wards. This training overlapped the speech training phase but was continued for an additional eight months. During part of this time he was living at home and his parents were helping with the training. Peter eventually learned to use language for his own purposes, but the process of teaching him was long and at times frustrating. He needed very highly structured building of basic associa-

tions before he could succeed in using language for himself.

Bereiter and Engelmann (1968) developed a systematic and intensive approach for improving language usage in disadvantaged four- and five-year-olds. Their subjects were selected from siblings of children who were having learning difficulties in a black ghetto school. For selection into the program the children had to produce some vocal response, not necessarily correct, on the Auditory-Vocal Automatic and the Auditory-Vocal Association subtests of ITPA. The training program lasted two hours a day, five days a week, and ran for two years. The schedule consisted of 10 minutes of free play; 20 minutes of intensive drill (either language, reading, or arithmetic); 30 minutes of toileting, snack, and music; 20 minutes of intensive drill; 20 minutes of story; and a final 20 minutes of intensive drill. Groups were limited to five children for the intensive instruction but operated as a whole for the other activities.

In language instruction a great deal of effort was spent on learning: "This is a . . . This is not a . . ." For the ablest students this chunk of learning took between two and three *months* and for the least able between six and seven *months*. Once the children were able to handle this bit of learning, they made rapid progress with active verbs, common tenses, personal pronouns, if-then statements, and all-only-some statements. During the second year the intensive language instruction was replaced by a unit on science reasoning. In spite of the presence of excellent models the improvement in language usage ceased when the direct instruction ceased. A major effort was made during the training to have the children think of the learning as work, to think of themselves as successful, and to build self-images as being able to undertake *hard* school tasks successfully. One critical facet of this study is the importance of a great deal of input in the form of basic associations. A second is the need to carry this learning beyond the initial success stage if progress is to continue to be made, and a third, the possibility of developing both affective associations and affective conceptualizations in a context of difficult learning.

Gray and associates (Gray and Ryan, 1972) at the Monterey Institute for Speech and Hearing developed a conditioning system for training language-deficient children. Groups of five were taught by paraprofessionals using programmed materials. Children who left the "is" out of sentences, as in "truck big," were asked to repeat "The truck is big." Learning to use "is" correctly took an average of 13 hours, 20 minutes. The children could then create new sentences that had not been taught directly in which "is" was used correctly. Although Skinner's operant conditioning paradigm was used by Gray, the children appear to have conceptualized an element of the structure of language.

At this point, when children use "is" in a new context to create their own sentences, they meet Chomsky's criterion for mastery of a rule (1965). In their programmed instruction the emphasis was on usage, but the children eventually conceptualized the semantic rules which form the deep structure of language. Although they could not explain the syntactical structure, they could use the rule to create sentences for their own purposes. It should be noted that a great many associations were used as input that reflected a single grammatical point but eventually conceptualization and creative self-direction were outcomes.

## Reading

Some of the reasons learning to speak is easier than learning to read are explained, at least in part, by the theory of association learning. First, speech is acquired very gradually, while reading instruction is comparatively compressed and intensive; essentially, the child himself structures the length of the accretions in learning to talk. Second, speech instruction is closely tied to strong reinforcement, including food and affection, while reading is associated with less direct, more obscure reinforcement. In the case of reading, the child who is expected to learn the cognitive associations of reading when he is still unready is likely to feel punished. Third, reinforcement for speech is applied individually and immediately after the response has been emitted, while in reading the child is usually one of a group of children, each of whom is unique in terms of the timing of his successful responses. Generally he should receive more individual reinforcement than is feasible in a group structure. Weak reinforcement tends to slow down the learning of the less able to increase the aversive characteristics of the total stimulus situation.

Children from two years old and up have been taught by conditioning to "read" (Doman, 1965). Word cards are used to help the child form associations with persons or subjects that are important to him—"Mommy," "toes," "shoe," "cookie." The method is explicit: Say the word clearly, show the card for no longer than ten seconds, and play with the child for a minute or two, repeating the procedure five times the first day and twice the second day. The effect of such teaching has not been evaluated with control subjects. Certainly the young child receives many forms of sensorimotor stimulation through these activities. It is hoped that the parent who tries this program will be perceptive of the child's responses in order to apply the most appropriate reinforcement. Doman's method for teaching babies to "read" requires that the mother-teacher make a fuss when the child learns a word, express her love physically, and then move on quickly. The sessions should end *before* the child wants them to.

Almost half the children in intellectually gifted groups as well as smaller percentages of children of average ability can read by the time they come to school (Durkin, 1972). Nearly all these preschool readers were taught by an older sibling or a parent in a one-to-one tutorial relationship, where the "teacher" was able to tell when a response was correct and to reinforce the learner immediately and selectively. Feelings of pleasure, interest, and satisfaction come to be associated with reading in order to reinforce the cognitive associations that are being formed.

The importance of the affective associations in beginning reading can hardly be stated too strongly. The school beginner has already learned from the culture to associate going to school and learning to read. The six-year-old is not likely to be influenced by an adult definition of when he is or is not reading, but the affective feedback from the classroom will indicate in a thousand ways whether he is succeeding in school or not. Most poor readers fail at the beginning of the process and associate punishment with reading. Nearly all children can succeed in beginning reading if taught through a sequence of associations that are pleasure-connected. The teacher needs to be sensitive to the feelings of the child and to find ways of helping him to make progress and to know when he succeeds.

### Foreign Language

Instruction in foreign language has undergone a revolution during the last few years aimed at making the language studied more functional. As a child learns his native language, he goes through a continuous process of associating meaning with a word sound, producing the sound himself in his speech development, learning to read written symbols for which he has both meaning and speech, and finally putting down meanings in the form of his own written symbols. In the traditional grammar-translation approach to teaching a foreign language, the student began at the reading stage and associated English meanings with the printed word. Intensive instruction was given in the rules of grammar as a means of coding the variations in verb forms, pronouns, and other parts of speech that vary systematically under specific conditions. However, the average high school student who learned by this method did not develop proficiency in reading, had very little facility in speech, and often had some negative associations with the process of learning a foreign language. The aural-oral approach was devised to remedy these defects by placing the emphasis on the development of skill in oral communication so that the language can be used in travel and study abroad.

**Basic Speech Phonemes**   Penfield and Roberts (1959) pointed out that during the first year of life most young children produce all the speech sounds found in all languages and some not found in any language. By a process of reinforcement and extinction, the phonemes—the basic units of speech—of the native tongue are developed, strengthened, and retained, while the phonemes not included in the native language are extinguished. These neurologists hypothesized that between nine and twelve years of age the organization of the brain makes it increasingly difficult to relearn the basic speech units. Someone should undertake the research to determine whether songs and games developed to give kindergartners practice in pronouncing the French "r" or the German "ch," for example, would establish these units as available mechanisms for later use. Success in correct pronunciation requires careful, intensive practice under supervision when the language is learned in the junior high school or later.

**Speech and Meaning**   The student comes to the learning of a new language with well-developed associations between concepts and English words. One of the main problems of early language instruction is to establish new associations between the concepts and the appropriate foreign word. The most obvious sequence is from the foreign word to the English word to the concept. Under some circumstances and with certain concepts, this double association—first with the English word and then with the idea—may be the most efficient approach. Whenever possible, the direct association of the foreign word with the concept should be established, thus eliminating a translation step. If the direct linkage is to be made in the school, extensive visual material must be provided, including study prints, filmstrips, and films. Short motion picture sequences, designed to portray a single concept, should be prepared and made available. This process involves a telescoping of many months of experience on the part of the learner, similar to the way he acquired his listening vocabulary in English as a child by associating the words he heard with a meaningful environment. In many classrooms, aural-oral language teaching has focused on the development of the speech patterns and has implicitly assumed that the association of meanings with new words would take care of itself.

The process of developing spoken French is primarily association learning. The words are heard and repeated, or as Cote, Levy, and O'Conner (1962) define the process, the sounds are imitated. The basic dialogue sentences are repeated in imitation and then in repetition, with increasing time intervals between hearing and repeating the sentences. After considerable practice, designed to make the associations secure, a series of questions and answers is used to vary the association linkages, followed by pattern practices that allow for moderate variations from associations that have already been established. The students use the associations they have developed to practice conversation. In this process, the grammar is taught as a simple process of associating usage with situation.

**Reading**  Under this approach to foreign language teaching, reading is deferred until after basic speech habits have been formed. The purpose of this deferral is to allow time for the establishment of speech patterns without the interference of having already-present English sound association patterns become linked with the written French symbols. By firmly establishing the sound patterns before introducing the visual word-form stimulus, it is more likely that associations will be formed between the French sound and the meaning. Thus the discriminations between French and English words are more certain to occur. As reading proficiency increases, it is possible to increase vocabulary by context clues and by other techniques similar to those by which children learn to read efficiently.

**Grammar**  Some research completed at the turn of the century, which should be replicated, indicated that people are never as fast or proficient in a second language as they are in their mother tongue, even after many years of working and thinking in the second language.

Cote, Levy, and O'Conner (1962) say:

> Ideally, the early stages of language learning should consist wholly of habit-forming through overlearning of basic sentences, followed by the guided development of grammatical habits through analogies in the stages of variation and selection. . . . [the] learner would acquire the grammatical habits of the French simply as habits without needing or desiring to formulate them as rules [p. xxv].

According to these authors the various grammatical constructions are learned as simple associations. However, Chomsky (1965) described language learning as primarily a conceptualization process in which children discovered the structure of the language and then creatively used this structure in new contexts for their own purposes (Chapter 6).

## Mathematics

The associations that students make with mathematics depend upon the affective associations of their teachers. Although mathematicians can see a beauty in the logical consistency and purity of mathematics, many teachers and most students have not acquired such a devotion to this subject. Brownell (1967) emphasized the teacher's dedication to a method of instruction as one of the most important variables in students' learning. He used an individual interview technique to explore the mathematical processes used to solve problems by 1,500 children in England and Scotland. They had been taught by the traditional approach, by the Cuisenaire system, or by Dienes structured materials. The design of his study was exemplary. The results obtained were disconcerting in that the findings from Scotland were the reverse of those from England. Of the three methods, the Cuisenaire system produced statistically superior results in Scottish children, while traditional methods proved superior in England. Later exploration indicated that these conflicting results reflected the commitment of the teachers, either to the traditional method or to the newer, structured method. For historical reasons, the separations were on national lines. From this and other studies, in which acceptance of a method by the teachers was crucial, it is probably safe to say that the learning done by students in mathematics depends more on the teacher's commitment than on the materials or the method.

Many research reports indicate that children acquire number associations early. Many children, including those from lower socioeconomic groups, come to kindergarten with skills in the use of numbers that have been acquired in their home and neighborhood environments. Long before a child is of school age, he knows when a sibling receives two pieces of cake and he receives only one. Deans (1954), who found that four- and five-year-olds need numbers to carry on their small affairs, concluded that arithmetic cannot be kept out of kindergarten if the needs of the children are to be the criteria for selecting kindergarten content. Bjonerud (1960) found that beginning kindergarten children in two communities, one in Michigan and one in California, came to school with the ability to do rote and objective counting to 19. Sussman (1962) found that kindergarten children start school with as much number skill as first graders did a few decades ago. Dutton (1964) found that at least one-third of a beginning kindergarten class were ready to start systematic work in counting, enumerating, grouping, reproducing numerals, and learning other mathematical concepts of size, shape, form, and measurement. This research has demonstrated the ability of most kindergarten-age children, when supported by careful teaching and suitable materials, to master both numerical concepts and the facts that they learn by association. A substantial number find their success so gratifying that they go on independently to creative activities as they work with numbers.

The following points seem important in a consideration of the psychological factors involved in mathematics: (1) The associations that the student develops before he comes to school and in his life outside school should be incorporated into the school learning experiences. (2) Modern mathematics is on a higher level of abstraction than Euclidean geometry, algebra, or arithmetic. Since mathematics is abstract, attention will need to be given to the teaching of associations that undergird the material if the conceptualizations with mathematical logic are to be developed. (3) Teachers should take the attitude that students can learn mathematics, and they should understand the distinction between associations and conceptualizations basic to learning.

## Science

Very young children have opportunities to learn many basic associations of scientific phenomena before they go to school, even in slum areas. They experience weight, sound, light, force, weather, and aroma in situations where they are reinforced for making new discriminations on the basis of their observations. They need to talk with someone who can help supply the vocabulary to facilitate communication. These are associations which can elicit response, and thus be reinforced, or which can be neglected. The sun shines and casts shadows in the slums just as it does in the suburbs, but the beginnings of scientific language are more likely to be nourished where adults have the time to listen to children's questions and have the resources with which to extend children's interests.

A good science program in the elementary school teaches pupils to observe selectively by reinforcing the discriminations they make. It also encourages them to develop new interests—for example, in simple tools or electricity. By extending children's interests, the schools assure that much association learning will occur in the physical world outside the classroom. Teachers who themselves have conceptualized science as a method of inquiry will be able to arrange sequences of associations that are basic to the use of the scientific method at the next levels of learning.

Scientific laws are conceptualizations for the one who formulates or reformulates them, but they become conceptualizatons for the secondary student only when he goes through the process of discovering these relationships himself. This distinction is crucial for the teacher and depends not upon the subject matter but upon what happens in the neurological systems of the learner. The required associations are of two major types: (1) awareness that the phenomenon exists and (2) knowledge that a logical and rational explanation is possible.

**Awareness That Phenomena Exist**   Roe (1958) pointed out that by selectively reinforcing a child's interest in a particular area he tends to develop that interest, while by neglecting or ignoring an interest it will diminish. Probably the differences among children from various socioeconomic backgrounds, as far as interest in science is concerned, can be traced to their early experiences when inquiring about environmental phenomena. No particular socioeconomic class has exclusive claim to success in stimulating scientific interests, although middle-class parents are probably least uncomfortable when confronted with questions about natural phenomena. Rural children seem to fare better than urban children, perhaps because their questions seem more normal to their parents and because the country setting offers relative freedom to explore the physical environment.

**Awareness of the Possibility of Rational Explanation**   Rational explanations of physical phenomena are nearly always conceptual in nature. Associations accumulate from successive experiences that indicate the existence of either a scientific or a magical explanation for them. Whether the magical or the scientific attitude is explored depends on the kinds of answers from adults that are associated with the initial questions.

Teachers will be increasingly proficient in developing both the basic cognitive associations in science and the favorable affective associations toward science if they are aware of precisely what they are trying to accomplish. For instance, in biology, in learning to use the microscope to see the field and to focus the machine are examples of association learning that can be facilitated by planned operant conditioning schedules. Much of the vocabulary is learned similarly by associations. Awareness, on the part of the teacher, of the learning process through which the student must go will enhance his chances for success.

In chemistry, as another example, after the periodic table of the elements has been taught and understood as a conceptualization, there are still many details of position and relationship that the student must learn as associations before he can use the information concentrated in the chart. In the laboratory, the use of the pipette, balance, and other pieces of apparatus is learned as a series of associations that have elements of conceptualization. Similar areas of conceptualization, built on chains of associations and later expanded by additional associations, exist in physics, geology, and astronomy. The teacher's analysis of the associative experiences that go into a conceptualization is reflected in the behavioral objectives for the course.

### History

Even in advanced university classes, much of the content of history is learned on an association level. The dates, names, and details that form the pegs on which the structure of history hangs have little inherent meaning. The secret in teaching history is to understand the interaction of the association and conceptualization processes in order to involve the students effectively in comprehending the past.

### Student Differences in Learning History

Some capable students appear to be memory-oriented, while others seem to be structure-oriented. Often the gifted youngster is able to grasp relationships more quickly than his less able classmate, to grasp them with fewer cues than most students require, and sometimes to develop new theories or hypotheses for events. However, there is a type of gifted student who is blessed with a particular facility to catalog information and to store it systematically in a manner that makes it readily retrievable when recall is important. Often the student with this type of learning pattern finds the systematic cumulative approach—the association approach—most beneficial. On many types of examinations, this student will do better than his structure-oriented competitor. If his ability to catalog is great enough and if history proves to be his major love, such a student may easily become the scholar who has read everything, remembers it well, and can reproduce and check myriad facts. The structure-oriented student who becomes a historian is likely to achieve his eminence for a new theory of history—almost always controversial—that is essentially a new structuring of temporal relationships.

Slow students, who need the lessons of history perhaps more than their more able peers, find both approaches difficult. Slow learners need many basic associations with steps that are close together and systematically presented. They need to have the relationships made very explicit and dramatically clear. They need specific guidance in order to generate or to discover relationships. From the teacher's point of view, they need much more help and of a different kind than the gifted student. As the teacher comes to understand the nature of the help that is needed, the success of the slower child in grasping the lessons of history is enhanced and made more permanent.

### SUMMARY

Association learning results when bits of information are linked together because they occur together in time. Thorndike described learning by *contiguity*, which results when events happen closely in time. He also described the facilitation or the retardation of learning as due to the *effect* of the learning experience.

Pavlov and Guthrie studied the nature of learning that is due to association in time. Skinner has shown how reinforcement of desired responses ensures the likelihood of their recurrence. His research with pigeons, rats, and Homo sapiens indicated that behavior which is not characteristic behavior of the species can be taught. Different patterns of work output were shown to be associated with *fixed interval, variable interval, fixed ratio,* and *variable ratio* schedules of reinforcement.

Classical conditioning differs from operant conditioning in that (1) one stimulus is substituted for another, rather than one response for another; (2) associations result from contiguity rather than from effect; and (3) the strengthening of neural connections is emphasized without particular attention to pleasure/punishment systems. The research of neurologists and others has established the unconscious nature of most learning by classical conditioning. Research was reviewed that indicates the importance of teaching for transfer and generalization of learning.

Language, according to S-R theorists, is developed by a series of associations that the child selects from his environment according to his readiness and the reinforcement he receives. In beginning reading the child associates printed (visual) words with known (auditory) words and graphemes with phonemes. Recent audio-lingual approaches to teaching foreign languages are based primarily on the association of phonemes with the appropriate meaning. The affective dimension in association learning of mathematical foundations determines whether future experiences will be colored positvely or negatively. Associations that lead to highly motivated work and to the students' discovery of generalizations in science should be developed. Association learning of historical information is basic to the student's successful comparison of sources, his ordering of temporal relationships, and his discovery of the factors that shape historical events. For the teacher, the crucial point to understand is that the level on which the student functions is determined not by the content of what he learns but by the thought process that he uses.

## SELF-DIRECTING ACTIVITIES

1 Make a list of the cognitive associations you expect to include in the curriculum guide you are teaching or expect to teach.
2 List a feeling, an attitude, or an appreciation you would hope the student would experience while learning.
3 Explain when and how you learned to read.
4 Record a child's spontaneous speech. Decide which expressions are imitative and which are creative.

# Chapter 5

Dr. Mildred Robeck reinforces children during a drawing activity.

# AFFECTIVE ASSOCIATIONS

This chapter is planned to clarify the use of affective loadings in making the classroom a happier and more productive place. With this in mind, you should be able to:

❦ State causes of student unrest, so that you can recognize them when teaching

❦ Remove causes of alienation from your teaching style

❦ Demonstrate that you can modify undesirable classroom behavior through positive reinforcement of desirable behavior

❦ Design ways to promote improved identity through experience in positive social interaction

❦ Use and interpret the following terms:
encounter group
behavior modification
base-line behavior
desensitization
aversion therapy
pecking order

The division between cognitive and affective learning is artificial, since there are elements of both in all experience. Another division might be between verbal and nonverbal learning, since affective learning is likely to be largely nonverbal. The traditional emphasis in schools has been on the verbal, cognitive side of the learning experience, although there has always been a necessity to deal with emotional and attitudinal responses of both the teachers and the pupils. Discipline, or getting pupils to do what the teacher feels they should do, has absorbed a great deal of teacher energy. In spite of the time and energy diverted to affective learning in school these elements have, until recently, been treated as though they were distractions and not part of the main theme of learning. A surge of interest in affective learning has come from two opposite and unrelated directions. (1) Students have become involved in the world of feelings, sometimes by exploring with meditation, yoga, encounter groups, introspection, old-fashioned religion, and even hallucinogenic drugs. (2) Psychologists and teachers have been using operant conditioning techniques to alter the environment and the emotional activities of students.

## ENCOUNTER GROUPS

One approach to increased affective learning has been through encounter groups. Included in this more or less systematic approach are diverse kinds of small-group experiences, including those designed to increase sensitivity to social reality, sensitivity to employer/employee interaction, openness, creativity-release, religious experience, and motivation shifts. In all these group interactions the emphasis is primarily on an awareness of the present emotional component in living. In many encounter groups understanding or conceptualization about the relationships within

these feelings is an important component of the total experience. These facets of affective conceptualization are reviewed in Chapter 7.

Maslow (1971), writing about peak experiences in self-actualization, described affective feelings that are part of such experiences. He described many people including himself who found their sense of humanness through the almost sensual awareness of the impact of an interaction with music, art, or creative production.

He suggested that the fundamental education for two- to four-year-olds should have, as its core, experience with art, music, and particularly dance as a way of helping them achieve understanding of who they are. The sheer involvement in the activity at a feeling level has a growth effect. Such elements provide the essential building blocks for self-actualizing people who thus are able to express themselves in their own terms. Such expression is explored in creative self-direction (Chapter 8). The motivation to try being oneself, what Maslow calls being fully human, comes from small and often seemingly inconsequential encounters with opportunities for joy.

Carl R. Rogers (1972) sees different kinds of encounter groups as opportunities for freedom in a world often restricting. The effect of the changed climate is to provide experience, in being expressive, spontaneous and aware of feelings or, as he calls it, in touch with one's feelings. New affective experiences tend to make people different from what they otherwise would be. Rogers points out that value-judgments of the therapist reflect his concern about the type of person most beneficial to society. Rogers does not want to see the judgments of the therapist replace the individual's own integrity, and he fears affective experiences used to condition a person to rely on authority, to mistrust his longings, or to operate on a rigid set of principles. Affective associations are important ingredients, according to Rogers, determining the kind of individuals who will grow up.

Schultz and Seashore (1972) described a microlab encounter group during which many different contacts, largely nonverbal, were made. The emphasis was on feeling reactions to other people, accentuated by short discussions of what had happened. The "sessions" lasted from one to ten minutes, during which the procedure included having each member stand, walk to another member, look him in the eye, touch him in some way, and tell him a first impression. This activity was continued around the circle until each person had interacted with all others. Other interaction techniques were described, each of which was designed to alter stereotyped modes of interacting with other people. The affective associations were new, and the result was learning new ways of responding to overtures from other people.

Lieberman (1972) analyzed clusters of behavior used by outstanding leaders who held different theoretical orientations to encounter groups. One of his main findings was that labels were not descriptive of the style of leadership used in encounter groups. The leaders trained in gestalt therapy by Fritz Perls, however, were close to each other in technique (Chapter 7). The format in gestalt therapy employs what is called a *hot seat*, in which there is a confrontation between the leader and a participant. This part of the group dynamics structure ensures that the leader has an intrusive role rather than the more obscure function common to many other group leaders.

Lieberman, Yalom, and Miles (1972) found that different leader styles led to different outcomes for the participants. In general, the participants of all groups (61 percent) felt that the group experience had changed them in beneficial ways; however, slightly over 9 percent of those that finished training sessions suffered some enduring psychological harm. The affects developed seemed to be related to the leadership style. The strongly directive leaders seemed to elicit high-intensity positive responses as well as a disproportionate share of damaging incidents. The laissez faire leaders produced relatively little effect of either a positive or a negative nature.

Bessell (1972) described a human development program (HDP) as a means of developing positive emotional responses in children. One root of the approach came from Harry Stack Sullivan (1950) and what he called the "delusion of uniqueness." The feeling that others are stronger, better informed, or less fearful than I am can be overcome by group experience in which each child grows in self-confidence, awareness, and understanding of interpersonal relationships. The magic circle of 8 to 14 children permits interaction among the children on a verbal level but also makes it possible to observe the nonverbal cues of interest or boredom that are part of being in the circle.

The Bessell techniques have been used with 500,000 children, preschool, kindergarten, first, second, and third grades, by 50,000 teachers. In developing awareness with the younger children a week is spent on pleasant feelings, on pleasant thoughts, and on positive behavior. The cycle is then repeated. As the children get older, negative aspects are explored as well as those that are positive. In dealing with social interaction a week is given to each of the topics: things we do that people like and dislike, things other people do that we like and dislike, and how to ask for and offer kind behavior. One by-product of the sessions was the involvement of even the shyest children in conversation. The positive affective experience of seeing other children with similar problems made them feel safe to participate. The teacher generalized explicitly about the children's experiences, putting them into context so that other children could see the meaning. This feedback provided the opportunity to develop affective learnings in a constructive and useful context and the children became better integrated human beings because of the experience.

All encounter groups are built on experience of awareness of feelings in the here and now. Different feelings are explored and different techniques are used to generate emotional responses, but the raw, affective associations are the key ingredients for growth in selfhood. The sessions help the participants to gain new insights into the way they respond to intrusion from other people.

## BEHAVIOR MODIFICATION

In contrast to the affective learnings that are largely self-initiated is a whole field of well-researched studies that focus on changing behavior patterns by manipulating the affective loadings that accompany either desirable or undesirable behaviors. This manipulation of the environment to facilitate learning has become one of the most effective teacher tools available. Some enthusiasts claim this is the ultimate way to teach. It is certainly true that behavior modification provides an excellent base for developing conceptualizations and creative self-direction. These higher levels of learning free the individual from the other-directedness that is characteristic of behavior modification schedules.

### Humanization in the Classroom

Rich (1971), among many others, speaks of classroom experience as dehumanization. It is his contention that many schools brutalize students, humiliate them, and cause them to lose their sense of identity by treating them as things rather than as individuals, thus causing

them to feel they are not in control of their own actions. Many schools and many teachers have these effects on children and adolescents due to the kinds of affects that become associated with learning. However, many young people, particularly those from disadvantaged groups, find the school an island where they can feel human and fulfilled. Teachers who strive to help their pupils find new levels of creative self-direction in each facet of the curriculum enable young people to become increasingly self-confident (Chapter 8).

Parents are more likely to be dehumanizing toward children than teachers are, if for no other reason than they have more privacy. They also are more likely than teachers to have experienced brutalizing treatment at home and to consider it normal behavior. Teachers who practice reinforcement approaches to teaching tend to build up a sense of worth on the part of the student who is reinforced for trying and for success. As a teacher tries to understand the kinds of reinforcers that are effective with a particular student, it is necessary to see him as an individual, and this focusing of attention on him helps strengthen his identity. There is some danger that teachers using behavior modification techniques can treat the student as an object to be manipulated when the modification is seen as the complete objective. If the goal is to help him become creatively self-directing, the student is automatically seen as a dynamic person to be nurtured and cherished for his own sake. Modification is an emphasis which accomplishes specified behavior changes, but for many practitioners manipulation can become intoxicating. B. F. Skinner (1971) in *Beyond Freedom and Dignity* made his belief in this potential for manipulation quite clear. However, individuals are also purposeful in their orientation to life from an extremely early age. Modification schedules work when they are able to fit into the dynamics of life for the individual but are unsuccessful when the selected reinforcements turn out to be punishing, as when the modification runs counter to strongly held goals of the individual.

## Nonverbal Communication

Reinforcement may be verbal, as when the teacher says "good work," but much more often it is conveyed by smiles, frowns, pats, hugs, or even tokens that can be traded for material items. Bernstein (1961b) found that British lower-class youth depend more on nonverbal communication by the teacher to grasp abstract symbols than do middle-class youth. They have become adept at interpreting the tone of voice and the distances that imply acceptance or rejection on the part of the teacher. In other words, they are adept at defining the positive or negative reinforcement that goes along with the teacher's instruction.

Young children are also able to understand the emotional toning of words and actions before they can interpret spoken words in a literal sense. Many of the difficulties children have in learning to read can be traced to instructional strategies that paid insufficient attention to the reinforcement dimensions that were being put forth. Rightly or wrongly, the children attributed to the teacher's activity the implication that they were not learning well. Since the process was a new one to them, with few positively loaded reinforcements built in, they built a wall of rejection to the activity. Few teachers would speak negatively to a child just beginning to learn to read, but the unspoken words were expressed by the way in which the teacher responded, the kind of emotional support offered, and the exasperation with failure to learn what had been taught. These affective associations were incorporated into the learning of reading.

The importance of nonverbal behavior in behavior modification is a two-edged sword. It means that the learners are very likely to get the message, but it also means that the message had better be helpful and intended. A case in point is the temptation to think, after some initial success has been gained, that it is comparatively easy to manipulate this student. This message will be relayed in a somewhat garbled form which is likely to result in rejection of both the process and the lesson, since children as well as adults resent being manipulated. Teachers can become sensitive to what is going on in the mind of the child by really attending to what he is trying to say, including the nonverbal utterances. This kind of listening, characteristic of able therapists and parents, as well as good teachers, goes a long way toward generating empathy for the young person.

## Brief History of Behavior Modification

Because of the important place behavior modification has attained in practical work with children in schools and clinics, some attention to the development of behavior modification seems important. Parents and teachers have used these principles since the dawn of organized society, although often with imprecise results and a lack of articulated rationale. The parent who smiles and hugs a youngster for saying "da da" is using behavior modification to shape verbal behavior. The teacher who praises a pupil for holding his temper when he has been accustomed to losing control is using behavior modification, even if it seems only good common sense. In the United States formal statements by E. L. Thorndike (1913) about the way in which events were influenced by their effects were an impetus for teachers to systematically try to modify behavior by intentional activities. When John B. Watson (Watson & Rayner, 1920) conditioned little Albert to fear white furry objects by making a loud noise behind him while a rat was brought near, and then reconditioned the learning by a method of gradual approach, he was using systematic behavior modification in an experimental setting. Watson's experiment drew on the conditioning work of Pavlov, who holds a special place in the history of behavior modification. Much of Guthrie's *Psychology of Learning* (1952) has been cited as basic to behavior modification. Skinner's research, in which pigeons learned to play table tennis, developed aggressive personalities, turned figure eights, and became superstitious, provided a research climate suitable for the development of behavior modification theory and experimentation.

Joseph Wolpe, working originally in South Africa, wrote an article, "Experimental Neurosis as Learned Behavior" (1952), in which he outlined a series of experiments that became influential in using behavior therapy to treat individuals who had a variety of adjustment problems. The use of formal behavior modification in the classroom seems to have started with the classroom interaction analysis developed by Flanders (1962). This instrument made it possible to count the numbers of positive or negative reinforcements being given to the class and to individual children.

## Assumptions Underlying Behavior Modification

Behavior modification can be defined as changing overt behavior through environmental manipulation. Franks (1967) claimed that behavior therapy, in order to be so classed, must involve three principles: (1) some associationistic learning framework; (2) delineation of some specific bonds, either of a conventional S-R nature or within a more general systematic, rigorous and (3) controlled

methodology which has become the hallmark of the good behavioral scientist. Eysenck (1959) tabulated the differences he saw between Freudian psychotherapy and behavior therapy (Table 5-1). His evaluations of psychotherapy seem biased negatively, while those of behavior therapy seem biased positively; however, the right-hand column of the tabulation is quite consonant with others in the behavior modification movement.

Sherman and Baer (1969) list the following assumptions as basic to behavior therapy: "(1) An individual may be viewed simply as the sum total of the behaviors which he emits. (2) There are general principles which describe the relationship of those behaviors to the environment; these principles emphasize the power of current environmental events. (3) Deviant problem behavior is not different in quality from behavior in general, and thus it can be changed by the techniques already known to be applicable to teaching ordinary behaviors. (4) It is neither necessary nor realistic to hypothesize a deeper level of behavioral function than the environmental events known to operate in current behavioral techniques" (p. 193). These ideas are quite straightforward but allow little room for any dynamic input from the learner.

Lazarus (1968), who worked with Wolpe in South Africa before coming to the United States, is seen by some behavior modifiers as, more or less, a heretic. He suggests that therapists should be eclectic by enriching behavioral approaches with other techniques such as interpretation, drug therapy, surgery, or electroconvulsive shock, when these have been found to be therapeutic under the prevailing conditions. He feels that therapists should do even more than that encompassed by complex S-R relationships.

On the other side of this ideological fence is Ullmann (1969), who argues forcefully that all

**Table 5-1  Eysenck's Tabulation of Differences between Psychotherapy and Behavior Therapy**

| Freudian psychotherapy | Behavior therapy |
|---|---|
| **1** It is based on inconsistent theory never properly formulated in postulate form. | **1** It is based on consistent, properly formulated theory leading to testable deductions. |
| **2** It is derived from clinical observations made without necessary control, observation, or experiments. | **2** It is derived from experimental studies specifically designed to test basic theory and deductions made therefrom. |
| **3** Symptoms are the visible upshot of unconscious causes ("complexes"). | **3** Symptoms are unadaptive CRs. |
| **4** Symptoms are evidence of repression. | **4** Symptoms are evidence of faulty learning. |
| **5** Symptomatology is determined by defense mechanism. | **5** Symptomatology is determined by individual differences in conditionability and autonomic lability, as well as accidental environmental circumstances. |
| **6** All treatment of neurotic disorders must be historically based. | **6** All treatment of neurotic disorders is concerned with habits existing at present; historical development is largely irrelevant. |
| **7** Cures are achieved by handling the underlying (unconscious) dynamics, not by treating the symptom itself. | **7** Cures are achieved by treating the symptom itself, i.e., by extinguishing unadaptive CRs and establishing desirable CRs. |
| **8** Interpretation of symptoms, dreams, acts, etc., is an important element of treatment. | **8** Interpretation, even if not completely subjective and erroneous, is irrelevant. |
| **9** Symptomatic treatment leads to the elaboration of new symptoms. | **9** Symptomatic treatment leads to permanent recovery, provided autonomic as well as skeletal surplus CRs are extinguished. |
| **10** Transference relations are essential for cures of neurotic disorders. | **10** Personal relations are not essential for cures of neurotic disorder, although they may be useful in certain circumstances. |

*Source:* H. J. Eysenck, Learning theory and behavior therapy, *Journal of Mental Science*, 1959, 105, p. 67, by permission of the author and publisher.

acts are environmentally determined. His position on freedom of choice is specific; there is none. What is classified as choice is just a cover for ignorance about the dynamics of the forces acting on the individual. Previously Chein (1962) had taken strong exception to a model of man as a robot, claiming that man is an active agent in the universe and able to influence the interplay of forces acting on him so that they are more nearly in accord with his purposes.

Buchwald and Young (1969) discuss the implicit meanings of some of the ideas basic to behavior modification. They point out that adaptation, in the biological meaning of the term, has very little to do with large areas of social learning. Inappropriate behavior, which Ullmann and Krasner (1965) put forward as a social definition of adaptation, was a highly flexible concept for parents, teachers, and significant others in the life of the individual. They also point out that whether a consequence of activity is positively or negatively reinforcing depends on the goals and interests of the subject as much as on the characteristics of the interaction viewed externally. They raise the question of whether symptoms are independent or are rooted in more fundamental etiologies; their interpretation could be summarized as having elements of both. Some symptoms, those which are independent and not deeply integrated into personality, are fairly easily corrected. Other symptoms have roots in complex personality structures and are less amenable to correction. Peterson and London (1965), writing in Ullmann and Krasner's *Case Studies in Behavior Modification*, point out with some vigor that while learning can take place without cognition, understanding can significantly facilitate the acquisition of adaptive skills.

Viewpoints change as difficult cases are encountered and interpreted. This section started with a 1967 review by Franks of the exclusive definition of behavior modification. In 1969 he wrote, "Historically, the short term progression (over the 60's) seems to be away from an emphasis by the behavior therapist upon the rather doctrinaire and simplistic thinking of the early 60's toward [a] broad spectrum behavioral management of more recent years (p. 20)."

## RESEARCH ON BEHAVIOR MODIFICATION

Behavior modification has been subjected to extensive research in part because measurable changes are possible in a relatively short time. The emphasis on observable behavior as a variable to be tested means that agreement can be reached as to the nature of the behavior before and after the treatment. For teachers the most interesting research concerns techniques for classroom control. Counselors and school psychologists may be more interested in studies of systematic desensitization, operant therapy, or even aversion therapy. Selected studies from each of these areas will be reviewed. In all these studies the affective loadings are manipulated to cause some activities to happen more frequently and other activities to be eliminated or made much less

common in the repertoire of particular individuals. Teachers and counselors need a base of communication in dealing with children with emotional problems.

### Classroom Control Experiments

**Madsen, Becker, and Thomas** Madsen, Becker, and Thomas (1971) found significantly fewer instances of inappropriate behavior when teachers systematically reinforced pupils positively than when rules of conduct were taught or when disruptive activities were ignored. The subjects were one kindergarten and two second-grade pupils. At the beginning of treatment one of the second-graders spent his time fiddling with objects, talking, doing nothing, walking around the room, and hitting other children. When kept in at recess to do his work, he was able to finish it correctly in a very short time. The other second-grader was noted for misbehavior in the classroom, intense fighting on the playground, and copying the activities for which other children had just been disciplined. The kindergarten child was described as "wild"; wandered around the room; pushed, hit, and grabbed youngsters and things; and destroyed his own work rather than taking it home.

Observers were trained to use coding scales for inappropriate and for appropriate behavior (Tables 5-2 and 5-3). Raters had developed a reliability beyond 80 percent before they started recording pretreatment data (Figure 5-1, base line 1). Ratings were obtained for a twenty-minute period for each of three days a week. Normally one rater checked the teacher's responses to the class as a whole, and the other rater recorded the activity of one of the children. During treatment the teacher stressed appropriate rules of behavior five times a day, for approximately three weeks (Rules). This was followed by stressing the rules of conduct and ignoring the inap-

## Table 5-2 Behavioral Coding Categories for Children

### 1 Inappropriate behaviors

**A** *Gross Motor* Getting out of seat, standing up, running, hopping, skipping, jumping, walking around, moving chair, etc.

**B** *Object Noise* Tapping pencil or other objects, clapping, tapping feet, rattling or tearing paper, throwing book on desk, slamming desk. Be conservative, only rate if you can hear the noise when eyes are closed. Do *not* include accidental dropping of objects.

**C** *Disturbance of Other's Property* Grabbing objects or work, knocking neighbor's books off desk, destroying another's property, pushing with desk (only rate if someone is there). Throwing objects at another person without hitting him.

**D** *Contact (high and low intensity)* Hitting, kicking, shoving, pinching, slapping, striking with object, throwing object which hits another person, poking with object, biting, pulling hair, touching, patting, etc. Any physical contact is rated.

**E** *Verbalization* Carrying on conversations with other children when it is not permitted. Answers teacher without raising hand or without being called on; making comments or calling out remarks when no questions have been asked; calling teacher's name to get her attention; crying, screaming, singing, whistling, laughing, coughing, or blowing loudly. These responses may be directed to teacher or children.

**F** *Turning Around* Turning head or head and body to look at another person, showing objects to another child, attending to another child. Must be of 4-second duration, or more than 90 degrees using desk as a reference. Not rated unless seated. If this response overlaps two time intervals and cannot be rated in the first because it is less than a 4-second duration, then rate in the interval in which the end of the response occurs.

**G** *Other Inappropriate Behavior* Ignores teacher's question or command. Does something different from that directed to do, including minor motor behavior such as playing with pencil or eraser when supposed to be writing, coloring while the record is on, doing spelling during the arithmetic lesson, playing with objects. *The child involves himself in a task that is not appropriate.* Not rated when other inappropriate behaviors are rated. Must be time off task.

**H** *Mouthing Objects* Bringing thumb, fingers, pencils, or any object in contact with the mouth.

**I** *Isolate Play* Limited to kindergarten free-play period. Child must be farther than 3 feet from any person, neither initiates nor responds to verbalizations with other people, engages in no interaction of a nonverbal nature with other children for the entire 10-second period.

### II Appropriate behavior

Time on task; e.g., answers question, listens, raises hand, works on assignment. Must include whole 10-second interval except for turning-around responses of less than a 4-second duration.

*Source:* W. C. Becker, C. H. Madsen, Jr., Carole R. Arnold, and D. R. Thomas, The contingent use of teacher attention and praise in reducing classroom behavior problems, *Journal of Special Education*, 1967, 1, pp. 287–307, by permission of the publisher.

propriate behavior in experimental pupils (Rules, Ignore). After behavior had been modified, by adding praise for appropriate behavior, an attempt was made to reverse the process and establish a causal relationship for the treatment. Following the return to base-line behavior (Base II), the modification was reestablished by using praise plus rules and ignoring inappropriate behavior. The results are shown in Figure 5-2 for the kindergarten child. Inspection of the figures indicates that inappropriate behavior was reduced to less

## Table 5-3  Coding Definitions for Teacher Behaviors

Appropriate child behavior is defined by the child rating categories. The teacher's rules for classroom behavior must be considered when judging whether the child's behavior is appropriate or inappropriate.

**I** Teacher approval following appropriate child behavior

   **A** *Contact.* Positive physical contact such as embracing, kissing, patting, holding arm or hand, sitting on lap.

   **B** *Praise.* Verbal comments indicating approval, commendation, or achievement. Examples: that's good, you are doing right, you are studying well, I like you, thank you, you make me happy.

   **C** *Facial attention.* Smiling at child.

**II** Teacher approval following inappropriate child behavior
Same codes as under I.

**III** Teacher disapproval following appropriate child behavior

   **A** *Holding the child.* Forcibly holding the child, putting child out in the hall, grabbing, hitting, spanking, slapping, shaking the child.

   **B** *Criticism.* Critical comments of high or low intensity, yelling, scolding, raising voice. Examples: that's wrong, don't do that, stop talking, did I call on you, you are wasting your time, don't laugh, you know what you are supposed to do.

   **C** *Threats.* Consequences mentioned by the teacher to be used at a later time. If _____ then _____ comments.

   **D** *Facial attention.* Frowning or grimacing at a child.

**IV** Teacher disapproval following inappropriate child behavior
Same codes as under III.

**V** "Timeout" procedures*

   **A** The teacher turns out the lights and says nothing.

   **B** The teacher turns her back and waits for silence.

   **C** The teacher stops talking and waits for quiet.

   **D** Keeping in for recess.

   **E** Sending child to office.

   **F** Depriving child in the classroom of some privilege.

**VI** Academic recognition
Calling on a child for an answer. Giving "feedback" for academic correctness.

---

*These are procedural definitions of teacher behaviors possibly involving the withdrawal of reinforcers as a consequence of disruptive behaviors which teacher could not ignore.

*Source:* W. C. Becker, C. H. Madsen, Jr., Carole R. Arnold, and D. R. Thomas, The contingent use of teacher attention and praise in reducing classroom behavior problems, *Journal of Special Education,* 1967, 1, pp. 287–307, by permission of the publisher.

than half the base-line levels when the children, who knew the rules, were being praised for doing the appropriate things and inappropriate behavior was being ignored. The changes are statistically significant even though the sample size is very small.

Subjectively the teachers found themselves looking for things to praise rather than things to criticize, and they felt better about their teaching experiences. The kindergarten teacher had been using a regimen of praise, but she often used it so that the child was reinforced for doing inappropriate things rather than for doing things that would make life in the classroom more desirable for him and for the other class members. The objective recording of what was actually taking place in the classroom seemed to be an important ingredient in changing teacher behavior under this form of modification. It was clear that the teacher's behavior needed to be modified in order to effect a change in the undesirable activities of the children.

**Thomas, Becker, and Armstrong** Thomas, Becker, and Armstrong (1971) used behavior modification techniques to disrupt the patterns of a well-behaved second-grade class and then to restore the desirable behavior. Analysis of the teacher behavior indicated that she was praising appropriate behavior and avoiding praising inappropriate behavior. For pupils, observers tallied the incidence of gross motor, noise making, orienting, talking, and aggressive disruptive behaviors. The teacher's disapproving behavior was also rated, including forcibly holding a child, grabbing, hitting, slapping, and pushing. Verbal disapproval included yelling, scolding, belittling, ridiculing, and threatening. Frowning, grimacing, shaking the head to indicate "no," and gesturing were also rated as disapproving activities. Approving behaviors including physically holding, patting, hugging, and kissing the child; verbal statements of approval, affection, or praise; and smiling, winking, or nodding were all considered reinforcing.

The disruptive treatment consisted of (1) discontinuing approving behaviors but continuing disapproval for inappropriate behavior, (2) return to base line, (3) removal of approval and increased disapproval to three times the former level, (4) return to moderate disapproval, and finally (5) return to base line.

The results showed an initial base line of 8.7 percent disruptive behavior followed by treatments: (1) 25.5 percent disruptive behavior upon withdrawal of approval, (2) 12.9 percent disruptive behavior for base line 2, (3) 19.4 percent disruptive withdrawal of approval, (4) 31.2 percent disruptive behavior for frequent disapproval, (5) 25.9 percent disruptive behavior for low disapproval, (6) 13.2 percent disruptive behavior upon return to base line 3

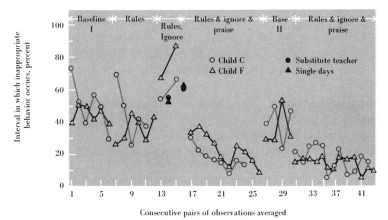

**Figure 5-1** Inappropriate behavior of two problem children in second grade as a function of experimental conditions. (*Source: Charles H. Madsen, Jr., Wesley C. Becker, and Don R. Thomas, Rules, praise, and ignoring: Elements of elementary classroom control, Journal of Applied Behavior Analyses I, Summer 1968, 139–50. Copyright 1968 by the Society for the Experimental Analysis of Behavior, Inc.*)

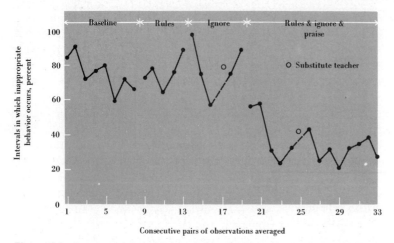

**Figure 5-2** Inappropriate behavior of one problem child in kindergarten as a function of experimental conditions. (*Source: Charles H. Madsen, Jr., Wesley C. Becker, and Don R. Thomas, Rules, praise, and ignoring: Elements of elementary classroom control, Journal of Applied Behavior Analyses I, Summer, 1968, 139–150. Copyright 1968 by the Society for the Experimental Analysis of Behavior, Inc.*)

(Figure 5-3.) As the disruptive behavior increased, the relevant behavior went down according to the tallies. The teacher commented that the major impact of the cessation of praise was greater than that recorded, since it came in the afternoon when recording was no longer being carried on.

Further analysis by inspection of the data indicated that positive response to undesirable behaviors increased the likelihood of those behaviors, that praise for desirable behaviors increased the incidence of the reinforced behavior, and finally that if the teacher did not supply enough approval for desirable activities, children looked for approval from their peers for disruptive behaviors or activities that annoyed the teacher.

**Schmidt and Ulrich**   Schmidt and Ulrich (1969) found that they could substantially decrease the noise level in a fourth-grade class during free-study time. The reinforcers were an anticipated extension of class gym period by two minutes and a two-minute break for

each completed ten minutes when the noise level did not go above 42 decibels, as recorded on a General Radio Corporation Model 710-A sound-level meter. The noise level in the room without students was between 36 and 37 decibels. If the 42-decibel level was exceeded by the class, the timer had to be reset and the ten minutes started over again.

A ten-day base-line period was established, followed by a seven-day conditioning period. The children were then told that the reinforcing conditions no longer existed, and after seven days the conditioning was reinstated. The results are shown in Figure 5-4. The noise level had changed from a range above 52 decibels to under 40 decibels.

In a somewhat similar experiment Schmidt and Ulrich found they could decrease the noise level in a first-grade classroom and that the achieved quietness was maintained over a summer and into the next year, when the teacher continued with the children into second grade. The experimenters also found that they could use this technique to reduce wandering around the room by students of these ages. Probably extra gym time was not particularly desired by all the children, but peer pressure was added to the other reinforcement to obtain a class response similar in nature to what would be expected from a single student for whom the reinforcement was rewarding.

**Karraker** Karraker (1971) reported the use of behavior modification techniques by a number of inner-city teachers who were graduate students in his program. In study hall, the 30-minute period was being largely wasted because most of the secondary students were talking; leaving their seats; and not bringing books, pencil, and paper. A contract was arranged that students who brought paper, pencil, and a book; who did not get out of their seats; and who did not talk for the first 20

minutes of the study hall period would be permitted to sit with a friend and talk quietly or read comic books for the last 10 minutes. The average changes from an 11-day base-line phase to a 15-day modification phase were reported: (1) students bringing study materials increased from 50 to 90 percent, (2) incidence of talking reduced from 64 to 25 percent, (3) time out of seats reduced from 28 to 0 percent. When the reinforcers were withdrawn, the behavior reverted toward base line, and when the program was reinstated, the desirable behaviors were reinstituted although not to the levels obtained in the first modification.

Karraker also reported instances where the attempt at behavior modification failed. In one case the teacher made a poor presentation, the reinforcement opportunities that were selected were ineffective with the students, and

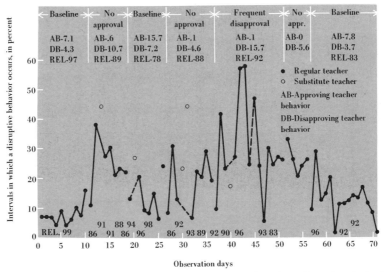

**Figure 5-3** Disruptive classroom behavior as a function of teacher behavior. Data points represent 2-minute samples on 10 children each day. Dotted lines cross observations where the regular teacher was absent due to a recurrent illness, including a 10-day hospitalization between days 39 and 41. The dotted line connecting days 44 and 45 represents the Easter vacation break. The data for day 26 were taken with the teacher out of the room. (*From Don R. Thomas, Wesley C. Becker, and Marianne Armstong, Production and elimination of disruptive classroom behavior by systematically varying teacher's behavior, 1971. Reproduced by permission of Thomas R. Crowell Publishers.*)

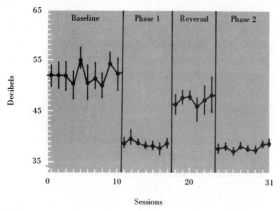

**Figure 5-4** The effects of sound control procedures on the classroom noise level. Each point represents the average sound-level reading for one session, with vertical lines denoting the mean deviation. (*Source: Gilbert W. Schmidt and Roger E. Ulrich, Effects of group contingent events upon classroom noise, Journal of Applied Behavior Analysis II, 1969, 171–179. Copyright 1969 by the Society for the Experimental Analysis of Behavior, Inc.*)

undesirable behaviors all increased. In another class the teacher used individualized teaching and was not in a position to recognize and reinforce the various behaviors differentially. A third teacher used comic books as the reinforcer but did not change them frequently enough to maintain reinforcement. Karraker also reported principals and school psychologists who resisted behavior modification as too Orwellian or as too much in a state of flux.

**Patterson** Patterson (1965b) worked with hyperactive nine- and ten-year-olds who had been diagnosed as brain-damaged. He was able to reduce the peer approval being given these children for inappropriate behavior by reinforcing the entire class for desirable responses on the part of the hyperactive students. The regimen increased the attending behavior of the brain-damaged children.

Teachers will find that using positive reinforcers for appropriate behavior, ignoring undesirable behavior, and distinguishing which is

which can improve the affective functioning of their students. They will also find that, as teachers, they are under reinforcing schedules from the class and that it is better to get started positively rather than to try to change negatively toned behavior patterns after they have been established.

### Systematic Desensitization

The early successes in behavior modification were developed in a clinical situation where the client was working with a psychiatrist. Obviously the problems were sufficiently troublesome to bring the client to seek help. As originally developed, behavior modification was only part of the procedure used by the psychiatrist and in the beginning was used on simple or uncomplicated phobias.

**Wolpe** Wolpe (1961) developed a desensitization package which consisted of (1) training in deep relaxation; (2) construction of hierarchies of anxiety-producing stimuli; and (3) gradual pairing, through imagery, of anxiety stimuli with the state of relaxation. Wolpe's clinical work for human patients had been preceded by experimental work on cats made neurotic by conditioning them to attempt discriminations that were too difficult in order to get fed. Wolpe's clinical procedure for *deep relaxation* teaches the client to relax the muscles in his toes, arches, ankles, calves of his legs, and so on until he is completely relaxed. One of the early uses for this process of relaxation was to help people sleep.

The *anxiety hierarchies* are produced by having the client tell about everything that makes him anxious, to create his own anxiety scale. Questionnaires can be used to help the individual think of areas that may be troublesome. The anxiety-producing stimuli are grouped into families such as anxieties about sex, about money, about religious beliefs, and so on. Within a family, a hierarchy is produced of stimuli that elicit anxiety. As nearly equal gradations as possible, working from very weak anxiety production to high anxiety production, are developed. Some of the strength differences are due to the closeness of the events in time or space and some are due to the differences between the events.

In the desensitization proper, *gradual pairing*, the individual is put into a completely relaxed state and the least anxiety-producing stimulus is suggested. When the stimulus can be imagined by the client without any feeling of tension, anxiety, or discomfort, the therapist suggests the next stimulus. If more than one family of anxieties has to be worked on, a switch is made after desensitization to stimuli in another family. This procedure can be seen as very much the same as that described under Guthrie (Chapter 4), where conditioning was carried out by bringing a troublesome stimulus gradually into the foreground in the presence of a very much enjoyed activity.

**Paul (1969a)**  Paul (1969a) analyzed eight of Wolpe's reports in order to determine that the behavior modification component of his treatment was causal. The problems treated included claustrophobia; agorophobia, or fear of being in an open space; inferiority feelings; exhibitionism; kleptomania; sexual impotence and frigidity; and obsessions. In order for the treatment to be considered a success, the patient had to place himself in either of the top two categories on a scale of 5 in treatment areas: improved productivity, better adjustment, pleasure in sex, interpersonal relationships, and ability to handle ordinary conflicts. On these criteria Paul rated 88 to 92 percent of the cases as successful. He pointed out that self-report scales are unreliable and concluded that Wolpe's work is historically interesting but not proof of the efficacy of behavior modification in treatment of neuroses.

**Lazarus**  Lazarus (1963) reported similar treatments for similar ailments in his own clients. He also used the 5-point rating scales but verified them with external reports from referring physicians, families, friends, and fellow workers. If a rating was in doubt, it was put in the lower category. Of 220 cases for whom systematic desensitization was the "therapy of record," 86 percent were reported as successfully treated. Of 30 cases rated failures, 26 had had previous treatment by other therapists for 10 or more years. In spite of extended clinical reports, Paul pointed out that these cases cannot be accepted as cause-and-effect relationships between systematic desensitization and reduction in distressing behavior.

**Paul (1969b)**  Paul (1969b) described a case of an eighteen-year-old girl who had suffered from test anxiety for six years. A test hierarchy of 10 items was constructed, and she was induced to relax and was desensitized. The whole treatment took four sessions spread over two weeks. The girl reported feeling "just grand" during her next examinations. Her grades raised from C's and D's before treatment to A's and B's after treatment and remained at this level for at least 13 months.

**Emery and Krumboltz**  Emery and Krumboltz (1967) reported a systematic study of the use of desensitization on college students who had high scores on an anxiety test designed for the experiment. The students were assigned on a random basis to one of three groups, an individualized desensitization group, a standardized desensitization group, and a control group. A hierarchy of 16 items was constructed from a pilot study, and the two desensitization groups differed only in that one group used the list in the order formulated, while in the other group each student decided which items should make up his intensity order. The total items remained consistent for both groups. Nine graduate students carried out the desensitization procedures with two students each, from each of the experimental groups. Criterion measures consisted of the anxiety test, self-ratings, and grades on a history examination, all given at the end of therapy.

Analysis of covariance was used for the history exam and the test anxiety scores. A one-way analysis of variance was performed on the self-rating scales. On the test anxiety scales the desensitization groups both showed significant improvement compared to the control group. Performance on the history exam was in the direction of improvement for the desensitization groups but was not statistically significant. The history test, incidentally, appeared highly unreliable because of the number of graders, the essay nature of the questions, and nonstandardization of grading procedures. In reviewing this experiment Paul (1969b) claimed that a cause and effect in favor of the desensitization is a valid interpretation although no definitive findings were available for standardized versus individualized hierarchy scales.

The requirements of research design often distort good therapy procedures because treatment must be the same for all subjects. As a result the validity of the treatment may be misrepresented. In order to satisfy the technical requirements of a statistical study, some of the essential features of treatment are sacrificed. The hierarchies of anxiety used by Emery and Krumboltz were kept the same rather than fitted to the individual's need for therapy. The number of treatments were kept uniform to avoid an error in comparability, although some patients may have needed *more* treatment and others *less*. Finally, the disability to be treated must be endemic in a large population in order to provide enough subjects to make up comparable treatment groups. It seems obvious that clinical research, which is not valued by some experimental psychologists, is needed to define the parameters that should be tested.

## Aversion Therapy

Another form of behavior modification of interest to clinicians is *aversion therapy*. The basic principle is that when an undesirable stimulus-response connection has been established, the connection can be broken by adding punishment to the connection system. As practiced, the punishments are usually either chemical or electrical in nature. The electrical punishment is more easily controlled and can be repeated more immediately than chemical punishments normally can. The emetics, such as Antabuse, given to alcoholics to make them deathly sick when they take alcohol, fall in the category of chemical aversion agents. Aversion therapy has been used primarily in the treatment of alcoholism and homosexuality, although it has also been used with smoking, obesity, and other problems. Because of the indeterminate effect of punishment connections, usually some positive therapy is also needed. In homosexual treatments this usually is in the form of positive reinforcements for approach reactions to female figures if approach reactions to male figures are being extinguished. Estes (1944) found that punishment for bar pressing in rats only suppressed the activity temporarily; however, Lichtenstein (1950) found that animals punished for eating would starve themselves to death in the presence of food. Many clients of aversion therapy have definitely changed their manner of acting after they had this form of treatment.

**Kimmel** Kimmel (1971) described the use of Antabuse (disulfiram) as a chemical aversion device for problem drinkers who were legally committed. After detoxification in a hospital, patients were given three tablets of Antabuse a day for four days. They were challenged with 1 ounce of whiskey which produced severe face flushing, racing pulse, drop in blood pressure, nausea or vomiting, and fainting or collapse. Emergency equipment was kept available during the aversion treatment. After the hospitalization phase, patients were required to come in for two to three tablets a week administered in the hospital. Patients who missed appointments were followed up and either continued on treatment, returned to the hospital, or confined to jail. After a year the report of 121 people who had completed the program indicated that 76 were functioning adequately, 8 were in prison, 8 were dead, 9 were drinking heavily again, 4 were in nursing homes, 1 was in a mental hospital, 7 had moved from the area, and 8 were unknown. It should be noted that the challenge to combine drinking and Antabuse constituted the only aversion application and this only happened once. Considering that the clientele were all hard-core alcoholics, the recovery rate seems excellent.

**Feldman and MacCulloch**  Feldman and MacCulloch (1969) developed a technique for treating male homosexuals by aversion therapy. Two series of slides were developed and classed by the patient in rank order as far as attractiveness was concerned. One series was of men in various poses and stages of undress; the other series was of women similarly unattired. Approximately eight slides of each sex were selected for the treatment sequences. The men's pictures were shown starting with the least attractive. The patient was asked to keep it on the screen as long as it appeared attractive. If he removed it within 8 seconds, nothing happened to him, but after that length of time he received a shock of sufficient voltage to be distinctly unpleasant. Pictures of

women were shown but not paired with shock. The intention was to eliminate the attractiveness of the males and increase the attractiveness of female figures. A follow-up evaluation of 43 patients who had been referred for treatment found that 25 were improved, 11 had not changed their sexual orientation, and 7 had quit treatment before completion. Patients who had some history of attraction for females tended to profit from the therapy while those who were complete homosexuals did not.

## Operant Therapy

All behavior modification contains elements of operant conditioning. Teachers are more likely to use operant therapy than systematic desensitization or aversion therapy. In contrast to aversion behavior control, therapy emphasizes the use of positive reinforcers to shape the desired behavior. Many studies have been conducted in this area, but only a few of them will be reviewed.

**Ferster**  Ferster (1967) analyzed the techniques of a skilled therapist in terms of behavior modification, so that other workers could understand the steps and become proficient in their use. Many teachers will be able to identify with her. Many kindergarten and first-grade teachers have rather distracting experiences with children who are bothered by being left alone with strangers when starting school and spend a great deal of time crying. The therapist in this study, Miss S., had a similar problem with a four-year-old autistic child in a residential center for disturbed children. Karen spent most of the first two weeks of her visit to the center clutching a doll and crying.

Miss S. put Karen on a rocking horse and sang to her. The crying stopped as long as the rocking and singing continued. After a few minutes Miss S. stopped rocking but kept the singing going; however, she restarted the rocking before Karen became bothered so as not to start the rocking in response to crying, which would have been reinforcement for crying and would have strengthened the probability of more crying taking place. Miss S. then waited until Karen was occupied with the handles of the horse and took the doll away, put it on a table, and moved the table close to Karen who reached down and picked up the doll. She also made movements that started the rocking. Miss S. reinforced this activity by singing when she moved and humming quietly when Karen stopped rocking the horse. The doll episode was repeated, and Karen was without the doll for a little longer but not long enough to cause her to cry. Again she was reinforced for rocking when Miss S. sang to her. Eventually Karen put the doll on the table in order to rock more easily. Next Miss S. stopped singing for short periods. During one of these Karen stopped rocking and reached for the doll, which fell from the table to the floor. Karen began to cry. Miss S. asked if she wanted to pick up the doll and helped her get off the horse. She reinforced Karen subtly for each effort at self help in getting back on the horse. On one occasion Miss S. picked up the doll and tapped a rhythm to which Karen rocked. Eventually Miss S. held Karen on her knee and sang to her even though Karen indicated she wanted to get back on the horse. Karen had been doing some things for herself, she had not been crying except for two brief periods, and she had been without the doll without crying.

The artistry in the treatment is in being sensitive to the involvement of the child in the ongoing processes, being acutely aware of the need for changes before the child cries, seeing opportunities to replace undesirable with more constructive activities, and sensing the steps that will move to the new activities a little at a time. In this sequence the reinforcers are friendly human contact which ebbed and flowed to strengthen desirable activities and to diminish undesirable responses. The difference between success and failure in building up highly productive attitudes and learning is largely one of sensitivity and timing. Failure can be changed to success by observing what is happening to the child or student and carefully reinforcing the desirable rather than the undesirable responses.

**Lovaas, Freitas, Nelson, and Whalen**
Lovaas, Freitas, Nelson, and Whalen (1967) combined behavior modification with modeling behaviors to work with autistic young children. The children were reinforced for imitating an adult by rewarding them each time they moved toward doing what the adult was doing. This process was extended over a number of activities, and it was possible to develop a generalized modeling response. After copying of a model had been established, the children were taught to make their beds, wash their hands, play games, brush their hair, and do other things that normally would have been learned. It was not necessary to teach each activity separately; once the general approach of modeling had been learned, the children were able to transfer it to new situations.

**Risley and Wolf**  Risley and Wolf (1967) used the modeling technique to teach language to retarded and autistic children who first were systematically reinforced with food and praise for mimicking the instructor. After the mimicking had been established, the use of words was transferred to naming objects and using words in phrases without the instructor saying the words. Parents were recruited to use the same procedures at home. After the use of words in a home context had been established, new vocabulary was taught by modeling, praise, and food reinforcement.

Teachers will find these studies particularly

encouraging, because it is much faster to teach by modeling, or instruction that requires imitation, than it is to shape responses from a non-existent base. If care is taken to ensure that the beginning learning is soundly established, later instruction can move forward more quickly. It is worth the time to establish basic patterns that are needed for later learning.

**Koegel and Covert** Koegel and Covert (1972) found autistic children needed a combination of punishment and positive reinforcement for learning and discrimination if progress was to be made. The three children, two age seven and one age five, had been diagnosed as autistic by agencies other than the researchers. All three were unresponsive to the environment, seemingly unaware of people trying to get their attention and walking into walls without any indication of pain. All three engaged in a great deal of self-stimulatory activity. For one this activity was rhythmic rocking and waving objects or hands before his eyes. A second gazed directly at the overhead houselight and rhythmically manipulated his fingers, flapped his hands or arms, and repetitively vocalized vowels.

The children showed no evidence of learning the discrimination while they were engaged in self-stimulation. Suppression of self-stimulation through punishment allowed learning to take place. It was as though only one sense modality was operative at a time. Lovaas and Schreibman (1972) found that autistic children responded to only one of two simultaneously presented cues, unlike normal children for whom different sensory modalities are often associated in standard classical conditioning. Additional work with autistic children may reveal the conditions under which attention to multichannel inputs can become established.

**Sherman and Baer** Sherman and Baer (1969) discussed the value of using tokens as reinforcers. Social approval and satisfaction in learning are definitely the most common and the most desirable ways of reinforcing young people for learning. Unfortunately a number of people have never found the usual systems of reinforcement effective; therefore, other more extrinsic rewards have been tried. In institutions food is quite regularly used in this way. Candies, essentially M&M's, have enjoyed a reputation as reinforcers. In the general society money is the commonest reinforcer besides approval and satisfaction. If a behavior modification schedule is to be successful, the reinforcers must be effective or the system will disintegrate. Not all individuals find the same things reinforcing so that the teacher needs to have a variety of possibilities available. A way of handling this problem that has been growing in popularity has been the use of tokens which can be exchanged for toys, privileges, food, trips, or rights.

Sherman and Baer list the following advantages of tokens as reinforcers: (1) They are easy to present and do not disrupt the ongoing activity. (2) Since there is normally a choice about what the tokens can be exchanged for, a strong probability exists that different tastes can be met. (3) Tokens can be used as fractions of a big reinforcer, such as a bicycle. (4) The timing of the reinforcement is simple. On the other hand, there are disadvantages to tokens. Sherman and Baer list these: (1) Tokens are not obviously reinforcing so that the student has to be taught the value of them. (2) They are no better than the backup materials or privileges for which they can be exchanged. (3) The person using the tokens must run a store which may involve considerable inconvenience, although this can be tied in with other school activities in a realistic way. (4) The token approach must be phased out so that intrinsic rewards will substitute.

In behavior modification the affective loadings are being manipulated to strengthen some responses and to weaken others that are counterproductive. Eventually the student must function in a satisfactory way after the therapist has gone home. The significance of this need will be discussed in Chapter 7, Affective Conceptualizations, and Chapter 8, Creative Self-Direction.

**Phillips**   Phillips (1971) used token reinforcement procedures with three predelinquent boys who were wards of the court and were housed in his home. The boys were aged twelve, thirteen, and fourteen years, with a range of reported IQ scores from 85 to 120. All the boys had poor reading scores, poor math scores, and social habits that were obnoxious to adults and students around them. The tokens were marks on a card that could be exchanged for privileges, such as permission to go downtown, permission to come home late from school, permission to watch TV. In addition, the boys could use points to buy—at auction—the right to choose where they would ride in the car, the right to be the manager in charge of cleaning the bathroom, and other similar activities. The boys could also lose points for speaking aggressively, being late, using poor grammar, receiving failing grades; and a very high loss would result from stealing, cheating, or lying. Points could be earned for watching news on TV, reading the newspaper, cleaning and maintaining one's room, being neatly dressed for evening meal, doing homework, aiding in various household tasks, etc. All these activities were required in any case; the points came for doing the work properly and up to well-defined standards.

One experiment on doing homework and another on removing "ain't" from spoken usage certainly had school-related overtones. Phillips established a base line over a 10-day period with regular observations during 3 hours a day. Then for a period of 5 days verbal correction, such as "That is no way to talk" or "Stop that kind of talk," was tried with very little effect. In the third period fines were imposed for each aggressive expression. The fine was minimal, amounting to approximately the bonus that could be earned by turning out a light when leaving a room. An immediate and stabilized drop in aggression occurred, which continued for 10 days. The boys were then told (in period four) there would be no fines, although semithreats were made during the 30-day period this was in order. The aggressive language returned to moderate strength on the part of two boys. Fines were again established and the aggressive speech was extinguished for a period of 20 days. Teachers frequently have students who speak in a manner that requires correction. A token approach would very likely remove this kind of speech.

Although Phillips' experiments used fines which could be considered punishments, he obtained similar results in some experiments in which the boys earned points rather than lost them. The fines seemed to work in the same way as positive reinforcers. By doing what was required in a detailed and measurable way, the boy could mentally earn points he wanted to use by not losing them. Teachers in school would normally find positive reinforcers more effective than fines or demerits since they do not ordinarily have the power to make the loss of points particularly meaningful.

## DISCIPLINE

Behavior modification was first used in schools to help teachers restore order to classrooms that had become chaotic. When many individuals are brought together—as in the school—to pursue goals that do not necessarily coincide with their needs as persons, external control is essential at times to the orderly conduct of work. However, the long-range purpose of discipline in schools is the gradual achievement of self-direction on the part of students.

The teacher's problems of class control result from the tremendous differences among class members in motivation to learn the designated curriculum, in degree of responsibility for self-control, in personal feelings of worth, and in ability to learn what is required to master the content. The specific needs of individual students differ from moment to moment, as does the relevance of a given task to prolonged deficit needs. This means that constructive approaches to discipline must be individualized in a setting where fairness to all is the first criterion for respect. Behavior modification, which requires different plans of reinforcement for different pupils, presumes a teacher with both emotional strength and professional expertise.

Repressive or punishing discipline is rarely needed when the good of the whole class has been accepted as important by the individual members. In such a classroom each individual is secure within himself. He knows where he fits into the organization, what his reponsibilities are, and what the limits and conventions are within which he can function most effectively. He expects few surprises about rules, and he knows that the rules apply equally to all members of the class. When the school is run as an efficient organization, effort is rarely expended in trying to remake it into some other image.

During times of radical change within the society as a whole, however, discipline is disrupted until new rules are established and new relationships are forged. Such times of change generate anxiety and lead many people to settle for stability by external control. Unable to tolerate a period of instability, they will relinquish their own chance for self-determination, perhaps out of fear of other people's use of freedom. Developing of discipline from a base of individual freedom

often seems hazardous to young teachers, but actually requires less energy than the use of repressive techniques.

## Adults as Disciplinarians

The quality of the social interaction that students learn affects the enjoyment that teachers derive from their work. When students work together, problems are solved, materials are shared, and teachers have a chance to finish lessons without disruption. When student disturbances are frequent, the most ingenious selection and arrangement of content will neither compensate the eager students for the disjointed, disrupted thinking processes they must endure nor prevent the teacher from having feelings of frustration. Ability to control the class is the single most important prerequisite to enjoyment of teaching.

### Discipline Failures Lead to Dismissal

University presidents, school superintendents, principals, and teachers all have been removed from their positions because the public or the board decided they were unable to discipline students in an acceptable manner. In many cases, the disruptive forces were beyond the control of the official or the teacher who was held responsible. Often public judgment has been based on ignorance of how the dynamics of working through roles leads students eventually to greater maturity. Often these lay boards have had a naive faith in exhortation and commands as a means of compelling obedience, with little understanding of the price in personality damage that primitive discipline often entails.

Although the teacher should not use discipline techniques which require abject obedience, he must be in control of his class. The teacher who cannot control a class cannot teach it. Students who are roaming around the room or talking or bickering with one another are learning what they are attending to, and not the lesson on the binomial theorem. Approximately half of all beginning teachers experience problems in class discipline that are serious enough to result in their dismissal, their resignation, or the intervention of the principal or supervisor. Many times the teacher himself requests help because he knows that the students in his class lack discipline, but he does not understand why they are so different from those he remembers from his student teaching experiences.

The teacher's role as disciplinarian is difficult and sensitive because he alone makes the continuous and immediate decisions involving the individual's need for support or action versus the group's need for protection in an environment conducive to schoolwork. Making such decisions is a teacher's professional responsibility. Teachers are restricted by state laws, district policy, and community notions of what school behavior should be like; more importantly, they are restricted by regulations regarding the techniques of discipline that may be used. A teacher who is new to a position should find out before school begins whether the district has a written statement of policy for his guidance. Typically, these district publications include goals for increasing self-direction in students, specifics of student conduct toward peers and teachers, procedures for referral of problem students to a guidance or counseling center, and conditions of corporal punishment. If a teacher thinks he must employ unusual tactics, the school principal and the parents of the students involved should be informed in advance of the process and of the expected behavior outcomes. Much misunderstanding of the actual functioning of the classroom results when students themselves describe disciplinary measures to their parents, who may interpret them in terms of their own school experiences even though the dynamics of the situation may be very different.

## Control Techniques Used by Parents

The discipline used in the home influences children's behavior in the school and the control devices that teachers will find effective. Devereux, Bronfenbrenner, and Suci (1962) reported changes in parental techniques of discipline over a 25-year period: (1) greater permissiveness toward the child's desires; (2) free expression of affection; (3) an increased reliance on indirect discipline, such as reasoning or appeal, as opposed to direct methods, such as physical punishment or threat; (4) a tendency toward use of middle-class values and discipline patterns by other social classes; and (5) an increasingly affectionate, less authoritarian attitude on the part of fathers, with an increasing importance of mothers as the agent of discipline. "Love-oriented" techniques for bringing about desired child behavior are still most widely used by middle-class parents, whose children are superior in self-control, achievement, responsibility, leadership, popularity, and adjustment to those children from homes where aversive controls are used.

Bronfenbrenner (1961), studying differential treatment of the sexes, found that girls are given more affection, are subject to more psychological controls, and are punished less than boys. The girls in the study were found to be more obedient, cooperative, and in general better socialized than boys of comparable age levels. They tended also to be more anxious, timid, dependent, and sensitive to rejection—characteristics that Bronfenbrenner called the risks of oversocialization. Individual personality differences among members of the same sex were considered evidence against a wholly genetic base for sex differences in response to discipline. First children, who receive more attention and indirect discipline, tend to be more anxious and dependent, whereas later children are more aggressive and self-confident. Analysis of teacher ratings has shown consistently greater responsibility traits in girls and greater leadership qualities in boys. In Bronfenbrenner's study, parental behavior toward girls was characterized by affection, praise, and companionship, while boys were subjected to more physical punishment and achievement demands. Bronfenbrenner found that extremes of either affection or discipline had deleterious effects on all children but that the socialization process seemed to entail somewhat different risks for the two sexes. Both parental affection and discipline appeared to facilitate the psychological functioning of boys, who needed love-oriented attention balanced by firm discipline. The girls showed unexpected susceptibility to the detrimental influences of overprotection; for them, a little discipline went a long way, and strong authority was constricting rather than constructive.

Class differences were apparent in the similar treatment of the sexes in upper-middle-class homes, with increasingly differential treatment of boys and girls by parents from lower socioeconomic groups. Girls from upper-middle-class homes seemed less vulnerable to psychological risks of socialization, while girls from lower-class families showed the debilitating effects of overprotection. Upper-middle-class boys revealed a risk of oversocialization in some loss of the capacity for independent aggressive accomplishment. Consistent with the changing patterns of parental discipline, analyses of Bronfenbrenner's data showed upper-middle-class girls excelling in *responsibility* and *social acceptance*, and lower-middle-class boys excelling in *leadership*, *level of aspiration*, and *competitiveness.*

In upper-middle-class homes fathers and mothers have tended to be alike in their treatment of siblings of both sexes, while in lower-middle-class homes sons and daughters are treated differently by the parents. Trends over three decades have shown little change in the disciplinary behavior of mothers; the changes have been primarily paternal. In low-er-middle-class homes fathers have continued to be more strict with boys, and mothers have continued to be more strict with girls.

The boys in these studies tended to thrive best in a patriarchal context, while the girls thrived in a matriarchal environment. The investigators tentatively concluded that families modeled after democratic, egalitarian standards—approved in professional circles—tended to produce young people who do not take initiative, who look to others for direction, and who cannot be counted on to fulfill obligations. High achievement motivation was identified, however, in a family atmosphere of cold democracy, in which initial high levels of maternal affection were followed by pressures for independence and accomplishment beyond early childhood. This study reported a marked slowing by the early 1960s of the rush toward permissiveness and indirect methods of discipline.

## Teachers as Disciplinarians

Until recently, teachers, who came primarily from the middle classes, regarded themselves as carriers of the American democracy. The job of teaching has always been strenuous, but the typical teacher readily subscribed to the values of his background, which in turn were those which a typical board of education wanted reinforced in students. Sputnik challenged the technology and economic structure of this country. Black, Chicano, and Indian people challenged American democracy through the courts and in the public schools, where exposure has been damaging to WASP values. Vietnam challenged American prestige among nations and diverted her intentions to remodel the domestic scene. Increasing numbers of teachers find themselves the unadmired symbol of the establishment, whose values are held in disdain by youth in revolt. In some secondary schools teachers put themselves in physical danger if they intervene in a playground fight. Friends of the authors, who have taught in slum areas of large cities for years, now travel to certain schools in pairs and leave before dusk. In many cases the teacher is caught between diverse standards of discipline in the homes and a universal expectation of success for each pupil at school. These pressures, uncertainties, and fears do not help the teacher become the secure person that an effective leader should be.

The strange ways in which hidden and often unknown teacher emotions can become involved is illustrated in the following anecdote. Miss McD. was an exceptionally dedicated teacher who thought of herself as just, competent, and kind to children. The authors thought her a little crisp, but many young boys from the houseboat side of the district did well under her precise tutelage. Corla, the first black student to move into the district, was promoted to Miss McD.'s room after successful achievement in second grade. In a few months, Miss McD. had accumulated a thick file on Corla consisting of psychological reports and anecdotal accounts of hostility, inappropriate dress, insubordination, and aggressiveness on the playground. The following year the fourth-grade teacher received Corla "on trial," along with the thick file, but the anticipated problem behavior did not emerge. One day Miss McD. was chatting in the teacher's room. "Say," she said, "did you get any of that new Wong family? I got one, but she's a nice little thing. When I took her to the nurse this morning, she put out her hand and I couldn't help taking it. You know, it felt just like a little *white* hand." Miss McD.'s racial prejudice, which she did not recognize, colored her treatment of certain children and created problems in classroom interaction that were destructive to her, the children, and the learning situation. Learning to live with one's own prejudices and still to avoid allowing

them to contaminate important relationships is very difficult.

### Genetic and Social Basis of Discipline

One reason for classroom tensions which create problems of discipline involves the phylogenic tendencies toward dominance of others. The drive to excel is an attribute of many species, including man. The human tendency to attempt to dominate others involves a concomitant pressure on the other members of the group to resist domination.

**The Pecking Order** Scientific observation of social structure in the barnyard shows that chickens, cows, and other animals set up a pecking order to define each member's place in the hierarchy of the flock or the herd. Only one member consistently dominates all others, and only one is pecked or pushed by all others. When a new member enters the group, he fights for his place with only a few others before his rank in the pecking order is established. Human society, rather than being crudely based on naked physical power, is structured on some form of enforceable leadership that is accepted down the line by the members of the social group.

One locates his station in a group through social interaction. Some of the trials are overt and some covert, but in all cases individuals compete for positions of status within the group. In mobile populations, classroom groups are in constant flux. Each addition to a class poses a potential threat to all the members, including the teacher, although he is much less likely to be challenged than the individuals further down the status ladder. As a result of this challenge, a strain is created that permeates the whole class. Once the positions in the pecking order have been reestablished, more complete attention can be directed to other problems. Teachers who recognize the inevitability of the trial of strength as new members are added to the class can anticipate the behavior and remain emotionally untouched. Some teachers keep abreast of shifts in the social hierarchy of the class by sociometrics, that is, by surveying and diagraming the students' friendship choices. The students' choices are based on affective associations, although the teacher's analysis of the social structure is a conceptualization. Most teachers consciously enhance the esteem of all students in the eyes of their classmates.

## Need Systems and Need Satisfactions

Maslow distinguished between deficiency needs, which must be satisfied by others, and self-actualization needs, which are satisfied from within, as the person seeks to become more complete. The discipline of the classroom in which creative work is the focus is based essentially on self-actualization needs. Most students are able to operate on this basis in part of their lives, although many find it difficult to function this way completely. When the student is satisfying himself from within, he is not likely to be disturbing the class, or at least this is not as likely to be the source of his satisfaction.

Alienated students, for whom the school is not well designed, are often deficit-need-motivated. They must derive their need satisfactions from the people around them. Their dependence and the demand characteristics of their personality structures tend toward rejection and toward refusal by others to satisfy their predominant needs for status, love, and affection. The nature of their needs makes them vulnerable in the pecking order, so that they are likely to struggle ever more violently and with increasing lack of success.

### Unfortunate Ways Students Get Reinforcement
Students who are not profiting

from classwork often establish systems of misbehavior that lead to recognition. Although no teacher does so consciously, the attention sometimes given a student for misbehavior is the only attention he earns. His misbehavior brings him into the group of those who are noticed. Even though the student may not be conscious of any attempt to seek the attention of others, he is likely to repeat those acts which he found rewarding. This unfortunate situation is self-perpetuating, since the teacher feels he must reprimand the student for his misbehavior, which the student finds more pleasant than being ignored.

Some deficit-need-driven children get reinforcement by tormenting the teacher. The fact that the agitation might lead to punishment is far less important than the fact that the provocation is effective. The teacher was focusing his attention on the tormentor, and the attention was reinforcing. The punishment, if it came, came later and was part of a different association sequence. Students who are reinforced in this way often obtain supplementary reinforcement from other class members who perhaps would like to torment the teacher but are restrained by various forms of conditioning. Both the adulation of these covert supporters and the exasperation of the teacher are rewarding to the student. The activities that led to the reinforcing conditions are likely to be repeated unless the sequence is broken. Whether the disruptive activities are on such a large scale that they make the headlines or are confined within the walls of a single classroom, the mechanism is much the same.

In some cases, discipline problems are learned mechanisms, originating in the home, where they have been socially generated. In *New Ways in Discipline*, Dorothy Baruch (1949) reminded teachers that the whole child comes to school—the pent-up emotions as well as the mind and the body. Successful teachers, she said, realize that a child must feel that he is understood and appreciated for what he is as well as for what he accomplishes. They know that it helps a child to study if he feels that he is *wanted* and *belongs* in his classroom. They know that emotional warmth and protection from coldness is just as important as protection from cold winds and draughts. They know that many a disciplinary problem has yielded when the old punitive disciplinary measures have stopped and the new acceptant measures have begun (p. 217).

The successful teacher encourages children to get rid of their unwelcome emotions through writing stories and poems and painting pictures. For example, Ronnie, aged eight, was making a Mother's Day card, along with 32 other third graders. He drew pink and red flowers on the front of the card and wrote, "To Mother." Inside he wrote as many "I hate you's" as the pages would hold. Then, without saying a word, he lined up with the other children, leaving his card on his desk.

Steve, aged seventeen, was a troublemaker in high school. He seldom did any work. He came to school without his books and told outlandish stories about why he did not bring them. The teachers were not surprised when an automobile was overturned at a football game and Steve was mentioned as the perpetrator. Later they were shocked to find that Steve's father had overturned the car. They began to understand that Steve was carrying forward habits that his father thought smart. Steve had gained parental approval for school misbehavior, including the embellishments that grew in their recounting at home. Some discipline problems require the modification of long-practiced personality structures, which is difficult, if not impossible, to accomplish at school.

**Constructive Alternatives and Reinforcement**  The patience with which many teachers accept socially illiterate children and teach them ways of becoming cooperative members of the class and community is heartening. The many children who enter school already adapted to respecting the rights of others provide a base from which teachers can build responsibility in those who are not so adapted. If 90 percent of the children in a class already know something about cooperative responsibility, the other 10 percent can be taught by example much more easily than if the proportions were reversed. Direct and specific attention should be given to changing some of the attitudes that children bring with them to school. Building attitudes of cooperation with the teacher, of respect for the advantages of school success, and of confidence in one's ability to be a productive person could be the key to social literacy.

Mr. D. was made principal of a school in an area that accounted for 38 percent of all arrests in a large port city. The population was made up primarily of black and Chicano families living in low-rent, single-family residences. The attendance area was isolated from the rest of the city by a power-generating plant, a foundry, and a cyclone fence. Although the school was the only attractive spot in the area, the grounds were locked to keep prowlers out when school was not in session.

Mr. D. arranged the transfer to his school of a few dedicated teachers who had worked with him previously and who shared his views about the school as a focal point of the community. Mr. D. opened the school to the people of the area after regular school hours. He organized playground activities for the children, English and citizenship classes for the parents, and shop classes for young men who had nothing in particular to do. He involved mothers in PTA and aide activities. He stayed at the school until ten o'clock at night and was back on the job by eight the next morning. Gradually he recruited parents in each block who would form welcoming committees for newcomers and tell them about school events. Block parents also took some responsibility for pupils whose parents both left for work before school opened. New ideas for better teaching were generated, and new materials were obtained that would help the teacher individualize instruction. The administration helped by keeping class sizes to the minimum for the district as a whole. Additional teachers were selected who were excited by Mr. D.'s accomplishments and were willing to work longer hours than was required in other schools.

Within three years, Mr. D. had this program well established, and the parents had come to have real pride in their school, in themselves, and in the accomplishments of their own children. Crime in the area dropped to 10 percent of the city total, and dropout rates in the high school went down. The percentage of children on Aid to Dependent Children (ADC) dropped as the people developed new skills and gained the personal strength to acquire employment. These changes were neither sudden nor dramatic, but the school did become a focus for upward mobility.

**Discipline from Within** It may come as a shock to experienced teachers to learn that class control comes from within the teacher rather than from the mechanics he uses. Such discipline is closely related to a quality called "face-to-face dominance" on the Bernreuter Personality Test. Mammy Yokum, in Al Capp's "Li'l Abner," has the determination and also the physical prowess to back up her role as disciplinarian. With her determination, she would be the "society leader" in any group. All readers of this book have known tiny women teachers who by their ego strength dominated male students (and principals) twice their size. This inner determination is the essence of control over groups.

**Inner Assurance of Leadership** Sometimes highly qualified teachers find their erudi-

tion a stumbling block to the assurance that is part of leadership. They cannot overlook qualifications or further explanations that they think are required. Students often subconsciously interpret this lack of assurance on the part of the teacher as evidence that the material being presented is not valid and should not be accepted. The condition of doubt, which is felt rather than known cognitively, seems to leave the teacher open to challenge. Teachers need to learn that no material can be presented in its entirety in one lesson; there must be a series of approximations to the truth. The intelligent teacher will settle for an honest approximation.

Often teachers who are quite ignorant of their material gain reputations as excellent teachers; they have come to terms with themselves, and so their presentations are clear and forceful. The students learn what is presented. Often these teachers teach what they know, error and all, more effectively than their more hesitant but better-informed colleagues who are sensitive to the limitations of their own knowledge and in whom the students detect a lack of self-assurance. Rogers (1958) defined inner assurance as the essence of trustworthiness in the eyes of an onlooker.

***Belief in the Importance of Content*** Belief in the importance of what is being taught can influence the classroom climate dramatically. Miss C. had been such an outstanding student teacher that she was hired on an emergency credential at midterm to finish her student teaching on an internship. The first reports of her new assignment were disturbing and rapidly deteriorated to the point where her college supervisor thought she should be withdrawn for the good of the students. This step seemed drastic to the director of interns, who undertook to find the source of her problems by visiting her class. One difficulty was an emotionally disturbed pupil, Billy, who was not easy to handle even for highly experienced teachers. Another problem was Miss C.'s own doubt about the importance of grammar in the lives of the students she was teaching. However, she felt strongly about teaching them to write and speak effectively. She also had some creative ideas about getting eighth-grade students to want to write. When it was suggested that Miss C. stop teaching grammar for awhile and spend the time on writing, she began to feel better about the possibility of success. She also accepted the idea of a reinforcement schedule for Billy that would change his activity on a five-minute basis. With these modest changes in her teaching program, she rapidly gained control of the class. The school principal accepted the minor changes in the curriculum and was very supportive of her teaching efforts. Because Miss C. was convinced of the importance of the material she was teaching in the lives of her students, she began to convey an urgency to which they responded.

### TEACHER'S ROLE IN AFFECTIVE ASSOCIATIONS

The most effective kinds of discipline are those that the student imposes upon himself. However, this self-control is built on a substructure of affective associations which must be experienced before the social reinforcement from the group can take place. Self-control has the further dimension of self-initiated activity. These aspects of discipline fit properly into the chapters on the conceptualization of affects and creative self-direction. Discipline is a topic of daily interest to teachers and a return to this topic in later chapters will reflect this importance in the world of teaching.

Affective loadings accompany and are part of all phases of ongoing experience. Whether these loadings will lead to the continuance of an activity, perhaps in a modified form, or will lead to replacement by some other activity depends on the nature of the affects. Teachers can and should structure learning so that beneficial habits will be facilitated and destructive habits will be eliminated. At the association level, intervention by the teacher is necessary and helpful. Experimentation in behavior modification is providing guides for the clearest ways of effecting that intervention with some assurance of the probable outcomes.

### SUMMARY

Affective and cognitive learning is interwoven. In schools most conscious attention has been paid to the cognitive sequences, although affective loadings determine whether teaching and learning will be pleasant and satisfying or stormy and frustrating. One way of exploring personal values has been through encounter groups of different types, all of which put emphasis on experience in the here and now.

Behavior modification is a system for using positive and/or negative reinforcement sequences to control behavior. Success in building conditioning schedules is dependent on an accurate determination of the kinds of responses by teachers or therapists that will be reinforcing to individual students. Tokens that can be exchanged for a variety of goods are easily distributed and often provide the breadth of choice necessary to satisfy nearly all the students. However, tokens require the teacher to operate a store or some system of exchange. This may be a nuisance, although under some circumstances the store can be incorporated into the school activities as part of the learning opportunities.

Many of the behavior modification studies have been related to improving classroom interaction. Therapists have used similar techniques to desensitize people suffering from phobias by associating the phobia with relaxation. Aversion therapy has been effective in the control of alcoholism and homosexuality in some patients by either chemical or electrical punishment. Operant therapy has been used to restore autistic and other psychotic individuals to normal behavior.

Whether or not the teacher uses behavior theory directly to establish rules of interaction, patterns of interaction will emerge as a result of inevitable classroom conditioning. Unless the teacher intervenes directly and with intention, some learning will take place which the teacher did not anticipate and which may be damaging to some of the children.

The teacher's feeling of success may be destroyed if the discipline in his classroom is allowed to become chaotic. Problems of discipline have their foundation in a genetically inherited need to achieve as much status as the social situation will permit. The dynamics of improved classroom and neighborhood interaction can be delineated.

Discipline comes from within the teacher rather than from the particular techniques or methods he uses. Self-discipline is the goal of all constructive teaching for any kind of discipline. The techniques for achieving self-discipline begin with the establishment of desirable associations concerning classroom manners, progress through a process of conceptualization about why these manners are functionally useful, and culminate in a self-directing, self-disciplined individual who can continue his own learning indefinitely.

## SELF-DIRECTING ACTIVITIES

1 Analyze annoying behavior in one of your associates and set up a schedule for modifying the behavior.
2 Do library research on sociograms including how to prepare and interpret the data.
3 Make a list of "things that bug you" and use Wolpe's techniques to desensitize yourself.
4 Identify a child who is at the bottom of the totem pole in the pecking order of his group and explore ways of enhancing his status in the group.

# Chapter 6

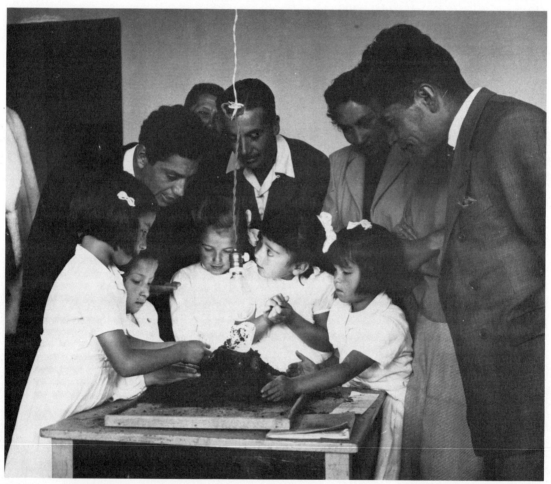

# COGNITIVE CONCEPTUALIZATIONS: GRASPING INHERENT RELATIONS

This chapter is planned to help you structure curriculum so that your students will learn relationships that are transferable to new situations. You will be able to:

◖ Observe when a student synthesizes knowledge, or associations, to form a conceptualization

◖ Plan a series of questions that point to conceptualizations

◖ Design a series of steps that lead to discovery

◖ Design learning situations to provide checks against which conceptualizations can be tested

◖ Analyze a unit of content into essential features

◖ Conceptualize the following terms:
intuition
inquiry process
gestalt
insight
intrinsic programming
inductive learning

Conceptualization, or level 2 learning, refers to the process by which the learner comes to understand inherent relationships. Conceptualization can be thought of as the grasping of connections within related bits of knowledge; the discovery of cause or significance; insight, or the "ah ha!" experience of the gestaltists; the formulation of a generalization from relevant specifics of experience; or the intuition of Bergson (1903). When level 2 learning is considered in these terms, the importance of the basic associations that undergird it is obvious. Although the critical event of conceptualization may require only a small amount of time, it is a vital segment of learning. In school learning situations, conceptualization lends meaning, permanence, and retrievability to the concepts that have been formed.

This chapter details, through the interpretation of research findings and the use of examples from classroom experience, some manifestations of level 2 learning—in other words, some forms in which conceptualization occurs and can be caused to occur in learners.

## THE NATURE OF CONCEPTUALIZATION

Conceptualization seems to require time, which may be short or long, depending on the complexity of the conceptualization being made. Newton had been storing information for years before he conceptualized the law of gravity. A simple conceptualization, such as the relationship between pieces of a design that have been broken apart, requires stored information about the elements that make up the design. Very young children create conceptualizations, but they are less likely to have the relevant information available in their memory storage and, thus, are more likely to need experiences over a period of time that will enable them to accumulate the necessary data to put the relationships together.

The exact nature of the conceptualization process is not known, but within the knowledge of the neural system are bits and pieces of data that help make the process seem real. In the retina of the eye are amacrine cells, flat bipolar cells, and horizontal cells, each of which collects data from many rods and cones. This consolidation of input is important in the perception of angles, movement, and changes in light and dark (Chapter 9). In the cerebral cortex are many stellate cells that have input from large numbers of other neurons from the cortical layers above and below. It seems reasonable to *hypothesize* that these cells are involved in synthesizing information to give meaning beyond mere accumulation of isolated messages. Within the core-brain a sorting process takes place that creates what Penfield (1969) calls the conceptual memories, distinguished from the experiential memories or the continuous storing of the experience of the ongoing present. Research is moving very rapidly in the exploration of the cellular functioning within the neural system, and definitive answers may soon be available about just how conceptualization takes place. At the moment the available data seem to support the thesis that there is a neural process of conceptualization that is different from the process of association.

Piaget (1970), in a book called *Structuralism*, explained the process of adaptation within the context of cognitive learning. According to this view, when a new idea is presented to an individual, he makes an accommodation in his ongoing thinking process in order to take in the idea. This accommodation may be slight or it may be complex. Along with, or perhaps subsequent to, the accommodation, a process of assimilation takes place during which the idea is fitted into the mental structure of the learner and, in the process, changes that structure so that the next adaptation takes place from a modified base. The process can be experienced during formal operations, when thinking about thinking takes place. Students whose basic psychology has been learned from an S-R point of view may find the accommodation of the idea of conceptualization as an integrating process difficult. As this concept is built within the thought matrix, a process of assimilation takes place in which S-R learning and conceptualization learning either are integrated or are held in separate compartments. However the assimilation takes place, the adaptation to the concept of conceptualization will require a new approach about learning to learn. In many instances of related assimilation, the process is one of conceptualization where related ideas are put together into a new whole. While the relationship of adaptation and that of conceptualization can be most easily seen during formal operations, the same cognitive structuring occurs during concrete operations and sensorimotor learning when children are learning to understand the interaction between real objects in a world external to themselves (Chapter 14).

### Designs for Conceptualization

Level 2 learning is easier to generate in some students than in others and is accomplished intuitively by some teachers more frequently than by others. However, the authors believe that learning efficiency is increased when the teacher is able to (1) discriminate which process the learner is using and (2) plan sequences that lead to conceptualization. Any of the manifestations of level 2 learning may be brought about in more than one way. Individual students will differ, as will individual students of teaching, in the number of association-level experiences they need in order to form a conceptualization. Some individuals develop a particular ability to generate structures of knowledge, just as some students have a particular facility for remembering or

unfiling learned discrete material. A few fortunate people have acquired strength in both areas. In part, the development of strength in both recall and conceptual thinking seems to involve successful practice; another factor appears to be the ease or difficulty with which one learns new and unfamiliar material.

### Step-by-Step versus Essential-Features Approaches

Different groups of psychologists have different orientations concerning the most effective way of grasping meanings. One school of thought is impressed with the value of a thorough and systematic approach that builds information gradually, so that only an additional small step in a carefully designed and well-contrived process is required for conceptualization to take place. The linear programmers, who structure difficult material into programmed instruction texts for eventual mastery by students, almost always see conceptualization as a result of a series of small steps. Little doubt exists that conceptualizations can be generated in this way, although the learner himself must complete the process.

In history, the teacher can build systematically through many steps so that the student comes, in the end, to understand the underlying trend of a historical era. The Westward movement, for example, may be taught as a series of episodes that include the Lewis and Clark expedition, the Indian wars, the discovery of gold in Placerville, the crude justice in the vigilantes, the conflicts between ranchers and farmers that followed the Homestead Act, the organization of the Texas Rangers, and the development of a system of independent banks. After many such events have been explored, the semester can be culminated with the thesis that the open frontier contributed to the growth of democracy in the United States. One of the problems in this approach is that the teacher and the students become so involved with the glamour of these minutiae that historical perspectives are sometimes subordinated.

Another route to grasping the idea that the open frontier made democracy the most viable way of organizing life is easier and more desirable for many students. To discover the underlying trend of a historical period, it is not always necessary to master initially all the details to support a thesis. A relatively small number of crucial facts can become the pegs on which the trends of an era can be hung. Once the pegs are in place, adroit questioning by the teacher can enable the students to formulate their private conceptualizations of the thesis and its importance to the history of the period.

The teacher who is seeking to have the students develop their own conceptualizations needs to plan his approaches at least as well as the one who uses a sequence approach. However, the intent of this teacher is different and is seen as different by the students when the conceptualizations are essentially their own. The learners are reinforced for skill in making conceptualizations rather than for mastery of details. A teacher who expects students to conceptualize the growth of democracy as an outcome of the Westward movement might concentrate on the need for cooperative action by the people to resolve the various conflicts between individual interests and the security of the group. To help students arrive at their private understanding of the need for a judicial process to handle conflict fairly—which is basic to political democracy—the teacher might first have them associate the necessity for protection and the crude justice meted out by vigilantes in the gold fields. The next conglomerate of associations might stress the development of local civil government in the frontier towns as the means by which the townspeople cooperatively sought

to meet common difficulties as they arose. Concentrating on particular incidents in particular towns would be one way to help students associate the idea of government with the idea of citizens meeting their common ends. A third peg on which the teacher might choose to hang the fabric of his thesis of the effect of frontier life on the evolution of American democracy could be the cooperative action of the people as they organized a school district and built a schoolhouse for their children.

When students are questioned concerning the common elements in such situations, they come to grasp the significance of cooperative action in solving problems, and further questioning can lead to the conceptualization that this necessity for working together to organize frontier society strengthened democracy. Once the idea of cooperative action as the essential element in democracy is established, many of the details of this period take on new meaning. Although they still need to be filled in as association learning, details at this point will help students evaluate the conceptualization previously formed. Facts that fit the conceptual framework are reinforcing for the learner, but details that conflict with an over-generalization should lead the student to rethink his conceptualizations.

Of course the teacher can also give the students the same information in a lecture. They may grasp this lecture material as a conceptualization, but more likely it will be absorbed as additional bits of association learning. The distinction is not in the material, but in what happens to the information as far as the learner is concerned. Under the circumstances of discovery, the closure, or conceptualization, is likely to involve a larger step than the student can take through association learning. When the student conceptualizes, his pleasure in having achieved an insight is reinforcing, and his goals become coordinated with those of the teacher. After the conceptualization of the relationship has been made, the additional factual content must still be learned, but by this time the facts are learned in context, rather than as isolated items. With this approach, the teacher's role is less deterministic, and the student then has more freedom to develop his own hypotheses than in closely directed sequences. Some teachers are unable to relinquish control over the formulation of major generalizations—a necessary price of intellectual integrity for the student. Both this essential-features approach and the step-by-step approach are possible, and both take place in classrooms.

An associative approach to presenting content—which the authors discourage—is as a series of episodes, facts, or information. For most students, facts presented in this way fail to come into focus as generalizations, relationships, or conceptualizations. Important conceptualizations must be identified and structured if they are to be grasped by many students. Only rarely will students conceptualize or discover relationships in a climate that precipitates learning as an unrelated progression of events.

The teacher who has mastered the relationship of association learning to conceptualization is able to keep in balance the need for key facts or information, the need for the framework of conceptualizations, and the need for attitudes toward this learning that have the potentiality for engendering creative and self-directed work by the students themselves.

## INTUITIVE THINKING AND DISCOVERY

The idea of conceptualization as a mode of thought has been described in various ways. Usually the terminology has differed from that used in this chapter, although the fundamental ideas expressed—upon analysis—fit into the structure of three levels of learning. Henri

Bergson described intuitive learning as a way of understanding time, space, and life that goes beyond ordinary thought and experience. The process in metaphysical terms can be thought of as conceptualization. His epistemology predated recent formations of the human thought process.

In 1903, Bergson first published "Introduction à la metaphysique," in which he explained some of the essential features of intuition as follows:

In conclusion, we may remark that there is nothing mysterious in this faculty. Everyone of us has had occasion to exercise it to a certain extent. Any one of us, for instance, who has attempted literary composition, knows that when the subject has been studied at length, the materials all collected, and the notes all made, something more is needed in order to set about the work of composition itself, and that it is often very painful to place ourselves directly at the heart of the subject, and to seek as deeply as possible an impulse, after which we need only let ourselves go. . . . Metaphysical intuition seems to be something of the same kind. What corresponds here to the documents and notes of literary composition is the sum of observations and experience gathered together by positive science. For we do not obtain an intuition from reality—that is, an intellectual sympathy with the most intimate part of it—unless we have won its confidence by a long fellowship with its superficial manifestations. And it is not merely a question of assimilating the most conspicuous facts; so immense a mass of facts must be accumulated and fused together, that in this fusion all the preconceived and premature ideas which observers may unwittingly have put into their observations will be certain to neutralize each other. In this way only can the bare materiality of the known facts be exposed to view (p. 21).

The importance that Bergson attaches to the acquisition of a tremendous background of facts, or associations, before it is possible intuitively to know the essence of the meaning of the world is often overlooked. Bergson's emphasis on the almost mystical function of intuition as a way of knowing, which he was at pains to distinguish from analysis, has often been noted without mention of his emphasis on experience. The authors interpret the amassing of background material described by Bergson as the intake of pertinent observations. He spoke of this process as "filling oneself with facts and details." The process of conceptualizing the relations inherent in associations leads to what some writers have called "intuition." These intuitive formulations are sometimes made by the person who was listening and observing while the more vocal person relayed the masses of detail.

### Bruner: The Process of Education

Bruner's *The Process of Education* (1963) emphasized the importance of basic information as a foundation on which to build intuitive thought:

> The good intuiter may have been born with something special, but his effectiveness rests upon solid knowledge of the subject, a familiarity that gives intuition something to work with. Certainly there are some experiments on learning that indicate the importance of a high degree of mastery of materials in order to operate effectively with them intuitively (p. 58).

His explanation of intuitive thinking is a good description of how conceptualization sometimes occurs:

> Intuitive thinking characteristically does not advance in careful, well-defined steps. Indeed, it tends to involve maneuvers based seemingly on an implicit perception of the total problem. The thinker arrives at an answer, which may be right or wrong, with little, if any, awareness of the process by which he reached it. He rarely can provide an adequate account of how he obtained

his answer, and he may be unaware of just what aspects of the problem situation he was responding to. Usually intuitive thinking rests on familiarity with the domain of knowledge involved and with its structure, which makes it possible for the thinker to leap about skipping steps and employing short cuts in a manner that requires a later rechecking of conclusions by more analytical means, whether deductive or inductive (pp. 56–57).

When Bruner distinguished analytic thinking as a step-by-step approach, he described the process of association learning. In the section of his book that dealt with the heuristics of discovery, Bruner spoke of the importance of familiarity with the material—"sheer knowing the stuff," as he put it—but coupled with this was knowledge of the proper ways in which things fit together.

In terms of the three levels of learning, "knowing the stuff" would refer to the basic associations; also in terms of the three levels, knowledge of the ways in which things fit together is an important element in the process of conceptualization. Bruner's emphasis on the importance of practice in problem solving and on the effort of discovery is similar to the importance the authors attach to structuring and reinforcing efforts to conceptualize. The distinction between discovery approaches and conceptualization is essentially the difference between knowledge as something to be discovered and apprehended and knowledge as built by the individual as he constructs his own private world. In Bruner's interpretation, the knowledge is static (it is there to be discovered), while in level 2 learning the knowledge is dynamic (it is built through the process of discovery).

### Suchman: Inquiry

Suchman (1962) developed in inductive method of teaching that he called the "inquiry process." Many teachers have been instructed in this technique, which improves students' abilities to form concepts by confronting them with a problem that is real and meaningful. For example, a film may be shown or a demonstration given of a discrepant event, such as the collapse of a paint can that is successively heated, sealed, and cooled. The students discover the reality of air pressure by asking questions that the teacher can answer with a "yes" or a "no," a situation Suchman characterizes as "freedom within a responsive environment." The teacher's role is described as that of information verifier; this technique has the advantage of rapid feedback, which enables the process of inquiry to continue and the excitement of inquiry to mount.

The essential harmony between this view and that of the authors concerning how conceptualization is taught is apparent at several points. First, the necessity for the learner to do his own thinking is a freedom that is a prerequisite to discovery. The step beyond "discovery," which is implied in conceptualization, consists in the learner doing his own thinking. His giving back information, data, or terminology is an indication of level 1 functioning, association. Second, in Suchman's method, the needed data are provided by means of a film or demonstration, teachers' answers, and experimental or library research. He, like Bergson and Bruner, stresses the importance of basic information. In the framework of the three levels of learning, the data that a student brings to the learning situation are critical to the conceptualization he makes. Suchman makes the important point that a person's conceptual systems should correspond as closely as possible to reality. Children who are given inquiry training have practice in selecting data that are relevant by having their topic of discussion defined.

Motivation in the responsive environment approach comes from the pleasure the learner derives from information gathering and from the feeling of power that accompanies the construction of new conceptual models. However, the subtle kinds of reinforcement inherent in the teacher's general responsiveness to the questions the children are asking cannot be ignored in an analysis of how learning is taking place during inquiry training. Inquiry, curiosity, and environmental exploration carry potential as self-reinforcing experience, but the potential comes to fruition in a reinforcing environment in which other persons share and respond to the discovery.

The New Nursery School in Greeley, Colorado, was begun in 1964 for children from educationally deprived homes and was designed as a responsive environment for three-to five-year-olds (Nimnicht, 1967). Although exploration and discovery by the children were emphasized and reinforcement from adults was deemphasized, a ratio of one adult for each four children ensured adult attention for child activity. The reinforcing effect of additional adults in the classroom is built into Head Start projects, financed by the U.S. Office of Economic Opportunity for preschool children from low-income homes. Preprofessional aides are brought into the classes with the expectation that master teachers will become engineers of a learning environment.

Children in slum areas have as many possibilities for inquiry as those in the suburbs, but in many cases, their parents are preoccupied with matters of survival or are involved in frequent crises, so that they have little time to attend to their children's explorations. Sometimes the parents punish rather than reward their children's curiosity, either by ignoring the question or by handling it in more overt ways. Sometimes the lack of adult interaction deprives the child of labels which he will need later to do abstract thinking. Gradually apathy replaces eagerness as the child's modus vivendi.

Inquiry methods utilize a structured situation in which students are certain to respond—to ask questions—for which they are reinforced, if only by the teacher's listening and answering the questions. Essentially, this is how skillful teachers launch the student in new directions or in new content: they structure a situation in which the students' responses may be anticipated and reinforced on a selective basis. The experienced kindergarten teacher cannot teach all the rules of school behavior during the first few days. The environment is arranged with a rug or chairs on which the children sit, a sequence of active and quiet activities is preplanned, and listening to directions is made a rewarding experience. The structuring assures pupil behavior which can be identified and reinforced, thus getting the desired behavior started.

As suggested earlier, assimilation and accommodation are the twin processes by which data from the environment are accepted and incorporated within the framework of the individual's intellectual structure (Piaget, 1954). An element of evaluation through which new knowledge becomes classified is basic to the acceptance of new data. Several alternative methods of handling the discordant bit of experience are possible. The first of these involves discarding the information, avoiding it, or disbelieving its validity as it has been presented. Sophisticated adults treat sleight-of-hand displays of magicians in these ways. The second method involves a sorting process by the midbrain for a category within which the new data will fit and, when necessary, the establishment of a new category. The third involves an expansion of present conceptual systems which makes possible the integration of new data as a refinement of old structures.

Johntz (1966) demonstrated the utility of both the discovery method and conceptual mathematics when used to work with culturally disadvantaged elementary children. The teaching assistants were nearly all doctoral candidates in mathematics from the University of California, who were able to analyze the mathematical reasoning that resulted in student error and to ask questions that moved from the child's error to a closer approximation of a basic understanding. Teachers need to be able to identify students' misconceptualizations that lead to error in order to help them restructure the direction of their inquiry.

Johntz found that fourth-grade students grouped as low to low-average regained self-respect, motivation, and the ability to work in other subjects as they were successful in the daily hour of conceptual mathematics. He became convinced that mathematics, in the framework of this teaching method and content structure, can be the key to upward social mobility for black students. The chief obstacle to large-scale testing of his hypothesis is the shortage of mathematicians.

Mathematics has some real values for the culturally disadvantaged as a high-status subject, having economic value, and not being affected by language deprivations which block efficient reading and hinder progress in subject matter based on reading. The language of mathematics and the concepts of mathematics offer a fresh starting point where everyone has an equal chance and where native endowment can be used to advantage. Also, young children seem to have a facility for thinking in mathematical terms that has not been generally appreciated.

### Problems in Discovery Approaches

Along with an awareness of the importance of teaching for discovery, considerable confusion has developed about the application of the discovery method in the classroom. Many people have become convinced that this method constitutes the whole teaching approach, forgetting that Bruner identified other steps in the learning sequence, *acquisition* and *evaluation*. The importance of learning basic associations sometimes becomes obscured by the emotional zeal that accompanies the descriptions of discovery techniques.

Some "purists" in the discovery method describe their approaches by saying, "We never answer a question except by asking another question." When asked how one extracts vocabulary that is obviously outside the child's experience, one advocate replied that vocabulary, such as "commutative," must be presented to the students. This foundation information—with its explanation of vocabulary—provides the necessary associations which the learner manipulates to form discoveries or conceptualizations.

Friedlander (1965) spoke of the danger that new innovations may become new orthodoxies, particularly with reference to the way children learn. In writing specifically about the act of discovery, he pointed out the problem of inappropriate discoveries. He cited the case of a pupil who "discovered" that the difference between the phonetic soft "c" in "cent," compared with the hard "c" in "cat," was due to the coincidence that the "c" in "cent" was a capital letter, while the "c" in "cat" was a lowercase letter. According to Friedlander, this discovery was accompanied by the glow of success normally associated with discoveries that are real and important. The teacher, or someone who knows the relationships inherent in material, needs to structure many discovery experiences so that an adequate sequence of instances becomes available for generalization.

A child's background is an important factor in the kinds of discovery that he is equipped to make; therefore, the problem of individual differences seems to require special attention. By "individual differences" is meant particularly the various ways in which different children are prepared in the classroom to make particular discoveries. The fact is that some children are ready and able to follow the sequence of associations and to grasp the conceptualization, while other children cannot do so for any one of a number of reasons. Perhaps they are not willing to make the necessary effort or have not attended sufficiently to the preparation. The possibility of an "ah ha" response from *all* class members during the same lesson is unlikely. What often happens is that the teacher gets such strong reinforcement from the children who are able to follow the reasoning that he misses or dismisses the nonconceptualizing of the others. These problems are compounded when the teacher has been seduced into thinking of discovery as *the* method. When conceptualization is seen as a high point toward which lessons develop and after which associations are supplied and learned, it is likely that the students who do not reach the conceptualization will substitute association learning.

## CONTRIBUTIONS OF GESTALT PSYCHOLOGY

Some of the earliest work on conceptualization was done by the German psychologists known as gestaltists. Christian von Ehrenfels (1890) introduced the idea of a gestalt which, without an exact English translation, means roughly "form quality" or "structure." Ehrenfels was interested in music and was impressed by the fact that a melody could be transposed and played on a different instrument in such a way that none of the notes and none of the overtones would be the same, and yet the melody would be readily recognizable. A tune seemed to have a wholeness that was more than the sum of its notes. According to the physics of music, a tune consists of a complex series of relationships of sounds to one another, which is preserved in transposition. The fact that the second note, for example, contains two-thirds as many vibrations as the first and the third contains twice as many as the first is the relationship to which the listener responds when he recognizes the tune. People are inherently able to learn to respond to the relationships in music that become meaningful to them.

Ehrenfels looked at a soap bubble and noted that its structure and beauty consisted of something more than particles of soap and water, which continued to exist after the bubble had burst. In most of life, the form of the materials and the relationship between them are more exciting than the elements themselves. A lady entered a millinery shop and asked the price of a certain hat. She was told that the hat cost $45. "But that hat is nothing but a piece of ribbon," she said. The milliner promptly took the hat apart, wound up the ribbon, and handed it to the woman, saying, "The ribbon, madam, is free." Sometimes the gestalt, or the form of the relationships, is the essence of the thing; reality consists in the relationships rather than in the components.

### Wertheimer: Concept of Gestalt

Wertheimer (1923) was the recognized founder of the gestalt school of psychology. He did a great deal of work on thought processes, but published very little. One volume, published in 1945 after his death, includes some illustrations of the way in which children are sometimes able to grasp concepts intuitively. He cited the case of a $5^1/_2$-year-old who had been taught the principles of finding the area of a rectangle and then was given a parallelogram to work (Figure 6-1).

> She said, "I certainly don't know how to do that," then after a moment of silence: "This is no good here," pointing at the region at the left end; "and no good here," pointing to the region at the right.
>
> "It's troublesome, here and there." Hesitantly she said: "I could make it right here . . . but . . ."

Suddenly she cried out, "May I have a scissors? What is bad there is just what is needed here. It fits." She took the scissors, cut vertically, and placed the left end at the right (p. 48).

Another child who was given a parallelogram cut out of a piece of paper remarked early in her deliberations that the middle was all right but that the ends were wrong. When she suddenly took the parallelogram and folded it into a ring, she saw that she could cut it anywhere and have a rectangle.

Some children seem to be able to perceive such relationships intuitively, unless they have had too much teaching that emphasizes following explicit directions and too little reinforcement for their own creative or insightful solutions. This conceptual reorganization, the recognition of relationships, illustrates level 2 learning.

### Kohler and Yerkes: Insight in Primates

Kohler (1925) spent the years of World War I on Tenerife Island in the Canary Islands chain, unable to return to Germany. He worked with the great apes and studied them more thoroughly than had been his original intent. Some of his observations of problem solving illustrate the meaning of insight.

In one series of experiments, he made available a box that the chimpanzees could use as a platform from which to jump and reach a banana at the top of the cage. Only Sultan, Kohler's smartest ape, was able to solve this problem without outside help. Once the other apes got the idea, they were able to reach the banana without any wasted motion. A more difficult variation involved two boxes, which needed to be stacked in order to reach a height from which to obtain a banana. The apes found this a difficult problem to solve, and although they managed to see what the solution was, they were never able to stack one box on top of the other so that it would make a stable pile. Occasionally they achieved this result, but by accident rather than by insight. Their lack of conceptualization was clear from the fact that they could not repeat the performance when they were faced with the same problem again.

Another series of Kohler's experiments (1925) involved the use of sticks or other materials as implements to extend the chimpanzees' reach so that they could obtain food that was otherwise beyond their grasp. The most difficult of these experiments required fitting two sticks together, like a fishing pole, in order to make an implement long enough to reach the food. This was a very difficult concept, and probably the first solution was achieved by chance. *However, this was shown to be insightful learning since Sultan was able to fit the sticks together without any particular difficulty at a later time.*

One experiment, reported by Yerkes (1926) in *The Mind of a Gorilla*, seems clearly to outline the learning involved at level 2. Congo, a gorilla, saw a banana placed in the center of a piece of sewer pipe that had been cemented to the floor of the cage. When she was let into the cage, she went over to the pipe and reached down to get the fruit, but her arm was too short. She went to the other end and tried from there, but again she was unable to reach the banana. She tried lifting the pipe to shake the banana out, but since the pipe was cemented to the floor this proved to be an inappropriate activity. She then gave up and started swinging on the bars of the cage. While she was swinging, she accidentally knocked over a common garden hoe, which fell between her and the sewer pipe. She picked up the hoe and poked out the banana. The next day she tried again, unsuccessfully, to reach the banana as she passed the pipe, but then went and got the hoe, came back, and poked the banana out of the pipe. Yerkes sums up the steps in the process of insightful learning as follows:

**Figure 6-1** A child's solution of the parallelogram problem using a pair of scissors. (*After Wertheimer, M. Productive thinking. New York: Harper & Row, 1945. Page 48. By permission of the publisher.*)

Insight in different organisms may reveal common characteristics.

**1** Survey, inspection, or persistent examination of common problematic situations. The process is not one of random effort but is focused on points that could be the key to the problem.

**2** Hesitation, pause, attitude of concentrated attention.

**3** Trial of more or less adequate mode of response. The gorilla's reaching down into the pipe to try to get the banana is a good example of this mode of response. She used a completely rational way of going about the problem.

**4** In case the initial mode of response proves inadequate, trial of some other mode of response, the transition from one method to the other being sharp and often sudden. [When the ape stopped reaching into the pipe and started trying to lift the end of the pipe, she gave a perfect example of this kind of transition. The change of approach was complete, but again it was reasonable considering the dimensions of the problem.]

**5** Persistent or frequently recurrent attention to the objective or goal and motivation thereby.

**6** Appearance of critical point at which the organism suddenly, directly, and definitely performs the adaptive act.

**7** Ready repetition of the adaptive response after once performed.

**8** Notable ability to discover and attend to the essential aspect or relation in the problematic situation and to neglect, relatively, variations in nonessentials (p. 156).

## GESTALT CONCEPT OF "AH HA!"

The development of gestalt psychology was welcomed 50 years ago by many educators. Their intuitive reaction to the ideas of wholeness and insight was a positive one, and they considered gestalt psychology to be more nearly in accord with experience than the cause and effect of behaviorist psychology, which some regarded as mechanistic and unhuman. The emotional appeal of the material led to a prostitution of the basic ideas on which the psychology was based. Since the discovery method of teaching seems in danger of suffering from similar distortion, it may be instructive to review some of the work in which the interpretation of gestalt psychology was questioned.

### Brown: Meaning of the Whole

Brown (1958) suggested that gestalt psychology could be used to defend the phonic approach to teaching reading as logically as it could be used to support the sight-word approach. By 1930, reading specialists had become impressed with the contention that rote memorization of meaningless parts is not an important kind of human learning. They drew support from the experiments on visual perception conducted by Cattell in 1885, in which he found that children could see whole words as quickly and easily as they could see either single letters or syllables of words, and in some cases more quickly and easily. The importance of meaning for learning that the gestaltists had emphasized was seen as additional support for the so-called look-and-say

method of teaching reading, in which whole words are learned rather than letters or phonetic parts. Hindsight makes obvious the value to most learners of developing word-attack skills, including phonic analysis, to make independent reading possible. This particular bit of hindsight was not available to those who were developing the new method of teaching reading. They argued logically that the new method dealt with words, which are meaningful wholes and of which the letters are meaningless parts; thus, on an a priori basis, they contended that the new method was intrinsically better than the old synthetic method, in which the words were built of phonetic parts, which are neither wholes nor meaningful.

Brown argued that the term "meaningful," as used by the gestaltists, had a systematic rather than a referential connotation. The meaning of a word, he said, is extraneous to the symbol. Essentially, meaning becomes attached to a word because of convention or agreement—a rather pure form of association—rather than because the meaning is inherent in the word itself. The meaning seen in the "ah ha!" experience—of which the gestaltists spoke—is meaning that is inherent in the structure of the material rather than meaning by reference.

To make his point, Brown cited an experiment conducted by Katona, who had his subjects learn series of numerals such as:

4 8 1 3 1 7 2 2 2 6 3 1

After a week, none of the subjects could repeat the numbers correctly. However, another group of subjects had little difficulty in remembering the series when it was presented in the following form:

4 8 13 17 22 26 31
 4 5 4 5 4 5

It was thus seen as a systematic additive set of relationships which could be reconstructed.

Brown contended that phonic analysis supplies this kind of meaning to reading, contaminated, however, by the oddities of the English language. Since there is more system in phonics than there is in a pure look-and-say approach, the work of the gestaltists could lend support to the proponents of phonics as well as to the proponents of the whole-word sight approach. The i/t/a system of teaching beginning reading was described in Chapter 2 as a logical association method in which the components maintain their individual values. Very few children will see i/t/a as a system, but conceptualization occurs when they become aware of a relationship between sounds and symbols.

### Snygg: An Experiment

Snygg (1935) performed a series of experiments that suggested the nature of conceptualization. In one he used mechanically equivalent tasks, in this case the learning of letter triads, to test the hypothesis that individual perception rather than external, or objective, similarities is critical in learning. The subjects were sixth-grade children who had studied Longfellow's "Village Blacksmith." In the experimental situation, the subjects were told that they were being tested to see who could learn the fastest, although they were assured that the scores would be kept secret. The following lists are half as long as those actually given. List 1 was used three times, list 2 was given twice, list 3 was given only once, and then list 2 was given twice more.

| List 1 | List 2 | List 3 |
|--------|--------|--------|
| era    | und    | for    |
| und    | era    | men    |

| | | |
|-----|-----|-----|
| ead | spr | may |
| spr | ead | com |
| che | ing | ean |
| ing | che | dme |
| utt | stn | nma |
| stn | utt | ygo |
| the | ree | but |
| ree | the | igo |

The children studied the lists for two minutes, and then were allowed one minute to reproduce as many triads as possible. After a week, they were again asked to reproduce as many of the triads as they could from memory and to tell of any devices they had used to help them learn the lists. Three youngsters had made up mnemonic devices of their own, eight had grasped the scrambled poetry structure, *seven learned of this structure between the testing and the retesting,* and twenty-three did not respond to the question.

On the retesting, the eight who had discovered the hidden structure produced 225 percent as many syllables as the other children and did 14 percent more syllables correctly than they had on their own last try. The seven students who picked up the principle during discussions of the material in the week between the tests did 98 percent as well as they had on their first test, while the other students did only 62 percent as well. In general, these results follow the pattern that most readers would anticipate. The conceptualization of the structure made recall of the syllables very much easier than when they had to be retrieved as individual items.

### GRASPING CONNECTIONS THAT RELATE KNOWLEDGE

Learning is a complex process, and many different ways have been devised to subdivide and name the elements that make up the transactions involved.

**Gagné: Hierarchy of Learning**

Gagné (1970) developed an eight-level hierarchy of learning which has become popular among teachers. The first five of these levels would be included within association learning in this volume and the other three within conceptualization (Table 6-1). In many cases Type 6, concept learning, could be built by association responses, but in others a conceptualization occurs that makes the abstraction more easily transferable to other situations. In Type 7, rule learning, Gagné distinguishes this level of learning as understanding rather than mere parroting a rule that has been memorized. In Type 8, problem solving, most of these formulations would be classed as conceptualizations, although some of them would be classed as creative production.

Gagné makes a strong case for the difference between the types of learning and an even stronger case for the need to develop *all* the lower levels before it is possible to move to a higher type of learning. In discussing foreign language learning Gagné (1970, p. 268) discussed the use of discovery techniques in learning rules. He pointed out that discovery may take longer but seems to have advantages. He stressed the importance of basic data on which rules are grounded if the rules are to be established. Gagné described teaching for problem solving almost exclusively in discovery terms.

Gagné's insistence on the need for building-in the preceding types of learning before attempting to achieve a more advanced level has lead to the analysis of the concepts that were necessary to form a rule, and the rules that were necessary to solve a problem. The teachers' attention to the necessary elements in practical application of these ideas has enabled them to structure lessons so that problem solving can occur. It may be that the

conceptualization of "a conceptualization being possible" is the most critical factor in increasing the effectiveness of classroom procedure. Those who are sure that insight, discovery, or conceptualization is impossible for children will almost never come across any evidence that contradicts their belief. They will not structure lesson sequences to bring forth conceptualizations they are sure cannot happen.

**Troubleshooting: A Form of Problem Solving**

A conceptualization of a system, such as a television set with inputs of various kinds and outputs to subsystems, makes the process of diagnosis manageable. With such a conceptualization as a basis, it is possible to set up a logical sequence for checking and isolating the problems that might be the source of a malfunctioning. The idea of the flow of the current and the way it works would lead logically to a check of the input of current to the set. Is it plugged into the wall outlet, and if so, is the wall outlet itself hot (sometimes it is controlled by a wall switch)? Other checks follow logically: Is the current entering the amplifier and leaving it, and is it entering the condensers and leaving them? The whole process is a system of checks to see what the cause of the stoppage might be, drawn from the conceptualization of what is happening to the current as it flows through the set. As in the example of learning an extended sequence, the teacher may have the conceptualization but teach the learners to follow a series of steps rather than to understand what is behind the steps—in other words, to learn at the association level rather than at the conceptualization level. Even after the major concept has been established, many sequences and steps will be essentially associations to be learned.

It was to teach the kind of problem solving

**Table 6-1   The Eight Types of Learning according to Gagné**

*Type 1:* Signal learning—the individual learns to make a *general* diffuse response to a signal. This is the classical conditioning response of Pavlov.

Conditions: 1 The stimulus produces a generalized reaction (contiguity).
2 The stimulus provides the signal.
3 The stimulus must precede the signal.

*Type 2:* Stimulus-response learning is a type of learning in which a very precise muscular movement in response to a very specific stimulus is formed. It involves operant conditioning, contiguity, and practice.

Conditions: 1 Learning is gradual.
2 Response becomes more sure and precise.
3 Controlling stimulus becomes more sure and precise.
4 Condition 2 plus 3 equals successive approximation.
5 Reinforcement follows the response.

*Type 3:* Chaining—what is acquired is a chain of two or more stimulus-response connections. (Example: the grip on a bat, the stance and swing in hitting a ball)

Conditions: 1 Individual links must be previously established.
2 There must be contiguity between links.

*Type 4:* Verbal associations—the learning of chains that are verbal. (Example: English word "match" from the French word "a*lum*ette"—illuminate—lum—light—match)

Conditions: 1 Learner must know what the word means.
2 He must make a connection between the words.
3 There must be a coding connection. (E.g., be able to associate *lum* with illuminate.)

*Type 5:* Multiple discrimination—the individual learns to make *n* different identifying responses to as many different stimuli (learning a French vocabulary list or symbols for the chemical elements). The learning of each stimulus-

response connection is a simple Type 2 occurrence; the connections tend to interfere with each other's retention.

Conditions: 1 Individual chains between each stimulus and each response must be learned.
2 Steps must be taken to reduce interference.

*Type 6:* Concept learning—the learner acquires a capability of making a common response to a class of stimuli which may differ widely in physical appearance (e.g., classifying a football, tennis ball, basketball, and baseball all as balls).

Conditions: 1 There is initial coding of property (ball-ness) plus a response capability.
2 Learner must be able to generalize to a variety of conditions.
3 Learning may be a gradual process. Therefore, there must be the possibility of multiple presentations of examples of the concept.

*Type 7:* Rule learning—the chaining of two or more concepts. (Example: when water freezes, its volume becomes larger. This principle embodies the concepts of freeze, volume, and larger.)

Conditions: 1 All concepts must have been previously learned.
2 Concepts must be brought together (not necessary that the *student* do this).
3 Learning takes place in one trial.

*Type 8:* Problem solving (thinking)—two or more previously acquired principles are somehow combined to produce a new capability that can be shown to depend on a "higher order" principle.

Conditions: 1 Learner must be able to identify the essentials of a solution.
2 He must be able to recall previously learned principles.
3 He must be able to combine the principles so that a new one is formed.
4 There is a sudden solution—repetition will add nothing.

involved in electronic troubleshooting that Norman Crowder (1960b) developed his intrinsic programming, which he distinguished from previous programmed learning. In *intrinsic programming* a concept is established or given and then test questions are asked to determine whether it has been understood; whereas in *linear programming* a sequence of discrete steps is designed to build toward a concept. In the *Tutor Texts* or on the Tutor Teaching Machine, a paragraph of information is provided that is written to help the learner master a concept. This is followed by a number of choice questions, each of which refers the learner to a page or a replica of a page (Figure 6-2). The choices represent understanding or common kinds of misunderstanding of the concept. If the student chooses the correct answer, a new paragraph of information is provided, and the process is continued. However, if the choice is incorrect, the student is referred to a page where additional information—including the probable cause of his misconception—is provided. He is again tested for his mastery of the material and sent on his way. The process of remediation can be quite short, or it can involve a large number of steps. Many kinds of material have been programmed in this way, including how to play bridge and how to interpret modern poetry. The success of the programs, like the success of other books and teaching materials, depends on the skill of execution of the writers as well as on the soundness of the theories on which the method is based. There is no doubt that the more quickly a student can conceptualize the relationships upon which complex systems depend, the more quickly and efficiently he will be able to handle the problems that will inevitably arise as the complex system breaks down.

An electronic system has certain advantages over a human system as a means of understanding troubleshooting problems and the kind of learning involved. However, the same principles are involved in the diagnosis of reading difficulties, in the diagnosis of physical illness, and in the diagnosis of the international problems that threaten world peace. In the electronic system, it is usually possible to replace the faulty part and to recheck the system to be sure that it now functions as intended. In some human situations, both the diagnosis of the difficulty and the remediation are more difficult, but a sound conceptualization of the nature of the system will help make troubleshooting more possible. Teachers will find that their own efficiency increases as they are able to help their students achieve the basic conceptualizations on which improvement in electronics, reading, or international affairs depends.

## Social Science: Problems in Teaching

Troubleshooting in an electronic system may seem far removed from the classroom; however, teaching for conceptualization in social studies can be valuable in the same way as it is in applied fields. In a report on California Project Talent, Robeck (1965) outlined a unit on anthropology in which fourth-grade children in gifted classes used scientific sources to study the Santa Barbara Indians. The children were systematically taught to work beyond associations for conceptualizations or generalizations. As gifted students, they learned the factual information primarily on their own. The teacher's role was to help them develop relationships: the impact of trade with other tribes on language, the effect of food availability on the kinds of tools people make, and the cultural changes that resulted from contact with the white man. The primary emphasis was on learning at the second and third levels.

Successful approaches to conceptualization for intellectually gifted children can be adapted to their more typical classmates by

### TEACHING MACHINES AND PROGRAMMED LEARNING

An example of such a step [from Page 101 of such a book] would be:

Page 101

Now, you recall that we had just defined

$$b^0 = 1$$

for any b except where b = 0. We had reached this definition by noting that our division rule,

$$\frac{b^m}{b^n} = b^{(m-n)}$$

will give $b^0$ as a result if we apply it to the case of dividing a number by itself. Thus,

$$\frac{b^3}{b^3} = b^{(3-3)} = b^0$$

but $\frac{b^3}{b^3}$, or any number (except 0), divided by itself equals 1, so we defined $b^0 = 1$.

We used a division process to find a meaning to attach to the exponent 0. Very well, let's see what other interesting results we can get with this division process. Let's apply our division rule to the case of $\frac{b^2}{b^3}$. What result do we get?

| ANSWER | Page |
|---|---|
| $\frac{b^2}{b^3} = b^1$ | 94 |
| $\frac{b^2}{b^3} = b^{(-1)}$ | 115 |
| The rule won't work in this case | 119 |

The student who elects to turn to Page 94 will find:

Page 94

YOUR ANSWER: $\frac{b^2}{b^3} = b^1$

Come, come, now. The rule is $\frac{b^m}{b^n} = b^{(m-n)}$

Now, in the case of $\frac{b^2}{b^3}$, we have m = 2 and n = 3, so we are going to get

$$\frac{b^2}{b^3} = b^{(2-3)}$$

So, 2 − 3 isn't 1, is it? It's − 1.

Return to Page 101, now, and quit fighting the problem.

The student who elects Page 119 will find:

Page 119

YOUR ANSWER: The rule won't work in this case.

Courage! The division rule got us through $b^0$, where m = n, and it will get us through the case where m is smaller than n. In this case we have

$$\frac{b^2}{b^3} = ?$$

and applying the rule

$$\frac{b^m}{b^n} = b^{(m-n)}$$

we get

$$\frac{b^2}{b^3} = b^{(2-3)}.$$

So the exponent of our quotient is (2 − 3) which is −1, isn't it? So just write

$$\frac{b^2}{b^3} = b^{(2-3)} = b^{(-1)}$$

as if you knew what it meant.

Now return to Page 101 and choose the right answer.

And the student who chooses the right answer will find:

Page 115

YOUR ANSWER: $\frac{b^2}{b^3} = b^{(-1)}$

You are correct. Using our rule for division

$$\frac{b^m}{b^n} = b^{(m-n)}$$

in the case of $\frac{b^2}{b^3}$ we get

$$\frac{b^2}{b^3} = b^{(2-3)} = b^{(-1)}.$$

Now, by ordinary arithmetic, we can see that

$$\frac{b^2}{b^3} = \frac{b \times b}{b \times b \times b} = \frac{b \times b}{b \times b \times b} = ?$$

So how shall we define $b^{(-1)}$ ?

| ANSWER | Page |
|---|---|
| $b^{(-1)} = \frac{0}{b}$ | 95 |
| $b^{(-1)} = \frac{1}{b}$ | 104 |

**Figure 6-2** Sample of intrinsic programming. (*From N. A., Crowder, The arithmetic of computers: An introduction to binary and octal mathematics, 1960, pp. 101, 94, 119, and 115, by permission of Sargent-Welch Scientific Company.*)

providing greater numbers of instances from which to generalize. Harrison (1934) found that high-intelligence children in kindergarten were as knowledgeable about social concepts as low-IQ third graders. These findings were also reported by Jersild (1954), who has shown that a child's experience background is of fundamental importance in determining the kind of concepts he is able to master. Eaton (1944) found that pupil achievement in social studies was not directly related to the amount of time devoted to the subject in school—that some of the learning was done almost exclusively at home. All these studies imply a heavy loading of association learning which is fundamental and which must be present before meaningful concepts can be developed.

Hilda Taba applied her concept of a learning hierarchy to develop a cyclical model for teaching the social studies. She believed that the quantity and quality of the ideas and concepts a person can use depends upon the quantity and quality of the stimulation he has had, plus the kind of active thinking experience. She recommended that teachers start with a generalization which has social significance and pursue both content and process objectives simultaneously. According to Taba, the acquisition of information is basic to conceptualization, generalization, and abstraction; but the coverage of specific content should be consciously reduced to a minimal number of instances from which the student can develop an understanding of the main idea. This selection and reduction of concrete experiences leaves time for conscious attention to higher levels of learning. Students are not expected to remember specific facts but to use them in conceptual processes. A three-step sequence is stimulated by the teacher's questions within a setting of what is real to the student: (1) acquisition of information, (2) conceptualization and generalization, and (3) use of concepts to make inferences and solve problems. For students who are disinterested in traditional social studies curricula, she would begin with emotional content, perhaps literature that "speaks to feelings," while exploring what they already knew, or needed to know, at the information level (Taba & Elkins, 1966, p. 77).

Preston (1957) suggested using such ideas as "when your father was a boy" and other personally relevant examples to help the student grasp the historical dimension of time. History obviously is meaningless until the student has some basic notions about sequence and duration of time. The same things may be said about knowledge of space and distance with regard to geography or about the nature of the people studied in sociology or cultural anthropology. The evidence seems to support the view that students can accelerate their acquisition of the basic associations that lead to conceptualizations if they are placed in learning situations—either in school or out—that make such acquisition normal and desirable.

On the other hand children and older persons find learning exciting only when they are probing outward from the fringes of what they presently know. McAulay (1952) found that many second graders considered social studies work boring because television, motor trips, living abroad, and other kinds of experiences had already provided them with the kinds of associations and many of the conceptualizations that the units were designed to teach. What was once a defensible approach, psychologically, to curriculum development —the expansion of the sequence outward in time and space from the child's immediate environment—has lost its relevance. Because of the associations built as a result of television and other extraschool experiences, there is no reason to think that the capital or the history of the state in which children live is nearer to them, as far as their life space is concerned, than events occurring in Washington, London, or Peking. There need be no problem of life-space orientation if the school recognizes the basic associations that the child has and builds from these to conceptualizations of major themes. The social studies have tended to stress the here and now and to neglect causal relationships—the essential difference between social studies and social science—with a resultant diminution of the individual's future effectiveness as a scholar. If the school were to teach systematically for level 2 functioning, average students and students whose home experience is limited to the here and now could probably learn social concepts as well as gifted students do at present.

### Ausubel: Subsumption Theory

Ausubel (1969) reviewed school learning, particularly that common to secondary and higher education, and concluded much of the research about learning was irrelevant there. Some teachers find his emphasis on mastering a large body of knowledge that has already been discovered and organized is very close to the goals they are trying to achieve. They tend to feel that Ausubel's material is relevant to them. He proposed a *subsumption theory* of learning and forgetting. His idea, stated very briefly, was that learning fits into, or is subsumed under, already existing frameworks of knowledge. The greater the degree of organization, clarity, and stability of new knowledge, the easier it will fit and the easier it will be retained because of more reference points or anchors under which the new material can be incorporated, imbedded, related, and thus transferred to subsequent learning situations. In the process of learning there is progressive differentiation from general patterns of organization to specific subconcepts and specific bits of information. During forgetting, the process moves from forgetting specific items of information to forgetting specific subconcepts until only global or highly general concepts remain that become part of the framework.

Ausubel distinguished between meaningful verbal learning, which can be incorporated into an ideational structure, and rote learning,

which usually is not structured. As an aid to subsumption, Ausubel prescribes the use of *advance organizers.* These are of two different types: (1) a *correlative* organizer, which provides the intellectual scaffolding necessary for the new material to fit, and (2) a *derivative* organizer, which is part of the cognitive structure into which the new learning fits. An example of a derivative organizer is the teacher's providing an overview of the new material or his showing how the new material is different from the old content. Ausubel also calls the correlative organizer an expository organizer.

Ausubel's research has usually been on the use of correlative organizers. In a 1962 study he used a passage that dealt with different kinds of uniformity and variability among primary and secondary sex characteristics. The passage, organized at a high level of abstraction, was introductory to reading about specific hormonal factors initiating and regulating pubescence. None of the "organizer" material could be used to answer test questions on the main passage. Presumably the reading at an abstract level and in the general area of sex produced a set or a framework that made later reading more meaningful. In this study the use of the organizer had a significant effect only on the lower third of the group when they were divided on a scale of verbal ability. Organizers that ask questions, provide overviews, or arrange contrasts with the new material would presumably be more effective than correlative organizers. However, it would be difficult or impossible to divorce the derivative organizer from its content which would be germane to the answers on the test questions.

Ausubel considers discovery learning particularly suitable for young children who do not have a highly organized body of information into which new material can fit. For older students—from junior high school on—he considers discovery learning a waste of time, therefore an inefficient approach to learning. In meaningful reception learning the learner is essentially given the answer in advance, whereas in discovery learning the learner is expected, largely through *inductive* processes involving formulation of numerous hypotheses, to find the answer for himself. Ausubel argues that presenting material in a highly organized and meaningful fashion will permit the realization of transfer, retention, and intrinsic motivation with much less time and effort than that required in discovery learning. In terms of the present chapter, an advanced organizer could provide a conceptualization in which the learning material built additional relationships. All organizers must be in terms that use knowledge already possessed by the learner, although this point is not stressed by Ausubel. He does emphasize that the material to be learned be meaningful and that it be understood rather than learned by rote. Students in college learn much of their course content from lectures that are organized to present lucidly a series of conceptualizations that will expand the student's knowledge base in a discipline. When these lectures are well organized and presented in a dramatic fashion, the students achieve conceptualizations that live and are effective in their thinking. When less skillful instructors present similar material, it is seen as a mass of details to be absorbed and regurgitated verbatim. Such learning is associative and often lacks intellectual structure. When Ausubel's subsumption theory is used well, it is efficient and even exciting. Many teachers find his ideas compatible with the image of "teacher" they have developed from their own experience.

## TRANSFER OF LEARNING

One of the perennial problems in learning has been to understand how transfer from one situation to another was possible. Very little of what is studied in school or on campus is used in exactly the form in which it is learned. Even on tests and examinations that ask for straight recall the form is changed in important ways. When school learning is used in life situations, it must be changed substantially to be functional. As one student said upon his return from France, "I did very well in first year French, but I found that nobody spoke first year French in Bordeaux." The stage play *La Plume de ma Tante* plays on this same theme of the need for more than the school forms of knowledge in a unique social milieu. In life, learning is continuously transformed to meet new situations, although just how the neurological changes take place is not entirely clear.

Thorndike (1924), who was interested in making school learning as useful as possible and found the prevailing theories about formal discipline distasteful, did extensive research in transfer of learning. *Formal discipline* viewed the mind as an organ that grew strong through exercise and improved in proportion to the difficulty of the exercise. The older disciplines of mathematics, Latin, and Greek were considered ideal forms of mental exercise partly because they were hard to learn for many students. Science was admitted grudgingly into the secondary schools as course content that had to be accommodated because of the growing importance of science in everyday life. Courses such as home economics and industrial arts were frowned upon as too utilitarian to be academically respectable. Thorndike's contention was that the basic premises of formal discipline were incorrect and that the learning elements that transferred from one situation to another were those that were identical within the situations. Among the ingenious experiments Thorndike designed to test his thesis was one in which Latin was contrasted with home economics in developing English usage. Group A studied Latin while group B studied domestic science, and both were tested on English. The comparative gain would show the efficiency of the different subject areas. According to his results, Latin was more productive than home economics but not startlingly so. He argued that home economics had value in itself, while Latin had very little utility for most students and that the difference between gains was not great enough to compensate.

### Identical Elements

In a variant of Thorndike's transfer studies, group A was taught Latin and tested on English while group B was taught English for the same period and tested on English. He found that teaching English was more productive than teaching Latin to produce scores on English tests. Partly as a result of his opposition, the study of Greek disappeared from the curricula of most secondary schools, and the study of Latin declined for a generation. The justification for mathematics shifted from its value as a formal discipline to its utility in science and technology.

Interest in transfer of training continued with Gibson (1940), who found that if a new response were needed to an old stimulus, the old response hindered learning. In other words, there was negative transfer because an established pattern was no longer appropriate. Mandler (1954) found that negative transfer could be overcome if the original task were highly overlearned. Under these conditions the new learning was facilitated, perhaps because the new task was discriminated as new. Hilgard and Bower (1966) reported a personal communication from Tanner in which his subjects were found to respond to minute aural differences accurately if practice were continued for many trials. Sounds that were so similar they could not be discriminated at the

beginning of the experiment were learned during approximately 350 exposures. The subjects were unable to explain how differentiation became possible during practice; in other words, they could not verbalize how they made the discriminations. Overlearning seems to be important in the transfer of identical elements associative in nature and made functional on a long-term basis through repetition.

### Generalization

Ausubel (1969) hypothesized that what are transferred are the major themes that become incorporated into the intellectual framework of the individual while the details of the learning decay. Reynolds (1966, 1968) found that learning nonsense words in a map setting substantially improved the ability of subjects to use the same nonsense words in sentences that were descriptive of the maps. His control subjects had been given map training, divorced from the nonsense words which were presented separately. Another control group were given the nonsense words in descriptive phrases without the map setting. He concluded that a cognitive structure during learning was critical for transfer to take place. In interpreting this research, Mathis, Cotton, and Sechrest (1970) hypothesized that students who learn words out of context may not transfer them to real-life situations. They suggested that school stores, school banks, and similar devices be provided as a framework for new vocabulary that would be meaningful in out-of-school settings. In other words, the probability of transfer would increase as the structural dynamics of the field became similar between school and utilitarian situations.

Thune (1950) studied aspects of learning how to learn as a cause of transfer. He found significant improvement over five days in learning three lists of equally difficult nonsense words. In addition there was an improvement from list to list during each day. On day 1 the subjects averaged 7 words for the first list, 14 for the second, and 18 for the third, indicating substantial improvements. By day 5 the learning had improved to a performance level of 14, 21, and 24 words. He concluded that people develop strategies for learning that transfer and make future learning more efficient.

Harlow (1949) found that monkeys could learn to solve the principle behind a system for hiding food in one of two cartons. In the beginning of the experiment the monkeys operated at approximately 50 percent correct, which is at the level of chance, but for the final 56 of 312 trials they were functioning at 97 percent level of correct choices. After only one error, the monkeys figured out the system and solved the problem at 100 percent efficiency. In a related experiment Harlow found that human children from two to five years old developed similar sets of efficient ways for solving the problem. The length of the trial sequence seems to be critical in experiments where complex transfer takes place.

Cooke (1973) used three different teaching strategies to compare the successes of first-grade children on block arrangements that depended on the transfer of an imbedded principle to the criterion task. The learning strategies were (1) rote, in which the attributes of the blocks (shape, color, thickness) were the focus for building a sequence, (2) principle, in which the teacher cued the child on the way the blocks were organized, and (3) discovery, in which an inquiry technique was used to encourage the child to discover the imbedded principle for himself (Figure 6-3). Cooke randomly assigned trials of subjects (matched for sex, chronological age, and IQ) to three strategy groups and carefully defined the interaction of teacher and subject. His "conceptualization" task, from which the total

scores were derived, was the number of blocks arranged from memory on a new design sequence that followed the same embedded principal as the child had built during the interaction. Two results were statistically significant: (1) The discovery group showed superior long-term memory (six weeks) over the rote group and (2) only the discovery group made significant gains after six weeks over their own initial scores. Although some individual children in each strategy group discovered the imbedded principle and transferred it to the "conceptualization" task, the investigator reported a tendency for them to conform to the teacher's guidance and not to discover the inherent structure in the design unless encouraged by questioning. Cooke speculated that improved scores over time were possible because the conceptualizers improved in the time they needed to learn how to learn the task.

## Application

As reported earlier, both Chomsky and Gray found that following an extended sequence of problems children developed verbal skills that enabled them to generate new and unique verbal patterns for expressing themselves freely. At this generative stage of language performance the transfer of learning has been transmuted into creative self-direction based on common principles that have been organized systematically.

Fluent reading exemplifies the transfer of many skills and meanings. After the code-breaking process has been completed, word identification occurs automatically at a high level of transfer. Word meanings are transformed to meet the demands of a new context and even the author's intent is explored at an empathic level.

An artist who has mastered the skills of his craft transfers his learnings to new productions that are unique for him and often for society as a whole. New responses are likewise generated from vestibular and muscle response mechanisms learned in running to those needed to learn the position and balance of the body when riding a bicycle. Most of this transfer is unconscious, and only when the skill or knowledge is lacking does the need become obvious.

Many instances of transfer are within the experience of the reader. In general, transfer of learning is a resultant of the nature of the learning and of its depth. When the material is new and the learning superficial, identical elements can be identified and transferred to similar kinds of tasks. However, even in the simplest learning there is some rather diffuse generalization, as Pavlov demonstrated in his work on the transferability of stimuli to evoke the same response. When overlearning is practiced experimentally, learning how to learn becomes evident in increased efficiency. In human learning, conceptualizations make the learned material available in many situations, some of which are quite remote from the original setting. At a high level of application, teaching may be viewed as the transfer of the principles of learning to remote and new situations. The transfer process has been highly developed.

## SUMMARY

Conceptualization, or level 2 learning, refers to the process by which the learner comes to understand inherent relationships. Conceptualization includes relating bits of knowledge, discovering cause or effect, gaining insight, or forming generalizations. Grasping the relationships between bits of experience enables the learner to see new experiences in context, thus increasing his learning efficiency and making the information more available at future times. Individual students differ in their

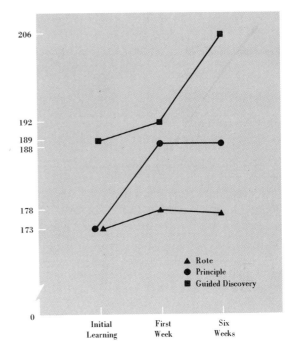

**Figure 6-3** Mean scores of three pupil-teacher interactions at three time intervals. *(From Gary E. Cooke, Conceptualization in young children: A comparison of the effects of rote, principle, and guided discovery strategies. Unpublished Doctoral Dissertation, University of Oregon, 1971. By permission of the author.*

relative ability to generate structures of knowledge as in their ability to accumulate and recall facts and/or information.

Two approaches to teaching conceptualizations are (1) the step-by-step introduction of a series of episodes that support a generalization and (2) the essential-features approach in which relevant experiences are analyzed by the student to formulate his own conceptualization. The greater the involvement of the student in structuring the relationships, the more likely the conceptualization will take place; the greater the inherent satisfaction for success in the process, the more likely the learner will continue to study this content on his own.

Information can be given in a lecture, including the principles or big ideas in a unit of knowledge, but for the student the process is likely to be the absorption of additional bits of association learning rather than insightful learning. The teacher can help students conceptualize by emphasizing inquiry techniques which encourage them to explore material and discover relationships within it.

Bergson described intuitive learning as emerging from masses of information which the individual himself orders in time and space. Bruner emphasized the importance of basic information as a foundation on which to build intuitive thought. Suchman devised and demonstrated a method of inductive thinking in which the teacher's role is to help the students conceptualize as a result of their questioning. An environment which is responsive to the exploration of young children can help them conceptualize the nature of their physical environment.

More than a generation ago, the founders of gestalt psychology emphasized the generative effect of the "ah ha!" experience, in which pieces are related to each other and to a whole that is greater than the sum of its parts. Gagné described learning situations which can be made more efficient when the student conceptualizes the processes on which the information is grounded. Ausubel developed a subsumption theory, in which advanced organizers helped the student structure meaningful verbal learning.

Students who discover a system of integrating otherwise discrete material remember it longer and more accurately than students who have studied the material but not conceptualized the relationships. It is hoped that somewhere through this chapter illumination appeared and the reader experienced the discovery, "Ah ha! So that is what conceptualization is all about!"

## SELF-DIRECTING ACTIVITIES

1 Identify an important conceptualization in another course. Decide whether you used a step-by-step or essential-features approach in arriving at it.
2 Plan a lesson that requires the use of inquiry techniques.
3 List the three most important things you have learned in the last 24 hours. Place them in Gagné's hierarchy.

# Chapter 7

Building affective conceptualizations about physical control in a teachers college in Jamaica. (*Courtesy of the United Nations*)

# AFFECTIVE CONCEPTUALIZATIONS

This chapter is designed to help you to modify emotional problems through an understanding of conceptualization of affects and to develop skills in motivating students. In order to accomplish these tasks, you should be able to:

◖ Explain how affective conceptualizations increase the effect of positive emotional responses

◖ Demonstrate ways to minimize the negative effects of emotional problems

◖ Explain why motivation techniques should be applied differentially with different ethnic groups and give examples

◖ Describe specific conceptualizations used to motivate gifted students

◖ List the types of incentives that would skillfully help built motivation

◖ Use the following terms correctly:
symbolization
free association
client-centered therapy
reality therapy
incentives

For many years therapists of different persuasions have worked with people to help them conceptualize the affective feelings that have disturbed their comfortable functioning as human beings. More recently teachers, counselors, and parents have come to realize that the way students and children feel about themselves and their interaction with other people influences the way in which they are able to learn. Helping people understand how they are feeling tends to allow them to become objective and detached about these emotional components and thus somewhat freed of their binding influence. This process of understanding is not automatic and is helped by the ministrations of an outside mediator who can avoid becoming emotionally involved in the interaction.

Even when the dynamics of the situation are understood, it is sometimes difficult to structure the learning situation so that conceptualization will take place. Amy was a bright, outgoing 3½-year-old whose sister was 6 months old. Amy was accepting and loving toward her little sister; however, because Amy had been the center of the universe for most of her life, emotional strains accompanied sharing attention with another. Little signs indicated her feelings. She was sometimes just a little rough in the way in which she cuddled her sister, and one day she said, "Christine won't like it when I get small again." She developed a negative set in her response to suggestions, probably as a way of asserting her uniqueness as a person. However, she could be manipulated by phrasing suggestions in the reverse. "Amy doesn't want to go downtown," or "You won't want cereal this morning." Helping Amy understand that sharing her parents' attention was not the same as losing it required both emotional support and subtle, but indirect, verbal probing that let her evaluate and express, in her own way and primarily to herself, the idea that there was enough affection for both. More typical insistence about eating and going to bed on the part of her parents would have deepened the trauma and confirmed her feeling of alienation. It is important for parents and teachers to break the ritual of negative responding toward negative behavior and to become conceptualizers of affective needs.

## NEED FOR CONCEPTUALIZATION IN SCHOOL

All learning situations carry affective loadings (Chapter 5). Both teachers and pupils can be more productive as they are able to anticipate these affects and to recognize their emotional importance in a conceptual way. In secondary school many academic courses get off to a bad start because adolescents find the beginning class sessions highly threatening, a condition which immobilizes them or generates negative responses toward the subjects. Once a negative emotional set has been established, the reaction system becomes self-perpetuating. Because the student is negative and fearful, he does not work well and subtly punishes the teacher just by his failure to learn. Normally the teacher responds by pressuring the student severely to induce him to work more, and the cycle repeats itself. These actions and reactions are at the association level. Escape from them usually requires (1) conceptualizing the dynamics of what is happening within the student; (2) restructuring the affective loadings so that the student can achieve some genuine progress, and (3) assisting the student to conceptualize why he is responding in the way he is and thereby helping him to free himself gradually from negative habits of response.

Teachers who are aware of the dynamics of affective learning can prestructure the classroom learning situation to avoid, as much as possible, the negative associations and to bring to the fore of the student's thinking the satisfactions he can get from mastery of learning. When classes are large (over three can sometimes be too large), it is difficult for the teacher to be successful with all the different individuals in the class. Recording sheets help by making it necessary to note accomplishments of each child. This review helps bring individual children into focus and reduces the chances of overlooking them before their behavior is reinforced. Success in cognitive endeavors usually carries pleasure loading. As these loadings are conceptualized, they become signposts that help structure the affective loadings of later learning. When teachers are first learning to use these ideas in their teaching, they will frequently believe that keeping track of each student's program is impossible, but as they persist, teaching will get easier and more pleasurable for the students as well as for the teacher.

### Cognitive and Affective Conceptualizations

The process of conceptualization seems to be similar for both affective and cognitive loadings. However, the contents are different because the associations out of which the conceptualizations emerge are different. Most people are aware of their cognitive thought content and examine their experience in different lights, thus aiding concepts to emerge. Affective loadings are more subtle and are much less likely to be known or understood. In many ways they are like the air that is breathed and are part of the world as it is. Because people are less aware of the affective reactions they have to a topic, it is much more difficult for them to conceptualize the nature and the causes of their feelings. Most people do not recognize their attitudes and prejudices

as being different from the attitudes of other people.

### Schools Stress Cognitive Conceptualizations

Probably because individuals have been relatively unaware of their affective feelings but have been conscious of the knowledge content, a vast amount of school time is given to trying to get students to conceptualize content with very little attention given to their feelings about the studies they are pursuing or about the teachers they have. Teachers share the common blindness about feelings and their importance. If emotions come to the surface, it is considered unfortunate, since they should have been under better control or, in other words, repressed so that they are not recognized by either the individual or those around him. However, since the affects have such a large influence on whether material will be repeated and thus learned, more attention should be given to affective learning in schools. Plans for stimulating awareness about how students are reacting and feeling should become part of the preparation for each class period. This change would modify school for both teachers and students. Since these ways of thinking about life are different from those which have been culturally sanctioned, many people will find this attention to emotional experience traumatic; however, since the changes will make learning more pleasurable, the reinforcement will rapidly establish the new approaches once they have passed a level of critical incidence.

## CONCEPTUALIZATIONS IN THERAPY

While schools have largely ignored the emotional dimensions of learning, the therapists who work with neurotic or psychotic people have been concentrating therapy on the affective side of human experience. Although therapists like Freud, Rogers, Glasser, and Perls represent a wide spectrum of theory orientation, they have been almost unaminous in helping their clients understand the emotional dynamics that were causing their difficulties. A great deal of the therapeutic effectiveness depended upon the skill with which clients were helped to understand the emotional forces that bothered them. In many cases it was not only the emotional forces but the reasons that these forces arose that made the conceptualization meaningful. Since a number of theories posited different causes for the emotional problems, it may be that the understanding of the problem itself generated the symptom removal.

### Sigmund Freud

Freud has had a massive influence on the thinking of psychiatrists. Although he established a system of psychoanalysis that was not made a basic part of the training of most psychiatrists, his ideas seeped into both the training and the practice of many of those who worked with the mentally disturbed. Freud's psychoanalytic theory is presented as background for the stages of affective development (Chapter 13). In this section cases from three periods in Freud's clinical procedure will be analyzed in order to show the constancy of the process of conceptualization across the different themes of psychoanalysis. Stone (1971) traced Freud's development in a sympathetic and perceptive way that is exciting reading for students.

*Hypnosis* was one of the early tools Freud used to help patients explore buried incidents in the past that were surfacing to trouble them in the form of physical illnesses. The problems were resolved only when the patient conceptualized a relationship of the buried insults to the present difficulties. Cacilie, a patient who

had an unusually complex set of problems, helped Freud develop the idea of *symbolization.* She was a highly intelligent, artistic, and sensitive woman who had been married years earlier in order to consolidate two fortunes. Her husband was frightened by her talents and disliked her, probably because he feared she was more able than he. After their second child he stopped having sexual intercourse with her and became notorious for his affairs with other women. Cacilie's first severe illness, explored under hypnosis, was a raging neuralgia of the teeth which would incapacitate her for five to ten days, then disappear for an indefinite time. Three sessions of hypnosis with strong posthypnotic suggestion cleared up this problem for a year, but then the pain returned as a nervous attack centered around the teeth. This time Freud explored the background of the initial attack, which had been a violent quarrel during her first pregnancy when her husband violently insulted her. Under hypnosis she revealed the quarrel, saying it was like a slap in the face. After awakening Cacilie, Freud discussed the causes of her problem and helped her understand the symbolism and the way her unconscious had used symbolic attack to initiate physical illness.

Cacilie's next illness centered around an inability to swallow. Under hypnosis this difficulty was traced to another quarrel during which Cacilie felt she had to swallow her husband's insult. Her unconscious set up conditions which prevented her from swallowing anything. Again the discussion and understanding of the symbolism helped clear up the problem. Another of her problems was a pain in her right foot which turned out to be symbolically related to her fear that she might not get off on the right foot with the other patients in a sanatorium. Other problems kept cropping up until Cacilie developed a serious illness that involved a piercing headache with a pain that made her half blind. During this exploration Freud helped Cacilie to recall that she had felt her grandmother, who was the dominant female in her life, suspected her of masturbation which she, Cacilie, had been practicing. She also had developed guilt feelings that the failure of her marriage was punishment for her sins. As these insights were explored and conceptualized, they ceased to cause illness.

*Dreams* were studied intensively by Freud, who read all the extant literature on the topic, but developed most of his understanding through analysis and interpretation of his own dreams. He discovered wish fulfillment in the themes of the dreams, but found repressed problems in the frustration that made the dream abort. In one of his dreams he had been summoned to a police examination because an article was missing and he was suspected of having taken it. In the dream he was recognized as a consultant and ordered released since he "was a respectable person." However, he could not find his hat so could not leave after all. His analysis indicated that subconsciously he was not as honest as he had thought.

A young woman, who had a violent aversion for her mother whom she hit and abused, was referred to Freud because the doctors could find nothing organically wrong with her. The young woman's dreams were about her mother's funeral at which she was seated with her older sister, both dressed in mourning. She was also obsessed with phobias which made her fearful that something had happened to her mother anytime she was away from her for a short time. Freud helped the young woman see that the phobia was a counterreaction to her hostility toward her mother, which had led her to alternate between exaggerated affection and hostility. The conceptualization of her affective loadings of hostility and love freed the young woman from the phobias and let her live a more normal life. The dreams

provided the associations out of which conceptual interpretations could be made.

*Free association* is a name Freud gave to the process of having a patient tell of ideas that arose in his mind as they came up without any need to make logical order or sense from them. From the disjointed ideas Freud was able to see connections that were normally repressed but unconsciously important to the client. The understanding of the relationship between the ideas often helped clients overcome their neuroses.

Lertzing was a young man who had been incapacitated for ten years by his fears and his fantasies. He required nearly a full year of daily sessions before regaining his health sufficiently to complete his bar examinations and continue the practice of law. As the analysis progressed. Lertzing told about having wished his father dead many times so that he could inherit enough money to marry his fiancée of ten years. Another part of the story was that his father had beaten him severely for biting someone. An additional piece of the puzzle was that a wealthy relative had offered to set Lertzing up in the family business if he married the man's daughter. The position would have made him independently wealthy, which was attractive, but would separate him from his fiancée, which was distressing. The strain of trying to make difficult choices precipitated his illness. During the analysis Freud became a transference object so that he became in the mind of the client the cousin who wanted him to marry his daughter, the father beating him on his buttocks, a sadistic army captain who clamped rats to the buttocks of prisoners and had them eat their way into the anus, and finally a servant girl whom he had explored with his hands as a very young boy. Over the period of the analysis, the young man was able to hear himself make these outpourings and they helped him conceptualize his problems in his choice situation, but extended exploration and understandings were required before he was freed from the dark ideas that had bound him. He had to live through the ideas a number of times before the cognitive understanding became affective understanding.

In all the different modes of treatment that Freud developed, the conceptualization of the affective loadings was the element that freed the patient from his chains. The emotional ties were often very convoluted and difficult to trace, but as they were understood they were no longer destructive. Mental health came with self-knowledge.

## Carl R. Rogers

Working from a basis of present problems rather than understanding early childhood traumas, Rogers developed modern psychotherapy. One of the fundamental assumptions in his early work was a conviction that the client had the resources necessary to help himself if he were given support while he discovered them. Rogers was careful to test the theory he had developed both through clinical records and through controlled statistical studies. One of the findings that emerged was the importance of a counselor's having a fundamental belief in the worth and dignity of the individual. When the therapist expected the client to be able to solve his problems, he was more likely to do so than when he had doubts about his capability. The tone of voice in which the counselor reflects or restates what the client has said distinguishes between evaluation, empathy, and rejection since the same words can be used with slightly different intonations for each response.

*Client-centered therapy* came to be the name of the process by which clients learned to understand themselves and to change as their understanding grew. A young woman who was quite disturbed came in for counseling. Her account of the changes she saw in herself after she had completed her treatment reflected many significant conceptualizations (Rogers, 1951, pp. 38–39). Her first reaction was that she had not been acting like herself in her untidy, withdrawn patterns. As she reflected on her actions, she came to see that she was indeed the same person; however, to reach this understanding she needed to talk out her shame, self-rejection, and doubts to the counselor and to accept herself as he, acting as a catalyst, accepted her. As the young woman progressed in her treatment, she recognized that she wanted both independence and dependence, and the conflict was bothering her since she actually thought of herself as wanting independence and despising a need for dependence. It required an accepting climate, generated by the counselor, for her to verbalize her troubled thoughts and then to accept herself. In the acceptance, she grew more independent and worthwhile in her own eyes. The key component in the therapy was the ability to conceptualize her present state of development and accept herself as she was.

Although client-centered therapy takes time, it is not nearly as extended as psychoanalysis. Time is required for the client to grow into self-acceptance and then to see how conflicting feelings fit together. One of the main principles of Roger's approach has been that the client is free to use the time as he sees fit rather than as the counselor thinks it would be profitable for him to use it. This means that time is spent testing the reality of this freedom before much is accomplished in the client getting to know himself.

In *Man and the Science of Man* Rogers (1968) discussed the importance of the human experience as the basis for all scientific knowledge. He stressed the idea that the generation of scientific findings requires a great deal of input from a broad spectrum of experience. Out of this experiencing, a sense of pattern or of relationship gradually evolves. As this pattern is explored in the light of other information, it emerges more and more clearly as a gestalt. There is a need to keep ideas in suspension, and not to close out any of the options for putting material into a relationship too quickly, if the structure is to become as whole as possible. An analogy in nature is the formation of crystals in a supersaturated liquid where, if allowed to form slowly, they become bigger and more perfectly formed.

Rogers points out the need for testing hypotheses after they have been structured to see whether or not the idea stands up, in many cases by employing statistical measures and large groups of subjects. However, some theories require extensive exploration of a single case, as in studying the circulation of the blood. The science is the generation of the ideas rather than the testing, which is necessary but not sufficient. In a thesis it is the development of the hypotheses to be tested and the conceptualization of the ways the testing can be handled that is creative rather than the routine experiments and statistical treatment which is necessary as a test.

Not all psychologists are comfortable with Rogers' ideas of the nature of science; however, in the conference on Science and Man where he presented his ideas, some psychologists as well as some other participants were neither frustrated nor annoyed with the idea of inner man as the reality and science as a handmaiden to the creative personality. Rogers pointed out that even B. F. Skinner (1961), when discussing the way research is conducted, described the highly subjective searching procedure through which the avenues to be explored further are opened and how these had not been anticipated although general themes had been assumed. But to psychologists who have been trained to think of the science of psychology as a process through which an individual discovers an already existent reality by the manipulation of

variables, the idea that the reality is generated, like a spider web, from within the individual is unsettling. To Rogers and others who explore the world in his terms, the *idea* of the mechanization of human behavior is demeaning. Worse still, it becomes a self-fulfilling prophecy which causes individuals to act like robots because this is the way they are expected to act—and be rewarded for acting.

Teachers who structure their learning situations in such a way as to build from associations to conceptualizations and then to creative self-direction can have the best of both worlds. At the association level, inputs are organized in a structured way for both cognitive and affective features. At the conceptualization level, the individual is encouraged and helped to generate his own patterns within the associations and eventually to go beyond the given patterns to new ones of his own devising.

### Ralph S. Welsh

Welsh (1971), who worked within a behavior modification strategy framework, conditioned a seven-year-old boy not to light matches, even though the child had started the treatment with a strongly developed penchant for this kind of activity. The procedure consisted in having him take one match at a time from a paper match packet, close the cover, light the match, hold it over an ashtray at arm's length without support, and burn most of the match before extinguishing it. His mother was counseled briefly about the procedures. For the first three periods lasting 50 minutes each the boy continued to light matches with enthusiasm. The fourth session was doubled in length and the boy asked to stop 10 minutes before the allotted time. At this time the mother reported improvement in home activities unrelated to matches. After another three saturation sessions the boy said that he would rather not light matches. Even after six months the match-lighting behavior was still extinguished. Welsh considered the results to be examples of conditioning. It seems probable that the boy may have been expressing a conceptualization when he said, "I'd rather not light matches."

### Stewart B. Shapiro

Shapiro (1969), a humanist psychologist, described an encounter group which illustrates how conceptualization can be part of the culmination of new experiencing. Although some leaders of encounter group sessions avoid any attempt at insight, each person in an encounter group has the choice of keeping or discarding a symptom when he has established that the symptom blocks his fulfillment. While many of the emphases in encounter groups are upon experiencing the here and now, many participants also come to understand why their internal responses make a difference, and sometimes what that difference is, in their daily living.

One of the groups with whom Shapiro worked was composed of executives of the National Council of Churches. These men and women were deeply religious, liberal Christians who hesitated to be aggressive—since it was non-Christian—even though their work required aggressive leadership. The purpose of the encounter group sessions was to increase their positive feelings of joy, love, strength, and serenity and incidentally to reduce their constrictions in dealing adequately with hostility.

The group sessions began with a worship service, which Shapiro felt was helpful, and continued in a nonstructured encounter. As usual, the lack of structure was unsettling for many of the members but nonetheless prepared them to participate in subsequent sessions. The next activity, which was started

when strong feelings were generally beginning to emerge, involved pairing activities when the individuals were free to express their negative feelings about the procedure and about other participants. Some strong individuals were not very sympathetic to this activity. Shapiro changed the activities frequently by forming small T-groups in which unstructured, interpersonal encounters were arranged with one proviso, that only positive feelings would be expressed about themselves or about one another. In another session tensions were relaxed by learning to play games, such as thumb wrestling. Fantasy exercises were set up in which small groups of participants expressed their reaction to a request to demonstrate their fantasy to the larger group. As the week continued, the groups were asked to devise a new tradition, ritual, or ceremony which was presented to the whole group. Shapiro pointed out in his account that the exercises in openness with a few members at a time were necessary in order for them to be ready to participate in the more threatening presentation to the whole group. The presentation activity deepened and extended trust bonds that had begun in the small T-groups. During the process of giving feedback after each exercise, the participants were verbalizing their perception of the changes that were taking place within them. The new affective experiences provided associative bonds that, for many individuals, formed the matrix from which understandings could grow.

### William Glasser

Many teachers find the basic premises of Glasser (1965) compatible with their feelings about teaching. In *Reality Therapy* he suggests that the therapist become involved with the client, help him build experiences of acting responsibly, and help him accept responsibility for his actions. In contrast to Freud, Glasser does not delve into the past and the client is accepted as a responsible human being who must, himself, be held responsible. Before much improvement can be expected, a feeling of trust must be built in the relationship between the therapist and the client, which usually is most effectively established by acting as though such a trust were already in existence. The beginning of this relationship is signaled in a greeting, a smile, or a glance. Usually the therapist has already done a number of things to indicate that he is sincere about holding the client responsible for what happens. Many excellent teachers treat students in just this way. The difficulty is in accepting the person when his activities are undesirable from the teacher's or therapist's point of view. Without this acceptance, the teacher or therapist shows disapproval and often causes the student, who is held accountable for his actions, to feel rejected. Usually these students have already had more rejection from parents and other teachers than they can manage. Building Glasser's form of involvement means that the teacher or therapist can be hurt by the students because he truly cares what happens to them. On the other hand, the affective associations that come from having someone really care about them are essential for deviants and delinquents, if conceptualizations about their responsibility are to take place. Glasser pointed out that his brand of reality therapy takes time and a great deal of effort. It is expedited, as is behavior therapy, when the total living environment can be organized to reinforce the same patterns of activity or belief.

Glasser (1969) discussed the application of his principles of reality therapy to regular classrooms in *Schools without Failure*. The importance of requiring responsibility on the part of the students, and correlatively insisting on performance by the teachers, is clearly outlined in one Upward Bound Program in which he participated. Although this particular program was good in many respects (the instruction was good, the classes were small, and grades were not important), fewer than half of the students attended class or did the required work. Apparently the lack of insistence by the instructors on performance was interpreted by the students as a lack of caring for them as people, even though the teachers were deeply anxious to help these young people who were literally throwing away their final chance to improve their future. In Glasser's therapy, the student must conceptualize his own responsibility for what happens to him. This is a departure from intervention strategies which assume the environment to be the critical factor.

### Peter A. Olsson and Irving L. Myers

Olsson and Myers (1972) described therapeutic work with fourteen-to-sixteen-year-old upper-class and upper-middle-class adolescents who were in therapy because of acting out their hostilities at home or school. Much of the acting out included the use of drugs, such as speed, LSD, and marijuana. The therapy involved nonverbal techniques, including modified sensitivity training and role playing. The setting was a comfortable room with carpeting on which the therapists and group members sat with their shoes removed. An important part of the therapy involved the here-and-now meaning of the nonverbal actions. These discussions avoided symbolic interpretation normal to Freudian-oriented therapists.

In one sequence of sessions, Chuck came to the group suffering from a residual drug effect, or "flashback." Group members chided him for not being with them and, at the suggestion of a leader, moved on to try to help include Chuck by putting hands on his head.

Chuck resented and resisted this approach but was moved when one of the more withdrawn members said, "Help is an intangible thing, but how can you expect us to help you in the group if you don't believe in our ability to help you."

Chuck struggled to describe his interpersonal relationships and his agonies with drugs. In the next session he described a scene in the bathroom at his home where he and a friend and a seductive friend of the mother's were smoking some of the mother's marijuana. The mother came in and scolded the group for smoking pot and smelling up the house. After a role-playing scene, one of the girls in the group pointed out that the mother was not mad about the "grass" but about her friend "putting the make on the two boys." Chuck denied this idea but intragroup discussion explored the possibility. The role playing made the verbal interpretation and a conceptualization of interpersonal dynamics, which were disturbing, possible for Chuck. The interpretation had an effect of freeing him from pressures that otherwise were insurmountable.

**Federick S. Perls**

Perls (1969) was originally trained as a psychoanalyst in Germany, He escaped from Hitler's gestapo and eventually settled in the United States. He became disenchanted with psychoanalysis and developed what he called gestalt therapy, a form of therapy which stresses the here and now rather than the past. In his work at the Esalin Institute, Big Sur, California, he evolved his ideas in the years just before his death in 1969.

Perls considered frustration as a stimulus to growth, and in the transcriptions of his workshops he provided his clients with a liberal supply of frustration. He claimed that learning was merely discovering the possible. In prac-

tice the individual experiences his difficulty, conceptualizes the nature of the stresses involved within him with the indirect help of the therapist, and goes on to make a more integrated response to the pressures that have made life difficult for him. By holding his conversations with a client in the presence of a dozen or two people—the so-called hot seat—Perls made it difficult for the individual who was preoccupied with himself to hide from himself. This therapy was done by noting the kind of response that the person had to others. For instance, a person who thinks everyone is looking at him has projected his eyes outside himself. One who thinks everyone is listening to him isn't using his ears to listen to anyone else. A person who has no center has no soul or spirit or no inner core. Perls analyzed much of a person's difficulties by observing his body movements. The way a person sat, stood, and moved indicated the body parts he was protecting or was not using and therefore were nonexistent. The holes in the personality were indicated by avoidance. Recovery consisted of getting the person to reown the disowned parts of the personality.

Perls thought of character as stereotyped responses or as roles that had been assumed to handle situations without growing. He disdained the crybaby (who acted like a three-year-old). He scorned the flatterer who butters up another's self-esteem in order to get something in return. He spoke of the "good" boy as one who was hiding a brat buried deeply in his personality. Some people play stupid so that others will do things for them. Still others are slaves to their own need for self-esteem. He spoke of people being in love, not with their spouse, but with a fantasy that the spouse only touched tangentially and diverged from significantly enough to cause trauma.

Perls described insanity as taking fantasy for real. The insane person says, "I am Abraham Lincoln." The neurotic person says, "I wish I were Abraham Lincoln," but the healthy person says, "I am what I am and you are what you are." Perls was insistent about the importance of awareness which requires a sender and a receiver. People need to be aware of themselves, they need to be aware of the world, but they also need to be aware of the fantasy zone which prevents the person from being in touch with either himself or the world.

In much of Perl's therapy he used a person's dreams or fragments of his dreams as a vehicle to help the individual explore and accept himself. He had the individual play conflicting roles in the same interchange. In one dream the participant dreamed of a wheel that came closer and closer and got bigger and bigger. Perls asked the participant to be the wheel and to talk to the dreamer, then to be the dreamer and talk to the wheel. He regularly suggested that several sentences be repeated, louder, and in the process helped the individual realize, or conceptualize, that he was not helpless and could do something if he were willing to try. In the transcripts of his therapy interaction, Perls insisted on the participant being wheel, road, anger, dreamer, or therapist rather than talking about these parts of the private world of this individual. Within this therapy the insistence is on experiencing the affect rather than cognizing about aspects of the experience, thus making it a thing rather than a part of the experiencer. As affective associations accumulate, the relationships within them are put together as part of the living whole. Through the increased understanding, the individual recovers the parts of himself that had been separated by rejection of aspects of himself he did not like or that could not be accommodated within the dominant self-image. For instance, one young woman rejected her need for self-determination as selfish in order to accept her mother's love which was conditional upon obedience to her

wishes. Living through the roles of selfishness, self-determination, her mother, and her subservient self made it possible for her to accept herself in a role of independence for running her life. In the experiencing there was a strong tendency for her to talk about these ideas, to avoid feeling herself in uncomfortable roles. Perls had the participants play the role or actually be themselves and talk to themselves. The experience made it possible for them to continue their own therapeutic experience after leaving Esalin Institute. Perl's emphasis on understanding an emotion through experiencing it in the open, rather than by verbalization once removed from the problem, seems soundly based in the theory of affective conceptualization.

In each of these therapy strategies for treating emotional disturbances, with the exception of behavior modification, the healing effect of understanding emotional responses is emphasized. Wilson (1949), working in a technical high school, found that helping students make rational choices about future vocations during counseling lessened their anxiety. Settling the turmoil about what these students would do after leaving school enabled them to spend emotional energy in productive ways. The grade of students thus counseled increased approximately one-half point in English, mathematics, and social studies, even though these courses had little direct bearing on the future vocations that had been selected. Personal experience seems to indicate that when emotional anxiety is lessened about a problem that seems insoluble, energy becomes available to pursue other matters that need attention.

Understanding the nature of the tensions that have been interfering with life seems to have a freeing effect. Teachers can help students achieve this freedom as they help them understand and remove blocks to their progress within a certain subject. Students are likely to underachieve academically because of emotional blockage that suffuses their experience with punishment loading.

## COMPLEX MOTIVATION SYSTEMS

Motivation, which starts as simple association connections to the pleasure or punishment centers, is strengthened as the affective feelings are conceptualized. It culminates in self-direction that overcomes earlier thwartings which could have been completely destructive. Teachers who are able to build toward self-direction on the part of their students give them a priceless gift of freedom to live on their own terms. This section might logically culminate the chapter on creative self-direction, but many of the crucial turning points are related to the conceptualizations that take place about affective loadings.

Motivation has many ramifications. Some of the questions include: Why and how does punishment work as a motivation force? Why are some ethnic groups more motivated toward school than others? Why do some children and young persons regard certain situations as a challenge while others react to them by withdrawing or by dealing with them in ways that ensure defeat? How are people motivated to climb physical or symbolic mountains? Why do some people work to become the decision makers, while others settle for a life of routine tasks? Why do people become motivated to self-destruction? How do needs stimulate motivation? How are incentives internalized? Can the school build motivations toward such complex goals?

## INTERACTION OF PUNISHMENT AND PLEASURE

Most learning sequences consist neither of pure positive reinforcements nor of pure negative reinforcements, but involve a mixture of both punishing and pleasure-producing experiences. To this point the interaction of positive and negative reinforcement has been treated lightly, with a mere acknowledgment that complex forces constitute the total learning pattern.

In reviewing the physiological research concerning the activation of punishment centers, it has been found that three or four hours of consistent stimulation to a punishment center often leads to death and that a breakdown may follow a lesser amount of punishment, often requiring protracted treatment to overcome the damage done by the punishment. However, the stimulation of an active pleasure center, even at a stage when considerable damage has been done, leads to rapid recovery from the effects of punishment (Brady, 1958). This physiological relationship, or balance, between punishment and recovery from possible damage through pleasure stimulation provides a basis for understanding the nature of the interaction in complex motivation.

Very primitive motivations, such as those in eating and drinking, have been studied extensively and provide clues to the way in which the brain functions to turn behavior on and off. Electrode stimulation can be substituted for the normal means of activating hunger sensations and can also be used to activate feelings of satiation. The start mechanism that leads to eating—which also acts as a punishment stimulus when food is not available—is a dual sensory device located on both sides of the hypothalamus (Chapter 9). The need to eat is triggered by an increase in the electrolytic concentration in the mechanism, which thus increases the need for water. This increased osmotic pressure is transduced and becomes a signal of the need for food. The stop mechanism is located near the midline of the hypothalamus and acts to terminate eating. The pleasure-center stimulation related to eating normally operates only until satiation occurs, when eating becomes no longer pleasurable as a result of the activation of the satiation mechanism.

If the start mechanisms are destroyed by excision, an animal will refuse to eat and will starve to death in the presence of food. Rat subjects whose start mechanisms have been thwarted must be kept alive by tube feeding during the beginning stages of recovery because they spit out food placed in their mouths and refuse to drink. A rat with a destroyed or damaged hunger mechanism is so highly motivated not to eat that it will commit suicide by starvation even in the presence of food.

When the cells of the stop mechanism are destroyed or its functions are suspended by electrode stimulation, an animal continues to eat beyond normal satiation. Some laboratory rats continued to eat until they had doubled their normal weight. If the neurons connected to the cells of the stop mechanism are electrically stimulated, however, even a ravenously hungry rat ceases to eat.

## Learning from Pleasure and Punishment

The automatic interaction of punishment followed by pleasure in the context of hunger-feeding has functional relationships to school learning. Very early in life, associations are built between hunger, which leads to crying, which then becomes a stimulus for action by the parents. This stimulus, external to the infant, ends in his being fed, thus putting an end to the punishment. At this stage of life, anything that might be considered motivation would be at an unconscious level; however, an element of awareness soon becomes part of the association system. Observation of young children seems to indicate a "demand quality" in hunger-crying even when the child is only a few weeks old. The connections formed at this point are probably purely associational with no conceptualization of the relationship between hunger, crying, and feeding. The beginning of the baby's separation of himself from his environment probably has primary roots in the interaction of punishment and pleasure, with crying as an intermediate activity. Eventually the infant uses crying as a deliberate control mechanism. The basis of many motivational systems seems to be established when the child is able to use crying to control others.

By the time a child has learned to use crying as a means of obtaining attention from those around him, he is already exploring, at least visually, his immediate environment. Children less than six months old demonstrate boredom following a lack of novelty in the visual target area (Chapter 12).

Interest in visual novelty and boredom with visual sameness seem to be connected with positive and negative reinforcement. The novelty leads to additional exploration, while boredom leads to avoidance activities, which are typical of mild punishment connections. Mothers observe how very early their infants identify the source of food and try to keep out of sight of their babies near feeding time or to keep their babies from seeing the bottle before it is warmed. The visual exploration, coupled with the feeding experiences, tends to augment the child's differentiation of himself and his surroundings.

As the child starts to realize his power to influence events, first through crying and later by physical manipulation, he establishes the primitive structure that will induce him to check all his answers on arithmetic papers or organize the games on the playground and eventually lead him to explore the nature of the atom and to strive to be chairman of the board. In the interactions of the doubt or stress—which are inherently punishing—followed by success in exploration or control—which is inherently pleasure producing—lies much of the motivation apparent in human activities. The motivation of infants to continue to examine visual targets seems to be strongest when familiar targets are interspersed with novel ones. Babies of this age are too young to explain the mechanism they are using, but controlled observation seems to indicate they find pleasure in a cognitive process of identification or classification. Relative success or failure in these classification activities seems to help form a self-concept as one who is or is not able to dominate the environment.

## Punishment as Motivation

Punishment has been found successful often enough in stimulating others to do positive work so that it has become the common method used by many teachers to control a class, by foremen to increase output, and by college deans to stimulate research publication. It is critical for the person who must occasionally use punishment as motivation to have a knowledge of the conditions under which punishment operates to produce positive results rather than to generate a more common withdrawal or avoidance pattern. Essentially the student who can be motivated to work harder because of the threat of punishment may be avoiding the physical or psychological barbs directed at him. On the other hand, a teacher who is punished emotionally by the principal for not controlling a class reacts in a more complex way. He may see the punishment as a threat to his concept of self as a teacher, and he may act to reestablish his image. Under these circumstances, the teacher evaluates the punishment to extract the element of truth behind the criticism and readjusts his action patterns to incorporate new response mechanisms. He thus restores a pleasure-producing sense of self-satisfaction. Punishment can produce positive motivation when attention is focused on the problem area

and the punished individual can resolve the problem. In other words, the punishment, which acts as a signal, has less impact on the person's motivation than the pleasure he gains from resolving his difficulty.

The punishing activities of the teacher will often motivate the student to study when he is able to meet the expectations of the teacher by doing additional work, the completion of which he finds rewarding. Punishment is particularly damaging and leads directly to withdrawal from, or rejection of, the learning situation when the student cannot exert the necessary effort to meet the teacher's expectation. This condition of failure is most apt to exist when the teacher expects certain students not to do satisfactory work and thus removes the reward. When the teacher has failure expectations, moderately successful performance does not result in pleasure-producing stimuli that make the effort worthwhile. Early failure interferes with later learning whenever the content to be learned is sequential, as in reading, foreign language study, and computation. The student's continued lack of performance is likely to confirm the teacher in his negative evaluation of the student and to confirm the student's concept of himself as inept. Punishment of a whole class is likely to be destructive and ineffective because most of the students have no opportunity to change their behavior and gain satisfaction. The frustration is most likely to emerge as hostility toward the punisher.

## MOTIVATIONS COMMON TO GROUPS OF PEOPLE

Some groups within a school community regularly achieve a reputation for high performance, which is accentuated whenever native endowment is taken into consideration. Oriental and Jewish children have gained reputations with teachers as being likely to try very hard to master school assignments, while other groups, including black and Spanish-speaking children, are seen as needing much more attention if they are to work industriously at school learning. Over a period of time, school people as well as others tend to overgeneralize about any conspicuous ethnic group, rather than to see each group member as an individual with unique abilities and motivations. Some young people are given higher marks because they get the benefit of a favorable expectation and others may suffer because of a negative expectation.

## Ethnic-Group Motivation

Oriental and Jewish children come from ethnic groups in which family ties are strong and in which education has traditionally been valued as the most available means of achieving upward mobility. Most of them are effectively reinforced at home for successful school progress. Because the goals of the home and those of the teacher are congruent and support each other, a comparatively small effort is needed to motivate these children to succeed in school. On the other hand, a belief has persisted (with good reason) in a segment of the black community that their high school graduates do not earn appreciably more than high school dropouts—that the white community will not recognize their education. Therefore, until recently, many black families did not see school as an effective means of upward mobility. Often the parents expected reports of poor work, and when the parents' anticipation was confirmed, the child was accepted as a conforming member of the family group. In Mexican or Puerto Rican families, the goals of family solidarity and other positive motivations toward helping each other in the home tend to replace the Anglo middle-class emphasis on the value of school performance. When any home does not systemat-

ically reinforce the children for evidence of success in school, the motivation tasks of the teacher become more difficult.

Coleman, Campbell, Hobson, McPartland, Mood, Wienfield, and York (1966) found that a significant factor in poor school performance was the feeling on the part of the child of being unable to control what happens to him—a feeling of being pushed by blind and usually malevolent forces, such as teacher rules, over which he has little or no control. This attitude was most common in schools attended by children from predominantly lower-class homes. When such children were moved to schools with a middle-class structure—but not in sufficient numbers to change the middle-class character of the school—they became more highly motivated and the quality of their schoolwork improved. Teachers in slum areas are more likely to have discipline problems in the classroom, come to expect failing work and punish children for it, and have classes made up of children from homes where schooling is not particularly valued and in which the general expectation is one of failure. Students come to believe that whatever they do is not going to be good enough, and they operate on an expectancy level where punishment centers are those most commonly stimulated. When such children move into a middle-class school, two factors usually change. The general expectation of the other children is toward school success, and the teacher who anticipates success from pupils generally tends to reinforce evidence of success, which in turn tends to make the student believe that he can control his destiny. In the Coleman study, from which these findings were derived, one contributing factor toward the improved performance of children who were moved into middle-class schools may have been the value these particular parents placed on education, leading them to expend the necessary effort to have their children moved. The study was large and cross-sectional rather than individual and longitudinal, so that this kind of selective process, concerning who would be moved, could have been influential, although not identified.

## Motivation to Climb Mountains

When asked why he wanted to climb Mount Everest, a famous climber replied, "Because it is there." His answer told very little about his basic motivational patterns. A more comprehensive question would ask why people do things that are difficult and dangerous when the rewards are almost exclusively in terms of a sense of personal accomplishment.

Analysis of the behavior patterns of people who derive satisfaction from difficult accomplishments indicates that their motivations are rooted in the same mechanisms that are apparent as the infant explores his environment. Probably there is a linkage to the punishment center, or at least the recognized threat of such a linkage, but there is an overriding linkage to the pleasure centers in the sense of having overcome the potential punishment. The reward comes from domination of some aspect of the environment. The process is similar to that of the child who is threatened with punishment but is able to perform up to expectation and thus gain satisfaction. A certain amount of success, which may vary for different people, is necessary if the person is to remain motivated to work until he has accomplished his goal. Some of the tee shots on the golf round must be good, and some of the approach shots must be good, so that feedback indicates that mastery is possible even if not yet attained.

Teachers in the inner core of cities desperately need to rebuild student self-concepts to include the possibility that success in life can be a challenge they are able to meet. The answer lies not in removing the challenge for the children but in building the anticipation that the challenge can be accepted, with a real hope for success in overcoming the difficulties. Often a way of avoiding old patterns that lead to failure must be found in new learning experiences. Failing students need help in setting and attaining interim goals between their present status and the eventual goal of controlling their destinies. Children who doubt their own abilities need external reinforcement at many points in the learning sequence, a fact that is overlooked by many who attempt to use traditional teaching methods with inner-city children.

At the high school level, opportunities for bridging the gap between school life and life after graduation can change a student's self-concept. Paul, a senior, had a reputation for being willing but very slow mentally. He was given a job gardening on the weekends, which consisted of cutting the grass, weeding the flower beds, clipping ornamental shrubs, and doing related chores. For the first six months he was on the job, he said practically nothing, although a shy smile indicated some response toward the people who employed him. He was praised for trimming the lawn neatly and was given only general instructions about how he should weed. In other words, Paul was given an area of responsibility, some general guidelines. and some reinforcement, including money, for the things he did, and thus he was allowed to find in this work an area of life where he could control his environment. By the end of the year, he began to talk to his employer about taking a permanent job. When he found regular employment as an engraver, he introduced a friend who he hoped could carry on the gardening. He took responsibility for showing him around and explaining the work to be done. After work, he came around to see that the new boy was doing his job well. This "slow learner" had built a concept of self-respect that enabled him to become an asset to the community.

Work-experience programs make it possible

for high school students to spend part of their time in school and part of their time doing paid work in the community under school supervision. Students who are successful in their outside jobs often find that they need school learning, and they gain enough faith in themselves to try again. There are many variations in work-experience programs, but part of the structure includes a fresh start with reinforcement for the successes that have been achieved outside the school.

In the elementary school, the most common and the most disastrous failure is not learning to read well. When the child has built an image of himself as unable to learn to read, remedial teaching becomes difficult and frustrating. Drastically new approaches such as Pitman's i/t/a, Sullivan's programmed reading, and Fernald's kinesthetic techniques make possible learning situations that are sufficiently different from those in which the original failure occurred to give the child a new start in mastering his environment. In the process, he is able to rebuild his image of himself to include the acceptance of challenges. Reading may be viewed as the first mountain.

### Motivation to Become Decision Makers

Foremen, captains, managers, and deans tend to make decisions and then to persuade others to conform to them or implement them. Voting patterns suggest that many people seem willing to have major decisions made for them. In part, motivation seems to go back to the experiences infants have as they seek to exert control over those with whom they first come into contact, often by crying. Much of the attitude of being either the controller or the one who is controlled is learned as the child tries to establish his place in the pecking order within his family and peer groups. Those individuals who derive a substantial net stimulation of their pleasure centers, rather than of their punishment centers, in their attempts to

dominate others are likely to continue to practice this kind of activity.

The hormone balances shift as a result of experience in dominant rather than submissive roles. The relative secretion of adrenaline as compared with noradrenaline may be changed by a child's learning experiences (Selye, 1956). The secretion of noradrenaline tends to lead to anger responses rather than to flight responses, so the child who starts life with a hormone balance that encourages anger rather than fear is likely to be more successful in dominating other people than the child in whom the balance of these two hormones is reversed.

Teachers can promote either the tendency to submit or the tendency to dominate, depending on which response complexes they reinforce and which they punish. Such changes depend on changes in hormone balance, which usually take a considerable amount of time to establish. Very few teachers consciously set out to create students who will obtain their satisfactions as leaders, but many of the teacher's activities tend directly to encourage response patterns that are compatible with being an obedient follower. Few teachers intentionally pursue a discipline policy that produces submissive adults. Often what teachers are seeking is obedience to their own direction in the classroom, and they feel no conscious concern about the effect that these patterns of behavior will have on the later adult lives of their students.

### MOTIVATION TO SELF-DESTRUCTION

Each year many people commit acts that are self-destructive to a limited degree; some even commit suicide. What motivates people to damage themselves in these ways? In some cases the systematic punishment of the environment has become sufficient to make death their only visible path. In a few cases the punishment is physical pain that seems unendurable but even when severe pain is the punishment, there is a psychological conclusion on the part of the person that he has nothing left to give to the world. When compulsory retirement at age sixty-five was first introduced, many men died the first year or two after retirement. Some had physical defects, but others died because life, for them, had lost its meaning. They had found their justification for living in the work they did, and when this was gone so was their reason for continuing to live. The emotional responses are similar to those of the children in inner-city schools who feel that they have no control of the forces working on them. The normal result of this evaluation is psychological withdrawal from the contest.

However, there is a more rebellious reaction that consists of striking back to try to make one's influence felt. It seems as though this whole series of responses that lead to motivation for self-destruction comes from the accumulated experiences that start in babyhood with attempts to master the physical environment, although the experiences also contain elements of interpersonal relationships.

In the elementary school, the classroom teacher can usually provide some learning experience during the day that will make the self-destructive child start to feel that he has something of value to contribute to his classmates and that he may, after all, be of value in himself. Teachers must remember that the students who are self-punishing and who desperately need help are characterized by habits of work and demeanor that invite invidious comparisons. Building motivations to try to succeed in classwork often must await the prior building of attitudes of self-worth and of having something worthwhile to contribute to the class. Direct pressure for participation will often do nothing so much as confirm the youngster in his motivations toward self-destruction.

Some students who have had little success in academic classes are able to find a place in sports activities where they can excel and be valued for the contribution they can make to the group. In these same activities their conceptualization of themselves as failures, with nothing to contribute, can also be accentuated and made evident to the whole class.

## MOTIVATION IN GIFTED STUDENTS

When special classes for gifted children were organized for California Project Talent (Robeck, 1968b), teachers found one of the major problems to be motivation. A young science teacher said, "I thought everyone in the class would be enthusiastic about the projects we planned. It's harder to get some of these students to go along than most of those in the regular classes. When you do get them interested, though, the work they do is fantastic." Why are some intellectually gifted children underachievers?

Although there are as many combinations of causes as there are underachievers, one factor is that the highly gifted child is too often denied the intrinsically motivating satisfactions that come with the solution of a really challenging problem or the culmination of a project that required sustained and superior effort. An activity must be challenging if its completion is to bring a feeling of accomplishment.

Dick, an eighth grader, was a challenge to his teachers because of a persistent lack of interest in schoolwork, despite his predominance of A grades and a WISC IQ of 160 ±4.5. When his counselor asked him about his interests, Dick responded:

I usually don't have enough ambition to really go into school subjects very deeply. Of course when I become interested in a subject outside of school, such as slot-car racing, I can usually find enough time to participate in it. Some of my

interests at this time are slot-car racing, swimming, fishing, marine biology, beachcombing,
and sleeping.

Although he had a reputation in school for
being lazy and had a self-image as a lazy
student, Dick found time for a startling number of activities, including reading, outside
school. Gifted children are highly individual
about their goals and interests. Materials and
activities that constitute incentives for some
fail to arouse a glimmer of interest in others.
Nearly all very bright children become involved readily in schoolwork that allows for
self-direction, involves new ideas and information, and is discussed or shared with
peers—provided they are not forced to spend
too much of their time at tasks they already
know how to do.

## LINKING MOTIVATION AND NEED SYSTEMS

Most descriptions of motivation are really
descriptions of need systems. The rat in the
maze is motivated by being deprived of food
for varying lengths of time. In his work with
pigeons, Skinner (1957) kept them at 75 percent of their normal body weight to ensure
motivation to work at tasks when the reinforcement was food. The teacher, however,
cannot use hunger or other primitive needs as
a basis for reinforcement; if the pupil is hungry, most teachers are in no position to satisfy
his hunger. Esteem needs are acute sources of
drive for many students at all levels of school.
Many teachers find ways of using the student's need for status to aid his learning. The
need for self-actualization is the most productive force available to teachers.

### Needs: A Base for Reinforcement

One of the problems that the teacher faces is
locating the kinds of activities that will be
reinforcing to the student he is trying to

motivate. Since the "good" students are already motivated, the problem really becomes
one of finding ways of stimulating students
who are alienated in some way from the
regular school operation. Some have learned
that approval from peers is more satisfying
than approval from teachers. Many such students have built associations between the
teacher image and punishment. Usually the
process of establishing these connections was
unintentional on the part of the teachers and
arose because the child was more aggressive
than conforming. The teacher's differential
treatment is likely to be more obvious to the
children than to the teacher. Once a cycle of
punishment for misbehavior is started, the
associations between the teacher and the punishment are both self-perpetuating and continuous. If a subsequent teacher is to break the
chain of responses and build new association
patterns of response, strong needs must be
identified that can be used as a bridge around
the old attitude patterns. Normally these
needs will not be for safety and food, but will
be the human needs for status and success.

### Need Satisfaction as Motivation

The dispossessed and disappointed student
may be expected to seek satisfactions out of
school that accord him status and relative
importance. Insofar as his means of achieving
need satisfactions are in direct conflict with
the teacher's goals, each day makes the
teacher's task of bridging the established
habits that much harder. In school, an alienated student is likely to be defiant in a manner
that other class members may interpret as
"cool" and consider praiseworthy. The combination of negative reinforcement from the
teacher and positive reinforcement from other
students for misbehavior soon establishes a
system of undesirable school habits. Such a
student's needs are being better satisfied by
destructive techniques than by positive ap-

proaches. He has already learned and continues to learn that defiant and destructive attitudes within school are reinforcing to him, and the teacher, unhappily, is both the negative stimulus and the symbol of the negative motivation. Some teachers must conduct classes of 25 to 35 students, and they cannot spend all their time on any one child. The good of the majority must be considered. For these reasons, individual students are sometimes destroyed because the teacher does not have the time and cannot expend the effort necessary to reach them. Sometimes the teacher's control of his class is threatened to such an extent that, incident by incident, he makes choices that are in favor of what he conceives to be the greatest good for the greatest number of pupils but are damaging to particular students. Actually, teachers are reinforced continuously by the community for whatever methods of interaction they use to control recalcitrant behavior.

## RELATIONSHIP OF MOTIVES AND INCENTIVES

An incentive incites a person to action. There has been a tendency to equate incentives with extrinsic motivation or with bribery, although the term is broader than this and merges into intrinsic motivation. An incentive wage is one that depends on the worker's output. The more effectively the person works, the more he is paid. Commission schemes are a form of incentive wage scale, as are piecework rates. Gold stars, grades, and money for A's are all incentives to study, provided the student wants the stars, the grades, or the money. Many educators have a distaste for incentives in school because they have been misused as far as the student's learning is concerned. In many cases, the incentive itself has come to be important, rather than the learning that it was originally designed to stimulate. Many college students claim that their education has been

nothing but a series of hurdles they have had to clear in order to obtain units and grades.

Motive is the view from inside; it is internalized. A motive may be unconscious in its operation, but it is always a part of the functioning of the individual. An incentive is something external that can be held up with the expectation of stimulating an activity—it is the carrot dangled in front of the donkey's nose. Until the incentive has been interpreted and internalized, it has no motivating power.

### Internalized Incentives

Although a carrot can be held in front of a donkey as an incentive, no activity will occur unless the animal wants the carrot. He must see it, smell it, and also interpret the possibility of obtaining it in order for it to be effective. In other words, the desirability of an incentive must be internalized before it functions in the individual's life space. Lewin (1935) used the term "valence" to indicate that incentives can be of varying forces, from strongly positive to strongly negative in the same person at different times and for different people under different circumstances. The higher the positive valence, the more energetic the person's efforts to acquire the incentive. In the same way, the higher the negative valence, the more energetically the individual seeks to avoid the incentive.

A subtle relationship exists between incentives and reinforcements. Normally the obtaining of the incentive is reinforcing, but the reinforcement usually comes after the effort to do something has already taken place, whereas the incentive—which may be exactly the same thing—is made evident before the act in order to induce the person to make the required effort.

### Dangers in Overuse of Incentives

The most persistent danger in the use of incentives is that the student will focus his attention on the incentive as an end in itself, while it is designed only as a starting mechanism. Doug was doing satisfactory work as far as reports from school were concerned, but he found no joy in reading. He did not read in his free time just for the pleasure it gave him. His father agreed to pay him a nickel for each chapter that he read, and as a result of this incentive, Doug read to his father a book of 26 chapters, a chapter a night, and went halfway through a second book. Eventually his father was forced to spend an evening away from home, and it was agreed that Doug could read a chapter as usual, tell his father the story the next morning, and collect his nickel. This experiment was a success, and the same arrangement was made the next night, with the proviso that more than one chapter might be read. On this basis, Doug finished the book in one evening and collected 50 cents. Doug's father then suggested that he might like to read another book, just for the fun of it. Doug accepted this suggestion and read several books in the series. During this process he increased his reading rate, discovered the joys of reading, expanded his vocabulary, and profited generally from the experience of wide reading. The use of an incentive, the nickel, was effective in getting the process of reading started and in continuing it long enough to enable other kinds of motivation to become operative. Finally, when the inner motivation had become strong enough to overcome inertia and frustration, the incentive was dropped.

Using incentives in this way requires considerable care. It would be easy to develop a dependency on the money, so that no reading would ever be done unless it was paid for. Many people fear this kind of inducement for student activities that are desirable in themselves, fearing the formation of associations that link payment with doing what should be done on other grounds. These fears are often justified unless the parent or teacher is prepared to help the student make the transition

as soon as possible to inner motivations. The child needs to recognize the satisfactions of performing for his own pleasure rather than performing to satisfy someone else.

## Grades as Incentives

The most common incentive and possibly the most misused in school is grades. Graduate schools commonly require that students maintain a B average to stay in school as well as a B average to enter. Under this kind of pressure, the grade often becomes an end in itself. In courses which the student is required to take but which do not interest him particularly, obtaining the necessary grade by means such as cheating or other tactics often becomes a college game. Some students expend more energy carrying out these schemes than would have been necessary to learn the material and earn the grade on the basis of performance. The faculty can further increase the pressure and the tendency toward deviant behavior by grading to the probability curve under conditions where such grading is unjustified because of composition of the student body, smallness of the class, or atypical work characteristics of the group. In a school where the pressure for grades is intense, an individual faculty member cannot afford to abandon the grading system as a unilateral action. The reduction of pressure on the students in his class then encourages them to spend more time on other courses where the pressure is severe. The learning goes down in the permissive teacher's class.

The preoccupation with grades starts with the inception of their use as incentives. In the face of demands from parents for more informative report cards, many elementary schools are returning to grades of A, B, C, D, and F. At the same time, pass-fail grading in colleges and universities is becoming more common. The distortion of grades as incentives may eventually lead to some other way of judging student performance that puts the emphasis on the inner motivation rather than on the incentive.

### Praise and Blame

For people who teach, a clear distinction between motives and incentives is essential. Teachers use both praise and blame daily as incentives to students to increase their work output. On the whole, the ones who are successful are commended for their successes, and those who are unsuccessful are condemned for their lack of success. In the case of many teachers, the result is that certain pupils regularly receive the praise and others regularly receive a punishing kind of attention. A middle group falls in between, who are praised for some responses or productions and blamed for others.

Students come to develop self-concepts that reflect the patterns of reinforcement. Consistent praise can become stultifying, so that it ceases to be effective, but consistent blame is more likely to be damaging to the individual over very long periods of time. Hurlock (1925) found praise to be more desirable than blame and blame to be more desirable than being consistently ignored by the teacher. In her study, duller children—those least likely to have been praised—and older children responded most to praise. The bright student was more likely to respond positively to blame. Probably he was more accustomed to being commended for his efforts, and the blame was a bit of a shock. On the whole, boys were affected more significantly by both praise and blame than girls were.

Sears (1940) reported the effect of success and failure on the attitudes of children who anticipated their own future performance. In his study, Sears used upper elementary—fourth-, fifth-, and sixth-grade—children who had been successful over the years in reading

and arithmetic, another group who had been unsuccessful, and a third group who had been successful in reading but unsuccessful in arithmetic. The three groups were balanced in age, sex, and intelligence. In the experiment, the children were given common tasks in reading and arithmetic, were timed, and then were given the results. Then all groups were asked to estimate how long it would take them to do a similar task again. This was basically a nonthreatening situation, or at least it was similar to regular school experiences.

In estimating reading performance the group that had been regularly successful anticipated that they would improve slightly in their performance on the next try. The goals they set for themselves were realistic and probably attainable. The generally unsuccessful group were more variable in their expectations of themselves. Most of them expected to improve substantially—much more than the group with a consistent pattern of success expected to, although a few of them expected to do less well than they had already done. The mixed group, who had a history of success in reading but failure in arithmetic, fell in between the two other groups in their estimate of their own future success in reading. The generally successful were more variable in their anticipation of success in arithmetic than in their anticipation of success in reading. Both of the other groups were much more variable, with the generally unsuccessful being more variable than the mixed group, even though they had a history of nonsuccess in arithmetic.

In a further analysis of the same data, Sears concluded that some children set realistic goals that require a slight increase in effort. The generally successful group saw in the situation an incentive to work a little harder. The generally unsuccessful group took two attitudes. Some of the children set goals for themselves that were safe—that is, somewhat below their previous performance—so that they were not expecting as much of themselves as they were able to accomplish. For them the incentive value of the situation was minimal. They would not be likely either to try harder or to think they should. The rest of the unsuccessful group, those who set unreasonably high goals for themselves, tended to be self-punishing. Even if they approached their stated success expectation—which most of them did not—they immediately raised their sights to new unrealistic levels. Those who failed, as was almost inevitable, then tended to become sluggish and apathetic. The incentive value of the punishment for these children was very low.

G. G. Thompson and C. W. Hunnicutt (1944) investigated the differential effects of praise and blame on children classified as extroverts and introverts. The separation was on the basis of scores on one of the Pintner personality tests. The task for which the fifth-grade students were praised and blamed was crossing T's out of lines of letters, which was difficult enough so that the pupils could not finish it in the 30 seconds allowed for each test. The praise or blame was then given in the form of a G (meaning "good") or a P (meaning "poor") on the papers. Half of the "introverts" were praised, and half were blamed, and half of the "extroverts" were praised, and half blamed (Figure 7-1). The blamed extroverts and the praised introverts did substantially better than either the praised extroverts or the blamed introverts. Thompson and Hunnicutt concluded from their experiments that when introverts and extroverts are grouped together, no difference results from use of either praise or blame as a means of incentive. If praise or blame is continued over a period of time, the praise will improve the work of the introverts more than that of the extroverts or of the introverts who are blamed, whereas blame will improve the work

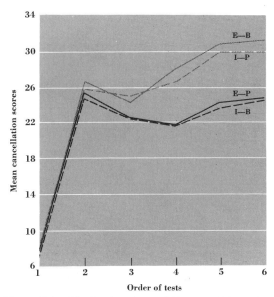

**Figure 7-1** Effects of praise and blame on introverts and extroverts. *(After G. G. Thompson & C. W. Hunnicutt, The effect of repeated praise or blame on the work achievement of "introverts" and "extroverts." Journal of Educational Pyschology, 1944, 35, 257–266. Copyright © 1944 by The American Psychological Association and reproduced by permission.)*

of the extroverts more than that of the introverts or that of the extroverts who are praised.

In general, the studies of praise and blame indicated that teachers should vary their techniques. They should not use the same techniques exclusively on any students, or the technique will lose its value as an incentive. Some students should be praised most of the time, while others will work harder if they are put under the pressure of considerable punishment. Completely reversing the techniques will tend to be unfortunate as far as work output is concerned.

The basic implication from this research is that the teacher should make every effort to think in terms of the student's view of life and to rely as little as possible on the more available teacher enticements. The learning is more likely to be enduring and to establish a firm base for later learning if the inner needs of the student are being satisfied, rather than the more superficial surface needs to avoid disapproval or to obtain rewards that are only temporary in interest or value.

## MOTIVATION AS THE KEY TO THE TEACHER'S EFFICIENCY

Most learning situations require that student attention be channeled away from a number of other possible avenues to the one that is relevant. Throughout a person's life, various facets of his surroundings compete for his attention. It is motivation that leads him to focus his attention in one direction rather than another. Openness to possible learning is implied in the idea of motivation, but exclusiveness is also implied. All the other possibilities that are screened out of the consciousness are opportunities for learning that must be ignored if success is to be achieved in the selected area. Since the teacher's function is to cause learning to take place, skill in the ordering of circumstances that make learning likely is of primary importance to his professional competence. One of the most important skills is that of developing motivation to attend to the material. The more skillful the teacher is as a motivator, the more successful he will be. In general, the more positive the teacher's approach, the more pleasure associations will be made and the higher the level of motivation is likely to be.

## SUMMARY

Counselors and therapists have worked for many years to help students and clients conceptualize their feelings. As these conceptualizations are developed, the emotional components of living become manageable. Although affective loadings are critical factors

in determining what will be learned, most schoolwork has focused on cognitive learning.

Freud worked systematically to have his patients understand the way in which their emotions were affecting them. He used hypnosis, dream interpretations, and free association to help individuals explore their pasts, and understand why they felt the way they did about critical facets of their lives. Carl Rogers used similar techniques but concentrated more on present feelings than on past ones. Welsh used a behavior modification structure to help a client conceptualize his feelings about lighting matches, after the propensity to do so had been extinguished. Shapiro developed conceptualizations about affective components as he used encounter group techniques to restructure experience. Glasser helped clients build conceptualizations through reality therapy. Olsson and Myers used similar techniques with diverse kinds of clients. Perls helped participants in encounter groups live through affective experiences and thus come to conceptualize their emotional problems.

Motivation is learned. Interactions of punishment and pleasure are observable in very young children, although the interactions seem to begin as associational reactions without any component of conceptualization. The group of motivations that focus on interpersonal control seems to have its genesis in the hunger-crying-feeding cycle and to be extended as the person develops through emotional crises. Motivations to control the physical environment seem to have their roots in the visual and tactile exploration of the environment, in which the unknown has the potential for punishment, while success in the exploration is pleasure-producing. Punishment can act to produce positive motivation by making alternative reactions to the one desired so unpleasant that the student conforms. However, a more constructive pattern seems to be one in which the punishment serves as an orienting and arousing device, which is followed by pleasure stimulation as the net effect of the interaction of punishment and pleasure. Two major kinds of motivation seem to be observable: One centers around interactions with people, and the other involves control of the physical environment. In life, neither of these is completely separated from the other.

Different ethnic groups find school activities motivating toward different ends, apparently depending on whether the expectations of the teacher and those of the home are congruent. Some people develop motivations toward self-destruction or self-punishment, which seem to have their roots in self-concepts of being worthless and deserving of punishment. On the other hand, when punishing habit patterns are based on motivations for self-punishment, treatment of the habit patterns is almost certain to be ineffective until after the basic motivations have been changed.

Teachers can change such destructive patterns—although with difficulty—by developing opportunities in which the student can contribute in a valuable way to the class, can be valued for his contribution by the class members, and can gradually come to think of himself as being a worthy class member. The teacher's task is made more difficult by the fact that these students have established personalities and habit patterns that are signals for punishing rather than rewarding responses on the part of the people with whom they come into contact.

Needs of one kind or another provide a substratum for motivation. The motivation pattern based on need fulfillment may be positive or negative from the viewpoint of the teacher, but it is always positive from the inner view of the student. The teacher can use incentives to induce action that may eventually lead to motivation of the student. Although incentives are normally external to the student, they have no effect on him until they have been internalized. The chief danger in using incentives is that they sometimes come to be the goal of the learning rather than a bridge to a sounder and more durable motivation pattern. The two most common incentives used by teachers are grades and praise or blame for the way work is done. Both of these techniques can be used constructively, but both of them also have a potential for mishandling.

## SELF-DIRECTING ACTIVITIES

1 Listen to the problems of a peer and help him to recognize what he is saying.
2 Choose a student who thinks highly of you. Try to make him face reality in the manner of Glasser's reality therapy.
3 Use a combination of challenge and success to build motivation in a particular student. Keep a record of the steps you use and the outcomes.
4 Set up a token economy and use the tokens as incentives to help students overcome problems in behavior they are having. Keep a record of your success.

# Chapter 8

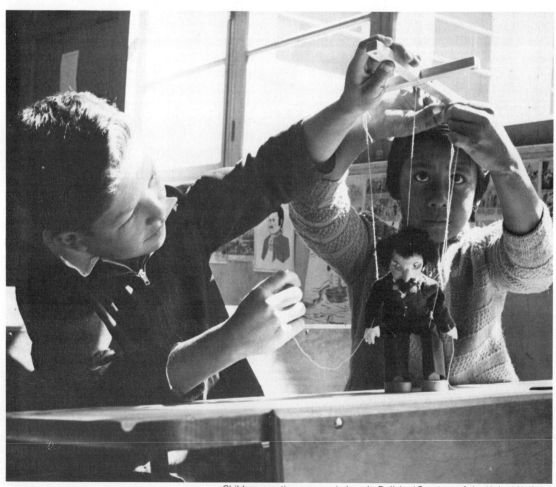

Children creating a puppet show in Bolivia. (*Courtesy of the United Nations*)

# LEVEL 3 LEARNING: CREATIVE SELF-DIRECTION

The purpose of this chapter is to provide the materials that can help you become creatively self-directing in your work with students so that you can help children establish a pattern of self-direction. To do this, you should be able to:

◖ Describe your own tendencies to creative self-direction

◖ Outline steps to reinforce your own creative self-direction

◖ Define the elements of creative responses in students

◖ Demonstrate ways to exhibit an acceptance of self-direction in students and explain how you would reinforce it

◖ Plan lessons that generate creative self-direction on the part of many students

◖ Explain the risks inherent in developing creative self-direction

◖ Define as used in the text:
   creativity
   determinism
   fluency
   flexibility
   elaboration
   deficiency needs
   being needs

The distinguishing feature of level 3 learning is an inner control or self-direction that enables the learner to formulate or create his own interpretations from the relationships that he has conceptualized. In both association learning and insightful learning, there is a quality of other-directedness. The teacher can set up conditions that almost ensure specific learning. But in creative learning, a quality of inner-directedness is involved. As conceived here, creative production includes such diverse activities as changing the way a class activity is done, writing a poem, developing consensus within a group, synthesizing a theory of mathematics, composing a fugue, inventing a machine to pick strawberries, breeding a variety of strawberries to withstand machine picking, painting a picture, or preparing a new chowder. Creative work cannot be forced; it can only be encouraged and permitted. In learners of any age, the important trait to be encouraged is not so much the determination to achieve the final goal as the push to go beyond organized contents, materials, or situations and to give something constructive of oneself. Children and youth who are reinforced for self-directed activity, which goes beyond performing specified tasks and discovering prestructured relationships, stand a good chance of eventually making a contribution that is considered creative by society. This chapter deals with five major topics: (1) freedom as the distinctive feature of creative self-direction, (2) the philosophic bases of freedom, (3) the relationship of creative self-direction to studies on creativity, (4) motivation in self-direction and self-actualization, and (5) creative self-direction in the classroom.

## FREEDOM AS THE DISTINCTIVE FEATURE OF CREATIVE SELF-DIRECTION

The definition of level 3 learning as inner-directed learning implies that creative activity involves uniqueness for the learner himself, motivation to be productive, self-discipline to culminate the creative process, and human potential for this kind of learning. Students learn to be creative when their efforts toward unique production are recognized and reinforced. When Mark, aged five, was praised for his rather cramped attempts to draw people, using a felt pen, he began almost at once to draw more expanded, bolder figures; he learned to be more creative. When the function of the school is conceived as the active encouragement of creative self-direction in students, the creative product becomes an integral part of the process rather than a separate entity. The creator has a need to complete his work in order to gain self-reinforcement as well as reinforcement from others. Within his private world, the satisfaction that a learner derives from completing creative tasks strengthens his framework of anticipation for success in future creative enterprises. The learning-motivation model shows how learning and motivation interact to generate creative, self-directed activity (Chapter 2).

## Assumption of Initiative by the Individual

Many home, school, and work environments actively discourage the individual from assuming initiative. The insistence that father and mother know best—that deviation from their pattern constitutes disobedience—actively discourages development of the freedom essential to creativity. The school in which the methods, answers to all questions, and programs are fully organized into a closed system has a similar restrictive effect on creative self-direction. Work environments that are highly structured for efficient production pay a price for productivity by delimiting initiative and innovation. Only the very strong, in such circumstances, are comfortable as they assert their independence and assume the responsibility for creating the framework within which they themselves will function. Such people are often seen as disruptive troublemakers by those within the authoritarian home, school, or work environment.

Even under regimented circumstances, in which self-direction is discouraged, most people need to find outlets that permit them to assume the initiative necessary to establish their identity as individuals. These outlets may take the form of hobbies, sibling rivalry, or subtle ways of defying the authority that imposes conformity upon the individual.

Sibling rivalry may be annoying to parents, but it is relatively safe for the individual child because his initiating and testing various forms of overt social behavior with his brothers and sisters carry less risk of alienation than if he displayed similar overtness toward more distant peers. In the adult world some individuals find ways to be personally assertive in highly authoritarian environments by following the details of a requirement handed down to them but reconstructing its original intent to suit their own needs.

### Process as the Determinant of Level 3 Learning

Although the product itself is important in creative self-expression, the creative process rather than the product is crucial in learning theory, particularly in the work of young children, whose creative efforts must be reinforced if this kind of activity is to continue. The process involved actually defines whether or not the act is creative self-expression. The imitator in art is downgraded, essentially because he allows himself to be controlled by the expression of another. William Carlos Williams, the great American poet, expressed this idea: "That which should be rare is trash; because it contains nothing of you." The

innovator is respected and appreciated because he assumes the responsibility of expressing the world from his own point of view. The imitator's work may be technically and aesthetically superior to that of the innovator, but it is not as acclaimed by those who recognize the source of his inspiration. The process of imitating others or repeating the work of oneself is crippling because the artist no longer functions at level 3 when he accepts from himself anything less than a new expression. Imitative behavior shifts his learning to level 1.

In spite of the ever-present danger of imitation, complete uniqueness is untenable as the sole criterion for judging creative production. Controversy still rages over whether Leibnitz or Newton—working at the same time in Germany and in Britain—first invented integral calculus. Since the invention was obviously creative, it is nonsense to claim that either Newton or Leibnitz was not creative because he had been predated by another in the independent production of this complicated system for processing infinitely small quantities. The quality of uniqueness is essential in a creation, but it is individually unique expression rather than uniqueness in society that counts. The satisfaction that comes from creative activity is self-reinforcing. Also, the recognition by others of innovation confirms and strengthens the image of oneself as a creative person.

### Escape from Control by Others

When the teacher is able to shift the student from functioning at associative and conceptual levels to functioning at level 3, he is providing the student with the means to escape from control by others, including the teacher himself. Self-direction means that a student moves beyond the content of the textbook and the scope of the lectures to knowledge that is restructured, extrapolated, synthesized, or in some way molded to his own world view. When freedom is given by the teacher, it can, it is hoped, be expected to unfold into creative self-direction; that is, the guideposts that were erected by association and conceptual learning will continue to be valued and used by the student as a means toward new and constructive ends. Maximum perception in teaching is required of the teacher if he is to know how much freedom an individual student can use productively.

Teaching for the freedom that is inherent in level 3 learning involves both difficulties and satisfactions for the teacher. Nearly always, he is under subtle pressure to keep the class disciplined and orderly. The teacher's responsibility is complicated by the knowledge that the finest possible development of each individual may itself create conflicts that no society has permanently and successfully resolved. The child who has not yet learned temper control may need to be ignored until he no longer derives satisfaction from this kind of activity. Sometimes, however, such an individual cannot be ignored and kept within a school group because his effect on the other pupils is injurious or because his behavior is widening the gulf between him and the other members of the group. As the teacher considers increasing the freedom of individual class members, there is always the threat that the freedom will be used to harm others. Most teachers have learned, sometimes through regretted experience, that certain students who are not controlled will use their freedom for ends that are inimical to themselves and those around them.

Increasing a student's freedom therefore involves an element of risk because of the possibility that instead of growing into positive self-control through freedom, he will tend toward negative excursions into anarchy. Some students become a menace to themselves and a distraction to other students; hence they quickly become a threat to the teacher. Individuals who have never experienced normal, satisfying relationships with others or conceptualized the give and take of social interaction need therapy outside the classroom to help them work out their frustrations. Other students become overly exuberant when they first experience freedom to work and learn on their own. Usually a quiet conversation about the effect of their abuse of freedom helps such students to bring their activity within tolerable limits.

Teachers who undertake to expand self-actualization or self-direction in their students are attempting the most sensitive and difficult aspect of a teacher's work. But the greatest reinforcement comes to a teacher when he effectively increases and can observe the freedom a student uses responsibly. The classroom climate becomes thoroughly constructive as both teacher and pupils reinforce each other for growth that is exciting and satisfying.

## Indeterminism in Level 3 Learning

The challenge to the teacher, as he evaluates the productions that represent creative learning, is that the outcomes are necessarily indeterminate. When students are stimulated to produce new or creative responses—when they are operating as self-determined individuals—there can be no predetermined set of answers against which their responses can be judged automatically. Guidelines in terms of time and space may be provided in the assignment—such as the medium to be used in an art project, the musical notation to be used in a transposition, the area of the world to be explored geographically, or other like limitations—but even these are not sacrosanct. The function of guidelines is to help rather than to restrict the student—the purpose is more important than the specifics of the assignment.

The production is evaluated in terms of whether or not it is creative for the student and on the basis of how completely it satisfies general guidelines. Even when the criterion for newness is the student's own, rather than that of the society, unexpected solutions to the problem are likely to emerge, with attendant problems of evaluation.

The teacher's response to any production that is personal—that is, to any work with which an individual identifies—is critical particularly in the learning stages. Often the child's or the student's first attempts in a new mode of expression are his clumsiest, and the teacher may find it difficult to respond in supportive but meaningful ways. Doug entered first grade without any kindergarten experience at easel painting. He was unusually curious, used advanced vocabulary and syntactical patterns, and showed exceptional motor coordination. Following the first class trip to the zoo, Doug rejected crayons, a medium he handled efficiently, and maneuvered a coveted place at an easel to record the experience. His painted animals ran together in an indistinguishable mess, and his lack of control of the paint resulted in numerous splotches on the floor. The teacher suppressed the dismay she felt when she realized that it would take him a long time to learn to handle this material. She smiled at him and said, "Doug, tell me about the animals you painted." His explanation helped the teacher realize what he had observed at the zoo and had tried to reproduce, even though his inability to handle the medium adequately obscured the representation. In subsequent lessons the teacher encouraged Doug to use dual media, drawings and words.

Often a teacher can help older students expand the ways they express themselves by encouraging them to discuss their own work. Many ideas are only germinal at first and need cultivation to come to fruition. By expressing them orally, the student can help the teacher make a more precise evaluation of his work. Oral expression also encourages the student to develop his rudimentary ideas into complex expressions. When a mature adult considers a creative product seriously, the student senses that it is valued and therefore that his own uniqueness is valued as well. His creation, and thus his view of himself as a creative person, is reinforced.

Unexpected dividends accrue to the teacher as he looks for creative value in students' work. *Psychology of Children's Art* (Kellogg & O'Dell, 1967) provides insights for teachers into the private world of the child which is important if the teacher is going to interact with the child about his work in meaningful ways. Sometimes this work has an element of humor that may not have been intentional. Teachers derive satisfaction from the realization that it is possible to live with indeterminism. This process of freeing students to express themselves carries with it the potential for the teacher to become more expressive and creative in his own right, both in teaching and in his personal life. Most teachers find that the compensations of this relationship with students outweigh the real difficulties associated with teaching for creative self-expression.

## PHILOSOPHIC BASES OF FREEDOM

Freedom is a logical extension of the concept of evolving complexity in organisms (Chapter 2). Association and conceptualization can be explained within a strict cause-and-effect system, but the crucial aspect of self-direction in level 3 learning is incompatible with a mechanical, deterministic universe. Because of the importance of freedom in creative self-direction, a review and an elaboration of the arguments for the reality of freedom are appropriate at this point.

## Subjective Experience as Evidence

Each person's experience of making choices forms the substrata on which the argument for freedom is based. Our knowledge of freedom is the knowledge of our own necessity to choose from among various alternatives in a moment-by-moment sequence. We choose to write with a pen or with a pencil, to put our feet on the desk or on the floor, and to read or to watch television. Although each choice is small, the cumulative effect is self-awareness as a decision maker when various alternatives are involved. This awareness of self as a choosing individual is freedom realized and carries with it the sense of responsibility that level 3 functioning demands.

An anecdote about a judge who was faced with the argument of determinism in a case he heard in Chicago in the 1920s seems relevant to this discussion of freedom in human interaction. The defendant, a man with a long record of convictions, was accused of robbing a bank. The defense attorney admitted the charge, but argued that the man had been helpless to do otherwise. To support his thesis, the lawyer called a noted psychologist as a witness, who clearly presented the theory of determinism and interpreted the slum environment in which the accused had grown up as the cause of the crime. The judge's wry response was that his own environment was such that he could not help but sentence the defendant to 20 years in jail. Readers instinctively reject both the prisoner's and the judge's helplessness. So many situations requiring decisions continually press in on us, each of which calls for an active, conscious response, that the experiences of decision making come to be learned as part of life.

Experiences are stored in the neurological system and can be retrieved—sometimes by the individual for his own purposes and sometimes through stimulation by electrodes in the neurologist's laboratory. The retrievability of experience establishes its reality in the objective world. The individual's own experiences constitute his private world, which to him is reality (Chapter 2). The class comprises individuals whose private view of reality represents the raison d'être of the teacher's professional world. The separate, aggregate private worlds of learners are each significant to the teacher, whether or not they correspond to the verifiable world of science. When a student sees gray rather than red as a response to a wavelength of 395 millimicrons, the experience is in his own perceptual terms. The student's indirect experiences—the experiences of others, about which he hears or reads—are stored as part of what he learns; therefore, these too become part of his reality. To some extent, the learner's experiences help him to predict the results of his own alternative actions and influence his decision making.

## Argument for Determinism

Many people, including many psychologists, are sincere in their belief that all organisms, including man, move in a world that is completely controlled by complex pushes and pulls of the environment. In this view, the controls operate on the organism in many and difficult ways, too complex to be set down and ordered in a neat construct, but nonetheless real. Thus the moment-by-moment awareness of decision making is illusory and is in violation of the laws of a universe that is fabricated on a cause-and-effect basis. That is, if the universe is governed by laws that can be known, it follows that predictability must, at least theoretically, be possible and that freedom of choice under these circumstances must, of necessity, be illusory.

**Predictability of Cause and Effect in the Universe** Modern science usually dates from the time of Bacon, who broke with the philosophic past to insist on the regularity of cause and effect. The educated world of the time was dominated by a system of thought based on premises that could not be questioned without heresy. Most scholars were locked into a climate of thought that excluded the concept of cause-and-effect as it has come to be understood in this century. Divine intervention in everyday experience was accepted as part of the private worlds that medieval scholars had built for themselves.

The development of the means to test private observations by objective criteria has led to refined control of the environment, reinforcement of the person whose view is different from the mainstream of thought but is provable, and accumulation of a body of verified empirical knowledge. Such developments as the periodic table in chemistry, the taxonomies in biology, and the structure of intellect in psychology have been postulated and elaborated by successive scientists.

During the twentieth century, a subtle transformation in the scientific method occurred as it was extended to the study of problems in the social sciences. Descriptive studies in anthropology, sociology, and political science were replaced by normative research employing quantified data. The shift in emphasis from description to measurement was made possible by the adaptation of mathematical probability theory to these fields. During the same period, probability theory was used to facilitate research on microparticles in chemistry, physics, and biology.

The success of the probability models as explanations of physical and social phenomena tends to obscure the activity of individuals within the mass. The electrons in atoms, the molecules in gases, and the voters in elections act in predictable ways when huge numbers are considered, although the mass action is frequently the result of very diverse kinds of individual activities. The molecules in a gas demonstrate clearly both mass action and individual action. In the aggregate, the molecules act as though they are pushing outward on the sides of a container with a force that depends upon their temperature and their number in a given space. Statistically, the pressure is a function of the speed and density of the molecules. The individual molecules, however, may be moving in the statistically indicated direction, in the opposite direction, at right angles, or in any possible oblique direction. The molecules may be moving at the average speed, faster or slower than average, or not at all at a particular moment. The action of the mass is predictable, but the direction and speed of an individual molecule are not.

**Extension of Determinism to People**
Experimental and social psychologists explore the conditions under which individuals act in predictable ways. Sociologists are developing laws that describe the predictable reactions of groups of people. Sampling techniques have been devised that make it possible to predict the behavior of a population by surveying a relatively small but carefully chosen group of people. On this basis, social scientists predict the outcome of an election, the gross sales of a new brand of laundry soap, or the number of suicides a metropolitan police force may expect in a given year. Political scientists can determine which of the candidates will be chosen by most voters, but the election often hinges on the undecided voter. The sociologist does not suggest *which* individuals will succumb to the environmental and endocrine forces that precede suicide, but given certain data, he can make fairly accurate generalizations about suicidal types, as well as predict other aspects of human life.

During man's evolution, the neurological and glandular structures that improved the probability of his survival have been preserved. Imprinting makes possible an inherited neurological system that dictates, at a predetermined point in the development of a duckling, for example, a compulsion (in most infant duck environments) to follow the mother duck (Chapter 2). The relatively simple code system that has made this kind of control functional has opened the way for baby ducks to follow gray mother ducks, white mother ducks, Rhode Island Red hens, or even a red wagon or a fox. This code system, which has been successful through generations of ducks, has elements of both control and freedom. Habits and predictable actions are extensions of the programmed aspect of "following," and the beginning of freedom is evident in the indeterminism of what will be followed. This primitive trace of freedom opens the possibility that the organism can be attracted by alternatives as it seeks to meet its needs for protection and shelter.

### Argument for the Reality of Human Freedom

Several different but related ideas (each detailed elsewhere) validate the argument for some freedom of choice making that all people have and critical amounts of freedom necessary for creative, independent, and productive people. One thread of thought that supports the reality of human freedom has to do with the cumulative experience of decision making. A second thread concerns the emergence of new functions when atoms, molecules, and organisms become more complex. A third idea is the variability of individual activity within valid predictions of mass action. A fourth thread of argument, explained in Chapter 9, involves the physiological evidence that less detailed, more generalized neurological coding systems develop in organisms to enable them to function in more varied and less predictable life-space environments. The arguments for the existence of freedom in choice making discussed here are (1) the element of flexibility in habit formation, (2) multiple choice

in decision making, and (3) the evidence of need for identity.

**Flexibility in Habit Formation**  Primarily, habits are formed by conditioning, with reinforcement from the environment, and represent level 1 learning. Some examples are smoking a pipe, screening out the teacher's voice to concentrate on a daydream, and attending to italicized words in print. When the learning represented by habit formation is contrasted with imprinting or instinctive activities, the potential for alternative action in habitual behavior becomes obvious. The determinism is apparent when environmentally controlled conditioning is contrasted with self-expression. The fact that habits can be and often are broken is evidence of the existence of an inherent freedom, which is subverted whenever a person gives up self-determination for the security of conditioned responses.

An example of action that clearly defies physiologically reinforced conditioning is the reformation of some addicts. An alcoholic has a thoroughly established set of conditioned responses. He has practiced them in the presence of certain stimuli over a considerable period of time, so that it becomes easy to predict what will happen in serial order if the first stimulus of the pattern in presented. The first step that must be taken in the rehabilitation of the alcoholic involves his acceptance of the need for rehabilitation and his resolve to do something about it. This resolve is crucial. Essentially, it involves the decision that when the stimulus situation is next presented, the response is going to be the opposite of that which is so well established. Many times the resolution is made, but when the actual situation arises, the old conditioned response takes over. The fact that this happens so often has no bearing on the validity of the idea that the new learning is possible. That people go against the stream of habit in the presence of the stimulus is sufficient to establish this kind of thinking as real and possible. Breaking this stimulus-response pattern as an outcome of decision making is evidence for the presence of freedom in habitual actions.

### Multiple Choices in Decision Making

The moment-by-moment decisions that help the individual to think of himself as a decision maker involve choices among various alternative actions. In life, the necessity for choosing a line of action may involve a decision that excludes several potential opportunities. The decision of whether to go to college and study one's favorite subject in depth, to balance one's studies in general education, or to take a full-time job, for example, involves multiple choices. A student may usually choose whether his term paper will summarize the sources listed in someone else's bibliography, develop the relationships between relevant sources and some important theme, or extend his own ideas through a new interpretation of the material.

Sometimes the individual can increase the number of choices open to him by retrieving from his stored experience various different but possible actions. Initially, many of the retrieved experiences may seem to be completely irrelevant, but obscure relationships become clear as various possible combinations are explored. This idea is explicit in the divergent production category of Guilford's structure of intellect (Chapter 15). Creative thinking is the goal of the brainstorming or hypothesis-producing sessions that are common procedure for research teams. Items to measure fluency as a facet of creative potential have been included in standardized tests for both adults and children. This aspect of behavioral science is reviewed in the subsequent section on the relationship of creative self-direction to studies on creativity. The

essential conceptualization for the reader at this point is the awareness of flexibility in the process of facing problems and seeking solutions that go beyond automatic or alternative responses.

### Evidence of Need for Identity

The efforts that individuals make to establish their own identity as someone special and unique are evidence of the reality of self-determination and freedom. Children, almost from the time of birth, seem to be engaged in a continuous experiment to define themselves in contrast to other people and to inanimate parts of their environment. The crying and smiling that are associated with hunger or with wet and uncomfortable clothes, and the repair of these deficiencies, seem to have elements of identity development. The crying stops before the feeding and changing are completed. Some young children have learned to use their primitive response systems to establish a tyranny over their parents well before they can sit up.

The following observation illustrates the probability that infants form a definition of self as different from surrounding adults. Two babies, both of whom had been living in completely adult environments, were first brought together when one was ten weeks and the other fourteen weeks old. When placed on a bed facing each other, they both started to laugh, to flail their arms, and to show other evidence that each recognized his novel situation in which there was another individual, who was small like himself and different from the many adults he saw but did not respond to in this way.

Frequent reference is made to negativism in two-year-olds. Such children are making a clear assertion of themselves, even at the risk of alienating the people who satisfy their need for food, shelter, clothing, love, and affection. The child who says "no" as he holds out his hand for a cookie seems to be asserting himself for the purpose of establishing his identity and defying the authority of others.

This need for self-identification leads many people to develop hobbies. In one survey more than three-quarters of the members of a fourth-grade class for gifted children had already independently established themselves as enthusiasts in one or more hobbies. From their account of why and how they had come to be interested in their particular activity, most of them seemed to want something of their own that they could do in their own way. Adults often find similar outlets for self-expression in hobbies and in the activities of lodges, unions, or other groups where they feel free to express themselves in their own terms. The docile and conforming person is usually in a state of anxiety for no other reason than because irreconcilable and conflicting demands are made upon him. It is impossible to have stability unless there is also an individual frame of reference against which decisions can be structured. The members of many research teams have found they need both joint and individual projects on which to work simultaneously in order to remain productive. They seem to need a purely personal outlet to *enable* them to be productive in the group situation.

## RELATIONSHIP OF CREATIVE SELF-DIRECTION TO STUDIES ON CREATIVITY

Theoretical and experimental work on the nature of creativity has become an important facet of educational and psychological thought. In this book, creative self-direction is defined as a level of learning that extends cognitive and affective conceptualizations to generate self-determined experiences that are creative for the individual. Although the idea of creativity as a form of learning is not yet common, the term "genius" was applied to highly intelligent, highly creative people within the memory of many people presently teaching. Many writers now distinguish between intellectual and creative abilities. Intelligence tests, developed to predict school success, necessitated high reliability and validation coefficients, and thus test items were selected that emphasized memory and abstract thinking abilities. These kinds of thinking could be tested, and objective scores could be obtained—raters could all agree on whether the answers were right or wrong. The antithesis of such testing would be to have students execute a painting, which some raters might think excellent and others might think worthless. Evaluations of this kind tended to be dropped as having low reliability. In time, attention was focused on the facile learner who did well on the factual items. The creative aspect of genius reoccurred as a central focus for investigation in the works of MacKinnon (1965), Guilford (1966), Torrance (1965), Wallas (1945), Getzels and Jackson (1962), and others. The role of motivation in creative production was explored and outlined by Maslow, Krathwohl, and others. The results of their studies are reported in the following sections.

### MacKinnon: Criteria of Creativity

At the Institute of Personality Assessment and Research at the University of California, MacKinnon studied several hundred creative individuals from many fields, including architects, writers, research scientists, mathematicians, engineers, and students. His subjects were brought together at Berkeley in groups of about 10 for intensive weekends of interviews, tests, and interaction with one another. The interviews covered such areas as life history, personal philosophy, orientation to work, and openness to new lines of thought. The tests included intelligence measures, projective and standardized personality inventories, scales to assess value structures, and tasks of creative representation such as designing with tiles. The similarities in the characteristics of creatively productive people in widely different professions led the investigators to some important conclusions about creative people in general.

**Identification by Productivity** MacKinnon chose individuals for study who had already proved themselves as outstanding and creative in their respective fields. The architects, for instance, had designed buildings that were recognized as masterpieces by their fellow architects. The essence of the requirement for nomination was original productions already achieved. This approach developed from MacKinnon's tripartite definition of creativity: (1) involving the production of something new or rare; (2) fitting the reality dimensions of the world in terms of some recognizable goal, such as designing a building that is efficient as a work space; and (3) carrying through to completion. In MacKinnon's terms, the facile dilettante who does not pursue his ideas to completion is not creative, nor is the madman who is out of touch with reality.

**Description of Creative People** The people selected for highly creative production were found to be in the upper levels of intelligence, beginning at a minimum IQ of about 120 when the intelligence measured was highly verbal. Beyond this minimum, the correlation between intelligence and creativity was almost nonexistent. The relationship for creative architects was .08 and that for research scientists was −.07, according to MacKinnon (1965). A factor contributing to the low correlation was the tendency of these creative people to be penalized for a willingness to take a chance with the knowledge they had and an

ability to interpret questions flexibly, so that the answers they chose varied from those given in the keys. The creative people in the Berkeley sample were high on tests of originality. Generally, those who were most fluent in suggesting new solutions tended also to have the better solutions. However, there were people in the sample who had relatively few ideas, each of which was of high quality. Others had numerous ideas of generally lesser quality. The creative people had an independence of spirit, although their attitude was not one of revolt just for the sake of being different. The extent of this independence was shown in one test, in which the creative architects indicated less desire for group activities than did the personnel who had been selected to go to the South Pole for the winter of the geophysical year.

Besides being highly original and having an independence of spirit, creative people were found by MacKinnon to be characterized by an openness to new experience. They tended to be curious and nonjudgmental in their approaches to life, characteristics that imposed on them the necessity of living with considerable confusion and disorder in the experiential array that made up their inner worlds. Their ability to hold in suspension large numbers of parts of experience, while the key to their integration was being found, put a subtle pressure on them to integrate complex experiences into simpler systems. Creative people were more than ordinarily intuitive in their responses to their environment. They tended to see what could be, as well as what was. One somewhat surprising finding was that the values of the creative people tended to be both aesthetic and theoretical; strong emphasis on both these scales tended to emerge from the Allport-Vernon-Lindzey *Study of Values*. MacKinnon speculated that this emphasis on both aesthetic and theoretical values indicated a need for solutions to problems that were correct, but also elegant. He expressed the importance to creative people of the aesthetic values in mathematics, history, and shop-work—subjects in which such values are not usually considered important by many people.

According to MacKinnon, most creative adults have solved the problem of their identity; they know who they are. They tend to have a strong sense of destiny, accompanied by a measure of egotism and a sense of the worth of their creative efforts. Often they are not particularly well rounded; they are intensely interested in some areas and make no effort to participate in others. When this facet of personality is supported by a tendency to be nonconforming in judgment, there is a possibility that such individuals have difficulty in meeting requirements for entry into graduate schools. The creative individual may not follow routine regulations because they have little significance in his value patterns.

**Importance of Inner-Directedness** From his studies of the common characteristics of adults who were highly creative in certain fields, MacKinnon developed suggestions for nurturing creativity in young people. Parents and teachers can contribute to this growth most effectively if they help students build a sense of identity, of purpose, and of drive to accomplish their private goals. Teachers who learn that highly creative students are not necessarily the ones with very high IQ test scores (although they may be creative also) and who come to understand the students' need for autonomy are likely to be successful in building for their inner-directedness. Adults can help develop creative abilities in young people by relaxing pressure on them to participate in group activities that put a premium on conformity to group goals and mores. Both parents and teachers must accept the possibility of a child's being so intensely interested in the area of his creative ability that he becomes somewhat lopsided in his develop-

ment. Young people can also be helped by giving them understanding support in their struggle to bring order out of their multivaried experiences and by giving some consideration to the aesthetic dimension of their environment.

MacKinnon's research on creative adults supports and reinforces the concept of creative self-direction in the learning-motivation model. Although he worked with mature, productive adults and used substantial visible output as a criterion of creativity, the kinds of school and home experience that may be expected to eventuate in creative production are almost identical to those suggested for level 3 learning, in which the self-directing facet leads almost certainly to productive output. The chief difference between MacKinnon's definition of creative output and that of the authors concerns whether the production is unique to the individual or unique to his society. All that should be expected of a child or a young student is that the production be unique to him.

### Guilford: Divergent and Convergent Production

Guilford's lectures and articles have stimulated great interest among professional groups in the creative and intellectual growth of students. Guilford's structure of intellect is presented in Chapter 15, Intelligence: Structure and Function. In the present chapter, those aspects of his work which are relevant to creativity are considered. Guilford, whose emphasis is somewhat different from that of MacKinnon, is much concerned with the inner process of creativity; thus he emphasizes intellectual operations rather than the societal value of the output.

**Shift from "Thinking" to "Production" in the Operations** Guilford (1966) stated that all problem solving that genuinely finds a solution is creative, although not all creative thinking is necessarily problem solving. Both are forms of learning. If an individual is completely ready to deal with a situation, there is no problem; when difficulties arise, the creative person finds novel ways of handling them. This devising of a novel solution is the *sine qua non* of creativity. This concept of creative ability as a facet of intellectual ability implies that practically everyone is creative to a degree. Guilford (1966) touched on the pervasive aspect of creativity:

I have sometimes said that a cognitive ability is an ability to know or to recognize or to discover a kind of information, where the kind of information is specified by its kind of content and its kind of product. The use of the term "discover" in this connection should be restricted to instances of prompt or immediate discovery. Where cognition is not immediately forthcoming, some productive operations, in the form of divergent or convergent thinking, or both, may well be required [p. 72].

Production can be roughly equated with creativity and is a form of intellectual functioning. Guilford is interested in what might be called "microcreativity"; that is, the elemental structure of creativity emerges as the retrieval and restructuring of knowledge, including an evaluation of the product in a very narrow experience. Guilford theorizes that evaluation is the general basis of reinforcement in learning and is involved at each substep of the creative or problem-solving sequence.

Three aspects of the creative process, each of which can be improved by learning, have a major importance in determining the refinement of the production. These are fluency, flexibility, and elaboration. *Fluency* is concerned primarily with efficient retrieval of many items of information that fulfill certain specifications. The individual examines many different kinds of items that are stored, and the wider the range of ideas called out of storage, the greater the fluency. The individual who is fluent has numerous diverse associations available to build new ideas or materials—in other words, the greater is his potential for productive thinking.

Guilford sees two main kinds of *flexibility*: that dealing with classes, such as round or square, and that dealing with transformations, such as selecting the letters of a sentence to form the name of a game. The ability to try many different possible ways of combining information is the essential characteristic of flexibility. Some people tend to work in a single class at a time and to work through all the possibilities before moving on to another class. In generating new ideas, this approach is usually less fertile than that of examining many classes in a more perfunctory way because in the former the range of diversity is more restricted. The development of these abilities is enhanced by practice which provides variety and by observation of others making transformations.

*Elaboration* is the process of developing a system or theory, once the basic outlines have been determined. In Guilford's terms, elaboration is the divergent production of implications. To summarize the present interpretation of Guilford's theory of divergent thinking operations, fluency involves output in units, relations, and systems; flexibility involves classes and transformations; and elaboration involves the production of implications.

**Relation to Three-Level Model** Guilford's emphasis on divergent thinking has led many teachers to transform their teaching to stress creative production and to put less emphasis on the acquisition of knowledge for its own sake. Because school people have been made aware of the possibility of creative responses in all subjects and in all content, teachers can now arrange their lessons so that divergent thinking and learning are likely to occur. Guilford's emphasis on microcreativity is similar to the position taken by the authors, as is his multifacet system of learned differential abilities that evolve from experiences.

### Torrance; Identification of Creativity in Children

At the Bureau of Educational Research in Minnesota, Torrance (1965) and his associates developed a variety of tasks that involved the creative process, and then examined the products for evidences of divergent thinking as defined in the Guilford structure. Experimental tasks were devised for students from kindergarten to graduate school age, but the forms for middle-grade children were used most widely—perhaps because there was a paucity of other valid and reliable instruments to identify creative children and because the early tests were relatively successful as low as fifth grade.

**Tests That Identify Creative Potential** To validate the early forms of the Minnesota Tests of Creative Thinking, a determination was made by the test constructors of item ability to differentiate children who were imaginative, humorous, playful, relaxed, and nonrigid in their viewpoints. Some examples of tasks that were developed and retained as tests of imagination were listing "unusual uses" (of tin cans); "impossibilities" (scored for fluency, flexibility, and originality); "consequences" (what would happen if animals could talk); "just suppose" (that shadows became real); "situations" (handling a friend who likes to kid others but cannot stand to be kidded); "common problems" (such as in taking a bath); and "improvements" (how to make a toy dog more fun to play with). Later forms of the creativity tests included the use of nonverbal figural tasks such as drawing objects suggested by circles and squares, writing imaginative stories, making up titles for pictures, and filling in gaps between illustrated events. Some of the Minnesota studies have been directed toward motivational patterns of creative individuals in an attempt to distinguish between creatively motivated and critically motivated personality structures. Torrance's finding of statistically significant differences in favor of high creatives over low creatives in motivation and of a trend toward greater critical motivation in low than in high creatives both tended to support Guilford's early separation of divergent and evaluative thinking operations.

**Personality Characteristics of Creative Children** Torrance found three characteristics that differentiated highly creative children from less creative but equally intelligent children: (1) they had a reputation among peers for having "wild or silly ideas," (2) their productions were outside the mold or anticipated standards, and (3) their work was characterized by humor, playfulness, lack of rigidity, and relaxation. Torrance (1963) summarized his findings and those of other investigators as follows:

> In spite of the fact that these children have many excellent ideas, they readily achieve a reputation for having silly, wild, or naughty ideas. It is difficult to determine what effect this derogation of their ideas has on their personality development, as well as upon the future development of their creative talents. The uniqueness of their ideas makes this a really difficult problem, because there are no standards, as in answer books and manuals. Although their humor and playfulness may win some friends for them, it doesn't always make them "easier to live with." In fact, it may make their behavior even more unpredictable than otherwise and this probably makes their presence in a group upsetting. Recognizing and understanding these three characteristics are important and each apparently has an important role in making an individual "creative [p. 81]."

In a follow-up study of 200 children originally identified as highly creative, Torrance (1969) concluded that four-fifths of them persisted in their creative activities over several years. How the child or student learns to interrelate with the others in his social environment may be a crucial factor in the development of his self-image as a creator.

## Tumin: Teaching Creative Behavior

Tumin (1954) published a theoretical article in which he proposed a list of *obstacles to creativity*, including (1) an excessive quest for certainty, (2) an excessive quest for power, (3) an excessive quest for meanings, (4) an excessive quest for social relations, and (5) a pathological or excessive rejection of social relations. This constructive or destructive interaction between the social environment and an individual's creative production may be established within the time-space limitations of the school. Tumin's rationale suggests that the individual needs to find a balance in his social interactions between overresponsiveness to the wishes of others, overconformity in an effort to gain the approval of others, and a pathological withdrawal from social relationships and communication. Stated positively, the personal-social need of the creative individual seems to involve freedom to seek and interact with other people, accompanied by freedom to assert one's own identity.

Teachers and counselors, beginning when the child first comes to school, can help creative potential to flourish by reinforcing, as frequently as possible, each child's efforts to find the freedom to choose or to reject social pressures. This teaching of social interaction is much more complicated, more critical, and more vital than teaching children to get along well with others. The sequence of conceptualizations in this research that are basic to teaching (and learning) creative self-direction may be summarized as follows: (1) Creative children may be identified in school groups by productions that demonstrate fluency, flexibility, and originality; (2) their responses are so far removed from the model patterns that they, personally, may be misinterpreted and rejected by others; (3) creative motivation may be related to the kind of reinforcement they get from a personal-social balance between excessive dependence on, or pathological withdrawal from, social relations; and (4) teaching constructive social interaction may help to give each student the freedom he requires to become self-directing and productive.

## Getzels and Jackson: Relationship of Creativity and Intelligence

In a project that received widespread attention, Getzels and Jackson (1962) compared high school students who were high on creativity tests (upper 20 percent) but comparatively low on IQ with students who were high on IQ (upper 20 percent) but not as high on tests of creativity. Students who were high on both tests were not included in the comparison. Researchers found (1) an average differential between the two groups of 23 points on IQ, (2) no significant differences between the two groups on standard achievement test scores, and (3) teacher preference for the high-IQ group rather than the high-creative group. The highly creative group appeared not to value the qualities they recognized as contributing to success in the eyes of the teacher as much as the comparison group did. The highly creative group showed greater imagination and originality in their writing style and valued humor more in themselves than the high-IQ low-creative group did.

Since both groups were chosen from a school population with an average IQ of approximately 132, the data should not be interpreted as a denial of positive correlation between creativity scores and IQ. This research does indicate, however, that instruments developed to measure intelligence may tap different abilities from those revealed by tests developed to measure creativity, especially when the school population being tested is superior in academic ability, as was that of Getzels and Jackson.

To the extent that IQ tests measure potential for learning, they should indicate potential for learning creative behavior as well as potential for learning associations and conceptualizations. Probably high-IQ students who are not also highly creative have received their reinforcement from conforming school behavior, while the highly creative students have learned the satisfactions of self-determined, often nonconforming, responses. The evidence between the value systems of the two groups suggests they had been motivated to seek different goals. The personal pleasure that is inherent in self-expression was apparently sufficient to compensate highly creative students for lack of teacher reinforcement whenever they had a choice between following their own or the school's goals. As the teachers come to value and to reinforce creative self-direction, the conforming high-IQ students will tend to become more creative, and the highly creative students will tend to find school goals compatible with their own needs.

### Wallach and Kogan: Separations between Creativity and Intelligence

Wallach and Kogan (1965) reanalyzed the data of Getzels and Jackson and found very similar intercorrelations within the various creativity measures and between the creativity measures and IQ scores. These comparisons are shown in Figure 8-1. Wallach and Kogan made a similar analysis of scores used by Cline,

| SCORES | BOYS | GIRLS |
|---|---|---|
| Intracreativity | .21 | .24 |
| Intercreativity—IQ | .35 | .33 |

**Figure 8-1** Comparison of correlations between part scores on creativity tests and between creativity and IQ scores. (*From Wallach & Kogan's reworking of Getzels & Jackson's data. In M. A. Wallach and N. Kogan, A new look at the creativity-intelligence distinction, Journal of Personality, 1965, 33, 348–369. By permission of the authors.*)

Richards, and Needham (1963) to support the hypothesis that creative children are different from high-IQ children. The analysis produced findings similar to those of Getzels and Jackson (Figure 8-2). The correlations between creativity and IQ appear higher than the correlations between subtests of the creativity test.

Wallach and Kogan agreed with Getzels and Jackson that there are differences between creative children and others, even though they were careful to indicate that the given data were not adequate to support the interpretations either of Getzels and Jackson or of Cline, Richards, and Needham. Wallach and Kogan operated on the assumption that a critical element in creativity is the absence of pressure, which they saw operating in nearly all test situations. In their own experimental studies, they arranged for initial observation of the students to classify their level of creativity in classroom, interpersonal, and intrapersonal situations. They gave a block of IQ-related measures consisting of WISC, School and College Aptitude Tests (SCAT), and Sequential Tests of Educational Progress (STEP). They also gave a series of 10 creativity tests covering uniqueness and productivity, which were administered individually in a game setting and with unlimited time. It should be pointed out that all these tests were in the area of fluency, and that no tests of flexibility or elaboration were given. Wallach and Kogan obtained correlations of .4 for intracreativity tests, .5 for intraintelligence tests, and .1 for intercreativity-IQ tests. This low correlation (.1) is not surprising when the intelligence tests used were loaded with association learning and eliminated the creativity tests that require a high proportion level 2 and level 3 functioning. In spite of the restricted coverage of the tests, Wallace and Kogan were able to separate their data into high-creativity–high-IQ (H-H), high-creativity–low-IQ (H-L), low-creativity–high-IQ (L-H), and low-creativity–low-IQ (L-L) groups. The characteristics of girls in different patterns are shown in Figure 8-3.

## Jackson and Messick: Identifying Creative Persons

Jackson and Messick (1965) developed a theoretical model of creativity in which they outlined the relationships between the cognitive styles of the creative person, his noncognitive psychological qualities, the characteristics of his product, and society's responses toward products that are accepted as creative

| SCORES | BOYS | GIRLS |
|---|---|---|
| Intracreativity | .26 | .27 |
| Intercreativity—IQ | .28 | .32 |

**Figure 8-2** Comparison of correlations between part scores on creativity tests and between creativity and IQ scores. (*From Wallach & Kogan's reworking of Cline, Richards, & Needham's data. In M. A. Wallach and N. Kogan, A new look at the creativity-intelligence distinction, Journal of Personality, 1965, 33, 358–369. By permission of the authors.*)

(Figure 8-4). Response properties (the central column) may be thought of as criteria of the creative product. Widely accepted characteristics of creative work, *unusualness* and *appropriateness*, have been extended to include *transformation*, the property that forces the observer to transcend some conventional view of reality, and *condensation*, the characteristic of restraint, economy, selection, or central truth.

According to this conceptualization, the corresponding personality, or affective, characteristics from which highly creative products emerge are originality, sensitivity, flex-

### HIGH CREATIVITY–HIGH IQ

Least doubt, least hesitation about answering. Highest level of self-confidence. Least tendency to deprecate work. Sought out by peers and seek companionship. Highest attention span, concentration. Interest in academic work. High in disruptive attention-seeking behavior. Apparently eager to propose novel divergent possibilities in classroom. May be nuisances in some types of classrooms.

### LOW CREATIVITY–HIGH IQ

High confidence and assurance. Sought by others, but do not actively seek companionship themselves. High attention span, high concentration, hesitant about expressing opinions. High interest in academic achievement. Least likely to seek attention in disruptive ways. Show a basic reserve.

### HIGH CREATIVITY–LOW IQ

Cautious and hesitant about expressing themselves in class. Least confident and assured. Seem to be the group at greatest disadvantage in the classroom. Tend to deprecate their work. Least able to concentrate and maintain attention. Least sought after by their peers and tend to avoid companionship of others. Tend to be disruptive to classroom routine and to be high in attention-seeking activities. Seem to be in incoherent protest against plight.

### LOW CREATIVITY–LOW IQ

Greater confidence and assurance than high creativity–low IQ. Less hesitant and subdued than high creativity–low IQ. More outgoing toward peers than high creativity–low IQ. Seem to compensate for poor academic performance by activities in social sphere.

**Figure 8-3** Wallach and Kogan's four-way separation of creative and high-IQ scoring girls.

| Predisposing cognitive styles | Personal qualities | Response properties | Judgmental standards | Aesthetic responses |
|---|---|---|---|---|
| Tolerance of incongruity, inconsistency, etc. | Original | Unusualness | Norms | Surprise |
| Analytic and intuitive | Sensitive | Appropriateness | Context | Satisfaction |
| Open-minded | Flexible | Transformation | Constraints | Stimulation |
| Reflective and spontaneous | Poetic | Condensation | Summary power | Savoring |

**Figure 8-4** Jackson and Messick's characteristics of creative producers and products. (*From P. W. Jackson and S. Messick, The person, the product, and the response: Conceptual problems in the assessment of creativity, Journal of Personality, 1965, 33, 309–329. By permission of the authors.*)

ibility, and poetic impulse. Jackson and Messick consider cognitive styles to be closely related to intelligence and therefore subject to measures of "correctness," as opposed to "goodness," which is closely related to affective characteristics. The creative qualities of the product and the person are verified by the objective judgments of others (column 4, Fig. 8.4) and by their subjective aesthetic responses (column 5, Fig. 8.4). This elaboration of creative functioning is helpful to teachers in setting criteria with students for their productions.

## Maddi: Creativity and Motivation

Maddi (1965) emphasized the factor of high motivation among creative people. He was quick to point out that many highly creative people can be extremely productive in a very frustrating and restricting environment if they are sufficiently motivated. Persons who are both creative and productive show strong needs for quality and novelty, in their own terms, even more than they need peer recognition or physical comforts. Maddi urged further

research on the relationships of motive power and likes or dislikes to determine whether creative people (compared to noncreative people) enjoy experiencing quality and novelty to the extent that they learn on the basis of these satisfactions. Although Maddi speaks of his creative people in these terms, he stressed the element of self-direction, which permits the creator to work in spite of hardships such as hunger, cold, or want.

## Wallas: Steps in the Creative Process

Wallas (1945) postulated four steps in the creative process: preparation, incubation, illumination, and elaboration. He discussed these processes in reference to macrocreativity rather than the smaller acts of creative self-direction, which have been emphasized in this text. Since there is often a telescoping of large-scale processes in the minute segments from which they are built, a brief examination of these stages seems desirable.

Wallas describes *preparation* as a process of intense study of the problem at hand. It involves assembling all the available information, marshaling it, organizing it, and working through it so that it is clearly understood. It is a process of building as many complex association chains as possible. The period of *incubation* is discussed more often in popular writing than in psychological texts. Many creative scientists and authors have reported that their creative ideas come to them after they have worked very hard on a project and have left it for a time to undertake some mild physical activity, such as taking a walk, going for a drive in a car, or even playing with their children. The *illumination* or the flash of insight that puts the various elements into their proper relationship seems, in many people, to be preceded by an intimation—a feeling or an awareness—that the pieces are falling into place. Distractions at this time seem particularly unfortunate, if not disastrous. It is as though the conceptualization were partly formed and only the final sections needed to be added in order to complete a pattern. During this very brief period, a distraction can disrupt fragile linkages. The fourth stage, *elaboration*, is one of intense, systematic work during which the poem is written down and polished, the theory is tested, or the machine is built.

The relationship of these four stages to the model of learning presented in this book is clear and precise: preparation corresponds to the process of building associations, incubation to the period of consolidation of chains of associations and the beginning of their linkage into grids, illumination to the conceptualization that occurs when the grid forms, and elaboration to the period of creative self-direction.

## MOTIVATION IN SELF-DIRECTION AND SELF-ACTUALIZATION

Learning at level 3 contains elements of inner-directedness, of motivation, and of un-

predictability regarding what will be produced (learned). Associations and conceptualizations learned in school are directed primarily by someone else or dictated by the structure of the material itself, but creative activity occurs when the learner directs himself and determines when his own learning has been successful. Repetitions occur in all levels of learning, but in creative self-direction they seem to have greater variability because of slight, but progressive, changes in the neurological linkages (Chapter 9).

The significance of the emotional or attitudinal dimension in school learning has long been reflected in curriculum guides, teaching goals, and reviews of children's and adolescents' books. In Chapter 2 the essential fusion of a learner's previous cognitive and affective experience in creative, self-directed activity was explained. The teacher who recognizes the necessity to cope with students' attitudes, interests, and values may decide to direct his teaching toward affective goals. Self-actualizing students and teachers are both busy putting their value structures to work to meet their needs as human beings. Krathwohl, Maslow, and others have suggested some steps in the sequence of a learner's development of values and value systems.

## Krathwohl, Bloom, and Masia: Characterization by a Value

One aspect of motivation—perhaps the major one—concerns the student's interest in, and attitude toward, the material being studied. The student who likes French, history, or mathematics is nearly always motivated to learn more about it than he already knows. Teachers find these students easy to teach and responsive to suggestions for broadening their knowledge. Krathwohl, Bloom, and Masia (1964) defined the stages of the development of this value structure and provided test questions that illustrate ways of measuring them (Chapter 3).

Everyone has varying degrees of favorable or unfavorable attitudes toward different phases of life. Similarly, the intensity of interest in the subject matter being taught varies from student to student. Krathwohl and his coworkers sought to order these intensities or degrees in some meaningful way. They summarized their search as follows:

> The more we carefully studied the components, however, the clearer it became that a continuum progressed from a level at which the individual is merely *aware* of a phenomenon, being able to *perceive* it. At the next level he is *willing to attend* to the phenomena. At the next level he *responds* to the phenomena with a *positive feeling.* Eventually he may feel strongly enough to *go out of his way* to respond. At some point in the process he conceptualizes his behavior and feelings and *organizes* these conceptualizations into a structure. This structure grows in complexity as it *becomes his life outlook* [Krathwohl et al., 1964, p. 27].

The attitudes related to school learning, and the emphasis was on a classification after the fact, rather than a description of a process under way. The highest category, "character-ization by a value," applies to a person who has become self-actualizing in some aspect of his life to the extent that others can observe and remark on the intensity of his dedication to the value under consideration (Figure 3-2).

## Maslow: Theory of Self-Actualization

Maslow first became important in psychology with the publication in the *Psychological Review* (1943) of a 26-page article entitled "A Theory of Human Motivation." His principal points concerned the existence of a hierarchy of needs, the most basic of which must be satisfied, at least to a minimal degree, before the higher ones can be attended to. His list begins with basic or preemptive needs and continues through successively higher ones, as follows:

1 Physiological needs (hunger, thirst, etc.)
2 Safety needs
3 Love and belonging needs
4 Esteem needs (needs for achievement and recognition)
5 Self-actualization needs
6 Need to know and understand

In *Toward a Psychology of Being*, Maslow (1968) expressed very clearly the difference

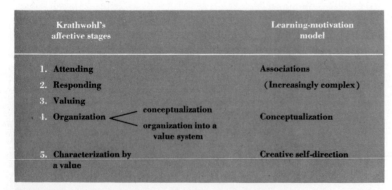

**Figure 8-5·** Relationship of Krathwohl's affective stages to the learning-motivation model.

between the inner dynamics of the creative learner and the forces that are basic to other-directed individuals. He distinguished between the first four needs, which he termed *deficiency needs*, and the last two self-actualization needs, which he termed *being needs*. He wrote:

The needs for safety, belongingness, love relations and for respect can be satisfied only by other people, i.e., only from outside of the person. This means considerable dependence on the environment.

A person in this dependent position cannot really be said to be governing himself, or in control of his fate. He must be beholden to the sources of supply of needed gratifications. Their wishes, their whims, their rules and laws govern him and must be appeased lest he jeopardize his sources of supply. He must be, to an extent, "other directed," and must be sensitive to other people's approval, affection, and good will. This is the same as saying that he must adapt and adjust by being flexible and responsive and by changing himself to fit the external situation. *He is the dependent variable; the environment is the fixed, independent variable.* . . .

In contrast, the self-actualizing individual, by definition gratified in his basic needs, is far less dependent, far less beholden, far more autonomous and self-directed. Far from needing other people, growth motivated people may actually be hampered by them. I have already reported their special liking for privacy, for detachment and meditativeness.

Such people become far more self-sufficient and self-contained. The determinants which govern them are now primarily inner ones rather than social or environmental. They are the laws of their own inner nature, their potentialities and their capacities, their talents, their latent resources, their creative impulses, their needs to know themselves and to become more and more integrated and unified, more and more aware of what they really are, of what they really want, of what their call or vocation or fate is to be.

Since they depend less on other people, they

are less ambivalent about them, less anxious and less hostile, less needful of their praise and of their affection. . . .

This *relative* independence of the outside world and its wishes and pressures, does not mean, of course, lack of intercourse with it or respect for its "demand character." It means only that in these contacts, the self-actualizer's wishes and plans are the primary determiners, rather than stresses from the environment. This I have called psychological freedom, contrasting it with geographical freedom [p. 34–35].

Children come to school with their more basic needs satisfied or unsatisfied to various degrees. Today, not many children are hungry or afraid for their safety, and not many teachers find it necessary to attend to these primitive needs. A number of children, however, are deficient in the areas of love, belonging, esteem, achievement, and recognition.

Very often, the children who are deficient in belonging and esteem needs are the hardest to satisfy, for two reasons. First, they are more deprived, and so their needs are greater; second, usually they are deprived because they have learned response mechanisms that call forth derisive action rather than love, recognition, and praise.

The pretty, well-dressed little girl who is open and friendly and thinks her teacher is perfectly wonderful tends to call forth responses of affection, praise, and understanding. The ragged little boy who is socially hostile and calls the teacher an old bitch finds little in the school environment to make his needs less pressing, diminish his hostility, or set him free from himself or from his environment. In many cases, the schools add to the harm done to children who have a history of poor psychological adjustment.

Maslow points out that a need-deficient person tends to see others in terms of the ways they can be of use, which is often resented. The self-actualizing person, who is freer and more disinterested, is able to stand off and see others as they are—unique people with their own problems, who can be helped in various ways by various means.

Maslow illustrates what he means by the difference between the self-actualizing and the deficit-need aspects of motivation by a comparison of selfless and selfish love. He points out the importance of satisfying love needs at critical times in the child's development sequence. Individuals who are seriously deprived in this way become emotionally crippled, so that later remediation may be quite difficult and occasionally impossible. However, people who have been surrounded by affection and love have these deficiency needs pretty well satisfied and need only small amounts of love to remain healthy. They are much more capable of giving love than their more deficient brethren. They are able to be nonpossessive, admiring, other-fulfilling, less jealous, and more disinterested, and at the same time they are more eager to help others toward self-actualization in their relations with them. The giving of this kind of love satisfies the deficit needs of the unfulfilled individual and makes it possible for him to become a whole person and to accept himself. Teachers need to be whole people who can help certain children to fill their need deficits.

### Reinforcement in Need Satisfaction

The private world of the individual is the product of the choices he makes and the effects of these choices on his subsequent well-being (Chapter 2). Learning is a by-product of this process of making choices. In the child's early years particularly, he has a need for safety. If those around him respond to his attempts at exploration of various kinds by withdrawing security whenever he investigates new possibilities, he is likely to learn a fear of exploration. The young child who first

attempts to walk has a great tolerance for falls and bumps. He may fall two dozen times each day, but as long as there is encouragement or even neutrality, he is likely to continue to master the complicated art of walking. If there is hostility toward his attempts to walk—as is sometimes the case when ornaments are knocked over and broken—he may learn that this activity is dangerous and regress to crawling. If parents or teachers attempt too often to control the actions of children, they can rob them of the experience of internal delight at success in a new step taken. When the child must continuously find his reinforcement in the approval of others, he is learning to live in a disaster world rather than in a success world.

Maslow pointed out that a comparatively small number of people live in the realm of positive mental health and are able to see others in relation to their self-actualizing potentials, rather than in terms of the others' possible utility in meeting their own deficiency needs. However, many people come to this kind of detachment from self-interest in moments of peak experiences. In the moments that change their lives or give them fresh insights into aesthetic opportunities, people find themselves freed from themselves.

### Problems in Self-Actualization

Certain difficulties are involved in the generally desirable state of being a self-actualizer, some of which are important to teachers. The self-actualizer tends to be freed from some of the drives that plague the deficit-need person. The self-actualizing teacher tends to be able to see what motivates other people's actions because he understands these drives and is not upset by them. He is a bit indulgent; he does not insist that things be done in just this or that way. When the class is large, allowing pupils this kind of freedom can make discipline difficult.

The classroom teacher who insists that students learn specifically whatever is being taught must himself feel certain that the answers he knows are the only ones to be considered. This assurance seems to be characteristic of strong leadership. However, it seems important to point out the fallacy of this approach in teaching children to be creative, and perhaps in teaching them to be self-actualizers. It is relatively easy for an extremely efficient teacher to stifle creative learning merely by insisting on systematic learning of so much factual material that there is no time or energy left for anything else. Some ideas about ways in which creative thinking and learning can be fostered will be presented, not as a rigid format to be followed precisely, but as a theme on which each teacher can play his own variation.

## CREATIVE SELF-DIRECTION IN THE CLASSROOM

The term "self-actualization" is used to describe the human need for coming into selfhood—that is, for becoming a full person. Creative self-direction is a process through which a person reaches self-actualization. As he expresses himself in creative works with which he can identify, he fulfills this need. The following sections describe the teacher's role in helping young people experience self-directed learning and increasing the likelihood that functioning at level 3 will reoccur.

### Freeing the Restricted Student

Liliane was born in France to an American Army officer and his very attractive French wife. She registered the highest IQ in her fourth-grade class, was an average reader, never volunteered answers other than those which were certain and factual, spoke excellent English, and had exemplary manners. During choice period, she made elaborate but stilted little paintings of flowers. One day she wrote a story about a girl named Sally who was pretty—which Liliane was not—but seemed to have some of her own interests and problems. The teacher was delighted with the story and asked to keep it until she had a chance to make a copy. Liliane said, "Yes, but don't show it to my mother, please." During succeeding weeks, many Sally stories were slipped under the green blotter on the teacher's desk.

One day the class made a trip to the local museum. On the way to the Indian collection, they stopped to inspect a temporary exhibit—a large dollhouse. Back in the classroom, the pupils busied themselves writing reports of their visit—all except Liliane, who toyed with her pencil for five or six minutes. When the teacher went to Liliane's desk, she said, "I can't write a report." The teacher attempted several motivating questions before one brought a light to Liliane's eyes. "Suppose Sally had gone to the museum. What would she have done?"

Liliane wrote for 20 minutes and then brought the following story to the teacher:

*Sally at the Museum*
One day Sally's mother said, "I thought you would like it if I took you to the Museum of History and Industry." So Sally went to the museum.

*What happened at the museum*
   As soon as Sally and her mother got there her mother said, "Don't run, don't touch."

   It happens that Sally's mother meets a friend, Miss Hollon. Miss Hollon took Sally's mother and started showing her some things. Sally already saw the dollhouse and started playing with it. She changed everything around. She called to her mother, "Come here." When Sally's mother saw what Sally did to the dollhouse, Sally's mother took Sally right home and gave Sally a spanking. As for the dollhouse it was put back just like it was when they came. The End.

This episode illustrates the way in which a responsive teacher was able to use a child's first tentative offering to help her grow. When Liliane's teacher accepted the first Sally story, praised her for it, and reinforced the praise by asking to keep a copy, she took one of the first steps toward freeing the inhibited little girl. There must have been earlier encouragement and evidence of personal acceptance, or the first story would probably not have been written. Success encouraged further attempts. The youngster displayed the beginnings of belief in herself as she shyly took the initiative to ask, "Did you read my story?" When the teacher used Liliane's ability to express herself through Sally to help her accomplish the difficult task of writing a report, she took the next major step in freeing the child. Liliane was able to progress to factual reports soon afterward. The Sally stories had a therapeutic value for the very restricted little girl. Writing them helped her become more like the self she wanted to be, and they provided a successful start in classroom composition at a rather crucial time in her school life.

Sensitive teachers can see the signs of emerging self-confidence and reinforce them delicately. From these early beginnings, later creative endeavors spring. The results are sometimes slow, but their coming is rewarding, to both the student and the teacher.

## Knowing When to Reinforce

The Kindergarten Evaluation of Learning Potential (KELP) was designed to help children shift from association-building experience, to pattern discovery or conceptualization, and finally to creative, self-initiated learning. Achievement levels on the bolt-board item require that, at the association level, the child remove, scramble, and reassemble nine bolts of decreasing size in the proper holes of a wooden stand. To score at level 2, he must explain his understanding of size-order sequence for replacing the bolts. At

level 3, he must, on his own initiative, pre-structure the task by sorting or otherwise organizing the bolts for assembly. Mark, who had chosen the bolt board for his independent activity one morning, called out to the kindergarten teacher to say, "Look, I did it, I did it." She noted that he had taken the bolt board apart and had arranged the bolts in order of size, with the appropriate nuts lined up beside them. When she suggested that he scramble the bolts, he replied, "That would just be wasting my time."

The teacher recognized that Mark had intellectually taken some steps that most five-year-olds need to take—those involving manipulations that build the chains of associations basic to the discovery of size order as the essential relationship involved in reassembly. This kindergarten teacher was quick to recognize and reinforce his initiative in going beyond the "rules of the game" because she knew the structure of the content and the levels of difficulty for the learner.

Perhaps more important was the teacher's flexibility in recognizing a growth pattern that differed from expected behavior. Many times innovative children are penalized for responses that may be superior to the standards but are unexpected and go unrecognized. The curriculum framework, when implemented without flexibility, provides some teachers with the means to evade personal responsibility for unlearned content and unconforming students. One creative young painter said that she made it a practice to break one rule in each picture. In the case of Mark, the teacher's acceptance of his individual high-level approach to the task and her perception of his thinking process increased the likelihood that he would again approach a task in his own way.

## Teaching Self-Direction in Social Relationships

The creative, self-directing person, as described in this book, is able to interact constructively with other people, has established his own identity sufficiently to tolerate differences in others, and finds satisfaction in supporting other individuals. The destructive person is not sufficiently integrated to risk damage to his inadequate self-identity through interaction with other people; therefore, he holds them at a psychological distance.

Even young children can be helped to become positive and constructive in their social relationships. Another item, "social interaction," in KELP was designed to develop this kind of competence through a progression from association learning and conceptualization to creative self-direction. Some observations written by three kindergarten teachers, which demonstrate level 3 functioning on the part of five-year-olds, follow:

Jimmy, a star in a cluster of the rowdier little boys, was asked to pass out balls for recess play. There were six balls. The first three were quickly distributed to three eager boys. There followed a rather long period of hesitation, and then the fourth ball was given to a little girl. As if to redeem himself, the boy looked up to his circle of friends and said, "Well, it *is* fair. The girls should get three balls too." (Jimmy had always made it a point to show a dislike for girls.) Since no rule had ever been established to govern the distribution of equipment, this perception of fair play had been Jimmy's own.

The morning class was playing dodge ball. Larry (very slow) did not get a chance to throw the ball because he had not once succeeded in recovering it. He pouted, stamped out of the game, and would not play. The next time Billy (very active) got the ball, he ran to Larry offering it to him. Larry was immediately all smiles again and joined in the game. I asked, "Billy, why did you do that?" He answered, "You're always talking to us about fair play and being kind and taking turns—so I just did."

After a trip to the bathroom, Chris came back to the circle with his shirt spotted by water. I went to the bathroom to find water all over the

floor and on the walls. I went to Chris and told him this was not the way to behave. He was all wet and the bathroom was a mess—which would mean extra work for Mr. Reidby, our custodian. I added that we must help Mr. Reidby and not cause him to work so hard.

Perhaps 20 minutes had gone by when Chris came up to me and said in a businesslike manner, "You won't have to send for Mr. Reidby. I cleaned up the water in the bathroom so he won't have so much work to do."

These children, each in his own way, demonstrated mature, understanding behavior. The appropriateness of their responses almost ensured that they would be reinforced by both companions and teachers and thus become a prototype for further growth in mature self-expression. Teachers, by example and by systematic teaching, can help students of all ages gain the insights and the motivation that combine to produce independent, socially constructive individuals.

### Using an Intellectual Approach to Creativity

Leland, a Chinese-American boy, was enrolled in the special class for intellectually gifted sixth graders. The teacher had observed his impressive array of information on many subjects, including the ability to identify selections from classical recordings and give biographical information about the composers. As part of the talent development program, Mr. L. wanted Leland and several others to try their hand at composing music; he had decided on an intellectual approach, beginning with music history and appreciation.

One day the teacher played a recording of Mozart's *Sonata in D Major for Violin and Pianoforte.* Leland raised his hand before the arm of the record player was lifted from the disc: "It's Mozart's—he composed more than 36 sonatas." Mr. L. asked, "And what is a sonata?" "Well," Leland replied, "it's a form of music they played in chambers—kind of like old-fashioned parlors—and a lot of composers wrote them—Bach, Haydn, Scarlatti, Beethoven."

In subsequent lessons, the class listened to other Mozart sonatas. Although Leland continued his documentary responses at level 1, the teacher was able to establish the three-movement form as the inherent structure of sonatas of the Haydn-Mozart period by teaching the class as a whole to listen and to put their discoveries into words. "There is a tune that they play over and over—I think it is called a theme." "I heard a fast part, then a slow part, then a fast part." "This music has a lot of harmony.

One day the teacher said, "What does Mozart usually do to make the second movement distinct from the first and third movements?" Leland said, "I think the central movements in the sonatas we've heard have been in a subdominant key." Leland had put the pieces of his experience together to make an important conceptualization.

The class was ready to analyze what the composer had done within the separate movements, and they began by listening to several first movements. "The theme was repeated several times." "It keeps changing keys." "The violin and the piano took turns." "It's strong and then sad, strong and then sad." "He kept alternating between tonic and dominant harmony." When the characteristic of contrast in the first movement had been established, new materials appeared in the music center of the classroom: recordings of sonatas by other composers, biographies about Mozart and others, paper lined for musical scores, and books about music by Aaron Copland and other modern composers.

During one music period, the teacher asked, "If you were writing a sonata, what are the different ways you might get this contrasting effect into the first movement?" Several students, including Leland, began exploring at the keyboard until they found themes they wanted to develop into first movements of a sonata form.

Several times, they played what they had written, and each explained to the class his plans for varying and developing his theme. Often the teacher responded with questions: "If you want it more playful, what instrumentation might do this for you?" "How can you alter the tempo?" "How did Mozart achieve a mood of gaiety?" The children would have a friend or two provide other instrumentation so that they could try the effects of different instruments in the development of a theme. After several weeks of homework and choice-time effort, Leland and four other students had each composed an elementary version of the first movement in a classical binary form. The satisfaction that Leland and his companions would derive from continuing to create their own music was evident to Mr. L. They already had the motivation and the experience to proceed with the slower, subdominant development of the central movement and the lively, climactic return to the tonic key in the recapitulation. Seeing them play, he realized they had not been hampered by the intellectual discovery of the art form, but had found a new mode of communication and expression. Many children who are talented aesthetically but not highly gifted intellectually will need to find different avenues to freedom in creative expression.

Five sixth-grade pupils in Mr. L.'s classroom composed their own sonatas. The teacher valued their knowledge, and they were encouraged by his interest. The reader may find it easier to engage in similar creative teaching with his own students by examining the key happenings in these pupils' attempts at musical composition. The crucial steps in the teaching seemed to include (1) the nurturing of an interest in music, already present; (2) the decision to use an intellectual approach; and (3) the choice of Mozart and the sonata form as vehicles for helping pupils conceptualize the structure of a musical composition, prior to their own attempts to create a sonata themselves. As Mr. L. asked the questions about the movements, particularly about the contrasts in the first movement, he drew their attention to relations they might otherwise have missed. The clarity of the form in Mozart's compositions and the rich reservoir of pieces helped clarify the relationships while keeping the pupils' interest alive with new experiences that were similar enough to the old ones to strengthen the lessons. Another crucial step to success in composing occurred when the children were asked how they thought they could achieve contrast if they were composing a sonata. No direct suggestion was made, but the implication was clear that they could write a sonata if they really wanted to. At this point they did.

### Using a Manipulative Approach to Creativity

Even for highly intellectual students, a manipulative approach to creative production in the arts may be the most direct and constructive avenue to original work. A manipulative approach is an introduction to creative work through direct exploratory experiences with the medium or material, which leads to an understanding of the possibilities in the material and finding an aesthetically satisfying way to self-expression. The material may be as concrete as clay, as symbolic as numerals, as empathic as a sociodrama, or as semantic as words that make up a poem. This diversity in the possible media implies a broad definition of manipulation to include kinesthetic, aesthetic, intellectual, or emotional experience. Basic associations are formed as the learner makes trial-and-error maneuvers, explores various arrangements, and puts objects and ideas into various juxtapositions. The relationships that are satisfying to him are identified and remembered as useful modes of self-expression.

An example of this process of learning through manipulation can be observed in the experiences of Donna, a high school art student, who became a creative painter and sculptor. Donna used her electives and most of her extra course privileges to study art with Miss F., who taught painting, crafts, and ceramics. This teacher began each new sequence with a different medium and allowed almost unlimited freedom in choice of subject matter and technique. Students who needed stimulation to get started were encouraged to arrange setups, but most students selected their own "models" or drew from memory. When the students had produced a collection of works, the class would evaluate them with the help of Miss F.'s constructive but analytical guidance. Because the subject of each painting was unique, the elements of art emerged as principles of artistic expression rather than as criticism of specific pieces.

One day the evaluation discussion concerned balance as an element of composition. "Does this mean," asked Donna, "that formal balance doesn't hold the viewer's interest because it is *too* obvious?"

This was a critical conceptualization for Donna, who had been troubled by a conflict between the conventional idea of balance and her own emerging taste. She knew she preferred asymmetrical and complicated design, but did not quite know why. The class discussion validated her preference and helped her understand the reason behind what she had considered to be an atypical taste.

In this way Donna conceptualized the contributions of color, texture, rhythm, light, and shape to the message or feeling she wanted to express. Reinforcement came primarily from the day-to-day growth in her power to communicate through her art, but it came also from Miss F.'s respected comments, from supportive interaction with fellow students, and from recognition in the form of awards in regional and national exhibits. These various kinds of reinforcement built the motivation to continue the cycle of association building, conceptualization, and creation. That Donna and several other classmates went on to become recognized painters and sculptors was evidence of the effectiveness of this approach toward developing creativity in students.

## ANALYSIS OF THE TEACHER'S ROLE

A number of examples of creative self-direction have been presented, ranging from the simple activities of a kindergarten child playing with a bolt board to the mature education of a painter and sculptor. The recurring theme has been the student's coming to control himself and his work through learning. In each example, the teacher's role was shown to be important and satisfying, even though it contained elements of uncertainty.

One of the first requisites, if creativity is to be fostered, is that the teacher have what amounts to dedication, or at least a passionate belief in the importance of whatever it is he is trying to teach. Equally important is his belief in the power of the young minds he may be influencing greatly.

Good teachers have learned to avoid thrusting students, head on, into situations with which they cannot cope. To get the process started, such teachers find ways to help students surmount the inevitable hurdles that come up and to meet frustrations that might otherwise be overpowering. At the same time, however, their assistance is such that the student remains free to express himself in his own way. These teachers raise the young person up to his own best possibilities. Sometimes they must begin with seeming nonessentials: "Where would you put the edge of the sea?" "How would you tell the story to your mother?" "How would Sally tell about the trip?" "Which foot do you move first?"

Many professional courses emphasize control and discipline—these are the materials out of which teachers' lives are fashioned. The teacher who can elevate his classes from the humdrum level of routine learning to the level of creativity will almost certainly move the problem of control to an entirely different plane. As a teacher, start on this basis before you know it is impossible. Remember the bumblebee, who does not know that according to the laws of aerodynamics he cannot fly, and so flies anyway.

Creative teaching is not aimless teaching, nor does it consist in letting students do as they please. Creative teaching has a pattern, as a poem or a play has structure, and has goals, as a research project or a novel has purpose. It can be evaluated, as a symphony or a bridge can be. Creative teachers are rewarded when they see their students' hidden talents unlocked, enabling them to do the creative work of which they are capable.

Often the creativity consists in the way students attack their learning. Sometimes reaching the goal is *not* so important as the progress, but it is important that there be some direction to the enterprise. A warning should be sounded that even the best creative teachers are not able to use these special techniques all day, every day. There are flat spots and low spots, when no one seems quite up to creative output. Sometimes it is necessary to come down off the mountaintop, but it is something to know that there is a mountain.

## SUMMARY

Freedom is the distinctive feature of creative self-direction; the individual assumes initiative for his own activity. When children or young people are permitted to assume this initiative, complications may develop for the teacher. In school, the process of creativity is more important than what is produced because these early efforts need reinforcement, even when they are less than superior when judged by adult standards. Related to the individual's assumption of initiative is his escape from control by others. One of the difficulties that confront the teacher who encourages freedom in students concerns the indeterminism of level 3 learning, which requires individualized evaluation criteria. However, teaching students to become self-directing is also richly rewarding in unexpected ways.

In this chapter, the reality of past experience, as evidenced by electrode retrieval of stored memories, was suggested as philosophic evidence of freedom. One of the contra-arguments presented concerned the orderliness of the universe and the predictability of cause and effect. However, the difference between individual action and mass action, of which the individual action is a part, blunts the argument, particularly when the orderliness relates to people. The emergence of more complex and less predictable facets of the universe, as the system became older, was suggested in support of the reality of human freedom. Examples of decision making were cited in the flexibility in habits and the possibility of breaking them. The need for nonconformity as a facet of identity creation was presented as further evidence for freedom.

MacKinnon studied eminent individuals who had already produced recognized creative works. He defined creativity as involving (1) the production of something new or rare, (2) some direction toward a recognizable goal, and (3) the completion of a product. The creative people in MacKinnon's study were of above-average intelligence, but beyond this point intelligence did not correlate significantly with creativity. They scored high on originality tests and were shown to be open to new experience. They were oriented to both theoretical and aesthetic values. In suggesting ways of teaching these characteristics, MacKinnon emphasized the kinds of experiences that would develop creatively self-directing people.

Guilford's emphasis on divergent and convergent production as aspects of creativity was examined in the context of three creative processes that can be improved by learning: (1) fluency, which is concerned primarily with retrieval of specific items of information; (2) flexibility, which can be in terms of classes, such as round or square, or transformations, such as rearranging elements into a new configuration; and (3) elaboration, which involves developing a system or theory from the basic outlines that have been determined.

Torrance developed test materials for identification of gifted children. Tumin listed obstacles to creativity. Getzels and Jackson studied the relationship between creativity and intelligence. Wallas's steps in the creative process were preparation, incubation, illumination, and elaboration.

The affective domain of Krathwohl, Bloom, and Masia was compared with the learning-motivation model. Maslow's theory of self-actualization for motivation indicates a distinction between deficit needs, which lead people to depend on others, and fulfillment needs, for which people depend on themselves. The final section of the chapter illustrated ways of developing creative self-direction in the classroom.

## SELF-DIRECTING ACTIVITIES

1 List 10 instances of activities in your own life in which your decisions were personal and individual rather than controlled by circumstance. This should be within a period of the last two days.
2 Provide a group of students an opportunity for creative experience. Record the different ways in which they responded to the opportunity.
3 Help a group of students develop a creative way of handling a problem of social interaction.
4 Use the steps in the learning-motivation model to help you achieve a creative experience for yourself.

# Chapter 9

Good nutrition is necessary for good brain function. (*Courtesy of the United Nations*)

# NEUROLOGY OF LEARNING

A knowledge of the biology of learning
will provide an understanding of how
experiences are stored and motivations
are learned. This chapter should enable
you to:

⬤ Define the anatomy of learning:
neuron, synapse, central nervous system

⬤ Trace the causes of some learning
difficulties to brain functioning

⬤ Identify the brain mechanisms that
receive process and respond to stimuli

⬤ State the physiological basis of
motivation

⬤ Conceptualize the evidence for
self-direction

⬤ Use the following terms correctly:
dendrites
axons
medulla oblongata
cerebellum
cortex
transduction
reticular formation
limbic system
slow wave potential
minimal brain dysfunction
aphasia
medial forebrain bundle

The interest of psychologists in the physical mechanisms of learning has fluctuated. There have been periods in the development of psychological thought when the principal theories emphasized the way in which the nervous system functions in the learning process. In the early studies of behaviorism, when the conditioned response was considered to be the model of the learning process, the reflex arc was thought to be the basic neural unit. The arc consisted of a sensory nerve, a connecting nerve, and a motor nerve, through which energy flowed, resulting in overt behavior. This conceptualization of the neurological process within the organism was supplemented by a statement that the model was oversimplified. Although the connecting nerve was described as a complex set of connections, the process was still considered to be a three-part mechanism.

At the same time, psychologists were adapting statistical techniques to the measurement and prediction of human behavior. Watson (1913) and others showed a disposition to emphasize external stimulus situations and the behavior that was associated with these stimuli. Influential psychologists advocated that neurology be left to the neurologists and that research time be spent on psychological problems. In this climate, the important work consisted of studying the responses that occurred when certain changes in the stimulus pattern were made. This approach has been productive. A great deal is now known about what will happen when stimuli are changed in certain ways. Predictions can be made about the outcomes of certain procedures. Such findings are particularly useful in studying and handling large groups of people. For example, a male student, aged nineteen, with a high school grade point average (GPA) of 3.2 in mathematics and physics and a GPA of 2.5 in English and history may be expected to fail in a foreign language major at a particular

university, but to maintain passing grades in the school of engineering. With this kind of information, students can be counseled into programs where they are likely to succeed. Mathematical curves can be graphed that project individual performances remarkably well.

In spite of the amazing successes that psychology has achieved in large-scale prediction, the teacher should understand the individual student who behaves differently from the way he is expected to. The teacher may have some nagging doubts about why Tommy does not quite fit the pattern, even though he may not matter in a statistical sense. If a procedure works 90 percent of the time with 90 percent of the students, a level of successful control has been attained that is so much better than the former level that it seems unrealistic to worry about either the 10 percent with whom the procedure does not work or the 10 percent of the time it fails. If a university, which has a dropout rate of 45 percent, applies the differential prediction data to reduce the dropout rate to 10 percent, the testing and counseling staff have cause for immense satisfaction. But for Tommy, who met the entrance criteria but became one of the 10 percent who flunked, the outcome is akin to disaster. The point is that whatever happens in school is happening to individuals. A decision that adversely affects even one student is important if you are that student or if he is one of your children.

Measurement and prediction of educational outcomes have stimulated much of the improvement in school programs. However, the increasing necessity to prevent the educational casualties that occur to some extent in all systems and at all levels compels the educational psychologist and the prospective teacher to try to understand the physiological processes that result in learning. Clinicians and others who diagnose learning difficulties have long been aware of a relationship between certain speech and reading problems and neurological dysfunctions. A knowledge of the biology of learning is convincing evidence that the changes that occur with learning are real. Neuropsychology and related sciences focus on the neurological growth that occurs during the learning-experience process.

## FUNCTION OF NEUROLOGICAL UNDERSTANDING

A look at the research in neurology, particularly that published during the last five years, shows how the statistically common individual operates and also how some individuals come to vary significantly from the usual pattern.

Understanding the processes that go on in the neurological system enables the teacher to plan for desired effects, rather than to function on a trial-and-error basis. When he overlooks some essential variable in a learner, the lesson plans go awry for that student. The teacher who works from a conceptualization of the neurological interaction of cognitive and emotional learning will find his errors with certain students to be instructive rather than merely negative.

Even the inexperienced teacher who tries a creative approach to a learning problem can analyze where a lesson went wrong and can refine his creative approach, rather than succumb to frustration, resort to a stereotype technique, or imitate the veteran across the hall. This systematic and intelligent modification of one's own teaching plans is the beginning of artistry in teaching. An understanding of the nature of learning as it takes place in the brain sets the professional apart from the amateur, no matter how skilled the latter may be.

The neurological system can be presented in a number of different ways. The authors have chosen to use a straightforward approach and to develop the content in terms of (1) the structure and functions of the neurological system, (2) selected research on how the brain functions in learning, and (3) an interpretation of the learning-motivation model within the framework of the physiological structure.

## PHYSIOLOGY OF THE NERVOUS SYSTEM

The nervous system of man is a complex network of electrochemical message carriers. The *neuron* is the basic energy unit, or message carrier, and the *synapse* is a gap or junction across which the connection to other neurons is made. Connection points impede or facilitate the flow of information between the neurons, which have a potential for accumulating and discharging electrochemical impulses. The synapse is a seperation point between the axons of one neuron and the dendrites or cell body of another, with an average distance of about one-millionth of an inch between them. In transmission, the gap is apparently bridged by chemical agents, often acetylcholine. The bridge is then removed by another chemical agent, probably cholinesterase. Synaptic knobs of one neuron terminate among the dendrites of other neurons (Figure 9-1). Recently a distinction was made between these chemical synapses and "electrical" junctions through which a continuation of electrical impulses flows from one neuron to another by direct contact (Handler, 1970). An additional system of *slow wave potentials* that move across rather than through the dendrites has also been postulated (Pribram, 1971).

### The Neuron

All neurons consist of an input system made up of the *dendrites;* a *cell body*; and an output system, the *axons*. Typically the current flows from the dendrites through the cell body and out the axons. A mnemonic device for remem-

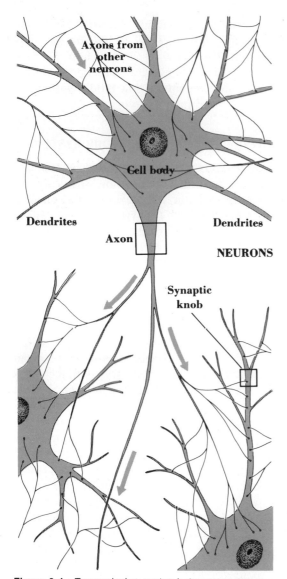

**Figure 9-1**  Transmission routes between neurons.

by changes in sound, heat, cold, light, or pressure; the *effector*, or output, neurons, whose axons terminate in muscle fibers or glands; and the *connector* neurons, which unite other neurons. The connector neurons are the most numerous by far and are the neurons with which this discussion is most concerned.

In the connector neurons, the dendrites receive electrical charges that accumulate in the cell body until the potential dissipates or until the charge grows large enough to trigger a discharge through the axon. The discharge of the axon is precipitated by a change in the electrical potential of the cell body from the normal 70-millivolt value to something on the order of 60 millivolts. (As electrons accumulate, the millivolt value decreases.) This change in electrical potential of the cell body extends into the axon a short distance. When the electrical potential changes to about 60 millivolts, the membrane of the axon changes character and allows sodium ions to enter and displace potassium ions (Figure 9-2). This change is progressive along the axon in the direction the current flows—that is, away from the cell body toward the end of the axon. Immediately after the discharge takes place, an excess of electrons enters the axon, creating a refractory period, during which time the axon will not fire. The electrons dissipate rapidly, leading to a period of partial refraction when the axon will fire only if the excitation of the cell body is unusually strong.

Whether a neuron fires or not is complicated by a fail-safe mechanism that usually requires input from two or more axons before activation takes place and by input from inhibitor axons. An inhibitor changes the permeability of the membrane around the cell body in such a way as to increase the flow of potassium ions into the cell body and to resist the flow of sodium ions. The possibilities are shown in Figure 9-3.

The nature of the flow of the current—the

bering the direction in which the current flows is to remember that the flow is in reverse of alphabetical order, from dendrites (D) to cell (C) body (B) to axon (A). There are at least three kinds of neurons: the *receptor*, or input, neurons in which the dendrites are equipped with sense detectors such as those activated exchanging of potassium ions for sodium ions —ensures that the strength of the current will not diminish no matter how long the axon may be. Axons vary from a fraction of a millimeter to a meter in length. The speed of the current flow is proportional to the diameter of the axon.

To summarize, the input of energy to the neuron comes through the dendrites into the cell body, where it accumulates and fires or where decay of the potential takes place. If the energy input accumulates sufficiently, the permeability of the membrane changes, allowing sodium ions to replace potassium ions and thus passing the change in potential to a new portion of the axon. This process continues until the end of the axon is reached at a synapse. The axons end in many branches with potential connections to many dendrites. The dendrites of the cell body are also numerous and are able to absorb energy from many different axons with connections to other cell bodies.

### The Synapse

As explained earlier, the gap, or separation point, between an axon of one neuron and the dendrites of another neuron is a chemical synapse. The physiology of the synapse is under intensive study. De Robertis (1964) has described the different kinds of synapses, the various ways in which they function, and the differential effects of certain ions—potassium ions encourage transmission, and calcium ions inhibit it. Krech, Rosenzweig, and Bennett (1958) indicated that the connections across some synapses are made by the bridging action of acetylcholine, which is then washed away by cholinesterase. The relationship between the enzymes acetylcholine and cholinesterase has been described in considerable detail by Eccles and Jaeger (1958). Handler (1970) includes norepinephrine and serotonin as enzymes that form bridges across synaptic

clefts. There is some indication that as the process becomes better stabilized—as more bridgings are made at one synapse—the distance across the synapse narrows and transmission becomes progressively easier. Since the space to be bridged is on the order of one-millionth of an inch, direct examination of the process is difficult (Figure 9-4). Flow of energy seems to be facilitated as learning of particular material takes place. This learning may be due to an increase in the electrical potential within a neuron, an increase in the number of neurons that are excited, a lowering of the resistance at the synapse by growth, a

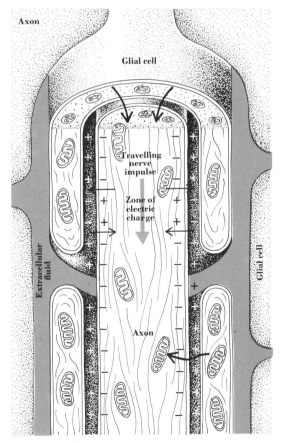

**Figure 9-2** Neural impulse in an axon.

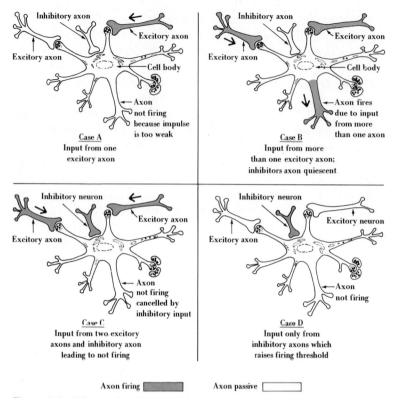

**Figure 9-3** Effects of excitory and inhibitory axon action.

chemically facilitated bridging, or some other mechanism.

Learning is more than changes in the synapse. Two other biological processes include changes in RNA or other complex molecules and slow wave potentials in the fine dendritic structures.

### The Central Nervous System

Most neural activity takes place in the central nervous system (CNS), which includes the spinal cord and the various parts of the brain. The nerves or neurons of the body are collected and sometimes coordinated in the spinal cord. At the top of the cord is the *medulla oblongata*, a collection of neurons that control

the respiratory, cardiovascular, and gastrointestinal reflexes (Figure 9-5). The *cerebellum* is a similar control center for proprioceptive information—muscle tone, balance, and body movement and position. With the *pons*, these constitute what is called the *lower brainstem* and are concerned primarily with the automatic aspects of living.

The *higher brainstem*, including the *midbrain*, and the *lower brainstem* constitute what is sometimes called the *old brain*, which phylogenetically predates the cortical areas. The cerebral hemispheres, which constitute the *cerebrum*, are the two large masses that make up the bulk of the brain, including their outer layer—the *cortex*. The cerebral hemispheres elaborate the functions of the higher brainstem and seem to be the area that distinguishes peculiarly human thought processes from those of other animals. Located in the upper brainstem are the coordinating and integrating centers that control consciousness and give the present, ongoing dimension to experience. The midbrain—which is associated with the reflex actions as well as with the voluntary functions of the higher brainstem—seems to be the center of consciousness. Sectioning through this area leaves an animal, after recovery from an anesthetic, without conscious reactions—as though it were still anesthetized.

Although the lower brainstem, the midbrain, and the cerebrum each have been given a name, it is inaccurate to think of them as discrete areas, separate from one another. All are collections of neurons that interact with one another in varying ways. The midbrain performs many of the functions of the lower and the upper brainstems. However, particular parts of the human brain have significance for certain functions that are well established, so that the location is the same in different individuals. Also, there are systems of redundancy in the brain; for example, at least six different areas are available and are used simultaneously to record information from a person's visual contact with the world outside himself. The characteristics of the mechanism for cross-linkages between visual areas of the brain are inherited. Except for a flexibility that allows some areas of the brain to take over the functions of damaged or sectioned areas, the location of a particular function in a particular part of the brain is also genetically ordered.

## EXPLORATIONS OF THE NERVOUS SYSTEM

Many scientists have contributed to the knowledge about the physiology of the nervous system. Brain surgeons have discovered the functions of various sections of the human brain as they attempted to alleviate diseases of the nervous system. Using laboratory animals, scientists have been able to conduct experiments that entail dissection and chemical analysis of the brain. Some studies, using animals as simple as planaria and as complex as apes, have pinpointed the neurological effects of learning experiences. Unusual accidents involving human brain injuries have led to serendipitous discoveries about the brain and individual behavior.

### Technique of Brain Charting

Penfield and Roberts, in *Speech and Brain Mechanisms* (1959), summarized case study data to explain their findings on the function-

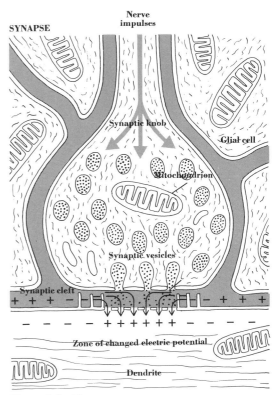

**Figure 9-4** The synapse.

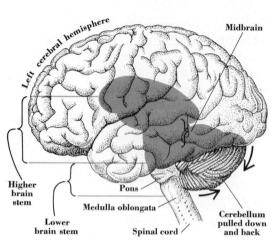

**Figure 9-5** The brain. (*From W. Penfield & L. Roberts, Speech and Brain Mechanisms, Princeton N.J.: Princeton University Press. © 1959. Reprinted by permission of Princeton University Press.*)

ing of the brain. Their work was done in the clinic of the Montreal Neurological Institute. People came to this clinic with serious illnesses: epilepsy, brain tumors, head injuries, and other diseases involving the nervous system. They had come to the medical practitioners to be cured. This was a practical rather than a theoretical situation, although theory played a definite part in the acceptance of treatment by the patients. The explorations that were made, the diagnoses that resulted, and the treatment that was carried out were directed toward the solution of problems that were afflicting particular individuals. Much of the surgery at Montreal was performed under conditions of local anesthesia so that the patient could continue to give information concerning the effects of particular operating procedures. The brain, protected by the skull, does not have pain nerves of its own, so that this kind of exploration is feasible.

One of the early procedures used by Penfield and Roberts involved mapping the affected area of the brain. Ordinarily, this was done with a very fine electrode, insulated except at the tip, which stimulated activity in

particular neurons. The reaction of the patient, such as motor or sensory responses, indicated to the operating team the function of the area stimulated by the electrode. The exposed area was mapped, ticketed, and photographed. As exploration progressed, the detailed information was dictated to and recorded by a secretary.

The effect of the electrode stimulation was to interfere with the normal functioning of the brain at the point of stimulation. The electrodes often elicited responses that surprised the patient, since his actions were not accompanied by the volition usually necessary to elicit them. When a patient saw his hand moving from here to there without his having willed to move it, the experience was probably unsettling. Even more disturbing was his wanting to move his hand and finding that nothing happened, no matter how much effort he exerted. Speech was most often inhibited by the electrodes, although in certain parts of the brain stimulation elicited involuntary speech sounds. Under these conditions, it was important for the patient and the doctor to understand the nature of what was being done and why the exploration was conducted as it was. By accumulating the carefully recorded data from many surgical patients, Penfield and Roberts were able to describe the functions of various areas of the brain and to predict where these areas would be located in the brains of future patients as well as normal human beings.

## Input Systems

Input to the sense organs is in the form of physical or chemical energy, which stimulates the receptors. In this initial phase of perception the acuity, the accuracy, and the intensity of the input are important in learning. Defects in acuity or in the physiological apparatus for conduction are called *organic defects*. Individuals differ in the range and effectiveness with which their sensory apparatus picks up information. There are established criteria for determining normal acuity of vision, audition, and other senses. One of the first distinctions that must be made in diagnosing learning difficulties is between acuity of sense-organ reception, which is organic in nature, and perceptual interpretation, which is functional.

## Transduction into Neural Impulses

Sense organs respond selectively within rather narrow ranges of sensitivity, and individual receptor neurons respond even more selectively. The normal human eye, for example, responds to electromagnetic radiation, or light energy, that falls between wavelengths of 400 and 800 millimicrons. Human beings with normal hearing are stimulated by sound vibrations that fall between 10 and 20,000 cycles per second (cps). Just as individuals differ in their sensitivity to auditory and visual stimuli, so do they differ in their sensitivity to tactile, kinesthetic, and olfactory cues. *Transduction* is the process by which stimulation of particular neural endings is changed into electrochemical messages for transmission through the neuron. Activation in a particular sense organ must be transduced and reach the brain before the person is aware of stimulation. In the sense of touch, for example, specialized dendrites terminate in minute spiral coils that, when compressed sufficiently, trigger an electrochemical flow in the neurons of which they are a part. After this differential compression has taken place in many dendrites and the messages have reached the brain, the person feels the roughness, smoothness, or resistance of the object touched. Specialized structures of the dendrites differentiate the kinds of stimulation transmitted. These include heat, cold, pain, and deep pressure sensations. In the senses of smell and taste, chemical changes initiate transductions into similar electrochemical codes.

## Transmission of Coded Sensations

The electrochemical codes from the transducers are transmitted through activated neurons to the brain. For instance, a sound vibration of 1,500 cps activates different nerve endings from those activated by a vibration of 70 cps. The message that arrives in the brain is translated on the basis of past learning or experience with this sound. This example is oversimplified, and the reader should try to appreciate the complexity of perceptual functions in hearing and speech. The neurons from particular sense organs lead to appropriate areas in the brain. Sometimes failure in a sensory system, such as hearing, occurs not in the sense organ itself but in some of the neurons that carry the message from the receiving mechanism to the CNS. Since it is unusual for all the neurons connected to the different auditory sense mechanisms to be defective at once, people suffering from "hearing nerve damage" are usually selectively deaf. They hear some voices better than others. Often teachers make adjustments in their classroom procedures to minimize their own handicaps or those of students. An examination of two input systems that have obvious importance in school learning will make some of the mechanisms more easily understood.

**Visual Input**   Most human beings are particularly oriented to input from optic sources. Normally this information is integrated with that coming from auditory, olfactory, or tactile senses. The eye provides vast quantities of information from both distant and near sources. The structure of the eye has been studied in detail, making it possible to be explicit about how information is processed.

The eye is a system of lenses and fluids designed to bring images of the external world to focus on the retina. It is important that the image be sharp since this is the only kind of data that the retina is prepared to handle without difficulty.

The retina is made up of three general layers (Figure 9-6). The layer on which the image is focused is made up of about 120 million rods and cones, which are photochemically sensitive. The layer closest to the brain, the inner layer, is made up of some 6 million ganglion cells, whose axons form the optic nerve to the brain. Between this layer of transmitters and the outer layer of receptors is a layer of interconnecting cells which combine sensations from many rods and cones. Although some of the rods and cones seem to be con-

nected directly with single ganglion cells, most second layer organizers form complex connections between rods and cones by means of flat bipolar, horizontal, and amacrine cells. This reduction from 120 million to 6 million cells between the three layers of the retina almost certainly has a bearing on the interpretation of the information supplied by the light sources. Certain brain cells respond to lines, others to angles, some to color, and still others to movement. Logically, a stimulus conveying information about a line would require input from a series of cells that were reported as a single unit. Rods and cones fire and then go through a period of inhibited refraction. Thus change from activation to inhibition provides temporal data that are part of the electrochemical code of the neurons (Pribram, 1971, p. 57).

The ganglion cells terminate at a relay point, the lateral geniculate nucleus, of the thalamus in the brainstem. Other neurons relay information both to the reticular formation and to various parts of the visual cortex. It is in the thalamic area that the integration of visual information with that from other senses takes place. This integrating mechanism will be explored further after a review of auditory input.

**Auditory Input**   Hearing is initiated when sound waves enter through the canal of the outer ear and vibrate the eardrum (Figure 9-7). This physical energy in the form of vibrations is amplified, as much as 90 times, by the lever action of the ossicles in the middle ear (Figure 9-8). The amplified vibrations are transferred to the organ of Corti in the inner ear, causing the membranes to move against one another. This differential movement activates specific hair cells, depending on the undulations of the waves in the membranes. As particular hair cells are activated, they transduce the mechanical energy of movement into electrochemical impulses characteristic of neural

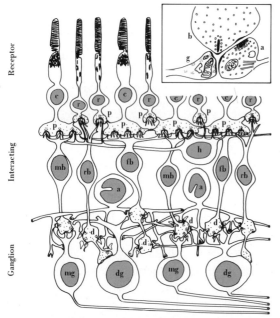

**Figure 9-6**  Receptor and connector neurons in the retina. (Note the contacts between receptors, the widespread connections of the horizontal cells and the amacrine cells, and the vertical arrangement of the bipolars. r-ro, c-cone, mb-midget bipolar, fb- flat bipolar, h-horizontal cell, a-amacrine cell, mg-midget ganglion cell, d-dyad synapse, dg-diffuse ganglion cell, p-pedicel. Inset shows details of a dyad synapse. (*By permission of the publisher and authors, J. E. Dowling & B. B. Boycott, Proceedings of the Royal Society B., copyright 1966, 92.*)

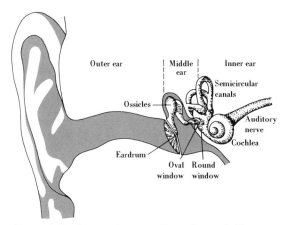

**Figure 9-7** Organs for reception of sound. The eardrum transmits sound vibrations to the ossicles, which set up waves in the fluid of the cochlea. The semicircular canals are the vestibular formation, which is not part of the ear, but initiates sensory data regarding body balance and position. (*From D. E. Broadbent, Attention and the reception of speech, Scientific American. Copyright © 1962 by Scientific American, Inc. All rights reserved.*)

firing. The coded messages are transmitted to the hearing areas of the brain through neurons of the auditory nerve that are selected by their sensitivity to particular hair cells (Figure 9-9). The frequency of the sound determines where along the membrane in the organ of Corti the sound wave will crest, thus determining which hair cells and related neurons will be activated.

The perception of sound intensity, which is related to loudness, depends upon the energy of the movement of the membrane in the organ of Corti but also on feedback from the middle ear, where automatic adjustments are made to dampen or increase extreme ranges of amplification.

The coded auditory sensations feed into junctions—which are collections of neuron bodies—that relay the messages to the hearing system and to other interconnecting systems. Even before birth, an individual begins to accumulate sound memories that have neural

connections with stored input from the other senses.

Related systems for other senses are traced in detail in the sections on growth and development of the perceptual systems. The integration of the ongoing present (Penfield, 1969) is concerned with arousal, attention, pleasure, and punishment loadings, as well as the putting together of inputs from diverse sensory systems.

## INTEGRATION IN THE OLD BRAIN

Much of life, even in human beings, is controlled and operated from centers in the old brain. Basically the old brain makes up the neural mechanisms between the spinal cord and the cortex, although the areas and the functioning are not always clear. The different sensory systems have axons that terminate in the brainstem before continuing to specialized areas of the cortex. From the synapses of the

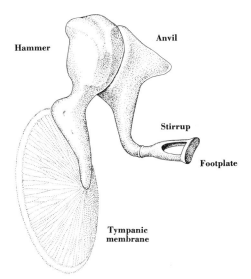

**Figure 9-8** Bones of the middle ear and tympanum. (*Adapted from G. von Békésy, The ear, Scientific American, 1957, 197, 68. Copyright © 1957 by Scientific American, Inc. All rights reserved.*)

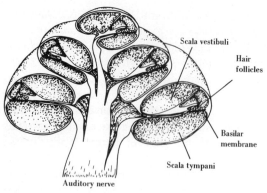

**Figure 9-9** Cross section of the cochlea. This organ looks like a snail from the outside and has chambers of decreasing size on the inside. Scala vestibuli and scala tympani are filled with fluid in which waves are set up. (*From D. E. Broadbent, Attention and the perception of speech, p. 144. Copyright © 1962 by Scientific American, Inc. All rights reserved.*)

transmitting neurons, lateral neurons go into the structures of the old brain, carrying the coded sensory information with them. Among the important parts of the old brain are (1) an ill-defined *reticular formation*, which seems to be the integrator system, as well as being involved in arousal and attention; (2) the *limbic system*, which is important because of its effect on emotional responses; (3) the *diencephalon*, including the thalamus and the hypothalamus, which controls temperature, blood pressure, heart rate, vascular dilation, sweating, salivating, weeping, shivering, hiccoughing, and yawning. Another way in which the old brain is sometimes divided is upper, mid, and lower brainstems.

Individuals do not separate what they see and hear during an experience, although, if required to do so, they are able to attend selectively and also to remember without confusion. The separate experiences are fed into the system discretely and then integrated. Nothing that stimulates the hearing has any noticeable effect on the eyes, and it is only when the sense materials have been integrated within the reticular formation that integrated

experience is possible. The mechanism by which this integration takes place involves the use of unspecialized neural cells that are able to respond to coded inputs from specialized sensory neurons.

## Pleasure and Punishment

Probably the most important function of the old brain, as far as school learning is concerned, is motivation for continuing or abandoning an activity. These affective functions are seated in the limbic system and have been studied by implanting electrodes in rats, monkeys, and men to stimulate neural centers associated with feelings of pleasure or punishment. The story of the initial discovery of these centers is one of the happy accidents that occasionally occurs in scientific work.

The story of how Olds (1956) discovered what he called pleasure centers has been told in Chapter 2. This finding of specific areas of the brain that control whether an activity will be repeated or will be avoided is fundamental to understanding the mechanics of motivation: Those connections that are linked to pleasure stimulation promote learning; those that are linked to punishment centers usually lead to avoidance. However, in individual experience the punishment may be overridden by pleasure that is derived from successfully overcoming the source of the psychological punishment.

The restrictions on research using human subjects makes it increasingly difficult to implant electrodes into the brains of children or adults. One of the published examples is work by Heath (1963) in New Orleans, who used pleasure stimulation to treat a man suffering from narcolepsy so severe that he would fall asleep every two minutes. By means of a portable device this man could stimulate himself frequently enough to be able to hold a position as a night club entertainer. The patient, who obviously was not falling asleep nearly as much under this treatment as he had previously, reported the stimulation as generating a feeling of mild euphoria.

Punishment is frowned upon as a way of treating both human beings and animals; however, most punishment studies have been on animals since they are unable to protest. The laboratory experiment is designed so that the animal works to avoid the stimulus. While continued unavoidable punishment will cause an animal to die, relatively protracted periods of punishment can be counteracted if the subject experiences brief episodes of pleasure stimulation. In school the punishment possibilities of having to work hard are usually counteracted when success is achieved and the person performs to a level of expectation that is satisfactory in his own as well as the teacher's eyes. The need to work long enough with a student so that he achieves the pleasure reinforcement from mastery of the task is obvious even though it may be difficult in practice.

## Arousal and Attention

When the environment changes in some way, an individual responds neurologically. The initial stimulation is general, with signals moving from the reticular formation to all parts of the cortex. This generalized response is called *arousal*, or sometimes the *startle reflex*. During arousal, control is vested in the mesencephalic portion of the reticular formation (Figure 9-10). Messages are cycled through different parts of the limbic or motivation system as well as to many parts of the sensory cortex. Not much learning takes place during this kind of brain activity, although the process is essential for selection of the sensory stimulation the organism will attend to.

The state of arousal shifts to one of *attention* as soon as the nature of the change in the

environment can be determined. Attention is a focused response to stimuli that have become relevant to the individual. Neurologically the control shifts from the mesencephalic to the thalamic portions of the reticular formation (Figure 9-11). Most of the stimulation to the different parts of the cortex is reduced and channeled to those areas that process the type of data selected. Interaction with the limbic system continues particularly with the pleasure/punishment centers. It is during attention that most learning takes place and that memory storage is initiated.

Attention is not ordinarily given to the same stimulus for a protracted period of time. Either new stimuli intrude, demanding attention, or habituation sets in. *Habituation* is automatic response to a stimulus situation. It can be likened to putting a plane on automatic pilot. Arousal reoccurs whenever a change in the stimulus pattern takes place. The change can be an increase in tempo or intensity, a decrease, or even a temporary cessation. Most students have experienced habituation as they

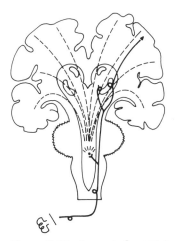

**Figure 9-10** Arousal: Control by the mesencephalic part of reticular formation. Stimuli are sent to all parts of the cortex and to the different parts of the limbic system. (*After Gastaut & Roger, 1960, 38.*)

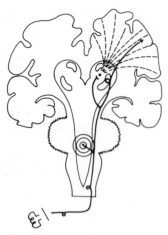

**Figure 9-11** Attention: Control shifts from mesencephalic to thalamic parts of reticular formation. The hypocampus of the limbic system is actively involved. Note the inhibition of most of the output to the cortex but the heavier involvement of one or two areas. (*After Gastaut & Roger, 1960, p. 38.*)

have listened to teachers who talked with little variety in intonation or mode of presentation. No matter how attentive the student is at the beginning, eventually habituation sets in and the words are heard but not attended to and not recorded.

Some highly distractible students, especially young children, behave as though they are constantly returning to an orienting response. They are affected by irrelevant stimuli and are unable to attend meaningfully to any of them for a sustained period of time. Feigenberg (1969) found that simple schizophrenics with well-developed psychoses (characterized by being out of touch with reality) often had no orienting reflex. Fifty-three percent of his subjects showed no orienting response, and only six percent had an adequate orienting reflex. The schizophrenic responds to an inner world that is divorced from the sensory world outside himself. This isolation cuts off the inputs necessary for the beginning of learning, and treatment is difficult.

### Building an Experiential Record

Penfield (1969) described that form of memory which records the ongoing present as an individual perceives it. This record seems to be formed as the multiple inputs from the different sense systems are integrated in the reticular formation with the pleasure or punishment loadings that come from the limbic system. "The strips of the stream of previous consciousness that we have been able to summon electrically are largely concerned with visual and auditory phenomena, together with previously attendant emotions and reactions" (p. 155). Only what is attended to seems to be stored "while other contemporary neural activity comes and goes without leaving a record."

A person whose memory was electronically stimulated had a "double-life" feeling, in which he watched himself live through experiences from the past. Frequently the episode that was recovered was a rather trivial one, and had long since been forgotten. Individualized records show that such patients actually heard and saw people—there was none of the confusion or vagueness that contaminates normal memory. They heard children playing in the street—specific children, as they were at a precise age, doing things at a precise time. The replay was unblurred by things that happened earlier or later. Events were relived such as conversations over a back fence about the PTA or a kind of curtain material being considered. The episodes involved nothing very important, but for a time they had been the focus of attention and were replayed in a state of vivid preservation. It is important to note that such trivial things as street noises were stored, while many important things were not. The experiential record of a particular day did not include the things to which the person was not paying attention at the time. If one were going to edit a slice of life, many of the things omitted from these experiential records would be considered worthy of notice, and much that was actually stored would be eliminated.

In these episodes, time moves forward. The record of experience does not play a bit of today and then switch to a bit of last week. If an episode out of the time sequence is called up, it is as something remembered during the sequence. The snatches of life that have been relived in this way have not been extensive. Most recorded observations have lasted less than half an hour. If the electrode is turned off and then switched on again—even a day later—the scene starts over again, beginning as it did at the first replay.

Sufficient evidence of storage of raw, unedited life experience has been reported to suggest that probably everything to which a person attends is stored in the neurological system, although "conscious effort gives any individual only limited access to this record" (p. 155). This storage material seems in some way to be available, at a subconscious level, for comparison of present and past experience. This experiential record, during its process of being formed, is the essence of perceiving. The details of the raw data of experience seem to be abstracted and form the substance of normal memory.

Most human activities involve interplay between the sense organs, the muscle systems, the old brain, and the cortex. Untangling the different strands of experience sometimes requires concentration on one aspect of an activity in order to understand it. It is hoped that the reader can hold these discrete chunks of information in suspension for later integration.

## The Physiology of Consciousness

It is interesting to note that consciousness and the integrative functions of the brain are not located in the cortex but are found in the old brain. Penfield and Roberts (1959) stated these ideas in this way:

There is evidence of a level of integration within the central nervous system that is higher than that to be found in the cerebral cortex. There is a regional localization of the neuronal mechanisms involved in this integration which is most intimately associated with the initiation of voluntary activity and with the sensory summation prerequisite to it. . . . All regions of the brain may well be involved in the normal conscious processes, but the indispensable substratum of consciousness lies outside the cerebral cortex . . . not in the new brain but in the old . . . probably in the diencephalon. . . .

There is a central integrating system situation in the higher brain stem. Integration reaches its highest level there . . . but it is presumably never divorced from the activity of some areas of the cortex and especially certain areas of the temporal lobes and the anterior portion of the frontal cortex.

Under normal circumstances, consciousness accompanies this combined activity. Consciousness disappears with the interruption of function in the centrencephalic system.

Bits of evidence which support this thesis are many. Any area of cortex may be removed on either side without loss of consciousness. All areas except those devoted to speech have been removed in our clinic at one time or another during the treatment of focal cortical epilepsy or for the control of involuntary movements. Whether or not the centrencephalic system could function at all if all areas could be removed at once in a single individual, is a question which cannot be answered. It must remain a matter of speculation as to the way in which the subject would still be considered to be conscious. On the other hand, any lesion, such as a tumor exerting pressure or some agent that interferes with the circulation in the higher brain stem, is accompanied by unconsciousness [pp. 20–22].

Consciousness is not limited to human beings. A moment's consideration suggests that no one would operate on a dog or a rat without an anesthetic, the purpose of which is to render the animal unconscious. What precisely is this consciousness that is important to human beings and presumably is shared by other higher animals?

Consciousness seems to include an element of the individual's awareness of self as distinct from everything else. The possibility of choice, at least among some alternatives, seems to be part of consciousness. A cat that has had the connections severed between the cortical hemispheres and the midbrain will still go on living. It will be able to swallow milk that is put into its mouth and withdraw its paw from a shock, but the responses will be automatic, with no flavor of decision. Such a cat is not considered to be conscious but is thought of as being unconscious and acting without volition. The cat is unaware of itself as a separate entity. Individual readers will define consciousness with their private variations, but a difference between a state of consciousness and a state of unconsciousness is easy to observe.

### MEMORY

The cortex is divided into two hemispheres which function together in memory. Visual images are stored in at least three parts of each, and auditory storage is similarly redundant. Motor responses can be initiated in either hemisphere from parallel locations. However, the hemispheres are different in definite ways. One hemisphere, usually the left, is dominant for speech. Similar areas in the nondominant hemisphere serve as the area of nonverbal interpretation of present experience or of perception (Penfield, 1969, p. 142).

In a normal event that leads to action of some kind, a sequence is followed from sensory stimulation, through neural processing, to a motor response (Figure 9-12). The sense organs receive and transduce information which is conveyed to the reticular formation and integrated with related information from other senses as well as with pleasure or punishment loadings. The ongoing experience is stored, but it also is separated and stored, with similar experiences already in storage, in the sensory input parts of the cortex; that is, the visual material goes to the visual areas of the cortex and the auditory data to the auditory cortex. The input then goes to the *ideation cortex*, to the *speech cortex*, or to both, depending on the nature of the input and the growth pattern of the individual. In any case, links to the opposite hemisphere are formed so that the ideation and the speech related to it are joined. Voluntary output originates in the higher brainstem in the medial forebrain bundle, and activates parts of the motor cortex where the response pattern is elaborated. Efferent neurons carry these directions, which stimulate appropriate muscle activity.

Memory is what the teacher's life is all about—both his own remembering of his content and that of the students who presumably are in school to learn. In daily living we are confronted with different memory needs, based on short- or long-term need for the information. Traditionally psychologists have distinguished between immediate recall and long-term memory. The temporal classification of memory forms is more complex than this dichotomy suggests, as is evident from neurological analyses of storage and retrieval.

The difference between storage and retrieval often confuses discussions of memory, because the observation and measurement of memory is usually based on successful retrieval. Penfield's "experiential record," retrieved in bits by electrode stimulation, logically indicates that even a telephone number attended to long enough for dialing is stored. Normally this information, like much of the experiential record, is unavailable for retrieval. The impinging environment that is not attended to does not become part of the ongoing experiential record and is not stored (Penfield, 1969). Students attend selectively to their lessons and store only the information on which they focus. When a person gets a new telephone number, it is processed into storage by frequent repetitions, analysis of numeral patterns within the sequence, and analogy to previous telephone numbers. The effect of these different experiences is to ensure that the new number is processed into conceptual storage where retrieval is possible. Retrieval is measured on most tests by recall and/or recognition questions. In the laboratory, retrieval is sometimes measured by the number of trials a subject needs in order to bring his performance to criterion level. *Retrieval* is available memory, whether elicited by artificial stimulation or by the requirements of living.

### Redundant Storage

Cortical areas for storage of particular sensory information have been explored extensively because of the availability of the cortex to electrode stimulation. The evidence of simultaneous storage in more then one area of the brain, or *redundancy*, helps to explain why damage to the brain may not result in loss of specific information. The idea that the left side of the body is controlled by the right hemisphere of the brain, and the right side by the left hemisphere, is an oversimplification of the complex neurological system for memory storage.

Sperry and his associates (1961) at California Institute of Technology taught cats by suitable operant conditioning schedules to discriminate between a door with a circle and a door with a square as identifying symbols. The position of the doors, at the end of a fairly long runway, was random, so that the cats had

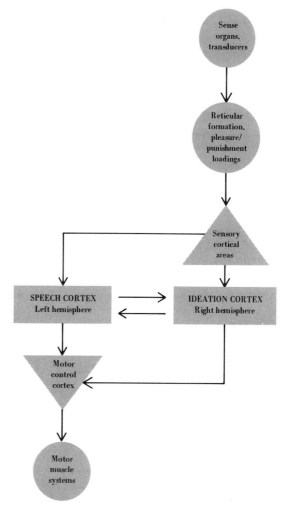

**Figure 9-12**  Input-output systems from sense organs to muscles.

to make a visual discrimination and not merely fall into the habit of turning either right or left. The cats wore an eye patch, so that they were seeing with only one eye at a time. In the first experiments, the cats were trained with the left eye. When they had learned to discriminate in a thoroughly reliable manner, the eye patch was put on the other eye, and they were tested to see whether they could continue to discriminate. As would be expected from introspection, there was no problem involved in switching from the trained left eye to the untrained right eye. Success was as frequent as if the trained eye had been used.

The experiment was then varied. The optic chiasma was cut to ensure that visual sensations from the left eye went only to the left hemisphere and sensations from the right eye only to the right hemisphere (Figure 9-13). The cats were trained in the same manner as before; that is, they were trained to discriminate between the doors with the right eye covered. When the cats were able to distinguish between the square and the circle, the

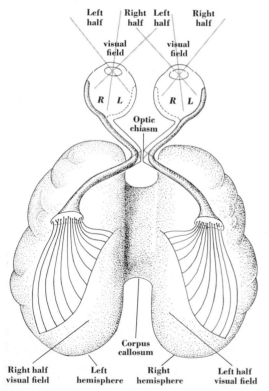

**Figure 9-13** Optic chiasma section in the brain of a cat. (*R. W. Sperry, Cerebral organization and behavior, Science, 1961, 133, 749. Copyright © 1961 by American Association for the Advancement of Science. By permission of the author and publisher.*)

eye patch was changed, and they were tested to see what effect the severing of the optic chiasma had had on learning. The experimenters had hypothesized that since cutting the optic chiasma the cats, when tested, would act as though no learning had taken place. The results, however, were the same as if no operation had been performed. The experiment indicated that the stored information was available in some way to the cats.

Two major explanations for the availability of the past learning were apparent. One involved the possibility that the sensations were transmitted to the brainstem and were actually compared there, and the other the possibility that the masses of nerve fibers that link the right and left hemispheres of the brain through the corpus callosum were providing the potential for comparison. The next step in the experiment was to sever both the optic chiasma and the corpus callosum, thus breaking all the connections between the two hemispheres except through the midbrain. This was done, and new groups of laboratory cats were trained as before. This time, when the untrained eye was tested, the result was the same as if a new untrained cat were being tested. No transfer was found from the training with the left-eye vision to the performance of cats using only right-eye vision.

A further experiment in this same series involved the question of whether storage occurred in both hemispheres or whether a comparison mechanism crossed hemispheres to check stored data. In this particular experiment the cats, who had one eye covered, had had the optic chiasma severed so that the information went to only one hemisphere—the one on the same side as the eye being used. After the cat had learned to discriminate, the axons in the corpus callosum were cut—an operation that had previously been effective in confining learning to one hemisphere. When these cats were tested with the untrained eye, they were able to discriminate, even though connections in both the optic chiasma and the corpus collosum had been cut off. Apparently the visual information was transferred and stored in both hemispheres through the corpus callosum.

Some important implications about human learning emerge from the Sperry research. The principle of redundancy explains why Gary, a fourth-grade pupil, recovered fully from an automobile accident in which a large section of his left frontal lobe was severed by glass. Although the scars on his forehead were conspicuous, he continued to play ball exceptionally well and to learn reading and number skills consistent with his second-grade mental ability tests, recorded prior to his accident. Experiences learned continue to be available in spite of severe insult to the individual.

**Consolidation of Learning**

Albert (1966a, 1966b, 1966c), in a series of experiments at McGill University, contributed important information about learning and retention. His basic method was to train one hemisphere of the brain of rats about avoidance of electric shock while the other hemisphere is rendered temporarily nonfunctional, as a result of a spreading depression from a laboratory injection of KC1 solution. The acquired learning was later transferred to the untrained hemisphere by using only one trial with both hemispheres operative. The efficiency of the initial learning was tested by depressing the transmitting hemisphere and, under varying conditions, finding the number of trials required to relearn the behavior to the criterion level of performance. When no learning had taken place, the number of trials required was on the order of $14 \pm 3$. Groups of rats that had previously learned or had retained the learning required approximately $4 \pm 3$ trials to avoid the grids where they would

be shocked. In all cases, control groups of animals were used to check the possibility that the change in learning facility was due to the experimental procedure. In many of the experiments, the tests were run blind as a check against bias by the experimenter. Albert's initial series of experiments established that when one hemisphere has been trained, it can transmit some of its information in one trial to the other, untrained hemisphere.

Albert also investigated the time required for *consolidation* or permanent storage of learning. The consolidation process was studied by depressing the receiving hemisphere at various times and for varying lengths of time to interfere with the storage process. Using this technique, consolidation was found to have the following characteristics under these experimental conditions: (1) A 2-minute period of interference reduced or disturbed retention only if applied within 1 minute of the transfer trial. (2) Periods of depression of 5 and 30 minutes were effective in disturbing retention when applied as much as 15 minutes and 2 hours after the transfer trial. As the periods of time following the learning trials were lengthened, the periods of depression had to be lengthened to disrupt learning. (3) The disturbing effect of a 2-minute period of interference, while not apparent when applied later than 1 or 2 minutes, lengthened the time during which a 5- or a 30-minute period of spreading depression was effective to 4 or 10 hours, respectively. He concluded that a short period of time is required for what he calls "acquisition of learning." This is followed by a period of several hours for consolidation of learning, during which time two processes of retention are functioning. One of these is used for recall during consolidation; the other serves as a template for permanent storage.

In addition to chemical disruption of learning, Albert found it was possible to enhance or to destroy learning with electrical pulsating currents. The effect of spreading depression by potassium chloride (KCl) was duplicated, in most respects, by a pulsating surface-negative electric current. A surface-positive pulsating current applied for 16 minutes, starting 5 minutes after transfer of learning from one hemisphere to the other, accelerated consolidation, so that 30 minutes completed the process as thoroughly as 2 hours had formerly. The effect of a surface-positive pulsating current as a means of speeding up the consolidation and permanent storage of learning opens interesting possibilities for research on improving the learning of students. The disruptive effect of a surface-negative pulsating current on the consolidation and storage of learning indicates important areas of research concerning the possibility of dramatically changing the learning abilities of mentally retarded persons. Changing the characteristics of the electrical potentials on the surface of their brains by mechanical means might make possible the learning and remembering of information that is critical to their functioning at normal levels.

In a very different experiment, using similar training procedures, Albert studied the role of RNA (ribonucleic acid) in memory storage. Instead of a transfer trial the medial cortex was removed, and parts of it were reinjected into the peritoneum (abdominal tissue) of the donor animal. The results were as follows: (1) The animals injected with the medial cortex tissue learned significantly faster than the control animals, which had the same surgery except for the injection. (2) The learning was specific to the kinds of responses for which the rats had been trained. (3) The time interval required for the formation of the molecules that conveyed the injected "learning" was 4 to 7 hours. These molecules seemed to be part of the permanent storage system of the animal. (4) The critical molecules were found in the

solid material of the nucleus of the cell. (5) The molecule that mediated the saving effect was RNA.

## RNA as Memory Storage

Although research on RNA as a storage mechanism has been severely criticized by many psychologists, Hydén (1969), among others, has presented convincing evidence of the reality of RNA production during learning. RNA molecules, several species of which have been identified in the mammal brain, are closely related to DNA (deoxyribonucleic acid), which carries the genetic memory that programs the development of individuals. Hydén's associates devised a procedure for separating RNA from surrounding brain tissue in the cortex of the motor control areas of rats. They made it necessary for right-handed rats to learn to use the left paw in retrieving food from deep into a narrow glass tube. A significant increase occurred in the amount of RNA per cell from the learning side of the cortex (right) when similar cells in the opposite hemisphere (left) were used as controls.

Handler (1970), who was critical of early RNA learning research, was convinced by the effectiveness of the antibiotic puromycin which inhibits protein synthesis to eliminate the memory of a learning experience in mice. This drug, when injected within two days in doses strong enough to inhibit 75 percent of the protein synthesis in the brain, destroyed learning. Protein synthesis is crucial to the formation of RNA molecules.

Fjerdingstad, Nissen, and Røgaard-Petersen (1965) extracted RNA from the brains of trained rats and injected it into the chest cavity of untrained rats. The learning of the same task was facilitated in experimental rats when compared with rats that received RNA from untrained animals or with rats that had not been injected. They found that the type of training was specific as far as the kind of learning facilitation that took place.

## Holographic Memory Structure

In recent times computer designers have come to recognize the enormous capacity for storage that is apparent in the human brain. These observations opened the way for a reexamination of the functioning of the neural system, leading to the postulation of a secondary system for processing and storing information. Pribram (1971) hypothesized a memory function in the *slow wave potential* formations in the fine mesh of dendritic fibers. Pribram's explanation in *Languages of the Brain* involves the evidence of a microstructure or interaction between the dendrites of different neurons which function somewhat like a hologram to process, store, and retrieve sensory images in three dimensions. His thesis is extrapolated primarily from research in neuropsychology. Pribram presents evidence that the lack of lifetime growth of the neurons in the human brain is more a lack of space in which to grow than of having exhausted their growth potential. The electron microscope shows the dendritic branches of the cortical layers crisscrossing each other as well as making synaptic connections with axons. The charges in the very fine dendrites are of a low voltage which is a function of the diameter of the nerve tissue carrying the current. Contact between the dendrites is facilitated by the absence of the myelin sheath, a neuron insulator which prevents interference between the larger nerve fibers. The result of the tangled matting effect seems to create a second interconnect system which is characterized by slow interference waves in the microstructure of the dendritic branches. Pribram compares the structure and the operation of

the system to the working of a complicated net of holographs.

Holographs are rapidly coming into prominence as a super storage and reproduction system (Lessing, 1971). The entire *Encyclopedia Britannica* can be stored on a square inch of thick photographic film. The reproduced holograph is completely three-dimensional so that the viewer can move his head in order to see around an obstructing object in the foreground of the hologram. Finally, each part of the hologram carries the whole message, which would help explain many difficult facts about storage of material in the brain, if a similar system were operating there.

The hologram is made by splitting a beam of monochromatic, or single wavelength, light; refracting part of the beam off the object; and combining the refracted and unrefracted light to produce an interference pattern which may be stored on a film. The image can be reconstructed by sending the monochromatic light through the film in the reverse direction and thus reconstructing the light waves which were the visible object in the original setting. The reproduced hologram is a decoding of the original light intensities and frequencies which were encoded from the settings. The fact that each part of the holograph can reproduce the whole scene from which it was made can be understood by thinking of a photographic picture so completely blurred that every point on the film has light from every point on the object photographed. This out-of-focus picture can be made quite easily; the problem is one of obtaining a recognizable image or readout from the result. The hologram simplifies the image by using monochromatic light, and by splitting this light to achieve an undistorted reference beam as well as a refracted beam, to produce the interference pattern. The image is pure enough to appear on the readout as it appeared in the original.

Colors are achieved by using more than one laser, which generates more than one picture, superimposed in layers within the film. In the brain the multi-input from many neurons in the microstructure seems to produce a similar effect. Auditory, as well as visual, holograms have been built, and somatic holograms have been conceptualized. The memory process is multifaceted and involves electrochemical action, cellular changes, and holographic arrangements of coded experience. Whether evanescent memory, the experiential record, or consolidated long-term memory is more closely related to one system of storage than another is yet to be determined.

## THE ENDOCRINE SYSTEM

The moods (e.g., depression, elation, and aggression) and the states (e.g., hunger, thirst, and sleepiness) of children affect the efficiency with which they learn in school. Feeling tones, such as these, also affect the satisfaction a teacher gains from working with children. Enough is now known about the neurological control of changes in these feelings to provide an introduction for teachers to the physiology of emotions and to some attempts to treat malfunctions in children.

### Autonomic Regulation within the Brain

Pribram (1971) pointed out that traditional division of the brain into frontal, medial, and posterior portions is arbitrary and that another view, more useful in understanding behavior, would be to think of layers from the inside out more or less on the model of an onion. He described the core-brain as made up of relatively short, hairy, dendritic, and fine-fibered neurons which have many contacts with neighboring neurons. These are the cells to which many different sensory neurons feed messages. They are responsive and reactive to

stimulation in the cortex. This fine network of neurons facilitates slow wave potential and renders the area sensitive to small changes in the chemical concentrations that form synaptic bridges.

Particular sites have been located within this core-brain area which control hunger and thirst, pleasure and punishment, sleeping and wakefulness, and depression and elation. Knowledge of these sites and of the chemical agents that affect them have made the effect of antidepressant and tranquilizing drugs understandable.

**Sleep and Wakefulness**  Four phases of sleep have been identified and labeled. The first of these, during which much active dreaming occurs, is characterized by rapid eye movements (REM). This phase of sleep is controlled by concentrations of norepinephrine, a catechole amine in the regulatory centers. The "deeper" phases of sleep, all of which are characterized by long, slow waves, are controlled from nuclei in the midbrain and involve the chemical transmitter, serotonin, which is an indole amine. Sleepiness seems to occur when sleep receptor sites are supplied with an accumulation of aminergic substances. This helps to explain the responsiveness to drug manipulation of wakefulness, sleepiness, and dream hallucinations.

**Hunger and Thirst**  Regulatory processes have been found to respond dramatically to both electrical stimulation of specific sites and to chemical agents induced into those centers. When the receptor sites that receive hunger information are stimulated, obese animals will continue to eat until they more than double their normal weight. Other animals, on opposite kinds of stimulation, will starve to death in the presence of food. Concentrated salt solution injected into the core of the brainstem caused goats to drink gallons of water, even though their body tissues were homeostatic (Anderson, 1953).

The important lesson from these studies is that biochemical solutions, produced within the organism, are stimulators or inhibitors of neural activity, which in turn regulates the interaction of body functions and emotions. The controls for release of these chemical agents are a function of the endocrine system, which is generally automatic and largely outside the immediate control of the person. A small bundle of neurons joins the pituitary gland to the hypothalamus. This neural connection is the anatomical relay station between the limbic, or motivation, system and the endocrine system. The pituitary receives coded information of visceral states from receptors in the brain and midbrain, and affective information from the limbic system, which is coordinated in the release of enzymes including adrenaline, insulin, and androgens.

**Children with Minimal Brain Dysfunction**  One of the interesting developments in drug therapy has been the discovery of a paradoxical effect of amphetamines on some children whose high-level motor activity and symbolic behavior suggest a lack of normal functioning in the central nervous system. Whereas adults are stimulated by taking amphetamines and typically experience a euphoric effect, some children under treatment for extreme hyperactivity show a quieting, even depressing, effect and rarely develop the tolerance to the drug that is observed in adults. Wender (1971) distinguished between minimal brain dysfunction, brain damage, and hyperactivity by suggesting that these conditions overlap in some patients and that any combination of problems may occur in an individual child. Wender stated that children with minimal brain dysfunction represent the largest group of patients seen by child psychiatrists. The problem is easily diagnosed in

gross forms, but difficult to diagnose when the condition is minimal. He suggested that the characteristic symptoms of minimal brain dysfunction become apparent when a neurophysiological cause interacts with social experience to generate a varied pattern of behavior—the psychological syndrome. He observed the child's reaction to amphetamines and considered the paradoxical affect of tranquility, along with other symptoms, as confirming a diagnosis of minimal brain dysfunction. The characteristics of children with this syndrome are complex and varied, although the basic patterns can be observed in their motor behavior, cognitive functioning, and impulse control.

*Motor Behavior*  Typically such a child is seen in the classroom as having a high activity level, shifting his attention constantly, and lacking goal direction. Although he wiggles a great deal and leaves his desk often, some research has found that the overall activity is no greater than normal, but that the child lacks the ability to inhibit motor activity at times when control is expected. Although his coordination is impaired, he sometimes has a history of early walking and sometimes is good at sports. More typically, high-level coordination is likely to be affected and he will be seen in the classroom as having poor visual-hand integration evidenced in poor handwriting.

*Cognitive Functions*  Teachers often describe this student as having a short attention span, as aimless and distractible, and as lacking in the ability to concentrate. Although he does not do well on his own, he is often seen as one who learns well on a one-to-one basis, which helps to explain why some do well in clinical or tutorial programs. In a group setting he is led astray by stimuli that should remain extraneous and may find it difficult to organize academic content or evaluate what is significant versus what is trivial. Extreme behaviors of perseveration are sometimes present in repetitive speech and stereotype imitations. Wender considers it important for teachers to distinguish between the "daydreaming" of these children, who are likely to explain their inattention by indicating they were anticipating out-of-school activities, in contrast to the student with schizoid behaviors who is likely to be caught up in a fantasy-reverie.

The characteristic that appears in the older child is underachievement in school. The largest subgroup of these show a discrepancy between their reading ability and their general intelligence. Some have had articulation difficulties when learning to speak. Most have a sense of guilt about their underachievement, which makes remediation difficult.

**Impulse Control**   These children typically show a decreased ability to inhibit disruptive behavior, a low tolerance for frustration, and an inability to defer gratification. They tend to do the things that draw negative attention from adults, such as untidy dressing, relatively late enuresis, and actions which threaten their own safety or that of others. They seem to need more than their share of teacher praise support, but because of their failure to act with regard to the consequences of their actions, they are likely to become the recipient of negative reinforcement from teachers and parents.

In personal relations such a child is not an introvert but becomes an unsuccessful extrovert who initiates friendships that do not last because of his unresponsiveness to social demands and his insensitivity to the needs of others. He tends to gravitate to younger children who are more likely to tolerate his bossiness and social aggression. Wender reported bimodal patterns of affection and dependence with unusual vacillation in physical expressions of love.

The emotional patterns are similarly vacillating, with reactivity changing daily from being impervious to being excessively sensitive. This lack of predictability in emotional response endangers any close relationship with peers. A high lability, or unpredictability, in behavior is frustrating to teachers who are unable to see consistent progress in any program they undertake to help the child, or to discover cause-effect relationships in their approaches to him. Although he is seen as aggressive in seeking personal ties, his unsocial behavior is characterized more by irritability than by hostility. Wender suggested that extreme unaggressiveness may characterize some children with integration dysfunctions, but that these are less likely to be referred to clinics than their more disruptive counterparts.

Of the possible neurophysiological causes of minimal brain dysfunction, the most significant is dysphoria, or reduced ability to experience pleasure. This inability to feel satisfaction in interpersonal relationships leads to lack of control by socially defined criteria, poor academic achievement, and low self-esteem. Wender summarized the primary abnormalities of their behavior as (1) a "diminished experience of pleasure and pain which is paralleled by a diminished susceptability to positive and negative reinforcement" and (2) an "excessive and poorly modulated level of activity" (1971, p. 165).

Wender hypothesized that diminished ability to learn through conditioning might be due to lowered monoaminergic levels in the positive reinforcement systems of the brain. Animal experiments had indicated the presence of neurohormones (dopamine, noradrenaline, and serotonin) when the reward system was stimulated. Complex motivation systems in rats were observed when a combination of positive and negative stimulation was applied. When the brain reward systems were stimulated electrically, behavior learned through punishment was enhanced. By this reasoning, managed doses of amphetamines given to patients should stimulate neural activity by raising the monoaminergic levels in the reinforcement system to increase *behavioral reactivity* and decrease interfering *emotional responsiveness.* By changing the monamine level with amphetamines, properly diagnosed children have shown decreased motor activity, increased attentiveness, and increased susceptability to social demands. Although most are quieted, an unwanted side effect sometimes occurs—increased wakefulness. In children with this form of minimal brain dysfunction the most significant reaction of amphetamine treatment is selective stimulation of the inhibitory system. Although the sedative effects of amphetamines on children with minimal brain dysfunction have been established clinically, Wender notes that his explanations of the etiology of the treatment are speculative and are being investigated.

## CONCEPTUALIZATION AND CREATIVE SELF-DIRECTION

The neurophysiology of the higher levels of intellectual functioning is less clearly established than the associative connections that explain conditioning. The evidence of human productivity is visible in the poems of William Carlos Williams, the architectural works of Frank Lloyd Wright, and the atomic fusion formuli of Oppenheimer. These creative men, each a subject of the extensive studies of the Institute of Personality Development at Berkeley, demonstrated the conceptual and motivational power to exceed any possible accumulation of input they might have received—to add 2 + 2 to get 5, as Koestler has stated. Piaget went beyond stimulus-response psychology to infer that an internal operation occurred with an observable external action, and used the behavior seen to infer intellectual functioning. With new knowledge becoming available about the workings of the brain of

men, scientists of humanist bent have postulated some tentative explanations of how known mechanisms function in conceptualization and self-initiated productivity.

Conceptualization occurs when the learner grasps a meaningful relationship between a number of sensory associations and bits from the experiential record. Information from several sources, usually gained over a period of time, is abstracted from the essential common characteristics and becomes a generalized idea. In learning to speak his native language the child generalizes how to form plurals by adding /s/ and demonstrates his conceptualization by using the plural form of new words, including some overgeneralizing to exceptional forms he has not learned by association.

Lorenz (1969) described the ideational breakthrough of conceptualization as a neurological short circuit in which one-way neuronal chains become linked into a closed circle. The effect of this closure is to establish a feedback cycle in cybernetic terms. He hypothesized that a linear chain is transformed into a schema which possesses entirely new systematic properties.

Lorenz traced the phylogenic evolution of thought process through his research on birds and mammals and extrapolated his findings to human beings. He theorized that conceptualization involves the process of abstracting from multitudinous and accidental data those patterns that are constantly characteristic of an object or an idea. The child who is just beginning to recognize dogs as different from other animals sees their common characteristics and begins to recognize them as a class. Lorenz considered neural functioning as basic to this abstracting process and basic to all conceptualization. He pointed out that scientists are involved in verifying the correctness of their conceptualizations when they state and test a hypothesis. He used the term "fulguration" to describe both the emerging cognitive structure and the joining of neural chains into a circuit.

Sarkisov (1966), a Russian neurologist, described neural structures through which associations are integrated and organized as "secondary reflections." The integrating characteristic of this neural activity is most prevalent in the areas of the cortex most recently evolved, the speech and perceptual areas. These areas consist of large concentrations of stellate neural cells, each of which has complex systems of dendrites and axons. Stellate neurons are concerned with intracortical connections rather than with connections between the cortex and other parts of the brain or with effector neural cells. The complexity of the stellate cells makes them highly efficient in relating facets of sensory experience into systems. These cells are most prevalent in layers 3 to 5 of the cortex, where extensive cortical comparisons take place. Sarkisov considered these stellate systems highly important in memory.

The extensive branching of the dendrites which interconnect the stellate cells, and their importance in conceptualization and memory, make them probable sites for the slow potential activity and microstructures described by Pribram (1971). The latticelike structure of the layers of cells in the cortex would provide anatomical structure for the holographic storage of information. The interrelationship of input from many sensory experiences, combined with inputs from stored experience, suggests the conditions for complex integration of past and present information that is the essence of conceptualization.

Even in lower mammals, neural activity has been identified with response to abstracted number. Thompson et al. (1970) found evidence for the activation of particular neurons in the cortex of cats conditioned to number codes. In the training period, repeated and simultaneous stimulation of three sensory modalities were used: shocks to the paw, light flashes, and bell sounds. After training, selected individual neurons responded to numerical abstractions of the different numbers 1, 5, 6, and 7 that were independent of sensory receptor neurons. The researchers hypothesized that the abstract property of number was learned by the cat and that this depended on particular classes of cells, apart from the separate sensory systems that were stimulated by the sense organs. Theoretically, complex thought processes can take place within the learner while bypassing the sensory neurons from which the percepts were initially derived.

## Separation of Concept and Word

The term "concept" refers to a generalized idea of a class of things. In behaviorist theory a concept is the result of the process of conceptualization, but many concepts are formed through a series of operantly reinforced discriminations—that is, associations in which a label, or word, becomes associated with an increasingly discriminate class of things (Skinner, 1968). Penfield (1969) believed that the memory storage of the experiential record and the memory storage of the abstracted concepts were separate. This idea is significant for the teacher, whose work consists largely of preparing students for retrieval—remembering of appropriate concepts in new situations.

Penfield described the concept unit as one of four functions that make up speech, the others being a sound unit, a motor pattern unit, and a motor expression unit. These four functions have been localized, and any one of them can cause misfunctioning of speech. In thinking about the relation of concepts to words, it is helpful to consider some of the inhibitions to speech that can be produced by electrode stimulation. Penfield found that the patient with *expressive aphasia* tries to speak but cannot summon the words he needs to express his images, although he does seem to have the images. On the other hand, the patient with *receptive aphasia* cannot turn the words that he hears into ideas. Although many patients experience *global aphasia*, or total inability to understand and use words, some people have one defect without the others. This disjunction demonstrates the separation of ideation or concept functions from the production of words, or labels, to express meaning.

C. H. was a patient in whom electrically induced aphasia was reported by Penfield (1969). An electrode was placed in one spot of the cortex, and C. H. was shown a picture of a human foot. He said that he knew what it was—it was the thing you put in your shoe. After the electrode was withdrawn, he said "foot". He was unable to find the word while the current was on, although he had a clear image of the object. The electrode was moved slightly, and he was shown a picture of a butterfly, but he was silent. A brief epileptic afterdischarge associated with this particular insertion was observed on the EEG. C. H. snapped his fingers in frustration at being unable to talk or to find the words he needed to answer the question. When the electrode had been withdrawn, he said "butterfly" and explained that he had been unable to get the word "butterfly" and had tried unsuccessfully for the word "moth." His speech mechanism was paralyzed, but the ideation that is usually associated with it was working.

The exploration of induced aphasia has provided the answer to one question that used to be important concerning whether or not thinking is merely subvocal speech. Seemingly, at least two steps were involved in thinking, even such simple thinking as recognizing and naming an object in a picture. One step involves the vocalization complex and the other step the concept behind the vocalization. Some almost automatic method of presenting a cue for a word that is associated with an idea seems to bring the word on demand—unless there is a block, which some normal people seem to develop when the desired word cannot be retrieved.

## Development of Conceptual Thought

Russian psychologists have given considerable attention to the possibility of enhancing conceptual thought, as contrasted with developing accumulative learning in children. Zaporozhets (1969) differentiated between the techniques used merely to give sensory experience to children and techniques used to teach them how to discover relationships within their sensory environment. He recommended that preschool children be taught to organize their sensory environment in order to improve their cognitive functioning. Venger (1965) found that infants of six months were able to distinguish shapes, sizes, and other characteristics. He concluded that school activity spent in mere discrimination of shapes was a waste of time for four- and five-year-olds. Sakulina (1963) found that when preschool children were taught to discriminate triangles and squares by observing the number of angles in each, they were then able to apply this principle to identify polygons, which were new and unfamiliar to them. In a study of children's drawings, Sakulina found that children's drawings improved markedly when they were taught to note the shape of the largest area of an object and then to note the relationship of the smaller shapes to the whole. The pattern of these and other studies reported by Zaporozhets indicates the improved effectiveness of the learner when the teacher focuses on exploration of the relationships within material, rather than on the bits of sensory information.

## Evidence for Affective Conceptualization

The pleasure/punishment associations are the basis for affective conceptualizations about the interrelationships of personal satisfaction, particularly activities, and self-involvement. Lorenz (1969) wrote about the importance of feedback from "self-exploration" as a critical element in human development. Somatic or deep-sense receptors in the core-brain continuously transduce information of the well-being of the organism into the reticular (activating) mechanisms, the limbic (motivating) mechanisms, and the endocrine (regulating) system. The theory of motivation suggests that this self-exploration usually carries a component of introspective analysis of personal feelings (motives, fears, and desires) as well as cognitive components. The thalamus, which caps the brainstem and integrates cognitive and affective information, probably has an important function in organizing the sensations of reinforcement for subsequent storage.

The conceptualization of affects is primarily conscious, meaning that generalized feelings can be retrieved in relationship to particular events and evaluated in relationship to self-concept or personal value. Conceptualizations such as these provide the psychological set that selects the specific kinds of stored information a person will remember in a given situation. The neurological evidence for psychological set was implied by Mahl (1964), who found that an implanted electrode, when stimulated by the same electrical charge, would retrieve different blocks of experience following conversations which differed in cognitive and affective content. An hour's conversation about childhood experience elicited different patterns than did similarly directed conversations about marital problems.

In infancy, the individual starts to build association chains that are linked to the pleasure and punishment centers. The mother's smiling or fondling as she feeds the baby leads to the formation of associations between the hunger satisfaction—stimulation of a pleasure center—and the smiling or fondling. This preconscious connection is an example of conditioning and is the basis of an emotional attachment to another person.

By the same process of conditioning, the very young child links the father's harsh voice, the mother's cross face, and the sibling's slap with the punishment centers. The mechanism is probably tied with temporary deprivation of some basic need. Years later, the teacher's fleeting frown as the child reads "was" instead of "saw" may link, at a preconscious level, with the established chains of mother's frown to the punishment centers. What constitutes punishment for an individual may depend not on the impact of the immediate environment on his senses but on connections with association chains that terminate in punishment areas of the limbic system.

The child who is brought up where most of the interpersonal relationships tend to link to punishment centers, rather than to pleasure centers, may arrive at school with a susceptibility to negative rather than positive connections. The teacher's remarks, intended to be pleasant, are linked to punishment chains. His aversive responses to the teacher's positive overtures, in the large-group situation of the classroom, will almost automatically elicit psychologically punishing activity from the teacher, who is also a learner with punishment centers of his own. Under these circumstances, the child will soon learn, by a process of conditioning, a generalized feeling of distaste for the whole school situation and a conceptualization that school has nothing constructive to offer.

The early life experience of children as they learn to associate psychological nearness to another person with the pleasure centers and psychological distance with the punishment centers can have fundamental effects within the school situation. The highly gifted child who deliberately underachieves in order to lessen the distance between himself and classmates is using these chains of neurons in ways that may not be to his long-term advantage. One effect of grouping highly able students together has been to release them from this necessity to discount their abilities and to give them the opportunity to build psychological nearness to peers by asserting a competitive interest in their studies. When interviewed, special-class children revealed sharp conceptualizations of their need for peer approval and the conscious distortion of their own image in order to achieve acceptance (Robeck, 1968b).

Sybil, an intellectually gifted student, was able to verbalize the feelings that led her to sacrifice academic performance for nearness to peers. Evidence of her conceptualization of self was transcribed as follows:

In school before [the special class] I found I had adjusted to the different abilities of students around me and the other students' interests had integrated into mine. Though my schoolwork was different from others', my interests were really the same. In HAPS I found that many students had not made this adjustment. They were sometimes more mature, and other times had let their interests go to pot, concentrating on the schoolwork they excelled in. I don't think we mutually came to understand each other except in one way. In regular classes I had sometimes come to be looked on as an "egghead" and different. In [the special class] I learned that most of us had had this problem. There I did not try to play down my abilities in school so as to conform because the "average" person now was up to my ability and the trend was not to be average but to excel in studies. Now, in junior high I try not to show off my abilities and not act too intelligent as long as it doesn't affect my schoolwork. At my age I am trying to conform with others, which I suppose is sad and I hope to outgrow this feeling. However, I think there is

hope for me because I realize I am different (as everyone really is) and know this is an asset.

### Bases for Creative Self-Direction

The neurophysiology of self-initiated and imaginative production involves (as the learning-motivation model suggests) an interaction of conceptualizations about self, including the sources of one's own satisfaction and feelings of well-being, and conceptualizations about the intellectual material being acted upon. To recap the neurology of basic learning, coded bits and pieces from the sensory analyzers are fed into the reticular formation. There the cognitive information is associated with stored sensory information and with affects from the pleasure/punishment centers, thus forming an ongoing record of experience. Elements of the ongoing experience are selected, abstracted, and stored to form holographic-like images in the perceptual/interpretive areas of the brain. At the same time in the opposite hemisphere, speech components from the same situations are being processed and stored. In neurophysical terms, images and words from the two hemispheres are linked by neurons. Under favorable levels of activation, neural chains are joined into circular and stable grids that characterize conceptualization. These conceptualizations may be organized in either the perceptual or the speech areas, and they may integrate cognitive or affective content but more probably elements of both.

When an individual forms a conceptualization of the relations within cognitive material and simultaneously forms a conceptualization of the pleasurable affects which accompany his cognitive activity, he tends to prolong the experience by manipulating the ideational systems, thus adding new associations and restructuring his conceptual framework. This drive to mentally manipulate a conceptualization is the self-directing aspect of level 3 learning. The constructive drive toward initiating behavior is *motivation.* The variations and modifications which occur in the conceptual structure when pleasurable experiences are repeated are the essence of creative production. This creativity, in the beginning, is restricted to small segments of experience, therefore to limited conceptualizations. As the individual is reinforced by success in his manipulating, altering, or creating small segments of cognitive content, he may generalize to see himself as a "creative" person. His self-image becomes that of a creator, and he functions as such. At this stage he may be seen by others in a role traditionally conceived as creative.

Piaget observed the beginnings of intention prior to age two, during the last stages of a sensorimotor period, as the "invention of new means through mental combination" (Chapter 14). Walter (1964) reported that potential waves (EEG patterns in the human brain) seemed to be associated with expectancy, attention, and decision making. He measured neural activity in the frontal areas, prior to activity, which he interpreted as indicating intention. Pribram (1969) tentatively located the neural mechanisms for self-initiated responses in the frontal areas of the brain. Penfield (1969) also located the function of initiative in the cortex of the anterior frontal lobes. He predicted that this area, largely unclassified, would someday be seen as important in the voluntary uses of attention.

Pribram (1971) described the neural mechanisms of reinforcement and commitment. Considerably simplified, his explanation distinguishes between the anatomical structures of the punishment and reward systems. The *punishment mechanism* is comparatively limited, having neural fiber interconnections through the core-brain, hypothalamus, and thalamus. Punishment mechanisms function in the release of inhibiting neurochemicals and are, therefore, important in stopping homeostatic processes and in avoidance behavior.

The *reward mechanism* is located in the *medial forebrain bundle* of long neurons which extend from the core-brain to the frontal areas of the cortex. They are nonspecific (as to sensory coding), but carry afferent messages. Changes in the level of norepinephrine in the extremes of these neurons are found responsive to the release of norepinephrine in the core-brain. The reward system is responsive to amphetamines, which are known to mediate activity in the synapses involved in goal-directed behavior. The reward system has a role in stimulating the secretion of RNA and in facilitating the protein synthesis required for the formation of memory structures. According to Pribram, "appetites and affects, feelings of interest, therefore, turn out to be the motivational and emotional (as contrasted with perceptual) stimuli" [p. 272].

Pribram (1971) pointed out that achievement is rewarding to an organism, as observed in monkeys who continue in a test situation while refusing the peanut rewards, or piling them on the table. (They will sometimes eat the rewards they have put aside following a failure in the testing sequence.) The sequence by which the neural mechanisms for achievement are explained: (1) the process of reinforcement progressively increases discrimination, (2) the process of discrimination (perceiving of meaning) is reinforcing, and (3) the learner builds a neural organization which constitutes an individual hierarchical commitment which guides his behavior. "The Image-of-Achievement is not informed by 'objects' or 'interests' but by the play of forces produced by the behaving organism" [p. 299]. Once the organism has become committed to a task, the activities of looking, sniffing, listening, and touching are in and of themselves rewarding.

Pribram reported a study by Mace (1962) in which he suggested that affluence provides examples of how means and ends become reversed when the man or the animal no longer needs to work for a living. The domestic cat who is provided with food, water, and protection prowls and kills for the enjoyment of it. Human beings "enjoy" life through activities that were work for their ancestors: hunting, rowing, gardening, weaving, and the like. Some persons invent, or participate in, games which demand a commitment of physical, temporal, and monetary resources with the expectation, based on past learning, that the *means* with its increments of pleasure in a faster mile run, or a lowered score in golf, is the end, rather than the comfort or appetitive goals usually exploited in reinforcement. "Thus, achievements rather than percepts or feelings become encoded by the motor mechanism" (Pribram, p. 301).

For self-guided behaviors to become stable, the outcomes of an activity must be consistent with the individual's commitment, and the processing must go on without distraction for a sufficient length of time for neural organization to occur. Pribram considers speech and communication to be the epitome of human self-actualization. Something momentous has happened in the psychology of learning when he, a neuropsychologist, and Maslow, a humanist psychologist, describe human behavior in like terms.

A basic treatment of the physiology of learning was unknown to teachers and laymen a generation ago. Although the neurology of conceptualization and self-direction is not fully understood, it is important to know that real and lasting changes occur in the learner with each interaction. It is also important to know that attention and motivation are learned in particular contexts and that both are related to the individual's own bias, or value structure. The responsibility a teacher has for helping students and children become self-directing and self-actualizing is marvelous to contemplate.

Apparently, very creative people have become highly sensitized to both pleasure and punishment; that is, they have established many feedlines into both the pleasure and the punishment centers of the brain. Such people seem to have conceptualized the manifestations of emotional elements in themselves and to have become sensitive to the same reactions in others. The poet who works to understand emotional dynamics extends his conceptualization of his own affects in much the same way that the biologist who analyzes the function of RNA extends his conceptualization from his cognitive knowledge. Each must hold in suspension many bits and many structures from which to forge his own explanation of previously unstructured phenomena.

Once the interrelationship between pleasure or punishment and the activity that stimulates the feeling has been recognized, the conceptualization tends to become both stable and dynamic. This affective conceptualization tends to strengthen the associations out of which it was formed, to become a strong reinforcing mechanism when linked to cognitive conceptualizations, and to force an image of self as a person with specific dynamic attributes. This concept of self as one who is unique and dynamic seems to be a crucial element in self-direction.

## SUMMARY

In recent years, independent research teams, working on diverse problems and with diverse species, have made important discoveries about the physiology of learning that necessitate a rethinking of the whole question of how learning takes place in the human brain. The teacher needs to understand the neurology of learning in order to plan curricula for the statistically common individuals in the class and also to identify any individuals who vary significantly from the usual pattern. To avoid becoming a trial-and-error teacher, one must understand the learning processes that go on in the neurological system.

The principal functions of the nervous system occur in the neurons and at the synapses and are integrated in the CNS. The areas in the human brain that deal with the various functions have been discovered and charted as an essential step in brain surgery. This information has been supplemented by brain research on laboratory animals. Learning in rats was found to result in chemical changes in the brain, which in turn increased the rats' potential for future learning. Experiments with cats established the redundancy of storage in the brain, meaning that identical information is stored in more than one part of the brain. Recent studies have indicated the following sequence in the learning of rats: (1) a short period of time required for acquisition, (2) a period of several hours for consolidation, and (3) permanent storage in an altered RNA molecule. The research done on animals has been verified in part through exploration of human brains, necessitated by neurological dysfunction such as that which occurs in epilepsy or results from accidents.

The crucial step in association learning is that neurons be joined together, which probably occurs with the repeated firing of a neural circuit, thus changing the structure of the synapse. Evidence of storage of connected experience, other than remembered experience, has been found through experiments in which the brain is stimulated with electrodes. Words (or labels) and concepts (or ideation) seem to be stored in different parts of the brain and the parts linked by conditioning. The unique characteristic of connections that occur in conceptualization is the internal structuring of related associations rather than a processing of new input.

Pleasure and punishment centers in the brain seem to be basic to the development of either positive or negative motivation. The essential element in creative self-direction is the interaction of conceptualizations about both the intellectual content of experiences and the emotional consequences of manipulating that content in unique ways. People begin to learn, as infants, to associate psychological nearness to another person with the pleasure centers and to link psychological distance (deprivation) with the punishment centers. When a learner conceptualizes the affects, he grasps the relationship between various emotional fragments of his experience. Creative production results when the learner comes to see himself as free to create and when he understands the inherent potential in certain materials for expressing his unique ideas about the universe.

Highly creative people apparently have well-established feedlines into both the pleasure and the punishment centers of the brain, have conceptualized the emotional elements in themselves, and have obtained reinforcement in their efforts to extend their private view of the universe through their work.

## SELF-DIRECTING ACTIVITIES

1 Develop a means of assessing whether a hyperactive student is in an arousal or an attending state.
2 Devise a biofeedback system designed to increase the amount of time a hyperkinetic youngster is attending to the instruction.
3 Formulate a way of assessing whether or not increasing the pulsating positive current on the surface of the cortex would improve the memory of mentally retarded youngsters.
4 Explore the relationship between temporal coding and spatial coding in perception.
5 Devise a system for testing the optimum proportion of psychological punishment and psychological pleasure to assure efficient learning.

# Chapter 10

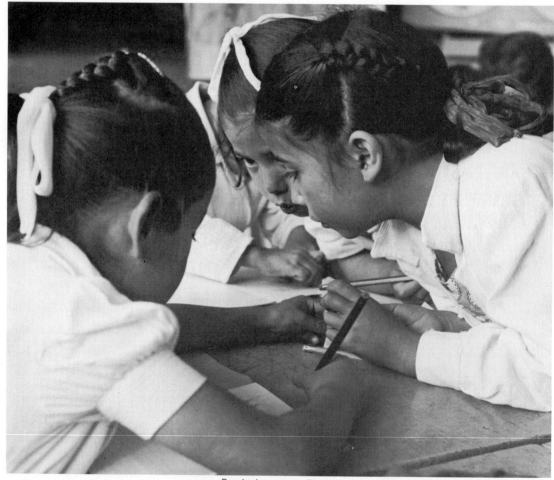

Developing personality through interaction. (*Courtesy of the United Nations*)

# PERSONALITY AND SOCIAL LEARNING

In this chapter, personality development is shown to be integral to all separate aspects of human development and learning. You need to conceptualize this fact and know the components of human development and learning. To do this, you should be able to:

◖   Explain your own responsibility for and impact on the self-concept of students

◖   Define the historical approaches to and classification of personality

◖   Illustrate ways to apply learning-motivation theory to personality change through the teaching relationship

◖   Discuss the value of your function in intelligent caring of students and in helping them achieve self-actualization

◖   Explain the following vocabulary:
   *persona*
   typologies
   role acceptance
   defense mechanisms
   projection
   logic-tight compartmentalization
   rationalization
   fixation
   regression

An individual's personality is the life signature by which he is known, the totality of all that sets him apart and makes him unique. People react to the personality of others in emotionally toned ways. Talented writers bring their characters to life by highlighting certain features of their personalities through their dialogue and action. The greater the depth of the treatment of personality facets, the more real and believable the character. Less gifted narrators restrict their characters to stereotypes by limiting their descriptions of them to the most obvious and common of their characteristics, thus making them less than real. The novelist or playwright selects with assiduous care the words he uses to project a personality. Despite the image the author attempts to project, the reader often evaluates the characters subjectively, in terms of his own world. Some readers see Hester, the heroine of Hawthorne's *Scarlet Letter* (1850), as beautiful, intelligent, warm, and responsible. But the community that branded her with the letter A for adultery saw her as bad and as a threat to the social order. Their judgment of Hester was based on one experience in her life, which blinded them to many other facets of her personality. Such is the personal nature of judgment that any interpretation of a personality reflects, to some extent, the personality of the observer.

The study of personality is complicated by differences in the typical modes of behavior that an individual exhibits under different circumstances. Superintendents and parents tend to evaluate a teacher's personality on the basis of conferences, interviews, or other interaction involving only adults. Children in the classroom usually see quite a different teacher, who may be more confident and supportive or more fearful and rigid than the person the adults see. On the other hand, the fully integrated person is likely to be seen as consistent by many different people because his own image of himself is stable and con-

sistent. The emphasis on wholeness in the description of people reflects some of the difficulty involved in the study of personality.

The nature of personality can be understood in part by tracing some facets of individuality to the primitive origins that preceded civilized human behavior. These elemental structures, unobscured by more recent societal overlays, provide cues for the adults who undertake to rear children. This chapter explores the interaction between the characteristics of the human species (which is unique in a zoological hierarchy) and the characteristics of the individual, who is unique in his society. Some determinants of personality are elements shared with other species, in a phylogenic sense; while other traits are the result of learning in the ontogenic sense. The theme of this chapter is the dynamics of the interaction between society and the individual in his struggle to become himself.

Part of the phylogenic inheritance is the necessity to assert oneself as an individual with rights and to become ontogenically unique. A model of the dynamics of personality patterns, based on learning, provides the basis for teacher intervention and/or guidance.

## GENESIS OF INDIVIDUALITY

Human personality has evolved to a complexity and individuality that is unmatched in any other species. Man has developed his ability to manipulate the personality patterns of lower animals through genetic breeding and the accentuation of inherited traits to produce individuals that serve his own purposes. The personality of a Pekingese differs from that of a bulldog, but either can be shaped into a schizophrenic by selective stress. People react differently toward a Pekingese and a bulldog, because of their appearance. Dogs act differently toward other dogs because of their size, their aggressiveness, and their ability to defend the territory they have defined as their own. Environmental manipulation was invented by man, who successfully teaches setters to retrieve birds but doesn't waste the same kind of training on poodles. Man gained this decisive control over animals when he learned to conceptualize the genetic and environmental forces that shaped response patterns.

The evolution of symbolic language increased man's control over himself as well as over other animals. Language enabled man to store and manipulate experience and so discover the forces that shaped development and to transmit these conceptualizations to other persons and other generations. Through understanding the determinants man has been able to escape, to some extent, the manipulation of others on what he does and therefore on what he becomes.

Historically men have sought to control other men by force and by psychological manipulation, which was intended to change their personality dynamics to make them submissive and conforming. Behavior modification is making this control scientific and is being used to eliminate undesirable personality patterns (Chapter 5). Humanist psychology is focusing on enabling people to achieve insights into their own personality and thus achieve self-control of their own lives. Understanding the forces that influence how a person feels and what he does makes it possible for him to avoid being manipulated. A knowledge of these forces increases the teacher's responsibility to use interaction for positive effects on personality growth.

## Primitive Urge toward Self-Assertion

Individuality is seen in the assertion of self in territorial imperatives. Although a strong individual may define his territory and keep out members of his species who threaten his individuality, the continuation of his species requires cooperation for mating and for rearing the young. So self-assertion must be tempered by accommodation to the needs of other individuals, including the young, who have their own needs for self-assertion.

The degree of social organization varies from species to species. Wolves share the territorial imperative with all the members of the pack. They proclaim their joint claim to territory with a medley of calls that has the constructive function of keeping the packs separated. When a social organization includes more than a single family, a pecking order develops that defines status among males, females, and often between siblings. In baboons, the pecking order is closely related to size, and the status of offspring tends to conform to that of the mother. A relatively stable identity of individuals within the troop tends to minimize the infighting and to enhance the survival potential of the group in competition with other groups and other species.

The tendency toward dominance is clearly seen within the family relationship, where the parents exert authority over the young, who test the limits of this authority as part of their own growing up. The personality characteristics of dominance are genetically rooted and transmitted both socially and phylogenically. However, excessive dominance is, of necessity, tempered by the constraints required if the family unit is to extend the individuals through offspring. For instance, fathers must allow a minimum level of independence to women and children if they are to survive and carry on the race. The beatings of primitive dominance control must stop short of killing or there is no continuity.

## Primitive Language

A breakthrough came in personality development when Homo sapiens developed language as a symbolic form of self-assertion, territorial imperative, aggression, and cooperation. Some cues to the function of language in personality growth can be teased out of a comparison of a bright chimpanzee, educated by an expert tutor, and the ordinary child. The chimp can learn to discriminate symbols and to follow directions communicated with visual symbols and can himself invent and communicate in American sign language. Washoe, a female chimpanzee, learned 150 signs to express such ideas as more, funny, please, shoes, clean, and go in 22 months of training. She also combined some of her signs to invent several new signs with which to communicate (Gardner & Gardner, 1969).

Other chimpanzees have learned to work, hoard, and even steal poker chips in a miniature economic system, and to spend them in a time of need (Jacobsen, Wolfe, & Jackson, 1935). Some investigators had trouble explaining why male chimps were working more vigorously than females at acquiring tokens until they found the females had learned how to acquire hoarded tokens for sexual favors. Premack (1970) applied operant conditioning methods to teach Sara, a chimpanzee, complicated stimulus-response associations, such as visual symbols for "Sara, insert, banana, pail, apple, dish" (Figure 10-1).

These remarkable feats of learning by chimpanzees are primitive by comparison with a typical child who learns to express in propositional terms how he sees the world. He learns this with only the normal social reinforcement that is characteristic of his species. Language gives the child freedom to manipulate ideas abstractly and to analyze consequences of actions. According to Pribram (1971) this anticipation of achievement is inherently reinforcing and forms a basis for self-actualization.

Pribram postulated that the token system, symbolism for the delayed reward, is the basis for human planning and self-realization. Having made a proposition, or commitment, in the form of a thought or a sentence, the person receives pleasurable sensations from his own actions in the direction of his goal. The sensations from sipping, running, listening, or talking become associated with the anticipation of success at the end of the activity and the personal rewards this entails. Language makes possible the individual's construction of a plan which reflects his own values and promotes a highly personal reinforcement from within.

Verbal language is what sets man apart from other species. The propensity to develop language is innate, and the use of language is a key to the way in which the person organizes his inner world and communicates it to others. It is an important facet of personality development.

## PERSONALITY

### Derivatives of "Personality"

Because personality is a complex effect of life forces, any single definition is both difficult to formulate and difficult to understand. The root of the word "personality" is the Latin *persona*, which originally meant "mask" and came to mean also the person behind the mask. Gradually other connotations were added, including "important people," from which came the English "personage" and "person."

### Descriptions That Focus on the Individual

Allport (1961) wrote: "Personality is the dynamic organization within the individual of those psychophysical systems that determine his characteristic behavior and thought [p. 28]." He expanded his definition by explaining six key terms used in it.

*Dynamic organization* includes the integrative aspect of the relationships between the parts. To Allport, personality was not static and finished but self-renewing and adjustive. *Psychophysical* denotes the dual aspects of the mental and physical properties of personality, just as *system* denotes the complex "potentials for activity," which often lie dormant but are capable of activation under the right circumstances. The word *determine*, an active verb, expresses the direction-giving or orienting quality inherent in personality. *Characteristic* refers to the individual, personal connotation of personality. Finally, *behavior and thought* mean the ways in which people react to the environment and internally reflect on the implications of their reactions. Allport's definition of personality has been reported at length because it interprets the individual nature of personality implied in the private-world concept presented in this book. Personality has been defined by some behaviorists as the total emergent, that is, the totality of observable behavior. Here the emphasis is on the "mask," or the externalization of personality. This and Allport's definition fall into the category of "individual-behavior definitions," as this term is used by Brand (1954). The emphasis is on the uniqueness of the individual, although one point of reference—Allport's—is inside the organism, while the other referent is outside the organism (MacKinnon, 1944).

McClelland (1951) defined personality as what is observable—the outside point of reference—"the most adequate conceptualization of a person's behavior in all its detail that the scientist can give at a moment in time [p. 69]."

Raven (1950) used a similar point of reference when he said: ". . . I propose to use the word personality to mean the qualities of a person's thought and conduct as they are apprehended by another person [p. 115]." In contrast to this global look was that of Churchman and Ackoff (1947), who saw personality as related only to the internal behavior of the individual, particularly the ways he goes about problem solving.

## Descriptions Based on Patterns of Behavior

Brand (1954) used "general-behavior conceptions of personality" as another classification of personality definitions. In this category are placed the definitions of such experimental investigators as Dollard and Miller (1950), Mowrer (1950), and Klein and Krech (1951), who see the study of personality as the derivation of general laws of behavior in which the individual is a chance variant who fits into the pattern. The pattern as a whole is important, and the individual is observed as a part of a class. In this context, personality is part of the general study of behavior, with particular emphasis placed on motives and perceptions as stimuli.

The definition, or type of definition, that a researcher accepts influences the kind of study that he is likely to make of the nature of personality. When the study is based on a general-behavior definition, different kinds of emphasis can be placed on different stimuli. Some scholars find a *neurological model* of behavior important; some find small *units of behavior* significant, and others *large units*; and some find a *conceptual model* necessary, while others consider it superfluous. All these may be grouped as problems under the general-behavior approach to personality.

## Descriptions Based on Typologies

Allport (1961) described another approach to personality that he called *typology*. This orientation is midway between an individual- and a general-behavior approach and has most of the disadvantages of both methods of studying personality.

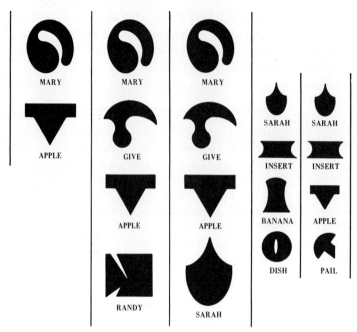

**Figure 10-1** A reading sequence of Sarah. Characters restructured from those read by Sara. (*Extrapolated from David Premack: A functional analysis of language, Journal of the Experimental Analysis of Behavior, 1970, 14, 107–125.*)

**Typologies Based on Emotional Handicaps** Freud (Chapter 13) typed many of his patients as fixated at the oral, anal, or phallic stage; in so doing, he defined their personalities. His classification was not as simple as this description may seem. The interaction of the id, ego, superego, conscious, preconscious, and unconscious forces is a complex way of determining individual reactions. Adler taught that personality was the result of the way people adjust to feelings of inferiority. This led to a typology including domination by inferiority complexes and compensation mechanisms. Superiority complexes, which may be manifested in masculine protest or in social-betterment drives, are forms of inverted inferiority. The personality comes, within this viewpoint, to be dominated by the characteristics of these response mechanisms. Jung typed people as introverts or extroverts. Popular literature classes people as criminal, literary, artistic, penurious, or athletic types. Allport (1961) pointed out the difficulties of typing individuals in this way. Most types cover only a relatively small segment ·of the personality—the person does not act in conformity to this pattern all the time or in all aspects of life. When additional types are added to cover different facets of life, the permutations and combinations of types become unmanageable to the student of personality structure. Typing, like stereotyping, is a way of avoiding the hard work of individual understanding. Although typologies are difficult to separate in application, people still type others and are typed in various ways by them.

**Typologies Based on Physical Development** Two of the best-known typologists were Kretschmer and Sheldon, who gained

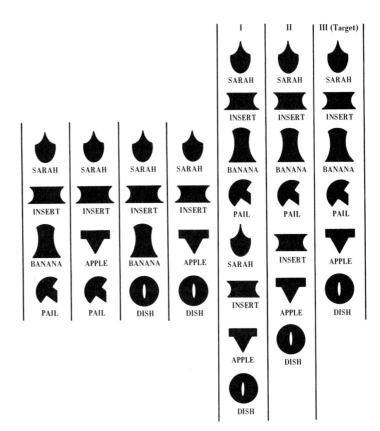

**Figure 10-1 (continued)**

their reputations for years of work on the relationships between physical structure and personality type. For many years, their work has been regarded with considerable skepticism, partly because there are difficulties in classifying individuals into physical types and partly because both investigators used methodological approaches that were vulnerable to criticism. Recently some of their findings have been partially corroborated (Child, 1950; Smith, 1949).

Kretschmer (1945) had originally classified men into three types, which he called the *pyknic*, the *asthenic*, and the *athletic*. He has since added a mixed type, which he calls the *dysplastic*. The pyknic individual tends to be somewhat obese with a large head, a full chest, and a generally chubby look. The as-

thenic person tends to be tall with long hands, narrow shoulders, and a thin face. The athletic type is broad-shouldered, big-chested, well-muscled, and generally powerful. The dysplastic individual is a mixture of the three other types, which provides a miscellaneous category. In temperament, the pyknic person tends to be social, outgoing, and good-natured. Both the asthenic and the athletic types tend, according to Kretschmer, to be fundamentally withdrawn, unsocial, morose, or peculiar.

Sheldon (1940) made a similar division into three body types, which he called *somatotypes*. The *endomorph* is similar to the pyknic individual. He tends to be fat, soft, and round with a well-developed digestive system but relatively poor muscle tone and bone system. Sheldon found a correlation (.79) between this physical build and a *viscerotonic* personality, which is characterized by a love of comfort, a gourmet relish for food and drink, and a tendency to derive pleasure from sociability.

Sheldon's *ectomorph* is described in terms directly transferable from Kretschmer's asthenic type. He is tall and thin with poor muscles and bones, a stooped posture, and a withdrawn expression. Sheldon has obtained a correlation of .83 between the ectomorph and a *cerebrotonic* personality, which is characterized by behavior that is restrained, inhibited, unsociable, and withdrawn. Even the bodily functioning of such an individual is overcontrolled.

The physique of the *mesomorph* is strong and hard, and his blood vessels are large, as are his hands and feet. He is "tall in the saddle" and generally resembles Kretschmer's athletic type. The mesomorph correlates highly (.82) with the *somatotonic* personality, which is vigorous, pushy, active, ambitious, and power-hungry; a somatotonic person generally shows a disregard for others because he is so busy pursuing his own ends that he is unaware of their feelings. All this work has been done with male subjects so that there is no cross-reference for studies of women in terms of either personality or body build.

One possible explanation of a correlation between physical and personality traits is the accommodation of the body to the life pattern of the individual. Men who drive bulldozers tend to be more muscular than men who write books. Physical activity is known to have tension-reducing effects, thus changing the endocrine balance in the body. Cultural expectations over many generations influence physical characteristics. The massive body build of early Hawaiian royalty colored the personality expectations of the natives, so that the obese person in that culture felt differently about himself and interacted differently with his peers from the way the typical obese

person does in the contemporary United States. The relationship between body build and personality is complex, involving hormone balance, social expectations, and self-images.

## Descriptions Based on Motivation

In contrast to the typologies of Kretschmer and Sheldon, which have their origin in physical characteristics, the authors have proposed four personality interactions that reflect motivation and are based on learning. (Figure 10–2).

Four patterns of behavior that tend to characterize the responses of individuals to others are outlined in the following sections: (1) independent, well-adjusted behavior, which dominates the activity of the person who has learned freedom in self-determination and enjoys being himself; (2) constructive and creative behavior, by which a person projects his individuality in creative productions; (3) personally and socially undesirable behavior, by which a trammeled, restricted person seeks to establish his identity in aggressive ways; and (4) submissive and conforming behavior, which is seen in the overwhelmed person who has succumbed to rejection of himself as a person in his own right and acceptance of the projection of another. None of these structures is present in consistent form in all areas of any individual's life, but people tend to develop a predisposition to follow one pattern over another in novel situations. (Frequently a student characterizes his own interactions with others differently from the way the teacher analyzes his personality.) People often assume roles for the sake of expediency which may be completely at variance with their self-ideation.

**Independent-Adjusted**    In some homes a child, from birth, is psychologically supported and rewarded as he explores and tries new approaches to life. He is not forced beyond his ability, but is encouraged to test, in many directions, his potential to cope with his environment. Baldwin, Kalhorn, and Breese (1945) at the Fels Institute found that children from such homes usually show an increasing IQ, more originality, more emotional security and control, and less excitability than children from other types of homes. There are some indications in Terman and Oden's book, *The Gifted Child Grows Up* (1959), that children from "unpressured backgrounds" grow up into well-adjusted adults and live serenely. An examination of the accomplishments of the well-adjusted adults in Terman's sample caused him to question whether these people contribute to the advancement of civilization as strikingly as their abilities indicate they might although they lived personally satisfying and useful lives.

**Determined-Creative** Goertzel and Goertzel (1962, p. xii), in the foreword to their *Cradles of Eminence*, say: "When we turn to biographies and autobiographies, we find exciting, experimental, creative men and women who in their childhood experienced trauma, deprivations, frustrations, and conflicts of the kind commonly thought to predispose one to mental illness or delinquency." If a commonality can be identified that operated in the lives of most of the people whom Goertzel and Goertzel studied, it seems to be a strong-willed parent or parents who tended to insist on performance they valued from their children. In order for the young person to survive and to find his own identity, he had to rebel—in effect, to become as strong-willed as his parents. Many of these eminent people continued throughout their lives to prove and reaffirm to themselves their worthiness and wholeness as individuals. Early in childhood they developed ways of expressing them-

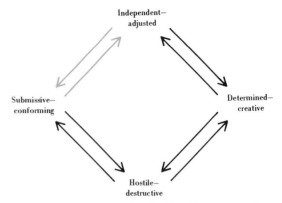

**Figure 10-2** Patterns of behavior. The arrows show the directions of probable changes or shifts in human behavior.

selves which were societally valuable and supported by someone close to them—an aunt, a grandfather, or a parent. Many of these men and women were driven throughout their days, seeking to express themselves and in the process leaving monuments of creative production that still reflect the effectiveness of their striving. Winston Churchill failed to learn Latin and Greek at Harrow and felt rejected by his father, Randolph Churchill. In spite of this start he learned to write and speak effectively.

**Hostile-Destructive** Not all young people who have driving and demanding parents are creative geniuses—the trauma, deprivations, and frustrations in many cases push them into delinquency or less conspicuous forms of rebellion. The biological or neurological mechanism seems to be much the same in the creative as in the destructive person; it is the form rebellion or self-assertion takes that makes the difference between productiveness and destructiveness. The ways in which each of these patterns of behavior finds reinforcement and success in the individual's struggle to establish his identity—his own self—make the difference. The delinquent finds his reinforcement in the approval and acceptance of peer groups, gangs, and other delinquents and develops increasing dependence on these associations. The exploits of Bonnie and Clyde detail a tragic example of striving that led to eventual destruction.

**Submissive-Conforming**   A pattern more undesirable than delinquency is described by Horney (1949) in a quotation from a letter:

> How is it possible to lose a self? . . . The loss begins with our secret psychic death in childhood—if and when we are not loved and are cut off from our spontaneous wishes! It is not just this simple murder of the psyche . . . the tiny self also gradually and unwittingly takes part. . . . He has not been accepted for himself, *as he is.* Oh, they "love" him, but they want him or force him or expect him to be different! Therefore, he *must be unacceptable.* He himself learns to believe it and at last even takes it for granted. He has truly given himself up. His center of gravity is in "them" not in himself [pp. 5–6].

The child who builds his orientation outside himself gives up his own identity. He does not struggle, but builds a pseudoself that is a reflection of the people around him.

Parents or teachers may be so successful in teaching conformity by rewarding "good" or submissive behavior that the child stifles his impulses to become independent. In some cases the dependence becomes so far-reaching that the child is unable to function on his own when he comes of age. Independence is built by small accretions, in which the responsible adult gives freedom and rewards independent behavior.

Not all personal development divides neatly into clear separations between independent-adjusted, determined-creative, hostile-destructive, and submissive-conforming behavior. One common situation seems to be a compromise that pushes an individual to continue an unproductive struggle to prove his identity. Individuals who struggled to assert themselves in the presence of dominating and domineering parents developed characteristics of obstinacy and self-will that were basic factors in their later success. Some individuals punish their parents, teachers, or mates as they seek through such punishment to prove the reality of their own individuality. In Ibsen's powerful drama, *A Doll's House* (1879), for example, Helmer pushes Nora into the imperative need to assert her individuality in ways that run counter to the mores of the community.

Three-fifths of the people selected by the Goertzels for inclusion in *Cradles of Eminence* (both destructive and productive) expressed dissatisfaction with school and were probably difficult students as far as their teachers were concerned. The abrasive ways of unconforming students can be exasperating to the teacher. An understanding of the dynamics that lead to the need for self-assertion can help the teacher accept the nonconforming behavior and direct it into constructive channels.

**Interaction of Personality Patterns**   Individuals whose primary focus is in any of these personality structures tend to move back and forth into forms of behavior that are related (Figure 10-2). Teachers can assist students to function in acceptable ways without discouraging independent thought and action as they provide motivation for the desired changes.

The person who tends to be independent-adjusted can move to determined-creative behavior under suitable drive conditions. In some areas of his life, the adjusted person may show submissive-conforming behavior, although usually in a different way from the person who has not established a well-defined selfhood. Some, but by no means all, business tycoons seem meek and submissive around home. The person who is basically determined-creative can move to independent-adjusted or to hostile-destructive behavior patterns, depending on the success of his creative efforts. Many successful artists have accepted themselves with their success, have relaxed, and have become independent, happy people. The energies of the hostile-destructive individual can be channeled into determined-creative modes of life when he is reinforced in this direction, or he can sink into submissive-conforming patterns as he gives up the struggle. Bill was constantly in trouble in school and was in and out of juvenile hall for shoplifting and street fighting. A Big Brother found he had a talent for sales and got him started in real estate. Success led to dedication and more success. People who tend to be submissive-conforming can become hostile-destructive as sparks of self-identity are fanned. They can learn to act as independent-adjusted persons, although this behavior would usually be an imitation of someone else's pattern of life.

This model, like the learning-motivation model, is most useful when seen as a dynamic relationship that identifies the person's projection of his self-image in a given situation. Probably the person is most fortunate who learns to adjust his pattern of interaction to one of creative-determination in some aspect of his life where a contribution is possible and important to him, while large areas of his life, such as in the routines of family life and perhaps even in earning a livelihood, are independent-adjusted.

## LEARNING PERSONALITY PATTERNS

Although differences exist at birth that are substrata for personality formation, environmental influences are also very important. The way in which the person interacts with the world outside himself is learned primarily by associations. The individual learns characteristic modes of response to stress situations that are variants of his inherited tendencies. In many cases, he is confirmed by reinforcement in the effectiveness of the response, which he learns to use habitually. This learning is usually at the unconscious level, unless a teacher or another sophisticated adult helps the young person conceptualize the personality dynamics of certain learning situations. Even in psychoanalysis or psychotherapy, both of which are designed to change personality patterns, much of the learning is conditioning at the unconscious level (Chapter 7).

### Classical and Operant Conditioning

Many of the young child's personality reactions are learned as a replacement of one stimulus by another that occurred at approximately the same time. Allport (1961) used as an example of early classical conditioning in personality development, the conditioning of the baby toward the mother, which results from food stimuli related to sucking, snuggling, or mouthing responses. The conditioning to the mother can be extended to the blue color she likes to wear and eventually to blue in other contexts.

The same result may occur as a reinforcement schedule from the mother's praising or otherwise rewarding the child for responses, such as smiling. Probably both classical and operant conditionings function under particular circumstances. Perhaps the personality patterns that are essentially maladaptive are built by classical conditioning, since the reinforcements for maladaptive responses are likely to be nonexistent, inverted, or negative, and adaptive responses may be built primarily by operant conditioning.

The difficulty of distinguishing between classical and operant conditioning a posteriori does not minimize the significant learning that takes place in personality formation on a conditioning basis. The pigeons that Skinner conditioned to be aggressive—when the hormone balance was shifted from adrenaline to increased noradrenaline output—were reinforced and conditioned to act in the new way. Young men who shift their hormone balance to adrenaline rather than noradrenaline output—to flight rather than fight responses—learn these mechanisms by conditioning with no intent or awareness of what they are doing. In an excerpt from a letter quoted earlier in this chapter, Horney (1949) described the loss of self and the attendant personality change. All such learning is by conditioning.

The process by which some individuals are induced to give up their identity for a pseudo-identity is the result of a long series of conditioned learnings toward submissive-conforming personality patterns. Some of the steps described below are illustrative of the effect of certain teaching techniques. Usually this kind of learning is started early in life. Each time the child moves toward obedience, he is rewarded. Each time he conforms to adult wishes, he is reinforced. On the other hand, each move toward independence is punished, and each trial in which he tries to express himself freely is negatively reinforced. Under these circumstances, the characteristics of conformity and submissiveness emerge and are strengthened, while impulses toward originality or creativity are construed as threatening or dangerous because of prior associations with punishment. The child comes to avoid initiative. If restrictive kinds of conditioning are started after independence has been positively reinforced, the confusion that results may resemble that of Pavlov's dogs who were driven mad while trying to choose between visual cues that they were not able to discriminate.

If the young child is reinforced for making small decisions on his own and then is reinforced for each evidence of independent activity, these responses will become increasingly common in his repertoire. If initiative is reinforced while acts of dependence or conformity are negatively reinforced in subtle ways—perhaps by being ignored—the child will move toward activities characteristic of an independent-adjusted personality. When the basic deficiency needs are also met during the process of reinforcing these independent responses, the child gradually emerges as an independent-adjusted personality.

The assumption is intended that a family or a school should find it easier to create an independent-adjusted individual than a submissive-conforming one. The basic energy flow in human beings is assumed to be toward independence rather than toward dependence and conformity. A conflicting pattern of forces results from the prevailing tendency of adults to express their own independence by requiring acquiescence and conformity from those around them, particularly those who are younger and weaker. Teachers and parents who understand the dynamics of learning can avail themselves of the potential strengths of their young charges and can gain their own sense of independence by exerting their influence from a conceptual rather than a conditioned base.

### Conceptualization of Roles

Learning can be made both easier and more efficient when the young person is helped to conceptualize the roles he is playing. This process should be started as soon as possible after the child enters school in order to avoid fixing habit patterns that are inimical to later school success.

Girls find their roles in school more like their accustomed practice in the home than boys do. Particularly in some subcultures boys are strongly reinforced for being aggressive, boisterous, and untidy. They imitate the male adult pattern to which they are exposed, and the females in their lives tend to reinforce them for developing "masculine" characteristics. When these young boys start school, they enter a society in which the response mechanisms they have evolved subtly over a number of years are signals for punishment rather than reinforcement by the teacher. Under such conditions, reaction patterns are likely to develop in the boys, which make their adjustment to school much less smooth than is true for girls. A male elementary school teacher or playground director can furnish such boys with a model of conformity to the school code of conduct. These boys can be helped to function more efficiently by linking conditioning to a conceptualization of a *difference between roles inside and outside the school.* They can be helped to see that in school males can be polite and helpful. The need for this kind of extra teaching for little boys is one that women teachers may understand but find difficult to accomplish because of their feminine personality expectations. All their school experience has usually been to negate the wisdom of reinforcing the boisterousness and untidiness of little boys (Figure 10-3).

To help an elementary school child develop an outgoing, supportive personality, another conceptualization that can be taught is the *uniqueness of each individual.* Everyone is different. All should be valued for what they are, rather than condemned for what they are not. Such a conceptualization can make the individual less vulnerable to peer pressure during adolescence, when uncertainty about self is likely to reach a climax. This conceptualization could be built on associations that come from the teacher's own valuing of the individual members of the class through his interactions with them, but most children will need guidance if the idea is to become explicit to them.

Another conceptualization that the teacher could help pupils to formulate is that of the *self as a free person.* This concept would be a function of, and basic to, teaching for the third level of learning in all the aspects of the school program. The student seldom functions on level 3 until he sees himself as free to innovate in a particular situation. When additional activities are brought into focus as possible areas of freedom, students can generalize the idea of themselves as free individuals. They must choose to use their freedom and potentiality if they are to develop as determined-creative individuals.

**Role Acquisition**

Allport (1961) described four different ways in which roles relate to personality structures (Figure 10-4). The first way is through what he calls *role expectation,* which is the prescription of the role that comes from the community. A father, for example, is expected to function in certain ways as a parent, and these expectations determine the role expectation of the father. The father is also a worker, perhaps a teacher, and the community has a role expectation of workers. Many communities are contained in each town or city, so that there are sometimes conflicting role expectations.

The second way in which roles relate to personality structures, according to Allport, is through *role conception,* which is the way the individual defines his role for himself. In part his definition depends on the community from which he comes, but in part he integrates a composite from many communities and interprets for himself what he thinks is the role. Role conception is an internalized, individual reaction, whereas role expectation is, in some ways, a public or social view.

Third is *role acceptance* or *rejection,* which is also an internalization. Having defined for

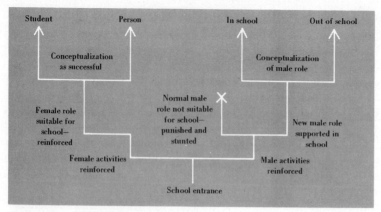

**Figure 10-3**  Conceptualization of roles.

himself the role of "teacher," for example, the individual finds that he either does or does not fit into the defined dimensions comfortably. In some cases, the comfort or discomfort associated with the role may be due to the individual's own definition of it rather than to community expectations.

Fourth and finally is *role performance*, which is the outward manifestation of one's role in society. Allport considered that those who are comfortable in their roles and whose definitions of their roles are in agreement with society's are likely to be conservative. They are not pushed into conflict situations that would motivate them to change either their definitions or their acceptance of their roles. On the other hand, persons who find their roles uncomfortable, either because they have interpreted them in an unfortunate manner or because they reject them, are likely to be rebels. Bill, who is a graduate student in theology, exemplifies the stress points in this model. The role expectation of a minister has traditionally been specifically defined to cover dress, mode of life, and attitudes which were supposed to be models of decorum. In certain subcultures, the role expectation has been

changing to accommodate ministers as activists for change in race relations and other areas of life. Bill's role conception stresses the role of a minister as an activist, although it is clouded by the more generalized role expectation. The tension within his role conception leads to difficulty in role acceptance—in other words, ambivalence about complete commitment to the role of a minister. In role performance, Bill tends to implement the activist rather than the traditional phases of the role of minister. Since he is still a student, he has time to try to bring the various roles into harmony with one another. He presents rather clearly the kinds of stress associated with changing role expectations within the society. The interpretation of role in people's lives is extremely complex because everyone lives in many roles each day. Some roles are more important to an individual's self-concept than others. Some roles are comfortable, and some are obnoxious—an individual may rebel with regard to his role as a worker while being conservative with regard to his role as a lover. Classification of people is never neat and simple because people are complex and live in complex environments.

**Sex Roles: Cultural Reinforcement of Inherited Tendencies** When describing a group of people, cultural anthropologists usually give considerable attention to characteristic sex roles, which are highly important determinants of personality. What kinds of tasks are relegated to, or reserved for, either sex is part of the value system that is taught through acculturation. In stable societies these roles persist through the generations, and an individual is punished in well-understood ways if he is found violating or circumscribing his proper sex role.

Some cultures, such as that of the native Hawaiians, valued inheritance so highly that blood strains were actively protected and supervised by the society. In these cases, the roles of nobility cut across sex barriers to the extent that the roles of both men and women of the nobility were determined more by status of the family than by sex. Hawaiian princesses could practice the arts as well as rule. In the course of many generations, members of the royal family became physically larger than the population generally, as a result of selective breeding, forced feeding, and imposed inactivity. In an island culture inbreeding was probable, so offspring were selectively eliminated by infanticide when maldevelopment appeared. Royal youth were closely supervised until after their marriage had been consummated, for the same reason that royal births were witnessed in medieval Europe, which was to ensure a lineal succession. The cultural expectations of royalty reinforced inherited tendencies and modified the sex roles enforced on the general populace.

Biological functions influence the sex roles that societies sanction. Among groups of people who desire a population increase—such as the Mormons in the nineteenth century, the settlers in rural America in the eighteenth century, and the Nazis in Germany in the

1930s—women are valued for childbearing and child-rearing functions. Such cultures are sometimes polygamous, and women may be unimportant in church, state, and commercial affairs or in the arts, even while exerting a dominant influence in the home. The reinforcement that little girls receive in such cultures is likely to make them feel valued because of their biological role. The societally sanctioned sex role overrides any native similarities between the sexes in intellectual or creative endowment, and the accepted role becomes associated with the idea of individual attainment, so that in the past it has been much easier for a young woman to become a nurse than a doctor.

Research and technology influence the sex roles of a culture. Consider the implications, for sex roles, of the "pill" or of any other readily accessible form of birth control. When nearly all children are wanted children, they will be both scarce and valued. Women, who have frequently controlled the family purse strings as compensation for the men's holding the valued occupational positions, will plan for motherhood and gain the kinds of freedom that biological inheritance in the past has reserved for males. Cultural changes will occur, perhaps more rapidly than many people will be able to cope with them. With the drop in the birthrate, reported and observed in the United States of the 1970s, the role of the teacher in society is changing toward more

| Without individual | Within individual | Without individual |
|---|---|---|
| Society viewpoint | Individual viewpoint | Society viewpoint |
| Role expectation | Role conception | Role acceptance | Role performance |

**Figure 10-4** Community and individual facets of roles.

individualized instruction. The high school counselor or dean of students may be less concerned with home study courses for pregnant girls and jobs for young fathers, but involved with problems associated with a declining population. Probably girls will be seen as much more career-oriented than is presently the case. Men and women are likely to be valued more for their human qualities and potential then for their biological functions. When people are valued, children will be valued, and many of the present problems associated with rejection may disappear.

### Group Roles: Tyranny for Individuals

Just as minority-group members have unpleasant role expectations thrust upon them, so also do members of majority groups find themselves in roles that are often uncomfortable. The members of the dominant middle-class group have a role of upward aspiration with a concomitant drive for upward mobility.

Coupled with the middle-class expectation of upward mobility is that of dominance. The unfortunate aspect of this dominance expectation is that it implies dominance over someone. In the struggle for status recognition, minority-group members are most likely to become the victims. Children make up a minority group that often suffers in this way. Parents who really have no base from which to dominate other adults are still usually bigger and stronger than their children and are able to dominate them. The potential damage to the personality structure of a child in such a situation would be hard to overestimate. Almost certainly the pressure is toward submission on his part, with the emerging personality shifted toward submissive-conforming or, if he is particularly strong, toward hostile-destructive patterns.

Another aspect of the role expectation of the dominant group is success, which comes to be appraised on the basis of status symbols that make the success obvious. Indians of the Pacific Northwest had a similar role expectation, which required them to be hosts at ceremonial feasts called *potlatches*, during which they lavishly destroyed their own personal property and bestowed gifts on their guests; often the expenses of the potlatch ruined them financially. Among contemporary symbols of success are possession of two or more cars, a bigger house in a better neighborhood, and a boat in the yacht harbor. As in the case of the Indians, success can sometimes be ruinous. An individual's personality structure can be subjected to a considerable amount of strain when his upward mobility falters because of conditions that are beyond his control.

## INDIVIDUALITY AND GROUP MEMBERSHIP

During the past decade, research on personality has focused less on the impact of society and culture on children and more on the dynamics of the individual's interaction within a particular social setting. Temperament may be highly important in shaping the quality of an individual's own social environment. In addition, some of this research has also concerned sex differences, suggesting that certain patterns of parent interaction may be beneficial for the emotional growth of a young boy but destructive for his sister and vice versa. Although siblings share an address there is growing evidence that their social environment may differ, according to sex or birth order, in ways that affect independence, cognitive style, and social aptitude.

### Temperament and Socialization

Temperament is the individual's style of interaction that excludes the motives and content of the action but characterizes his approach to people and things. Thomas, Chess, and Birch

(1968) studied the interaction of temperament and environment in the development of behavior disorders in young children. They identified nine temperamental characteristics on which children could be reliably observed: activity level, rhythmicity, approach or withdrawal, adaptability, intensity of reaction, threshold of responsiveness, quality of mood, distractibility, and attention span and persistence. Of 136 they followed from infancy into elementary school, 42 developed behavior disorders of sufficient intensity that clinical diagnosis and treatment procedures were established. One group, identified as "difficult children," were irregular in their biological functioning, withdrawing in new situations, intense in their reactions, and slow to adapt. Parents who developed consistent approaches in their nurturing of difficult infants were able to teach their children adaptive behavior by nursery school age or kindergarten that enabled the child to cope in the peer environment. On the other hand, parents of infants with similar temperament characteristics who were unable to meet the special demands of these children, found clinical help necessary at a later time. Other temperament factors that required special skill from parents and teachers were high intensity, hyperactivity, emotional irregularity, and persistence. Some adults were able to use the tendency toward persistence in productive ways for the child and to help him gradually learn to adapt to group demands and school schedules.

## Birth Order and Sex Differences

To a large extent the individuality that teachers see in school children and students has been established during the preschool years. Sears, Rau, and Alpert (1965) reported a study of masculinity and feminity of four-year-olds in relation to the adult-reaction patterns that were available in their homes for rein-

forcement and imitation. The data showed that children of both sexes adopted feminine behaviors when they were very young, but that boys developed a "cognitive map" of male behaviors by the third to fourth year of life. Further, this masculine behavior was influenced more by parental response to freedom of expression, control of sex and aggression, and nonpunitiveness in discipline than to the availability of male models in the home. Children of both sexes seemed to be harmed (in the sense that social maturity was retarded) by reinforcement for dependency on the part of the parent of the same sex, but not from the parent of the opposite sex.

Moss (1967) studied mother-infant interaction during the first three months of life by direct and carefully recorded observation. He found that mothers attended to and fondled boy babies, in the early months of life, significantly more than they did girl babies. Even when factors such as more crying and longer periods of wakefulness in boys were accounted for in statistical treatment, the time mothers attended the different sexes remained significantly greater for boys. They were encouraged more for musculature activity while girls were reinforced more frequently for cooing and babbling. To some extent the maternal behavior was responsive to infant individuality, while some differences in interaction were culturally derived and reinforced.

Rothbart (1971) studied mother-child interaction in which siblings of the same sex were paired with a five-year-old kindergarten child. Half of the pairs involved older sibs (age 7) and half involved younger sibs (age 3). All subjects were given picture-puzzle tasks in the presence of the mother. Rothbart discovered birth-order differences, including greater dependency on the part of older children, accompanied by higher standards of performance and higher school achievement. Mothers were more supportive and cautious in directing their sons and, of the four groups, mothers were most demanding, exacting, and intrusive toward their firstborn daughters, but they treated secondborn daughters with less pressure to achieve and were less likely to correct or to criticize them. Mothers did not interact more with older children of either sex, as had been anticipated.

Rosen and D'Andrade (1972) identified older boys who showed low achievement motivation and those who showed high achievement motivation. Their interactions with parents were compared in game situations where parents were able to participate in setting the standards of success imposed by the games. The evidence showed that independence training, although characteristic of working-class parents, was not related to high achievement motivation. However, achievement training was related, in this study, to the achievement motivation of the boys. The mothers of highly motivated boys became emotionally involved in the boys' success, they withdrew affection when the boys failed, they gave many options on how the game would be played, but they were clear in their expectation of what would be achieved. Apparently the boys were able to take more pressure from their mothers than from fathers whose domination had a negative effect on their sons' achievement motivation level.

Bronfenbrenner (1972) suggested that American parents of middle and low-middle classes are becoming more like upper-class parents in child-rearing practices, particularly in their showing affection, being more permissive, and using psychological (rather than physical) forms of discipline. On the basis of his extensive studies of adolescents, Bronfenbrenner suggested that daughters gain through this closing of the social gap by developing greater responsibility and achieving greater social acceptance while the sons become less sure of their leadership and their levels of aspiration are lowered. He observes some

signs of a general return to more explicit child-rearing practices in which paternal authority is stronger.

It is important for teachers to remember that these research conclusions are based on group results and that individuality is a complex of characteristics that overlap the trends observed for temperament, age, sex, or social class. Nevertheless, the research should give teachers pause for thought on the impact of their own interaction on the personality of the individual student.

## TEACHER'S ROLE IN SELF-ACTUALIZATION

The development of personality takes place much as physical development does. Just as children are dependent on adults for food and shelter in a physical sense, so they are dependent on adults for emotional support while they develop their own personality structure.

A gradual release of restraints while he is emotionally dependent enables the child to become a decision maker and his own person in specified areas of his life at each stage in his growth. Teachers, like parents, are authority figures who provide emotional stability while the young person learns roles of interaction, leadership, supportiveness, assertion, dependence, and affection. Much as the teacher might like to abdicate authority and free the student to make his own decisions, lessons from the evolution of human personality and classroom experience suggest that immature people will turn to the dominant members of the peer group for support in the absence of adult constraints. The human being must move gradually from the complete emotional dependence of infancy when he literally cannot differentiate himself from the rest of the world to a self-fulfilled person who is emotionally in command of himself. During this long period of attaining maturity, the young gradually assert themselves in expanding spheres of social activity. They must have resistance against which to assert the self in order to grow emotionally; constructive adult authority supplies this resistance tempered by love and experience. The self-actualizing teacher or parent has learned to subordinate some of the "I-me" in order to encourage the young to grow.

The study of personality is basically an attempt to understand how people got to be the way they are. The teacher's responsibility is to help students become better than they otherwise would be through helping them understand the forces that operate on them. Instead of waiting to see what happens to a child, the teacher intervenes constructively to help him in his struggle to resolve the crises of personality growth.

The teacher is able to see peer interaction from a detached and professional point of view. The emotions of young people are seen as real events. The detachment makes it possible to objectify, solidify, and externalize the affects that form the basis of behavior. As a member of the rearing generation the teacher has a responsibility to help the child conceptualize the dynamics of his own personality development and thus gain increasing control of the affective loadings that had been felt but not understood.

Accidental forces, when understood, can be subdued to minimize trial-and-error interaction. This rationalizing of otherwise subconscious forces helps the individual grow positively through his ability to manage those parts of his life that are subject to control. The teacher's role is to identify punitive constraints that are inherent in the culture and to create alternatives that have growth potential.

### Definition of Self-Actualization

Self-actualization may be defined as a state of development characterized by freedom to be oneself within a context of responsibility for the impact of one's actions on others (Maslow, 1971). All human beings seem to be compelled to seek self-fulfillment in response to a vital force that pushes each individual to be more than a passive reactor in his drive for individuality.

Self-concept is the person's self-evaluation in relation to other people. Concept of self consists of the person's own summation and interpretation of his personality. Self-concept reflects the level of attainment toward self-actualization. The concept that a person has of himself is often quite different from the concept that others have of him, even those who know him well. Part of the difference between the person's self-evaluation and the evaluations of others is a function of his aspirations—what he thinks he should be doing, as well as what he is doing. This aspiration is usually an unknown quantity to the outsider, who judges the person's success on the basis of role expectation and role performance; thus a student of low ability is thought to be doing well when he gets C grades. Fey (1957) found a number of relationships between self-acceptance and acceptance of others. In general, the student who is high in self-acceptance but low in acceptance of others is likely to impute base motives to other people concerning their evaluation of him; at the same time, he estimates that they rate him higher than they actually do. If acceptance of both self and others is high, the person tends to be responsible and well integrated. When both acceptances are low, the person tends to be anxious, dependent, impulsive, and accommodating to others. If the person is low in self-acceptance but high in acceptance of others, he is very unlikely to accept leadership roles. A review of some ways in which self-concept develops may be helpful.

### Protection of the Self-Concept

Most people who work professionally with young people have formed some assumptions about the durability of personality patterns that they try to develop and about the stability of some habits that they would eliminate. As a means of testing the stability of the self-concept, Kagan and Moss (1960) investigated the effect of gratification versus denial of children's dependency overtures when directed toward their parents. The investigators compared groups of males and females, observing the same individuals from ages three to six, six to ten, and twenty-one to twenty-nine. They rated childhood behavior on the Fels Research Institute 7-point scale of observations in school and at home. Ratings were on passivity when faced with obstacles, general dependence, and emotional support sought from female adults. Reliability checks were made against other raters' evaluations.

In independent evaluations, the same 54 subjects (then young adults) were rated on passive and dependent behavior: dependent gratifications in choice of vocation, dependent behavior toward love object, dependent behavior toward parents, withdrawal in the face of anticipated failure, and conflict over dependent behavior. For women, passive and dependent behavior was stable into adulthood, and the dependency was accepted with minimal anxiety. For men, however, dependency behavior at ages three to six tended not to correlate with dependency in adulthood. However, two measures at ages six to ten were correlated positively and significantly with adult dependency in males: (1) Boys who were high on instrumental behavior—seeking help with things—tended to turn to nonparental figures in adulthood, and (2) boys who showed a high degree of emotional dependence beyond early childhood tended to withdraw from possible failure situations as adults. Tachistoscopic studies—in which pictures are flashed on a screen for brief periods of time—involving the recognition of a conflict situation supported the data obtained during interviews indicating that the adult males were more conflicted over dependent behavior than the

women. Kagan and Moss noted that little social or geographic mobility had occurred in the lives of these subjects. Apparently the patterns of dependent and independent behavior stabilize in girls by the age of ten, at least when the environment remains unchanged. This study seems to indicate that young boys may be gratified when seeking emotional support, without fear that dependency will persist (Figure 10-5).

## Barriers to Self-Actualization

Self-actualization grows beyond psychological limitations that are imposed by unmet needs essential to continued growth. Hampering deficit needs are grounded in negative or nonexistent reinforcement at critical times during psychological growth. Self-actualization is moving upward in the need hierarchy, beyond restricting forces into an untrammeled level of existence.

Many aspects of personality are accidental. For some unfortunate people the chance factors of heredity and environment combine to fixate their development at restrictive levels. The fixations can be thought of in terms of Freud's infantile sexuality, Grave's lower levels of existence, or Maslow's deficit need hierarchy where love and affection were lacking at critical times in the development.

The person's phylogenic tendency to self-realization may be frustrated by punishing experiences in the attempt to grow up, by maladaptive solutions to the crises of growth. The young person chooses growth-destroying actions which are continued because they are reinforcing at a conditioning level (Figure 10-6).

The teacher will find evidence of how the self-concept is revealed in deficit need students through their defense mechanisms.

**Defense Mechanisms**   Havighurst (1949) described the ego defense mechanisms as the first part of the Freudian theory to be gener-

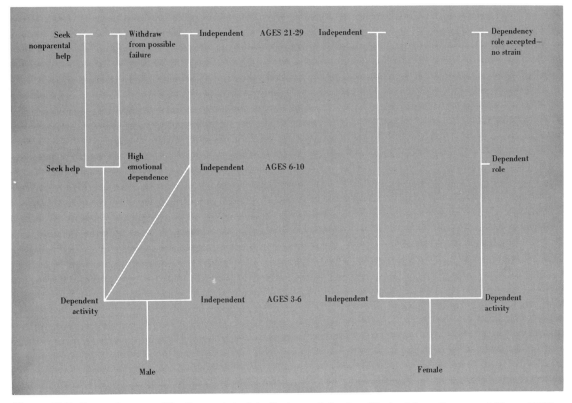

**Figure 10-5** Dependency gratification and denial effect on adult roles. (*Derived from Pagan and Moss, 1960.*)

ally accepted into American psychology, although there was little acknowledgment of the origin of the ideas. Freud was a naughty word for a long time. Defense mechanisms are means by which the ego modifies, suppresses, or otherwise deals with guilt feelings or fears that cannot be faced realistically. In terms of personality development, these mechanisms are the systematic ways in which a person handles disturbing data so that he can maintain an acceptable self-concept. All people use these mechanisms to some degree, but usually the smaller the individual's dependence on defense mechanisms, the more likely he is to have a strong ego and an integrated personality.

***Projection*** Of several common defense mechanisms, *projection*—in which the person projects his own problems or inadequacies to someone else—is most likely to have unfortunate consequences for beginning teachers. The manifestations of this mechanism in students are many and varied, but the following illustration shows why teachers should be aware of this form of expression. The fact that the person who is projecting is unaware of what he is doing makes the mechanism complicated for an adviser, principal, or teacher to handle.

After an outbreak of petty thieving from the lockers, Miss G., a gym teacher, announced that students should be sure to keep their things locked up. She made the class uncomfortably aware that one of the girls was

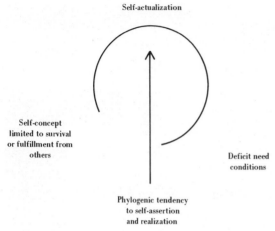

Self-actualization

Self-concept
limited to survival
or fulfillment from
others

Deficit need
conditions

Phylogenic tendency
to self-assertion
and realization

**Figure 10-6**  Restrictions to self-actualization.

probably a thief. Two days later Mary came to Miss G. to say that she had gone to the washroom and had seen Amy taking money out of a wallet that was in an unlocked locker.

Miss G. accused Amy of taking the money. Amy admitted that she had been off the gym floor at the time, but she said that she had not been feeling well and that Miss G. had excused her to go to the washroom. She denied having taken any money and burst into tears at the implication that she was a thief. Amy's parents came to see the principal to protest the incident, pointing out that Amy had always been scrupulously honest, even when money was kept in accessible places around the home. Ever since Amy was a little girl, she had readily admitted anything she had done wrong on her own volition or when they, the parents, had raised any question. They were thoroughly annoyed and showed their feelings to the principal.

Later investigation, which included catching Mary in the act of rifling a locker, proved almost conclusively that she had taken the money herself. Although she continued to deny any theft, she had more money to spend than the amount of her allowance. Other pieces of evidence pointed to Mary, who had

projected her own guilt on Amy. Apparently Mary went to the teacher really believing that she had seen Amy take the money. She accounted to herself for her own surplus money by telling herself that she had found it. The accusation of another is not always a projection, but it is often enough so that teachers should be wary of concluding that a child is guilty only on the basis of this kind of evidence. The safest approach for the teacher is to accept the story but to withhold judgment and include in the list of suspects the student who has made the accusation. Other courses of action can be embarrassing and humiliating both to the teacher and to the student accused unjustly.

***Logic-tight Compartmentalization***  Another defense mechanism that many people use to protect their egos is *logic-tight compartmentalization*, which consists in separating different roles so that there is little if any interrelationship between the various compartments of the person's life. He uses different value systems, or different forms of private logic, which are consistent within a role but not between roles. For example, a person may argue in favor of dedicating one's life to the service of others and thus become immune to the ravages of one's own poverty. The next day this person will boast of a family member because of the material possessions he has amassed and the easy life he has arranged for himself. This type of ego mechanism is applied almost universally as people evaluate themselves in different areas of responsibility.

***Rationalization***  An ego-protective device that many people use is *rationalization*, which involves changing the ground rules after failure to achieve a goal. A teacher puts a great deal of effort into obtaining a summer fellowship grant in Seaside University, only to see himself eliminated on the final list. At this point, especially if a scholarship offer comes from Inland, where Unknown State University is located, he can easily argue that the rain in Seaside would get depressing and that the clear air and bright sunshine of Inland would make life more pleasant. Many variations are played on this theme. Some come under the heading of "sour grapes," when what cannot be had is not wanted, while others, under the heading of "sweet lemons," consist in dwelling on the advantages of doing what had to be done anyway.

**Fixation and Regression** *Fixation* and *regression* are two other defense mechanisms. In these, the modus vivendi involves removing the ego from the threat by going back to a simpler stage in life where the threat did not exist. It is helpful to the teacher to realize that the person who uses these protective devices does not do so consciously.

Hilgard (1949) pointed out the element of self-deception in all defense mechanisms. Using reasons one knows are false to deceive someone else is not rationalization, but lying. The emphasis in defense mechanisms is protection of the self-concept. Amnesia is a form of ego protection. The victim does not forget all he has learned; if he did, he would lose his ability to function as a person. His memory loss is related to facets of his past life that have threat value to his psyche. Defense mechanisms enable a person to live with himself by creating psychological order and compatibility to resolve the disorder and conflict that occur when he fails in his attempt to have his self-concept verified by the world outside. He learns ways to defend his self-concept.

**Failure Syndrome** Unfortunately, some students have built a concept of themselves as such bad people that they deserve to be punished for their evildoing. Guilt is a substantial part of their self-concept. The most common source of this destructive force seems to be the acceptance of a parent's value system while feeling unable to live up to the accepted standard. In many cases, the value system is not one by which the parents live, but the child's idealization of a system. The failure to have role performance match role acceptance leads to feelings of guilt, worthlessness, and the necessity of atonement.

As this feeling of failure grows, it becomes generalized as a self-concept as an unworthy person. The next step is to feel a need for punishment that can only be self-imposed. In the real world, the person is often living an exemplary life, far beyond the level of performance expected by those around him. However, this person does not suffer from real sins, but from imagined ones. The mechanism deceives him, so that he is unaware of the role he has assumed. His method of self-punishment usually turns on failure to attain reasonable goals; he runs as fast as he can but always slowly enough to ensure defeat. He arranges outcomes so that punishment is attached to his effort. Usually no part of this mechanism is known to the person, who is both victim and perpetrator of the damage. He suffers from bad luck, but in reality is paying a penalty for his imagined sins.

### Changing the Self-Concept

The failure syndrome underlies the basic problem in changing the self-concept. The student does not know why he acts as he does. Usually he does not have a clear idea of himself. Although he habitually acts in predictable ways, he is unaware of the probability that he will act in these ways under certain definable circumstances, and analysis of his behavior is foreign to his normal level of thinking. A severely disturbed person may require psychiatric treatment to help him reconstitute his self-concept, a process that may involve psychotherapeutic or psychoanalytic sessions extending over months or years. As a general rule, serious emotional problems are associated with deeply hidden self-concepts involving guilt feelings for real or fancied acts which are so heinous that they cannot be accepted and which are buried so deeply in the unconscious that their recovery is difficult and time-consuming.

In most cases where school help is sufficient, the hidden part of the self-concept is easier to uncover and to examine than in the case of extremely disturbed persons who need more specialized help. Often the "sins" that the person has committed are serious only in terms of his own frame of reference. His role concept is often quite different from the role expectation of his community, but his stress point is the variance between his role concept and his role performance as he sees them, rather than between the role expectation and role performance as these are seen by others. Many highly moral and virtuous people suffer seriously from guilt complexes that their more deviant fellow citizens are unable to recognize or understand.

In serious cases, the skilled ministrations of a psychiatrist will be required to help the individual stand off and look at himself, but the teacher's response toward him at this time can be helpful or unfortunate. Literature courses can be starting points, using analysis of characters as nonthreatening springboards to later study of oneself. Questions that probe into the causes of specific forms of behavior, the reasons why a character felt misgivings about himself, and the kinds of childhood experience that lead to certain feelings about self all offer steps to self-understanding. Discussions based on such questions can provide students with the basic association learning that makes possible later conceptualizations about themselves. This kind of exploration can be extended to causes behind innocuous behavior of extroverted class members. Extroverts are less likely to be hurt by this kind of attention that introverts, who may search for hidden implications that do not exist. Further guidance toward conceptualization

can come later with similar—now familiar— help in examining students' self-concepts in individual conversation between the student and teacher. They can be helped to see themselves a little more clearly than before. Social science teachers can use historical figures as starting points for discussion, science teachers can use the lives of famous scientists in a similar way, and language teachers can illuminate the lives of writers or even use some national characteristics as the foundations for understanding people's self-concepts.

The steps a teacher uses are now familiar to the reader: First, provide the student with association bits to form a foundation; second, help him integrate these bits into a conceptual structure or relationship; and third, ask questions that bridge conceptualization and motivation. Choosing the foundation material is more difficult in the area of self-examination and change than in subject-matter areas.

A clearer knowledge of his self-concept may lead the student to desire to change or to develop a more comfortable acceptance of the roles he is living. Although many students would probably benefit from such analysis, the teacher is not likely to undertake extra and difficult work for this purpose alone. The need of some students to build a more dynamic self-image in order to succeed in class work is more likely to motivate a teacher to undertake the necessary work involved in helping them to explore the self-concept.

Once the individual has developed the ability to see himself with a degree of objectivity, change becomes possible. The direction that change might take and the personality loading of new self-orientations can be explored with some dispassion. Understanding motives will require the same kinds of underpinnings from association gained in literature and in real life that generated student ability to see the self. No shortcut three-minute discourse by the teacher can substitute for the gradual amassing of the fundamental information about possibilities and consequences. The need for the student to build basic knowledge rather than to accept it ready-made from a teacher makes teaching difficult. It is much more comfortable to think that the young person who can parrot the teacher's words has learned the ideas than to build up the necessary foundation. Understanding of the need for this basic preparation within the student makes it possible for teachers to provide opportunities to develop motivation and to avoid the assumption that it can be given ready-made.

The knowledge that self-concepts shape each person's life, coupled with the knowledge that other people influence a person's life-style, can lead to a belief in the possibility of change in oneself. Change then comes to depend on an assessment of the costs involved and the returns to be expected. The crucial point in building motive power for change seems to be the building of the conceptualization that change is possible under specified conditions of cost in personality effort.

### Effects of Value Structures in Building toward Self-Actualization

One of the cornerstones of self-actualization is self-acceptance. Integration, the key to both personality and character, involves the fitting together of the various aspects of the person's life and psychological makeup so that they are not in conflict with one another. It is sometimes possible to accomplish this with growing children, but it is not commonly done since many people act in many conflicting ways in building children's lives. More commonly, integration is achieved by analyzing and evaluating existing structures of the personality and by deliberately changing certain parts to restructure a harmonious result.

A general congruency between role conception and role acceptance is essential if the person is to be willing to live with himself and those around him. Essentially, this willingness

to do one's best with the character that has been built and discovered is a level 3 operation. The conceptualization consists of seeing what the personality mechanisms are and then moving on from this point to a determination to be willing to build upon this framework. The choice is one of self-direction.

One's value system is incorporated into his characterization of a life-style. Inasmuch as character carries with it the implication of outside judgment, the value system of the person who is evaluated by others as having a strong or a "good" character usually conforms to the mores of the society in which he lives. The incorporation of value systems into the personality is another way of explaining how the superego is built. By identification with parents and other adult figures whose behavior the community sanctions, the individual conceivably can live out his life in conformity while gaining a reputation for having a strong character. The reader may recognize this imitative activity, which is a functioning characteristic of the association level.

The individual acquires the material for conceptualizing a value system by abstracting basic ideas from the orders and requirements of his identity figures. When he incorporates these abstractions as an integral part of his judgment of the rightness or wrongness of his activities, he has identified with the model.

## DIMENSIONS OF PERSONALITY

The dimensions of personality are separated into the chapters that constitute the following section on human development and intelligence. The impact of physical characteristics on personality have already been suggested in the typologies. How these physical characteristics develop is discussed in Chapter 11. Perceptual development, which is basic to all school learning, is treated as an extension of neurology of learning in Chapter 12. The separate sensory systems provide input which the person integrates and acts upon in an increasingly idiosyncratic manner that is the cause of individual differences in the classroom. Emotional development, the content of Chapter 13, is a critical ingredient in the growth of personality. Erikson identified three processes of development that come together in each human life: the biological inheritance of the organism, the organization of experience in the individual ego, and the social coherence of family class and community. His stages of man, based on Freudian concepts of emotional development, provide the theme for one way of looking at emotional development. Piaget's theory of cognitive development, detailed in Chapter 14, provides a bridge from the developmentally oriented themes of Chapters 11 to 13 to the issues raised by the study of intelligence, including the relative influence of nature and nurture in Chapters 15 and 16.

## SUMMARY

Personality is the life signature by which an individual is known; it is the sum of all that sets him apart and makes him unique. Definitions of personality have stressed (1) an individual orientation, which may be concentrated on either inner operations or outer manifestations, and (2) a group understanding, in which the individual is a unique example of many interacting components.

Largely because of the impossibility of maintaining an infinite number of possibilities in focus, there has been a tendency to group personalities into stereotypes or typologies. Freud, Jung, and Adler segregated people into groups according to the kinds of emotional handicaps they suffer. Kretschmer and Sheldon grouped people into personality types that correlate with physical development. The authors have postulated descriptive patterns of personality that are based on motivation

and are subject to change through learning. The individuality of the student always takes precedence over the classifications. However, the classifications can be helpful as a starting point in work with the individual.

The teacher's role as an authority substitute supplies resistance to the child for irresponsible attempts on his part at self-assertion. As a professional adult, the teacher's role in helping the student achieve self-actualization includes: (1) conceptualizing the forces in the personality dynamic of the student, (2) remaining concerned but detached in helping the young person conceptualize his role, (3) observing growth and providing optimum amounts of authority and permissiveness.

Self-actualization is defined as a state of development characterized by freedom to be one's self within a context of responsibility for the impact of one's actions on others.

The self-concept is the internalized view of one's own personality. As the self-concept is formed, various ways are found to protect it from damage. These defense mechanisms—projection, compartmentalization, rationalization, fixation, and regression—are often sources of distortion away from a fully integrated and completely healthy personality. Learning can influence the rebuilding of the self-concept and of the personality.

## SELF-DIRECTING ACTIVITIES

1 Analyze and define the kinds of stereotypes you have been using as you thought of the personality of your associates.
2 Develop a plan for helping a student modify his self-concept.
3 Analyze the kinds of defense mechanisms you have used during a recent week. Accept the way you have been responding or work out a new way of dealing with the problems that led to the defense mechanisms.

# Chapter 11

An experiment in education in Ecuador. (*Courtesy of the United Nations*)

# GROWTH, DEVELOPMENT, AND LEARNING

When you have completed this chapter, you will have a conceptualization of human biology as the context of human learning. The goals of this chapter are to:

◖ Generalize the patterns of growth

◖ Differentiate the genetic and environment factors in prenatal development

◖ Relate early motor development with speech and cognitive growth

◖ Establish a knowledge base for empathy with adolescents and the aging

◖ Define correctly:
morphogenesis
cephalocaudal
proximodistal
idiographic
nomothetic
zygote
embryo
fetus
ectoderm
mesoderm
endoderm
anoxia
neonate
prehension

The protracted biological development of the human being predisposes him to gradual development of social, perceptual, emotional, and intellectual maturity. His prolonged periods of infancy, childhood, and adolescence give the human animal many advantages over other organisms in the mammalian species. During the months a human infant is dependent upon others to see that he is fed, carried, bathed, and changed, he experiences the close physical contact needed for his development as a social creature. By the time the human child is able to run about, he is also able to shout and laugh, to request or refuse food, and to seek or withdraw from new experiences. During these same two years of growth, the rhesus monkey has attained puberty, the laboratory kitten has produced two generations of cats, and the hooded rat has become senile. In the development of large muscles and the achievement of mobility, the typical child of two years is comparable to the chimpanzee of two months, the rabbit of two weeks, and the colt of two hours.

## DYNAMICS OF HUMAN GROWTH

Growth in an organism is that structural change which increases its level of functioning in specific ways, although the potential for some different but related function may be concomitantly decreased. While the toddler is learning to run, for example, his skill as a crawler may decline. The interlocking rise of one skill with the decline in a related skill has particular significance for teachers, who must sometimes wait for developmental readiness while at the same time avoid postposing learning opportunities past the time when optimum success can be expected. Growth is a process of patterning human behavior: physical, perceptual, emotional, and cognitive. Several important concepts regarding the nature of growth have been observed and verified by many investigators. Although authorities disagree on the emphasis a teacher or a counselor should place on various facets of growth in students, the authors consider those explanations most helpful which feature the dynamics of individual development and which encompass the lifetime of the human being.

Each successive moment in a person's life brings changes in his physical status, his drive or motivation, and his potential to cope with his environment. From this point of view, the human organism continues to grow, at least in some ways, until death. Growth patterns—which develop simultaneously and in relationship to one another—need to be considered separately if they are to be analyzed and defined. At the same time, the teacher works with the student as a whole person and not just one facet of him. Although the psychological effects of extreme physical or social deprivation are widely recognized, many less obvious interactions affect the growth patterns of students, including their intellectual growth. Dysfunction or regression in one aspect of development affects the total self.

Although each individual grows in his own way, the following generalizations suggest some dynamics of human growth:

Growth is continuous.
Growth is sequential.
Growth is integrated.
Growth is unique.
Growth is maturation.
Growth is learning.

### Growth Is Continuous

As a dynamic, energy-consuming system, the living organism must continually supply many needs besides growth by expansion. Through various degrees of activity or rest, the organism operates its own mechanisms to control temperature, rebuild cells, and produce enzymes. The blood courses through the body continuously, carrying at different times different amounts of the materials of change: oxygen, sugar, amino acids, antibodies, hormones, viruses, and wastes. The external evidence of internal physical change may be observed in every person. The infant wails loudly one moment and then nurses contentedly when given his bottle. On Tuesday, David's teacher recognized his first efforts to clean his table after painting. On Wednesday, she will look for an opportunity to reinforce the behavior again, but her standard for praise will be a little higher than before. Each time the center on the school's basketball team reports to the court, he is different in subtle ways because of his program of eating, resting, and practicing, which coaches call "training." These obvious examples of physical growth involve some of the structural changes of development, called *morphogenesis*, which occur continuously.

Some of the changes that occur continuously in the development of a mature person are more subtle and more difficult to observe than the growth of an infant or a basketball player. With each new perception, the individual's neurological structure is altered; with each personal contact, his pattern of social interaction is supplemented. Each evening that the student spends in intensive study enhances his fund of retrievable knowledge in measurable ways. The nature of the structural changes that occur in learning is not completely understood, and the concept of physical change in learning is not accepted by everyone. The nature of growth, however obscure it may be as a physical phenomenon, is easily observed in the changes in the individual's behavior. When the infant is given his bottle, he stops crying immediately, before the formula could have changed the sugar content of his blood, because he has learned that relief from hunger will follow. The *rate* of growth may change, as in adolescents whose height increases rapidly. Some growth patterns become complete, as in adults, whose skeletal height remains relatively constant. However, the growth of cells and neurological systems continues through life. A man is said to grow tall, to grow in wisdom, and even to grow old.

### Growth Is Sequential

Organisms, including human beings, tend to develop in an orderly and predictable sequence. In both prenatal and postnatal growth, two principles tend to operate simultaneously. First, the line of development from the head downward, called *cephalocaudal*, is seen in the early appearance of the head in the human fetus. At approximately two weeks into the gestation period, the head is about the same length as the rest of the body. When weight is the referent, the proportion of the head to the rest of the body decreases gradually, from one-fourth at birth, to one-eighth at age twelve, to one-twelfth at age twenty-one. The infant gradually becomes mobile by lifting first his head, then his chest, and then his abdomen. He sits, crawls, stands alone, and then walks, in that order. The sequence is orderly and predictable, but the timing is varied.

Shirley (1933) reported a longitudinal study of the development of the motor sequence from birth to age two. She observed 20 subjects in spontaneous as well as structured activity to determine whether the sequence of motor development remained consistent when various sequences (postural control, locomotion, and manipulation), each of which was dependent upon preceding acts within the sequence, were combined and observed in a single series. She determined the median age at which 42 items of controlled behavior were first observed and arranged them into a single developmental sequence. Items with an average developmental separation of approximately four weeks were paired and checked for reversals in the growth order of the individual babies. Of over 5,000 case comparisons, 85 percent were in conformity to the order established by the medians for the group. Rank-order correlations, when checked against the sequence based on medians, ranged between .93 and .97. Shirley interpreted the consistency of the babies as indicative of the reliability of the motor development sequence, and its harmony with accepted laws of growth order as evidence of validity. Teachers, however, should be alert to the 15 percent who do not conform to the predicted pattern and to the evidence they provide that variation in pattern is possible.

The second line of development, called *proximodistal*, progresses from the center of the organism outward to the periphery (Crow & Crow, 1956). In the human embryo, the stump of the upper arm appears in the trunk. During the next few weeks, the stumps of the limbs elongate, the outer segment broadens, five lobes appear, and finally the skeletal segments of fingers develop. Legs grow in the same order, but they follow the principle of cephalocaudal growth and hence they develop after the arms develop.

### Growth Is Integrated

The human being grows as an organized, integrated unit. He searches his environment for whatever is his uppermost need at the time: food, love, information, cigarettes, companionship, revenge, oxygen, sex, or aesthetic expression. The personal and environmental resources available to him at the moment will determine how he manipulates the environment to preserve his physiological or psychological entity: whether to eat, to turn on the radio, or to chase the neighbor's children from

the orchard. John returns home after his late-afternoon lecture to find three of the neighbor's children in his peach tree eating the fruit he has been zealously nurturing. John's value of the peach tree is uppermost at the moment, and this motivates him to the extent that he risks his neighbor's misunderstanding by ordering the young visitors out of the yard. Entering the back door, he sees his wife's frown as she serves the roast. Quickly he selects her favorite albums and starts the hi-fi. The pleasure she associates with the music shows in her expression, and a happy atmosphere is restored. In a few moments, John experiences the hunger pangs he felt as he left the campus, and soon his food is eaten. John's environment is altered. He has eliminated the internal stimuli for eating. He is no longer hungry, but thirsty for coffee. However, he must wait, unsatisfied, because Mary feels uneasy at the sight of dirty plates on the table. She must rinse the dishes before she can enjoy her coffee. John alleviates his tension by lighting his pipe. People go through life integrating their activities to attain equilibrium. Teachers can use the principle of integration by alternating tension and release or tension-satisfying experiences as students work through the hour or the day.

This tendency for the organism to operate its mechanisms so as to retain a steady state of well-being is called *homeostasis*. Lack of balance in the organism creates the tension of hunger, fatigue, chill, or fear. The restoration of physical comfort, through satisfaction of the need, constitutes reinforcement of the behavior that accompanied the gratification. During interaction with the environment, both the person and the environment are changed. Note how John has changed the internal and external world for his wife. When she meets her next-door neighbor in the market the next day, her emotional and physical being will not be the same as if the peach-tree incident had not occurred. Whatever Mary's feelings, she will respond as an organized unit to protect her psychological self from disruption or injury. Whether she upbraids Mrs. Smith for her children's actions, avoids Mrs. Smith, apologizes for her husband's behavior, or acts as if no incident had occurred, her interaction with the neighbor is likely to be much more intricate than her husband's response to frustration of his hunger for homegrown peaches. People are integrated, partly by their purposes, which move them through successive and interrelated forms of imbalance toward growth. Much of this growth consists in learning complex responses to multivariate stimuli.

In his book *The First Five Years of Life*, Gesell (1940) proposed a description of mental growth. He equated all human abilities, including intelligence, to the ability to grow. He described the mind as a growing system, undifferentiated from the "living organic complex." He stressed the "essential uniformity of the mechanisms of growth at all ages":

> From the standpoint of the mechanics of development, not only are the various ages similar, but the diverse fields of behavior are similar. Posture and locomotion, speech, adaptive behavior, and personal-social behavior are obedient to common laws. Accordingly it would improve our management of disciplinary problems if we could recognize in the field of personal-social behavior the same molding mechanisms which govern the development of creeping and walking [p. 8].

Although Gesell did not separate mental growth from physical growth per se, he did distinguish between major fields of behavior: motor characteristics, adaptive behavior, language, and personal-social behavior.

Behavior is organized in young children through the concomitant growth of neural, muscular, and other tissues. The uniformity and harmony so frequently noted in the development of infants give way to more varied, more complex, and more individualized growth as the child becomes older. Different facets of growth proceed at different rates as the individual develops. Teachers are probably most aware of differential growth as they note differences in physical and mental growth. Children who vary significantly from average intelligence (very bright or very dull) increase the gap gradually between their physical and their mental levels of maturity. Gifted students, for example, are far above the norms in intellectual development but tend to be only slightly above the norms in physical development.

### Growth Is Unique

When the characteristics common to a group are known, case studies and anecdotal records can be interpreted within the framework of group normative data. Systematic observations of the individual are extremely useful to the teacher, clinician, or counselor who works with people. A study of the individual, when conducted on a professional level, is called *idiographic* research (Mussen & Conger, 1956). By contrast, *nomothetic* research is conducted to establish general laws or statements. To teach individuals, the instructor must be concerned with observing the uniqueness or individuality that sets each one apart from the group.

**Uniqueness of the Species** Human beings differ from other mammals in important ways, including their ability to learn speech. In a carefully recorded study, the Kelloggs (1933) reared a young chimpanzee, Gua, with their son, Donald, aged ten months. By the time Gua was sixteen months old, she had learned to wear clothes, to sleep in a bed, to drink from a cup, to handle a spoon, and to use the toilet. Being relatively more mature than Donald, she was superior to him in mobility and in coordination. By the time Donald was beginning to talk, Gua had acquired a meaning vocabulary of 50 words, but she was unable to acquire human speech. Living in a superior human environment, the chimpanzee learned to walk upright much of the time. Donald learned some apelike behavior by imitating Gua, who did not provide a superior learning environment for the child. Although unable to communicate with words, Gua learned some empathic behavior. After being taken from the Kelloggs, she rejected other apes, languished in her cage, and died. Although some lower animals learn to obey verbal commands and respond to graphic symbols, the ability to use symbols as generative speech is a unique function of Homo sapiens. In spite of parallel rearing practices, the differences between the chimpanzee and the human child persisted.

The use of language enables a person to develop a psychological self, which is differentiated and maintained through mental processes involving language (Harris, 1963). The biological capacity of the organism to resist damage and to heal itself appears to have a psychological counterpart. People are able to perceive experience in such a way as to support their own private view of the world and to preserve the integrity of their own personalities. An understanding of history enables man to conceptualize the processes by which he has arrived at his present state and, in light of this, to reorganize some of the processes of personal development. The symbol system enables people to adjust to conflicts between their biological drives and social controls. Man is able to manipulate his future through goal-setting activities that change his drive organization, his external environment, or both.

Cole (1953) was impressed by the influence on an individual of his interaction with others. He saw this interaction as the process by which the individual, born with certain genetic reaction systems, is forced into patterns of action, habits of perceiving, and personal ways of adjusting to the expectations of others:

> Organisms become persons as they participate in human society. Without the environment of persons, the child could not even maintain himself at birth. He is equipped with reflexes and is reactive at the start, and the tensions of his homeostatic mechanisms arise promptly and automatically. In contrast to the precise and elaborate reflexes of insects . . . the human infant's responses seem random, diffuse, unpatterned, and his road to equilibrium is longer and more variable. Helpless as he is, his cry may prompt an adult to action; but the skill and continuing concern of the adult are what keep him alive. . . .
>
> In coming to terms with the vitally important world of persons, the child acquires a personality. He takes on the common patterns of action and belief, even as he organizes these into a unique life style [p. 42].

Usually the teacher is one of the significant adults who influence the individual's life-style. The school is concerned with how the child or youth develops within society, including how he develops differently from any other person.

**Uniqueness of the Individual** Developmental psychologists use two very useful terms, acquired from biologists, that distinguish between functions that are common to one's kind and functions that are learned through training. Functions common to the human race, such as crawling, sitting, and standing, are called *phylogenetic* functions. By definition, phylogeny is the evolutionary development of a species (Chapter 10). Ducklings take to the water and swim without training or practice, in spite of the frantic cluckings of a foster mother hen, who—like all her species—will not go into the water to save the babies she devotedly rears. The related term *ontogenetic* refers to the individual's biological development. Some writers classify swimming, skating, and bicycle riding as ontogenetic functions because they are acquired through training and practice.

Although this distinction between phylogenetic and ontogenetic functions is useful in understanding the difference between nature and nurture, or maturation and learning, this dichotomy is seldom if ever mutually exclusive. The long period of dependence of human babies and the fastidious care they receive make the distinction of racial versus individual functioning obscure. The duckling can swim as early as he can walk to the water. Walking upright may be assumed to be a phylogenetic function of human beings since all humans eventually walk upright, and swimming may be considered an ontogenetic function since many human beings do not learn to swim.

Gesell (1940) noted that the newborn is an individual—no two are alike:

Even newborn infants display significant individual differences in their physiological processes, in their reactions to internal and extrinsic stimuli, in their patterns of feeding, sleeping, and waking activity, and in perceptivity. These neonatal expressions of individuality are largely the end products of the primary mental growth which was accomplished in the long period of gestation [p. 12].

This long period of gestation is part of the mammalian inheritance that is mentioned frequently in the literature on child development.

The individuality in growth patterns that appears at an early age tends to be maintained. Ames (1940) reported the constancy of motor development: Children who show relative proficiency in behavior patterns continue to show a high level of proficiency in newly learned motor skills. Terman, in his classical

studies of the development of genetic intelligence (1925, 1926, 1930, 1947, 1959), found that IQs remain relatively stable over a 30-year period in most individuals. Bayley (1940) is among those who think the personality variations that are observable in young babies build into personality patterns that persist throughout life. Height curves for groups of children have shown that, over a period of years, the short and tall individuals in a population tend to remain the short and tall individuals in subsequent measures (Baldwin, 1922). These group data obscure individual exceptions to group patterns, and any pupil or student may be the exception.

With increasing age, the gap between an individual's measure of a trait and the group norm tends to increase because the rate of growth in individuals tends to be consistent. Children whose mental age is less than their chronological age tend to persist in the pattern of slower growth, and therefore the absolute gaps widen between mental age and chronological age. The slow child seldom catches up, and the gifted child becomes increasingly atypical mentally. The effects of environment, motivation, and learning tend to be stable in a given family and to accumulate and stabilize the child's individuality, unless some critical and severe change occurs in his life space, in which case his personality may change dramatically. For some deprived children, teachers provide the critical change force. Likewise, for advanced students, some schools develop stultified or resentful learners because activities that offer no new satisfactions are painful.

### Growth Is Maturation

The term "maturation" has varied and interesting usages in English: aging or ripening; incubation or gestation; suppuration, meaning festering; refinement or perfection; development, meaning elaboration; and "full development," meaning completion. In common usage, the term "maturity" often denotes a state of readiness for a particular responsibility. The kindergarten teacher selects Mark, a "mature" pupil, to deliver the milk money to the office. Much later in the school year, it becomes Jimmy's turn to deliver the money, but the teacher considers him so "immature" that she sends Susan along to be sure it is put into the hands of the school secretary. Both boys are able to carry the money bag, both can locate the office, and both can relay whatever information is needed. The teacher may really have in mind a certain dependability or social responsibility that has little to do with Jimmy's state of physical development or his level of speech. However, parents, teachers, and others seem to find the label "mature" or "immature" convenient for expressing undefined notions about pupil behavior. "Immature" is an objectionable term in educational psychology when used to explain misbehavior in a child or student, when the etiology of the behavior has not been established or when used by a person who lacks the necessary knowledge to be definitive.

In this book, the term *maturation* means the culminating state in any growth process. A growth stage can be distinguished by direct observation of physiological data or by the organism's ability to perform a function. Specific known and unknown physiological maturation is essential to each new step in psychological development. Cognitive growth accompanies and stimulates growth in the CNS. Known and unknown forms of deterioration probably occur in biological structures that mature but remain unused.

In the context of human development, maturation is the process by which an individual's inherited endowment comes to fruition. Maturation provides the necessary physiological structures or foundations for learning. The stimulation of maturation in a human organism leads him to try responses that are generally regarded as phylogenetic functions; thus the learning and maturation processes are interacting. Stimulation of the different kinds of neurons during mental, muscular, or visceral activity generally increases the individual's ability to perform related functions or to transfer his learning.

Babies in poor institutions, and some babies reared at home, who receive little personal attention or environmental stimulation learn to sit, stand, and walk later than would normally be expected, when compared with controls living in excellent institutions or in good family situations. Some of these babies learn to avoid eye contact and generally fail to thrive (Koch, 1968). Head Start programs for preschool children have recognized the need for teaching—that is, for learning—as well as for maturation. An example of intellectual stimulation for motor development was noted in Elyse, aged seven months, who was able to roll from her stomach to her back and back again—a typical developmental accomplishment for her age. Since she had never rolled off her blanket, her parents left her in the middle of the living room floor while they went into the kitchen to have lunch. Much to their surprise, Elyse rolled 12 feet across the living room floor and in through the kitchen door. When she was picked up and returned to the blanket, she cried loudly. Apparently Elyse wanted to get where the others had gone, and she demonstrated unusual growth in locomotion skills to reach her goal. Motivation, which is learned behavior, may be very important in the rate of development of locomotion abilities. Teachers can often stimulate improved use of a mature ability that has not functioned because there was no need to use it.

Most decisions in school concerning a child's readiness to function successfully in a specific situation should take into account whether or not he has had a previous opportunity to acquire and demonstrate the necessary abilities. Hurlock (1956) suggested three criteria that indicate a child's "state of readiness": (1) his interest in learning a function, (2) how sustained his interest is over a period of time, and (3) what progress he makes with practice. Readiness for reading is appraised by formal and informal observations of the child's level of development—including spoken language, perceptual integration, and motivation. Rather than introducing new activities at normatively derived chronological ages, the teacher should make skillful observations of day-to-day growth in order to determine the teachable moment.

In developmental psychology and in education, little attention has been paid to the obverse implication—which is inherent in the biological concept of maturation—that an organism's peak of physiological readiness is followed by a decline. An individual who is given no opportunity to learn the functions for which he has attained physiological and psychological maturity is handicapped, particularly if his culture had identified the function as a necessary part of growing up. Neuromuscular structures that are not used atrophy rather quickly. Similarly, when the organism does not utilize a structure for learning over a period of time, the structure does not remain "ready" and available for later use.

J. A. Harris (1930) compared the major forms of physical growth from birth to age twenty. Using the functional state of normal twenty-year-olds as a base at 100 percent, he measured various parts and organs of the body and plotted his measures in percentage of size or function at age twenty. The values of measures taken successively showed the rate and extent of lymphoid, neural, general, and genital development (Figure 11–1). Lymphoid masses, lymph nodes, and the hymus grow very rapidly until the age of approximately eleven; this growth rate is then reduced very rapidly, at which point these are

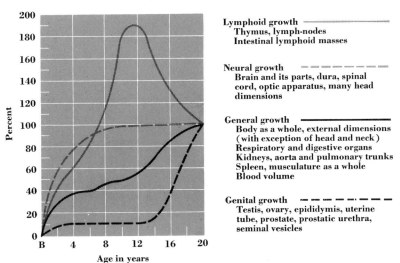

**Figure 11-1** Differential growth patterns. (*Adapted from J. A. Harris, The Measurement of Man. Minneapolis: University of Minnesota Press. By permission of the publisher, 1930.*)

little more than half their maximum size. The brain, the spinal cord, and other parts of the neurological system grow more rapidly than any of the other functions studied until the age of approximately six, when the system reaches about 90 percent of adult size. The body as a whole—external dimensions, respiratory and digestive organs, and blood volume—grows very rapidly during the early childhood and adolescent years, to attain full overall growth at about age twenty. The genital organs develop slowly until age six or seven, show little increase or slight decreases to the onset of puberty, and then grow more rapidly than any of the other physiological structures. Teachers may see in these data some biological explanations for the strains that accompany puberty, when the genital growth is accelerating rapidly, the growth of the lymphoid system is decreasing rapidly, and the hormone levels that are part of each system are changing dramatically. Balance between different forces is in a constant flux during this period of development.

During the early and middle adulthood years, the rhythmic curves of the physical dimension charts level off and remain relatively stable. Subtle biological changes continue to occur within the various systems, including the glandular, skeletal, neurological, muscular, digestive, and circulatory systems. This prolonged period of stability eases the extension, elaboration, and refinement of psychological systems and behavior patterns. The individual who enters his twenties emotionally prepared for adulthood can continue to grow in the characteristics that are essentially human: empathy, creativity, compassion, wisdom, courage, and individuality.

## Growth Is Learning

Earlier in this book, the major theories of learning were presented and the dimensions of the learning-motivation model were developed in detail. Research from diverse sources was assembled to support the thesis that physiological changes occur in the neurological systems of the brain when learning takes place. The close relationship between growth and learning may mean that when potential opportunities are missed or postponed, the person's potential effectiveness is reduced. Penfield and Roberts (1959) reported that damage to speech areas of the brain did not prevent recovery of the speech function in their patients but that full recovery was almost impossible in patients past the age range of nine to twelve. They hypothesized that the decline of potential for speech learning occurs when other uses preempt the unused areas of the alternative hemisphere of the brain, thus making subsequent changes in the use of a potential speech area more difficult. Apparently there are peaks in an individual's ability to do particular kinds of learning, after which time the foundations for this new learning are established with greater difficulty. Hurlock (1950) cited the disappearance of certain features with increasing age. Among the physical features that disappear gradually as the child grows older, the most important ones are the thymus gland, often called the "gland of babyhood," located in the throat; the pineal gland, at the base of the brain; the Babinski and Darwinian reflexes; "baby hair"; and the first set of teeth.

Babbling and infantile speech, including those phonemes which are absent from the language spoken, also disappear as more effective communication develops. Forms of locomotion such as crawling and creeping outlive their usefulness and are replaced by walking and running. Certain senses become less keen in adults than in young children, especially taste and smell. Various investigators have differed concerning the age at which maximal mental power is attained, depending upon the kinds of intellectual functioning being tested. This chapter focuses on the physiological growth patterns of human beings and, in the process, indicates some of the aberrations or abnormalities of physical growth that may limit or enhance intellectual growth.

## LIFE BEFORE BIRTH

New knowledge of the physiology of prenatal and postnatal growth has revised many notions about human learning before birth. Human life begins with the union of the sperm cell and the ovum. The new organism, called a *zygote*, develops according to a coded plan (DNA) inherited in the chromosomes. A zygote that survives the germinal period to attach itself to the mother's uterine wall is an *embryo*. When the embryo shows skeletal growth through calcification, it is defined as a *fetus*. Studies of prenatal development have identified many facets of intrauterine environment that affect the growth of the organism. Many factors related to intelligence that were formerly thought to be hereditary are now attributed to prenatal environment.

### Zygote: Multiplication of Cells

The newly conceived organism enters the uterus as a cluster of cells the size of a pinhead. According to the program in the DNA molecules, these cells separate into an inner cluster, which forms the embryo, and an outer circle, which forms a layer of protective tissue, the *trophoblast*. After drifting in the uterus for several days, tendrils of membrane grow out from the zygote and attach themselves to the receptive walls of the uterus. Estrogen and progesterone, released during ovulation into the mother's bloodstream, alter the hormone balance, causing a thickening of the walls of the uterus and making available

the nutrients for growth. When the zygote has attached itself to the mother, it begins to live as a parasite, drawing nourishment, oxygen, and hormones from her bloodstream indirectly through the placenta (Figure 11-2).

Early zygotic growth is characterized by rapid *differentiation*; that is, different cells develop into different organs and structures. This differentiation is based on the position of individual cells within the general mass and on the nature of the chemical environment around them. During the ten days or two weeks that the zygote drifts free, its life is extremely vulnerable to injury and discharge—in which case, the pregnancy is ordinarily terminated before being suspected. An estimated one-fourth of all fertilized ova are thought to be eliminated during this period, probably including many that are less than perfect. When the new organism becomes attached to the uterine wall, secretion of hormones is triggered that results in pregnancy symptoms. Under a microscope, the brain and the heart of the zygote are visible by the second week after conception.

Besides the genetic plan for a complete and unique human being, the DNA of the fertilized

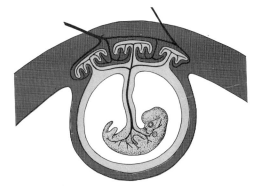

**Figure 11-2** Function of the placenta. A mass of fibers separates the uterine wall of the mother and the circulatory system of the new organism. (*From E. B. Hurlock, Child Development, 3d. ed. New York: McGraw-Hill, 1956, p. 43.*)

egg cell contains instructions on how to form a temporary anatomy for the protection and nourishment of the embryo during its growth—the amniotic sac, umbilical cord, and placenta. The *amniotic sac* envelops the expanding organism with a tough, transparent tissue. At first, this sac holds the various parts of the zygote together—brain, heart, and liver—while the external and connecting structures are growing. Similar in appearance to an inflated balloon, the sac remains filled with increasing amounts of salinelike fluid, or *amnion*, which suspends the embryo and protects it from physical shocks, temperature changes, and gravitational pull. This fluid is the gentle medium in which the organism will later practice its flexing movements and develop its reflex patterns. The amnion is the material which the fetus will swallow and eliminate, as part of its preparation for the postnatal digestive process, and which will be taken in and expelled during the development of the respiratory system.

The *umbilical cord* also begins to form during the zygotic stage. This cord is the lifeline of prenatal existence and is attached to the organism in the area of the liver. The cord floats and coils through the amnion, terminating in a network of blood vessels where the double walls of the amnionic sac and the placenta come together. Like a garden hose with three channels, the umbilical cord encloses the inward-flowing vein, which carries digested food, oxygen molecules, and hormones to supply the new organism, and two outward-flowing arteries, which carry away waste materials.

Knowing the functions of the placenta helps scientists to discriminate between the effects of genetic inheritance and prenatal environment on growth. The *placenta* is a fibrous, blood-laden mass that contains the terminating capillary systems of both the parasite organism and the mother. Between the two organisms is a semipermeable wall of membrane, which is part of the placenta; this membrane separates the two circulatory systems but makes possible an exchange of molecules of food and waste. Also exchanged through the filter are certain immunities in the form of antibodies, a small number of poisons if available in the mother's bloodstream, and certain hormones that trigger growth and control many activities in both the offspring and the mother. The separation of their individual bloodstreams in the placenta enables the mother to tolerate a foreign body during the 200 to 300 days, usually about 252 days, of the pregnancy.

The first major differentiation in the growth of a zygote is the three-layer development of cells. First, the outer layer, or *ectoderm*, forms the nervous system and the skin—the beginning of a system of sensory input. Second, the middle layer, or *mesoderm*, forms the heart and circulatory system and the muscles and lymphatic systems. Third, the inner layer, or *endoderm*, develops into stomach, pancreas, and respiratory system. This early differentiation can be observed under a miscoscope as the brain, heart, and liver of the zygote.

**Multiple Births** Several times in each 100 conceptions, multiple births occur. When two or three ova are produced, fertilized, and attached to the wall of the uterus at the same time, two or three amniotic sacs and two or three placentas grow to sustain the organisms, and fraternal twins or triplets, called *dizygotic* or *trizygotic* births, are produced. If in the early stages of cell division a single fertilized ovum splits into identical but separate organisms, identical or *monozygotic*, twins result. Frequently research scientists have compared groups of identical twins with groups of fraternal twins as one way of investigating hereditary versus environmental influences on growth.

Some of these studies of nature versus nurture based on twins have been contaminated because of inaccurate classification or undifferented environment. Often fraternal twins are inaccurately labeled identical twins because data about the placentas are not established at birth. Another source of contamination is the lack of consideration given to the greater similarity in the environments of identical twins, who look so much alike that they tend to be treated alike, while fraternal twins may be so dissimilar as to stimulate a dissimilar environment, even though they share the same home. Some investigators have avoided most of this problem by using siblings reared together or twins reared apart as comparison groups.

**Inherited Physical Traits** Newman, Freeman, and Holzinger (1937) studied a group of identical twins who had been reared in different homes to discover whether there are inherited tendencies in physical growth patterns, aside from the obvious similarity of identical twins in terms of physical features. The study revealed that identical twins reared apart are more like each other than nonidentical twins in terms of anatomical traits such as height, hand length, and hand width. Of many physical characteristics measured, only weight—which is subject to family dietary patterns and to psychological needs—showed greater similarity in sets of fraternal twins reared together than in identical twins reared apart.

Aside from the known influence of environmental factors on physiological functions, heredity has been shown in twin studies to be a factor in such diverse measures as blood pressure, age of first menstruation, longevity, and motor ability (Mussen & Conger, 1956). In an investigation that included neurological development, Jost and Sontag (1944) combined factors such as breathing rate, blood pressure,

pulse rate, salivation, and perspiration measures to obtain an "index of autonomic stability." Their comparison groups were identical twins, siblings, and other children who were raised together in the same family but were unrelated genetically. Their group of identical twins was found to be more similar on the autonomic characteristics than either of their other groups. These studies indicate the kinds of traits that are highly related to inheritance. Extreme environmental conditions that alter physical growth characteristics include nutritional deprivation, serious diseases, and crippling accidents. Given a moderately stable environment, heredity determines physical growth to a very great extent. The relatively greater influence of environment on intellectual, emotional, and perceptual characteristics, as compared with physical traits, will be considered in subsequent chapters.

### Embryo: Organization of Systems

The embryonic period extends from the time the organism becomes attached to the uterine wall to the time the permanent formation of the bones begins, when layers of calcium begin to replace the cartilage mold of the skeleton, usually from the end of the second week following conception to about the end of the eighth week. During this period, the organism increases in weight by 2 million percent and grows in length from about 1/10 inch to about $1\frac{1}{4}$ inches, when measured according to the technique of embryologists, from the crown of the head to the bottom of the rump. Until recently, knowledge of the growth of the human fetus was accumulated almost entirely from pathological evidence; embryologists studied the organisms that miscarried or were removed by surgery. Laboratory techniques are being developed that include internal photography, sound amplification, and blood analyses. One important breakthrough has been the use of blood tests to diagnose pregnancy within hours of its occurrence. Certainty of the time of conception enables researchers to refine and elaborate the timetable of embryonic development. Because observations are made of live, healthy organisms, the findings reflect normal development, undistorted by pathological factors. This research has tended to establish earlier development of reflex systems than was previously suspected.

During the third and fourth weeks after conception, a fold develops in the ectoderm at the base of the brain that is the beginning of the spinal column and extension of the nervous system to receptor areas throughout the body. Eventually this outer layer will make up the sensory system, including receptors in the skin, the retina, and the core-brain. The heart (formed from the mesoderm layer) pumps blood through a rudimentary circulatory system. Buds of arms become visible (Nilsson, 1965). The heart and organs from the endoderm system (liver, stomach, kidneys, and intestines) are gathered together and contained. By the end of the fourth week the embryo is intact and is identifiable as a vertebrate, but it is not easily distinguished from the embryos of other mammals.

During the fifth and sixth weeks, the embryo develops various bodily systems rapidly, so that the head now constitutes only one-third of the body volume, compared with one-half at the zygotic stage. Development can be observed in the iris and lens of its lidless eyes, in the cartilage formations of its lower jaw and vertebrae, and in the elongated and jointed limbs. The organism begins to swallow and to expel amnion, eliminating its own waste into the sac in addition to its elimination through the liver into the umbilical cord. Still lacking the bone-marrow structure for the manufacture of its own blood cells, the organism relies in part on the yolk sac to perform this function. All the internal organs

of the adult are present in some stage of development, and the embryo is clearly distinguishable as human. Processes such as swallowing and other reflexive behavior are stimulating and developing new neural patterns—an example of early learning by association (Figure 11-3).

**Sex Differentiation**  Genetic sex is established in the DNA at the time of fertilization, but the influence of sex genes is not apparent until the fetal gonads develop and produce their own hormones, beginning in the fifth or sixth week. During the zygotic and most of the embryonic periods all human organisms are anatomically female in structure (Sherfey, 1972). Differentiation of sex in males involves inducing the development of internal and external genital structures and suppressing the development structures that characterize females. The male fetus must be strong enough to produce fetal androgens in sufficient amounts to maintain sexual differentiation but also enough to overcome the hormonal balance of the mother. By the end of the third month the male growth pattern is established and sex reversals in these tissues are considered no longer possible. If the fetal gonads are destroyed at or before the beginning of sex differentiation, a normal female develops from both male and female embryos, providing only that hormones are injested at the time of puberty.

The xy and xx chromosomes that determine sex have a direct bearing on the learning incapacities of certain males. Sex-linked characteristics such as color defects and hemophilia are masked in the female by the second x chromosome which gives the organism a double chance of having a strong, healthy, and usually dominant inheritance pattern. Not all the learning difficulties that boys share in much greater proportions than girls are sex-linked in a genetic sense. Some unfavorable conditions arise in the uterine environment, where hormone conflicts must be resolved, and others are societal in nature.

By the time the organism has reached a congenital age of eight weeks, it has lips, tongue, and buds for 20 "baby" teeth. The trunk straightens and curves; the head moves sidewise and vertically; the limbs flex, straighten, and rotate in patterns that indicate control by the central neurological system. The hands and feet are formed, including fingers and somewhat knobby toes. Fetal movement begins very early, but is not felt by the mother because the organism is small and is protected by the amniotic fluid and sac. When the fetus becomes more crowded, its thrusts distort the wall of the sac, and the mother can feel the movements. The tiny embryo practices and learns many patterns of muscular reaction and the associated sensations from the proprioceptors.

**Malformation from Maternal Deprivation**  Detrimental environmental conditions can affect the embryo in two ways: (1) by depriving it of elements essential to sustain life and (2) by allowing destructive molecules to penetrate the walls of the placenta. Damage occurs to that part of the anatomy which has priority in the development sequence at the moment (Hurlock, 1956).

The most common form of harmful deprivation and the most frequent cause of prenatal injury is *anoxia*, a condition resulting from insufficient oxygen. Many conditions, including some that are relatively minor for the mother, cut off or reduce the amount of oxygen supplied to the embryo through the umbilical cord. Anesthesia, shock, or metabolic upset to the mother may cause severe damage to the organ that is genetically programmed to begin development at that moment. Damage at the appointed time of origin may result in elimination of an organ. Later

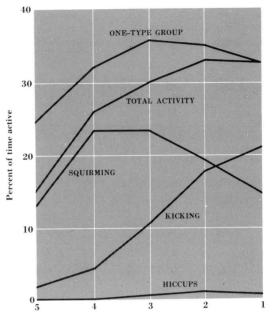

**Figure 11-3**  Developmental trends in three types of fetal activity. (*From H. Newberry, The measurement of three types of fetal activity, Journal of Comparative Psychology, 1941, 32, 521–530.* © *The Williams & Wilkens Co., Baltimore, Maryland, 1941.*)

damage may stunt it, but does not destroy it. In the third week of development, any severe injury may leave the heart or some part of the viscera outside the body. During the fourth week, the limbs can be blighted, or an opening from the outside into the throat may result. Malformations that occur during the fifth week are often to the eye lenses, the upper lip, or the hands and feet. Insults during the sixth week may result in abnormally small eyes, heart and vascular disease, or malformation of the lower jaw. After the seventh week, gross abnormalities are less likely than earlier in the pregnancy, but growth of a rapidly developing part can be halted or retarded. The eighth week is critical in brain development. Abnormally small heads or the development of a Mongoloid child has frequently been traced to damaging events at this stage of pregnancy.

Other parts that seem to be affected are the fingers and toes, the palate, and the lungs. Parts of the body that are fully formed at the time of the insult or those which have not begun to grow are usually normal.

Other kinds of deprivation are severe malnutrition, thyroid deficiency, and progesterone deficiency. These tend to affect an unborn child in more obscure ways, although when severe, they may cause early miscarriage. Poor general health of the mother at a late stage in pregnancy, when the demands of the fetus are great, may produce a neonate less robust and responsive than normal.

**Detrimental Invasions through the Placenta** The placenta allows the passage of digested food molecules, antibodies, hormones, oxygen molecules, and other materials. Apparently some detrimental molecules, such as very small viruses, can also pass through membranes that protect the embryo from most potential invaders. Some drugs or diseases may attack the placenta itself.

In 1941 an Australian eye specialist, Dr. N. McAllister Gregg, noticed a phenomenal increase in the number of infants with cataracts who were brought to his office for treatment. Of 78 babies he diagnosed in a relatively short span of time, 44 also had heart defects. His investigation showed that 68 of the mothers had a common history of German measles, or rubella, during their first or second month of pregnancy. Aware that the epidemic had been widespread, Dr. Gregg contacted other Australian physicians and located 350 other babies whose histories and symptoms were similar. The relationship between German measles in early pregnancy and malformation in the embryo has since been so thoroughly documented that many physicians urge mass immunization for rubella (Schultz, 1956). Teachers who study to become specialists in learning difficulties will learn much more about the physiological hazards to neurological growth.

Biological development and learning are integrated. Teachers need to be able to distinguish between hereditary factors, which neither they nor the students can do anything about, and environmental forces, which potentially they and society can hope to alter with adequate knowledge and motivation.

An understanding of the multiple causality of handicaps helps the teacher to accept the child's problem. For example, Mrs. Y. brought her second child, a mentally retarded boy, to an elementary school that incorporated special classes for mentally retarded children. Mrs. Y. showed relief and gratitude when the principal revealed early in the interview that she knew about the conditions in the prenatal environment that caused Carlton's disability (Joffe, 1969). The principal, through staff meetings and conferences with normal pupils, was able to create a school climate in which mentally retarded pupils were seldom subjected to additional and unnecessary injury to their personal and social development.

In another school in the same district, Mrs. D. enrolled her only daughter, Marilee, two years late because she had not been able to face the outside world with a partially hearing child. If the mother had known at the time what was later to emerge as the probable cause—a case of measles at a critical time in pregnancy—she might not have been ashamed of Marilee's disability or afraid to have another child. Actually, the little girl responded to good teaching and was almost ecstatic to discover the world of sound through her hearing aid. Mrs. D., however, was counseled more than a year before she became willing to allow her daughter to wear the amplifier outside the classroom.

Miss E., a young teacher, was traumatized on her first day of teaching in a junior high school when she glanced up from her class lists to see an armless youth, wearing prostheses, approaching her desk. Recognizing the teacher's fright, he tried to get nearer to explain, but Miss E. screamed and ran toward the teachers' room. Too late, Miss E. read in the cumulative file that Kevin's mother had had oral surgery in her third week of pregnancy, which had resulted in his being born with stumps where his arms should have been. Miss E. was so disturbed by what she had done, she left the teaching profession. These pupils—Carlton with his retarded mind, Marilee with her loss of hearing, and Kevin with his artificial arms—all began life normally, and each will be able to transmit normal, healthy genes and should be accepted for their strengths. Each was subjected to physical injury, environmental in nature, at a particular and critical time in embryonic development.

### Fetus: Organization of Behavior

When the cartilage skeleton of the embryo begins to be replaced by calcium formations, or bone structure, the organism is technically known from this point to birth as a *fetus*. The growth rate is slower than during earlier periods, but remains spectacularly rapid compared with postnatal growth. The average fetus grows to 19 or 20 inches in length—measured by pediatricians from the top of the head to the sole of the extended feet—and weighs from $6\frac{1}{2}$ to $8\frac{1}{2}$ pounds. This growth is accompanied by learning of complex behavior patterns. Gesell (1940) described normal ontogenetic behavior in the fetal stage as both adaptive behavior and motor development.

The fetus of eight weeks is able to respond to oral stimulation. By fourteen weeks—approximately one-third through the gestation period—he swallows amniotic fluid and makes facial contortions. Taste buds are distributed over his tongue, hard palate, tonsils, and esophagus (Hurlock, 1956).

Reinforcement theory strongly implies that pleasure stimulation of the taste receptors probably occurs when the amnion is swallowed and contributes to the establishment of the sucking-swallowing pattern within the neurological system of the fetus. At sixteen weeks he inhales and expels amnion through his nose. At eighteen weeks he makes crying movements and sucks his thumb (Nilsson, 1965). These systems form the basis for speech. Systems of comparable complexity develop throughout the body.

### Development of the Nervous System

The reflex movements of the fetus demonstrate the development of a nervous system capable of directing the movement. The early appearance of the brain and spinal column would seem to indicate a developmental load for the neurological system. The axons and dendrites appear very early in the fetal period as threadlike prolongations. These systems are extended, and modifications occur in the synapses, so that some systems are mature even before birth. According to Carmichael (1970), the neural systems that control motor activities develop earlier than other areas. The midbrain develops in advance of the cerebral cortex, although apparently the brain develops before the spinal column.

A study was reported by Korr, Wilkinson, and Chornock (1967) in which they were able to trace the delivery of neuroplasmic material, such as cytoplasm, from the nerve cell along the axon to the peripheral cells. They labeled nerve cells in rabbits with isotopes, so that the movement on the cells could be detected autoradiographically. They found that the neuroplasmic material was carried in a proximodistal direction although the circulatory system was not involved. When selected nerves were severed, but the blood circulatory system remained intact, the affected muscle deteriorated. The researchers suggest that nerve-cell substances in addition to electrochemical charges are conveyed down the axons and cross the neuromuscular junction into the cells of the muscles. They suggest an influence from this transfer of neural substance on the metabolism, function, development, differentiation, growth, and regeneration of the structures that they innervate. It would seem likely that the physical structure of the neurological systems and the establishment of behavior patterns through a primitive form of learning all proceed together in a mutually stimulating interaction.

**Preterm Viability**   Shirley (1939) studied groups of children who had been born prematurely. She described a "prematurity syndrome" of infantile speech, poor motor coordination, delayed sphincter control, activity extremes, and other characteristic physical and emotional responses. Unfortunate characteristics in the prematurely born may be due not to the prematurity itself but to the conditions that brought on the early birth, the possible overprotection of the frail infant by his parents, and the possible pressures that may be exerted on him later to catch up. His lack of physical maturity at birth is certainly a disadvantage in terms of making the difficult adjustment to the cold, bright, loud, hungry world outside the uterus. According to Mussen and Conger (1956), prematurity deprives the infant of his accustomed sources of protection, support, and nourishment at a time when he is less capable physiologically of coping with radical changes in his environment than the full-term baby is. As the child grows older, one or two months of his life become a decreasing fraction of his total experiences, which may explain Shirley's finding that premature children tend to fade into the normal population.

It is usually a disadvantage for the fetus to remain inside the uterus past the normal period of gestation. Degeneration of the placenta is thought to have occurred in about 90 percent of late deliveries. Other factors being equal, the newborn child who has the normal nine calendar months for interuterine development is more fortunate than early or late babies. This is one further indication of a peak of readiness in the developmental sequence.

Gravitational pull is thought to cause the relatively weighty head of the fetus to up-end him and to cause his head to settle into position for birth. Some pediatricians have said that the 20 minutes before and the 20 minutes after birth are the most important moments in the individual's life. The first stage of labor dilates the cervix. The strong contractions of the second stage culminate in the expulsion of the fetus. The infant whose birth is natural, or spontaneous, generally has a better chance to survive the critical moments immediately following birth than one who is assisted surgically or born by Caesarean section. Infants who emerge head first by normal delivery and whose delivery is neither unduly prolonged nor extremely rapid are least likely to be injured in the process.

The period of the *partunate* is the 20 minutes or so between the newborn's existence as a parasite and his existence as an independent life when the umbilical cord is severed (Hurlock, 1956). His first imperative function is breathing because the oxygen supply through the umbilical cord is cut off shortly after the cord is exposed to air. The birth cry helps the infant inflate his lungs.

The period of the *neonate* lasts approximately two weeks; during this time, the navel heals and the infant adjusts to extrauterine life. He must survive the temperature change from about 100 to about 70° Fahrenheit. Although sucking and swallowing reflexes are well developed, taking his nourishment through the mouth and at intervals is new to him.

**Birth Injury** The parts of the body most commonly affected by prolonged labor or difficult births are the brain, other parts of the CNS, sense organs, and limbs. The most common disabilities resulting from birth injury are motor dysfunctions, cerebral palsy, and low-grade intelligence (Pratt, 1954). Drugs administered to the mother during labor have in some cases caused deprivation to the parturnate of oxygen by chemical means, resulting in the symptoms of anoxia. Pasamanick and Knoblock (1966) reported evidence that cerebral palsy, mental deficiency, epilepsy, reading disability, and childhood tics are associated with pregnancy difficulties involving hypertension and bleeding in the mother or prematurity in the child. However, their evidence seemed to exclude speech disorders as being due to pregnancy problems unless they accompany cerebral palsy or mental deficiency.

Teachers are not likely to receive the victims of severe prenatal or birth damage because most communities provide full or partial care for them in special classes or institutions. However, they are likely to work with children suffering from the effects of minimal damage to the neurological or neuromuscular systems (Chapter 9).

## BIOLOGICAL DEVELOPMENT
## IN THE FIRST TWO YEARS

The body proportions of the infant continue to change along the same general patterns that obtained during the prenatal stages. His head becomes smaller in relation to his total body weight, and his legs become longer in relation to his total height. The infant rapidly takes on the skin and eye color determined by his genes.

The baby requires less and less sleep as he grows older, usually about 18 hours the first day after birth, decreasing to approximately 10 hours a day by the end of the first year. Great variation has been noted among individual babies in hours of sleep (Pratt, 1954), demand for feeding (Olmstead & Jackson, 1950), frequency of elimination (Halverson, 1940), pulse rate (Pratt, 1954), and respiration rate (Halverson, 1941). Neuromuscular growth continues to proceed as an interaction of the organism with his environment and becomes evident both in learning and in physiological growth. Asleep or awake, the infant continues to perform many of the same functions of the prenatal period: hiccoughing, squirming, reflex smiling, and swallowing. His transitions from waking to sleeping are less abrupt than in older children; in fact, researchers must define carefully the sleeping-waking state prior to investigations of infants. The accomplished learning displayed by the newly born has established the need for attention to their learning environment.

### Sensory Acuity

The sensory systems of taste, vision, audition, smell, and touch have been studied extensively to determine the nature of the discrimination processes. Sensitivity to taste is the most highly developed of the senses; however, individual babies differ widely in their taste thresholds. Groups of infants studied have shown positive reactions to sweet stimuli and negative reactions to salty, sour, or bitter tastes (Pratt, 1954). The retina of the eye at birth is smaller than that of the adult eye, but the number of cones per area unit is the same. The pupillary reflex is well established within 30 hours after birth. By the time the infant is ten days old, he can track moving objects by making horizontal, vertical, or circular movements with his eyes.

Some infants respond to sound stimulations minutes after birth, while others seem to be deaf for several hours or several days. Apparently, the amniotic fluid must drain from the middle ear before the hearing mechanisms, already formed, can receive stimulation and function outside the uterus. The sense of smell is highly developed and can be observed within an hour after birth. Sensitivity to touch, temperature, and pain is present in all parts of the body at birth. The lips and the area around the mouth are the body parts most sensitive to touch. The soles of the feet, the skin of the forehead, and the membrane of the nose are most sensitive to pain. The surfaces of the body, legs, underarms, and hands are less sensitive to touch stimulation than the same areas in adults (Hurlock, 1956).

One of the problems involved in discovering how much babies can distinguish is similar to a problem encountered in work with animals—neither babies nor animals are good at answering questions unless the questions are put into special forms. Mussen and Conger (1956) report that infants can distinguish colors, although they do not pay a great deal of attention to them. They seem to prefer complex patterns and distinguish these from simple patterns, preferring a checkered pattern to a simple square or circle. A six-month-old child can demonstrate his discrimination of color by choosing a blue bottle that contains a sweet-tasting liquid over a similarly shaped red bottle that previously contained a bitter liquid. In order for this kind of learning to take place, the infant must be able not only to distinguish between the two colors but also to associate the blue color with pleasantness and the red with unpleasantness. This kind of learning takes time; hence the child who can indicate that he recognizes the color difference must have been able to distinguish that difference considerably earlier.

Children between six and fifteen months of age have been tested for the ability to discriminate shapes (Mussen, 1963). Circles, crosses, and triangles that the children could handle and put into their mouths were used. One of the shapes was sweetened with saccharine, and the test involved having the child reach for this particular shape reliably more often than chance would allow. Six-month-old babies were able to demonstrate this discrimination even when the shapes were moved into different positions. Teaching designed to improve young children's skill in visual discrimination should be otherwise enjoyable to them and should be conducted at the level of their ability.

Mussen (1963) reported that infants as young as two months of age smile at patterns of a human face moving toward them. By six months, the child clearly differentiates between his parents and strangers by smiling at the former and not smiling at the latter. Undoubtedly a large element of learning is present, although cues in addition to visual discrimination of face patterns are probably also involved in this recognition. Children of six months are already able to discriminate size constancy and apparently have developed some depth perception. In one experiment, two rattles were presented to children from ten to fifty weeks of age. One was close to the children, and the other, which was three times as large, was three times as far away, so that they both appeared to be the same size. Six-month-old children reached for the nearer rattle significantly more often than they did for the one that looked to be the same size but was actually farther away.

**Speech Sounds** Intensive studies have been made of the speech of young children. New equipment makes it possible to visualize the nature of their speech sounds by converting them into electronic impulses that can be portrayed pictorially. Young infants, under two months of age, use about seven phonemes, although in the course of speech development they use and later drop a number of phonemes that are not in their language. In English-speaking children, these include the French nasals, the German vowels, and the Yiddish "ch." These sounds are very difficult to recover once they are discarded.

The fact that the different phonemes appear in the speech of children of different countries at approximately the same time and in approximately the same order has been taken to indicate that speech is primarily a motor function that evolves on a maturational basis. The young child at the babbling stage may well be repeating and practicing sounds for his own satisfaction and amusement. Around the sixth month, the child seems ready to respond to parents and others who talk to him by "talking" back to them, although he may not imitate accurately the sounds of those around him until about the ninth month.

The imitation process in speech seems to involve making a selection from among the sounds that already exist in the baby's repertoire and repeating these sounds after one of his parents, then being reinforced. Parents tend to reward such imitation with signs of extreme affection, bordering at times on delirium. These rewards include picking the baby up, smiling or cooing at him, and making other signs of approbation. Parental attention to early speech may account for some of the verbal superiority of groups of first children over siblings and twins. Mowrer (1954) has suggested that these imitations of parental sounds acquire a secondary reward value; that is, the baby hears himself sounding like the parents who succor him and, by a conditioning mechanism, comes to reward himself for these sounds by reminding himself in this way of the pleasant things that have been associated with them in the past. During the first year, the baby starts to associate definite sounds with definite meanings, although individual babies vary greatly regarding the age at which they begin to understand words.

Penfield and Roberts (1959), in *Speech and Brain Mechanisms*, identified four separate and distinguishable sets of neural circuits that develop with learning to understand and to produce language. The baby shows understanding when the neural connections are established between the *sound reception unit* and the *concept mechanism.* His babbling sounds originate in a *motor pattern unit* and are articulated through a *motor expression unit.*

### Prehension

Among the reflex patterns the normal infant has developed before birth is the grasping reflex. When stimulated in the palm of the hand, he will grasp a finger or another small object, holding it tightly. By four months of age, the baby's grasping reflex has disappeared and does not emerge again until he learns to manipulate objects. *Prehension*, the ability to seize and grasp, is basic to much psychomotor learning. Halverson (1931) analyzed motion pictures to identify 10 stages in the development of prehension, beginning at 16 weeks of age and culminating at 60 weeks when attractive objects were reached and grasped without unwarranted motions (Figure 11-4). Neural patterns, apparent at birth, must be retained and extended in a meaningful context or the function will disappear.

### Mobility

Ames (1937) analyzed motion pictures of 20 infants and identified 14 stages of prone progression, from the forward thrust of one knee to the creeping on hands and feet by the age of 49 weeks. She reported that two of the stages are skipped by some youngsters. Shirley (1933) reported 16 stages from "fetal posture" to walking alone. Merry and Merry (1958) considered the ability to run the most out-

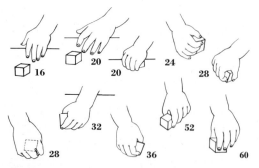

**Figure 11-4** The development of prehension. (*From H. M. Halverson, An experimental study of prehension in infants by means of systematic cinema records, Genetic Psychological Monographs, 1931, 10, 107–286. 1931. With permission of the Journal Press.*)

standing achievement of the four-year-old because of the complicated control and accurate timing that are required. When one sees the colt stand and walk within minutes after birth and gallop and frisk within hours, the achievement of the human being in gross motor development is not impressive.

Apparently, biological maturation is a major factor in the child's rate of development from one stage of mobility to another. Differences between children who are restricted (Dennis, 1940) and those who are neglected (Dennis, 1941) seem to show that maturation occurs during periods of relative inactivity but that progress occurs very rapidly when the child is given the opportunity to practice. Some investigators believe that restricted children catch up, but the evidence seems to be rather flimsy on this point. How does the investigator know what the performance would have been had the restriction or deprivation not occurred?

In contrast to observations based on restriction placed on mobility were the Czechoslovakian studies in which experimental and control groups of 120 infants each were observed in systematic training (experimental) versus spontaneous mobility (control). Training consisted of ladder climbing in which the

infant could support his own weight earlier than normal by using his arms as well as his legs. Trained physical therapists taught the experimental subjects to roll over large balls, swim, and swing in a blanket. The infants who were stimulated beyond the normal infant environment learned to crawl one to two months earlier than controls; learned to walk two to four months earlier than controls; and registered significantly greater amounts of cooing, babbling, and laughing. They appeared more alert and happier than children cared for in the same center with similar routines of feeding and affection.

The role of learning in motor development takes on significance as embryologists, neurologists, cultural biologists, cultural anthropologists, and others discover the growth patterns of the CNS.

## MOTOR DEVELOPMENT OF CHILDREN BEYOND TWO

After the age of two, the child's rate of physical growth continues to decline until the onset of puberty (Figure 11-5). During this time, phylogenetic growth patterns are such that clothing and desks can be ordered in advance with the expectation that they will fit. Ontogenetic growth patterns assure that most children will show increasing uniqueness within their chronological age groups. At a time when the child is trying to reduce his identity with adults and to establish his identity with peer groups, extreme variations in size or physique are likely to be painful to him. Even minor characteristics, such as freckles, red hair, enormous eyes, or a pug nose, may be the source of extreme discomfort to a child whose relatives think the characteristic appealing enough to mention in his presence. As a rule, teachers and other adults need to be restrained and sensitive in their remarks about unique characteristics when talking to or about older children. Probably the time to teach children to value uniqueness in others is the early childhood period, prior to their common preoccupation with peer identification, which begins at about the third or fourth grade.

## Skeletal Age

Accurate predictions of growth must be based on both the growth cycles of the species and the growth pattern of the individual. Skeletal growth occurs through ossification, a process in which calcium phosphate and other minerals are deposited in a structure that was initially cartilage. Ossification begins near the midsection of the large bones. These centers, called *epiphyses*, number over 800; their appearance marks the beginning of the fetal period, and they continue to appear through the teen years. In the growth of the skeleton, the epiphyses extend until they grow together, at which time the size of that bone is complete (Merry & Merry, 1950).

Flory (1936) devised an index of anatomical growth that was based on the degree of ossification as shown in an x-ray of the individual's hand and wrist. He developed scales to indicate the individual's skeletal age in months and in percentage of final adult status achieved. He reported a close relationship

between sexual maturity and skeletal development.

Individual variations from group norms are not considered significant unless the deviation is greater than a year. Children from underprivileged environments show delayed anatomical growth compared with children from superior homes. Girls attain full skeletal growth at about sixteen years and boys at about eighteen years, although the ossification process continues in both for several years after the length of the large bones is established. Some school systems keep records of skeletal maturity in form of wrist x-rays, which are helpful to the teacher in appraising the physical maturation of students.

Most of the permanent teeth erupt between the ages of five or six and approximately twelve (eruption of the wisdom teeth is delayed until the full dimensions of the skeleton have been attained). The shape of the face changes as the jaw grows to accommodate large, adult-size teeth. The upper part of the head grows relatively little during this period, the brain having attained 90 percent of its adult weight by the age of six.

## Developmental Age

Ilg and Ames advocated the placement of children in school on the basis of develop-

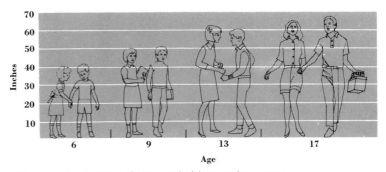

**Figure 11-5** Heights of boys and girls at various ages.

mental age rather than chronological age. Both were Gesell proteges, contributed to his classic book, *The First Five Years of Life* (1940), and were staff members of the Gesell Institute of Child Development at the time *School Readiness* was published (1965). They studied children from the ages of five to ten to describe typical developmental age characteristics during this period. Although they recognized individual differences, their major work has been to describe "the recurring similarities of behavioral patterning as it changed from age to age." Their viewpoints were extended from the early works of Gesell to their test materials. Their concept of readiness includes a commitment to stages and cycles of growth, the implied judgment of normality as desirable, the close tie between physiological and mental growth, and the need for adjustment downward in grouping children who are "highly individual"—that is, out of balance in their development. Their major contribution is the concept of the child's *developmental level*, rather than chronological age, for determining readiness for school learning.

Ilg and Ames represented the "flow of development" as reoccurring waves of stormy reorganization followed by calm and integra-

tion (Figure 11-6). The level line stage A, represents the calm stability of the "twos," "fives," and "tens," their terminology for these age groups. Stage B is described as stormy and vacillating. Stage C represents the "organization of opposites," in which successive evidence of maturity is noted. At the next stages, D and E, the dynamics of inwardizing, or withdrawal, are followed by expression and release, seen in the outgoing behavior of these age groups. A time of high effort and reorganization, stage F, completes the cycle, at which point the child is ready to repeat the sequence at a higher level.

The Weston Connecticut study (Ilg & Ames, 1965), conducted under a grant from the Fund for Advancement of Education, classified kindergarten and first- and second-grade children according to a developmental appraisal, which these investigators later refined as the "school readiness" tests. According to their criteria of readiness for a particular grade placement, 35 to 59 percent of the children studied were classified as "ready," 30 to 40 percent were classified as "questionable," and 9 to 31 percent were classified as "unready." The developmental examination includes (1) an interview to obtain data and establish rapport, (2) copying geometric forms and completing a picture of a man, (3) verbal and motor response to distinguish left and right, (4) memory for designs (delayed response), (5) naming animals (fluency), (6) an interview on interests, and (7) an examination of teeth. In developing their test materials, a chronological age comparison showed that "unready" kindergartners were less bright (99.3 IQ) than "questionable" (114.3 IQ) and "ready" groups (116.5 IQ).

An examination of the criteria and a careful reading of their individuality "types" suggest that some very bright children were being included in their "questionable" groups and recommended for a junior-first type of grade

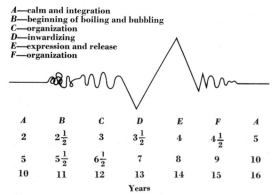

A—calm and integration
B—beginning of boiling and bubbling
C—organization
D—inwardizing
E—expression and release
F—organization

| A | B | C | D | E | F | A |
|---|---|---|---|---|---|---|
| 2 | $2\frac{1}{2}$ | 3 | $3\frac{1}{2}$ | 4 | $4\frac{1}{2}$ | 5 |
| 5 | $5\frac{1}{2}$ | $6\frac{1}{2}$ | 7 | 8 | 9 | 10 |
| 10 | 11 | 12 | 13 | 14 | 15 | 16 |

Years

**Figure 11-6**  A point of view. (*From F. L. Ilg & L. B. Ames, School Readiness. New York: Harper and Row, 1965, p. 31. By permission of the publisher.*)

placement, a school organization designed to retard the child's formal schoolwork. On the basis of our longitudinal studies of bright children, acceleration might better have been recommended for some of these subjects than retardation (Robeck, 1968a; Wilson, 1959). Successful schoolwork is much more highly correlated with mental age than with either physiological or social age (Robeck, 1968a). Mass school retardation, done on the basis of an Ilg-Ames developmental analysis, does not seem as good a solution to the problem as curriculum adjustment. If 50 percent of a group is below the readiness level for school learning, then one would think the course of wisdom is to plan the program to the growth stage and capacity of the individual child, rather than to retard high percentages of children in their progress through school. Considering that two years of junior college is becoming the standard minimum and that retardation increases the chance that a child will drop out, schools should be extremely reluctant to undertake mass retardation. Since the mentally retarded have already been removed from our classes, any system of evaluation that retards more pupils than it accelerates should be questioned. Physical growth is related to changes during the same period (ages two to eleven) in the cognitive development described in Piaget's period of preoperational and operational thought (Chapter 14) and the emotional development described in Erikson's latency stage (Chapter 13).

## PHYSICAL CHANGES IN ADOLESCENCE

The growth spurt of puberty is triggered by a series of complex activities within the individual's *endocrine system.* According to endocrinologists, the hormones are chemical substances produced in one organ of the body and carried to another organ or tissue, where some specific activity is stimulated. The thy-

roid, adrenal, and pituitary glands are endocrine glands. Of several different hormone secretions from the pituitary, three apparently control sex and reproduction.

The most complex molecule of the pituitary secretions is the human growth hormone (HGH), which stimulates growth and the regeneration of tissues. Choh Hao Li and Dixon, of the University of California, identified 188 amino acids—each very complex—that make up this molecule (1966). Clinical uses of HGH injections include the successful treatment of dwarfed children.

### Rate of Maturing

The rate of maturing is significant because of differences between the sexes and differences among individuals within chronological age groups. Referring to anatomical size, Mussen and Conger (1956) report that boys, on the average, are slightly taller than girls until about age ten and are heavier until about age eleven. By age thirteen, girls, who attain puberty earlier than boys, are both taller and heavier. By age sixteen or seventeen, these trends have reversed, and boys are stronger, taller, and heavier.

However, the growth spurt of adolescence, like other characteristics, shows such great individual variability that the sexes overlap in time of coming of age. The criterion frequently used to judge maturation in girls is the occurrence of the *menarche,* or first menstruation—which in turn corresponds closely with the development of the mammary glands and with calcification of the skeleton. The menarche occurs at an average age of thirteen, with an age range of from about ten to sixteen years, although teachers of nine-year-olds occasionally find cases of menstruation among their pupils. Maturation in boys is judged by various investigators according to one or more criteria such as increase in growth rate, appearance of pubic hair, and first seminal ejaculation. By these criteria, the onset of puberty in individual boys may occur from eleven to seventeen years. Teachers can help the mental health of late maturers by assuring them that these differences are perfectly normal and temporary. Girls find the menarche a traumatic experience and often need reassurance from teachers as well as parents. This experience is particularly trying for the early-maturing girl, who is usually not prepared psychologically for it. Sherfey (1972) attributes premenstrual depression in adult females to the fear conditioning that most girls experience during puberty.

Relatively little is known about the relationship of the development of the CNS, or other physiological bases for learning, and skeletal or developmental age scales. Stott (1967) suggested skeletal age, rather than skeletal size, as an index of development age. At the age of six, boys are generally about one year behind girls in skeletal age; at age thirteen, they are about two years behind girls; and at about age eighteen, the sex group norms are comparable. The schools at present do not provide realistic ways of meeting the different needs of girls and boys, whose growth spurts differ, nor does society allow for the social problems of late and early maturers.

Little, if any, difference has been found between late-maturing (LM) and early-maturing (EM) groups of school adolescents at any given chronological age in IQ, grade placement, or socioeconomic status (Eichorn, 1963). However, several investigators have found important personality differences related to rate of maturation and to sex. Jones and Bayley (1950) selected two groups of extreme types from among 90 public school boys. They were rated by the Institute of Child Welfare observers in boy-group playground situations and mixed-group social situations. They were rated by peers on the

"guess-who" instrument devised at the University of California. The study covered six years, from the late sixth to the twelfth grade. On most adult ratings, the LMs were equal to group means, except in "relaxed versus tense" and "attention-getting" behavior. Early maturers were consistently rated above average on most traits, including physical attractiveness. Peer groups tended to distinguish the EMs for athletic distinction, and they were elected to student offices more frequently than the LMs. Both late and early maturers were differentiated less in boy groups than in mixed groups.

Mussen and Jones (1958), in groups of males drawn from a large high school, and More (1953), in a small sample of boys studied from age ten, found differences on projective and personality tests. The EMs were more popular, exerted more self-control, and were more likely to support the mores of the culture. The LMs showed little overt interest in girls and described heroes in negative terms. Kinsey, Pomeroy, and Martin (1948) reported an average difference of five years in maturation between their EM and LM groups. Over half of their EMs were described as socially extroverted, vivacious, and physically active, while only one-third of their LMs were categorized in this way. The reverse proportions—one-third of the EMs and one-half of the LMs—were found to be socially inept, reserved, and taciturn. At adulthood, males in the Kinsey sample did not differ in educational level, socioeconomic rating, incidence of marriage, or number of children.

Jones (1957) found significant differences on personality inventories favoring EMs when contrasted with LMs. Eichorn (1963) attributes many behavior differences between LM and EM males to differential experience rather than to endocrinological variables. She says that adults and peers may first react to physical appearance by assigning responsibilities; if the EM is "able to meet the challenge," he confirms their favorable impression, "increases his own skill, and derives personal satisfaction." The reader should note that in personality structure, where the differences were greatest, one out of two EM individuals was likely to emerge as characteristically personable, while one out of three LM individuals showed constructive personality traits. Perhaps teachers need to begin early to help pupils see individual worth in others and to counter the cultural tendency to overvalue physical maturation during a limited period in the lives of males.

The favorable versus unfavorable reinforcement for EM and LM female adolescents is quite the opposite, according to research. Everett (1943) stated that EM girls were rated below the group average by adults on personal and sociability traits, while LM girls were consistently rated above average. Jones (1958) found peer nominations to be the opposite of those for boys—favorable for LM girls and unfavorable for EM girls. On personality tests, however, the LM rather than the EM girls showed negative characteristics and the need for recognition.

Some of the discrepancy in research on girls may be explained by comparative shifts in social status during the preadult period. In a large sample of 731 girls, Faust (1960) found a shift in prestige within different school age groups. Elementary school sixth-grade girls who were still immature sexually had a significantly greater chance of a prestige rating on the "guess-who" peer rating instruments. Early maturation became an advantage during junior high school, fell off in importance during grades 10 and 11, and again enhanced popularity in late senior high school. Kinsey (1953) reported little differentiation among females on the basis of age of onset of puberty. He found the self-concept of status of married women to be more closely related to their

husbands' occupation than to their own. From these studies, it would appear that the disadvantages that accrue from late maturing are related to personality characteristics developed through environmental or cultural artifacts and not to inadequacies of intelligence, size at maturity, or socioeconomic status. Girls appear to lack prestige on a rather broad base with both adults and peers when they mature ahead of the norm, especially at elementary and senior high school levels. The implication for schools might be that bright mature girls, if accelerated to an older chronological age group, would have a better chance to establish positive interpersonal relations with boys, other girls, and adults.

The stresses and strains of the period of adolescence seriously complicate teaching. This is a difficult period for the student, particularly for the boy. His voice changes; occasionally the change is gradual, but more than likely it is uneven. He is going along with his new, rather startling deep voice, when suddenly, often in the middle of a word and always in the middle of an important statement, the voice betrays him and skids off into a falsetto. If the people around him do not laugh openly, they look as though remaining straightfaced requires superhuman effort. The sense of what the adolescent is saying is lost in the accident of the voice change. His audience responds not to his meaning but to his *lack of control.*

The adolescent's bodily mechanisms betray him in many ways. A boy may grow as much as 4 inches in a single year. The dress shoes he bought only last month are too small even though they are hardly worn. His trousers have crawled high above his ankles, and his stomach is constantly an aching void. The family, who should know better, treat him as though he grew out of his shoes on purpose and as though he had washed his clothes in hot water to shrink them and make remarks about his eating as though he were selling food on the side.

Glandular imbalance causes his face to break out in acne at a time when he wants to impress a girl he has been scared to talk to. He says bizarre things that disgrace him with his teachers, and he cannot figure out why he said them in the first place. The stupid things he has done depress him. These are years of uncertainty, with intervals of joy between the periods of self-doubt and frustration.

The effect of puberty on girls is likely to be as hard psychologically as it is on boys. The development of sexual maturity is accompanied by upsetting and trying changes. The glandular secretion system is thrown out of balance for a time, generating emotional turmoil that is hard for the adolescent to cope with and hard for her family to tolerate. Most of these physical changes are determined fundamentally by genetic heredity.

The age of puberty, on the average, has gone steadily downward for both boys and girls for the last 50 years. Increased height and earlier maturity seem to be a reflection of the better diets and health care that most children growing up in the American culture enjoy. The influence of diet on body growth is rather dramatically demonstrated in the case of Japanese immigrants. Those who came to this country as adults, two generations ago, had of course already attained their basic growth. Their children grew somewhat larger than they, but not dramatically so. Investigation indicates a considerable tendency to carry most of the dietary practices learned in the old country into life in the new country. However, the second generation of Japanese grew both taller and heavier than their parents and their grandparents. Their diets were markedly influenced by general knowledge about vitamin and mineral intake and a broader acceptance of protein foods including milk.

Much of the credit for the spread of this kind of knowledge must be given to the schools, especially to home economics classes during the junior high school years. Large segments of our population still need information about nutrition and food preparation, particularly the residents of the inner city.

## ADULTHOOD AND AGING

Growth continues beyond adolescence, although the patterns of change have different characteristics from those most obvious during earlier periods. Physical size and strength increase in early adulthood even though no large gains in height are made. The muscle systems increase their potential so that athletes of both sexes ordinarily reach their peak during their twenties. Calcification of the bones continues more slowly than was true earlier and shows up in brittle bones that do not mend easily during old age.

Women go through a period of childbearing fertility which ends for most women between the ages of forty and fifty with the onset of the menopause. This cessation of the menstrual cycle causes changes in the patterns of hormonal balances that often trigger adjustment problems. Many women become depressed because of resulting physical stresses. The cessation of production of estrogen seems to signal other changes that are often visible as symptoms of aging. The skin becomes drier and tends to wrinkle as it loses its resiliency. Men go through similar hormonal changes although theirs are not as dramatic or obvious. Muscle tone decreases in most people as a result of both a slowdown in physical activity and changes in hormonal balances. Many of these changes can be accelerated or retarded by accompanying psychological attitudes.

During early adulthood most people are expectant about the future. They are gaining physical and mental vigor and are increasingly able to assume leadership roles in the groups with whom they associate. This buoyant happy approach to life is fortified by hormonal balances that are self-perpetuating and self-feeding. With middle age most people find that they have reached a plateau in the kind of success they can expect and gradually lose their expectation about the future. As they lose their anticipation, they become less active physically and mentally and thus set in motion adjustments in hormonal balance that are different from those established during more active years.

Many people have found accidentally that if they start a new life for themselves in their middle years, they may experience a resurgence of expectation about the promise of the future. There are new questions to which the answers are not completely known and anticipation continues to give zest to life. These people seem to age less rapidly than do their companions who remain in their old positions. Some people are able to stay in the same working environment and move to more challenging positions periodically. Unfortunately there are limited opportunities in this direction for the vast majority of people.

Retirement can be disastrous for many people, primarily because of the psychological implications implicit in no longer being needed. As a retardant to aging it probably is desirable to change jobs or retire before it is mandatory and move into an activity that can be carried forward indefinitely. This may be in volunteer work, self-employment, or leisure activities that are meaningful to the person. If at all possible, people should try to arrange their lives at any age so that tomorrow can be approached as a challenge with an element of uncertainty. It keeps the juices flowing.

## SUMMARY

The protracted biological development of the human being predisposes him to gradual development of social, perceptual, emotional, and intellectual maturity. Maturation means the final process in any of the various forms of growth. Although each individual grows in his own way, the following generalizations have come out of the study of human growth: Growth is continuous in a biological sense from conception to death. Growth is sequential and orderly, but individuals vary in the time required for characteristics to become evident and in the extent to which they appear. Growth is integrated within each individual in biological, perceptual, emotional, and cognitive functions. Growth is unique to the species and to each individual. Growth is maturation that readies the individual for a function; if the function is unused, it declines. Growth is learning.

Life begins with the union of male and female cells which join to create the plan of development. The new organism, the zygote, is extremely vulnerable to accident and discharge as it drifts down to the uterus. Very rapidly its cells multiply, organize, and attach intact to the uterine walls of the mother. The embryonic period is the time between its attachment and the beginning of bone formation, at about the eighth week after conception. All the organs and limbs of the adult are present and are in some stage of development at the time the organism becomes technically a fetus. Insults resulting in severe abnormalities occasionally occur when a virus, drug, or other agent that is small in molecular structure penetrates the membranes in the placenta that separate the bloodstream of the mother and the bloodstream of the embryo. Anoxia, or deprivation of oxygen, can also have serious consequences during prenatal growth.

During the fetal period, the organism grows more rapidly in length and weight than at any later period in life. The brain directs the growth of the nervous system, which develops with the many reflex systems that emerge and are practiced prenatally. The new organism learns to flex the trunk, make fists, kick, turn, and stretch. By the seventh month, he is also quite proficient at swallowing, hiccoughing, sucking, exhaling, and eliminating. In fact, the biological development, including the sense organs, is adequate for survival if premature birth should occur.

The body proportions of the newborn infant continue to change in accordance with the same general pattern that obtained during the prenatal stages. Apparently, the neonate discriminates and likes sweet tastes at birth and is sensitive to touch, particularly around the mouth. He sees within minutes or hours after birth, and when the amniotic fluid drains from his ears, he can also hear. Many infant reflexes, present at birth, go unused and disappear.

After age two, the child's rate of growth slows markedly, but continues steadily until the growth spurt of puberty. Skeletal age is an index of development based on the extent of ossification of the bones. Many researchers have found skeletal age to be more closely related to percentage of full growth and to onset of puberty than chronological age is. Developmental age is an index based on a combination of factors such as anatomical age, visual perception, motor coordination, and language development. Some authorities recommend a developmental index rather than chronological age for grade placement in school. The elementary school years mark a latent period in the biological growth scheme; these are fruitful years for school learning since they are relatively free of sexual and social upheavals.

Puberty is triggered by an influx of secretions from the pituitary and other endocrine glands. Early-maturing boys seem to receive important positive reinforcement from the culture that enhances their social development. Early-maturing girls seem to be penalized by unfavorable adult and peer interaction when the maturity is apparent as early as the elementary school years. Adolescents need adult understanding during the years when radical physical changes are causing them to make adjustments more rapidly than they can manage without stress.

## SELF-DIRECTING ACTIVITIES

1 Work out the interaction pattern between maturation and experience as a young child learns an activity.
2 Obtain x-ray photographs of calcification of the wrists and become adept at interpreting the information available on them.
3 Develop a system of instruction that will ease the trauma of the menarche.
4 Assess your satisfaction in teaching after you have been in the profession twenty years, and decide where you want to go from there.
5 Devise a way to help an elderly person find a renewed purpose in life and observe the evidence of renewed physical vigor.

# Chapter 12

Young people learn to see small differences.

# DEVELOPMENT OF PERCEPTUAL ABILITIES

After studying this chapter, you should comprehend the different sensory systems, the way they interrelate, and the impact of defects on school performance. You should be able to:

❪ Distinguish between internal and external sensory systems

❪ Compensate for defects in visual perception

❪ Emphasize the tasks that enhance auditory perception

❪ Devise tasks that promote integration of sensory information

❪ Use the following terms correctly:
  percepts
  affects
  concepts
  proprioceptors
  interoceptors
  vestibular sense
  strabismus
  astereopsis
  aniseikonia
  saccadic movements
  hyperkinesis

Each person perceives and builds his world through internal organization of sensory stimulation. *Perception* is the individual's immediate interpretation of his sensory environment. Perception begins with neural responses to the activation of the sense organs and ends when the input is selected and coded for storage. *Percepts* are the coded bits and pieces of input from the separate sense organs. *Affects* are the bits of punishment or pleasure that are associated with particular information or knowledge. *Concepts* are the result of the learner's integration of relevant and related percepts. Repeated sensory input leads to the formation of images that retain the common features of many experiences. By this definition perception is the flow of neural action during the initial process of learning, but stops short of the consolidation of learning.

The perceptual process includes the coding of stimuli received by the sense organs, the transmission of this coded information to the CNS, and the individual's mode of processing that information in the CNS. In the context of neurology, percepts are the coded sensory data that the brain or the CNS handles at the moment of perception. Perception involves the activation of already existent neural structures to make an immediate individual interpretation of data. Concepts, on the other hand, are generalized ideas of classes of things and may be manipulated in the brain, independent of external stimuli. Concepts provide the individual with an efficient way of manipulating remembered percepts. Affects are important because they help to determine the kinds of selection a person makes when he perceives his environment.

The sequence in the perceptual process is as follows: (1) transduction or initial coding of sense-organ stimulation, (2) transmission of the coded messages to the CNS by way of selected neurons, (3) reception of the coded messages into the CNS, and (4) immediate differentiations made by the learner. This selective interpretation of relayed information is the final step in the perceptual sequence (Chapter 9). This chapter looks at perception as part of the developmental sequence and builds on the neurological foundation already explained.

Since before birth, the individual has been accumulating perceptual information, which is usually associated with affective concomitants of satisfaction or dissatisfaction. This past learning of perceptual content is the context both for thinking and for adaptive behavior. The individual modifies relayed sensory information by intervention, selection, and distortion. What he consolidates becomes the context of future perceptual selections and the base of percepts from which future conceptualizations will be built.

Perception can be thought of as the neurological activation that leads to association learning. The learning process requires time for the consolidation of sensory data that were perceived very quickly. Perception determines the form and content of association learning. Punishing or pleasure-producing affects are part of the perceptual syndrome. Affects may enhance a perceptual experience, distort comparisons, influence the selected response, or disrupt the learning of discriminations. The child learns to discriminate "man" from "men" by comparing the new coded stimulus with the percepts already stored or learned. Similar discriminations are made, for example, between different musical forms, art styles, cooking odors, chemical symbols, and golf shots. This chapter outlines human sensory systems, emphasizing the forms of input to the systems from outside the organism because of their significance in communication and learning. The way an individual learner perceives, including his perceptual distortions and his selective attention, is the facet of the perceptual process with which the teacher deals most directly.

## SENSORY SYSTEMS

Perception is built from the information received from the senses. Some sensory information originates in the environment and is received similarly by different individuals if their functioning is normal. Internal sensory systems provide information to the individual about his own somatic state. These stimuli are internal and cannot be experienced directly by anyone except the subject.

### External Systems

Sensory stimulations produced by external objects are transmitted to the brain as visual, auditory, cutaneous, gustatory, and olfactory perceptions (Table 12-1). In visual perception, light energy from external sources is transduced and conveyed to the individual's visual sorting and storage areas. In auditory perception, sound waves from the environment are transduced into electrochemical impulses that the brain can process. For a long time, teachers and psychologists have observed a relationship between visual perception and reading efficiency. Poor visual acuity and faulty visual interpretation have long been regarded as major causes of school learning problems. The child who cannot discriminate "walk" from "wait" probably has other perceptual difficulties also, although psychological research on perception has dealt predominantly with visual perception. Until recently, interest in auditory perception has been primarily clinical and stems from attempts to correct speech and reading problems. Though less obvious, auditory perception is as important to the teacher as visual perception. The importance

**Table 12-1  Classification of Sensory Systems Based on Objective-Subjective Dichotomy**

**External: Stimulation or activation by external object**

Visual: response to light waves

Auditory: response to sound waves

Cutaneous: response to pressure, heat, cold, texture on skin

Olfactory: response to volatile substances in nose

Gustatory: response to soluble substances on tongue; taste of sweet, salty, sour, and bitter flavors and combinations thereof

**Internal: Stimulation or activation perceptible only to subject himself; not connected to external object**

*Proprioceptor: Information about balance and body position*

Labyrinth: response in semicircular canals to body movement

Kinesthetic: response to muscle tension

Articular: response to contact of moving joint surfaces

*Interoceptor: Information from organs in the viscera*

of the integration of these two systems in learning the communication skills is beginning to capture the attention of researchers, particularly those interested in special education and early childhood education.

The *near senses* are the cutaneous, gustatory, and olfactory systems. The cutaneous sensations include touch, pressure, warmth, cold, and pain. Another of the near senses is taste, which transduces the chemical stimulation taken into the mouth to neural impulses. Chapter 11 notes how the infant has taste buds distributed throughout his mouth, on his hard palate, and in his esophagus; in the adult, however, the taste buds have deteriorated except in the area of the tongue.

Sweet, sour, salty, and bitter flavors are combined in various ways in the innumerable gourmet foods that adults relish. The sense of taste interacts with the sense of smell and with stored affects to produce the sensations that people associate with different foods.

Another of the near senses is the sense of smell, which is closely related to the sense of taste. People associate the different odors of food with specific tastes. Many of the near senses are of particular importance in the areas of home economics, physical education, and industrial arts, where specialized discriminations must be made.

### Internal Systems

The *deep senses* include *proprioceptors* that give information about balance and body position and *interoceptors* that produce information from organs in the viscera. The proprioceptors transduce the stimulations from changes in body position and the motion of muscles, tendons, and joints. When learning to run or skip, the young child associates cues from his kinesthetic sense organs to coordinate his body positions. In a similar way, students learning to pole-vault, run the high hurdles, or broad-jump must learn complicated series of associations related to their interoceptor inputs. Another system is the static, or *vestibular*, sense, which transduces stimulation from changes in body balance. Even if a person is blindfolded, is wrapped in gauze, and has his nostrils plugged and muffs put over his ears, he still knows his position with reference to gravity. One of the problems in space travel involves the maintenance of the vestibular sense in the absence of gravity. The interoceptors are the *organic* senses which transduce stimulations from changes related to the regulation of organic functions such as sexual activity or digestion. The infant may have a generalized feeling of discomfort

when he wants to be fed, but he does not distinguish between hunger and thirst. The young child can say "I want a drink" when he is thirsty and "Cookie now!" when he is hungry. In other words, he has learned to differentiate such closely related organic sensations as those of hunger and thirst.

## VISUAL PERCEPTION

Visual exploration is basic to much of the infant's learning before he becomes mobile or able to handle objects. White (1971) compiled a group of longitudinal studies in which an enriched visual environment was provided for infants over an extended period of time. Visual exploration was increased by extra handling, head rearing to allow child to look around, and giving interesting objects to the child. White concluded that these experiences played an important role in the development of hand regard and visually guided reaching, which was earlier for experimental children over comparison norms.

Optimal acuity changes from near-point accommodation in young babies to far-point accommodation in young children. Visual acuity is the degree of accuracy with which the eyes receive light-wave information from the external environment. Usually, "normal" human vision is described as the visual image seen by young adults who have no optic defects. The person with 20/20 vision in both eyes sees at a distance of 20 feet with a clarity that is typical of individuals with mature, undistorted corneas and otherwise normal eyes. People see in three dimensions and with a sensation of space because the two eyes see the same object from a slightly different angle and because the left and right hemispheres of each eye transmit visual data to the left and right hemispheres of the brain (Pribram, 1971). Through many associations of exteroceptor, proprioceptor, and interoceptor sensations, the individual learns the characteristics of familiar objects. He is later able to "perceive" the shape and weight of many objects by means of vision alone, even when he is just shown a picture of them.

Some visual problems are due to the fact that a person receives slightly different images from the two eyes. The eyeballs may be slightly different in size or shape. Vertical imbalance and horizontal imbalance, for example, result in the lack of fusion of the two visual images. The person's visual acuity is impaired—he may see blurred print, or he may need to put unusual strain on the muscles that focus his eyes, which leads him to fall asleep over his books. Screening tests for pupils' visual acuity should include a telebinocular test, such as the Keystone Visual Survey Test. This device enables the school nurse, or someone properly trained, to screen for close vision and to determine whether the two eyes are working together. Screening tests made at 20 feet are not adequate for analyses of the organic efficiency of potential readers. A few schools provide ophthalmological examinations for all pupils. The reports to the teacher from such examinations should include descriptions of fusion irregularities even when minor or otherwise not amenable to correction. This knowledge enables the teacher to adapt seating arrangements and formats of reading materials to minimize visual deficiencies. If teachers are to make adjustments for individual discrepancies, they need to understand the reports from ophthalmologists.

Many emotional loadings become associated with difficulties in near-point vision that make reading books a strain. One of the ways in which the body meets this difficulty is to make the person tired and unable to read anymore. If this difficulty is associated with failure in a task that is important for the student's self-concept, reading may become a punishing activity. On the other hand, a sub-stantial number of students cannot see the chalkboard because of faulty far-point vision. These students often have difficulty catching balls and judging other distances that are important for success in the eyes of their peers. Most of these problems can be solved by the use of glasses, but often teachers have to reinforce young people for wearing the glasses they need. Many students associate wearing glasses with punishing emotional affects, which can be removed only through careful help from teachers and other significant adults.

The eyes make constant visual adjustments during waking hours. A *pupillary reflex* adjusts the amount of light received on the retina. An *accommodation reflex* shapes the lens for far- or near-point focus. A *convergence reflex* turns the eyes inward for viewing a close object. In order for an individual to see clearly, these reflexes require the continuous coordination of six pairs of fine muscles. Student activities that allow for frequent change from near- to far-point focusing minimize eyestrain for most students.

Extreme lack of fusion can be observed in children with *strabismus*, or overconvergence of the two eyes. Slight defects may be detected only on professional examination. Faulty depth perception, called *astereopsis*, may result when one eye is very dominant, while the other is very weak. Sometimes the ophthalmologist decides to cover the dominant eye so that with use the weak eye will develop and function normally. When the eyeballs differ slightly in size or shape, images of different sizes may be transmitted to the brain and cause a fusion defect called *aniseikonia*. After extended periods of near-point work, some children demonstrate possible eye defects by holding their books in unusual positions, rubbing their eyes, or assuming unusual head postures. Such children should be referred to the school nurse or physician.

## Development of Visual Discrimination

Freud (1953) reported that infants can follow moving objects with their eyes, and many research studies have since substantiated his observation that neonates can see. Gesell (1949) emphasized the importance of maturation and practice in the interaction of systems for discrimination. Piaget (1956) emphasized the role of experience in which action is transformed to perception and cognition, through increasingly complex stages. The evidence of color discrimination in infants has been documented (Chapter 9).

Fantz (1966) took the position that perception precedes action and that early perceptual experience is necessary for normal development of visually directed behavior. He based his findings on a series of investigations in which he found evidence that infants can see at birth, that action is initiated by what the infant perceives, and that oculomotor coordination improves with learning. The development of sensorimotor coordination allowed his infant subjects to increase their perception, which in turn directed more active forms of behavior. Feedback and reinforcement from past responses altered what was attended to and therefore what would be perceived in the future.

In experimental work with human infants, Fantz placed a shield over the crib, through which he could see into the baby's pupil and iris (Figure 12-1). Thus the infant's visual fixation target was apparent to the observer and could be timed. In most of his experiments, two objects were presented for the selective attention of the infant. The baby could look at one or the other target, or he could look at neither. Using selective attention to patterns as a criterion, Fantz showed in the first of these studies that newborn infants can discriminate $1/8$-inch stripes at a distance of 9 inches above the eyes. His subjects, 83 in

number, showed increasing improvement with age to six months in the selection of a striped pattern over a gray pattern of about the same overall light reflectance.

Perception means more than the presence of sensory capacity; it implies the use of sensory data to direct behavior or to make contact with the environment. To determine whether selection indicates merely the receiving and transmitting of sensory data. Fantz designed another study (1963) in which the visual preference of newborn and older infants was examined; again fixation times were the criteria. His subjects were one group of 25 infants ranging in age from two to six months and another group of 18 infants ranging in age from ten hours to five days. The target objects were 6-inch discs. One showed a face printed in black and white, one showed a bull's-eye printed in black and white, and one was covered with newsprint; the three remaining discs were in plain colors of white, fluorescent yellow, and red. Both neonates and older infants gave the greatest amount of selective attention to the figure of the face, next to the bull's eye, next to the newsprint, and last to the three colors. Little difference was found in attention given to any particular color. Fantz found that his subjects, usually thought to be farsighted, accommodated visually to objects about 9 to 12 inches from their eyes. He interpreted this near-range accommodation as being helpful to the newborn infant in making selective exploration of his environment—his mother's face, sources of food, and the like.

Fantz's next studies (1963) were concerned with the hypothesis that facial features—eye, nose, and mouth shapes—attract the attention of infants. He therefore presented his subjects with two-dimensional discs, some showing features in the regular positions and others showing the same features in scrambled positions. In one study, infant subjects from less than one week to six months old attended selectively to the discs showing the regular arrangement of features over those showing scrambled features or plain discs (Figure 12-2). After the age of one week, this selection was significant beyond .001 probability. The investigator suggests that the preference for correct arrangement of facial features was neither instinctive nor genetic but was associated with learned social stimuli, that is, that the infants had learned to recognize human facial arrangements visually.

Fantz (1963) next tested selective attention to a three-dimensional head compared with that to a flat disc showing a head. Subjects were 40 infants from less than one month to six months of age. Up to about two months of age, his infant subjects tended to prefer the flat form, while beyond three months they preferred the three-dimensional head form. These results indicated both depth discrimination and solidarity preference, after the age of approximately two months. This visual perception ability on the part of very young children is important background for their subsequent manipulation of a three-dimensional environment. These infants showed a preference for three-dimensional forms prior to their having manipulated a three-dimensional world.

Fantz (1964) hypothesized that the changes he observed in infants could have been due to maturation or oculomotor practice rather than to visual experience—that is, learning. To test this hypothesis, he used rhesus monkey infants that he reared in controlled laboratory conditions that would have been unsuitable as an arranged environment for human infants. He restricted the visual experience of the young monkeys by keeping them in total darkness for varying periods of time. His monkeys who were kept in darkness for six weeks or less showed poorer differential responses to patterned over plain discs, and solid over flat objects, than monkeys reared normally. Many

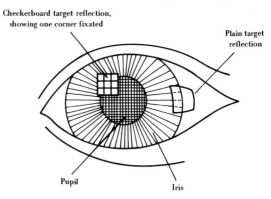

**Figure 12-1** Schematic drawing of an infant's eye as seen in a test chamber. The experimenter observes where checked and plain squares are exposed. This illustrates the limiting condition for satisfying the criterion of fixation; more generally, the target reflection would overlap the pupil to a greater degree. (*After R. L. Fantz, Pattern Discrimination and Selective Attention as Determinants of Perceptual Development from Birth. In Aline H. Kidd and Jeanne L. Rivoire (Eds.), Perceptual Development in Children, New York: International Universities Press, 1966, p. 148.*)

months later, the monkeys raised in a prolonged environment of darkness showed poor visual performance and were very slow in learning to use visual cues to direct locomotion and to recognize objects. The investigator concluded that some maturation had occurred during the period of darkness, as evidenced by the pattern preferences of monkeys who had been reared in darkness for up to four weeks. Preference for pattern or fixation of patterns increased during the first three or four weeks, even though the young monkey's life included very little visual experience. However, this initial increase changed to a downward trend when the dark rearing was continued beyond five weeks. The less deprived animals gradually developed the expected visual discrimination, while those who had undergone prolonged deprivation failed to catch up when provided with typical visual experiences.

Fantz (1964) finally experimented with 14 infants from two to six months of age who

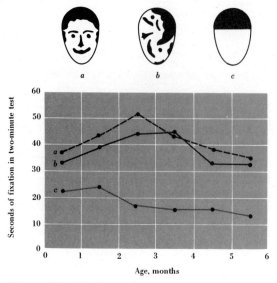

Figure 12-2 Facelike and control patterns shown to infants. (*After R. L. Fantz, In Eleanor J. Gibson, "Perceptual Development, in H. W. Stevenson, J. Kagan, and C. Spiker (Eds.), Child Psychology: The Sixty-second Yearbook of the National Society for the Study of Education, Chicago: University of Chicago Press, 1963, p. 181.*)

were given successive exposures to the same patterns. With this repeated exposure, fixation time increased at first and then generally decreased throughout the test. With another group of infants from two to six months of age, the investigator used one constant pattern in different positions paired with 10 variations. In this situation, the level of interest remained high through 10 successive exposures, the duration of the study. This greater visual attention to a novel pattern implies that infants over two months can recognize a pattern they have seen before and may lose interest in repetitions of visual experiences. Fantz suggests that visual experience changes the infant's selectiveness of future visual experience. These studies show that (1) from birth, human infants can see and discriminate patterns, (2) visual patterning is intrinsically more stimulating than color or brightness alone, (3)

selective attention allows the infant to explore his environment visually, (4) visual selectiveness is modified by visual experience at two months or earlier, and (5) visual perception precedes action in the sequence of child development. The studies showed that there is a deterioration of mechanisms for learning visual discrimination when the mechanisms are not used during critical times of development.

Fantz's studies, together with Platt's reports (1962) on the need for novelty in adults, emphasize the importance of variety in the visual and other perceptual experiences provided by the school. Class materials should be arranged to build necessary discriminations on a basis of rotating variety within a generally familiar content. Teachers can contribute to the same result by varying materials even when they have not been prestructured to produce the desired effect.

## Perception and the Private World

A person's value structure alters his visual perception. In an investigation by Lambert, Solomon, and Watson (1963), subjects changed their estimation of the size of tokens when the conversion value of the tokens was changed. Two groups of children—one from a highly educated, high socioeconomic background and the other from a low socioeconomic background—were divided into experimental and control subjects. The children were taught to work a machine and then were rewarded by a plastic token.

The experimental group had available to them a machine into which they could put a token and receive a candy reward. After 10 days, the candy reward was removed, but on the twelfth day it was reinstated. Following these experiences of work with tokens and reward with candy and work with tokens only, the children were asked to estimate the size of the token. Experimental subjects overestimated the size of the token when it was represented graphically. At the point of extinction—the point at which children received no reward after learning to expect one—their estimation of the size of the token dropped below that of the control group. Their estimation of the size of the token increased significantly after reinstatement of the candy reward, when compared with that of the control group. In interpreting this study, the investigator suggested that the size of the object may have been overestimated because of its social value.

Some of the research on visual discrimination of color was conducted by Cook (1931). He asked 110 children from seventeen months to six years to match squares in four colors, using variations of color brightness and saturation. By age two, his subjects could match specimens with 45 percent accuracy, and by age six their color matching was 97 percent accurate. Color naming, on the other hand, was 45 percent accurate in the two-year-olds and 62 percent accurate in the six-year-olds. This and other studies have shown that children discriminate color at a very early age but that the color-naming ability, which also requires vocabulary learning, develops later. Probably children can be taught to name colors as early as they can speak and have some need for color names.

Some early studies of the interpretation of photographs and pictures created the impression that experience with two-dimensional representations was necessary, in addition to experience with the three-dimensional world, before interpretation of pictures in readers was to be anticipated. In an attempt to test the effect of picture deprivation, Hochberg and Brooks (1960) reared a child to nineteen months of age in an environment without pictures, providing him, however, with real objects along with their names and other associations for them. At nineteen months of age, he was shown a set of 21 pictures presented on 3- by 5-inch cards. The pictures included outline drawings, photographs, and realistic drawings of objects and people. The child was able to identify pictorial representations, both in photographs and in line drawings. Hudson (1960) was interested in testing earlier observations that primitive people cannot identify pictures—that is, two-dimensional representations of familiar three-dimensional objects. He tested 11 samples of Africans, including some who attended school and some who did not and also including children and adults, both black and white, representing various territories. His subjects were able to identify correctly nearly all the pictures presented, both line drawings and photographs. These results do not indicate that teaching is without value in the perception of pictures and drawings, but they do show that both children and adults are able to relate experience in a three-dimensional world to a two-dimensional representation.

## Perception of the Panoramic Field

The panoramic field is the whole view that the two eyes can take in simultaneously. Some vertebrates view the left and right fields, but have an optic chiasma in the central portion of the panoramic field. Man's phylogenetic status is such that he has an uninterrupted field of vision and can make the near-point accommodation that is necessary for many tasks, including reading. This aspect of visual perception has implications for unsolved problems in the potential rate of reading, the diagnosis of laterality problems in reading, and the selectivity of visual detail from the panoramic field.

## Eye Movements in Reading

A reader's eyes move across a line of print in a series of fixations (when clear visual images are received) interspaced by sweeps when little or no input data are being received through the eyes. These jerky eye movements are called *saccadic movements.* The movement of the eyes to the next line of print is called the *return sweep.* The backward movements of the eyes to reread are called *regressions.* Eye movements can be observed accurately by a camera, designed for the purpose, which photographs the reflection of a beam of light on the cornea. The beam of light is interrupted at regular intervals—often 1/100 second—to create a series of dots on the film, which locate the fixation pauses and indicate the duration of each pause. Tinker (1965) reported that in most situations, 90 to 95 percent of reading time is devoted to fixation pauses, when the eyes are motionless (Table 12.2). He defines the sum of the fixation pauses as perception time, or speed of reading. Saccadic movements consume about 9 percent of the reader's time when the material is very easy and only about 3 percent when the material consists of mathematical formulas. Oculomotor behavior in reading is extremely complex, involving different rates of move-

ment for the two eyes during the saccadic movements and motor adjustments during fixations. However, some knowledge of the time limits of visual perception is useful to all teachers and to college students who are interested in their own rates of reading.

Most students read more slowly than they would like to and much more slowly than they are capable of reading without the use of special gimmicks. Moore (1970) reviewed the research on the effectiveness of different machines designed to increase reading rate. She concluded that mechanical devices are useful for increasing eye span for common words and phrases. She stressed the motivational value of devices for some students but suggested that nonmechanical methods could also accomplish similar improvement by systematically pushing oneself to get the sense more quickly. To some extent this speed-up is gained by limiting oneself to acceptance of ideas rather than by evaluating them.

Extreme differences of opinion exist regarding the rate at which the human eye can

**Table 12-2   Percentage of Movement Time and of Pause Time in Reading**

| Kind of material read in various line widths | Percentage of reading time | |
|---|---|---|
| | Movements | Pauses |
| Very easy prose: | | |
|   Silent reading, 25-pica line | 9.6 | 90.4 |
|   Oral reading, 25-pica line | 6.2 | 93.8 |
| Easy narrative prose: | | |
|   9-pica line | 6.4 | 93.6 |
|   19-pica line | 8.1 | 91.9 |
|   40-pica line | 8.5 | 91.5 |
| Hard scientific prose, 25-pica line | 7.3 | 92.7 |
| Algebra problems with formulas, 20-pica line | 5.3 | 94.7 |
| Easy speed-of-reading test, 19-pica line | 7.9 | 92.1 |
| Multiple-choice examination questions, 25-pica line | 6.2 | 93.8 |
| Overall mean | 7.3 | 92.7 |

*SOURCE:* Tinker, M. A., *Bases for effective reading,* Minneapolis: University of Minnesota Press, 1965. By permission of the publisher.

take in printed material. Evelyn Wood advertises that her training techniques will enable enrollees to triple their rate of reading. Some claims mention about 30 pages of text a minute. Spache (1962) summarized the time-limit data on reading perception: A short fixation requires $1/6$ to $1/5$ second, a saccadic movement requires $1/25$ second, a return sweep requires approximately $1/25$ second, and the maximum number of words per fixation in continuous reading is 2.5 to 3. By these limitations, maximal reader performance on 10-word lines would be .66 seconds per line, 15 words per second (wps), or 900 wpm. S. E. Taylor (1962) analyzed the oculomotor patterns of college students who had recently taken training in speed reading. He found their pattern of saccadic movements and fixations to be similar to normal readers' when skimming. Responsible researchers, at this time, set the maximum rate of taking in all the words of printed material, line by line, at about 1,000 wpm. Until laboratory tests can verify the oculomotor pattern that speed reading programs supposedly develop, a rate of comprehension much greater than 1,000 words per minute is open to question. If skimming fits the reader's purpose, then speed reading techniques might be worth his investigation.

## Selectivity of Visual Detail

Normally students learn to focus on panoramic aspects of the visual environment or on details, according to teacher direction or their own purposes. Some children are very distractible. They seem unable to screen out irrelevant stimuli, perhaps because of some dysfunction in the neurological feedback to the sense organ. Such children need to have their visual stimulation limited as nearly as possible to the materials that are needed for a particular learning situation. Most students, however, take in information from a visually

stimulating classroom environment and organize and store the information for future use.

## Problems of Laterality in Reading

Directional confusion is observed in readers whose problem is the reversal or inversion of letters, words, or whole pages of material. Many beginning readers occasionally reverse letters such as "b" and "d" and words such as "was" and "saw." Experience in reading from left to right usually eliminates this confusion within a few months. In extreme cases, the problem may persist to the extent that the individual eventually learns to read the mirror reflection of printed material and also learns to write in reverse form. Leonardo da Vinci, for example, persisted throughout his life to write and read in reverse form. Albert Harris (1957) found that the tendency to mix left and right dominates the activities of greater numbers of young children with reading problems than of typical learners. This tendency toward mixed dominance is not found to a significant extent in preadolescents with reading problems (Baylow, 1963).

Lateral confusion shows up when the child first works in two-dimensional material, which denies him the opportunity to use the deep senses for orientation and verification. This tendency is usually considered perceptual in nature and disappears with maturity. The learning problems that seem to be correlated with lack of dominance by one hemisphere of the brain are not typical of the population in general, as indicated by the ability of naive populations and normal child subjects to interpret pictures. Young children who show mixed dominance probably need three-dimensional manipulation materials that will help them form associations with letter and numeral shapes.

Physiological evidence of left-right asymmetry in the human brain was reported by Geschwind and Levitsky (1968). They examined 100 human brains (obtained at postmortem) and found the left temporal speech area markedly larger in 65 percent of their sample and the right side larger in 11 percent. Since the importance of this area for speech is well established, as is the predominance of right-handed people in the population the finding has significant implications for the unanswered questions about lateral dominance. Educational researchers will need early data on the left-right functioning of individuals, predating the reading problem, before the relationship of laterality and reading ability is determined.

## AUDITORY PERCEPTION

Until recently American psychologists have paid very little attention to the development of auditory perception (Kidd & Rivoire, 1966). Most of the knowledge in this field has accrued from practice-oriented research in medicine and neurology, speech correction, and the clinical teaching of reading. Case histories have shown extreme variability in the audition of individuals of a given age and in the audition of the same individual over a period of time.

### Auditory Acuity and Speech Development

As a result of clinical observations, the functional lack of discrimination of specific speech sounds has been established, the mechanisms of the auditory system that are affected have been determined, the probable causes of these dysfunctions have been identified, and evidence of successful teaching has been recorded. The pure-tone audiometer has made it possible to control and measure the intensity, or volume, of sound in decibels (db) and to control and measure the pitch, or frequency of

sound vibrations, in cycles per second (cps). The problem of feedback from the subject is difficult in the case of the unborn, infants, and those with sensory dysfunctions. Research in speech and hearing has contributed enormously to the current ability of clinicians to distinguish between lack of hearing acuity and auditory perception.

Communication skills normally develop in the following sequence: (1) understanding speech, (2) speaking, (3) reading, and (4) writing to communicate. Although some methods of teaching the native language introduce reading and writing skills simultaneously, the reading level of the typical child quickly surpasses his writing fluency. Learning a second language poses different problems from those involved in learning to read the mother tongue, but learning to read and write in any language requires the building of many associations between visual and auditory cues.

### Discrimination of Phonemes

Several investigators have found a positive relationship between auditory perception and reading success. Wepman (1960) noted a positive correlation between poor auditory discrimination and accuracy of articulation. Teachers can improve both these skills by systematic instruction. Both auditory and articulation abilities were related to reading failure in Wepman's studies. Epstein, Giolas, and Owens (1968) found that normal hearing subjects could learn to identify familiar words undisturbed even when the enunciation of them was distorted mechanically. In studying children with neurological disabilities, Zoepfel (1964) found a positive correlation between faulty auditory discrimination and the learning difficulties. From the results of his longitudinal study, B. Thompson (1963) recommended that those who score low on auditory discrimination tests be given extended training in aural perception, prior to instruction in phonics. He further recommended that those who score high on tests of auditory discrimination be started early in reading.

In working with black children from lower socioeconomic areas, Chall, Roswell, and Blumenthal (1963) observed that auditory blending—the ability to unite different letters into a simple pattern—correlated more highly with first-grade reading success than IQ did when independent variables were held constant. Certain children need special help in developing these auditory perception abilities before they are taught word-attack skills. Fortunately, this instruction can be supplied readily by a classroom teacher who knows how to develop this kind of discrimination.

In her Reading Aptitude Tests, M. Monroe (1935) included three auditory subtests—sound blending, sound discrimination, and memory for details of a story presented orally. These subtests involve what appear to be discrete abilities on the part of the subjects. In the test for sound blending, the child must identify a picture with its label when the word is presented by the teacher in sound phonemes. Sound discrimination is measured by the child's ability to identify which of three words is the correct name of a pictured object. These words are presented orally and differ in one sound element only. The test for memory for story detail hinges on the child's ability to hear whole words in context and to reproduce them orally. The uniqueness of these three activities in the auditory battery points up the diverse nature of auditory perception.

Durrell and Murphy (1963) reported an earlier study in which four groups, made up of a total of 540 pupils, were equated for mental age, learning rate, speaking vocabulary, and auditory discrimination. Each group was given one of four treatments: auditory training, visual training, both auditory and visual training, or the regular kindergarten program. The differences that favored the girls in the control groups were eliminated for the boys who had had training in both visual and auditory discrimination. They noted that the kindergarten child who found reading easy discovered the sound likeness at the beginning of words such as "cake," "cookies," and "corn." They told of a ten-year-old boy with an IQ of 166, an MA of 17, five years of schooling, and a reading vocabulary of 66 words. After the boy had conceptualized the relationship of beginning sounds to one another—that is, discovered sound-letter patterns—he made eight years of reading progress in three months.

A. J. Harris (1968) summarized the research on causes of reading disability, citing many studies in which auditory discrimination was significantly related to success in learning to read. Reading failure was found to be related to perceptual difficulties, lack of auditory discrimination, articulation defects, and neurological disorganization. All these studies emphasize the close relationship of auditory perception and reading success. One implication of this research has been the possibility of improving auditory perception abilities through teaching, which would increase reading potential.

### Perception of Compressed Speech

Research on the ability to understand compressed speech is a good example of how incomplete signals can be understood. Witkin (1969) was able to increase the speed of speech without changing the pitch by cutting periods of silence from the tape or by excising bits of the message at random from the tape. Lecture material could be speeded 50 percent without loss of comprehension. Foulke (1968) found no serious decline in STEP Listening Test Scores when the rate of reading was increased from 175 to 250 words per minute (wpm). However, when the rate was increased an additional 25 wpm to 275 wpm, scores of college subjects fell off significantly. He suggested perception time became inadequate at the higher speed if listeners were required to make interpretations of the material to answer the questions. Woodcock and Clark (1968) found significant differences between children of low, average, and high intelligence in their ability to comprehend compressed speech. The ability to perceive incomplete messages depends on the ability of the listener to fill out an auditory image from past experience.

### Selective Listening

The auditory organization of the individual is important in what he will hear. Witkin (1969) reported improvement in the skill of elementary school children in listening to one voice and screening out another. Lesson sequences involving progressively more difficult discriminations were designed in which earphones fed one voice into one ear and another voice into the other ear. Children were instructed on which voice to attend and which to disregard. In the first lesson the voices were far apart in pitch, loudness, and timbre. In successive lessons voices were brought together progressively and eventually crossed over so that the subordinate voice became the one that was heard and followed. Children learned to selectively perceive what they were motivated to hear.

### INTEGRATION OF SENSORY SYSTEMS

Some systems of education, such as the Montessori method, stress the importance of a foundation of sensorimotor learning as preparation for reading and mathematics. Visual, auditory, tactile, proprioceptor, and other sensations must be integrated if an individual is to function adequately in any school task. Human beings are born with sensory functions linked to primitive interpretations, which operate as reflex systems. Although some coordination of the perceptual systems has already been established by birth, a critical phase of infant learning involves the further integration of the different sensory systems. Held and Bauer (1967) studied the effect of the separation of visual perception and kinesthetic learning in infant macaque monkeys. The baby monkeys wore aprons that prevented them from seeing their body parts. Care was taken to provide the established needs for feeding, attention, and exercise. Fur-covered props were provided for them to cling to, and amusing things to handle were available. After 30 days—the established period of time for the grasping skill to have developed—one arm was exposed. At first the monkey examined its free hand. Even when hungry, it would ignore the bottle in favor of hand watching. Grasping objects was retarded. After the second arm was exposed, very little, if any, transfer of learning to coordinate hand-eye activities had occurred. From this study, it can be concluded that opportunities to manipulate teaching materials that provide multisensory input help to stimulate integration in perception (Figure 12-3).

Neurologically, much of the integration of multisensory experience, so important in basic learning experience, is provided by the reticular formation. This system receives impulses from many sense organs operating simultaneously and incorporates these data to generate an awareness of the present (Penfield & Roberts, 1959). Apparently, data that signal change are processed, while static data are ignored. When substantial changes in input from one sensory system, or less substantial impulses from several systems, reach a critical level, attention is aroused. Appropriate senses are then focused, and perception is initiated. Consciousness is the integration of perceptual awareness.

A particular level of sensory stimulation may become the new norm for an individual's state, so that the sensations no longer initiate his attention. The noise level in an over-crowded home can become the condition for inattention. The habit of turning off or ignoring human voices in the home can be carried over to become inattention at school. This behavior can be altered by rewarding the child for paying attention and by gradually extending the time that his attention is required. The use of attention-getting techniques is probably essential in the beginning of the reteaching program. The need for reteaching habits of attention may be as urgent in high school as in kindergarten.

Pribram (1971) identified cross-cortical linkages of neurons that integrate auditory and visual signals with somatic-proprioceptor tactile information. Ayers (1968) suggested that the somatic and vestibular systems preceded the visual and auditory systems in the phylogenic development of the species. Reading requires the highly integrated activity of all the primitive systems on which vision and hearing are built.

Rock (1966) tested the relative importance of visual- and tactile-related cues in adaptive behavior. His subjects were all fitted with lenses, some image-distorting, and given objects to manipulate inside a black-curtained cage. Rock found (1) most human beings are vision-dominated, (2) body position and texture are learned by establishing harmony of visual and proprioceptive systems, and (3) space knowledge is a conceptualization of visual patterns. It is important to note that one-fifth of Rock's subjects reversed the normal pattern and adapted to proprioceptor cues rather than visual cues when the input from the different systems was conflicting. Because of generally normal language abilities, instructional games were suggested which associated verbal labels to left-right sequencing and visual symbols (Robeck & Wilson, 1973).

Lovell and Gorton (1968) compared backward readers with normal readers on an exten-

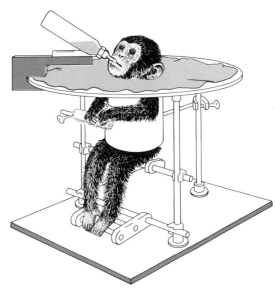

**Figure 12-3** Apparatus for rearing an infant monkey without sight of its limbs. (*From R. Held & J. A. Bauer, Jr., Visually guided reaching in infant monkeys after restricted rearing. Science, 1967, 155, 719. Copyright 1967 by American Association for the Advancement of Science.*)

sive battery of perceptual intelligence and achievement tests. Their 100 subjects ages nine and ten were all in the average range on individual intelligence tests. On non-reading tasks which required auditory-visual integration and sound-symbol association, the backward readers were significantly lower than the normal readers. On visual-motor integration, retarded readers were low in spatial orientation and left-right discrimination. The investigators found a common factor of items suggesting poor sensory integration in a high proportion of the poor readers.

Katz and Deutsch (1963) compared the reaction time to auditory versus visual stimuli of groups of good and poor black readers in New York City schools. Their subjects were first-, third-, and fifth-grade boys, divided into six groups of twenty-eight each. All groups took longer to respond to visual or auditory stimuli when alternative modality stimuli were presented first than they did when like modality stimuli were presented consecutively. Poor readers took significantly longer to shift from one modality to the other than good readers did. IQ was not significant in the reaction times to either visual or auditory stimuli. Older children shifted modality reaction more rapidly than younger children. These findings suggest the importance of practice in perceptual integration in learning.

In *Kindergarten Evaluation of Learning Potential,* Wilson and Robeck (1967) devised items, including bead design, that cited integration of sensory systems as a learning goal. For example, the child strings beads from left to right, and he matches designs and builds associations between the shapes and colors of the object he feels and sees. By working from left to right, he begins to pattern a mode of progression in the direction required for reading in English.

## CAUSES OF FAULTY PERCEPTION

Faulty perception is a cause of low achievement in some school learners. One of the problems of diagnosing perceptual dysfunction involves the difficulty of determining whether the sense organ is not functioning properly, as in the case of myopia; whether the transmission is faulty, as in the case of damage to the auditory nerve; or whether the CNS has some physiological dysfunction. Children with severe damage to the CNS with afflictions such as some forms of cerebral palsy, Mongolism, or epilepsy, for example, will have been identified long before they reach school age. Milder forms of neurological damage, such as those caused by anoxia, may not be discovered until the child comes to school. Many students, perhaps 5 to 10 percent, are handicapped in their ability to deal with symbolic material because of slight malfunction in the neurological system. The causes of faulty or inadequate perception are many, but the most important are the follow-

ing: low mental ability, meager store of basic associations, lack of motivation, and neurological damage.

### Low Mental Ability

Students whose general intellectual capacity is low are generally less alert—less easily aroused. They extract fewer sensory data from the environment. The quality and quantity of the data perceived and stored have not been clearly measured, but research on intellectual functioning clearly shows wide individual differences in the ability to retrieve and use the data from past experience.

### Meager Store of Basic Associations

Children from deprived environments lack a variety of experiences, and therefore it can be assumed that they lack a large store of basic associations. For example, a child who has never seen a daffodil is not likely to respond to a poem about daffodils as enthusiastically as a child who has seen, smelled, felt, or even grown daffodils. The student who has seen a live tiger experiences Blake's famous poem "The Tiger" differently from the child who has seen only black-and-white pictures of a tiger. Some experiences negatively influence the kind of learning a child does in school. The student who suffers from asthma may not enjoy the poem "The Golden Rod Is Yellow." Basic associations, including perceptions, are the bits and pieces from which conceptualizations or abstractions are formed. An impoverished store of basic associations results in lowered mental functioning and a downward spiral of school achievement.

### Lack of Motivation

Lack of motivation is a common characteristic of students who drop out of school or who wish they could drop out. A student's lack of motivation is often assumed to be an artifact of a cultural environment in which school learning is unimportant. Such acculturation has an impact but is not definitive. When a student first comes to school, transfers to a new school, or begins a new type of course, the teacher has the opportunity to provide a fresh start as far as motivation is concerned. Motivations are formed from the satisfaction or lack of satisfaction that the learner associates with particular sensory and cognitive experiences. Each new teacher whom a student encounters can help him associate the affects of pleasure rather than punishment with each experience in the new class.

### Neurological Damage

Cerebral dysfunctions in mild forms are difficult to diagnose even for the neurologist, who has the electroencephalograph (EEG) from which to study electromagnetic impulses in the brain. The student with minimal neurological dysfunction (Wender, 1971) is seldom identified before he comes to school. Although his disability ordinarily disappears by puberty, the confusion he experiences in trying to read is likely to live with him forever in the form of affective associations. Many functions important in learning are not readily accessible to neurological examination: perception, cognition, judgment, concentration, impulse control, visual memory, auditory memory, and symbol organization. For these reasons, it is important that teachers know the characteristics of children with this kind of impairment.

The student with minimal brain dysfunction is likely to exhibit two or more of the following characteristics: (1) *hyperkinesis,* or hyperactivity (is restless, impulsive, disorganized, and disruptive), (2) *distractibility* (cannot screen out inconsequential stimuli), (3) *lowered emotional thresholds* (cries and laughs more readily than is typical for his age), (4)

*poor motor coordination* (awkwardness in running, retardation in skipping), (5) *mixed laterality* (lack of left or right dominance in motor abilities), (6) time and space disorientation (doesn't anticipate the schedule at school), (7) *adiadochokinesis* (inability to perform rapid alternative movements), (8) *inappropriate displays of affection* (excessive hugging and kissing, or intolerance for body contact) (Clemmens, 1961). Children who are experiencing learning difficulties and frequently show two or more of these characteristics should be referred to the appropriate physician or neurologist.

### SEX DIFFERENCES

Hansen (1967) compared the differences between the sexes in reading achievement when two types of supplementary instruction were added to the regular reading program in the primary grades. Experimental and control schools were selected that were socioeconomically comparable. Control and experimental groups in grades 1, 2, and 3 were matched on scholastic aptitude, age, and sex. The experimental school used a phonic system that was characterized by training in auditory perception (ear training) prior to and during association of sound and visual forms of letters. The control school used four types of district-prepared guides on phonics instruction, a planned sequence of learning in phonics, supplementary materials in the curriculum guide, and reading worksheets for grades 1 to 3. Both schools used the same cobasal reading series, provided 20-minute supplementary periods for instruction, put like emphasis on the research aspects of the program, and made available comparable in-service training for teachers. Achievement tests showed significant differences in favor of the experimental phonics program in all grade and sex groups. Differences in favor of girls over boys prevailed. By the third-grade level, however, boys in the experimental groups exceeded the mean scores for both boy and girl groups in the control school. The teaching materials that emphasized simultaneous auditory and visual cues tended to eliminate differences between the sexes in beginning reading success.

Slobodian (1966) studied the reading achievement of about 250 first-grade children from the suburbs. She found no significant differences between boys and girls in this cultural group and suggests that value systems in the subculture may have contributed to the boys' educational motivation. This study might be interpreted as reflecting the increasing similarity in the perceptual experiences of boys and girls in the preschool environment of the modern suburb, as compared with the experiences of children from rural areas, the inner city, or lower-class groups. Typically, boys in the suburbs are kept as close to home as girls, see the same television programs, have comparable verbal interaction with the mother, go on similar kinds of family outings, and play with many of the same educational toys. Their perceptual integration patterns are similar. Frequently, writers suggest that the school progress of a whole sex or age group should be retarded; such suggestions should be resisted on the basis of evidence of individual differences in perceptual development.

## SUMMARY

Perception is the individual's immediate interpretation of sensory information. *Percepts* are bits of data that the learner organizes to make up chains of cognitive associations. *Affects* are bits of data from the learner's own internal or emotional structures. *Concepts* are generalized or abstracted ideas which may be stimulated by affective as well as cognitive associations but which involve awareness on the part of the learner. Conceptualization is based on

perceptual data, but represents learning beyond the perceptual process.

Sensory systems may be classified as *external* when the stimulation comes from outside the person, and *internal* when the stimulation comes from within the body structures. External systems are visual, auditory, cutaneous, olfactory, and gustatory senses. Internal systems are the *proprioceptors* that produce sensations of body balance and position (inner ear, muscle and joint senses) and the *interoceptors* (visceral organic senses). Generally, the sense organs of a full-term infant are relatively well developed at birth.

The perception process in initiated by the stimulation of a sense organ. Perception includes the coding of stimuli, the transmission of coded messages via selected neurons, the reception of coded messages into the CNS, and the immediate differentiations made by the learner.

The human organism explores his environment first with his eyes; then, when he is visually oriented, motor activity is initiated. Studies of perceptual development have shown that infant performances improve with maturation, but experience (learning) has been found to be necessary for continuous development. In studies of visual deprivation, the perceptual development of infant monkeys did not fully recover from early and prolonged deprivation.

Loss in auditory acuity handicaps an individual in his development of auditory discrimination and auditory perceptiveness. Skills in a person's native language develop in the following sequence: understanding of speech, speaking, reading, and writing to communicate. Audition skills that have been found to correlate with reading success in school are articulating accurately, blending phonemes, discriminating sound parts, and recalling stories or information perceived aurally. Children who are trained systematically in the perception of sounds and the association of appropriate sounds with letter symbols do better in reading than children without such training.

Integration of sensory systems is necessary for an individual to function adequately in any school task. The reticular formation receives and integrates the impulses received simultaneously from the various sense organs. The awareness of the ongoing present, or consciousness, is the result of multisensory integration. The integration of visual and auditory perception is essential to successful school learning.

Groups of boys and girls have been found to differ in various sensorimotor and perceptual skills, usually in favor of the girls. There is some evidence that girls have more experience in language-related activities and in two-dimensional tasks. Boys frequently have more experience in exploration and manipulation of a three-dimensional environment. Boys and girls who have similar learning experiences, including acculturation, show similar abilities in early school tasks.

## SELF-DIRECTING ACTIVITIES

1 Devise an experiment that will test the fineness of discriminations made by six-month-old babies with regard to colors.
2 Check to see if any children with a tendency to reverse words such as "was" and "saw" also reverse words that are not words when reversed. Develop a minitheory to account for your findings.
3 Devise a way of testing whether comprehension is better or worse for compressed speech as a means of communication compared to reading at the same speed. Develop guidelines for determining who would profit from the speech rather than the reading.
4 Develop a way of determining whether there are sex differences in the perception of two-dimensional and three-dimensional representations of visual forms.

# Chapter **13**

Emotional development through mastery of learning tasks. (*Courtesy Sally Cahur*)

# EMOTIONAL DEVELOPMENT

This chapter is designed to help teachers use their knowledge of emotional development to improve learning in the classroom. When you have finished studying it, you should be able to:

◖ Read the literature relating to Freud's work

◖ Toilet-train children without producing trauma

◖ Build a sense of industry and avoid a sense of inferiority on the part of elementary school pupils

◖ Define steps in a developing sense of identity

◖ Avoid a sense of isolation in your relationship with peers

◖ Understand and be able to use the following terms:

    anal stage
    phallic stage
    id
    ego
    superego
    unconscious
    preconscious
    pleasure principle

The progressive changes in the individual's physiological growth influence other aspects of his development, even though emotional growth and cognitive growth proceed with some independence of physical maturation. Originally, the biological term "development" was used primarily in relation to physiological maturation. Gradually, the emotional, cognitive, and social dimensions of human growth have become incorporated into the idea of development and have tended to be emphasized selectively. Emotional development is an important aspect of psychosocial growth.

Initially, child growth and development was organized as an interdisciplinary study. Psychiatrists, pediatricians, psychologists, home economists, social workers, and teachers all had information to contribute, and all had insights to gain from joint studies of the nature of the growing child. To some extent, the early promise of this interdisciplinary approach has been thwarted by the inevitable tendency of each group of specialists to concentrate on the phases of development that were most compatible with their specific background and training. Current research, which has located important physiological functions of learning and of motivation in the CNS, has reverified the essential unity of the human organism. The disciplinarian, whatever his field, has rediscovered the necessity for considering the contributions of others concerned with human development. Emotional growth has been highly important to the psychiatrist and the social worker, while cognitive growth has seemed most significant to the psychologist and the teacher. In America, psychiatrists and social workers have been much more conversant with psychoanalysis than psychologists and teachers have. In this chapter, the most important theories of Erik Erikson form the basic information on which the study of emotional growth is structured. A synthesis of psychoanalytic work with the learning-

motivation model is included to help the prospective teacher understand the significance of psychosocial growth in terms of learning.

## A PSYCHOANALYTIC FRAMEWORK FOR GROWTH

The theoretical structures and the therapy techniques in psychoanalysis are largely the product of Freud's clinical experience and insight. During the 40 years that he wrote on this topic, his views continued to evolve, so that it is difficult to say precisely what his theories were except in reference to a specific time in his career (Freud, 1953). Several of Freud's most influential disciples evolved variations of their own and disengaged themselves from the team. Jung, Adler, and (a dozen years later) Rank were among this group of dissenters, who were broadly classed as analysts. The ideas on which Freud worked have continued to evolve since his death in 1939. Anna Freud, his daughter, extended analytic work to children (1965). New understandings of normal people have also been conceived, particularly by Erikson.

### Freud's Libido

Libidinal energy—the driving force behind all human activity—is an inherited generic drive of enormous importance, according to Freud (1949). This is the pure primordial source of racial survival—the energy that blindly seeks to ensure the continuing existence of the race. In Freud's view, the libido is the prime mover of all human life and the instigator of all activity. The libidinal force dwells in (or constitutes part of) the unconscious, that area of which we are unaware but which activates much of our living. Opposed to this drive is a resistance that is polar to the libido and tends toward regression of a person to less complicated states of existence. The residual strength of these two interacting forces determines the developmental phase at which the individual will function at any particular time. The Freudian concepts of both the regression tendency and the libido are based essentially on punishment avoidance rather than on reward or reinforcement.

## Freud's Stages of Development

Freud's description of development during infancy shows more marked changes over the years than his descriptions of later periods. Eventually, he divided this period into three independently important stages, each of which will be discussed briefly. Infancy is followed by the latent and the puberty stages. Although the earliest childhood stage, the oral, was the last to be described by Freud, this discussion will proceed from earliest childhood to adulthood. Freud's information about these stages came from clinical analyses, including his own self-analyses—a process that took approximately five years and continued sporadically for the rest of his life.

**Oral stage**   Normally the oral stage lasts from birth to eighteen months. The child's earliest contact with the world outside himself is through his mouth. This oral contact with the mother's nipple is stimulating to the infant in the broad Freudian concept of sexuality. Many kinds of acceptance—including holding, cooing, singing, and other pleasantly toned reactions on the part of the mother—are associated with the oral stimulation of the very young child. Freud's contention is supported by the later discovery of the extension of taste buds in the neonate to the hard palate and the esophagus and by the finding that cutaneous senses around the mouth provide his most active stimulation. Exploration, by free association or by memory in a form that involves the use of words, is difficult during the oral period. This impossibility that adults have

in reaching back to the happenings of the first eighteen months of their childhood explains why the oral stage, which has come to be considered of crucial importance, was so long delayed in Freud's order of investigation.

The child's first aggressive acts—biting— are also oral in nature and bring the first rejection responses from the mother or mother substitute. Regressions that fixate at the oral stage of development result in psychotic rather than neurotic symptoms. One of the reasons psychotics are so hard to reach is that they have regressed to the prespeech era of their lives, and contact becomes very difficult.

**Anal Stage**   This period, sometimes called the *anal-sadistic* stage, covers the ages from about eighteen months to four years. Sensual sensitivities are thought to shift from the mouth to the anus. Attention is focused on the process and product of elimination. The anal and the phallic, or genital, stages tend to merge or overlap. The importance of the anal phase in emotional development became clear to Freud during his own self-analysis after the death of his father. The two years following his father's death were a period of depression for Freud, then in his twenties. He came to understand his own feelings of competition with his father and to understand the significance of his early childhood in terms of his own development. As a result of this self-analysis, Freud's interpretation of dreams widened to incorporate the principle that in dreams, events that occurred during the previous several days become involved with some residue from the distant past. During the spring and summer of 1898, Freud relived the period of his own toilet training. He dreamed of excrement, experienced digestive difficulties, and recalled images of elimination processes.

During the anal stage, the child develops his first independence of locomotion, along with the related feelings of power. Most neuroses are fixated at this stage of development. Current ideas about perception suggest that attention to new events in the life of the child, as well as sensory stimulation, is significant in the associations he makes. This view offers hope of teaching positive attitudes to young children regarding toilet training and independence.

**Phallic Stage**  The last of the infantile phases of sexuality is the phallic stage, which extends from the ages of about three to five years. During this period, the child obtains the sensual satisfactions from manipulation of, and attention to, his genital regions that he previously derived from oral or anal stimulation.

The Oedipus complex emerges during the phallic stage as a strongly motivating force that is closely tied to sexual development. The Oedipus complex comes from a sense of competition with the parent of the same sex for the love and attention of the parent of the opposite sex. This competitive drive is suppressed into the unconscious, but remains as one of the most important residual causes of later neurotic functioning. In Freud's formulation, the Oedipus complex is the single most pervasive and most significant cause of neurotic disorders and is associated with dreams of erotic behavior that involve fantasies of either the anal or the phallic region.

**Latent Stage**  Freud considered the sexual urges to be either quiescent or reduced to a minimum during the period in a child's life corresponding roughly to the elementary school years. The oedipal conflicts have been brought under control, and the stirrings of adolescence are not yet in evidence.

**Pubertal Stage**  With the coming of puberty the instinctual forces move the in-dividual toward the choice of a love object. Normally this is a member of the opposite sex, and in Freud's view it is likely to be someone bearing a great similarity to the mother or the father, depending on the sex of the child. Feelings of tenderness form part of the complex of sexual emotions that emerge, incorporating an element of outgoingness that was absent in the phallic stage of childhood. All stages of development overlap, so that different aspects of one can be present along with characteristics of earlier or later stages. Freud considered these different developments to be the result of maturation rather than learning—the person grows into them rather than learning them. Growth is inclined to be uneven and to generate weak spots. Later when the person regresses, these weak spots become focal points for fixations.

In terms of growth and development, Freud's insights concerned the step-by-step development of the individual through the oral, anal, phallic, latent, and pubertal stages. He conceptualized the possibility of regression to one of these early stages under conditions of threat or aggression. Successful therapy enabled the individual to accept himself and to resume his proper level of development; he was helped to escape from the fixations that had bound him.

### Freud's Terminology

A number of terms developed by Freud have passed into the vocabulary common to educated people. A brief mention of the ways in which Freud used these words seems desirable.

**Id**  The *id* is the name Freud gave to the primordial libidinal force that is the prime mover of people—the driving force that functions to ensure the continuation of the race. sexual energy is both the' root of all the neuroses and the force that makes man push out from himself. In some ways, the id is a divisive force in the world since it has a strident, demanding quality, and leads to aggression and insistence.

**Ego**  Separated from the id is the *ego*, which tends to civilize and unite people rather than to push them toward aggression. The ego has been described as the force that tends to keep the individual, rather than the race, alive. The ego deals with reality and sanity; it screens the incoming sensations and acts as a protector against too much stress. Freud saw the ego as a composite of defense mechanisms including sublimation, reaction formation, regression, repression, isolation, and "undoing." A strong ego is better able to handle reality, both internal and external, than a weak ego. The ego has components of both hereditary and environmental influences. Essentially the ego's energy comes from desexualized libido.

**Superego**  The *superego* is formed through a differentiation from the conscious ego and the unconscious id, called at first by Freud the *ego-ideal.* It arises out of parental images and stabilizes during the period after the Oedipus conflict has been resolved. In some ways the superego is the internalization of the teaching of parents and parent substitutes. The superego has been thought of as the conscience.

**Unconscious**  The dynamic unconscious, which should be understood as a short way of saying the "unconscious mental processes," does not have an independent existence. In Freud's terminology, the *unconscious* consists of different wishes that seek expression. In origin these wishes are instinctual, but usually have become complicated by environmental elaboration. The unconscious, or parts of it, can become known in dreams or fantasies or through neurotic symptoms where wishes find expression.

**Preconscious**  Certain parts of the unconscious are admissible to consciousness. This group of thought processes Freud called the *preconscious.* The most important difference between the preconscious and the unconscious is the amount of threat to the ego contained in each.

**Conscious**  According to Freud, the *conscious* has two parts. One part is the perceptual intake from outside the person that leads to memory or memory traces. Essentially the memory traces are in the unconscious and are admissible to the conscious only through the preconscious, which acts as a screening barrier to protect the ego from overwhelming threat. In dreams the progression is a reverse of normal wakefulness. Some kind of motor activity during sleep sets up energy to operate both the preconscious and the unconscious. The energy at this level activates the memory traces and eventuates in perceptions. Freud thought of psychoanalysis as the psychology of the "depths," or psychology of the unconscious. Freud believed that much of his contemporaries' resistance to these theories was due to his emphasis on the unconscious. In his opinion, people resisted the idea of the unconscious because it indicated they were not in complete control of their thoughts. Dark, unknown forces pushed and pulled them into doing things and thinking things they would not consider on a conscious level. At the time, many people could not accept the idea that they had dreams and fantasies or indulged in aggressive and infantile ways of handling problems that resulted from their bondage to the unconscious. Freud considered that much of the threat in such an idea was transferred from the idea to Freud himself as a person.

**Pleasure Principle**  For Freud, the basis of the *pleasure principle* was the discharge of tension that accompanies sexual gratification, when sex is used in the broadest sense to include infant sexuality and associated satisfactions. He considered the pleasure principle to be deep-seated and to be based on the id. The normal healthy person, in contrast to the neurotic person, satisfies the pleasure principle by a discharge of his tensions, and then he forgets the whole matter. The neurotic, on the other hand, does not release the tension and builds up unbearable ideas, which remain in his unconscious to haunt and to frustrate him. These unbearable ideas and the mechanisms that grow like barnacles around them constitute neuroses.

**Death Wish** The regressive force that tends toward masochism was termed by Freud the *death wish.* This force is opposed to the libido forces, which tend toward pleasure. The idea of the death wish has been modified over the years since Freud interpreted it as the destructive instinct and has been set in contrast to sex as the constructive force. Freud considered the two major driving forces in human life to be the libido and aggression. The destructive instinct is closely allied with aggression and has come to be almost synonymous with the "death wish" in psychoanalytic psychology.

Careful reading of Freud seems to indicate that he considered everyone more or less neurotic. The question of neuroticism is one of degree. Everyone must defend himself against some unbearable ideas, and his defenses constitute the struggle between the id, ego, and superego.

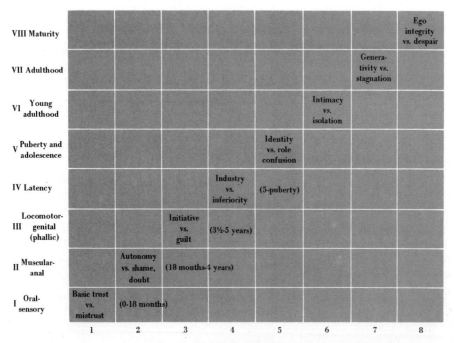

**Figure 13-1** Eight Ages of Man. Erikson's conception of emotional development. The box represents the psychoanalytic stages: oral (birth to 18 months), anal (18 months to 4 years), phallic (3½ to 5 years) and puberty (5 years). (*Adapted from Erik Erikson, Childhood and society, pp. 272–273, by permission of W. W. Norton,* © *1963 and Chattow and Windus.*)

## Deviationists: Adler, Jung, and Rank

A number of the men who worked closely with Freud eventually broke with him to found their own schools of analytic thought. In general, the deviationists came to differ with Freud on the primacy of the psychosexual drive as the basic motive power in all aspects of life. There is evidence that part of the bitterness of the various breaks had to do with the patriarchal relationship of Freud to his associates. The struggles were reminiscent of the cultural struggles grown sons have with their fathers to assert themselves as individuals.

**Adler** Abraham Adler (1959) worked closely with Freud in Vienna and was the official head of the Vienna group when he broke with Freud. Adler substituted an instinct toward power, or an instinct toward aggression, as the principal driving force. Unsuccessful operation of this force, he said, leads to inferiority feelings, and much of his writing concentrated on the nature of inferiority and superiority complexes. Eventually Freud incorporated aggression as one of the basic drives into his own theoretical structure.

**Jung** Carl Jung (1957) was another member of the inner circle who broke with Freud about the same time Adler did. At the time of the break, Jung was president of the International Psychoanalytic Association. He substituted a creative impulse in place of the sex drive as the fundamental instinctual force on which development occurs throughout life. He classified people as *introverts* or *extroverts*. He developed the process of word association, which was later adopted in modified form to build lie-detector tests. He postulated the "racial unconscious," by which he meant the influence of millennia of racial experience as the creator of a genetic inheritance. Probably his emphasis on the idea of the racial uncon-

scious was less acceptable to his critics than his other innovations.

**Rank** Otto Rank was Freud's protege; Freud helped him with his early education and included him in his inner circle from an early period. Rank broke with Freud over the publication of *The Trauma of Birth* (1929), although the book was dedicated to Freud, who in turn accepted the dedication with a cordial note of thanks. Rank moved to the idea of "will" as the central force that drives all human development. Schopenhauer, author of *The World as Will and Idea* (1819), had been one of Rank's heroes before his contact with Freud.

All these defectors rejected psychosexuality as the primary moving force and substituted an alternative primary principle. Although each made contributions to the understanding of emotional development, Freud's work has survived as the most significant formulation in psychoanalysis.

## EMOTIONAL GROWTH AS A LEARNING PROCESS

Erik H. Erikson met the Freuds at a critical time in his own life when he was twenty-five years old, uncommitted, and indecisive about his own future. He was born in 1902 in Frankfurt, Germany, of Danish parents who were separated. During an early illness his mother took him to a Jewish pediatrician who cured the child and married the patient's mother. His stepfather, Dr. Homburger, whose name he used while going to the *Vorschule* and the *Gymnasium*, had a tremendous influence on him. When Erik left the *Gymnasium* at age eighteen he spent the next several years roaming Europe as an itinerant artist (Coles, 1970).

At the request of a school friend, who knew biology and mathematics, he formed a free school in which he taught art and literature to the children of wealthy Americans who had come to Vienna to be psychoanalyzed by Freud. Anna Freud had, at this time, become interested in applying psychoanalytic principles to child development. Erikson spent two relatively relaxed years of analysis with Anna while observing the children in his classroom. At this time he was more committed to teaching than to analysis and earned a certificate as a Montessori teacher. He married the English teacher in the school, a Canadian American, who had a B.A. in education from Columbia and a master's in sociology from Pennsylvania, and had been analyzed by Dr. Jekels. This marriage and the arrival of his two children had a settling effect on him. His wife tutored him in English and helped him with his manuscripts written in English. Erikson first came to America in 1933 to practice psychoanalysis and to lecture in Boston. He has since been associated with the Harvard Medical School, the University of California Child Guidance Study Clinic, the Menninger Foundation, and other institutions.

After early research with Harvard students using play materials, Erikson turned to the study of American Indians to observe whether Freud's sequence of emotional development and his own eight stages of man could be generalized to humanity.

A comparison of Erikson and Freud shows an increasing emphasis on cultural influences over instinctual forces. The change is in part a reflection of the transition from an id psychology to an emphasis on growth with its locus in the conscious. Erikson continued a trend already evident in Freudian thought as a basis for understanding human growth. This section outlines the ways in which human beings learn to resolve the polarities that are the crux of Erikson's developmental sequences. An understanding of some of the unconscious id forces that were of primary interest to Freud makes these aspects of human behavior more intelligible to the teacher. The last section of

this chapter suggests ways in which adults can help change emotional forces to alter student behavior. When a teacher understands how young people learn the emotional patterns by which they live and the crisis points at which significant changes take place, he is able to enter into his transactions with students in a meaningful way.

## ERIKSON'S TRICHOTOMY OF INTERACTION

Erikson (1963) identified three interacting forces as particularly important in the successful development of the individual: the individual's ego, the somatic stages of growth, and the societal forces of parent and culture. The biological process is an accepted pattern with characteristics that define the growth stages and are a positive factor in development when the individual is able to overcome the tensions of change and emerge as more mature. Biological growth is a negative factor when disease strikes or when changes converge in psychosomatic illness. Cultural forces, family, school, and community support him in times of stress when he acts in conformity to group mores but tend to punish him when he deviates from the value structure of the group. The ego process is the inner development of identity of self within society. The ego expands when the libidinal, biological, and societal dynamics are in harmony. The ego is damaged when realities of biological limitations and societal forces combine to traumatize the individual, who then regresses to an earlier stage where the stress and crises of the period have already been resolved.

## ERIKSON'S DEVELOPMENTAL STAGES

Erikson's Eight Ages of Man describe the ego qualities which emerge from critical periods of development when the individual integrates the timetable of his biological self and the structure of social institutions. His first five stages parallel those of Freud; however, his structure extends through three additional adult phases of life (Figure 13-1). Although the importance of the id, ego, and superego is retained, each stage deals with a crisis, having particular polarities to be resolved as healthy growth takes place. The demand character of the society in which the person lives—first the whole family and later the wider social group—is seen as a powerful force in shaping his emotional growth. Erikson stresses the adaptive and creative strength of the individual and is optimistic in his hope for positive growth. The individual needs trust and respect from those around him in order to develop his potential. The major motivating force for Erikson, as it was for Freud, is the libido. Explicit in Erikson's work is the polarity of the drive toward moving out, counterbalanced by the drive to regress to simpler levels. Play is one way the ego can deal with reality situations that might otherwise be too difficult to manage. Play situations are, for Erikson, important developmental tools in the individual's repertoire of learning. They function in much the same way that dreams do for the id; in other words, they make meanings overt that would otherwise remain hidden.

## Stage 1

The child first has the necessity to develop a sense of trust and to avoid the reverse sense of mistrust—the polarity of the phase. In Western culture, one source of crisis is the weaning process. The basic trust is already partly established through the communion of the mother with the child as he is fed and handled. Most of his contacts with the outside world are through intake mechanisms, not only for food but also for light, sound, and air. In this stage, the basic feelings of the mother or the mother substitute are communicated to the child. In almost all relationships, the mother cares about the infant's security feelings and communicates the depth of her caring through the regularity of her attention, thus developing the beginnings of his faith in the regularity of the universe. Not all the child's wishes or desires can be met immediately, and the need to wait is part of the reason that a basic distrust may develop. If the mother is not trustworthy and is irregular in her attention to the child's needs, a basic distrust is likely to prevail, making progress to the next stage difficult.

As the child grows through his first oral stage, he becomes somewhat more active in his intake by grasping the parts of his environment within reach. This stage comes to a climax as the teeth develop. Childhood insecurities can be intensified by biting, which is a painful experience for the mother and leads to temporary exclusion or denial. When exclusion is not too prolonged and is terminated by supportive behavior, the experience can be constructive. In this way, the child discovers that isolation is temporary and not disastrous. The experience is the beginning of a separation that will eventually mean independence. The dependability of the child's relationship with the mother lays the foundation for his later identification with her. For the child, this dependability provides the basis of faith in the mother and, eventually, in the world.

If, within the concept of the learning-motivation model, he is fed and attended to only after he has cried violently, these violent activities will be associated with hunger satisfaction. The violent crying is associated physiologically with increases of adrenaline in the bloodstream, among other changes, and the conditioning process comes to include the emotional overtones related to pain and anger. In other words, the child learns to be angry and demanding in order to be fed or otherwise cared for.

The infant's most obvious need is for food, and the satisfaction of this need is basic to his well-being. Usually, the contact of the mother and the child during feeding is mutually satisfying, whether the feeding is by breast or by bottle. Even the inattentive mother, who is made aware of the child's need by violent means on his part, probably finds the peace of the feeding period comforting and rewarding. The infant's oral stimulation is conditioned to other pleasurable need satisfactions; thus both the child and the mother learn generally pleasurable associations from the experience.

When the mother starts the weaning process, the patterns that have been established are disrupted. The transition may be made in a context of pleasure-related activity to a new food. Under these conditions, the new routine for need satisfaction becomes associated with pleasure. When much of the feeding routine has been accompanied by adrenaline-induced responses, however, the transition is likely to be incorporated into a framework of distrust or threat. Most of this learning occurs at an unconscious level. Many of the emotional patterns of a child's responses to his mother become associated with responses to his father and later to adults outside the home. Emotional patterns persist over long periods of the individual's life. Probably replacement of early patterns that are unsatisfactory or undesirable can be accomplished by restructuring the responses to needs that are basic to the person at his particular age.

### Stage 2

In the period between approximately eighteen months and four years, the anal stage in Freud's structure, the child gains his beginnings of a sense of autonomy and combats a sense of doubt and shame. According to Erikson, the developing sense of autonomy is primarily a function of the ego rather than the id or the superego. This period marks the development of holding and letting go. The child practices these processes with his hands, eyes, mouth, and sphincters. In most of the Western cultures, the crisis situation during this phase is likely to center around toilet training. One concomitant of successful toilet training is the mother's own feeling of worth as she is able to teach the child acceptable modes of handling elimination problems. The obverse is the mother's distress when failure results from her best efforts. Failure tends to be associated with subtle forms of self-rejection and child rejection on the part of the mother, thus leading to a decrease in the child's trust in himself and an increase in his sense of doubt about his own competence. The child may feel the need to regress to a dependence typical of the oral stage.

Play in this period is important and is marked by alternating swings from joy and assurance to despair and hopelessness. Play helps to develop a sense of self-control without the loss of self-esteem since it is only play. Adults other than parents come into importance as the child becomes more mobile. They in turn broaden the base, for good or ill, that the child uses to determine his success or failure in his reach for autonomy.

This is the period during which the child first becomes ambulatory and first masters the art of talking. Parents usually find themselves less completely in control during the learning experience of toilet training than they have been in any former situation. The problem stems from an overestimation of the child's understanding of change in expectation, from not knowing whether the child has control of his sphincters, and from parents' inability to analyze the small steps in conditioning that will lead to the behavior they desire. The emotional learning that is injected into this sequence usually has its genesis in the parents' emotional reaction to the child's failure.

Sometimes the signals of need may not be noticed. Since the child cannot manage bathroom mechanics, an emotional scene follows, which often confuses the child. He has done what he has been taught, and the result is punishment. In the context of conditioning theory it is clear why he interprets his signals for bathroom help as a mistake. The result may be extinction to a state of no training or regression to an earlier stage. Primarily, the responses that are learned are those which are reinforced. When the wrong things have been learned, the parent should examine exactly what he has been reinforcing in his day-to-day interaction with the child.

Toilet training is only one aspect of the changes characteristic of this age. Many of the small deeds that herald the child's emerging autonomy contain elements of emotional learning, in the same way that toilet training is invested with emotional overtones. The constructive and/or destructive patterns that build the child's feelings about himself come from the conditioning that the parents use to make him conform to their own image of what a son or daughter should be like. Parents use conditioning unconsciously and continuously—and often with unintended effects.

## Stage 3

Erikson's locomotor-genital age is the period during which the child acquires a sense of initiative. This is the time when the child learns to make contacts on his own with other children and adults. This stage has flexible age boundaries. Although many children acquire this kind of initiative between the ages of 4 and 6, some may begin as early as $2^{1}/_{2}$, and others may prolong initiative acquisition through age 8.

For Erikson, as for Freud, the crisis of stage 3 is the resolution of the Oedipus complex. The genital zones replace the anal and oral

areas as those most sensitive to stimulation, but Erikson sees the nature of the Oedipus conflict somewhat differently from the way Freud did. The mother (or father) becomes the love object of the son (or daughter), primarily because there is no other real love object available. Erikson considers the problem one of propinquity, rather than of incest. These romantic attachments lead to mistrust of anyone who might interfere with the relationship, even while the child is using his parent of the same sex as an identification figure after whom to mold himself. The father is a boy's ever-present model for behavior toward the mother, while the mother is the singular example of female behavior toward the father. The emerging romantic attachment for the parent of the opposite sex is part of developing initiative and willingness to assume responsibility for one's own acts. At least two kinds of emotional learning take place during this period: The child learns that caring brings its own reward, and he also learns that competition brings rewards that are not exclusively pleasant. Gradually the attachment shifts to a more attainable love object; some reality ideas develop about the inequality of the competition between a five-year-old son and his father for the sexual affections of the mother. The relinquishing of the romantic attachment to the parent is easier if the child has been able to establish his autonomy. The parent of the same sex becomes the model for the superego.

Children of both sexes are interested in the sex organs, and both have an idea that the girl somehow lost her genitals and that the boy could suffer a similar disaster. This imaginary problem causes fears or guilt feelings that may persist. Play activity is important to the child in establishing himself as a person. He needs time and opportunity for both solitary and associated play when he can explore in a play situation some of these disturbing thoughts about himself. The resolution of the doubts and fears of this age and the concomitant growth in security and initiative are fundamental to the child's later growth into an integrated, healthy individual.

Erikson considers this period to be dominated by the ego, which is becoming strong enough to control even the more restless id. He also considers this to be a time when the conscience, or developing superego, assumes some of the supporting and controlling functions of the parents and parent substitutes. The child's conscience is built from the interpretation of the social heritage of the culture as he sees beliefs of parents and other influential adults reflected in their acts.

Much of his time is spent with other children of his own age, from whom he gains new insights about the world around him. He tests himself against these others in new ways and expands his universe in doing so. He becomes very conscious of the fact that he is a boy and of the roles he is supposed to assume. However, he feels comfortable much of the time in returning to the former stage, in which sex roles were less highly differentiated.

During the nursery school and kindergarten years, the child moves out as an independent person and explores snails, tool sheds, and the neighbor's flower beds—either on his own or in concert with other children. He takes more responsibility for himself and his things—including his toys, clothes, and pets. This brings him recognition as a person in his own right. In some of his striving, he overreaches, to find himself intruding on the autonomy of others, who are often brusque with him. These reprimands encourage feelings of guilt, of having gone too far, which are one aspect of the polarity of this stage. The other pole, or pull in the opposite direction, is the initiative that got him into trouble but also satisfied his urge to explore. At four and five, the child reaches out with language and imagination as well as with the locomotion that his developing physical mastery provides.

## Stage 4

During the years from six to eleven or twelve, the child is busily acquiring a sense of industry, is warding off a sense of inferiority, and is building his self-image as a person of worth. Erikson writes that during this period, the child has temporarily resolved the oedipal problem and is freed from concentration on the sex role he has to play. He agrees with Freud in describing this period as latent in sexual development. During the elementary school years, the child is building habits of industry and is attaining perfection in the performance of many skills. He sees his contacts with peers, usually of his own sex, as opportunities for measuring and evaluating himself. As he succeeds in his own eyes, the child is able to accept himself; as he fails, he develops a sense of inferiority and a strong urge to regress to a less threatening stage of development.

It is important that the child enter the elementary school years with the affective and cognitive background to participate with peers with the kind of industry which society has defined for them—playing ball, reading, calculating, swimming. The boy who enters the latency period feeling confident in body contact games is in a good position to cope with the industry versus inferiority struggle as it relates to peers. The boy who has the readiness abilities for success in the classroom is likely to resolve his tendency toward industry in becoming a good student. The elementary teacher has an unusual opportunity to help the child build constructive motivations at a time when his biological stresses are relatively quiescent.

## Stage 5

During the early adolescent period, the young person builds a sense of identity, as opposed to that side of the polarity concept in which the individual succumbs to a sense of identity diffusion. During the early research years Erikson studied the adolescent age group more thoroughly than any other. As a result, his schema is more complete for adolescents than for children or adult groups. The sense of identity—a feeling of wholeness—is important if the young person is to make independent, adult decisions. This identity is different from identifications of younger children with significant adults. Self-identity is a fusion of inner stability and outer-directedness that is polarized with a sense of instability or lack of a framework to resolve inner and outer demands. Erikson calls this instability *identity diffusion* when the adolescent doesn't know who he is.

Securities about mastery of the body mechanisms that had been built up in the previous period are shaken. Growth is irregular, balance of the physiological development is poor, and muscles and bones grow at different rates. The result of this imbalanced growth is an awkwardness and clumsiness. The voice in particular is likely to betray boys.

The id forces, which renew their strength with puberty, have to be harnessed in much the same way that physical action must again be brought under control. This whole process of upheaval must be stabilized under the control of the ego, which must synthesize the past and the future. Among the essential functions that must be incorporated into the identity are the sexual urges, the occupational goals, and kinesthetic mastery. In current American society, unusual strain is put on the adolescent, particularly in respect to the occupational goals, so that he is likely to suffer identity diffusion longer than is healthy or desirable.

Erikson sees positive advantages in the adolescent's delay of occupational decision that is characteristic of American society, even though emotional costs are involved. Because the society sanctions and expects indecision and identity diffusion, this pro-tracted delay is not as traumatic as similar delay in other cultures. Erikson sees the long adolescence of American culture as an opportunity to develop greater variety and flexibility in personality outcomes. The long adolescence allows the youth to explore tentatively various potential facets of adulthood without being required to commit himself permanently.

Erikson described seven possible subpolarities that often form crises during adolescence.

**Time Perspective versus Time Diffusion** This dichotomy is between self-insistence on immediate decision and self-immobility accompanied by a hope that the need for decision will evaporate. When the young person is able to develop a perspective of time and to see reality in terms of extended periods of time, he has matured to the point where his decisions can be made in a meaningful context. The adolescent who plans ahead for class papers and tests shows the development of a perspective of time, while the student who has to complete his entire paper the night before it is due has not matured to control time realistically.

Emotional learning about time centers in the youth's need to reach a mature view of understanding that changes take time and that time brings both intended and unintended changes. Emotional security comes as the young person is able to conceptualize from his own experience—that is, from observing the time dimensions of living—that time provides a sequence in which events are ordered. This conceptualization of the flow of life events brings emotional security.

**Self-Certainty versus Apathy** Here the dichotomy is between awareness of self and the impression that others convey back about oneself. When these coincide, self-confidence and a sense of identity are increased. However, when self-perception and the perception conveyed by others are disparate, the resulting self-consciousness tends to project an air of vanity or an attitude of not caring about the impression one makes on others.

The youth learns to accept himself as he is conditioned by the acceptance of those around him, usually his peers, that he can do what he decides to do. To some extent, he relearns the lessons of the latent period. He overcomes his self-consciousness; his security increases. On the other hand, his present failures tend to accentuate the emotional insecurities that are the basis of self-consciousness.

In school as he sets and reaches goals, he grows in assurance and in willingness to make further attempts. Teachers can be of particular help by structuring genuine learning situations in which the youth can succeed and also feel secure in his success.

**Role Experimentation versus Negative Identity**    This dichotomy is between the need for experimentation to find identity and the danger of premature commitment to an unsuitable role. Experimentation with extreme ideas has two major dangers—the possibility of being labeled and the possibility of overt acts that are irreversible. However, it is necessary for the adolescent to try out various roles to see how comfortable they are before he can find his identity. Much of this investigation is in imagination and fantasy, but some requires close approximations to actual commitment to the role, at least for a brief time.

Many boys try out the role of juvenile delinquent, perhaps going as far as stealing cars for joy rides. If they are caught, justice is often unequal as it attempts to appraise the reality of the role being assumed. The student from a professional or managerial home is more likely to be bailed out at a critical time and thus finds it easier to retreat from this role than the student from a less favored background. Both boys and girls must explore many roles before they accept an image of themselves as real.

As the youth tries varied roles, he experiences the emotional concomitants. When these emotional experiences are pleasurable, the role is seen as desirable, and the individual is drawn to this mode of living. If the role is emotionally unpleasant, it is avoided and becomes extinct. During the role experimentation, some adolescents learn to find negative roles desirable. To be ignored is emotionally intolerable; being an entity in a rejected group may be desired over being a nonentity. Parents and teachers find it difficult not to enhance the emotional attractiveness of certain roles by increasing the attention they pay to young people who are experimenting in antisocial ways. The attention of significant adults—even though negative—tends to reinforce the role positively at times when attention is needed.

**Anticipation of Achievement versus Work Paralysis**    This dichotomy is between the need to develop habits of work and the development of habits of task postponement for fear of failure. Occupational identity requires a commitment to start and finish a task, even when continuation of the task may have become distasteful. Negative forces that hinder commitment include unexpected difficulty of the work, leading to abandonment of the task before achievement, and the temporary attractiveness of other opportunities, leading to no commitment. Under these circumstances, no occupation identity becomes established.

Teachers are often able to help reluctant students complete tasks and eventually come to think of themselves as able to persist in a job that needs to be done. Allowing students to be sloppy and ineffectual tends to undermine their anticipation of achievement and to allow them to build concepts of themselves as unable to complete a job. Emotional associations develop from expected achievement learned by the feedback from small achievements that succeeded. The anticipation of failure comes with emotional feedback of negative kinds from small tasks undertaken but unrealized.

**Sexual Identity versus Bisexual Diffusion** Here the dichotomy is between male or female identity and the uncertainty of a mixed role. Adolescents need to establish themselves in their own eyes in the appropriate sex role. Part of this sexual identity is formed from contacts that contrast the roles. The young person must learn to be comfortable in situations that his own culture defines as appropriate for his sex. The diffusion that results from uncertainty as to what role will be accepted causes instability and uneasiness. If the adolescent continues too long in activities of the opposite sex, alienation from both his own and the opposite sex may result.

Perhaps because the culture is fearful of sex-role experimentation, more emotional tension is related to this aspect of maturing than to any other during adolescent development. The sex role is further emphasized by physiological changes. Security in the appropriate sex role is gradually achieved by operant conditioning. Everyone makes repeated small tests of his sexual status, and feedback comes from the reaction of others, including members of the opposite sex. Tests involving the opposite sex are more crucial in adolescence than during the latency period.

**Leadership Polarization versus Authority Diffusion** This dichotomy is between acceptance of both leadership and followership roles and vacillation, which results in neither good leadership nor good followership. Authority diffusion brings the discomfort of in-

security. Identity requires the clarification of roles in this area of human relationships.

Roles as leader, follower, individualist, or maverick are accompanied by emotional learning. The first two are usually positively reinforced by the dominant culture, while the individualist and maverick get their reinforcement in atypical ways.

**Ideological Polarization versus Diffusion of Ideals** The last of the adolescent conflicts is the dichotomy between commitment to a religion, philosophy, or ideology and the insecurity of noncommitment. Part of the ideological commitment involves a rather belligerent attack on those who are not equally committed. The action that accompanies the adolescent's strong prejudice and loyalty to ideas provides him with a means for testing the ramifications of his positions.

Apart from sexual identity, ideological commitment probably has the strongest emotional loading of any aspect of adolescent development. To some extent, the exploration is noncommitted, but any ideological choice the adolescent makes has strong affective influence on his self-concept. Commitments are emotional in tone because identity is implied. During adolescence, much emotional learning comes from feedback from the peer group as the youth experiments with ideological concepts through discussions, reading, reflection, and term papers. Self-concept as an ideological commitment begins with conditioned responses to the environment without awareness on the part of the learner that a pattern is being established.

**Stage 6**

In the young adulthood period the individual acquires a sense of intimacy and solidarity and avoids a sense of isolation. The first of three adult stages of development described by Erikson is the courtship phase, which is followed by the young married and by the older adult stages. The chief aims of the sixth stage are the selection of a mate and the establishment of an occupational pattern. Failure in either endeavor leads to a sense of isolation and exclusion from the mainstream of society. The search for a mate involves the development of a psychological readiness for, and an emotional commitment to, the shared relationships of marriage. Part of the readiness involves the development of mutual trust; part of the commitment concerns the willingness to adjust work patterns, recreation, and living arrangements to the mutual benefit of both parties. Exploration in many of these adjustments is verbal, with evidence of commitment in terms of adaptability to the other person during the courtship period. The sense of identity expands to include another person.

## Stage 7

The young married adult acquires a sense of generativity and avoids a sense of self-absorption. The dichotomy in this stage is between providing the growth potential for the new generation and regressing to self-centered living. The identities that both husband and wife have been developing throughout their lifetimes make their commitment to provide a suitable environment for children either easy or difficult. If an individual has established himself as a whole person, the progression by which he becomes a provider is easy. If he is diffused in many of his identity areas, he is likely to find it difficult to accept the responsibility for providing a healthy environment for a new life.

## Stage 8

During the final stage of adult development described by Erikson, the individual acquires a sense of integrity and avoids a sense of despair. The integrity comes from having provided the necessary framework for the continuity of the next generation. It overcomes the alternative sense of despair and fear of death that seems to accompany a feeling of failure in the previous stages.

In young adulthood, the primary learning focus is on reaching out beyond the self to accept responsibility for others. First is the association with the prospective mate, later with a chosen mate, and eventually with responsibility for children. The emotional learning involved is an outgoingness, which requires awareness of the needs of other individuals. This shift from self is usually possible because the maturing individual is able to identify with his mate and his children. He learns to project feelings of need and well-being to others.

For Erikson, the individual forms his identity through exploration of these possible roles. Some aspects of the adolescent's search are troublesome to adults who are concerned that the exploration may result in unintended commitment. Other adults tend to label the young person on the basis of one phase of his exploration, thus making it more difficult for him to explore alternative, and possibly opposite, roles. Much of the adolescent's testing is accomplished through long conversations, friendly competition, or rivalry with peers. One of the problems that teachers and parents face is allowing enough exploration to take place and at the same time making the adolescent feel that the adult trusts him to conduct his search successfully. The young person needs to explore for himself, but he also needs the support from adults that trust implies.

## EMOTIONAL GROWTH IN SCHOOL

The concept that emotional growth in children is largely a product of the interaction of learning emotional responses and physical growth makes the teacher's role in the process apparent. Affective learning can be aided or accelerated by suitable strategies of reinforcement on the part of the teacher. Within circumstances of balanced support and stimulation of affective response, the process of emotional growth will continue to take place in much the same order as that observed by competent analysts. The process can be smoother and more pleasant for the growing person and more reinforcing for those around him if emotional growth is understood and given conscious attention. The learning-motivation model provides a framework within which the teacher can operate with considerable security to reinforce mature responses and to avoid unintended reinforcement of regressive emotional behavior. By using constructive strategies, regressions can be reversed and the probability of their recurrence can be minimized (Chapter 5).

## Teaching Trust and Mistrust

In the Freudian framework, trust and mistrust develop in the first eighteen months of life. Occasional regressive behavior is typical, rather than abnormal, in the growth pattern of children, and certain aspects of school life often contribute to these insecurities.

Hour-by-hour teacher functions require reinforcement such as comments on written assignments, selection of pupil products for display, recognition of one student among several who want to talk, and selective praise for unique ideas. When a teacher is capricious in his grading or evaluation practices, he contributes to the lack of order in the young person's universe. When the dependability of any significant adult is missing, the student's distrust of both the system and himself is likely to grow, even though the disparities might be directed toward another student. The

better established the young person's trust in the orderliness of the world, the more likely he is to come to resolve discrepancy by distrusting himself. The subconscious argument goes more or less as follows: "The world is well run and orderly; therefore, the weakness must be in me." Distrust in oneself is probably more damaging than distrust in others. The teacher can avoid this kind of strain on students by using a consistent appraisal system and by making evaluation explicit and understandable to them.

Mistrust syndromes can be generated in children who find themselves in schools where prejudice exists or where there are double standards of reward and punishment. It is not enough to have both black and white students in the same room—each individual must be accepted for himself if any are to feel secure. The probability that the insecure person will slip into a generalized mistrust of the social order is great whenever he observes specific evidence of unfair and capricious treatment. Regression to infantile responses becomes understandable in such circumstances, although the manifestation of the regression is dictated by the level of growth of the individual and the social milieu to which he responds. Teachers can remedy such situations by learning to avoid prejudicial behavior themselves, by interpreting on a conceptual level the evidences of prejudice so that the prejudiced person will not be seen to represent the whole world, and by helping the individual discriminated against to function on his own initiative despite known discrimination. The child needs to be shielded from discrimination in any of its forms until he has gained enough emotional and cognitive learning to cope with the situation as a challenge. Faith in the worth of every person is built by separating what students "are" from what they "do." Such a climate reduces the competition for attention and recognition and enlists the support of peers in helping certain classmates overcome their infantile habits of distrust.

## Teaching Self-Control

Increasing numbers of children are being sent to nursery schools or enrolled in Head Start programs. Typically the nursery school staff requires that the child have independence of locomotion and be toilet-trained, prior to his acceptance.

By age five, an individual child may be expected to act in mature ways at some times and in some situations, but to regress when he cannot do what seems to be expected of him. The observant teacher will reinforce mature responses with the expectation they will be learned as the pattern. However, the dynamics of a typical kindergarten class on a typical day will encompass each of the crises of self-rejection, dependence, feelings of guilt, or an uncontrolled ego.

To maintain status among his preschool peers, the child must have learned to control his elimination functions. Closely related emotionally, according to the Freudian scheme, is his letting go of the parent who brings him to the play center and his holding and letting go of favored toys, which he must share at school. The child who has not learned to separate self from parent, from possessions, and from wastes that come from his body is at a disadvantage.

Extended periods of crying may leave a child so upset that negative emotions are associated with the people who try to help him or with the objects he is given for diversion. A sense of autonomy, which children normally acquire during this period, will let him trust himself with new people, but often help is needed from the teacher. The teacher builds autonomy when he arranges for each child to have some things which are his own and with which he can identify; when he values the things the child makes, such as his paintings; and when the child is allowed to take home the things he has made. These steps help bridge the transition from egocentricity to sharing in the school.

Children who lack control over elimination are likely to receive the disdainful attention of their peers, who enhance a sense of guilt when they say, for example, "Tad is a baby—he still wets his pants." The teacher must intervene to prevent the emotional damage that may result from this kind of taunting. The child who has frequent "accidents" should be observed for three possibilities: (1) lack of physical control of the sphincters, (2) need for more frequent elimination than the school routines provide, and (3) overt defiance. In the first instance, the prevention of an emotional problem is crucial while the necessary acquisition of control takes place. The other children in the class need to learn a constructive social response, like that of the four-year-old who was found with an arm around the shoulders of a wet, unhappy playmate, saying, "I'll get the teacher—and don't cry, I won't tell anyone." In the second instance, the child must be taken to the bathroom more frequently than other children his age, while maintaining a matter-of-fact attitude about the interruptions in his play and making sure that he is able to resume his place in the activities. In the case of defiance, the adults in the situation need to identify what the child is rejecting so that reteaching or restructuring of the environment can be undertaken.

When the child joins a group of peers, at school or in the neighborhood, he acquires models from outside the family for the development of his superego. One or more significant adults are added to the child's life experience. Usually nursery school or kindergarten teachers assume the role of "teacher" rather than parent substitute, but they try to be available to give physical comfort to the young child whenever this is his essential need at the time. Having adults outside the family to comfort the child in times of stress and to reinforce his efforts toward independence can help him resolve the conflicts of the oedipal-phallic phase.

## HELPING THE FEARFUL STUDENT

Modern psychoanalysts tend to believe that psychosexual development encompasses all facets of mental and emotional development (Peller, 1965):

> Libidinal development opens the path for all development; without adequate libidinal development, there can be no adequate growth in any other area. Perception, cognition, reasoning, memory, body control, etc.—all these are predicated upon development in the realm of affects. Furthermore, developmental phases do not follow each other like kings or presidents. There is an overlap, indeed a slow infiltration, leading to eventual dominance of the new phase. The earlier organization is by no means destroyed, it merely recedes; disturbances can bring it to the fore again, at any time.[pp. 53–54].

The elementary school student who has successfully resolved the "libidinal organizations" of infancy and early childhood during his preschool years is fortunate.

Infantile behavior may be observed frequently in the student whose early efforts to reach beyond himself and his familiar attachments have been blocked or frustrated. Excessive restriction, limitation, and protection on the part of the parents produce a child who arrives at school without having developed emotional autonomy. Such a child lacks initiative, is self-centered, shows overconformity to peer or adult wishes, and lacks the control needed to defer pleasure gratification. Whether aggressive or submissive, he has a weak ego. The school must do the hard work

of overcoming regressive behavior by teaching in specific ways the control and confidence that such a child lacks.

When a child has a temper tantrum, the teacher must respond in such a way as to remove him from the stress situation without reinforcing his loss of control. Isolation, calmly executed, is usually a safe procedure, whether his removal be to the principal's office, the library table, the nurse's room, or a cot at the back of the classroom. If the teacher can anticipate his loss of control, he can send the child on an errand or suggest a run around the building. After a number of removals have taken place, the teacher can discuss with the child whether he is able to anticipate and handle the problem. He and the teacher can start a chart to keep track of the growing number of days between the times he slips back into baby ways. Positive reinforcement for nonaction is the difficult thing that the teacher achieves through his procedure of consciously rewarding a display of control. The child who has learned to resort to crying when frustrated can be retrained by this same constructive procedure. Children who lack emotional control often need firm and consistent control by the teacher while they are learning to understand and to handle their problem.

A child's unrealistic estimation of his own abilities is another manifestation of regression to a preschool stage of emotional development. He may tell things that he imagined without knowing they are not true. In school these stories may bring him emotionally satisfying attention from the other children. The teacher can help pupils separate the real from the unreal by having them read and discuss children's literature. A conceptualization of what fantasy means in literature is within the cognitive abilities of elementary school children. They may have fun with fairy stories while discussing what does or does not happen in real life. They need to learn the distinction between reporting factual material and writing imaginative stories.

In the upper elementary grades, the problems of regression to infantile behavior become rare; however, experimentation with adolescent roles becomes a common emotional deviation. Children who begin the physical maturation of adolescence early or children who yearn for this status are particularly likely to try out these roles. Diversions need to be developed which are acceptable within the community and which permit heterosexual activities under supervision. Examples of possible activities include outdoor education, organized games, student government, and folk dancing. It is difficult to see how the emotional development of the child in the latency period can be aided by premature entry into the turbulent emotional period of adolescence.

Children in the elementary school age group are generally a joy to teach. They tend to identify with the things they produce and give much of themselves to do the best they can. They are not yet closed to the suggestions of adults, although they have become independent as persons. One of the difficulties for the teacher is the need to reinforce differentially. Each child needs to be accepted and reinforced for the best he can produce. Although the elementary school child is never freed from what he learned during the infant period, he can still learn new emotional patterns as he comes into contact with the new social milieu of the school.

## GUIDANCE FOR ADOLESCENTS

If the child has learned during the elementary years to analyze and conceptualize the dynamics of his emotions and to initiate the activities that help him control his emotional life, he can use these patterns when the stresses of adolescence descend upon him. Many of the students whom the teacher meets

in his classes or whom the counselor meets in his office will not have learned these self-actualizing approaches to emotional problems. Two choices are available to the teacher or counselor. He can try to help the student conceptualize, or understand, his emotional problems, or he can try to ease the tensions associated with each problem as it arises. Although direct instruction in the conceptualization of emotional concomitants seems at first glance the obvious way to guide the development of youth, the instabilities of the adolescent period make such an approach difficult. The sequence for teaching level 2 ways of responding to emotional stimuli can be devised for students who need this help (Chapter 7). The Erikson subpolarity classification of this age group provides some guidelines for teaching and counseling.

**Time Perspective** The understanding of the orderliness of time is basic to a youth's understanding of his own emotional impatience with the inflexibility of time; cognitive understanding, however, is an easier step toward accomplishing this goal than understanding of the related emotions. Understanding the emotional accompaniments requires definite intent on the part of the counselor or teacher. Questions such as "How did you *feel* about having to wait for a job?" followed by "Why?" can help the youth attend to the time order and also to his own emotional reactions to waiting. The difficulties in a structured approach center around the impatience of both the youth and the teacher, who are tempted to short-circuit the program and thus to obscure a clear resolution. If a particular problem is alleviated short of conceptualization of the affects, the counseling effort has little transfer value to new situations.

**Self-Certainty** The teacher or counselor can increase the youth's self-certainty by planning situations in which he chooses tasks that he will probably perform successfully. By examining the feelings that attach to the successful completion of these tasks, considered as a whole, the student comes to appreciate the emotional concomitants of success-producing choices. Then he is likely to be able to initiate deliberate selections that will further reinforce him. His knowledge about the emotional loading of achievement helps to reduce the negative emotional content of failure. The principal problem, as far as the teacher is concerned, is the erratic choices of the unstable young person, which makes his success uncertain for the adult who tries to structure his opportunities. The difficulty of conceptualizing cause-and-effect relationships between achievement and pleasant emotions increases as the frequency of the successes decreases.

**Role Experimentation** Teachers have two main concerns about role experimentation in adolescence. First, they must stabilize the role identifications that are socially acceptable; second, they must see that the young person finds negative roles undesirable and allows them to dissipate. Awareness that young people are going to experiment with different roles makes it easier for the teacher to select reinforcements toward positive roles and later to aid the student in conceptualizing the emotional gain from roles that are not antagonistic to society. At the same time, the teacher of adolescents should usually restrain himself from making negative comments about role experimentation, with the knowledge that some students perceive such comments as reinforcing. The dividing line between positive reinforcement and objective analysis is very fine and requires acute perception on the part of the counseling adult if the intrusion into the emotional life of the student is to be constructive.

**Anticipation of Achievement** The meth-

ods of structuring learning situations to help adolescents build positive self-expectations are like those for developing self-certainty. Respectable tasks are assigned at which each young person can achieve success. The pleasure in the anticipation of achievement becomes associated with the sensory experiences involved in the activity, and self-directed action becomes self-reinforcing. Students are helped to conceptualize the positive emotional rewards of achievement and to seek out opportunities for success of various kinds.

**Sexual Identity** The school provides for sex-role identification through separate competitive athletics for boys and girls; school dances, with the need for refreshment committees and decorating committees; and joint participation in school government. Not all the students who need these opportunities pursue them, and not all the possibilities are exploited by the schools. Independent dating and the automobile provide other opportunities for testing sex roles. Sex roles are in a state of flux, and many secondary students seek to expand the established roles of their parents. Secondary school faculties have learned that these explorations in sex identity can be facilitated by acceptance and understanding.

**Leadership Polarization** Teachers can provide meaningful opportunities for leadership and followership roles for students. The difficulty comes in providing worthwhile experiences for the students who need leadership opportunities the most. Ingenuity must be used to find suitable leadership roles that are not too costly for other members of the group. As these opportunities are provided and accepted, a youth can be helped to conceptualize about the relationship between good followership when he is a leader and his own followership when someone else has the leadership role. At the same time, attention can be paid to the emotional contents of success or frustration as the followers act cooperatively or noncooperatively. The young person, it is hoped, can go on from there to function independently as an autonomous individual realizing at a conscious level the pleasure or punishment associated with success or failure.

**Ideological Polarization** The emotional content of ideological choices is important to young people, although affects are likely to remain unconscious unless emphasized in some systematic way. To some extent, the testing of various ideologies is similar to the testing of roles. The teacher can help the process of making overt the emotional concomitants of ideological positions by allowing the student an opportunity to talk about his ideas and to express how he feels about them. The time that such conversations require is a very real barrier to providing students with this kind of help. Aiding only one or two students each year to understand themselves and the choices they are making can be taxing in terms of time for the teacher, but it is highly desirable for the students who need the help.

During the adolescent period, the teacher can assist emotional growth by structuring learning situations in which the emotional concomitants of changing one's habits are explored. In general, the pattern of instruction contains (1) opportunities for success and positive emotional toning accompanying success, (2) guidance in making the emotional changes that accompany different patterns of activity obvious to the student, and (3) stimulation of the adolescent to form a self-concept as a person who enjoys functioning within a positive emotional climate. The teacher can move the learning of emotional content from the unconscious to the conscious level. This intervention can shorten the time required for learning new affects. Finally, the teacher can help extend the situations in which the student

is more definitely the master of his emotional functioning.

**School and Marriage** Counseling for marriage (or avoidance of marriage) at the high school level might begin by identifying the responsibilities of establishing a home. Adolescents know the stress points in family living from their own observations of their parents. One successful approach is through role playing, paying attention to the ways each participant would probably feel about his responses to various kinds of conduct by the role partner. Such learning situations should be structured to emphasize the importance of each partner's accepting responsibility for the other. Although this point can be made relatively easily on an intellectual level, attention must be paid to the emotional result of giving up much of one's autonomy.

A course in child rearing, particularly for young people ending their education, should be encouraged, including a practicum on the intellectual stimulation and emotional growth of the young child. The teaching should be aimed at developing an understanding of the emotional implications inherent in changing from an egocentric to an ethnocentric approach to family problems.

**SUMMARY**

The progressive changes in an individual's physiological growth influence other aspects of his development; both emotional and cognitive growth, however, proceed somewhat independently of physical maturation. The pioneer explorer in emotional growth was Sigmund Freud, whose ideas have become part of general psychoanalytic knowledge. Freud considered libidinal or sexual energy to be the driving force behind all human activity. According to him, distortions of this force are the basis for neuroses and possible psychoses, but smooth development ensures the survival of the race and the happiness of the individual. Freud traced the growth of the individual through five stages—the oral, anal, phallic, latent, and pubertal—during which variations in the sexual stimulation take place. The terminology he developed has persisted into the common vocabulary, often without the profound meanings that Freud ascribed to the words and phrases.

Erikson, among others, carried forward the basic principles that Freud enunciated. He has continued to evolve his theories. One of Erikson's important contributions is the notion of the various stages of development, which parallel and extend those of Freud, as a series of characteristic crises in psychosocial life that are resolved for healthy growth. Erikson is positive in his approaches and optimistic about normal development, although he believes that the child must have the trust and respect of those around him in order to develop normally. Erikson carried the Ages of Man through later adolescence, a period that particularly interested him, into adulthood and on to old age.

One of the transitions from Freud's to Erikson's thought involves an increasing emphasis on the importance of learning in emotional growth. For the teacher, the mechanics of this learning is probably more useful than a complete understanding of Freud's original position. The learning progresses initially by operant conditioning, but eventually many associations can become conceptualized. In emotionally healthy people, creative self-direction evolves in important segments of life. Teachers have a powerful impact on the emotional growth of students at all stages of development.

## SELF-DIRECTING ACTIVITIES

1 Plan a course outline for family living as taught in the high school.
2 Help high school students work with young parents to create trust and avoid distrust on the part of their young children.
3 Read Stone's *Emotions of the Mind* and visualize the pressures on Freud as a young man.
4 Develop a behavior modification program to help a student overcome his fears.
5 Explain to a parent the basis for a phobia that is bothering an elementary school pupil.

# Chapter 14

Young people developing cognitively in Ecuador. (*Courtesy of the United Nations*)

# COGNITIVE GROWTH: PIAGET'S THEORY

When you have completed this chapter, you will be able to:

⊂  Describe the age-stage framework of Piaget, including the variations which have appeared during 50 years of elaboration

⊂  Conceptualize the intellectual functioning that distinguishes sensori-motor intelligence, preoperational thinking, concrete operations, and logical thinking

⊂  Practice the Piagetian techniques of interviewing children or youth at the period of development that is consistent with professional goals: infancy, early childhood, and later childhood or adolescence

⊂  Evaluate the points of application in Piagetian theory for a particular situation: to identify Piagetian generalizations which are not appropriate

⊂  Use Piagetian concepts with understanding:
  adaptation
  assimilation
  accommodation

Jean Piaget began his studies of cognitive development in Paris more than 50 years ago. His early books on intellectual functioning in infants and children were published in French during the early twenties and became available in English translations during the late twenties. Recently a spectacular increase in Piaget's following has occurred in the United States along several fronts simultaneously. He has been studied seriously by educational psychologists who supported his efforts in going beyond stimulus-response psychology to discuss the cognitive events within the learner as well as his external behavior. Curriculum experts in early childhood education implemented his theory in designing learning-teaching strategies for disadvantaged children. Laymen, and some teachers, found that Piagetian interview techniques and the everyday objects that were used were directly applicable to their interactions with children, in contrast to the laboratory research on animals which had less meaning for them. Secondary teachers wanted to know how their students differed intellectually from children and from adults. Health and physical educationists, under pressure to produce scholarly work that would be valued in the academic world, found status in the Piagetian concept of sensorimotor intelligence as basic to operational and logical thought. These and many other groups combined their interest in psychological development to create a cognitive/conceptual renaissance in education.

## DEVELOPMENT OF PIAGET'S THEORIES

Piaget considered the problem of knowledge (epistemology) as a problem of the relationship between the subject and the object. As a biologist he translated this problem into studies of how the human organism adapts to its cognitive environment. Piaget and Inhelder (1956) devised the problem of the three mountains to study how children develop the ability to perceive how an object looks from another point of view. The child sits at the side of the table where the photograph was taken (Figure 14-1). The child is asked to identify the diagram that represents what he sees. Then a doll is presented who walks around the mountains and the child is asked to find the picture of the mountains as the doll is seeing them. In several variations of this experiment the typical child of four to six years makes random choices, but by age seven or eight he makes some transformations correctly. Not until about age ten can the child perform the mental operations which enable him to select or draw the doll's view with confidence. The younger children were *egocentric* in their representation of objects. *Egocentrism* in the epistemological context means that the child considers his one view the only one possible and cannot put himself in another person's place. Piaget's usage of egocentrism is different from the affective meaning of ego-centered and devoid of the morality of self-centeredness. This interview situation illustrates how direct, child-oriented problems were used to derive the data from which abstract generalizations were deduced.

Piaget was born in Neuchâtel, Switzerland, in 1896. His first scientific paper, written at the age of ten, consisted of his observations of an albino sparrow. On the basis of his publications he was offered, while still in high school, a position as curator of the mollusk collection at the Geneva museum, but the offer was withdrawn when his age became known. He received his doctorate in natural science when he was twenty-two. At a time when it was still possible to be well-read in many areas, he mastered philosophy, religion, biology, sociology, and psychology. As he read Bergson, Piaget became stimulated by the idea that

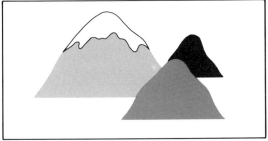

Mountains as seen from doll position 1.

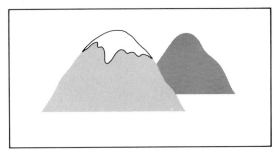

Mountains as seen from doll position 2.

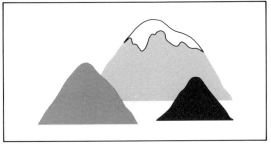

Interviewer asks child to sit at table where model of mountains is seen in relationship shown here. Child is asked to select one of eight drawings of mountains as he sees them.

Note in test pictures are also shown from corners.

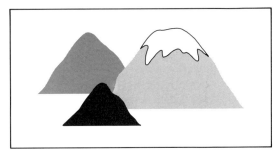

Mountains as seen from doll position 3.

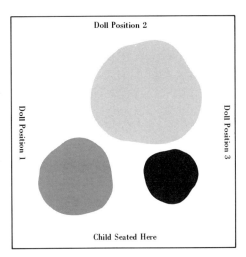

Mountains are arranged on a square board in this relationship, shown from above.

**Figure 14-1**  Example of Piaget's Cognitive egocentrism.

biology could be the key to understanding the nature of knowledge.

Piaget developed the belief that actions as well as thought are organized spontaneously and logically. He began his work as a psychologist in Binet's old laboratory in an elementary school in Paris. From the beginning of his work with children he had little interest in normative research, but was intrigued with the processes by which children arrive at their answers, particularly incorrect ones. For over 40 years he taught each week at the Sorbonne in Paris and the University of Geneva in Switzerland, as well as being director of the International Office of Education and holding other onerous administrative positions. Typically at the end of summer session he headed for his cabin in the Alps to write, taking along the sagging briefcase that holds his data.

Reading Piaget in translation is difficult; the task becomes more manageable when one first becomes acquainted with the structure of the developmental periods, so that the separate studies (books) can be understood in the context of the total theory. Also, the terminology which is unique to Piaget needs to be conceptualized as ideas which apply simultaneously to biological, psychological, and epistemological principles. To a large extent, Piaget needed new terms for the unique dynamics of his theory, and the student reads him effectively only after some of the critical language has become internalized. Many of Piaget's insights can be experienced in the kinds of interactions with children which he himself used to learn about learning. These observations can be conducted almost anywhere there are children. This chapter is designed to help the reader become a student of Piaget by (1) outlining the periods of cognitive development and the stages within those periods, (2) explaining the concepts that are basic to his structuralism, (3) describing several Piagetian interviews with children, and (4) evaluating

the developmental theory in a context of the learning-motivation theory that is familiar to the reader.

Piaget described five phases of cognitive development, which roughly parallel Freud's phases of emotional development. Independently and apparently without collaboration, these two innovators analyzed related human functions. Freud and Piaget, whose careers overlapped, have been compared to explorers who walked opposite sides of a river, but never came together. (Figure 14-2.)

## PIAGET'S PERIODS OF COGNITIVE DEVELOPMENT

Over the years Piaget modified, elaborated, and altered his subperiods of cognitive development. His impact on American educational thought falls into two intervals. During the first interval, from 1926 to 1932, five of his books were translated into English. The second interval dates roughly from 1950 when *The Psychology of Intelligence* was published in English, to the present, when several titles appear each year. Piaget's stages, outlined in this text, are based on Flavell (1963) and the more recent translations of books and articles that were originally written with Inhelder.

Piaget and Inhelder (1956) defined the development sequence into three major periods: (1) the period of *sensorimotor development* (birth to 2 years); (2) the period of *preparation for, and organization of, concrete operations* (2 to 11 years; and (3) the period of *formal operations* (11 to 15 years). The middle period is often subdivided to create a total of four to six periods.

The three-phase organization is a logical format for Piaget's view that operational structures develop first as sensorimotor, preverbal substructures which vary in their complexity from reflexive actions to actions show-

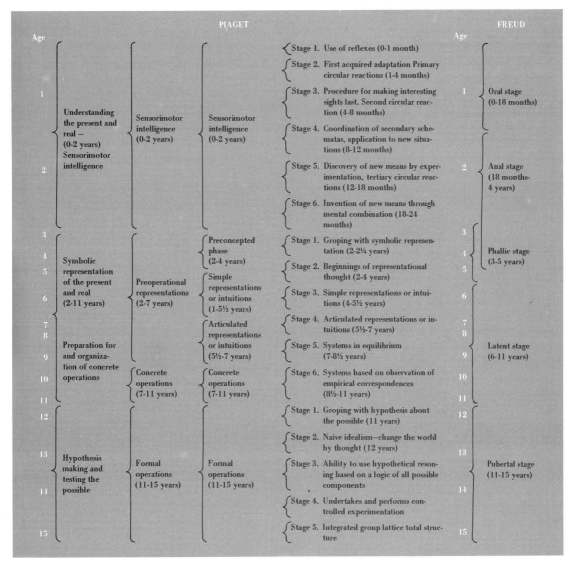

**Figure 14-2** Age similarities of Piaget's and Freud's stages.

ing intent and a "practical knowledge" of cause and effect. During the second period representational thought, including language and other symbolic functions, emerges from the practical sensorimotor structures of the earlier period, and a symbolic reconstruction takes place as children operate on objects until finally they manipulate these representations intellectually, independent of perceptual discrepancies. They can order things by size, numerate, and reverse a process intellectually. During the third period the adolescent repeats the developmental sequence at a higher level of abstraction by grouping, hypothesizing, and experimenting. In this final period his operations are on symbolic abstractions and he develops a logical sequence for solving problems.

In 1969 Piaget defined the cognitive developmental sequence in four periods: (1) *sensorimotor intelligence*, which he then defined as performances that show spatial organizations, a notion of the permanence of objects, and causal relationships; (2) *preoperational thought*, wherein the child becomes capable of having representational thought by means of symbols; (3) *concrete operations*, which result in the child's ability to classify and order objects or use numerical operations on them; and (4) *formal operations*, wherein abstract hypotheses and deductions come to be employed systematically. This four-period framework, shown in the second column of Figure 14-2, has been widely used in curriculum planning whenever a distinction is needed between the early childhood and the later childhood years. Preoperational representations were in turn subdivided into beginnings of representational thought (2 to 4 years), simple representations or intuitions (4 to 5½ years), and articulated representations or intuitions (5½ to 7 years) resulting in five and six periods, depending on where the age stage lines are drawn.

A five-period division was used in some of the early publications which corresponded closely to Freud's emotional phases of development. Translations have not been consistent in the use of the terms periods, subperiods, and stages; therefore the reader may find it useful to associate the age designations that are used throughout the table. Piaget was a voluminous writer; Flavell (1963) listed more than 125 books and articles in his bib-

liography, and scores more have been published since then. Certain major theses of Piaget are basic to an understanding of the framework he elaborated.

## PIAGET'S BASIC THESES

Over the years Piaget changed his research methods for studying cognitive development. Much of his very early work was severely criticized in America because he made generalizations on the basis of samples of four or five children. Since 1956 his studies have been based on as many as 1,500 children. Inhelder (1969) explained this shift in methodology as a sequence which began with explorations of the whole range of reasoning at different ages. These observations are clinical rather than experimental. For instance, when interviewing a child on what he thought about the sun, Piaget would ask a question and then follow this with other questions that seemed appropriate in terms of the child's answer to the opening question. Such interaction ensured that no two children were asked exactly the same things in precisely the same way. Because of Piaget's technique, statistical treatment of his early results is obviously not justifiable.

Piaget used data from his early observations to build a theoretical position. The evidence from the data provided hints that he wove together to form the theoretical structure. The empirical evidence did not contain the structure within itself, but was necessary for two purposes: (1) to provide material for thought and (2) to furnish a means of checking the theory being constructed. His earlier checking system, however, was not empirical but logical. Inhelder outlined the step-by-step procedures that follow the initial interviews: (a) classification of the different types of reasoning, (b) comparison with the logical model, (c) analysis of frequencies of response, and (d) hierarchical analysis by means of ordinal scales. This procedure will be recognized in the large-group studies published since 1956 (Furth, 1969). During the years of criticism from American psychologists, Piaget tended to focus on his philosophy, rather than his psychology. He claimed that symbolic logic could function as a research tool as well as the more usual statistical approaches can.

Another of the fundamental beliefs on which Piaget has built his work is the interrelatedness of all living and nonliving parts of the universe. The laws that apply to one apply to all, and thus a small sample of one or two can represent the modality of the entire world system. The accidents of cultural or hereditary deviation are seen as minor and of small import to the overall developmental scheme. This interpretation of the nature of the universe from a small number of individual cases assumes a tremendously great ability to distinguish between the basic and the accidental information that the individual under study conveys to the investigator.

A third major assumption basic to Piaget's work is that mental processes are a continuation of inborn motor processes. In other words, the child comes biologically equipped to make certain motor responses, which in turn provide the structure of the mental processes that come later. Prenatal learning (Chapter 11) provides some support for this assumption. Another assumption is that the person interacts with the world and that he discovers the existence of the world he experiences in the process of his interaction with it. The private-world concept (Chapter 2) is based on a similar thesis. Time, space, objects, and causality are all inescapable aspects of the world with which the person must come into contact as he lives. From this contact the person structures his intellect. In other words, he learns the world and in the process of learning becomes a more competent learner.

Thus there are biological necessities that impose an inescapable direction. Piaget uses the example of time, which always flows from the past to the future. These essential functions interact with the incidents of experience that fall within the purview and attention of the individual and provide the acquired characteristics of the particular person.

Piaget (1929) clearly understood some of the hazards of leading his subject by the questioning techniques used. He was also concerned that since no hypothesis was being tested at the "exploratory" step, his techniques would bring nothing important to light. As part of the training of a child interviewer, he recommended daily practice with children for at least a year; only then would the interviewer be likely to have acquired the ability to allow the child to talk freely and at the same time to be alert for definitive responses. When students attempt interviews on the Piagetian model, they quickly learn to appreciate the skill required to elicit the child's view without leading his thinking.

## Adaptation

To Piaget, the development of knowledge is a spontaneous process that concerns the total biological-psychological complex of body, nervous system, and mental functions. The structures of knowledge are neural structures which change systematically with experience and growth. The *functions* by which knowledge develops are invariant processes. They are species-specific and determine the way human beings organize their interactions with the environment. Some invariant functions are adaptation, organization, and equilibration.

Two opposing forces to which individuals must adapt are assimilation and accommodation. In meeting the environment, the individual can incorporate into his thinking only those facets which he can conceive. At the same time, he is compelled to react to the impact of the real, external world. Piaget defined *adaptation* as the process by which people find a balance between the opposing forces in their lives. *Assimilation* is the process of incorporating or taking in external reality, not in a causal sense, but by the person's natural seeking for material from the environment. *Accommodation* is the adjustment required of the individual imposed by a characteristic in the external environment which leads to differential of a previous structure, and thus the emergence of a new structure. One factor in Piaget's thinking is that knowledge is not a copy of environment, but the individual's action on an object or an event. Experience must be assimilated in some way. Assimilation and accommodation are the subjective and objective sides of the same process. Assimilation is the subjective incorporation of reality, whereas accommodation is the outgoing action on a particular demand of reality.

Adaptation results from the interaction of assimilation (the taking in of experience within the limitation of the organism's cognitive abilities at the moment) and accommodation (the organism's change to the reality of the environment). *Adaptation* is the human tendency to strive for equilibrium or balance between self and the environment. This dynamic characteristic is central to Piaget's developmental concepts; the pull to act in old patterns is balanced by a pull to fit the individual's cognitive world to new situations. Balance did not mean homeostasis in the traditional sense, and so equilibration was conceptualized as a dynamic and growth-producing process.

*Equilibration* is the person's own active regulation of cognitive adaptation. This regulatory factor is based in the active compensation of intellectual systems that leads to a knowledge of reversibility. Equilibration must be achieved at each intellectual stage before a person reaches the next level of cognitive functioning.

An *aliment* is the property or element of an object or problem situation which activates the schema—that is, which sets in motion the adaptation process.

## Organization

Piaget (1952) placed *organization* along with adaptation as an invariant that determines the ways in which the organism can function. Organization is a force that penetrates every aspect of an organism's life processes. Organization refers to the inescapable way an individual must come to terms with the environment. Human beings do not inherit cognitive structures, although they do inherit necessary ways of functioning that produce cognitive structures. This necessity to organize experience in specific ways is a key facet of growth and development. The direction of development is imposed on the organism by its necessity to conform to the organizational structure that is particular to its genetic inheritance. Organization is a form of interaction with the environment. Adaptation is the change in the organism that occurs as a result of its organization of life experiences. Piaget's concept of functions as invariant is in contrast to his concept of internal structures which change systematically.

## PERIOD OF SENSORIMOTOR DEVELOPMENT (Birth to 2 Years)

In his writing over the years, Piaget divided his periods of cognitive growth in various ways. However, in all his works the sensorimotor phase (birth to age 2) is distinct. The cognitive thought phase (approximately 11 years and older) is also identifiable. The intermediate period (ages 2 to 11) is variously treated as one period with subdivisions (Piaget & Inhelder, 1956) or is separated into as many as four equal phases. In the discussion that follows, the total span will be divided into three periods with subdivisions from birth to age 2, ages 2 to 11, and ages 11 to 15.

In Piaget's dynamic conception of growth each phase of development interpenetrates subsequent phases. Much of what was learned in earlier periods continues to function as a mode of thought in the later periods. The highest forms of thinking observed in children at a certain period tend to be the behavior that Piaget used to characterize that period. Obviously these age boundaries are fluid, although Piaget is insistent that the sequence is inflexible and follows the described pattern from genetic necessity. Each stage is built upon and incorporates the earlier developments within a new *modus operandi.* Each stage begins with a period of preparation, during which the child's reaction pattern is loose and somewhat unstable as he begins to deal with new problems characteristic of the phase. This period of preparation gradually merges into a period of achievement, when the functioning becomes integrated and characteristic of the age level. At these times growth is accomplished by extension within a phase when the individual learns to handle a number of horizontal problems using similar techniques. The child's cognitive growth is extended vertically to comparable but harder problems when the same general approach to the environment is used, but at an intellectual level above that of the earlier experience. For instance, "object constancy"—the idea that the object remains the same even when out of view—can be replicated in the later phase with "concepts of the object" remaining the same, even under processes that temporarily obscure vital characteristics of the object.

Piaget developed his understanding of the period from birth to age 2 primarily from observations of his own three children. His accounts reveal the thoroughness and care with which he observed each of the developing children. He built tentative hypotheses on the basis of cues and then checked the logical consistency of the hypotheses within the framework of a theory that had already been produced. Once this step was taken, new implications of his hypotheses became visible, which then were tested by reobservation of the child. Through this step-by-tested-step approach, the theory was created.

### Stage 1: The Use of Reflexes (Birth to 1 Month)

Piaget (1954) interpreted the child's functioning during this time as being based on inherited reflexes. The child is unable to distinguish himself from the world around him; his assimilation and accommodation are antagonistic but undifferentiated. There is organization to his activities, which keeps the infant alive and functioning. The reflex responses of sucking, seeing, and grasping have no differentiation, as far as the child is concerned, from the act of sucking and the object being sucked. However, his accommodation to the object carries with it the first faint stirrings of a later conceptualization of a "me" and an "other than me."

Piaget believed these stirrings to be implicit in the adjustments that accommodation requires for assimilation to take place. The undifferentiation of this period he called *egocentrism,* by which he meant that, although the infant sees the world from his own point of view, he does not distinguish between the world and himself. Consciousness of self can come only with the experience of accommodation and with the growing awareness of a necessity to adapt one's activity in order to assimilate food or other intake materials. Intelligence begins with knowledge of the interaction of the self with things outside the self; this knowledge starts to develop on a very primitive level soon after birth.

### Stage 2: Primary Circular Reactions—First Acquired Adaptations (1 to 4 Months)

During this very early period of life, changes occur that indicate the nature of the child's cognitive development. The interaction of assimilation and accommodation results in an improved act of sucking, building what Piaget calls a "schema of sucking." In the course of stage 2, different schemata are coordinated or assimilated to one another. This accommodation brings the beginnings of a separation of self from not-self, which is crucial for cognitive development. The child of 4 months has learned to smile at his mother, a behavior that is distinct from his smiling reflex. The main difference between the reflex schema characteristic of stage 1 and the schema characteristic of stage 2 is the slight possibility of modification of the behavior beyond the immediate changes necessitated by the characteristics of the object of interaction. A slight breaking apart of assimilation and accommodation begins. The assimilation provides the initial organization and direction, while the accommodation changes the schema so that future assimilations start from a somewhat different base. These changes in both assimilation and accommodation are a result derived from experience and are described by Piaget as *circular reactions.* The initial response is new to the child, but is followed by repetition of the action again and again. In the process, the new response establishes a modified schema or pattern by which future responses in this context will be made.

An example from Piaget (1952)—in which he discussed the way his son functioned at the age of 2 months—may clarify this circular reaction. Laurent, 3 days after he was 2 months old, began a series of activities that ended in a systematic grasping. His first efforts were scratching and trying to grasp and then letting go and trying to grasp again. By the end of 10 days, he had developed a well-defined habit of scratching, grasping, holding, and letting go. This series of actions would continue for 15 minutes at a time. Essentially this process seemed to be a modification of reflex actions, but the modifications were being learned so that they could be repeated at a later time. In modern child development sources, this learning to grasp and to let go is called *prehension* (Chapter 11).

During stage 2, coordination of two different modes of response to the environment begins to take place. Halfway through her second month, Piaget's daughter, Jacqueline, stopped crying merely to show hunger or discomfort and started crying to indicate expectation or disappointment. The changes in type and time of crying became expressive of anticipations, rather than solely of discomfort. Shortly after this development, she showed an interest in crying for the sound of it, repeating and listening to the different patterns. The processes of hearing and vocalization were being coordinated. The integration of sound with sight followed shortly after. She again went through a series of circular modifications that gradually coordinated the two schemata.

At this stage, Piaget's children started a primitive kind of imitation in which they responded to an outside person who first initiated contact by imitating the baby. Apparently a child assimilates the external sound as though it were a variation he had produced himself. Play seems to begin with repetition of novel adaptations that have been mastered and are now repeated for the sheer pleasure of the repetition of some act that has come under the child's control. In the period from 1 to 4 months, the child still lacks awareness of an outside world separate from himself. However, he is already differentiating reactions and practicing new responses, which indicates that learning has taken place. The changes Piaget noted are inferences and indicate both the strength and the weakness in his work.

### Stage 3: Secondary Circular Reactions— Making Interesting Sights Last (4 to 8 Months)

According to Piaget's observations, children establish the distinction between themselves and the world beyond themselves during this period. As in stage 2, much of the activity is centered around accidental or fortuitous new responses to the environment, which are then repeated with increasing fluency, so that greater stability is generated in the performance of the activity. The child's awareness of the environment is displayed as he performs motor acts that produce effects in that environment, performs reduced versions of the acts to the objects, and performs symbolic acts related to objects with the apparent intention of continuing the previous effect. Thus the child's activity displays the beginnings of intention or goal orientation.

One of the principal differences between this and the previous stage is that the infant at stage 2 is almost completely oriented to his own bodily actions for the sake of the actions, while in stage 3 his interest has turned to the effect of his actions on the environment. He strikes a rattle and hears the sound; eventually he strikes the rattle for the purpose of hearing the sound. Visually guided manual activity, or the coordination of the visual schema with the motor schema, is an important bridge between the stages.

Piaget's (1952) observations of the times when certain activities occurred indicates the adventitious nature of many of these activities—for instance, rubbing an object along the wicker of the bassinet. Laurent discovered this method of producing sound 1 month earlier than one of his sisters and 2 months earlier than the other. He seems to have accomplished this activity earlier because of the fortunate circumstance of his having a paper knife, which made the sound as he waved it around, while his sisters used dolls or other less noise-producing toys.

During stage 3, children also come to recognize objects at a distance and to display the recognition by making small-scale movements previously associated with use of the objects when close at hand. Piaget describes these as *symbolic motions*; the infant seemingly indicates recognition of an object itself, rather than attempting to move the object itself. Similar large-scale or symbolic motions are made with the intent of making interesting sights continue. The intentionality of this period is displayed in activities that move toward a visible goal; these activities should be distinguished from later activities that move toward more distant goals.

### Stage 4: Coordination of Secondary Schemata—Their Application to New Situations (8 to 12 Months)

During this period, the child develops increasingly complex actions that now clearly show intention. He also increasingly anticipates events from signs that predict their imminence. He reacts to the novelty value of new objects rather than to their utility value. As long as a part of an object is visible, the child will make deliberate attempts to remove other objects that hinder his attainment of it. He coordinates complex visual, motor, and tactile schemata in order to achieve a result that has clearly been premeditated. His goal is obvious from the beginning and is not incorporated as a goal after accidental attainment, as in the previous stage.

This schema shows the adaptation from

rather crude and fairly ineffective ways of dealing with problems to more direct and effective ways of reaching desired goals. In terms of cognitive development, the child is becoming increasingly independent of the objects in his environment and more concerned with ideation about them. He moves toward the subordination of means to ends, which will become increasingly characteristic in the stages ahead. The effectiveness of signals as heralding coming events is seen in his crying when his mother puts on a hat. He has learned on earlier occasions that this signifies that the mother is going out. This signaling does not imply the existence of imagery or symbolic analysis, but rather is direct cuing from past associations of events.

Piaget (1952) interprets the child's approach at this age to novel objects as subtly different from his actions in stage 3. The overt acts are quite similar, but stage 4 reveals evidence of the child's trying to understand the object. He uses a more exploratory approach, as though he were attempting to understand the functional value of the object. Piaget's explanation in this instance may be more sophisticated than the activity justifies.

During this period, the child will imitate others while sometimes using other effectors than the one used by the experimenter. Lucienne at one point imitated Piaget's opening and closing his eyes, first by opening and closing her hands and then her mouth. Play during this period is amusing to the child, who laughs while doing a task he has mastered, especially when shared with a parent or other adult. The child also shows a tendency to imitate his own actions when he encounters stimuli that are associated with specific actions. For instance, a pillow can stimulate play actions of going to sleep. One aspect of play activity that Piaget noted is a tendency to look for a hidden object in the place where it was first hidden, rather than in a later hiding place,

even though the child watches the hiding both times. Other play activities show an increasing awareness of space. Balls are hidden and found and are rolled to see how they behave. Objects are sought in locations that indicate the child's primitive space orientation. Laurent would follow with his eyes as Piaget moved behind the buggy and then would swing around with the obvious expectation of seeing his father emerge on the far side. Both causality and time emerge as realities. During this period, the child will push an observer's hand to set in motion some action which the hand had already performed but which the child cannot perform for himself. The seeking for hidden objects is an example of sequencing before and after. These developments lead eventually to understanding cause and effect.

### Stage 5: Tertiary Circular Reactions—the Discovery of New Means by Experimentation (12 to 18 Months)

The emergence of experimentation occurs during the first half of the second year. This third cycle varies from and extends its earlier counterparts, both of which had elements of exploration and beginnings of intention. The child learns new ways of controlling the environment by active experimentation. The repetition, which is characteristic of all circular reactions, differs from earlier forms in that now the child's repetitions are varied with each operation. He seems to express an attitude that emerges as "What will happen if?" as his interest shifts from the action itself to the effect of actions on external objects. This continuing circular reaction shifts from assimilation to attention to accommodation. With each repetition of the circular pattern, the child incorporates some modification in order to discover the possibilities in the object to which he next adapts.

Cognitive development at this stage is characterized by the beginning of true trial-and-error activity, with the emphasis on means rather than ends. The means are new to the child, and to achieve this kind of learning he must move out of himself in order to discover various possibilities. The child's understanding of causality takes a large step toward reality during this period.

### Stage 6: Invention of New Means through Mental Combinations (18 to 24 Months)

The major development in this stage over the previous one is that experimentation now becomes internal and mental rather than physical. The child sees a goal he wants to attain and for which he has no ready-made approach. The trial-and-error approach of the former period gives way to immediate appropriate activity. Piaget considered the mental functioning, in this process of finding a solution, to be covert or mental trial and error. A number of examples Piaget (1952) used may help to clarify the nature of the stage 6 operations.

Lucienne, at about 19 months, pushed a doll carriage across the rug and against the far wall. At this point she turned and started pulling the carriage, but found this mode awkward. She paused, went around the carriage, and without any learning period started pushing from the other side. The important facet of this endeavor was the lack of need for experimentation. At about the same age, Jacqueline arrived at a closed door with a blade of grass in each hand. As she went to open the door, she saw that she could crush the grass, so she placed it on the ground, opened the door, picked up the grass, and went inside. On going outside again, she repeated the operation in reverse, except that she put the grass down, saw that the door was going to cover it when opened, and then stooped and moved the grass before opening the door.

In another observation Lucienne, who had already learned to dump a pail of sand to empty it, used the same technique for emptying a chain from an open matchbox. Later she was given a partly open matchbox, and was able to reach her finger inside to pull the chain out. Finally she was given a box that was almost closed, with the chain inside. She tried the former technique of reaching her finger inside to pull out the chain, but without success. After studying the narrow slit, she opened her mouth several times. Finally she put her finger in the slit, pulled the box open, and retrieved the chain. Piaget explains the mouth opening as a symbolic aid to the child's thinking of the need for increasing the size of the box opening; he considers this activity a demonstration of the existence of motor or visual symbolism prior to the development of language. Interpreting the activity in terms of schema, Piaget concluded that the patterns in the brain that control activity are combined with one another before overt activities of the kind described can take place. Stage 6 of the sensorimotor period begins the transition to the conceptual-symbolic period of development.

By age 2, children are able to imitate many things, both present and remembered. Piaget tells of Jacqueline's imitating a temper tantrum the day after she saw one displayed by a young visitor. Make-believe play also emerges during this stage. From play that requires realistic stimulus mechanisms, the child changes to play activities that use attenuated symbolic representations or stimulators.

During the last half of the second year, the child is able to follow the hiding of objects and to make deductions about the location in which an article could be found. His search is from one likely spot to another, but if neither of these searches is successful, he tries the third possible location. Piaget considered the child to have developed a conceptualization of space-object relations. During this sixth stage, the understanding of causality has also matured markedly. The child can now infer causes from results and can infer probable results from events, as Jacqueline demonstrated after being taken from a game and placed in her playpen. She called, but no one took her. Next she expressed a need to go to the bathroom. Although she had just been there, the maneuver was successful. Once out of the playpen she moved to continue the game that had been interrupted. She had apparently reasoned that a request to go to the bathroom would get her out of the playpen and that she could arrange events from there.

### Relation of the Sensorimotor Period to the Learning-Motivation Model

The child begins life as an egocentric organism with no distinction between assimilation and accommodation. Gradually he learns to distinguish the outside world from himself; begins experimentation, with its attendant focus on the object; and moves to trial-and-error activities. Finally his trial and error is mental, which seems to involve rudimentary conceptualizations.

Schemata—as Piaget defines them—seem to consist of association chains as described in Chapter 9. Many of these associations are already developed and are able to function at birth. Extension and elaboration of the schemata take place as the child interacts with his environment. Piaget's twin processes of assimilation (taking in) and accommodation (adjusting to) often form the stimuli and conditioning of level 1 learning.

Gradual development of the ability to distinguish between the self and the not-self— which is first visible in stage 3 as intention—is one aspect of the affective sequence in the learning-motivation model. Almost all learning during Piaget's first four stages is associational in nature. The beginnings of trial and error

(stage 5) build on experiences that were started accidentally and modified genetically but were refined as they were practiced. The intention—an aspect of motivation—becomes increasingly important through variations in these trials to produce new effects. The child starts a shift from dealing with concrete objects to dealing with mental representations of the objects. Trial and error within the framework of this ideation leads to actions that seem to be explained as conceptualizations, or gestalt formations, in the learning-motivation model. At stage 6 the explorations of the child have elements of self-determination and originality at a sensorimotor level.

### PERIOD OF PREPARATION FOR, AND ORGANIZATION OF, CONCRETE OPERATIONS (2 to 11 Years)

Piaget used the term "concrete operations" as the intellectual accomplishment over this period of development. His descriptions are of representational thought, including the images and symbols that are associated with mental abstractions. The cognitive growth that Piaget described—such as *establishing systems of classification*, *enforcing rules and disciplinary action*, and *time constancy*—involved internalized structures that corresponded with the functions observed. The period of concrete experience is distinct from the sensorimotor period in that the child deals with the representations of objects. During these 9 years of the child's life, he is mastering the ability to think symbolically. Preoperational and operational thought differs from the period following in that the older child, from 11 to 15, is mastering the art of thinking about thinking. In other words, the concreteness of the period from 2 to 11 suggests a direct tie between vocabulary, or ideation, and the child's objective world, while the later formal operations suggest a second-order removal from concrete reality to abstract relationships.

In each of the three developmental periods, Piaget has discerned a similar cyclical growth from relative inability to function in the materials of thought—objects, words, formulas—through increasing differentiation to a transitional level that forms the springboard for the next cognitive period. During the sensorimotor phase the child begins to distinguish between himself and the world apart from himself, achieves knowledge of the permanence of objects, develops intention, and proceeds through trial and error to the emergence of ideational representations, which forms the transition to the next period. During the second period the child develops cognitively through five phases in his use of symbolism: (1) beginnings of representational thought, (2) language associated with this thought, (3) the use of language for egocentric purposes, (4) the use of language for social purposes, and finally (5) the use of semantic and symbolic functions for dealing with abstractions about the environment (Piaget, 1926). This last stage of emerging abstractions forms the bridge to the third period of formal thought, in which an analogous series of steps leads to the ability to think in terms that have no counterpart in the immediate, visible world.

The persistence of earlier kinds of intellectual functioning during the development of new stages of cognitive behavior provides a source of confusion to an observer of children and to the student of Piaget's work. The use of nonverbal imagery persists as an important facet of children's thoughts for many years, at least, and is easily overlooked by adults because they tend to interpret the child's behavior within their own integration of verbal and representational forms.

Piaget (1926) explained that the child's cognitive structure is expressed in his language, which develops and expands during the second period. The child's use of language, however, differs from that of adults. By eliciting explanations from the child, the interviewer can gain an understanding of the underlying processes in much the same way that careful observation of physical action can explain the mental processes that develop during the sensorimotor period.

Inhelder (1969) explained the stages of the child's conceptualization of seriation with a sequence of pictures children drew and the words they typically used to explain their reasoning (Figure 14-3). The seriation experiments consisted of the child's ordering of a series of sticks from the shortest one to the longest. At the beginning of the preoperational period the children tended to see all the sticks as similar, without differentiating them for length. By age 3 or 4, her subjects divided the sticks into two categories and referred to them as long and short sticks. At the third stage, ages 4 to 5, the children drew sticks in an organized arrangement and referred to them as tiny, medium, and long. By age 5 to 6 most children constructed the series correctly by trial and error and explained their ordering as short, longer, longer. By the beginning of the concrete operational stage, ages 7 to 8, most children discovered a method of choosing the longest stick (or the shortest) and working systematically to the end of the series without hesitation. The typical explanation corresponded to Piaget's definition of seriation, and the child could reverse the action or insert an additional stick in the correct position. Piaget and Inhelder's memory studies provided many similar problems in which the typical stages of accomplishment varied according to the conceptualization to be discovered, but the stages remained consistent in developmental sequence.

## Preconceptual Phase (2 to 4 Years)

The 2-year-old child has already learned to think in sensorimotor terms about cause and effect, objects in space, and relations between objects. His beginnings as an operator in the

| | Child's behavior during interview | | |
|---|---|---|---|
| Age stage | Memory drawing | Linguistic interaction | Piaget's description |
| 2-3 A | | | "They are sticks" | Child maintains that all sticks are of equal length. |
| 3-4 B | | | Sticks are "long" and "short" | Child divides sticks into two categories; no ordering. |
| 4-5 C | | | "Tiny, middle-long, and long" | Child talks of three lengths or categories. |
| 5-6 D | | | "Short, longer, longer" | Child constructs empirically, arrives by trial, error. |
| 6-7 E | | | "longest to shortest" or "shortest to longest" | Child discovers a method; orders without hesitation; can reverse. |

**Figure 14-3** Five stages in memory for seriation. Seriation tasks consisted of ordering a series of sticks (dowling from approximately 4 to 10 inches in equal increments) from the smallest to the tallest. *(From a lecture by Barbel Inhelder, Los Angeles, 1969.)*

realm of representational thought are built on this earlier background, but are still chaotic with regard to symbolism. Piaget (1954) pointed out that during the second period the obstacles to understanding the child's development reappear in the same sequence in which they were observed in the sensorimotor period.

One of the problems in the years from 2 to 4 is the development of the facility for distinguishing between a signifier and that which is signified, or the ability to understand the difference between the cue for an idea and the idea itself. Piaget (1951) discussed the relationship between imitation and play as "building blocks" for representation in language. The reduction in the child's imitation and play activities assists in the establishment of representations that are less than the complete object. The early use of language often involves the child's experimentally talking to himself almost as much as he talks to others. Command language that often involves only one word is closely connected to the sen-

sorimotor world of the first 2 years, although it persists much later. The child is most likely to practice the language that deals with things not here and now when he is alone and then try it on others.

Piaget described the change from the sensorimotor phase as a change from an individual world to one that is based on social organization. The child experiences all the difficulties in learning to be a social person —that is, a self among others—that he did in learning to be a person in the physical world. The first stage is one of exploration almost without guideposts, and much effort is devoted to finding meaningful landmarks. This is followed by increasing awareness and assurance as he finds the language to function as both a cognitive and a social individual.

### Intuitive Thought (4 to 7 Years)

Two phases of intuitive thought—simple representations (4 to $5\frac{1}{2}$ years) and articulated representations ($5\frac{1}{2}$ to 7 years)—are treated together here for purposes of contrast. Piaget (1926) described a series of experiments that illustrate growth in language during this period. In his first pilot study, the speech of two 6-year-old boys was studied and classified into two main divisions: egocentric and socialized speech. *Egocentric speech* was described as that which may be used in the presence of others or in solitude, but which has as its primary function the communication of the child with himself. *Socialized speech* has as its function communication with others.

In a follow-up study to test these observations, Piaget observed 20 children, of an average age of 6, and found that nearly half their utterances were of the egocentric type. A third study in this series involved conversations between two or more children who ranged in age from 4 to 7 years. Piaget found that the youngest group used what he called *collective monologues*, in which children stimulated each other to speech but did not engage in dialogue. The response of the second child to the first was unrelated to the stimulus since both children were essentially talking to themselves. By the age of 7, the children were engaging in a genuine exchange of information. In *arguments* the intent of the initiator and of the reactor was to convince the other; in *agreements* the interchange was supportive and elaborative. The children between the youngest and the oldest age groups were observed to engage in a mixture of each kind of communication. These experiments indicate the sequence of language development in children's social interaction.

The child who is developing intuitive thought patterns uses increasingly appropriate language, but not always with the meaning that the adult assumes. In many ways the child is going through a sequence of changes in assimilation and accommodation of ideas that he went through earlier in his interactions with concrete objects.

In *causality*, the concept of cause-effect relationship, there is a steady shift toward accommodation to an external reality and away from the internal orientation that characterizes assimilation. The idea that two separate properties, such as height and width, can operate separately and can interact with each other is only beginning to form by the end of this period.

The classification of the ages 2 to 7 as the years of intuitive thought reflects Piaget's findings that the process of arriving at answers concerning causality and rightness or wrongness is based on incomplete thinking. Children make these and similar kinds of decisions on the basis of intuition, whereas the adult depends on logical reasoning. Piaget's subjects from 4 to 7 tended to make an immediate leap to a perception-bound conclusion rather than to reason out a logical answer. The child becomes capable of representational thought by means of symbolic-semantic functions by which he goes beyond immediate perceptions and internally manipulates the concrete world (Piaget, 1969).

### Concrete Operations (7 to 11 Years)

The last subperiod of childhood, from 7 to 11 years, encompasses most of the child's elementary school life. As in the last stage of the sensorimotor period, the cognitive development of concrete operations blossoms because of the preparatory growth that has been emerging during the previous 5 years. This middle period is devoted to interaction with representations, as contrasted with the direct action of the earlier sensorimotor period; however, the changes that take place during the final phase of middle childhood are nearly as dramatic as those which occur in the final phase of infant life.

The term "operations" holds the key to understanding Piaget's own conceptualization of the nature of mental activity during these years. Operations involve the use of cognitive systems or integrated sets of patterns for handling new data. In terms of the learning-motivation model, Piaget's operations would constitute a whole series of complex conceptualizations. As new data are incorporated into a system by the learner, the system is modified—the new data become a part of the whole. The operations persist, but they continually expand and become ever more inclusive. The past learning provides a framework into which the present information can be fitted without distortion. Assimilation occurs at this stage also, but the "taking in" builds a storehouse of diversity and rich potential. Accommodation has become highly discriminatory and selective in function.

The shift from the externalized and observable actions of the subject during the sensorimotor period to the internalized, schematic, and flexible actions of the middle period is epitomized in the systems of the concrete operations. Now the integration of the cognitive processes is relational and not additive. These totalities, characterized by specific organization, are what Piaget calls *operations*. The phase just prior to concrete operations, wherein the representations have the character of loose aggregations rather than of systems, is sometimes called *preoperational* by Piaget. The adolescent-adult period of cognitive development is called the period of *formal operations* to indicate the systematic structure that permeates all facets of the developing thought processes.

In order for a system to develop or for an operation to be possible, there must exist a complex series of interrelationships into which the operation can fit. The possibility of identifying and describing a group of individuals as a class involves the preexistence of a classification system that includes, at least potentially, the categories being suggested.

The emergence of the operations as functions seems to depend upon both maturation and practice. Apparently Piaget conceives no way of providing these cognitive structures much earlier than the predetermined age at which they appear; however, he does note a possibility of retarding the operational functions by removing stimulation from the environment. Children in any age group need the opportunities to produce that which their environments commonly provide.

Much of Piaget's writing about the age group from 7 to 11 years consists of a classification of the operations that can be observed and describes his methods of observation. However, Piaget has gone beyond classification to build a theoretical model of the kinds of operations that should be possible. Not all these operations categories have yet been established as functional, but remain for later testing by his associates or by other researchers. There are five general properties in his theoretical structure for this period: (1) composition, (2) associativity, (3) general identity, (4) reversibility, and (5) special identities. Each of the general properties may apply to nine variations or groupings in the structure. The most important of the five properties is reversibility.

A look at some experiments that illustrate the emerging concepts may clarify some of the interpretations that Piaget gave to the intellectual structuring, or the process of operations. Piaget (1928) described a series of two experiments designed to investigate the child's understanding of relations. In one experiment, 40 boys ranging in age from 9 to 12 years were given the absurdity sentences from the Simon-Binet Intelligence Test and were asked to find the absurdity. Seventy percent of the subjects failed to detect the absurdity in the sentence "I have three brothers: Paul, Ernest, and myself." Piaget claims that their difficulty hinged on distinguishing between brother as a class and brother as a relation—"We *are* three brothers" or "I *have* three brothers." In Piaget's analysis, he finds relations a more difficult operation to handle than classification. Piaget did not distinguish between intellectual operations or processes and the products of thought in the way Guilford did (Chapter 15).

In a more elaborate investigation, Piaget (1928) explored the brother concept with a group of 240 children between the ages of 4 and 12. The following questions (rephrased appropriately for girls) were asked:

**1** How many brothers have you? And how many sisters? If the child had a brother A and a sister B, the questioning was continued: How many brothers has A? How many sisters? How many brothers has B? How many sisters?
**2** How many brothers are there in the family? How many sisters? How many brothers and sisters altogether?
**3** There are three brothers in a family: Alfred, Auguste, and Raymond. How many brothers has Alfred? Auguste? Raymond?
**4** Are you a brother? What is a brother?
**5** Ernest has three brothers, Paul, Henry, and Charles. How many brothers has Paul? Henry? Charles?
**6** How many brothers are there in this family?

The more important findings of this study include:

**1** It is difficult for children to see themselves as brothers to their own siblings.
**2** They often have difficulty including themselves in the pool of brothers.
**3** The difficulty increases when the question concerns a hypothetical family.
**4** The definition of brother goes through a sequence of development—
   **4.1** A brother is a boy;
   **4.2** There must be two or more children to have a brother but the answer is not completely rational.

Piaget illustrates with a response that hinged on the brother being the younger member of the group:

   **4.3** A roughly correct definition was achieved by about 60% of the 7-year-olds and by 75% of the 9-year-olds.

These same children were given a series of questions to investigate their knowledge of right and left. At the preoperational level (ages 4 to 7), they knew their own right and left, but could not transfer their knowledge to the experimenter facing them. When somewhat older, the children could distinguish this relationship, but could not incorporate the idea in the case of the second in a row of three blocks, which was both right and left of the other blocks in the group. This relationship was manageable only at a later age.

Piaget (1929) investigated causality in a number of areas. Many of these studies have been reported by other writers, and they will be only briefly reviewed here. Piaget was particularly careful to structure the questions used from recorded questions that children of the ages under study asked one another. He was also careful in his interpretation of the results to indicate that the children's answers provided hints about their own thinking, rather than that their thinking showed a logically organized conceptualization of cosmology. In a way their answers were more indicative of what they still did not know than of what they did understand.

In discussing dreams, Piaget's investigators asked children whether they dreamed, whether they knew what a dream was, where the dream was, where dreams came from, and what they used to dream with. In general he found that 5- and 6-year-olds believe that dreams come from outside, take place in the room, and are seen with the eyes. Children of 7 and 8 years think of the dream as being unreal—as taking place outside themselves, in the room, but as originating in their heads. To a degree, they see their dream as a projection. By 9 or 10, the child thinks of the dream as a mental image inside his head, although he believes that dreaming may involve an inward viewing by the eyes. Children of this age express a definite progression in a logical structure that relates dreaming to other experience.

Piaget studied the child's concept of animism, or the aliveness of various objects. In general, young children consider things that move to be alive; by the late concrete operational period, they restrict their idea of aliveness to animals and people. Children tend to show more instability in their ideas about animism than in most areas Piaget investigated.

Piaget (1930) continued his study of causality into the child's conception of the world. He found a progression in their thinking about the movements of clouds, from their being moved by an individual, to being moved by men or God, to moving themselves. At about 8 years of age, the children in the study explained that clouds are moved by the wind; this impression is, in part at least, created by the movement of the clouds. Finally, at about age 9, Swiss children gave a correct explanation. In general Piaget found a transition from the idea of moving bodies being pushed by individuals, to the idea of the object willing the movement, to the idea of external, mechanical causation. A force could will its own movement at the same time it is moved by outside forces having psychic elements—for example, a river moves because the rocks will it to. The prevalent causation theory of a culture is expressed by children in the final concrete operational phase.

This sequence in the development of mature thinking has an interesting parallel in the early philosophical explanations of these same phenomena by the Greeks. The effect of the cultural teaching is apparent in the increasingly sophisticated explanations given by modern children to these same questions. They cease at an early age to think of clouds being moved by the gods.

In the study of machines, the child develops cognitively from assuming that the most prominent feature of the machine is the cause of its movement to being able to search out the points of contact that cause mechanical action. Piaget suggests that the changes in animistic explanations of the physical world may depend on the child's acquaintance with simple machines—his understanding of mechanical causation is facilitated and then seems to be transferred to more distant objects.

Piaget and his associates have done literally hundreds of experiments since 1920. Their investigations cover moral judgment, quantity, logic, time, movement, space, geometry, probability, and perception, in addition to the other areas already mentioned. The growth pattern in the school-age child (7 to 11 years) is developed from a form of egocentricity in which the self is confused with the external world and with other individuals. A period of objectification follows, which involves socialization and interaction with other people. The development during this social age depends on contact with other people who force the individual to take cognizance of them and of their views. The process is divided by Piaget into three main stages. The first involves automism, which precedes the clear awareness of self. The second is a magical period in which wishing can make it so—desire can influence objects, even inanimate objects. Finally, the desire to make logical justification of one's ideas leads to rational causality and ontology. To summarize the period of operational intelligence, the child can classify concrete objects, put them in serial order, establish correspondences between them, use numerical operations on them, and analyze spatial relationships.

## PERIOD OF FORMAL OPERATIONS (11 to 15 Years)

Last in the developmental sequence is the period of formal operations, in which the individual comes to think at the level of adults when they are functioning at their best. The experimentation was conducted with subjects from 11 to 15 years of age, by which time Piaget considers mature thought processes to be stabilized. In *Discussions on Child Development*, Piaget (1958) put forth the thesis that between the ages of 11 and 15, the nature of thought undergoes a change that he links to the maturation of cerebral structures—the youth enters the world of ideas per se, in which his cognition is based on abstract symbolism, rather than on representations of reality. Piaget points out that during this period reality becomes secondary to possibility. Reversibility has been well established; thus the student is able to think in logical terms and to return to the original point in his thinking to check the results of his theory against logical consistency. The youth is able to bring opposing or contradictory positions into new syntheses by logical reasoning.

### Stage of Egocentrism

In the analysis of three periods of intellectual development as unities, one of the characteristics that emerged was the return of the individual to a form of egocentrism at the beginning of each period. The formal operations period is no exception (Inhelder & Piaget, 1958). In the sensorimotor period, the egocentrism is complete, and the individual is involved in an unawareness of the difference between himself and the world around him.

The beginning of the concrete representational period involves another rise in egocentrism when the child assumes that everyone represents the world to himself in exactly the same way—the way the child knows. In the third period, the egocentrism has been described by Flavell (1963) as being on a higher level, in the form of naïve idealism rather than the egocentrism of the two previous levels. The young person is likely to become immersed in theories for reshaping world conditions. His emphasis is likely to be on thought as the effective instrument, without due regard for the brutal realities of other intransigent individuals.

### Later Stages

In the same way that experience with objects and with representational ideas evolves into stable and workable systems for using new cognitive tools, so the adolescent gradually accommodates his cognitive processes to the realities of the world of ideas and their limitations. Piaget considers the ability of the youth to think in terms of the possible—of which the real constitutes a special kind of possibility—to be the most critical delineation of this age group. During this period of cognitive development, the youth takes the results of concrete operations, casts them in the form of propositions, and then proceeds to operate on them in terms of implications, identity, disjunction, conjunction, and other logical processes.

A brief summary from Inhelder and Piaget (1958) of an experimental situation shows the difference between *concrete operational* and *logical operational* thought. The materials used in the experiment were four flasks containing sulfuric acid, water, oxygenated water, and thiosulfate, plus a bottle of potassium iodide and a dropper. The experimenter, who had previously prepared a mixture of sulfuric acid and oxygenated water and another glass containing water, added a few drops of potassium iodide to each and then asked a child to duplicate the yellow color that was produced in one of the glasses. According to Inhelder's account of the observations, the child from the concrete operational age group tried adding potassium iodide to each of the bottles in turn. This failed to produce the yellow color, and he was unable to proceed further without help. After questioning about other things that could be tried, he mixed two bottles and added potassium iodide, but these were exclusive pairs and did not represent all the possible combinations. The student even tried mixing three bottles and adding the potassium iodide. In the trial and error, the child did not hit on the proper combination, which he might well have done accidentally. The point Piaget made is that the problem was not conceived in terms of all possible combinations, but in terms of an incomplete system. The child did use a definite system that in many cases would have produced the required results.

A youth, faced with the same problem, started in the same way. When the result was negative, he assumed that mixing them might be necessary. He then established a system that involved all possible combinations. After some further questioning, the youth went on to explore more complex combinations, including the effect of thiosulfate in removing the color. Even under questioning designed to shake his conclusions, the youth based his reasoning on the results of the experimental situation and maintained his position. In the formal operational period, the young person builds a system and in a logical manner proceeds to test all the possible ramifications. He is displaying his cognitive system as different from that of the younger child, even though the concrete operation might have accidentally provided a means for solving the particular problem. The more sophisticated mental process of the older student would enable him to reach a correct solution necessarily because of the cognitive processes he had at his command.

During this period, the adolescent masters the mental processes that are basic to a controlled experiment. In specifying the ways of distinguishing between the concrete operational and the formal operational levels of functioning, Piaget (1958) recognizes that a few isolated bits of behavior are not adequate evidence. The actions and the statements of each subject need to be examined in a global fashion; the nature of the proofs offered by the student also needs to be examined. When he is functioning on the formal operational level, the individual will be consistent in his way of dealing with data. For Piaget this level represents a general orientation to problem solving. The adolescent theorizes, but checks his theories by careful analysis and by accommodation to detail. Logical operations cover propositions that the student can use as abstract hypotheses to reach deductions by formal logic (Piaget, 1969).

## CRITIQUE OF PIAGET'S CONTRIBUTIONS

The major contributions of Piaget's work include:

1 The clear delineation of learning as different in kind from the additive accumulation of associative chains of information to the individual's discovery of inherent structure of knowledge in cognizing (Piaget, 1970).

2 The sheer volume of his observations of children at different periods of intellectual development, and the ingenuity with which he enabled them to communicate their view of the world.

3 The analytical thoroughness by which he organized his observations, thus making clinical-type research respectable again.

4 A description of the sequence of cognitive development in the human species.

Much of Piaget and Inhelder's work has been exploratory rather than definitive, although the cumulative effect is supportive of the general framework within which all their studies have been conducted. The interaction of assimilation-accommodation factors with one another and with the environment has provided a thread of continuity in cognitive development from birth to adult scientific thinking. The progressive elaboration of schemata into more and more complicated operations provides a consistent strand that gives form to the mental operations even though the biological nature of the processes remains veiled in obscurity. Probably Piaget's self-concept as primarily an epistemologist has contributed to the systematic nature in which he explored cognitive growth.

Piaget has not claimed inflexibility for his age groups. He has been much more insistent on the serial progression of cognitive development than on age characteristics. Many of the criticisms of Piaget's interpretation of the thought processes of the elementary school years have been due to misunderstanding of his view of their significance. In some cases these confusions can be laid, justly, to the obscurity that veils some of his publications.

One of the main contributions that Piaget has made to the study of cognitive development is the value of a theoretical position as a stimulus for research. His work has been described by Flavell (1963) as a prime example of a developmental-descriptive approach to research in the field and one that may very well contribute to the renaissance of respectability for clinical studies. Although Piaget's work has certainly been developmentally descriptive, it has more importantly been theory-based, with forceful stimulation for new research projects to test hypotheses that continually emerge from research findings based on theory.

Piaget found evidence of cognitive growth that is sequential, continuing, and integrated with other aspects of growth. Piaget observed differences in kind, that is, qualitative differences that were more significant than his findings of differences in amount or quantitative differences in learning. Piaget demonstrated that observers with training can do descriptive work that is detached and analytical. When Piaget himself observed individual children, his organization of the data was profound. The work in recent years has extended his audience and increased his prestige by involving many others in the studies of cognitive growth.

Many of Piaget's experiments might have been structured to have facilitated an understanding of his results. Piaget's descriptions of sensorimotor understanding, of conceptual organization, and of formal abstract thinking are extremely useful in planning learning sequences in the school. The prospective teacher needs to remember that the ages at which these phenomena occur are likely to differ from one culture to another, from one teaching situation to another, and from individual to individual. The differences in levels of intellectual functioning are more important than the age designations observed by Piaget. The authors place less emphasis on the maturational aspects of learning and more emphasis on the teaching-learning sequence than Piaget did.

A number of specific complaints regarding Piaget's techniques will be mentioned in the next section. Related studies of cognitive development, which include a number of validations of Piaget's work, will be reviewed. Piaget's ideas become more meaningful in the context of these related investigations.

Piaget has been criticized regularly for almost all aspects of his work: delineation of stages, methods of sampling, and lack of statistical verification. Much of the criticism of his experimental design applies to his description of infant development. Piaget ignored the impact of teaching and reinforce-

ment on his children, while using his observations of them to generalize on the development of all children. Systematic and
constructive teaching, extended over a long
period of time, tends to change the learning
potential of children. However, his keen and
systematic observations provided an understanding of a sequence of cognitive development of children that is a classic.

Much of Piaget's writing is obscure. The
sentences are difficult. His use of mathemat-
icological symbols to explain verbal functioning increases the difficulty unnecessarily.
Flavell (1963) suggests that Piaget sometimes
operates according to a system of rules that
differ from those which the reader expects or
understands. The authors found a key to the
translation of Piaget through an understanding
of his belief in the unitary nature of the
universe. Piaget's belief in the cosmic unity of
all things makes rational his use of small,
select samples. Once this variation in the
rules has been grasped—even if not accepted—much of his presentation becomes
exciting.

## OTHER STUDIES OF COGNITIVE GROWTH

Researchers in the United States and other
countries have replicated the studies of Piaget
and his associates. Some of these later studies
have used research designs that incorporate
hypothesis testing, statistical evaluation, and
randomized grouping of subjects. The findings
tend to support Piaget's major postulations
concerning the nature and sequence of cognitive development in children.

### Conservation of Number

Piaget's work with children on the conservation of number has been replicated. According
to Piaget's definition, conservation of number

means the way in which children are able to
understand (1) the effects of adding or subtracting pieces on the number in a group or (2)
the effects of concentrating or expanding the
arrangement of pieces in a group.

Mehler and Bever (1967) examined number
conservation in over 200 children aged 2 years
4 months to 4 years 7 months. In Piaget's
research, children younger than 4 years were
not assumed to be able to work with conservation of number since his 4-year-olds did not
demonstrate this ability.

Mehler and Bever divided their children
into seven age groups, the youngest ranging
from 2-4 to 2-7 and the oldest ranging from
4-4 to 4-7. When asked to choose the row with
*more* clay pellets, the youngest group of 22
children performed at 100 percent accuracy,
even though the row with fewer pellets was
longer. In this part of the experiment, the
performance dropped off significantly to age 4,
when fewer than 20 percent responded correctly. The oldest group improved performance to almost 70 percent accuracy.

When pieces of candy were substituted for
clay pellets and the children were instructed to
"take the row you want to eat and eat all the
candy in that row," the youngest group
dropped to 80 percent accuracy, the 4-year-
olds were about 60 percent accurate, and the
oldest group was about 90 percent accurate
(Figure 14-4).

Complex interrelationships of age, motivation, and verbal instructions complicate interpretation of these findings, but they do indicate that Piaget's linear developmental growth
sequence needs further empirical study. These
results demonstrate the need for caution in
extending results to age-level groups (younger
or older) that were not tested.

Wohlwill and Lowe (1962) experimented
with three procedures designed to test the
possibility of accelerating the mastery of con-

servation of number. Seventy-two kindergarten children were divided into four groups of eighteen each. One group was given repeated practice in counting sets of objects before and after the objects were rearranged. The anticipated effect was to teach the irrelevance of the arrangement of the pieces as far as the number of pieces was concerned. The second group was given practice in counting the number of pieces in a group before and after pieces had been added or subtracted. The anticipated learning was the effect of adding to, or subtracting from, the number of pieces in a group. The third group was given practice in shifting pieces in the same group around, so that the child could observe the possibility of using the same elements to make a long or a short row; a small, tight pile or a large, loose pile; and other similar rearrangements. The fourth group of pupils were controls enrolled in the regular kindergarten program with no special emphasis on number conservation.

All groups were given nonverbal and verbal pretests and posttests. The verbal test was similar to one used by Piaget. All four groups improved on the performance test as a result of the training period, although there were no significant differences between any of the groups. None of the groups made significant improvement during the training as measured by the verbal test. Interpretation of these results is difficult, but they seem to substantiate Piaget's claim that verbal ability to explain conservation of number does not emerge this early in a child's life. The Wohlwill and Lowe experiments can, of course, be criticized on the same basis as other methodology research studies that involve teacher variables of undetermined force and direction. What the control group was being taught about numbers is not indicated in the report. The lack of expected change in verbal organization may

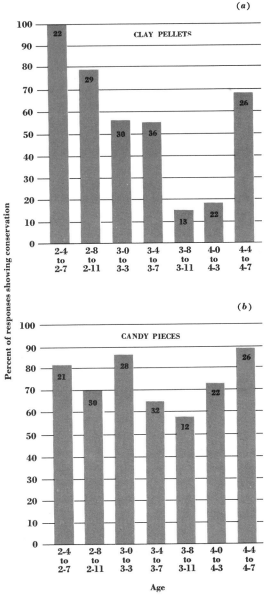

**Figure 14-4** The proportion by age of responses choosing the row with more members. Numbers inside bars indicate the total number of subjects of that age. (*Adapted from J. Mehler and T. G. Bever, Cognitive capacity of very young children, Science, 1967, 158, 141-142. By permission of the publishers.*)

have been due to the nature of the verbal associations incorporated in the instruction.

## Conceptualizations about Weight

In a series of studies, Smedslund (1961a, 1961b, 1961c, 1961d) explored conservation of weight as understood by 5- to 7-year-old children. In his first experiment, Smedslund (1961a) divided 48 subjects into three groups. One group was given reinforced practice in changing the shape of a mass of Plasticine and then weighing the new shape against a comparison piece of the same weight on a balance scale. The training of the second group consisted in having them add bits of Plasticine and then weighing the mass and subtracting bits and then weighing it. The control group had no training. The results showed small gains from pretest to posttest, but no statistically significant differences between groups were obtained.

In his second experiment, Smedslund (1961b) compared a group of 13 children who demonstrated thorough knowledge of the conservation of weigh on his pretests with a group of 11 children who showed no evidence of understanding the conservation principle on the pretest but who have only correct answers on the posttest after two training sessions. Both groups were then subjected to training designed to destroy their concept of conservation of weight. One of two masses was changed in shape and then weighed; however, the experimenter had surreptitiously added or subtracted additional Plasticine during the shape changing. Before the weighing took place, the children made estimates as to whether the new shape would weigh the same as the control shape. Under the pressure of the false evidence the newly trained children gave up their new ideas about conservation without hesitation. Six of the thirteen children who had established the concept of conserva-

tion of weight prior to the experiment argued that the experimenter had been adding or subtracting material and did not change their interpretations. Smedslund argued that this experiment supported the thesis that the children who had acquired the idea of conservation of weight by operant conditioning had only a superficial learning, whereas the children who brought the knowledge to the experimental situation had developed a logical certitude about the conservation of weight. The authors are inclined to think that the six who continued to trust their own judgment had probably conceptualized the relationship between the mass and weight of the clay, while the others of both groups had developed no such generalized principle to support their observations.

In two other related experiments, Smedslund (1961c, 1961d) explored the thesis that cognitive conflict—which is considered to require that the subject reorganize his thinking pattern to resolve the conflict—rather than reinforcement leads to thought development in this context of mass and shape versus weight. In these experiments, the children were asked questions designed to elicit their ideas about changes in shape and about adding material to, or subtracting it from, a ball of clay. The ball of clay was adjusted in two conflicting ways. For instance, if the child thought that making the ball longer and thinner increased its weight and that subtracting material decreased it, both operations were performed at once. A conflict was emphasized by asking the child what the results would be now. Four of the thirteen children in the first of two experiments came to an addition-subtraction rationale logically stated. The second experiment was repeated, using a control group, and the experimental group made statistically significant gains over the control group. Smedslund considered this result to be tentatively supportive of his cognitive conflict theory over a reinforcement theory. These studies demonstrate qualitative changes, due to teaching, in children's thought processes. Piaget believed that these changes occurred as a result of increasing age.

## Conservation of Area

Beilin and Franklin (1961) conducted an experiment in which first and third graders were taught to apply the conservation principle to areas. The important result of this study was that the third graders improved significantly in their handling of area, while the first graders made no observable progress. The implication of this investigation is that age per se is a critical factor in developing this kind of ability in large groups of children.

## Sequence of Cardinal-Ordinal Conceptualization

Dodwell (1960, 1961) made two large studies of number conservation. In the first he used individual tests with kindergarten, first-grade, and second-grade Canadian children. In the second study he used group presentations of the materials and obtained results similar to those obtained in individually administered tests. In his tasks he used diverse levels of difficulty—for instance, one-to-one matching of eggs to eggcups as a simple combination, contrasted with differently shaped flasks containing the same number of beads as a complex task. The difficult tasks gave better age separations than the simpler ones. The same child gave different levels of responses, such as preoperational rather than concrete operational responses, depending on the difficulty of the task he faced.

Dodwell's scalogram analysis generally supported Piaget's thesis that a child who solves ordinal-cardinal problems can also solve seriation and one-to-one correspondence pro-

blems. The reverse relationship is not necessarily true. Dodwell reported individual variation in which reversals of successes in the different tasks were obtained from those expected, although the majority of the subjects conformed to the expected pattern. He concluded that the three stages Piaget had specified in number conservation had been shown to exist, that in general the progress was from stage to stage as postulated, but that there were individual variations that raised some doubts about Piaget's sequence of development in all children.

## Relationship of IQ and Conservation

Elkind (1961a, 1961b, 1961c) reported experiments in the conservation of various measures for age groups 4 to 7, 5 to 11, and 12 to 15. With the youngest age group (1961a), he used conservation of number, of discontinuous quantity, and of continuous quantity. He also ran correlations with Wechsler Intelligence Scale for Children (WISC) scores and success with different measures. The results showed chronological age dependence on all the tests and higher mean age for continuous than for discontinuous quantity. Low positive correlations were obtained with subtest scores on the WISC, some of which were significant.

With a 5- to 11-year-old group of 175 children, Elkind (1961b) used tests for the conservation of global quantity, weight, and volume. The materials were balls of clay. The results were age-dependent, with more successes at higher levels of cognitive functioning as the children became older. Conservation of mass was mastered at an earlier age than weight, which was easier than volume. No report was made of individual variations from the sequence as learned by the group. Some of the older children appealed to general laws to support their judgments of conservations, thus supporting Piaget's findings that this kind of reasoning is a function of the older but not the younger age group.

In his oldest group, using 469 subjects, Elkind (1961c) found that a 75 percent accuracy of volume did not show up until 15 years of age, when students were asked to demonstrate the knowledge that volumes remain equivalent when liquids are transferred from a container of one shape to one of another shape. The volume test was based on immersion of an object in water, with a consequent rise in the water level. The commonest explanation was that the rise was due to the weight of the object. The means for boys were consistently higher than those for girls on this task at the age levels represented. A low, positive, but significant, correlation with IQ scores on the Kuhlmann-Anderson scale was noted.

### Abstract versus Concrete Operation

Keats (1955) used 1,358 subjects ranging in age from 9 to 15 years for a comparison of abilities to use concrete operational versus formal operational strategies in solving problems. Three kinds of problems were used: arithmetic, probability, and inequality. The problems to be solved were given in two forms. One was presented in concrete terms, and the other was more abstract and required formal operational thought for its solution. For instance, in arithmetic the problem could be posed as "$6 + 3 = ? - 3$," where a number of choices for the value of "?" would be given. The correct answer at the concrete level would be "? will never be 6." In the formal operational phrasing of the question, the numerals would be replaced by algebraic letter symbols and the "$+$" and "$-$" would become generalized so that the question would become "$A \pm B = ? \mp B$." In this case the answer among those given would be "? will never be $A$." The hypothesis was that the more abstract formulation would be achieved

only by students who had already been able to solve the more concrete example. The hypothesis was substantiated for arithmetic and probabilities but not for inequalities tasks. Keats interpreted the lack of support in the problems of inequality to have been due to an artifact of the questions. In discussing this experiment, Flavell (1963) claims that this experiment, which was meant to test Piaget's theory, did in fact do so, but in structures other than those which Keats assumed he was using.

The authors have misgivings about the extent to which formal operational thought as described by Piaget governs the day-to-day lives of adolescents. Many graduate students in selective universities seem to have trouble casting thesis outlines in terms that reflect formal operational thought in their habitual interaction with their environments. Intellectual ability seems to be an important variable when the material of the thought is in any way esoteric. Possibly, college aptitude could be defined as a student's ability to function at the formal operational level.

### Changes in Learning Mode with Age

Kendler and Kendler (1962), working from a pretheoretical model of learning, produced experimental evidence that seems to support certain aspects of the Piaget formulations and also of the learning-motivation model. One part of their experimentation involved the comparative ease of making a reversal shift as opposed to a nonreversal shift (Figure 14-5). The subjects were reinforced for making a discrimination of one of two factors, size or brightness, when the other factor varied independently. If the subject had been reinforced for discrimination of largeness, regardless of brightness, and then was switched to reinforcement for discrimination of smallness, regardless of brightness, this was defined as a *reversal shift.* If, however, he was switched from reinforcement for largeness, regardless of brightness, to reinforcement for brightness, regardless of size, this was defined as a *nonreversal shift.* In the reversal shift, the same cue in the subject's former training required a response that was opposite to the one previously rewarded. In the nonreversal shift, the irrelevant cue of the possible choices became relevant (Figure 14-5).

In this series of experiments, the Kendlers found that for rats a reversal shift was more difficult than a nonreversal shift, whereas for college students the opposite was true—they found the reversal shift easier than the nonreversal shift. The Kendlers suggest that the rats were performing as would be expected on the basis of a single-unit theory of learning, while the performance of the college students could be explained best in terms of a mediational theory of learning (Figure 14-6). In the mediational shift, the student could be thought of as saying to himself, "The brightness of this stimulus is the key to the problem." If he used some such mediation, it would be easier to shift from bright to black than from bright to large, which is not part of this particular system of thought. The responses of kindergarten children were mixed between the characteristic behavior of the rats and that of the college students as to their difficulty in learning the reversal or the nonreversal shift. The Kendlers hypothesize that the kindergarten children were in the process of changing from a single-unit to a mediational mode of handling this kind of experience. The fact that these changes seem to occur at the age that Piaget designated as the time of change from preoperational to concrete operational thinking lends credence to his findings.

The Kendlers found further support for their interpretation that a shift in thinking process occurs when they studied the age groups below and above kindergarten age.

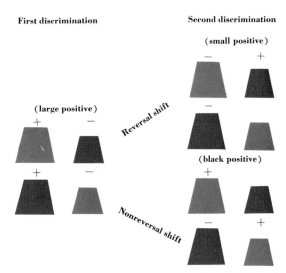

**Figure 14-5** Successive discriminations in reversal and nonreversal shifts. The plus sign represents positive reinforcement, and the minus sign represents nonreinforcement. A reversal shift involved a change from reinforcement for discrimination of largeness to reinforcement for discrimination of smallness when brightness had no relevance. A nonreversal shift involved a change from reinforcement for discrimination of largeness, regardless of brightness, to reinforcement for discrimination of brightness, regardless of size. (From H. H. Kendler and T. S. Kendler, Vertical and horizontal processes in problem solving, *Psychological Review*, 1962, 69, 5. Copyright 1962 by The American Psychological Association, reprinted by permission.)

Their hypothesis held that smaller numbers of subjects use a mediation approach at the younger age and that a larger number of subjects use mediation processes by the first and second grades. A similar division occurred when their kindergarten children were divided into groups of brighter and slower students. A high percentage of the slower students used thought processes like those of the rats, and a high percentage of the bright kindergarten children used processes like those of the college students.

The Kendlers found evidence of a change in the function of verbalization that accom-

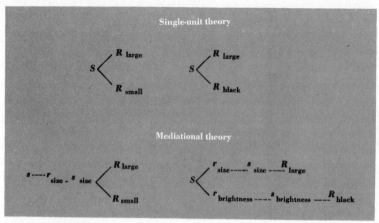

**Figure 14-6** Possible connections in reversal and nonreversal shifts. *(From H. H. Kendler, and T. S. Kendler, Vertical and horizontal processes in problem solving, Psychological Review, 1962, 69, 5. Copyright 1962 by The American Psychological Association, reprinted by permission.)*

panied the differentiation between large, small, light, and dark objects used in the reversal shift and nonreversal shift while learning new responses. Many of the children would talk to themselves as they were going through the activities of selecting the answers. A number of subjects made the correct verbal response and at the same time made an incorrect overt response. The Kendlers interpret the lack of verbal and choice coordination as indicating separate behavioral chains for the verbal and operational tasks. These chains apparently fuse during the period in which Piaget observed a shift from the preoperational to the concrete operational phase.

In an extension of this study, the Kendlers found verbal cuing helpful to 4-year-olds but damaging to the response success of 7-year-olds when inappropriate cues were included. They interpreted the results of this experiment to indicate that when the child has switched to using words as effective mediators in problem solving, inappropriate words will effectively hinder problem solving that otherwise would have been accomplished.

The Kendler research, conducted from an S-R base to test their own theories, supported Piaget's findings that qualitative changes occur in the nature of the thought process that children use. Cognitive functioning changes with age—both in nature and in complexity. The relationship of verbal responses to other facets of behavior changes. The questions that remain to be answered concern why these changes take place and whether the changes that Piaget found at the beginning of adolescence and at about 2 years of age can be demonstrated as clearly as the changes shown in 5- to 7-year-olds. Finally, the possibility that structured precedures—such as those projected from the learning-motivation model—can expedite these changes to the advantage of the learner needs to be tested. Individuals may not conform to the pattern because they have been subjected to learning protocols that differ from those of typical environments. The authors find mediational learning easier to interpret in terms of conceptualization than in terms of associational learning.

## REALITY OF COGNITIVE STAGES

Hofstaetter (1954) analyzed the changing composition of intelligence by factoring the longitudinal intelligence test data from the Berkeley growth studies. Factor I, which he identified as sensorimotor alertness, peaked sharply at age 8 to 9 months and fell off sharply soon afterward. Factor II, which he called persistence in provisional activity, showed a high positive loading from 2 years 8 months to about 3½ years. Factor III had negligible influence until 1 year 9 months when the ability emerged very rapidly to .68 loading at age 4, .90 loading at age 6, and .97 loading at age 9. (Figure 14-7). Factor I corresponds closely to the development of concrete operations in Piaget. Hofstaetter found no factor to explain the emergence of formal operations at ages 11 to 14.

Wallace (1967) suggested that the intelligence measures used in the Berkeley studies probably contained few items to challenge the logical thinking capabilities of their subjects in the way Piaget defined and presented problems and probed for hypothesizing, systematic deduction, and inferences. Wallace, however, credited Piaget, his collaborators, and other researchers who have replicated them with most of the Western world's research on conceptualization. Wallace cites a number of unresolved problems in the psychological research on conceptualization, including the lack of a clear separation between the development of conceptualization as an internalized structure and the use of symbolism by which the child explains his thinking. Wallace says that the process of conceptualization will be fully understood only when "neurophysiological research provides a reliable description of the neural bases of conceptual behavior" (p. 235). In the meantime, learning theory and research will suggest the framework for neurological exploration.

## SUMMARY

Since most of the work of teachers concerns learning in intellectual areas, cognitive growth has priority among their interests. No system of thought has been so specifically and so prodigiously directed to the study of how children come to know their world as that developed by Piaget and his associates. They are known best for a framework of stages in cognitive functioning—periods of development when the learner functions differently from the way he does during earlier or later periods but when he interacts with his environment in ways that are characteristic of his general age group. Piaget's major contribution was a genetic epistemology that explained how knowledge develops and changes within individuals. He used clinical methods to observe, record, and structure the intellectual activities of infants, children, and adolescents

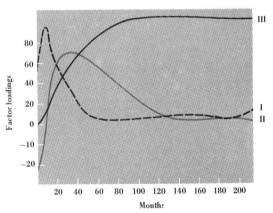

**Figure 14-7** Factors in intellectual development. Factor I peaked at 9 months of age and dropped sharply until approximately 4 years of age when the functioning leveled off to maturity. Factor II peaked at 3½ years. Factor III did not become operational until about 1 year 9 months of age and peaked at approximately 8 years. (From P. R. Hofstaetter, The changing composition of "intelligence": A study in T-technique, *Journal of Genetic Psychology, 1954, 159-164.* By permission of the authors and publishers.)

as they acquire the strategies for coping with their world.

Piaget's terminology evolved as he attempted to interpret his observations and to postulate his theory, and therefore certain terms need to be understood within the context of his work. A reflex *schema* is an innate, mental organization that becomes stabilized with repeated activations brought about by motor activity and sensory perception. Schemata are extended and modified as a result of experience. When two or more schemata are integrated, complex intellectual *operations* are possible. To Piaget, intelligence is the dynamic process by which experience extends the existing mental organization, thus making the person more adaptive. *Adaptation* results from the parallel functioning of assimilation and accommodation. *Assimilation* includes such variant processes as taking in milk, which the biological structure is prepared to receive, incorporating selected visual stimuli into the appropriate reflex schema, and integrating an idea into a related system of thought schemata. *Accommodation* is the process by which the individual is changed in ways that help him adapt to reality. *Aliment* is the property or element of an object or problem situation that activates the schema or activates the adaptation process. *Equilibrium* is the state of the organism that results when repeated actions, with their accompanying interaction of assimilation and accommodation, have completed the adaptation.

Piaget divided the stages of intellectual growth differently at different times in his career. This chapter summarized a three-stage classification. During the period of *sensorimotor development* (birth to 2 years) the child develops (1) from undifferentiated reflexive activity, (2) to primitive adaptation to his environment, (3) to separation of himself from the objective world, (4) to intentional modifi-

cation of conditions in the physical world, (5) to the emergence of experimentation with the physical world, and finally (6) to objective representation of relations between parts of the physical world. Between the ages of 2 and 11, the child learns to handle language by developmental steps that are comparable to those of the sensorimotor period. In this period of *concrete operations,* the child first uses language for egocentric ends; second, language becomes a tool for social ends; and finally it becomes a means of representing relationships within the physical world. The period of *formal operations* (ages 11 to 15) is the stage in cognitive development during which the youth learns to use language to think about abstract ideas.

Piaget was concerned with describing typical intellectual development; he did not concern himself with the range of individual differences at the various age levels. He was interested in how the child builds his conceptual world but not in the measurement of abilities at a specific time. His sequence of cognitive developmemt has been verified in part by the replicating research on conservation of number by Wohlwill and Lowe, conceptualizations about weight by Smedslund, and the sequence in development of cardinal-ordinal concepts by Dodwell. Elkind found a low but consistent correlation between IQ and conceptual development in three age groups: 4 to 7, 5 to 11, and 12 to 15. Keats verified the importance of age in the development of concrete and formal operations. Kendler and Kendler found a change in the nature of thought processes employed by 4- to 7-year-old children.

The typical intellectual behavior of a group, which Piaget worked assiduously to describe, may not characterize the individual student. Piaget's idea that a reflexive or a potential schema needs stimulation for development has tremendous implication for a neglected area of research in America. Piaget believed that the child comes into the world biologically equipped to make certain motor responses, which in turn provide the structure of the mental processes that come later.

## SELF-DIRECTING ACTIVITIES

1 Analyze the process of assimilation and accommodation that you went through as you became interested in a new topic, field, or area.

2 Try out an experiment with young elementary school age children on the conservation of liquids. Choose a liquid that the child would like to drink and let him drink it when he develops the concept.

3 Record the way in which a young child (4 to 8 months) makes interesting sights last.

4 Devise a way of improving the formal operations of high school students who are starting science.

5 Devise a way of recording evidence of a shift from concrete operations to formal operations for students leaving elementary school or starting junior high.

# Chapter 15

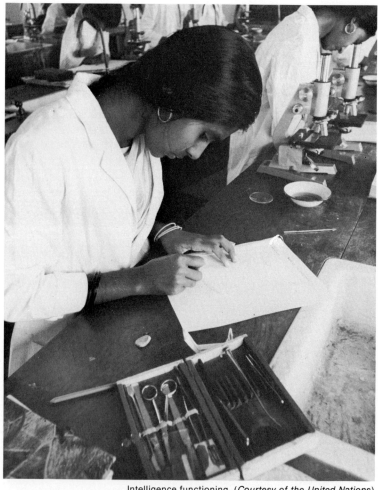

Intelligence functioning. (*Courtesy of the United Nations*)

# INTELLIGENCE: STRUCTURE AND FUNCTION

This chapter provides a basis for utilizing the values of intelligence scores and avoiding the pitfalls of overconfidence. This information will enable you to:

- Recognize the relationship of theory and test construction
- Select tests for specific uses
- Interpret scores on different tests as having different meanings
- Form behavioral objectives based on Guilford's structure of intellect
- Classify different productive activities as divergent or convergent production
- Be aware of the neural efficiency analyzer as an alternative to intelligence tests
- Use the terms:
  symbolic
  semantic
  behavioral (in the sense that Guilford defines the term)

Intelligence is a component of successful living. One indicator of the difficulty involved in understanding intelligence is the variety of the definitions used in its measurement. Intelligence refers to the ease or difficulty with which people are able to learn various things. On the basis of this working definition, people of high intelligence in a particular function learn new behavior in that area with comparative ease, while people with low intelligence find it difficult to learn the same things. Most people fall somewhere between these extremes. When attempts are made to apply this definition in school situations, problems begin to develop for teachers. The nature of learning is unspecified or assumed, the way in which ease or difficulty can be determined is not made clear, and the meaninig of "various things" is indeterminate. This definition would be more respectable if it were based on a solid theoretical concept of intelligence, and it would be more acceptable to many psychologists if it were stated in behavioral terms that were subject to precise measurement. More precise definitions will be considered shortly, but as these definitions become more precise, they tend to exclude important facets of intellectual functioning. Even a casual perusal of the above definition indicates a relationship between a theory of intelligence and an assumption of a theory of learning on which it is based. An examination of the meaning of intelligence in the context of the learning-motivation model may help to clarify the relationship between learning and intelligence.

The first level of learning has been presented as one of associations in which neural chains are formed within various areas of the brain and linked together (Chapter 2). Associations may include visual, auditory, speech, and tactile components. These chains or circuits may be extremely complex, but are thought to depend upon systematic connections made by the learner. Whether this described the exact nature of the association process or not is immaterial to this argument. In some way, associations are made that link the sight of an apple with the sound of the word "apple," the feeling of firmness, and the odor as the apple is bitten. The person who makes this linkage easily and who thus can learn several of these connections at the same time is more intelligent than the person who can manage only one or two connections. If greater ease of learning is due, in fact, to a lower firing potential in the individual neurons, then a low potential makes for brightness and a high potential for dullness (Chapter 9). If the ease of forming connections is due to the bridging and debridging facility at the synapses and if this facility is based on the comparative levels of production and excretion of acetylcholine and cholinesterase, then the enzyme balance that forms the bridges most effectively is associated with high intelligence, and the condition that makes bridging difficult is associated with lower intelligence (Rosenzweig, Krech, & Bennett, 1961). If the stabilization of the circuits is due to a surface-positive pulsing current on the cortex, the mechanism that produces such a current is a factor in high intelligence, and the mechanism that produces a surface-negative potential is a factor in low intelligence (Albert, 1966b). When the learning is easy and rapid, the intelligence is higher than when it is difficult and slow.

The second, or conceptualization, level of learning has been presented as consisting in the grasping of inherent relations or the structuring of associations into interlocking patterns. If these structures are formed by the linkage of separate circuits into grids, the smaller the number of circuits required to form a grid, the more intelligent the functioning of the student at the second level (Chapter 6). Similarly, the greater the ease with which the linkages can take place, the greater the intelligence. In this same vein, the less the student needs complete contiguity in space and time in order to grasp the relationships, the higher his intelligence. As discussed in Chapter 6, Congo, the ape, had to have the hoe, the sewer pipe, and himself in a line of vision before he could grasp the relationship (Yerkes, 1928). A comparatively young child can hold one or more elements in memory and still grasp a similar relationship, and therefore he functions more effectively at level 2 than the ape. Newton carried many elements in suspension before he grasped their relationship as a gravitational law. He was brighter and more intelligent than the young child, who must have closer contiguity in space and time to conceptualize.

Level 3 learning has been presented as a fusion of motivation and cognitive structures to produce creative self-direction (Chapter 8). Those who are most effective in functioning as creators or as motivated self-starters are more intelligent at this level than less able individuals who generate new ideas with difficulty or depend on external stimulation for their energy. If the energy necessary for self-directing activities comes from the efficient interpretation of pleasure or punishment connections—positive or negative reinforcing effects—whatever leads to simpler or more direct connections and interpretations will increase level 3 intelligence, and whatever confuses this interpretation will decrease this aspect of intelligence. In the same way, if creativity or production of new knowledge depends on an accumulation of small changes in reverberatory circuits, whatever leads to systematic modification will increase the creative aspect of level 3 intelligence. Whatever tends toward routinized, inflexible patterns of circuits will produce a lower level of this aspect of intelligence. An understanding of the exact nature of the neural connections is not essential to an appreciation of the validity of the illustration. Whatever neurological substructure facilitates learning at the different levels increases intelligence, and whatever inhibits learning decreases it.

The definitions of intelligence discussed in the following sections are representative of the varied conceptualizations one finds among experts on human learning ability. Measures of intelligence need to be interpreted according to the particular author's concept of the nature of intelligence.

## DEFINITIONS OF INTELLIGENCE

### Thorndike's Definition

Edward L. Thorndike, the founder of educational psychology, wrote extensively on its many phases (Chapter 4). Thorndike defined intelligence as the power to make good responses from the point of view of truth or fact (1913). The intelligent person is the one who is able to come up with the right answers to difficult problems. The answers may not be popular—sometimes the truth hurts—but a long view in history eventually vindicates the point taken. Occasionally the right answers lead to eminence during the intelligent person's lifetime.

Thorndike believed there were three different kinds of intelligence: the abstract, the mechanical, and the social. These kinds of intelligence are neither mutually exclusive nor necessarily correlated in an individual. Personal experience indicates, as Thorndike points out, that it is quite possible to find a select group of people who are very adept at dealing with abstract ideas. Any reasonably selective university is populated with people high in this kind of intelligence. There are many gradations within these people's abilities, so that some seem even brighter than others, and some may seem brighter than all the rest put together. However, as a group, university professors and students are well above average in their ability to deal with symbolic and verbal ideas.

Within the highly selective university community are individuals who are as adept in mechanical intelligence as they are in abstract ability. However, within this highly selective community there are also mechanical morons, as well as people with all the possible gradations of this type of intelligence. In the same university community there are social geniuses who are able to manage the right social response at the critical time, but within the group of those gifted in abstract intelligence are many who might be classed as social morons. Sometimes it may seem as though an inverse correlation exists between abstract intelligence and social skill, although this is not true. In a similar way, if people were grouped into a community that selected them because of their mechanical intelligence, so that only the mechanically gifted were included, some of the group would be abstractly intelligent and some would not, and some would be socially intelligent and some would not.

Occasionally one finds a person who is endowed with great ability in all three areas, and it is also possible to find less fortunate people who seem to be quite devoid of ability in any of the areas. Most people are more or less average, with additional strength in some area and weakness in others.

Thorndike believed that the level of intelligence depended on the number of bonds or nerve connections that had been made. He taught that learning new material was facilitated by being able to use connections that had already been formed. Thus the person who had already built many bonds in the area of mechanical intelligence, for example, would find adding to this skill comparatively easy and would go on adding to the already considerable strength in this facet of his intellect. People who had their original strengths in the abstract or social facets of their intelligence would strengthen these areas in similar ways and for similar reasons.

## Terman's Definition

Lewis M. Terman (1916) developed the popular revision of the Binet-Simon tests for use in America. He defined intelligence as the ability to think in abstract terms. An examination of the Stanford-Binet reveals the emphasis on this particular kind of intelligence. Many of Terman's later studies were related to his monumental work—a five-volume series that spanned 35 years—on the characteristics and the teaching of the intellectually gifted (1925, 1926, 1930, 1947, 1959). The importance of the ability to think in abstract or nonconcrete terms is paramount in Terman.

## Henmon's Definition

V. A. C. Henmon, who was one of the authors of the Henmon-Nelson group intelligence test (Henmon & Nelson, 1931), wrote that intelligence involves two factors: the capacity for knowledge and the knowledge possessed. This concept of intelligence had an obvious bearing on the nature of the test he developed. Because of Henmon's attempt to measure "knowledge possessed," some parts of the test look more like an achievement test than an intelligence scale.

## Stoddard's Definition

George D. Stoddard developed an excellent descriptive definition of intelligence that was *operational* in that intellectual behavior was conceived as being demonstrated in the many and varied facets of the person's life. He says (1943):

> Intelligence is the ability to undertake activities that are characterized by difficulty, complexity, and abstractness, and to perform these activities with economy or speed, and with adaptiveness to a goal, so that they show social value, and the emergence of originals or inventiveness, and to maintain these activities under conditions that

demand a concentration of energy and a resistance to emotional forces [p.4].

A closer look at this definition may aid the reader in understanding intelligence.

The idea is prevalent that the intelligent person, as contrasted with the less intelligent, is able to do difficult mental tasks that are complex and abstract. Most people reach a point beyond which ideas become too complicated; they are not able to think past a certain level. A fact that may not be obvious to many is that extremely bright individuals can manipulate ideas that are abstract, complex, and difficult, and they can do so quickly, with little wasted effort. The intelligent person gets through more work with less effort and in less time than a dull person. Some college students seem to be able to read an article once and have a better grasp of it than others who read it several times, outline it, and study the outline.

To include social values in a definition of intelligence may bother some readers. Consider, however, an intelligent criminal who operates in reverse as far as generating social values is concerned—he actually destroys the competences on which living depends. Such a person, by his activities, shows himself to be less intelligent than he would be if he had a better social orientation. Either he spends a considerable amount of time in jail or in the law courts or expends much of his talent in efforts to avoid being caught. Insofar as he uses his time in a wasteful fashion he is functioning on the level of a less able person. With a more benign attitude toward society and its mores, he could have functioned more efficiently, that is, more intelligently.

The ability to develop original ideas or to be inventive is a facet of intelligence that is generally accepted in principle. Great store is placed on this creative ability by the general populace. Einstein, Newton, and Madame Curie are thought of as intelligent people because they were able to see reality in new ways. The ability to carry on activities under conditions that demand a concentration of energy and a resistance to emotional forces may not be as immediately apparent in the innovator. Young children are thought to display the opposite characteristics. They are easily distracted, have a short attention span (unless it involves watching television), and generally do not work for sustained periods of time. Children vary in these characteristics, the bright children having greater powers of concentration than their duller companions. The reader may wish to try Stoddard's definition on himself and note his own areas of strength and weakness.

### Stephens' Definition

J. M. Stephens' (1952) approach to defining intelligence is different from the descriptive technique that has been followed to this point. He says that intelligence is whatever the intelligence tests measure. At first glance this seems an odious way to define intelligence. Stephens, however, points out that very little is known about the nature of electricity but that this does not prevent its use. The definitions that are related to electricity are in terms of the ways in which it can be measured. For instance, the international ohm is defined as the resistance offered to an unvarying current by a column of mercury at 0°C, 14.4521 grams in mass, of constant cross-sectional area, and 106.300 centimeters in length. This definition does not describe an ohm very well. A person has no feeling for an ohm after reading the definition, but ohms have the advantages of being measurable and of being constant from one sample to the next. In the same way, according to Stephens, teachers would be better off if the definition of intelligence were pinned down to whatever the tests measure. A substantial number of studies have been made to discover precisely what it is the tests are measuring in the expectation that this knowledge will be useful to teachers. Most of these studies have been carried out by a technique called *factor analysis*.

## ANALYSIS OF WHAT TESTS MEASURE

The process of analyzing intelligence is somewhat formidable. Each subtest must be compared with each other subtest to determine which are measuring the same things. The computer has made this kind of comparison very much simpler, although factor analysis is still a complex process. In essence, the methodology is to give a number of different tests to the same group of examinees. After some data have been collected, an intercorrelation matrix is computed in which each subtest is compared with each other subtest to see how much correlation or relationship there is between each of the pairs. The factor analysis consists of treating this information statistically to see how many different discrete groupings are necessary in order to accommodate all the items in the smallest number of dimensions. The process of breaking the measures within a test battery into the factors is somewhat like taking a complex number and breaking it into the prime numbers from which it has been composed. For instance, if the number 75,600 is factored, it becomes 2/2/2/ 2/3/3/3/5/5/7. The prime numbers can be gathered into piles with four 2s, three 3s, two 5s, and one 7 in separated piles. One of the important points about factor analysis is that one gets out of the factoring only what has been included in the original input, although unexpected patterns or combinations of test variables may arise. The analogy to factoring numbers is clear. In the 75,600, no 11, 13, 17, 19, or 23 is found, but this does not mean that no such numbers exist. This principle also obtains with regard to factoring tests, although the volume and difficulty of the work required to make the analysis tend to obscure this fundamental point.

### Spearman

Charles Spearman, a British psychologist, came to the conclusion that intelligence was composed of a *G* (general intellectual ability) factor and a large number of *s* (specific intellectual ability) factors (1927). Later he amended his position to include group factors that resulted from overlapped specific factors. He was one of the first to use factor analysis and developed what is called the *tetrad equation*. In this approach, the intercorrelations between four tests give three tetrad equations, which when equal to zero indicate that the intercorrelations are due to a common factor. The battery of tests is analyzed by keeping two anchor tests and adding two new tests at a time. Low intercorrelations are assumed to be due to specifics and sampling errors. This approach puts the primary emphasis on the discovery of the general factor. Applying this principle in the school situation, a student who learned a subject easily would be equally capable in all subjects, and a student who could not learn algebra would probably be slow in all areas.

On the basis of these studies. Spearman proposed the thesis that the most important part of intelligence was the *G* factor. A bright person would be generally bright in all directions, and a dull person would be dull in many ways. There were specific areas in which this formulation did not hold, but Spearman considered these variations comparatively unimportant. He continued to refine his techniques of analysis and gradually found more and more overlapping among specific factors that could not be attributed to the general factor; that is, they were not highly correlated with the *G* factor in many individuals. These group factors were identified as verbal ability, numerical ability, mechanical ability, attention, and imagination.

Bischof (1954) depicted the evolution of Spearman's ideas in two illustrations (Figure 15-1). In the first, the *G* factor has three specific factors emerging from the *G* ($s_1$, $s_2$, $s_3$). The amount of commonality is roughly represented by the shaded area that is common to the specific and the general. The later Spearman position shows additional factors in which $s_4$ and $s_5$ have been added with overlapping between them in both the *G* area and the non-*G* realm (Figure 15-2). The overlapping in the non-*G* area became the "group" factor.

Spearman's work has influenced British psychology much more than American psychology, which has been dominated by the factorial approaches of Kelley, the Thurstones, and later Guilford. Although Kelley predated the Thurstones by roughly a decade and generally came to many of the same conclusions by quite similar methods, the Thurstones' work, which was translated into intelligence tests, will be presented to cover both positions.

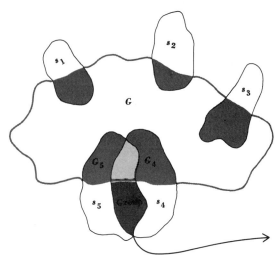

**Figure 15-2** Spearman's two-factor theory, according to which intelligence consists of a general capacity factor (*G*), specific factors ($s_1$, $s_2$, $s_3$, $s_4$, $s_5$), and group factors (shown as exterior overlay $s_4$ and $s_5$). (*Redrawn with permission of the publisher from Intelligence by L. J. Bischof, p. 9. Copyright, 1954 by Random House.*)

## L. L. Thurstone and Thelma Gwinn Thurstone

The Thurstones developed the centroid method of factor analysis, which made it possible to analyze the intercorrelations within a large group of subtests in one operation. In one analysis, they used 56 subtests, and in another 60. It would be a more formidable job to analyze such a mass of material by the tetrad method than by the centroid approach. The correlations can be depicted graphically (Figure 15-3) in terms of the angles separating vectors that represent tests. These vectors are plotted with reference to pairs of perpendicular (centroid) axes in a plane much as the *x* and *y* are portrayed as reference dimensions in the geometric representation of a linear two-variable equation in algebra. The patterns the vectors describe are the ways in which certain

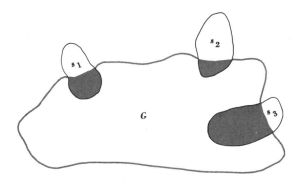

**Figure 15-1** Spearman's two-factor theory (*Redrawn with permission of the publisher from Intelligence by L. J. Bischof, p. 7. Copyright, 1954 by Random House.*)

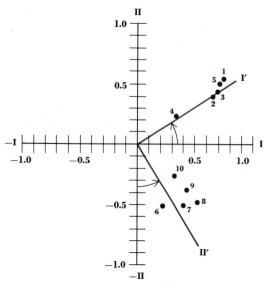

**Figure 15-3** A hypothetical factor pattern, showing weights of two group factors in each of ten tests. (*From Anne Anastasi, Psychological testing, New York: Macmillan , 1954, p 355. By permission of the publishers.*)

subtests are related to one another and different from others, which in turn may cluster together in one or more other groups. The effect of this kind of analysis is to emphasize the separations between groups of subtests rather than to focus, as the tetrad approach does, on the commonalities of the tests. By examining the content of tests that make up a cluster (factor) and by noting ways in which the content of tests not involved in the cluster differs, one can make inferences concerning the psychological nature of the factor. It should be noted that there are residual bits of information that do not quite fit under either system. Ordinarily this leftover material is interpreted as being due to sampling error. A judgment also has to be made as to the point of deviation that means a subtest is or is not to be included within a group of factors. The

graphical representation makes the decision making more obvious than the numerical symbolism does. Thurstone (1947) described factor analysis as a preliminary means of bringing order out of an unordered complex so that hypotheses might be developed and tested on the basis of the preliminary findings of the factor analysis.

The analysis of 56 tests given to 218 University of Chicago students led to tentative findings about the factors contained in the different tests. Checks were run on several of these factors using several samples of high school students. In a second study, 710 eighth-grade students were given 60 tests, and the results were analyzed. Twenty-one of the tests were selected to form a battery for use with a second sample of 437 eighth-grade students, after which the results were again subjected to analysis. As a result of these investigations, Thurstone concluded that intelligence consisted of seven "primary mental abilities": number ability, word-fluency ability, verbal-meaning ability, associative-memory ability, reasoning ability, space ability, and perceptual-speed ability. All these abilities were modestly correlated with one another and with the total battery. Bischof (1954) illustrated the correlations of these factors with one another and with the total test performance, although he did not include any coefficients of correlation for perceptual-speed ability (Figure 15-4).

The correlation of reasoning ability with the total score of which it is a part is .84, which is very high, and the correlations of reasoning ability with number and verbal-meaning abilities are both .54, which is somewhat high. Generally the correlations of space ability with the other factors are low. Of course if the primary mental abilities were pure factors measuring different psychological functions, the interfactor correlations would be close to .00. The implication is that these primary

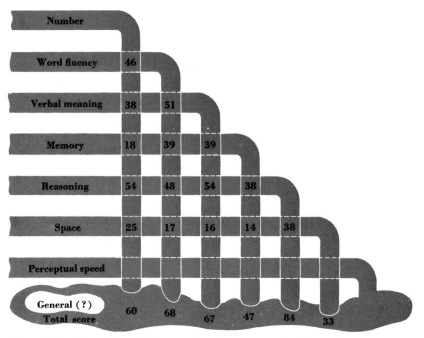

**Figure 15-4** Correlation of Thurstone's primary mental abilities with each other and with total scores (*Redrawn with permission of the publisher from Intelligence by L. J. Bischof, p. 14. Copyright 1954 by Random House.*)

mental abilities are complexes that might be further broken down and might have a common loading that gives the high correlations.

A look at the different primary mental abilities and the kind of test in which they are located may be informative concerning the nature of the separate abilities and the possible ways in which they may be similar in content:

*Number* ability appears to be primarily a factor of speed and accuracy in routine arithmetic computation such as addition and multiplication.

*Word-fluency* ability is demonstrated in the speed with which a person can give words of certain characteristics. The fast radio announcer, the hack writer, and the auctioneer display this kind of ability. It shows up in tests involving anagrams, rhyming, giving words that begin with a certain letter, and like activities.

*Verbal-meaning* ability has been described as the principal characteristic of the ability to function in a setting of higher education. Tests involving vocabulary, verbal analogies, disarranged sentences, and matching proverbs for similar meanings are highly loaded with verbal meaning.

*Associative-memory* ability has been described as the ability to have details stick in the memory. It involves the ability to remember birthdates and addresses, as well as historical facts. In Thurstone's work there appear to be many different memory factors, although this one is most clearly delineated.

*Reasoning* ability is highly associated with the total score on the test battery and also seems to be a common factor in most of the subfactors since it is highly correlated with all the abilities except space ability. The tests most commonly used to identify reasoning ability are arithmetic-reasoning and series-completion tests.

*Space* ability is particularly important to sheetmetal workers, architects, tool and die makers, and others who need to translate two-dimensional drawings into objects in space. Tests such as the Minnesota Paper Form Board or variations seem to be the most common way of measuring this ability.

*Perceptual-speed* ability is important to proofreaders, account checkers, and those who must spot deviations from a model. The most common tests of this ability are those in which lists of names or numbers that are the same or nearly the same are set up in pairs. The test involves spotting those which are not the same in the shortest possible time.

The Thurstones constructed the Primary Mental Abilities (PMA) tests on the basis of their previous factor-analysis work. The first edition of this battery contained three tests for each factor, and the series required six hours to administer. Two years later, the test was shortened in two ways: (1) Only two tests were given for each factor, and (2) the tests themselves were reduced in length so that the battery could be administered in two hours. School test administrators found two hours more onerous than valuable, and the battery was again shortened by reducing the number of tests for each factor to one, eliminating the test for memory, and shortening the individual tests so that the whole battery could be administered in one regular 50-minute class period. Forms of the test were provided for ages

seven to eleven and also for ages five to seven. Publicity for the tests in the shortened form suggested their value for counseling students into the areas of their greatest strength in order to maximize these strengths and minimize weaknesses. Anastasi (1954) pointed to two difficulties in using the tests in this way. The intercorrelations between the factors are relatively high, indicating unreliable separations between the factors; also, the reliabilities found on independent research were about .72 to .75, which is too low for these tests to be used as a basis for individual advising. (See Figure 15-4.)

Wilson and Stier (1962) made a longitudinal study involving a sample of 700 students who were administered the PMA test at the beginning of third grade and again at the end of sixth grade. They found an average variation of 15 IQ points on each factor from one testing to another, although the mean total scores for the total group moved only 2 points. The IQ ratings of some of the students changed greatly on individual factors, going from 85 to as much as 135. Such a variation means that a particular student's rating on a particular factor went from dull to gifted. The large variability in factor scores over $3\frac{1}{2}$ years emphasizes the unsuitability of this test for differential teaching between the ages involved in this research project.

## Wechsler's Verbal and Performance Scales

The subtests of the Wechsler Intelligence Scale for Children (WISC) are stable enough to make differential diagnosis of reading problems possible (Robeck, 1960, 1964, 1971). Although Wechsler did not develop his tests on the basis of factor analysis, Cohen (1959) found the WISC subtest to be separated into four factors. Wechsler (1944) specifically disavows the idea that intelligence is whatever the intelligence tests measure when he says,

"Intelligence is the aggregate or global capacity of the individual to act purposefully, to think rationally and to deal effectively with his environment" [p.3]. He goes on to explain that intelligence is global since it characterizes the totality of the person's behavior. Wechsler uses the word "aggregate" in the sense that it is used in classifying a rock that is composed of rock fragments of different sizes and shapes. In Wechsler's view, the individual's drive and persistence are as much a part of his intelligence as his retentive memory or his ability to reason. Intelligence is more than the sum of the parts; it includes the way in which the parts fit together into a mutually supporting whole. The performance items were incorporated into the scales for the purpose of getting at some of the drive mechanisms. In Wechsler's understanding of intelligence, the possibility that a test can get at all the diverse variations of intelligence is very slight. The older a person becomes, the more diverse are the forces that are important in his life and the less likely he is to show his ability on a test. These limitations are minimized by providing a battery of test items, by ensuring that the items are likely to seem sensible to an adult, and by giving weightings to results that reflect changing abilities.

### Guilford: 120 Factors

J. P. Guilford has almost certainly provided the most complete factorial approach to understanding the intellect available at this time. He organized all the factors that had been discovered up until 1954, some 40 in number, into a pattern involving *contents, operations,* and *products* of thought. As a result of his ordering, he came to the conclusion that there were some 120 possible ways of being intelligent. Many of the missing factors have been located since he first proposed this hypothetical structure. After a consideration of the

effect that different definitions of intelligence have on intelligence ratings, Guilford's findings will be discussed in detail in a subsequent section.

### DEFINITIONS OF INTELLIGENCE INFLUENCE TEST CONTENT

J. A. R. Wilson (1959), working with low-achieving eighth-grade gifted students, found considerable variability in their test scores, depending on the intelligence test used for measurement. Tom, who showed the greatest variability in a group of 20, had the second highest score on one test of intelligence and the second lowest on another. Both were widely used and well-respected tests for measuring scholastic aptitude. His high test score was 140, and his low score 105. Two counselors, each of whom had only one of these scores available to him, would counsel Tom very differently. The counselor who had only the high score available to him might, on the basis of Tom's ability, respond positively to the idea of his attending a school such as the California Institute of Technology, which is highly selective and has high performance requirements. However, the counselor who had only the low score, with supporting evidence from the same family of tests, as evidence of Tom's intellectual capacity would recommend a less demanding institution, if higher education was being seriously considered at all. This counselor would want to help him find an institution that emphasized efforts rather than ability.

Tom was given the WISC including two alternative subtests. He obtained a score of 127 for the total test, but the important finding was the large variability of some of the subtests. In two of them he had scores that could be extrapolated to an IQ of 82 and 85. An examination of the content of the group tests indicated that the one on which Tom had done badly had many items that tested the same factors as the subtests on the WISC on which he had done poorly. The other tests drew almost no items from these factors. About one-third of the group of 20 students had similar irregular profiles on the WISC with less pronounced variability in the total scores on the group tests they had been given. Further research is needed into the relationship between irregular ability profiles and classification as gifted nonachievers. Teachers need to be aware of the possible variability of recorded scores for IQ, which may be artifacts of the test maker's conception of the nature of intelligence.

### Henmon and Terman: A Contrast

Henmon defined intelligence as being composed of the capacity for knowledge and the knowledge possessed, whereas Terman defined it as the ability to think in abstract terms. An examination of the tests composed by the two men indicates the variation that would be expected from this difference in their definitions. Many of the questions on the Henmon-Nelson test (1931) involve primarily achievement test materials, such as arithmetic computation, information about such things as family relations, and other similar knowledge that he assumed is picked up in the course of living. The Terman test stresses abstract thinking to a greater extent. The sets of questions for eight-year-olds cover vocabulary, defining abstract words, analogies, tracing the search for a hypothetical lost ball in a square, and counting backward (Terman, 1916). Although the general ability that both tests seek to determine is such that most people who have learned the material covered in one set of tests will be able to reason equally well about the material covered in the other, individuals are still likely to vary to a substantial

degree in the success they have on one test or the other. It is not necessarily that one test is right and the other wrong, but that they are designed to measure different behavior and different facets of intelligence, and thus a person could reasonably be expected to score differently on them.

### Thorndike and Thurstone: A Contrast

The Thorndike and Thurstone tests have subsections with similar names, and superficially they might be assumed to be measuring the same kind of intelligence. Examination of the contents of the tests, however, indicates that they are tapping different abilities. Teachers need to study the tests that are administered to their students in order to know what abilities are being sampled.

The intelligence test with which Thorndike is most commonly associated is the CAVD (Completion, Arithmetic, Vocabulary, Direction), which is a test of abstract reasoning and does not touch the social or mechanical aspects of intelligence. Thurstone was involved in making other tests besides the PMA tests, most notably the Scholastic Aptitude Tests (SAT) of the College Entrance Examination, which give verbal and numerical factors as well as a total score. However, the PMA tests most clearly reflect the factor-analysis imprint of his work.

The first part of the CAVD requires sentence completion. The second, arithmetic, is heavily loaded with arithmetic reasoning and numerical relationships. The third is a traditional vocabulary recognition test, and the fourth tests understanding of sentences and paragraphs, which is the kind of understanding commonly measured in reading achievement tests. The CAVD was published in 17 levels, ranging in difficulty from the level at which half the three-year-old group passed half the items through a top form on which half the items would be passed by 20 percent of college graduates.

The Science Research Associates PMA tests for high school age consist of a page of simple addition to cover number, a vocabulary test to cover verbal meanings, a choice of four shapes to complete a figure to cover space, writing as many words beginning with "s" as possible in one minute to cover verbal fluency, and a test of similarities to cover the reasoning factor. The number test on the PMA and the arithmetic test on the CAVD are sampling quite different kinds of thought processes. The vocabulary tests are similar in function on the two tests. None of the parts of the CAVD taps the same factors as the verbal fluency or the space. The sentence completion and the reasoning seem to be testing similar abilities, at least partially. Finally, there is no part of the PMA that taps the abilities in the understanding of directions in sentences and paragraphs. Under the circumstances, a comparison of the two sets of tests leads to the conclusion that comparability of scores on the two batteries would be only moderately better than chance (Figure 15-5). The sections on arithmetic and number are particularly noteworthy since the labels would tend to indicate that the tests were similar, although very different abilities are being investigated. Names do not always convey the intellectual ability being measured.

## Binet and WISC: A Contrast

California Project Talent evaluated several educational programs for intellectually gifted children (Robeck, 1968a, 1968b). One of these programs, for fifth- and sixth-grade children, was located in a university community. A high percentage of highly verbal youngsters were identified, nearly all of whom were from cul-

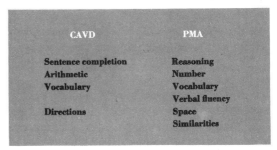

| CAVD | PMA |
| --- | --- |
| Sentence completion | Reasoning |
| Arithmetic | Number |
| Vocabulary | Vocabulary |
| | Verbal fluency |
| Directions | Space |
| | Similarities |

**Figure 15-5** Comparison of the CAVD and the PMA tests.

turally rich, verbal homes. Over a period of several years, the school psychologist observed that verbally skilled youngsters were not necessarily superior in all intellectual tasks. In order adequately to distinguish children who needed a special educational program, the psychologist for this project gave the WISC and required high scores (130+) on both the *performance* and the *verbal* scales. In work with less privileged children—particularly the culturally deprived—a high verbal score was needed to identify the child who could survive in a special class for gifted children. In order to get a high score on the Stanford-Binet Revised Intelligence Scales, a child must be able to manipulate concepts and words well, which favors children from verbal homes. Youngsters with perceptual handicaps or those who had motor difficulties often did better on the Binet than on the WISC, which tends to penalize for these handicaps while testing for energy output.

The observation of gifted high-achievers indicated two groups of talented or creative children—those creative in humanistic endeavors and those creative in science and mathematics. By the middle grades, the former are already distinctive in their compositions, drawings, paintings, and creative drama, while the latter are showing their creativity in testing scientific hypotheses and solving mathematical puzzles. In special programs with "true peers," talented children became more open in talking, sharing, and encountering other people's ideas. At the lower age levels, neither the WISC nor the Binet test measures adequately the mathematical or quantitative reasoning of highly intelligent youngsters. Also, some children who were openly creative gave unconventional responses and depressed their potential scores in this way.

### Implications for Teachers

The differences in the concepts of the test makers regarding the nature of intelligence have influenced the kinds of items selected for the tests. When using IQ scores to appraise an individual's ability, more than one score is desirable. Although nearly all these tests are standardized to have a mean of approximately 100 and so would appear to be equivalent, they have different emphases. Different students with different intellectual strengths may seem especially capable or especially incapable on one test but not on another. Intelligence is a complex phenomenon, from which most of the tests take comparatively small samples, which leads to variation in results. A particular test may predict student performance for a particular classroom situation, but not for another. In general, the tests that are semantically oriented—that put a premium on vocabulary, memory, and sentence interpretation—tend to predict success in the humanities and social sciences well. On the other hand, tests that stress structure and symbolism tend to be most efficient in selecting students who will do well in the fields of mathematics and science, where convergent intellectual production is of primary importance. The net effect of these implications is that teachers should not take recorded scores at face value, but should look behind the scores to the significance they have for particular pupils in particular courses.

## GUILFORD'S MODEL OF INTELLECT

The studies in factor analysis of intelligence traits, started by Thurstone, were carried on by others, who located a number of other identifiable factors. Much of this work has been done under contracts with the armed services in the expectation that understanding of human abilities would be improved, the various abilities would be strengthened, and thus the various talents possessed by individuals could be used to better advantage by both the service and the men themselves. J. P. Guilford, at the University of Southern California, was one of the leaders in this field of investigation. His primary contracts were with the Air Force and have been part of the overall search for ways of identifying young officers who have special leadership talents needed for difficult assignments. The nature of the contracts sometimes made the investigation of some aspects of ability more urgent than others. For this reason, some facets of intelligence have been more thoroughly studied than other components.

Guilford (1956) arrived at his conceptualization of the nature of the intellect as he was preparing an address for the semicentennial of Binet's work. He had been asked to present a paper on the results of factor analysis in intelligence testing to a Paris gathering of psychologists. From his description of the events leading up to his first formulation of his model of intellect, the result seems to have been a classic example of a conceptualization. He had been working over the approximately 40 factors that had already been discovered to bring some order out of the variety within the factors themselves. Finally he saw a way in which all the pieces might fit together into a rather simple pattern. To some extent, his ordering was a little like Mendelejeff's original work on the periodic table, although in Guilford's case the model was in three dimensions (Figure 15-6). The address in Paris was a success, marking a new milestone in the understanding of the nature of the intellect.

Guilford and his associates went on to investigate the possible existence of factors which should have fit into specific locations in the model but which had not as yet been identified. New tests have been developed to probe abilities that the model indicated should exist. These were put into a factor-analysis matrix into which were also placed tests with known loadings. These tests provided reference points against which to check the analysis of the new tests. In this work, the model provided a theoretical framework for the analysis, and the results, as they emerged, strengthened the model. As in the original periodic table, there were more holes than filled-in spaces, but also, as in the case of the table, each time a space was filled, using the chart as a guide, the value and worth of the model became a little surer and a little stronger. The framework becomes more secure and trustworthy with each conformation of a projected ability. Guilford's exploration had to be fitted into the pattern of the research that was being financed, so some areas have been easier to explore than others. Some factors seem to be more germane to the search for ways to identify potentially able leaders than others do.

Guilford's model, structure of intellect (1967), gives three major dimensions to the intellect. Each of these major dimensions is composed of subdivisions, giving a possible 120 factors ($4 \times 5 \times 6$) when all the combinations are made. The major dimensions are (1) the contents or materials of thought; (2) the kind of functions, operations, or processes involved in thought; and (3) the products of

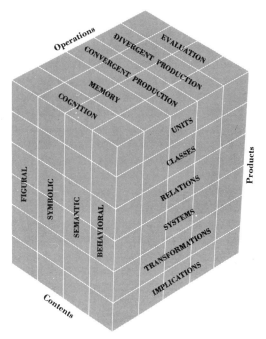

**Figure 15-6** Theoretical model for the complete structure of intellect. Redrawn from J. P. Guilford, *The nature of human intelligence*, p. 63. New York, McGraw-Hill, 1967. By permission of the publishers.

the operations on the contents of thought. Careful examination of each of these subdivisions is necessary for a thorough understanding of Guilford's model.

### Contents of Thought

Guilford (1967) has compared this major dimension of the intellect with Thorndike's subdivision into abstract, mechanical, and social intelligence. Factor analysis has confirmed the existence of true separations of this type involving the kinds of materials or *contents* by means of which people think. Guilford identified four major subdivisions rather than the three that Thorndike had hypothesized. There are differences between Guilford's subdivisions and those described by Thorndike, but on the whole they fit together quite well. Thorndike's mechanical content is now called the *figural;* his abstract dimension is divided into *symbolic* and *semantic* content; and the social category becomes a broader *behavioral* material of thought, which Guilford has also called *empathic.*

**Figural**   This content has to do with the way people think in terms of concrete, tangible, real things. Abilities in this area are manifested differently by different people. Some, hearing a motor hum and falter, are able to visualize the parts interacting and the cause of the falter; they can reach into the engine and make a small change, and the falter ceases. Another person can look at a block of marble and see within it a statue so completely formed that all he has to do is chip away the excess marble. Still another is able to see a new sweater in some skeins of yarn or a new dress in a piece of cloth. Some field commanders, by observing the terrain and their men, see the possibilities of tactical assault. There are hundreds of manifestations of such thinking, but they all relate to the concrete, real materials with which the thought is concerned. People perform many different operations of thought and evolve different kinds of products when they use figural materials of thought. The range of competence in using figural materials stretches all the way from those who seem to have almost no skill to those who are geniuses.

**Symbolic**   Some people who think clearly and precisely in figural terms have great difficulty thinking in highly symbolic terms. Symbolic content involves material in the form of signs that have no significance in and of themselves, such as letters, numerals, musical notations, chemical symbols, and other code elements. Probably symbolic thinking involves the most abstract material of the four possible kinds. Many people slip into thinking of numbers as belonging to the figural category rather than the symbolic, where they certainly belong. The thinking of a field commander in terms of men and terrain was given as an illustration of figural content. Other equally competent commanders may reduce their men to symbols and the terrain to lines on a topographical map, so that they manipulate the different symbols in relation to one another. The symbols have meaning attached to them, but when thought is in symbolic terms, the meaning is removed and the symbols are used as though they were real things. After the operations have been completed, there may be or may not be a translation of the symbols back into the objects for which they stand.

**Semantic**   Guilford found a definite factorial separation between symbolic and semantic materials of thought. Semantic content is material in the form of meanings to which words have commonly become attached, so that semantic content consists largely of verbal thinking and verbal communication. On logical grounds, it is difficult to justify a separation between semantic and symbolic content since they are both abstractions in which symbols are used, but analysis reveals the difference between them. Intelligence tests such as the SAT that give a quantitative and a verbal score usually tap symbolic thinking for the quantitative score and semantic thinking for the verbal score. The number "4" can perhaps be used to illustrate the differences between the figural, semantic, and symbolic materials of thought. In the figural category, 4 is tied to various manipulations of 4 objects, number boards, wheels, or children, for example. At the semantic level, 4 is involved with the meaning of 4 as a set of relations. At the symbolic level, 4 is manipulated as a symbol in computation, with the meaning held in abeyance until it may be needed later.

An illustration from logic may indicate the difference between symbolic and semantic phrasing of an idea. A proposition may be stated as follows: "All S is P. J is S. Therefore, J is P." This is a symbolic statement. One may also write: "All men are mortal. John is a man. Therefore, John is mortal." This is a semantic statement.

**Behavioral**  Originally, Guilford's model consisted of three contents of thought: the figural, the symbolic, and the semantic. The behavioral category was added on logical grounds as the model was compared with Thorndike's kinds of intelligence. Factorial studies have since justified the addition. Behavioral content refers to essentially nonverbal contents that are involved in human interaction or social intercourse. Awareness of the attitudes, needs, desires, moods, intentions, perceptions, and thoughts of other persons and of ourselves makes up the material in this category. In some early writing, Guilford used the term "empathic" to designate this area of functioning. It conveys, perhaps better than the term "behavioral," the sensitivity to others that is basic to this kind of thinking.

### Operations of Thought

A different way of looking at the functioning of the intellect is in terms of the operations of thought. Essentially, the term "operations" refers to the method of treatment or intervening psychological process—what is done—to the materials being thought about. The genesis of these operations in factor analysis should be kept in mind. The separations of the statistical process give clusters of factors, but they do not bring with them names. An examina-

tion of the cluster usually suggests a name —an influence—that is appropriate, but usually other meanings in other contexts have attached themselves to the name selected. The attachment of the name does not bring with it the additional meanings the word carries. For example, Guilford uses the term "evaluation" differently from the way Bloom does and from the way teachers normally do. The five thinking operations Guilford has located are cognition, memory, divergent production, convergent production, and evaluation.

**Cognition**  This is the immediate discovery, awareness, rediscovery, or recognition of information in various forms. Cognition is also comprehension or understanding. Confusion with other operations is quite possible, particularly with production, in which given information is processed, and with memory, in which material is brought out of storage. Figural, symbolic, semantic, and behavioral materials can all be known at the cognition level. A child knows that a ball is round, red, smooth, and slightly soft—a cognition of figural materials. A student can use $H_2O$ in a chemical formula to represent one of the products of the interaction of a base and an acid. Semantically, he knows that water is made up of two atoms of hydrogen and one of oxygen, that it is a liquid, that the oxygen and the hydrogen are joined in some vague way (the cognition is not very good here), and that it is good for washing, drinking, and hosing the garden. These are all cognitions of semantic material. The same student is aware that if he insults another person, the result will be hurt feelings, even though a smile accompanies the response. In the same way, he senses that he is disliked or liked, even though he may have no conscious explanation for the liking or the disliking. Cognition is the base from which other operations develop.

**Memory** This is the process of retention or storage, with some degree of availability, of information in the same form in which it was committed to storage. Recall from storage is in response to the same or similar cues that were available when storage took place. Memory is for material that has already been cognized, evaluated, or produced. Some 24 different specific kinds of memory exist, including memory for figural, symbolic, semantic, and behavioral materials.

**Divergent Production** Information available from cognition is transformed, combined, and treated to produce *new information.* In divergent thinking the production is diverse, new, novel, or original. This is production of many possible combinations. There are many possible solutions to the problem posed, and usually many different ways in which it can be solved. Many answers are wanted or needed, although they must meet certain requirements. Given the facts that China is a Communist country oriented to the idea of world revolution and that it has developed atomic devices and at least preliminary rockets for delivery, what should America's policy be toward China? This question should lead to divergent thinking, and it has probably occupied some of the best brains available to Washington. There is no clear-cut answer to the problem. The answers are incommensurable. Creative producers in the humanities are primarily people who use divergent thinking. Schools can help promote divergent thinking, but the process is difficult because evaluation of the student's work is difficult and sometimes may be unfair.

**Convergent Production** Generating new information from given information is also the characteristic of convergent thinking. The problem focuses on the production of an answer that is determinate or is desired by another, as in the instance of making the correct choices on a multiple-choice test. In social behavior, a conforming response to social expectations represents convergent thinking. However, the answer may not have been available when the question was asked. Einstein's theory of relativity is a very advanced example of convergent thinking. A large part of the creative production in science, mathematics, and engineering is convergent production. Evaluation of this kind of productive thinking is much easier than evaluation of divergent thinking. Even when the thinking is completely new, the step-by-step process can be followed and evaluated on logical grounds.

**Evaluation** This is the process by which decisions or judgments are made concerning the goodness, suitability, adequacy, or success of information in terms of identity, consistency, and goal satisfactions. Evaluation is made as to whether convergent production has met the specified criteria, whether the information retrieved from memory is correct or complete, and whether divergent or convergent production is the best approach to a problem.

**Interactions within Operations** The operations of thought do not function on a one-at-a-time basis. Interaction occurs during the ongoing process of thinking (Figure 15-7). Evaluation operations interact continually with the other operations. Raw data, from the environment and from the body functions or soma, are processed by cognition, which is evaluated, stored in the memory bank, and transferred to convergent production, or the outcome is added to input from the memory bank and from outside the system, evaluated, and run through further production processes, which are also evaluated, stored, modified, and removed from the system either to the

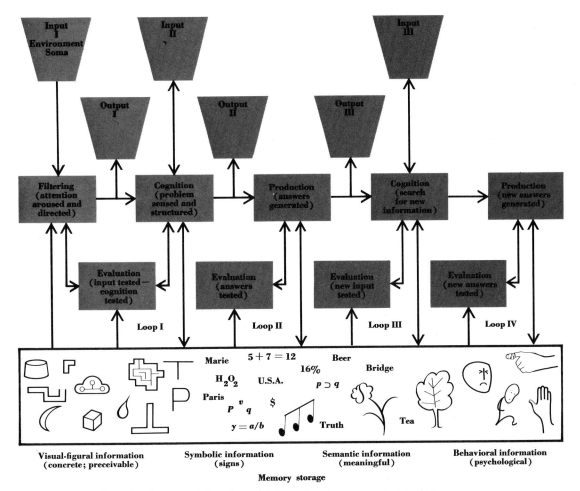

**Figure 15-7** Schematic diagram of the flow of information in a somewhat typical instance of problem solving, from input (from the environment and from soma) to output of accepted information. Redrawn from J. P. Guilford, *The Nature of Human Intelligence*, p. 315. New York, McGraw-Hill, 1967. By permission of the publishers.

memory bank or to external output. One difficulty in analyzing the nature of the operations is the change in the process that occurs as the information is handled by the system. Convergent production will probably be retrievable from memory storage after repeated experiences in which the same material is incorporated into a system.

**Products of Thought**

The third dimension of the model structure of intellect is the products, or the forms that information takes in the organism's processing of it. The various forms the products may take are units or elements, classes, relations, systems, transformations, and implications.

**Units**  Elements are relatively segregated bits of items of information. Units are products of the interaction between various materials of thought and the different operations. Units can be words, ideas, forms, figures, symbols, bits of verbal comprehension, or feelings. Units are the simplest form that a product may assume.

**Classes**  Originally, classes were thought of as groupings, often set in contrast to something outside the class. For instance, a ball, an orange, a circle, and a bicycle wheel are all round, as contrasted with a checkerboard, a book, an envelope, and a box, all of which are rectangular. Classes were originally assumed to be made up of units. Classes have also been shown to be formed from relations, from systems, and possibly from transformations, implications, and classes. A special relation of similarity is the *sine qua non* of a class. Testing for classes is a very common part of group intelligence tests.

**Relations**  Relations exist between units, but there may be similar interaction between classes, or between transformations. An example of what Guilford means by "relations" is seen in the demand to produce the word that is the opposite of high, or flat, or ephemeral, or complex. Tests of analogies are tests of relations: "A *hand* is to an *arm* as a *foot* is to a . . . ."

**Systems**  These products involve internally consistent groupings of figural, symbolic, semantic, or behavioral items. The following letter triangle is a system that involves symbolic elements:

```
        -
     d  -
   b e  -
 a c f  ?
```

What is the letter that belongs where the "?" is?

In a test of a subject's understanding of systems, he may be asked to tell what is wrong with a picture in which the wind is blowing the smoke in one direction and the clothes in the opposite direction or in which a tree casts no shadow although other objects cast strong shadows.

**Transformations**  Changes of various kinds, including modification in arrangement, organization, or meaning, are called *transformations*. The similarities test, in which the student is asked to tell in what way an apple and an orange are alike, demonstrates the cognition of semantic transformations. Guilford pointed out that it is only by shifting the meaning of both that the examinee is able to give many responses to such an item. Such transformations often underlie much creative thinking and problem solving.

**Implications**  This type of product requires the individual to go beyond the given information and by extrapolation or interpolation to see certain consequences. As a figural exercise, the person may be presented with a piece of paper showing a small line and asked to elaborate it. The more elaborate the drawing that results, the more implications the individual has seen. According to a technique used to classify items within the total structure, this task would be designated DFI, to mean divergent production of figural implications.

### Implications of Guilford's Model

In defining any particular mental operation, one facet from the contents, one from the operations, and one from the products are needed. Thus there are $4 \times 5 \times 6$, or 120, different ways to be intelligent. According to this model, when all the missing links have been located, there will be 120 different mental abilities. One of the most significant ideas to grow out of the work on the model is the possibility of isolating the particular phase of the intellect that should be improved and then concentrating on this aspect, much in the way Benjamin Franklin sought to eradicate his vices, that is, one at a time.

Think for a moment of trying to improve memory per se, as contrasted with trying to improve memory for figural classes, semantic transformations, or behavioral relations. When the problem is posed in this way, it becomes obvious that success is much more likely when one of these special memories is singled out for attention than when a shotgun approach is used, which hits many memories, with very little force expended to improve any particular one of the 24 different types. When the large function is seen as made up of many small segments, each of which could be improved with practice, the eventual possibility of improving memory as a whole seems rational. The improvements in intelligence related to greater attendance at school are probably due to small advances in each of several different, discrete abilities, so that the cumulative effect is very marked.

One of the principal changes that Guilford foresees as a result of serious consideration of his model is a move away from the conception of the learner as a "stimulus-response mechanism," built more or less on the vending-machine principle, where a coin (stimulus) is inserted, and out comes a package of cigarettes (predetermined response). In his thinking, the model is an agent for dealing with information somewhat as a computer does, which stores the information that is fed into it, uses it to generate new information on either a convergent or a divergent basis, and finally evaluates its own results. Guilford conceives of the student as learning by the discovery of information rather than by the formation of associations.

A renewed interest in creativity, at least partially resulting from Guilford's model of intellect, has resulted in the creation of tests that stress divergent production. A number of these tests were discarded by Terman as he built and revised the Stanford-Binet because they did not show a consistent pattern of increased scores with increased age. One artifact of the removal of these items has been the research finding that students who were judged to be particularly able as creative students were not necessarily equally able when judged by intelligence test scores.

As far as curriculum practices and materials are concerned, any serious consideration of the Guilford model emphasizes the need to assess just what factors of the intellect are being developed by present school practices and, further, whether other factors should be given more attention, thus providing the student with the chance to expand in new and significant ways. Even a very cursory look at the normal school practice of a few years ago indicates that the bulk of the teaching was concentrated in the areas of cognition, memory, convergent production, and evaluation, to the almost complete exclusion of divergent thinking. This has been so because of both the prevalent concepts of learning and the traditional functions of the schools. It may be worthwhile to point out in passing that this statement is even more true of European than of American schools.

Changes are not likely to come about through a reversal of curricular patterns; they are much more likely to develop rather slowly, as teachers—one by one—gradually change their test and examination questions to give their students a greater opportunity to show their own ability in divergent thinking and, in the process, as they develop new ways of presenting materials that will strengthen the possibility that these students will become able to answer the questions. Indeed, changes of this type are already evident in a number of school districts and in the course structures of some university classes.

## RELATIONSHIP OF THE LEARNING-MOTIVATION MODEL TO GUILFORD'S MODEL

The factors of the Guilford model can be explained in terms of the learning-motivation model. Neurologically speaking, cognition of units for figural, symbolic, semantic, and behavioral materials must be very similar processes of association involving different regions of the brain. These association chains must be based on the formation of circuits laid down in nearly the same way for different sensory experiences. The question immediately arises of how there can be gross differences in the strengths and weaknesses of these different areas. The answer seems to lie in the fact that greater interest and greater practice in one of these areas, as compared with the others, have led to the establishment of many more circuits in this area than in the others. The availability of already-established circuits makes possible the establishment of grids, or, in Guilford's terms, makes feasible convergent or divergent thinking in the areas where the greatest concentration of units is stored. The "reward" and "drive" aspects included in the learning-motivation model help to explain the differential strengths that Guilford found in mature learners.

The learning-motivation model is concerned with the process of learning. How are things learned from the beginning? What can the teacher do to facilitate this process? In the structure of intellect, the emphasis is on what has been learned. The teacher needs to know what the strengths and weaknesses are in the various patterns of thinking that have been laid down and how these strengths can be used to the greatest advantage.

Probably memory is a good example of the contrast between the two approaches. In the three levels of learning, the establishment of memory is a concomitant part of each act of learning. Memory is the result of the establishment of neural circuits or grids. If the reverberation persists long enough to establish the circuits or grids, learning is stored. In the Guilford model cognition, memory, convergent production, divergent production, and evaluation are processes of thought, but they are processes for using knowledge rather than the initial acquisition of knowledge. Memory is the retrieval of the knowledge that has been acquired at some earlier time, and what was convergent thinking or conceptualization yesterday will probably turn out to be memory today. Guilford's structure of intellect provides many factors that can be examined and strengthened. The learning-motivation model provides ideas about how the strengthening might be accomplished.

## INTELLIGENCE AND CURRICULUM PLANNING

### Use of Guilford's Model in Writing Objectives

Guilford's structure of intellect model affords a means for developing and stating inferred process objectives that allow for the complexity of cognitive functioning. What the objective constitutes is a statement that the learner *processes* (carries out psychological operations on) *content* (given information) to obtain *products* (new information). These objectives actually reflect the 120 cells in the model. In other words, any one of the five psychological operations, functions, or processes can be permuted with any one of four kinds of contents to yield any one of six types of products.

For example, a traditional multiple-choice vocabulary test involving the pairing of a stimulus word with one of five alternative response words represents the ability to cognize (process) semantic (content) units to yield new products. Thus in the development of word power or vocabulary skills, an objective for the learner could be stated as the "ability to recognize or comprehend (inferred process) the meanings of several familiar words (semantic content involving given information) by identifying or selecting (observable process) an appropriate synonym among a list of alternative words (product units involving new information)." If the task is slightly altered so that the student must generate several synonyms as in an open-ended question involving the filling in of several blanks, one could hypothesize that the objective would be the divergent production of semantic units (a creative task involving word fluency). When extreme restraints are imposed on the task, such as finding a synonym starting with a given letter and having a specified number of letters, the objective could be hypothesized as the convergent production of semantic units.

It should be emphasized that many learning tasks involve the simultaneous use of several abilities and thus reflect the existence of more than one process-oriented objective. Thus it can be expected that complex learning experiences will require several abilities that can be classified in terms of many process objectives derived from Guilford's model. (For evaluation purposes the items of teacher-made tests can be designated to sample these inferred process objectives that have been chosen in curriculum planning.)

In Figure 15-8 the implementation of Guilford's model in the formulation of objectives is set forth. The emphasis is upon the processing of four kinds of content through the use of five different psychological functions to obtain one of six possible types of products. This paradigm could assist curriculum workers in developing objectives, provided that these specialists are thoroughly familiar with Guilford's constructs that are derived from the basic dimensions of contents, operations, and products.

## Basis for Grouping

The preceding sections have emphasized the possible variability of intelligence within one individual and the probability that he will score differently on different tests used to measure brightness. The implication is that scores should be used with caution and in connection with other information when an individual is being considered. Although Wilson and Stier (1962) found great variability in individual subscores on the PMA tests over a

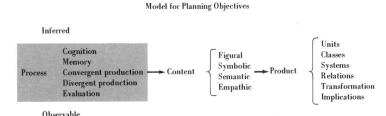

**Model for Planning Objectives**

**Figure 15-8** Paradigm for the formulation of objectives within the framework of Guilford's structure-of-intellect model.

3$\frac{1}{2}$-year period, the group as a whole remained quite stable on total scores over the same period. In schools where classes are selected and grouped on an ability basis, after six years a class with a mean IQ score of 120 points will probably show a 30-point difference, as a group, from another class with a beginning mean IQ score of 90. The level of achievement that can be expected from the two classes is very different and will remain very different.

### Range of Learning Rate within a Class

The separation of classes into bright, average, and dull groups provides an opportunity for the more able groups to move ahead more quickly. The effect of the division on the average students is not so clear-cut. There is some evidence to support the contention that in a class containing students of all levels of ability, the stimulation of the brighter students helps the average to perform at a higher level of competence than they would otherwise be capable of. On the other hand, separation of students into ability groups makes possible the development of special curricular features for both the less able and the more able. The school can thus become better adapted to the strengths and interests of the various groups of students, who may find school more enjoyable as a result. Even after grouping, any class will contain students with a wide range of abilities, on the basis of both a total score and the individual profile. A class of intellectually gifted students typically show an IQ range of 130 to 160 or higher (Barbe, 1959). Any subsequent ability test, especially a different test, will show significant changes in score for about one-third of the individuals in the class.

Differences within individuals—that is, the strengths and weaknesses of a particular learner—are a fact of life in school. Even abilities in all areas of a student's life are the exception. Donald, for example, had a WISC IQ score of 132 and a Binet score of 129. He had particular strengths on the WISC subtests of comprehension, vocabulary, similarities, picture completion, object assembly, block design, and picture arrangement. He was comparatively weak on information, arithmetic, digit span, and coding. In addition, he was weak in auditory perception. With this information, his teacher was able to select appropriate diagnostic materials and plan a teaching sequence that raised his reading level from the 1st to the 50th percentile in seven months.

### Interpersonal and Intrapersonal Differences

Ability grouping enables the teacher to plan a course to suit the students' general level of ability. One of Mr. A.'s high school history classes had a mean IQ of 130. The class as a whole could work on historiography much as university classes do. However, the mean IQ in his third-period class was 90. In order to make history meaningful in the lives of these students, Mr. A.'s emphasis was on a practical, immediate utilization of historical knowledge in day-to-day events. Within each of these groups were individuals who did not fit the class median. Some students had arrived in one class because there was no room in the other class, where they really belonged. Sectioning the students did not eliminate intrapersonal differences, which still required different approaches for different students. However, Mr. A. did not want to abolish ability grouping since he was able to use course content in which most of the students could function most of the time. The adjustments for individual differences were made more easily than would have been the case if the classes had been made up of students of all levels of ability.

## NEURAL EFFICIENCY ANALYZER

An exciting and potentially valuable way of testing mental ability without the use of language has been developed by John Ertl, who was born in Hungary and educated in England and Canada. He once scored 77 on an IQ test when he was a graduate student in psychology. He had a feeling this score was incorrect and has since spent a dozen years developing a better way to measure brain power. Before there were intelligence tests, physiological measures were considered the best indicators; however, it remained impossible to get good measures until after the development of the electroencephalogram (EEG) and a computer which could analyze masses of data efficiently.

Ertl's neural efficiency analyzer works by placing small silver discs on the scalp of the subject with conductive jelly—the same material that is used for a cardiogram or an EEG. The discs are placed on top of the head, one on each side of the midline, and a clip is attached as a ground to the right earlobe. A light flashes on a random basis for 200 times. The spacing averages once per second. The procedure is purely automatic. An operator checks an oscilloscope to make sure the EEG pattern is normal, to indicate that the discs are properly attached, and pushes a button. The machine catches the rhythm of the brain's chemical-electrical firing and flashes a light at the same point in the rhythm of each subject. While the brain processes information, the neural activity is indicated in a series of spikes on the EEG. (In the alpha waves there are no spikes and the brain is at rest). The third and fourth spikes seem to be indicative of conceptual thinking, and so the critical measure is the average time it takes for the subject to generate the third and fourth peaks following each of the 200 flashes of light. These means are calculated by a computer. The shorter the time needed, the more efficiently the brain is functioning (Ertl, 1968).

Correlations with the Wechsler Intelligence Scale for Children, Primary Mental Abilities Test, and Otis IQ Test have been reported. In one sample of 300 children the correlations between IQ and the time required for brain rhythm spikes to form ranged from .28 to .51. When compared with correlations of .67 and .68 for the IQ tests with each other, the new device shows promise of being useful for subjects who do not produce valid scores on traditional IQ tests. The neural analyzer correlates better with IQ measures in the extreme ranges than when most of the sample is average.

The difference in average times required by three subjects of different intellectual abilities for processing the light stimulation is shown in Figure 15-9. For the subject with the Otis IQ of 137 it took about 30 milliseconds to reach spike 3 and about 100 milliseconds to reach spike 4. For the subject with an Otis IQ of 100 the spiking times were 150 and 260 milliseconds, and for the subject with the Otis IQ of 73 the millisecond averages were 280 and 460. These illustrations indicate that the individual brains functioned at different rates, one taking four times as long to process the same information as another.

The analyzer has also been used to determine the comparable activity of the two brain hemispheres of the same subject. In children who have severe reading problems, some of the analyses have shown unbalanced functioning of the two sides. The possibility of being able to distinguish between children who are functionally different and in need of particular treatment and those who are suffer-

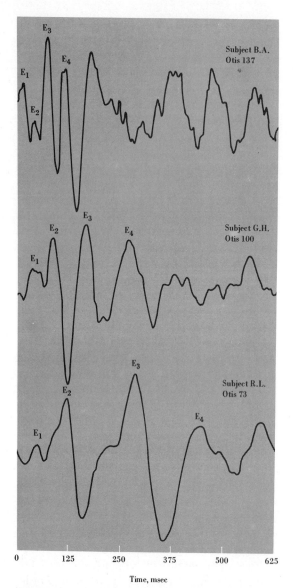

Time, msec

**Figure 15-9** Average evoked cortical potentials to 400 photic stimuli for 3 subjects: Subject B. A. IQ 137, Subject G. H. IQ 100, Subject R. L. IQ 73. Redrawn from J. Ertl, "Evoked potentials, neural efficiency and I.Q., p. 10, paper presented at the International Symposium for Biocybernetics, Washington, D. C., February 8, 1968. (*By permission of the author.*)

ing from motivational problems which require retraining would be important in learning and reading clinics.

Ertl found his efficiency test useful with very young children and infants less than one month old. When used with non-English-speaking children, he could study brain functioning in ways that were impossible with standard tests. Ertl believed that functional ability is stable by the age of five years. This hypothesis should be checked against other theories, particularly the cognitive stages of Piaget. The higher thought processes seem to be more closely related to spikes 3 and 4 than to spikes 1 and 2. Much more work needs to be done to establish the meaning of these differences.

Ertl (1972) reported that efficiency scores remain relatively stable for an individual, apart from drug effects, which, with one exception, lowered the efficiency index. The loss from the effects of alcohol was recovered by the following day. The exception to lowered efficiency from drugs was found in one case, his secretary, who showed a 20 percent increase in efficiency when she took the vitamin niacimide. Although these results occurred in ten repeated tests, they did not occur in other subjects who took the same drug.

The testing equipment is relatively easy to operate. The normal testing period is about five minutes. The scores are read from two windows on the face of the computer. One window shows the efficiency rating and the other an IQ estimate. The lowest score obtained to date was 85 milliseconds, indicating efficient neural processing on the part of the subject, a belly dancer, who also scored 186 IQ on a conventional test. According to her record she spoke ten languages.

The neural efficiency index needs further testing in many contexts, but much of this work will take place, now that the machines are available in a revised form through Associates International in Louisiana. Direct measures of the speed of neural transmission of sensory signals should, logically, be a good indicator of intellectual functioning. When it appears that researchers might soon distinguish between different kinds of intellectual processing, the tool for their research will take on increased value.

## STUDENT'S USE OF HIS INTELLIGENCE

Most students do not make the greatest possible use of their intellectual ability. Many of them lack the motivation or drive to exert themselves as fully as they might reasonably do. The learning-motivation model emphasizes the relationship between emotional and intellectual performance. With this model, the teacher can learn to schedule experiences that will develop the concept of self as learner that is needed to sustain motivation. Even if the teacher is interested primarily in teaching factual knowledge and sees this as his first responsibility, he still needs to understand that maximal cognitive learning will not occur unless appropriate motivation sequences are set in motion. Even very bright students will not learn if they do not see the possibility of success in what the teacher is asking them to learn. The personality structure, which involves much more than intelligence, is a major factor in the success a teacher will have in generating learning by the individual students. Successful teachers have always found means to motivate students to use their intellectual potential as fully as possible.

## SUMMARY

Intelligence is a component of successful living. Different test makers have defined it in various ways, depending on their conception of how learning takes place. The learning-motivation model assumes that intelligence is related to the ease with which associations are formed, the ease with which conceptualizations emerge from the associations, and the ease with which the individual is able to make the transition to a self-directing, creative approach to a problem.

Formal definitions of intelligence include (1) Thorndike's, that intelligence is the power to make good responses from the point of view of truth or fact; (2) Terman's, that it is the ability to think in abstract terms; (3) Henmon's, that it is made up of two factors: the capacity for knowledge and the knowledge possessed; (4) Stoddard's, that it is the ability to undertake activities characterized by difficulty, complexity, and abstractness; to perform these activities with economy or speed and with adaptiveness to a goal so that they show social value and the emergence of originals or inventiveness; and to maintain these activities under conditions that demand a concentration of energy and a resistance to emotional forces; and (5) Stephens', that it is whatever the intelligence tests measure.

The most common way of discovering what intelligence tests measure is based on factor analysis, in which commonalities are grouped together and separated from other factors by mathematical analysis. One of the most important figures in this process is Spearman, who concluded that intelligence was composed of a $G$ (general intellectual ability) factor and a large number of $s$ (specific intellectual ability) factors. Later he amended his position to include group factors that were more general than the $s$ but less comprehensive than the $G$. Kelley, Thurstone, and Guilford each developed factor-analysis approaches to discovering what intelligence tests measure. Thurstone listed seven primary mental abilities: number, word fluency, verbal meaning, associative memory, reasoning, space, and perceptual speed. Intercorrelations between his factors tend to indicate considerable commonality between them.

Wechsler developed an individual intelligence scale, which Robeck found could be used for differential diagnosis of reading problems. Wilson found that students score differently on different intelligence tests and that sometimes these differences are dramatic, leading to possible miscounseling, if the test used fails to tap the relevant abilities.

Guilford developed a model of intellect, which indicates that there are some 120 ways to be intelligent. The model has three dimensions: (1) the contents of thought, including figural, symbolic, semantic, and behavioral; (2) operations, including cognition, memory, convergent thinking, divergent thinking, and evaluation; and (3) products, including units, classes, relations, systems, transformations, and implications. The interaction is tripartite: One part comes from materials, one from operations, and one from products. The model of intellect focuses on the implications for future learning of the kinds of learning that have already taken place, whereas the learning-motivation model stresses the process of learning.

Ertl developed a neural efficiency analyzer to obtain a physiological measure of intelligence. The analyzer shows promise not only for measuring intelligence but also for distinguishing between types of reading disabilities.

The kinds and the range of intelligence that a teacher has to accommodate within a given class complicate the problems of teaching. This range is both intrapersonal and interpersonal. As a teacher masters the implications of variable strengths and weaknesses in learning ability, he can help each student capitalize on his strengths and minimize his weaknesses.

## SELF-DIRECTING ACTIVITIES

1 Look for evidence of high intelligence in the activities of your four grandparents.
2 Devise a systematic environment that would or should improve intellectual functioning. Test the system over a period of time to see whether IQ scores improve.
3 Develop a lesson sequence that is based on symbolic information and another based on semantic information. See whether there are different students who do outstanding work on one or the other of these sequences.
4 Pick one of the twenty-four kinds of memory and spend 15 minutes a day trying to improve it in yourself. Test yourself at the end of two weeks for improvement.

# Chapter 16

Nurturing intelligence in Bangladesh through teaching. (*Courtesy of the United Nations*)

# INTELLIGENCE: NATURE AND NURTURE

As a result of reading this chapter, you should be able to:

❰  Provide enriched environments for young children

❰  Work consistently, over a long period of time, to improve the intellectual functioning of students

❰  Understand that chemical factors change human functioning

❰  Help students keep channels open to learning

❰  Understand the following terms:
   capacity
   ability
   achievement
   glutamic acid
   phenylketonuria
   IQ

The controversy over children's scholastic ability and over the school's responsibility for improving this ability and for destroying, revealing, and using information about it will probably become more virulent and menacing in the immediate future. Teachers have been caught in these conflicts regarding intelligence. Minority groups claim that intelligence test scores lead to discrimination. Parents claim the right to know what scores are recorded by the school in their children's cumulative folders. Teachers doubt that most parents have enough technical background to understand the scores and what they mean. Many school psychologists feel the same way about teachers and administrators. Students placed in classes for the gifted on the basis of their intelligence test scores often complain about the grading practices of the teachers— sometimes they receive grades of B or C when they would be making A's with little effort in nonsectioned classes. Some parents will not allow their children to be placed in a class for the mentally retarded even when their failure in regular classes is inevitable. An examination of some of the problems involved in using information about intelligence may help prospective teachers to gain perspective on the differences of opinion that are prevalent and assurance from a consideration of alternative actions that are usually open to them.

Most professionals are in agreement about the following points:

**1** Some people learn more easily than others. In general, the person who learns easily as a child continues to learn easily as an adult, and the person who has great difficulty learning as a child continues to have difficulty learning as an adult. However, the adult may not need to learn as many new things and should be able to choose his areas of activity.

**2** The differences in ability to learn are a continuous function rather than being separated into clusters. The difference between an educable mentally retarded person and a high-ly gifted individual is real and obvious, but most people fit somewhere between these extremes, with the great majority differing only slightly in their level of intelligence.

**3** Not all people are equally intelligent in all areas. Some people learn music easily and mathematics with difficulty, while others find foreign languages easy to learn and physics difficult.

**4** Very young children and infants show differences in their ability to learn, indicating that inherited factors are involved in the development of intelligence.

**5** Evidence of changes of intelligence with radical changes of the environment indicates that intelligence is partly dependent on environment.

Although these points are generally conceded to be true, a genuine difference of opinion exists about the causes of variability of intelligence, the extent of variability within the same person, the amount of change that differences in the environment could be expected to contribute, and the dominance of inheritance as a contributing factor in intelligence. Some of the bitterness in the controversy has been due to differences in definitions of intelligence and, more particularly, to differences in interpretation of intelligence test scores.

The terms "capacity," "ability," and "achievement" have been used with regard to intelligence. Capacity is the most inclusive of the three. *Capacity* is potential ability—the inherited potential an individual receives from his parents through genes. Capacity refers to maximum ability with perfect training, which means that capacity is never quite attained as an operating function. Capacity may be measured and inferred from various kinds of test sequences that give more or less valid indications of intellectual ability. When intelligence is defined as the inherited capacity to learn, environmental forces are necessarily excluded.

Ability is simpler to measure than capacity. *Ability* is the power to perform a designated responsive act; it may be potential or actual, native or acquired. Ability implies that the act can be performed now, without further training, if the necessary conditions exist. In terms of intelligence, ability is capacity diminished by the effect of the actual environment, in contrast to the perfect environment, which would have made complete attainment of the capacity possible. Many psychologists refer to intelligence tests as tests of "scholastic ability"—a term that tends to underline the interaction of environment and heredity in the intellectual potential at any given time.

*Achievement* is the individual's output. It is the actual performance on a given test at a given point in time. Achievement tests are usually used to determine the degree of mastery of subject-matter content or skills. However, the score on an intelligence test—which attempts to measure mental ability—is of necessity a measure of past learning or, by definition, a measure of achievement. In other words, complete separation of a student's capacity, ability, and achievement is not possible in test situations. In this chapter, the discussion will focus on the evidence regarding diverse capacities among individuals and on the forces that cause people to perform below their capacities, or potential level of ability. Attention will be paid to misunderstandings about the differential strengths of heredity and environment in effecting changes in the functional efficiency of students' intelligence.

The most dramatic evidence of the existence of a problem in communication about intelligence is the edict issued on February 26, 1964, that banned the use of group tests of intelligence and the use of IQ scores in New York City schools. J. O. Loretan (1965) explained that the ban was imposed because of the effect that knowledge of students' IQ scores has on teachers. When a child is given an IQ rating, the teacher tends to see him in terms of this rating. Teachers come to expect the child to perform as his score indicates that he should, and as a consequence many children are not given the extra pushes that could enhance their ability to do schoolwork. Loretan interpreted Binet as stating that intelligence could be increased with instruction. He claimed that this viewpoint had been lost as intelligence became identified with something fixed and immutable—partly because it was defined for a long time as an inherited capacity. Loretan pointed out that in the New York Demonstration Guidance Project, the students showed an average gain of 8 IQ points between 1956 and 1957. In the years from 1957 to 1960, the average gain of the students in this project was 15 IQ points, with a range in gains from 5 to 40 points. He also noted that Haryou, in a different project, reported to the U.S. Office of Education a median IQ drop of 4 points as children progressed from grade 3 to grade 6 in 25 central Harlem schools. Loretan raised the question of whether attendance at school was making these children less able to learn. Loretan reported that New York was replacing the intelligence tests with a system of achievement tests that stressed reading and arithmetic and by an observation schedule developed jointly with the Educational Testing Service called *Let's Look at First Graders* (1965). When the nation's largest school system bans the use of intelligence tests, prospective teachers should be alerted to the idea that the use of intelligence data in school is likely to be connected with certain problems.

## SELECTIVE BREEDING FOR INHERITED TRAITS

One of the factors in the interaction that produces functional intelligence is inherited capacity. Some spokesmen are beginning to sound as though they think that environment is the only important variable in functional intelligence. However, powerful evidence exists that heredity can be controlled to produce distinctive characteristics, including intelligence.

## Genetic Control in Agriculture

The science of agriculture has developed experimental techniques for separating the effects of environment and heredity as causes of differences in both plants and animals. Briefly, the methods used to establish genetic inheritance involve inbreeding to produce a stable trait and then crossbreeding to test whether the trait can be transmitted genetically. For instance, corn has been inbred to produce pure strains. In the process, many of the strains that emerged were discarded as undesirable if, among a host of other reasons, they grew small ears, grew few ears, or were subject to diseases. Out of this long series of studies emerged a few strains that had strong, consistent, and desirable characteristics. Inbreeding is accomplished by covering the tassels and the silk, pollenating each plant manually with its own pollen, and re-covering the silk to avoid contamination. Crossbreeding requires the same technique, except that pollen from one pure strain is used to fertilize another pure strain. Crossbreeding of these strains has led to commercial seed that produces many times as much corn as the original stock. Each generation, new crossbred seed from the pure strains must be reproduced if the genetic inheritance is to remain clear and the original productivity is to continue.

To test the effect of environmental factors such as moisture, fertilizer, cultivation, and space, these are varied systematically. From this kind of experimentation, agriculturists have been able to establish the environmental factors that are most important in the productive growth of corn of a given genetic inheritance. The agriculturist can determine, for example, that a particular strain of corn yields best when grown in an environment in which it is fertilized with VX3 mixture, watered $m$ times and in $n$ amounts, planted at $d$ depth and $c$ inches apart with $b$ number of seeds in each hill, and cultivated $q$ times to a prescribed depth. A steadily declining farm population, working on a diminishing amount of acreage, has been enabled to produce increased yields as a result of the control of both the genetic inheritance and the environmental factors that together result in optimum production.

The experimentation in animal husbandry has been less complete because the costs involved per individual produced are much higher and the reproduction of generations often requires more time than in plant breeding. A complete breeding program has been followed on certain stud farms that raise racehorses. Long-loined pigs have been bred for bacon yield with specified characteristics of fat and lean meat. Chickens have been bred for egg yield, while the environmental factors of feed, water, and illumination have been systematically studied to establish the greatest possible productivity. Other chickens and turkeys have been similarly bred and fed for yield of white meat. Dogs have been bred for size and personality characteristics. Cattle have been selectively bred for milk or beef production. Santa Gertrudis cattle were deliberately created to thrive in hot climates where other cattle had had only meager success. Thorough experimentation has not been carried on with human being, although Hitler made an attempt during one period of German history to create a pure Aryan strain.

## Breeding for Intelligence in Rats

In his work with rats, Tryon (1940) noticed that some animals made more mistakes in mazes than others. The range was 7 to 214 errors in 19 trials (Figure 16-1). He selected a group of the brightest rats, those having low error scores, and a group of the dullest rats, those having high error scores, and bred selectively for 22 generations. By the third generation, the separation of brightness and dullness was already observable, although there was still considerable overlap between the groups (Figure 16-2). By the seventh generation, a bimodal curve had been established with almost no overlap in the ranges of abilities. At this point in the experiment, the bright group had a mean score of approximately 20 errors, and the dull group had a mean score of about 120 errors (Figure 16-3).

After 22 generations, the bright and dull rats were allowed to mate freely. The test scores of offspring fell into a normal curve that resembled the learning abilities of the unselected original group of forebears (Figures 16-4 and 16-5). When a characteristic can be selectively bred to increase or to diminish and when that same trait can be removed by crossbreeding, the evidence for genetic importance is very strong. Tolman (1949), Krech (1961), and others used strains of bright and dull rats for differential studies of learning.

Searle (1949) did a follow-up study using Tryon's rat strains and found that (1) brightness in one maze situation did not guarantee equal brightness in other learning situations; (2) bright rats were food-driven, economical of distance, low in motivation to escape from water, and timid in response to open spaces; and (3) dull rats were relatively uninterested in food, average or better in water motivation, and timid of mechanical features.

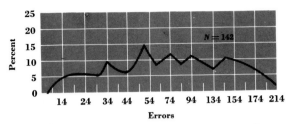

**Figure 16-1** Maze ability of parent stock of rats. (Redrawn from R. C. Tryon, Genetic differences in maze-learning ability in rats, p. 113, 39th Yearbook of the National Society for the Study of Education, Bloomington, Ill., Public School Publishing Co., 1940. By permission of the publishers.)

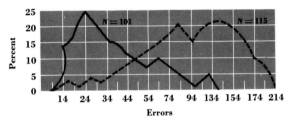

**Figure 16-2** Maze ability after three generations of selected breeding. R. C. Tryon, op. cit., p. 113.

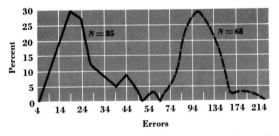

**Figure 16-3** Maze ability after seven generations of selected breeding. R. C. Tryon, op. cit., p. 113.

## ENVIRONMENTAL FACTORS AFFECTING INTELLIGENCE

The most dramatic evidence of the effect of environment on intelligence comes from studies of certain diseases caused by an over-supply or undersupply of certain chemicals that are essential to the efficient functioning of the organism. The most common disaster, as far as learning is concerned, is a shortage of oxygen being supplied to the brain. Critical

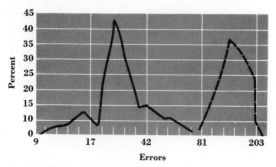

**Figure 16-4** Maze ability after 22 generations of selected breeding. R. C. Tryon, op. cit., p. 115.

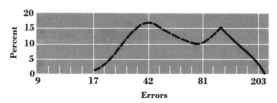

**Figure 16-5** Maze ability of crossbred bright and dull rats. R. C. Tryon, op. cit., p. 115.

periods in the life of a human being occur just before, during, and just after birth, when the infant first assumes the breathing function for himself (Chapter 11). Other major evidence about the effect of environment includes the physiological changes in the neural system that result from sensory stimulation or learning experiences, a decline in the IQ scores of school-age children as a result of deprivation of learning experiences, and a reversal of an expected decline as a result of special-opportunity experiences.

### Chemical Imbalance: Diseases

The development of the field of neurochemistry has increased the understanding of the manner in which certain deficiencies in critical foods or enzymes can have disastrous results

as far as the intelligence is concerned. Tower (1958) indicated that much of the chemical transformation of food materials that is necessary before the food can nourish the brain takes place in the brain area itself, rather than the food being reconstructed in other body organs for assimilation later by the brain. A number of vitamins, particularly of the B complex, seem to be critically important as coenzymes that act as intermediaries in the reconstruction of the needed nutrition components. The element magnesium also seems to have a critical role as a catalyst, at least in some brain nourishment. Deficiencies of any of these critical molecules may impair the development of the organism to some degree. The following sections discuss various substances that are known to affect intelligence.

**Glutamic Acid**   A group of borderline subnormal children who were fed glutamic acid, one of the amino acids that make up proteins, increased their intellectual functioning by approximately 5 to 10 IQ points (Tower, 1958). The change was sufficient to enable these subjects to function in the community, whereas they had been problem learners before the treatment. Similar feeding of glutamic acid to more able children had no observable effect. Tower pointed out that glutamic acid—like blood corpuscles—will not pass through certain brain tissues, although glutamine—a compound that forms glutamic acid by the addition of ammonia—does pass the blood brain barrier.

Gilgash (1967) reported treatment with glutamic acid of mentally retarded adult males. They showed a mean gain of 8.54 IQ points during a 30-day treatment period. This gain was increased to 9.32 points by the end of 90 days after treatment ceased. Matched pairs who were given cornstarch in orange juice as a placebo gained .30 IQ points during the same period. These differences in gain were highly significant and persisted over a substantial period of time.

The nature of the mechanism that provides ingested material for the brain area is not clearly defined. The function of the glutamic acid in the brain is apparently that of a substrate for respiration; that is, it provides a basis for energy production in the brain area. The importance of this function could explain the increase in intellectual ability, if the disability in intellectual functioning were due to lack of glutamic acid as a source of brain energy. A second function of the glutamic acid seems to be related to the production of $CO_2$, which in turn may have a function in maintaining the acid-alkaline balance in the brain. Teachers are not expected to rush out and provide their less able students with food supplements containing glutamic acid, although a knowledge that such a deficiency could be an effective agent in subnormal performance may sensitize them to other problems these children encounter.

**Tranquilizing Agents** Serotonin acts in complex ways to regulate neural activity. Serotonin is normally produced in the brain area and has a regulating function related to transmission in the neural system. Both hyperactivity and underactivity create less than optimal conditions for learning. The serotonin balance in the neurological system is maintained by amine oxidase, which rapidly changes the serotonin to a form of acetic acid that is excreted in the urine. Serotonin acts as a tranquilizer or inhibitor of activity, and if it is not broken down and discharged, neural activity is inhibited. The effect of tranquilizers is to reduce hyperactivity. Reserpine, one of the most common active ingredients in tranquilizers administered to psychotics, seems to interfere with the serotonin cycle, resulting in the increased freeing of the serotonin and thus slowing brain activity. Lysergic acid diethylamide (LSD), a member of the same family as reserpine and serotonin, has an effect opposite to that of reserpine. It speeds up transmission, and the brain tends to produce hallucinations and paranoid-type reactions. Tower (1958) compares the effects of LSD to those of sensory deprivation studied by Hebb (1961).

**Phenylketonuria** Phenylketonuria (PKU) is a disease for which a standard check is now made on newborn infants by treating the urine with a reagent and checking the color. If untreated, the disease leads to severe mental retardation, seizures, and spastic reactions. The cause is apparently a defective gene in the hereditary system that makes impossible a needed breakdown of an amino acid, phenylalanine, thus creating a toxic effect and destroying neural tissue. Treatment is through diet, avoiding the amino acid in question. If the disease is caught early, the symptoms can be reversed. Baumeister (1967) compared the effects of diet treatment for an average period of 27 months on 22 phenylketonuric children. All these children had lower IQ scores than their unaffected siblings at both the beginning and the end of treatment. Treatment led to an improved rate of development of intelligence at a slower pace than that of the unaffected siblings. Also studied were six children who were not treated through diet. Their IQs steadily declined.

The possibility of compensating for a genetic defect by a substantial change in environment, in this case in diet, demonstrates the very complex relationships involved in intelligence. Teachers can use their knowledge to do what is possible on their own to improve the functioning of the intelligence. Also, they can be aware that other specialists may be able to help in ways that require very different skills, and they can refer the parents to other resources when help is needed.

**Hypoparathyroidism** Another disease that leads to extreme behavior problems—convulsions, loss of alertness, and irritability—is hypoparathyroidism. Money and Ehrenhardt (1966) reported clinical evidence indicating that although the disease lowers effective intelligence while it is in progress, treatment that raises the low calcium levels effects a rise in IQ score. The investigators interpreted their findings as evidence that intelligence survives this very debilitating disease. Mental ability is masked but not destroyed. Caspari (1968), a geneticist, inferred that a large number of genes influence intelligence since almost all chromosomal aberrations result in mental deficiency. Extending his information from the need for interaction of two genes to produce "hygienic behavior" in the honeybee, Caspari deduces that " . . . high intelligence would depend not on one pair of genes, or even a few which act additively, but on particular combinations and combinations of several independent genes" [p. 52]. Caspari points out the very important role of the environment, not only in terms of the development of human intelligence but also in terms of the more tightly genetically controlled growth of plants and animals.

### Physiological Changes: Learning

Rosenzweig, Krech, and Bennett (1961) used bright and dull strains of rats from Tryon's selective breeding to analyze physiological differences in the brain chemistry of the two strains (Chapter 9). In later experiments, they found a thickening of the gray layer of the cortex in rats raised in an environment in which they were provided with designed, systematic learning experiences, and no such thickening in the cortexes of control littermates who had had the same diet but lived in a restricted and less stimulating environment. This thickening of the gray layer was accompanied by increased ability to learn new tasks as well as accumulated learning.

To summarize these studies of intelligence in rats, (1) the hereditary factor in intelligence was shown to exist in selectively bred strains of bright and dull rats, and (2) the environmental factor in the development of intelligence was established through measurable changes in overt behavior, which correlated with physical changes in the structure of the brain.

### IQ Decline: Environmental Deprivation

Gilbert (1966) illustrated some of the problems involved in defining environmental deprivation. In New York City's Special Service Schools, the children who stayed in the same school from grade 3 to grade 6 showed an increase in average IQ test scores from 100.8 at grade 3 to 102.4 in grade 6. However, children who moved about showed declining scores over the three-year period, from 94.2 in grade 3 to 92.9 in grade 6. Those who moved most—four or more admissions—had more accentuated declines from 88.0 in grade 3 to 84.0 in grade 6 (Table 16-1).

All the children were living in environments that have commonly been classed as intellectually depriving. Gilbert points out, however, that some of the homes within the area were

**Table 16-1  Changes in IQ Scores of Children from New York Mobile Disadvantaged Families** (*From Gilbert, 1966*)

|  | Mean IQ scores | |
|---|---|---|
|  | Grade 3 | Grade 6 |
| No moves | 100.8 | 102.4 |
| All who changed schools | 94.2 | 92.9 |
| Changed schools four or more times | 88.0 | 84.0 |

much more intellectually stimulating than others. He points out that the moving itself was probably not depriving but was symptomatic of complex family relationships that were intellectually destructive.

The generally destructive effect of a poor environment can be gauged by the Haryou report quoted by J. O. Loretan (1965) that showed a median drop of 4 IQ points in 25 central Harlem schools during the period from grade 3 to grade 6. The unfortunate effects of environmental deprivation on special groups of children have been discussed in the literature for a long time.

**Canalboat Children**   Gordon (1923) studied canalboat children in England to see what effect their environment had on intelligence. These children lived on houseboats with their families and traveled up and down the same stretch of canal while the boats hauled goods back and forth. The speed of the journey was slow enough so that the children could run along the banks, pick berries, look for birds' nests, and pursue other kinds of activities related to life outdoors, although within a restricted environment. While the boat was tied up waiting for another tow the children would go to school. Their attendance averaged only one or two days a month.

The parents of these children were, on the whole, not intellectually very capable. They found their jobs neither very stimulating nor very profitable, but they continued in them, often because their parents had had similar jobs before them, so that this was the only world they knew. Gordon made a comprehensive study of the long-term effect of this way of life on the mental functioning of children from ages four to fourteen. The four-year-olds had an average IQ of about 90, which dropped systematically over the years to about 65 at age fourteen. Apparently the drabness of this life coupled with the lack of the stimulus of

regular school attendance combined to produce individuals who were mental defectives, as compared with children who grow up in normal environments.

**Hollow Folk from the Appalachian Mountains**   Wheeler (1942), Edwards and Jones (1938), Asher (1935), Sherman and Key (1932), and Hirsch (1928) made studies of children brought up in isolated communities in the Appalachian Mountain areas. In general, the results were similar to those which Gordon found for the canalboat children of England, although some critics have questioned the validity of the instruments used to test intelligence in these children. These communities were settled by British stock at approximately the time of the Revolutionary War. The ridges are steep and the valleys quite small. The original settlers were apparently self-sufficient, independent, and able to establish themselves in rather complete isolation. Entry into the valleys was by trail rather than road. They made a living by hunting, trapping, and primitive farming, and they had little contact with the outside world except for occasional trips to the store "over the mountain" and feuds with people in neighboring valleys. In some of these communities there was much intermarriage and inbreeding. Very few of the inhabitants could read or write—for that matter, few of them needed to. The interpersonal relations within the home tended to be permissive and accepting. Their diets appeared to be poorly balanced, but their physical growth was more normal than one might expect from an analysis of their eating habits. Intelligence tests indicated a steady erosion of intelligence between the ages of seven and fourteen, as intelligence is measured on these mental scales. Roads, federal parks, school services, draft calls, and other modern ways have tended to disturb this subculture. Many of the inhabitants have moved north to Chicago,

Detroit, and other industrial areas. Their lack of schooling and the differences in their social mores have made assimilation into the rest of the Anglo-American culture very difficult. Both heredity and environment combined to lower the effective intelligence of these people.

**Maria: A Longitudinal Study** The mechanics of environmental deprivation can be seen in the case of an intellectually gifted child whose home was not able to support her intellectual needs. Maria was a gifted girl from a Spanish-speaking background. As a seven-year-old in a supportive school environment, she showed great promise and had a Binet IQ score of 125. She was included in a special program for gifted children on the assumption that her score was probably depressed by a lack of preschool opportunity. The school provided a planned acceleration program with a summer session to make the transition as smooth as possible from grade 2 to grade 4. Maria's parents were proud to have her attend the summer session, and she was accelerated. Although the home situation was affectionate, the family failed increasingly to provide the materials and experiences for an educationally supportive environment as Maria advanced to upper elementary classes. Neither of the parents was able to counsel the child, nor could any of her siblings serve as a model for academic achievement. Owing to district policy, which allowed each teacher to have a turn teaching the cluster groups of gifted children, Maria was assigned to a fourth-grade teacher who opposed acceleration on a doctrinaire basis. He apparently also considered Mexican-American children less able to learn than children from Anglo-American homes. As a result of the teacher's expectation, her failure, and her family's inability to help her, Maria's school achievement deteriorated. She withdrew from voluntary activities, did poorly in

daily assignments, and had no friends in school except her sister. She began to avoid reading assignments, but continued to read widely outside school in materials beyond her grade level. In other words, in school she conformed to the expectations of her teacher, who was repeatedly reinforced in his negative conceptions about acceleration and about this particular minority group. By the fifth grade, Maria was a poor student. On a retest her IQ score dropped 10 points. Her school grades dropped from exceptional to below average. In addition, she had lost confidence in herself as an able learner, and her drive to succeed in school was less than average. What might have been a developmental opportunity became an unhappy and destructive experience. After lengthy discussion about whether she should be retained in the fifth grade, Maria was promoted to a sixth-grade teacher who began the slow and patient process of rebuilding her confidence and teaching her the study skills she had missed. Although he could not provide the books, records, equipment, and educational stimulation that other children in the accelerated group received at home, he was able to send her on to the junior high school as a successful if not outstanding student. Some bright children are not so fortunate in getting the necessary help at the critical time and slide into mediocrity.

## ATTEMPTS TO EDUCATE INTELLIGENCE

Studies of intellectual differences between ethnic groups, socioeconomic groups, and cultural groups have led to the attempt on the part of government and social agencies to improve learning opportunities for young people. Most of the programs for disadvantaged youth have involved adolescents or young children prior to, or shortly after, their entrance into public school. Programs for adolescents have attempted to change attitudes by counseling, to improve basic communication skills, and to train for jobs. The goal has been the rather specific one of raising students' abilities to perform in job-hunting and wage-earning situations. On a different front, programs in early childhood education have been directed toward raising the school learning potential of young children. The target group for government agencies has been disadvantaged youngsters, primarily because desperation about persistent poverty has made the American society willing to intervene in the learning environment of these preschool children, with the idea that early intervention is necessary to reverse the depressing effects of poverty on intellectual growth. The goal has been to raise each child's ability—his power to perform in a given situation—as nearly as possible to his capacity, or potential ability. When the "given situation" in which the child must perform is the total school setting, the implication is that intelligence as well as other abilities will be improved. When the disadvantaged child's capacity is seen as comparable to that of other children his age and when differences in his intelligence are seen as a reflection of his handicapping environment, the use of pretests and posttests of intelligence is necessary for evaluation of the program. The expected improvement in IQ scores of nursery school children has so far been negligible.

Blatt and Garfunkel (1967) reported experimental research in which the effect of a two-year intervention on preschool disadvantaged children was studied over a one-year period of follow-up. The nursery school program for the pilot and two experimental groups included (1) social functioning, (2) experiences to promote curiosity and inquisitiveness, and (3) preacademic skills such as language development and visual-auditory discrimination. The Moore version of the responsive environment, including his typewriter for preschool children

(discussed in the next section), was added to a nursery school environment enhanced by staff training, curriculum development, and new materials. The curriculum was described as teacher-developed for individual children. The nonexperimental groups were from similarly poor and culturally deprived homes. They had no intervention program (nursery school), but participated in the testing, which was done "blind"—that is, by testers who did not know which were experimental subjects. The Stanford-Binet (L-M) was administered, plus a list of aptitude, language, achievement, personality, and social scales and measures. The investigators concluded: "Analysis of the data led to the unequivocal conclusion that there was no more difference between the groups at the end of the study than there had been at the beginning."

Although this particular curriculum pattern failed to produce measurable results, the investigators did not consider that the question of whether intelligence can be improved by practice and training had been answered. The failure of the intervention program may have been due to a lack of real differences in cognitive learning opportunities between the home and the nursery school, a lack of control of the experimental program, or a lack of instruments to measure the changes that took place.

## MOVEMENTS AIMED AT IMPROVING INTELLIGENCE

At present, two movements aimed at improving the intellectual functioning of young children are under way. They tend to be expensive programs and require low ratios of teachers to learners. One is financed primarily by the federal government through Head Start and Follow Through projects for disadvantaged preschool, kindergarten, and primary school children. The other is financed primarily by parents who can afford to send their children to expensive, innovative private or experimental schools. The stimulation for change in the young child's learning program has come from research in neurobiology and neuropsychology. Although the schools have remained largely outside this movement, parents are reading such books as *Revolution in Learning: The Child from One to Six* (Pines, 1967) and *How to Raise a Brighter Child* (Beck, 1967). These books describe the work of Bereiter and Engelmann (1966), Hunt (1961), Moore and Anderson (1967), Montessori (1909), and Loretan (1965). Many parents are reading these and other sources that suggest that young children are capable of cognitive learning far beyond that which is introduced in the typical nursery school or kindergarten. They cite research that implies that a child may fail to develop his maximum potential for some kinds of learning if his early environment is restricted.

Bereiter and Engelmann (1966) questioned the relevance of the middle-class nursery school programs for impoverished or disadvantaged children. They insisted that because of the brief time (ages four to five) available during which to prepare deprived nursery school age children for entrance into the public school, an immediate and direct approach in language development and quantitative thought is necessary. These writers reported gains in vocabulary, syntax, number concepts, and response to group instruction as a result of specific learning sequences taught in a prescribed order and manner. They are best known for their pressure techniques designed to force attention and response by the children.

Omar K. Moore (Moore & Anderson, 1968) invented a typewriter that is used by children from ages two to five to explore letter and word relationships. The machines are electric or are operated by an observer to give im-mediate feedback to the child explorer. After a period during which the child punches keys to see what comes up, the machine is controlled to print only when the letter that matches a model is punched. The child first learns to write letters, then words, and then sentences and paragraphs. Because the paragraphs are of the child's invention, he also learns to read. Crucial to Moore's method is the absence of pressure on the child from an adult and the reinforcement and feedback from the learning environment. In Moore's experimental school, children between the ages of two and five learned to read and write.

Maria Montessori (1909) designed teaching materials and sequences for her relatively untrained helpers to use in teaching slum children in Italy. These materials stressed the development of conceptual thinking through the manipulation of carefully designed materials, letters, maps, puzzles, shells, form boards, and other objects. Montessori observed the effectiveness of multisensory approaches. Her subjects were primarily children between the ages of two and five in child care centers for poor working mothers. After a quiescent period of about 40 years, due primarily to the opposition of Kilpatrick who believed that the system led to a stunting of creativity and imaginative expression, her methods and materials were revived in the 1950s for use in well-financed private schools. Her philosophy stressed the freedom of the child to explore with a minimum of adult direction. In American schools, little evidence has been offered that this method results in improved intellectual development. There has been a tendency in this country to provide these materials to advantaged children who are somewaht older than the children in Montessori's groups. The lack of affirming data may be due to the timing of the experiences in the children's lives.

Deutsch (1964) also devised materials for sensorimotor and perceptual development.

His major contribution has been to identify perceptual differences between deprived and normal school populations (Chapter 12).

Nimnicht, Meier, McAfee, and Rogers (1967) designed and evaluated a nursery school program in which they extended the responsive-environment concept to all the learning activities in the school day. Their subjects were 51 children from welfare homes most of whom were of Indian or Spanish descent. The program employed a ratio of one adult to four children, and the environment included Moore's typewriter and a large collection of self-informing devices with which the children could interact. The adults were available to help if they were asked and to tell or read stories, which the children could listen to or not as they wished.

Preliminary results with small numbers of children using the Peabody Picture Vocabulary Test showed mean gains during the first-year program equivalent to those made by advantaged bright normal children who attended a regular nursery school. A small pilot group who were in the program for two years made somewhat larger gains.

Taken together, the results of these various programs seem to suggest that young children, like older children, learn what they are taught. Programs designed to enhance social development need to be evaluated in terms of improvement in social interaction, whereas programs that are evaluated for cognitive growth should stress cognitive learning if gains in this area of development are to be expected.

## GROUP DIFFERENCES IN INTELLIGENCE

One source of hostility toward schools has been a feeling on the part of many minority groups that teachers consider minority-group children less able to do schoolwork than they actually are. Often the intelligence tests have been considered unfair—they have been thought to be biased in favor of Anglo-American middle-class culture and not constructed to allow children from other backgrounds to show their abilities. Teachers often become unwilling participants in these disputes, which affect the once-harmonious atmosphere of the classroom.

Many studies have shown differences in the IQ scores of black and white children when tested either individually or in a group setting. The results have consistently favored white children. Although the range of scores has nearly always been approximately the same, the mean scores have shown statistically significant differences. Most of the studies have not partialed out the socioeconomic status of the parents. A number of investigators have interpreted these differences as being due to psychocultural factors (Dreger & Miller, 1960), and others have suggested genetic causes (Garrett, 1967; Shuey, 1958).

Adler (1968) reviewed studies of intellectually gifted children with regard to race. When race identification was incorporated into the studies concerned, people of Jewish descent were most commonly highest, followed by those of German and then British descent. Negroes, Italians, Portuguese, Mexicans, and American Indians were most commonly mentioned at the low end of the scale. However, he reported a study by Jenkins (1950) in which there was the statistically normal number of black youth above 130 and also above 140.

Lesser, Fifer, and Clark (1965) compared children of four ethnic groups in New York City schools: Chinese, Jews, Negroes, and Puerto Ricans (Figure 16-6). The children were compared on verbal, reasoning, number, and space scores. Each nationality had a distinctive profile that was maintained when middle- and lower-class children were compared, although in all cases the profiles for the children from lower-class homes were substantially below those of their racially similar

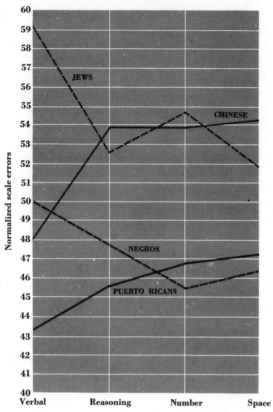

**Figure 16-6** Patterns of normalized mental ability scores for different ethnic groups. (*Redrawn from G. S. Lesser, G. Fifer, and D. H. Clark, Mental abilities of children from different social class and cultural groups. Monographs of the Society for Research in Child Development, 1965. (Ser. no. 102), Fig. 2, p. 64. By permission of the publishers. Copyright © 1965, Society For Research and Child Development.)*

the lower the socioeconomic standing of the family, the lower the IQ scores. A number of the studies, particularly those of Jenkins (1968) and Semler and Iscoe (1966), indicated that the test instruments did not discriminate well between children from lower socioeconomic backgrounds.

Bond (1960) studied the families of students from among whom the National Merit Scholars of 1956 were selected. He found that 45 percent of them came from homes of professional and technical workers, who constitute 8.5 percent of the population, while only .2 percent came from homes of laborers, who make up 8.5 percent of the population. In numerical terms, there were 12,649 talented students whose parents were laborers. Eson (1964) finds it difficult to believe that the genes of the human race can have been so segregated that such a discrepancy could be due to inheritance. Although it is likely that the environment provided by the laborer tends to stultify high native ability, the aptitudes of children who are raised in such an environment are probably not comparable to the high potential of students from academically oriented homes. In other words, an increase would probably occur in the abilities of children from families low on the socioeconomic scale if they were moved at birth to be brought up as sons and daughters of professional families. It is also probable that many would go on to college who do not do so now, but it is doubtful that a vastly increased number would have ranked as Merit Scholars. The scholarships go to those who have both the genetic background and the environment to exploit it.

Semler and Iscoe (1966) found that the differences in favor of white as compared with black seven-, eight-, and nine-year-old children on WISC scores did not show up for the eight- and nine-year-old children when tested with the culture-controlled Raven Progressive Matrices test. Jensen (1968) reported a study involving white, black, and Mexican-

middle-class neighbors. Ethnic backgrounds apparently make a difference in intelligence test scores, but the basis for the difference is obscure.

**Socioeconomic Status and Children's Intelligence**

In the previous section on ethnic differences in intelligence, the effect of socioeconomic status was repeatedly mentioned. In general,

American children of low socioeconomic status. The correlations between their IQ scores and a test involving free recall and serial and paired associate learning were low in all cases. On the other hand, children from middle-class backgrounds had high correlations between their IQ scores and the same tests. Jensen pointed out that learning tests for children from families low on the socioeconomic scale are correlated at nonsignificant levels with IQ scores. He interpreted the studies as showing that IQ scores are not good indicators of learning ability for children from socioeconomically disadvantaged backgrounds.

Garrett (1967) reported mean IQ scores of 100 for white children and 80 for black children, and then argued against the feasibility of integration because of this difference. Kennedy, Van de Riet, and White (1963) found approximately the same differences when a sample of 1,800 black children from Southern states were compared with the norming sample for the Stanford-Binet. Jensen restudied these data and pointed out that the scores from black and white children were far apart on vocabulary but quite similar on digit span. He implied that the differences between the group scores were an artifact of the tests and reflected differences in learning opportunities rather than a difference in native abilities.

## Genetic and Environmental Factors

Jensen (1969) published a long article, "How Much Can We Boost IQ and Scholastic Achievement?," which has become a focus for new controversy about the relative importance of heredity and environment in intelligence. Most of the rage that has been generated by the article has been triggered by two sections on implications of the findings: (1) that concerning the relative levels of black and white intelligence and (2) the success or probability of success of compensatory education programs. Within the framework of the study, it is possible for both Jensen and his critics to be correct in their statements.

Jensen's calculation of heredity is based on particular scores from particular tests given to specific populations. Cronbach (1969) pointed out that the heredity factor would be substantially lower for height than that generally reported and accepted if a group of 1940 Japanese males were pooled with a similar sized group of 1970 Japanese males than would be the result if heredity were calculated for each group separately. Extreme changes in the environments of these two groups occurred, and these changes made probable larger physical stature than would have been possible in the old environment. Jensen (pp. 42, 43) is quite precise in his definition of heritability and states it is not a constant, like $\pi$. He also said, "H will be higher in a population in which environmental variation relative to the trait in question is small, than in a population in which there is great environmental variation." Massive changes in the environment of children could be expected to have significant impact on their intelligence, although the improvement would probably be greater for those with superior genetic potential than for less endowed individuals.

Heritability is calculated by analyzing the variance that is attributable to different factors. In trying to calculate the impact of environment on intelligence, monozygotic and dyzygotic twins, siblings, and unrelated children can be studied in closely similar and in widely different environments. Monozygotic twins have the same genes, and differences between them can be attributed to environmental factors which include the prenatal environment. Unrelated children who are reared in the same household have more similarity in their environments than do other unrelated children reared in different households. The variance due to environment can be calculated for these groups. More complicated calculations can be made for cousins, grandparents, and other relatives. In a number of studies, mostly involving white Anglo Saxon populations, the variance due to environment is approximately .25 and that due to inheritance approximately .75 (Table 16-2, Figure 16-7).

Hunt (1969) reacted to Jensen's article with substantial praise, but he pointed out (p. 290) that significant improvements can be made in the schemata for looking, if young children are given practice in differentiating visual patterns. He related this finding to an average height of sailors (5 foot 2 inches) at the time of the War of 1812 and the subsequent increase in average height of United States sailors. The implications are that the distribution of intelligence between subgroups of the general population might very well change. Hunt suggested that child-rearing practices for the low-income groups could be improved by successful intervention in the patterns of interaction with children.

Jensen's analysis, the reaction of his critics, and experience with compensatory programs can be interpreted to mean that change in intellectual ability is possible. All children can function intellectually better than they do. Substantial changes will require more skill and more effort than has been typical of most early childhood programs. More time for longitudinal intervention will be required than many parents and teachers are willing to wait. Height has increased 10 inches in American males in 160 years; intelligence can improve but this will happen as a result of sustained effort over a long period of time. Teachers will probably provide the energy that makes the difference. They need to accept the low view and not to become discouraged when progress seems slow. As long as teaching increases the

**Table 16-2   Correlations for Intellectual Ability: Obtained and Theoretical Values**

| Correlation between | Number of studies | Obtained median r* | Theoretical value† |
|---|---|---|---|
| Unrelated Persons | | | |
| Children reared apart | 4 | −.01 | .00 |
| Foster parent and child | 3 | +.20 | .00 |
| Children reared together | 5 | +.24 | .00 |
| Collaterals | | | |
| Second cousins | 1 | +.16 | + .14 |
| First cousins | 3 | +.26 | + .18 |
| Uncle (or aunt) and nephew (or niece) | 1 | +.34 | + .31 |
| Siblings, reared apart | 33 | +.47 | + .52 |
| Siblings, reared together | 36 | +.55 | + .52 |
| Dizygotic twins, different sex | 9 | +.49 | + .50 |
| Dizygotic twins, same sex | 11 | +.56 | + .54 |
| Monozygotic twins, reared apart | 4 | +.75 | +1.00 |
| Monozygotic twins, reared together | 14 | +.87 | +1.00 |
| Direct Line | | | |
| Grandparent and grandchild | 3 | +.27 | + .31 |
| Parent (as adult) and child | 13 | +.50 | + .49 |
| Parent (as child) and child | 1 | +.56 | + .49 |

\* Correlations not corrected for attenuation (unreliability).
† Assuming assortative mating and partial dominance.

ability to learn, it will be effective in raising competence when viewed in terms of decades.

### Gifted Students

Platt (1962) described the differences between a person with an IQ of 140 and one whose IQ is on the order of 170. Both have abilities that are beyond those of the average individual, in much the same way that the average person who can jump 4¹/₂ feet is surpassed by one who can clear 6 feet but not 6¹/₂ feet. By exceptional training from his earliest days, coupled with a better diet, the average person might learn to jump 5¹/₂ feet—a substantial increase over his present best performance—but he would not match the exceptional performers, who had the best training coupled with a better kinesthetic inheritance.

Platt commented upon the effects of selective breeding brought about by large concentrations of exceptionally able individuals in university communities and the contiguous satellite research communities that gather around universities. In the public schools of these communities, some unsegregated classes are found where the mean IQ is 120 or above. As these children grow up and marry the people with whom they have always been in contact and with whom they feel comfortable intellectually, the result may be a younger generation that contains more exceptionally intelligent individuals than the present one. Considerable evidence is available that musicians, poets, and mathematicians tend to be drawn to others of the same interests and to develop strains that are unusually capable in music, poetry, or mathematics. Children whose parents are intellectually able and intensely interested in a particular activity are likely to have environmental advantages in that area. The temptation to ascribe the extraordinary success of such individuals to environmental influences should be resisted, as a few years ago, some psychologists should

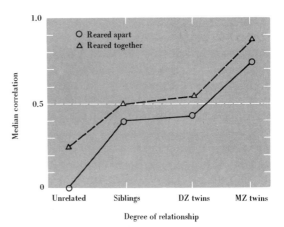

**Figure 16-7**  Effects of heredity and environment on growth of intelligence. (Redrawn from A. R. Jensen. How much can we boost IQ and scholastic achievement? *Harvard Educational Review*, Winter 1969, 39(1) p. 50. By permission of publishers.)

have resisted the temptation to interpret similar data in purely hereditary terms. In the extreme ranges of performance, such as the upper 170s, an exceptional genetic system must be matched with an exceptional environment. At less esoteric levels, an exceptional environment may combine with poor inheritance to produce above-normal development, just as a poor environment may combine with exceptional potential to produce an above-average product. Teachers can do very little about genetic inheritance, but there are many ways in which they can influence the environmental forces that determine how the genetic potentialities will be used.

Terman and Merrill (1937) made an extensive study of the relationship between the scores made by children on the Revised Stanford-Binet Intelligence Scale and the occupations of their parents. In their sample, a systematic relationship was found between the level of intelligence of the children and the occupational level of the parents when means were compared. The children of the day laborers averaged about 20 IQ points below the children whose parents were in the professions. These differences were very similar in the group of children from 2 to 5½ years of age and in that of children from 15 to 18 (Table 16-3). Two explanations of these differentials have been given, based on two different theories. The first, which is essentially genetic, asserts that the parents move as far upward on the socioeconomic scale as their ability permits and find marriage partners of genetically superior stock, so that their children inherit the better genes as far as intelligence is concerned and show up to better advantage on tests. The other explanation is basically environmental in nature and interprets the differences as being due to the inferior home backgrounds of the children who score less well. The truth probably lies somewhere between these two views. Very able people tend to migrate upward socially, to marry others of similar general ability, to transmit somewhat better genes to their offspring, and then to provide a favorable environment for these children when they arrive. Less capable adults are pushed downward in their initial job opportunities, find their marriage partners within their new economic and social environment, pass on the relatively poorer genes, and then provide a less stimulating environment for their children. No condemnation should be construed from this statement. These people have less opportunity, time, and money to create a stimulating environment in the home.

The conclusion to be drawn is that different levels of genetic potential combined with markedly enriched or deprived environments result in divergent patterns of development. It should also be stressed that these findings are based on means and that the range of ability in all groups is so large as to make prejudgments of individuals indefensible. Some children from professional homes are born so retarded that they must be institutionalized all their lives. Membership in a group does not determine the individual's intelligence.

## Comparisons of Boys and Girls

Teachers must vary their teaching if they are to deal effectively with the host of different children. Although the IQ scores of boys and girls are very similar, some characteristics are more common to one sex in our society than to the other. In school, boys are expected to excel in subjects that require convergent, structural thinking such as mathematics and science, while girls are expected to do well in the humanities and social sciences, where memory and divergent thinking are important. Probably the schools should reinforce mem-

**Table 16-3   Mean Scores on Stanford-Binet at Two Ages by Occupation of Parents** (*After Terman and Merrill, 1937*)

| Parental occupation | Average IQ | |
|---|---|---|
| | 2–5½ years | 15–18 years |
| Professional | 114.8 | 116.8 |
| Semiprofessional and managerial | 112.4 | 116.7 |
| Clerical, skilled trade, retail business | 108.0 | 109.6 |
| Semiskilled, minor clerical, business | 104.3 | 106.7 |
| Slightly skilled | 97.2 | 96.2 |
| Day laborers | 93.8 | 97.6 |

bers of both sexes for using appropriate intellectual operations over the entire spectrum of the school curriculum (Broderick, 1966).

On the average, girls receive higher grades than boys through the elementary school years. More boys drop out of school than girls, more nonreaders are boys than girls, and in general more boys fail in school than girls. These results may be due in part to a greater disparity in role expectancy for boys than for girls inside the school and out. Although evidence is inconclusive, some observers think that girls are often better treated in school than boys, perhaps because their relationships with teachers, who must preserve and maintain the cultural expectation of school behavior, are mutually reinforcing.

Kuznets and McNemar (1940) summarized comparisons of the sexes on total scores of intelligence tests. They restricted their report to studies in which (1) more than 100 subjects were involved, (2) tests of statistical significance could be applied, (3) wide variations in the ages of subjects were avoided, and (4) there was no selective bias in favor of one sex or the other. On the basis of this approach, they reported general agreement that no apparent differences existed between the sexes in IQ scores. This report was amended by the following subfindings: Pressy (1918) found all the mean differences favored girls, with three of them being significant; Whitmire (1920) and Whipple (1927) using the National Intelligence Test both found a similar superiority for girls; and Thorndike (1926) and Commins (1928) both found systematic differences in favor of boys, although their research involved older students. Kuznets and McNemar considered the differences that appeared to be more closely related to the content of the tests than to differences in the individuals tested.

Rusk (1940) reported on the intelligence of Scottish children. In the first of these studies, undertaken in 1932, all eleven-year-old children in both public and private schools and in institutions were given an intelligence test. There were 87,498 individuals in the sample. In order to check against the group test, a random sample of approximately 1,000 children born on June 1, 1921, were tested with the 1916 Stanford revision of the Binet test. A further test was made between 1935 and 1937, when all the children born on February 1, May 1, August 1, and November 1 of the year 1926 were tested with the same form of the Stanford-Binet scale. Rusk was able to locate all but one of the children born on these dates. Since the group was the universe of possible cases, the sampling error disappeared. All this testing was done by one test administrator. This series of tests still ranks as the most carefully executed and comprehensive examination of a total population ever undertaken.

The mean of the group test (1932) was 103 for boys and 100 for girls. The mean of the Stanford-Binet sample (1935 to 1937) was 100.51 for boys and 99.7 for girls. The boys were somewhat more variable in their spread than the girls, and the standard deviation of the sample was higher than Terman had obtained in his original norming data. The results are shown in Table 16-4.

Rusk makes the point in his article (1940) that intelligence tests are basically very poor ways of separating differences between boys and girls since questions that favor either sex are regularly discarded by the test maker. The result is that any indication of separation means that the test is not quite as good as it was intended to be. He makes the same point about environmental differences. Since they are intentionally excluded during test construction, they should not show up during test usage.

## GROWTH OF INTELLECTUAL POWER

Teachers are able to vary their instruction to take advantage of changing abilities if they

**Table 16-4  Distribution of Scores for Boys and Girls on the Scottish Survey** (*After Rusk, 1940*)

| | Group test (1932 survey) | | Stanford-Binet 1916 revision (1935–1937 survey) | | |
| | Boys | Girls | Boys | Girls | Total |
|---|---|---|---|---|---|
| Mean | 103 | 100 | 100.51 | 99.7 | 100.11 |
| Standard deviation | 17 | 17 | 15.58 | 15.26 | 15.58 |
| Number | 44,210 | 43,288 | 444 | 430 | 874 |

| IQ | Percent calculated from the standard deviation | | | | |
|---|---|---|---|---|---|
| 129+ | 4 | 3 | 5.4 | 3.9 | 4.7 |
| 110–128 | 24 | 24 | 22.3 | 20. | 21.2 |
| 90–109 | 44 | 46 | 46.2 | 51.2 | 48.6 |
| 70–89 | 24 | 24 | 25.5 | 23.0 | 24.2 |
| 0–70 | 4 | 3 | 0.7 | 1.9 | 1.3 |

know what can be expected in the rate of growth of intelligence. If, as has been commonly thought, growth of intelligence stops at about age 16, a normal high school sophomore is as intelligent as he will ever be and presumably can be expected to learn as complex material at that age as he will be able to learn when he is older. Some recent studies indicate that 16 may be an unrealistically low age to designate as the top of the developmental period. Bradway and Robinson (1961) found continuous growth to approximately age 18½ as they studied IQ changes in a 25-year follow-up.

Burt (1939) studied different groups of English children and found that the more intelligent children had already established their intellectual superiority by the time they were 4 years old. Not only did they continue to increase in intelligence more quickly than their less favored peers, but they also kept on growing for a longer period of time. The mental defectives in his sample reached their full growth by the time they were 12 years old, at which point they had an average MA of 8

years (Figure 16-8). The scholarship winners—the mentally gifted group in his study—continued to improve or to grow intellectually until they were nearly 20 years old, at which time they had an MA of about 20 years. The inadequacy of the mental age—chronological age ratio when used to describe intelligence in subjects older than 11 or 12 is seen clearly in this report. However, the data indicated that the normal group grew mentally until they were about 15, when they had reached an MA of about the same level. The dull and backward grew mentally until they were 13 or 14 and reached an MA of about 11. From these figures it is apparent that those most richly endowed at the start grow both faster and longer intellectually, perhaps because their intellectual activities are very different from those of the less gifted.

The individual growth curves, which are consolidated and smoothed to arrive at these figures, show considerably more variability and irregularity in the year-by-year fluctuations. Some of the average students spurted ahead and surpassed some of the mentally gifted students, at least for part of the growth period. For teachers, the focus of attention should be on the possibilities apparent after maximum growth has been attained. Even seriously retarded children have the mental capacity to learn to read simple material by the time they have reached the height of their mental capacity. Many mentally slow children do not learn to use their abilities because of early frustrations they suffer while trying unsuccessfully to learn school tasks for which they are not yet mature enough intellectually.

Burt's data indicated that the development of intellectual power levels off for normal or average students by about 16 years of age, while the more able student continues to gain in ability until about age 20. The age at which full growth of intelligence is reported to be achieved has tended to increase over the years. This increase may reflect more years of schooling, better testing instruments for adult populations, more stimulating mental occupations for the majority of the populations studied, or perhaps even increasing age of the investigators.

Binet considered 15 to be the age at which intelligence stops increasing in the average person. Terman, in *Measurement of Intelligence* (1916), says that intellectual growth continues to 15 or 16, and he used 16 as the divisor in finding the IQs of all those older than that. Wechsler (1955) used a cross-sectional technique in standardizing the Wechsler Adult Intelligence Scale (WAIS) and found increased intellectual power to age 30, with a gradual drop off after that until age 60. Anastasi (1956) criticized these data on the grounds that the younger individuals had had more education than the older subjects, leading to the possibility that their higher scores were an artifact of their longer education. Bayley (1955), working from longitudinal studies, found evidence that individuals continue to grow intellectually until at least 50 years of age. The probability that strenuous mental exercise increases the functional abili-

ty should be considered. The average person who drops out of school at age 14 to work at routine tasks for long hours finds little in his environment to stimulate growth of his intelligence. A judge might be expected to have a different pattern of intellectual functioning from that of the lumber piler because the mental activity in which he engages is different.

Thurstone (1955) reported that the primary mental abilities develop at different rates. Reasoning, space aptitude, and perceptual speed are among the abilities he found to grow more quickly than the average. He found that memory and numerical ability largely overlap but are somewhat slower in their development, while the verbal factors are the last to attain their full growth. This pattern of intellectual growth can be compared with that outlined by Piaget (Chapter 14), who describes growth as being spiral, with functioning in the world of things followed by the ability to function in the world of purely abstract ideas. Reasoning is part of all three cycles in Piaget's account and tends to be the end of the cycle. Piaget's concept of verbalization is the factor that distinguishes the second and third cycles from the first. In general, Thurstone's findings

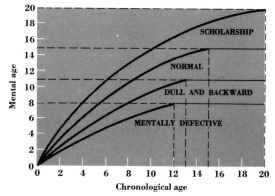

**Figure 16-8** Eight differences in speed and length of mental growth period for English children of different abilities. (*Redrawn from C. Burt, The latest revision of the Binet Intelligence Tests, Eugenics Review, 1939, 30, 255–260. By permission of the author and publisher.*)

agree with those of Piaget, although pertinent questions arise about the kind of reasoning ability and the kind of numerical ability they tested.

It seems fair to conclude that those who have and use their abilities increase their holdings. Those who have few abilities are likely to have even these diminish, at least on a comparative basis. Those who are well endowed genetically also seem to need to use their abilities or else lose them.

## MECHANISMS THAT AFFECT INTELLIGENCE

Gifted students sometimes do not work up to the intellectual levels of which they are capable. Some students with comparatively poor ability use their strengths to great advantage, while others give up and let the world pass them by. These deficient ways of responding to life's expectations affect functional intelligence. Mr. W., a high school English teacher, observed the subtle changes in the intellectual functioning of two students from the same family when the father was promoted to bank manager. They made indefinable attempts to measure up to their new role as sons of an executive. The upward mobility manifested itself in an assumption that an executive's son should be able to solve certain problems, which six months earlier had been too difficult to attempt. Much of the greater success of children from professional and managerial families probably springs from a self-image that leads to extra effort and extra persistence. When applied over a period of time, the extra push leads to accomplishments just out of the reach of individuals with equal intellectual ability but lower aspirations.

### Slum Children Who Close Out Noise and Information

Some aspects of the environment influence students in negative ways. Silberman (1964) described life in a slum, in which too many people are crowded into two or three rooms and all are creating noise of one kind or another. Under such circumstances, people come to stop discriminating among subtle sounds. They close out as much of the noise that bombards them as they can, much as people who work in a saw mill close out the noise, which would otherwise be unbearable. As slum children close out the sound of other people, they are also shutting down the communication channels that bring needed information and auditory discriminations. Reactivating the reception channels is difficult once they have been programmed to exclude incoming information.

### Dropouts Who Close Out School

Most of the young people who drop out of school give socially acceptable reasons for doing so. These include a need to help with the family finances, the desire to get started on a career, and other excuses. They usually do not admit that they must escape from the punishment that school represents to them. Many of these youths have cut school off their input systems years earlier. They sit in class and often play the role of a listener. Sometimes they even try to attend to a teacher they admire, but often the habits of inattention, built up over the years, keep them from success. Semester after semester, starting in kindergarten, the information that came in assured them that they were not satisfactory learners. Under the circumstances, they stopped listening to or hearing these bits of speech from the teachers. When the quantity of information shut out passed a critical point, they were effectively lost to further education; only a drastic change could have brought them back into communication with the classroom dialogue. In most cases, their inattentive roles brought only further aversive remarks and another drop on the falling scale of their intelligences. Such young people have become truly alienated from school and from school learning. Their *abilities* and *capacities* as students have systematically diverged.

### Adults Who Close Out New Experiences

Many adults, as they become older, close down mechanisms by which new experiences can reach them. They grow tired of trying new things; they lose confidence in themselves as being able to accomplish much that is important, and they give up. They are doing precisely what the school dropout does, only at later stages in life. Often they start to look and act elderly when they reach this point of decision. The young in heart are still open to new experiences at ninety-five, while some have become old men and women at thirty-five because this is the image they have built of themselves. Whatever his age, intellectual growth stops when the individual comes to reject learning.

### SUMMARY

*Intelligence* is the degree of ease or difficulty with which various kinds of things are learned. *Ability* is the power to perform a designated responsive act, native or acquired. *Capacity* is potential ability—that is, genetic ability. *Achievement* is the individual's actual performance on a given test at a point in time. Intelligence tests reflect the opportunities the individual has had to learn information, skills, discriminations, or other functions, as well as the potential with which he was endowed.

Genetic inheritance has a significant effect on the individual's intelligence. Rats have been selectively bred for intelligence, and it has been possible to develop new strains that are distinct in this ability. The environment also has an observable and measurable effect on intelligence. The interaction of environment and heredity has been shown in twin studies and is evident in the histories of families. Certain drugs act as special environmental effects that may increase or decrease intellectual abilities under specific conditions.

Intelligence is distributed uniformly from the very high to the very low ranges, with most people falling somewhere in the middle. The very able differ from the less able in the kinds of thinking they can do as well as in the amount of thinking they can do on a given level; the able are superior in both realms. The highly intelligent grow more quickly and continue to grow for a longer period of time than the dull. In unfavorable environments, the person's mental abilities can deteriorate, so that he becomes progressively less able to function intellectually than he had been. Boys and girls develop at the same rates, although cultural effects seem to influence a differential set of abilities to a limited extent. Groups of individuals vary in their intellectual abilities depending on selective breeding and on environmental opportunities. Black children are found with all ranges of ability, although the concentration of blacks in the lower socioeconomic groups tends to depress their intelligence level as an overall group, as does the poor environment of white children from laboring-class homes.

Self-expectations and rewarding or punishing experiences can, over a prolonged period of time, markedly increase or decrease the functioning level of intelligence. Teachers are efficient agents in effecting changes of this type in the functioning of children.

### SELF-DIRECTING ACTIVITIES

1 Explain the causes for a decline in the general IQ of the canalboat children as they got older.
2 Look for evidence that the intellectual level of a particular group may have been improving since the Second World War.
3 Devise a learning situation that would be as likely to raise the IQ of gifted students as another learning situation would improve the performance of slower students.
4 Find an adult who has stopped growing intellectually and devise a motivation system that will restart him. Test over a period of time to see how effective your efforts have been.

# Chapter **17**

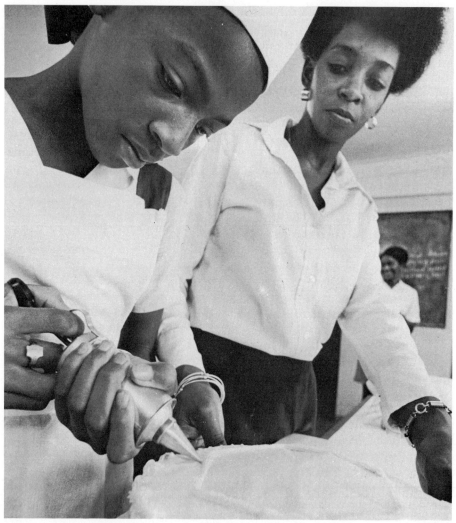

Performance evaluation. (*Courtesy of the United Nations*)

# EVALUATION OF OBJECTIVES

In this chapter, you will see how teachers can use evaluation in the context of decision making as a means of helping them and school administrators to improve the teaching-learning process and to enhance the realization of desired educational outcomes. Specifically, you should be able to:

◖ Differentiate between evaluation and measurement

◖ Delineate principles underlying criteria necessary for evaluation

◖ Describe steps required in evaluation procedures

◖ Explain the interrelationships of key concepts underlying a comprehensive model for evaluation that involves four types of decisions

◖ Relate educational accountability to evaluation

◖ Demonstrate how tests and observations can be used in the evaluation process

◖ Use and identify such terms as:
   evaluation (including context, input, process, and product evaluation)
   measurement
   accountability
   test
   scale
   reliability
   content validity
   criterion-related validity
   construct validity

Teachers and administrators often find it both desirable and necessary to judge the quality and effectiveness of instruction by comparing student performance against behavioral standards so that appropriate decisions can be made to effect changes in teaching procedures, in selection and use of instructional materials, and sometimes in the objectives themselves, especially if they appear inappropriate to the abilities and interests of students. Such judging activities that are aimed toward establishing the value or worth of individual learning endeavors in relation to the goals of the school community and to the specific behavioral objectives developed by teachers and administrators constitute evaluation. Once information is obtained regarding how closely student performances correspond to standards or criteria incorporated within specific behavioral objectives, additional judgments are needed in choosing among alternative strategies that would most likely bring about desired behavioral changes within the constraints imposed by available human and physical resources and by previously established school district priorities.

Evaluation is significant in learning when it encourages the student to see how he can improve in his educational endeavor and when it permits the teacher to interrelate all kinds of evidence about student behaviors and to do a bit of soul-searching to ascertain how his teaching might be improved. In evaluation, every effort is also made to locate major forms of inadequate behavior as well as possible causal factors underlying what may be judged to be inadequate learning. Of course, inadequate learning itself is defined in terms of certain standards that have been set by the teacher, the administrators, and the governing personnel of the school district—in fact, by all those implementing the program. Thus, in short, evaluation is concerned with the whole individual—with all forms of learning experience that may contribute to his intellectual,

physical, emotional, aesthetic, and social development, and thus to his finding a useful place in society.

## DEFINITION OF EVALUATION

In general terms, educational evaluation may be described or defined as an ongoing process for generating relevant information that can be used in identifying and judging according to certain value criteria alternative courses of action (decision alternatives) in response to a question or problem situation requiring planned change. The individual who is responsible for delineating, obtaining, and providing the information required for formulating decision alternatives is the *evaluator*, whereas the user of evaluative data who judges the relative advantages or disadvantages of alternative courses of action and then chooses one of them is the *decision maker.* In the continual modification of instructional strategies and in the varied uses of instructional materials in the classroom setting to meet individual student needs, the teacher is typically both the evaluator and decision maker, but in a districtwide educational program or in a federally funded project in which the roles of personnel are well defined, the evaluator is often a trained specialist. He supplies information to and consults with project directors, administrators, or board members, who in turn are expected to act as decision makers and to accept responsibility for (to be held accountable for) their decisions.

## DISTINGUISHING BETWEEN MEASUREMENT AND EVALUATION

Many school personnel, as well as students of educational psychology, have difficulty differentiating between measurement and evaluation. *Measurement* is the process of using a test, scale, or instrument to obtain a relatively objective and quantified indication of a person's standing on a characteristic (such as achievement in arithmetic or language ability) represented by the device employed. Customarily in the measurement process individuals are ranked along a scale from high to low, or in psychological terminology, are "ordered" along a scale from high to low. There are different degrees of performance, and if individual differences did not exist, there would be little point in giving tests or examinations. Thus in an arithmetic test consisting of 50 items, the range of scores might vary from 8 to 49 items answered correctly. Such a range of scores would afford a teacher a basis for measuring the level of achievement. If scores on a comparable form of the test administered at an earlier time were available, the teacher would have a basis for determining the amount of change in standing and for making an inference about the degree of progress.

*Evaluation* involves the use of measurement as a tool for obtaining information that can be employed in decision-making activities as in assigning marks, retaining or promoting a pupil, diagnosing learning disabilities, modifying course objectives and/or instructional strategies, grouping students, or providing (or not providing) remedial instruction or counseling services. Test scores furnish evidence regarding (a) a student's initial level of standing on selected behaviors such as reading comprehension, arithmetic skills, or interests; (b) subsequent level of placement on these same behaviors; (c) amount of change in such behaviors from one testing session to another; and (d) discrepancies between actual outcomes and intended outcomes of instruction that have been previously specified by behavioral objectives. These four kinds of evidence permit a partial basis for making judgments regarding how effectively instructional objectives have been attained and for drawing inferences concerning how effective instructional strategies have been in changing student

behaviors. In short, the score from the measurement procedure represents a fact or bit of relatively objective information; the judgment concerning the meaning and value of the score represents an evaluation.

## Criteria Relative to the Evaluation Process

The determination of meaningful criteria or standards concerning what are acceptable or appropriate amounts of change in behavior is a highly subjective and complex undertaking that is influenced by the philosophy of teachers, administrators, school boards, and citizens of the community. Conflicts frequently arise where there is a contradiction between a school district's policy and a teacher's judgment. For example, in a lower-middle-class community, John, according to test norms, might be reading at only the beginning of the third-grade level when he is at the end of the fifth grade. For promotion the district requires that a pupil be reading not more than $1^1/_2$ years below his grade level. Yet John may have shown a gain of one full grade level in reading performance since he was tested almost one year before. In terms of evidence concerning his intellectual capacity, he might have shown about as much growth in reading as could be reasonably expected under the most favorable learning environments. Any evaluation of his performance would obviously need to take into account the gain in reading level in terms of his intellectual capacity as well as in terms of a possibly barren or disadvantaged home environment. Decisions concerning his promotion to sixth grade might be quite complicated for a teacher or even an administrator if district policy required a reading level equivalent to what the average student would attain at the beginning of his second semester in the fourth grade. In order not to impair the social development of a child such as John who relates well to his peers or to handicap him in intellectual endeavors in nonverbal areas where he has shown some special strength, the teacher might advisably wish to appeal any decision of retention to the principal. When additional sources of information are evaluated by the school psychologist regarding John's performance potential and when his achievement level in other subjects is looked at with care, an insightful administrator might well make an exception to the rule and recommend promotion. In any event, the decision would be based on an evaluation of as much information as could be obtained and of a whole complex of factors on which data were available. Obviously the decision would be reached on the basis of an evaluation that would be admittedly highly subjective and strongly value-laden.

The following principles are important in defining the nature of criteria for evaluation if evaluation is to be helpful in the promotion of future learning:

**1** The dimensions of behavior to be evaluated must first be clearly described, preferably in operational terms that are amenable to measurement.

**2** The level of standing on the measure (test or scale) that represents a criterion of performance or behavior (the criterion measure) should be explicitly and sharply defined, preferably in terms of a quantitative index such as a cutting score. For example, a carefully constructed 40-item test in mathematics achievement that supposedly reflects the objectives of the curriculum might furnish scores ranging from 0 to 40. In terms of logical considerations based on the teacher's prior experience, a score of 25 or higher might be declared adequate for going on to the next unit of work.

**3** Customarily, differences in the degree of appropriateness of criterion behavior that the test or scale supposedly represents should be specified relative to certain scores or intervals of scores or in terms of explicit descriptions of observable behaviors such as those appearing on a rating scale. In the instance of the mathematics test just cited, the teacher might decide in terms of some rationale that a score between 35 and 40 would be considered "outstanding"; a score between 30 and 34, "superior"; a score between 25 and 29, "satisfactory"; and any score at or below 24, "unsatisfactory." [It should be emphasized that absolute standards for marking simply do not exist. In the final analysis, all grades are arbitrary indicators of relative standing. In the instance of criterion-referenced tests, however, standards do exist in relation to whether a student can or cannot demonstrate his competence in a skill as reflected by his response to a test item which corresponds to a specific behavioral objective. Thus a criterion-referenced test affords a basis for each student to demonstrate whether he has mastered a given set of competencies (objectives) irrespective of how he has achieved relative to his peers. The "criterion" in the term "criterion-referenced" designates the standard of mastery or competence that is defined by the behavioral objective and is incorporated within one or more items representing performance required for that objective.]

**4** The standards for making judgments concerning the adequacy of behaviors should be applied in a relatively consistent and stable manner. A feeling on the part of the pupils that they are being treated fairly and that certain of their peers are not receiving favored consideration is important for sustaining motivation in the class and for maintaining the respect of the class for the teacher. Such consistency or stability, which will subsequently be defined as *reliability of measurement*, is essential if student behaviors are to be evaluated accurately and if educational research is to be conducted with the data from which evaluations are derived.

**5** The sampling of behaviors for most evaluative criteria should be broad and representative of the domains of behavior judged to be important in learning. In other words, the evaluation needs to be made on multiple dimensions of behavior so that the validity of the evaluation process can be assured by a sampling that allows many facets of behavior to appear in the proportions in which they are judged significant. Both cognitive and noncognitive outcomes need to be covered. For example, in language arts in the junior high school, the mechanics of written expression, teacher assigned compositions, self-initiated papers, oral presentations in class, outside pleasure-reading experiences involving self-selection of books and magazines, library research, and other dimensions need to be sampled frequently and representatively so that a total, valid picture of achievement in language arts may be realized.

**6** The meaningful application of evaluative criteria in decision making requires cognizance of the fact that the particular behaviors to be sampled and measured should be those which are consistent with the principles of child development relative to variables of age, sex, intellectual level, physical maturity, and levels of social and personal adjustment.

Finally in evaluation a distinction should be made between the terms "norm" and "standard"—between "what is" and "what should be or ought to be." The term "norm" refers to typical performance such as that found in reading at a given age or grade level. Thus the child in any grade who reads at the average level of children in the fourth grade would fall at the fourth-grade norm. On the other hand, the term "standard" pertains to a criterion measure that is judged to be appropriate, adequate, or desirable in light of the value system held by the teacher, administrator, or counselor. Although teachers and administrative personnel often believe that a statewide or national norm should represent the expected standard, such an assumption is not necessarily realistic, as ability levels of students and curricular objectives vary widely from one school or community to another. Thus norms refer to descriptive characteristics of test data, but interpretations or judgments regarding what is satisfactory, adequate, or appropriate performance constitute

potential standards for the procedure of evaluation.

## STEPS IN THE EVALUATION PROCEDURE

In formal evaluation studies, several steps are involved that are relevant even in less formal evaluation activities. Michael and Metfessel (1967) described in a paradigm the basic steps for the more formal types of evaluation. The essential phases are as follows:

**1** Developing broad goals or broad objectives that are anchored to the philosophic framework of the teacher, administrator, school board, or community. These are illustrated by three examples given by Michael and Metfessel (1967):

(1) To develop an understanding of the nature of the scientific method.

(2) To write and speak correctly and effectively.

(3) To gain appreciation of the heritage of music and art of Western civilization [p. 378].

**2** Formulating specific behavioral objectives that satisfy numerous criteria such as (a) relevancy to the basic philosophic tenets and values of the school and community concerning what is important to learn; (b) satisfaction of both immediate and long-range needs within and outside the culture of the school; (c) compatibility with students' psychological readiness and prior preparation; (d) realistic correspondence to what can be effectively learned in terms of available physical plant, staff qualifications, library resources, and physical capability; and (e) opportunity for student-teacher interaction to provide for continuous two-way feedback that can motivate and direct learning. Michael and Metfessel (1967) have given some illustrative examples of specific behavioral objectives that correspond to the broad objectives just cited:

(1) (a) To draw accurate inferences concerning possible cause-and-effect relationships from tabulated data on an

experiment in photosynthesis; (b) to design an experiment intended to test the validity of Newton's second law; or (c) to predict the tensile strength of a piece of metal from a measure of its hardness.

(2) (a) To show accurate use of noun and verb forms; (b) to punctuate a paragraph correctly; (c) to compose a letter of job application correct in form and free of grammatical errors.

(3) (a) To attend five or more musical events (without compulsion) held on the college campus; (b) to read for pleasure three or more books during the school year on the history and theory of visual art; (c) to participate in the campus choir at least one evening per week without receiving unit credit [p. 378].

3 Devising instructional strategies, designing the curriculum, and selecting or putting together instructional materials so as to facilitate attainment of the specific behavioral objectives through appropriate learning experience.

4 Developing a variety of measuring instruments and scales as well as observational procedures to furnish data that will permit inferences to be made concerning the extent to which specific behaviorally expressed objectives have been attained. [In another article in which they elaborated upon this paradigm, Metfessel and Michael (1967) listed more than 80 different criterion measures that can be used in evaluating selected characteristics or objectives of the program that are judged to be both relevant and important.]

5 Carrying out periodic observations and administrations of tests and scales to establish base lines and subsequently sufficient data to assess changes in behaviors judged to be related to the specific objectives.

6 Analyzing data gathered from observations and testing so that (a) comparisons of performance of individuals or student groups against norms can be made, (b) amounts of change can be determined and examined, and (c) patterns of interrelationships between various measures can be found.

7 Interpreting data obtained from measures with reference to specific behaviorally stated objectives to ascertain how closely several of the outcome (or criterion) measures conform to previously valued judgmental standards of what would be minimum levels of satisfactory performance or standing in other measurable characteristics such as personal and social adjustment—the step that actually represents the act of evaluation itself.

8 Making recommendations (subsequent to the feedback of information to the teacher, student, counselor, parents, and other individuals at different stages of the evaluation process) that lead to further implementation of, or modification in, the instructional strategies and curriculum, as well as at times to revisions in the specific behavioral objectives or the broad goals from which these objectives were derived—decisions in the instance of evaluating school programs that often lead both to substantial changes, not only in the specific objectives and broad goals of the school program but also in district policy, and to repetition of the cycle of evaluation.

## A COMPREHENSIVE MODEL FOR EVALUATION

The decision-making approach to evaluation that has been already described is not inconsistent with what is probably the most comprehensive model of evaluation to date—namely, the one developed by Stufflebeam and his coworkers as the culmination of nearly four years of work by the Phi Delta Kappa National Study Committee of Evaluation (Stufflebeam, Foley, Gephart, Guba, Hammond, Merriam, and Provus, 1971). Whereas the paradigm proposed by Michael and Metfessel (1967), which was just described, outlined the basic procedural steps in carrying out an evaluation that was oriented toward comparing actual or observable products (measured performances) with behavioral standards (intended outcomes), the Stufflebeam model is a dynamic system that defines, obtains, and provides information necessary for executing four types of decisions—planning, structuring, implementing, and recycling—respectively served by four kinds of evaluation—context, input, process, and product. From the first letters corresponding to each kind of evaluation, the acronym CIPP is formed to stand for the Stufflebeam model.

Closely approximating the definition already given for evaluation, the CIPP model defines educational evaluation as "the process of delineating, obtaining, and providing useful information for judging decision alternatives." This definition embraces three fundamental points. First, evaluation is a systematic, ongoing process. Second, this process incorporates three key steps: (1) detailing questions to be answered and information to be found, (2) obtaining pertinent information, and (3) making information available to decision makers for their considering and weighing the potential impact of alternative decisions upon improving ongoing educational programs or activities. Third, evaluation serves the decision-making process itself of selecting an alternative and following up on its consequences (Stufflebeam, 1971).

Evaluation serves four types of decisions specified by the CIPP model: (1) *planning* decisions, which determine goals and objectives; (2) *structuring* decisions, which set forth procedural designs and strategies for accomplishing the objectives derived from planning decisions; (3) *implementing* decisions, which offer ways for carrying out and refining the execution of previously selected designs or strategies; and (4) *recycling* decisions, which ascertain whether to continue, modify, or terminate a project or activity. These four decision types are served, respectively, by four kinds of evaluation. *Context* evaluation furnishes information about needs (discrepancies

between what is and what should be in terms of certain value expectations), difficulties, and opportunities, in order to identify and state goals and objectives. *Input* evaluation yields information regarding strengths and weaknesses of alternative designs and strategies for effecting specified objectives. *Process* evaluation affords monitoring information concerning strong points and weak points of a selected procedure or strategy during its implementation so that either the strategy or its application might be improved. *Product* evaluation provides information to ascertain to what degree the objectives are being attained and whether the procedure or strategies being implemented to realize the objectives should be continued, altered, or terminated. In a trial project a continual simultaneous interplay between process and product evaluation takes place so that the feedback gained from the level or quality of product attainments can be used in process evaluation for improving or refining defects in implementing decisions. Feedback can be possibly employed in input evaluation for redesigning the procedures so as to achieve more nearly acceptable products. In short, the CIPP model serves to answer four questions: (1) Which objective should be achieved? (2) Which procedures should be tried? (3) How well are these procedures working? and (4) How effectively are the objectives being attained?

Additional descriptive information regarding the CIPP model may be found in Figure 17-1, and information regarding the dynamic action of the CIPP model is portrayed in Figure 17-2. It should be noted that in Figure 17-1 the planning and recycling decisions are directed toward attainment of *ends* (goals or objectives), whereas structuring and implementing decisions are oriented toward the *means* of realizing these ends. Furthermore, planning decisions and structuring decisions reflect *intentions*, whereas implementing and recycling decisions pertain to *actualities*. In-

|  | **Intentions**<br>*Phase 1* | **Actualities**<br>*Phase 4* |
|---|---|---|
| **Ends**<br>(consequential<br>goals or<br>objectives) | Intended ends (objectives)<br><br>*Planning decisions*—choice of alternative change-oriented objectives (existing, modified, or new improvement-oriented objectives) in an educational system represented by a project or program<br><br>served by<br><br>*Context evaluation*—provides information to develop systematic rationale for objectives largely through analysis of unrealized needs and unused opportunities and through diagnosis of those difficulties preventing needs being met and contributing to discrepancies between intentions and actualities | Actual ends (attainments)<br><br>*Recycling decisions*—choice of alternative interpretations of how well objectives have been attained in relation to context, input, and process information and the judging of alternatives to continue, terminate, develop, or modify activities intended to solve problems posed by an educational system<br><br>served by<br><br>*Product evaluation*—provides information from which reactions and judgments of program or project attainments (products) can be made regarding extent to which objectives (change efforts) have been met either at the end or at any temporal point in a project cycle |
|  | *Phase 2* | *Phase 3* |
| **Means**<br>(instrumental<br>objectives) | Intended means (procedural designs)<br><br>*Structuring decisions*—choice of alternative designs, strategies, and procedures arising from planning decisions<br><br>served by<br><br>*Input evaluation*—provides information for identifying and assessing relevance and capabilities of designs, strategies, and procedures in light of human and material resources for achieving those objectives arising from planning decisions | Actual means (procedures in use)<br><br>*Implementing decisions*—choice of alternative courses of action involved in operationalizing, carrying out, controlling, and refining a previously chosen project design or strategy of known specifications<br><br>served by<br><br>*Process evaluation*—provides information (feedback) for monitoring by personnel responsible in implementing previously chosen procedures—information that allows (1) detection of existing or potential defects, (2) data generation for programmed decisions, and (3) record keeping of activities as they occur |

**Figure 17-1**   Four types of decisions in relation to four types of evaluation: A typology in a given educational system or framework.

spection of Figure 17-2 shows how each of the four types of decisions served by each of the four kinds of evaluations interact in a dynamic way. The schematic representation of the CIPP model indicates through the use of lines and arrows the feedback functions that take place continually between a given type of decision and its immediately supportive or servicing kind of evaluation as well as the feedback functions that occur from decisions of any type or evaluation of any kind to another type of decision and its corresponding kind of evaluation. In other words, as the feedback loops show in Figure 17-2, information can be transmitted from any stage of the decision-making process to a prior stage, with the result that modifications can be made in the kind of evaluations made and in the resulting decisions arising from these altered evaluations. Although the CIPP model was devised largely for the evaluation of educational programs, the insightful classroom teacher can and probably does make use of it, albeit unconsciously, in making decisions in teaching-learning activities underlying a given unit of instruction. (It is suggested that the reader might take a given instructional unit and try to apply the essential characteristics of the CIPP model to decision-making processes that might arise in teaching a curricular unit.)

## EDUCATIONAL ACCOUNTABILITY

Closely related to educational evaluation is educational accountability, which has received national, if not international, attention during the past few years. During the 1960s considerable money was spent on special programs with the view of improving the quality of education. Many educational leaders propagandized the educational community into believing that vast expenditures of money especially in disadvantaged areas would do much to improve educational outcomes and to effect substantial gains in learning. Unfortunately, most evaluation studies revealed that experimental groups receiving innovative programs did not achieve at a significantly higher level than did groups exposed to more traditional and conventional programs. Meanwhile, taxpayers whose annual bills showed staggering increases not only became resistant to spending more money on education but were demanding an accounting of how effectively their money was being expended. The public became concerned when published information from statewide testing programs revealed that their children were showing what critics declared to be unsatisfactory progress. Citizens often concluded that their tax moneys were being wasted and that teachers were not

bringing about a level of achievement commensurate with the investment being made in education. Taxpayers displayed a distrust in the competencies of teachers and demanded through their legislators an accounting for the not altogether satisfactory outcomes which teachers were judged to be producing. Hence in many states legislation was enacted in which teachers as well as administrators were to be held accountable for setting up objectives, for attaining them, and for taking corrective actions when objectives were not met. Provisions in legislation were included for censoring or dismissing teachers whose students did not perform at expected levels and for rewarding teachers those students exceeded expectations.

Educational accountability may be roughly defined as the designation of responsibility to educational personnel for the attainment or lack of attainment of educational outcomes

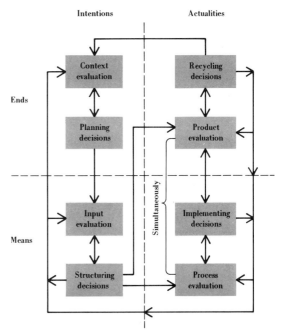

**Figure 17-2** Dynamic action and an evaluation model.

that are desired (but often not too well defined) by the educational community. In a definitive article, Alkin (1972, p. 2) described accountability as a "negotiated relationship in which the participants agree in advance to accept specified rewards and costs on the basis of evaluation findings as to the attainment of specified ends." Negotiation is used in the sense of an ongoing dialogue which leads to a mutual acceptance of a position of responsibility in meeting certain desired and carefully specified ends within a set of allowable constraints such as those imposed by the availability of certain instructional materials, time allocations, size of class, or access to teacher aides. Alkin has proposed three types of accountability: goal, program, and outcome. In *goal* accountability the school board is responsible to the public for setting goals and selecting objectives. In *program* accountability the administrators of the school district are responsible to the school board for the formation and/or selection of instructional programs that are considered appropriate for realizing or attaining the stated objectives. *Outcome* accountability is the task of the teacher, or instructional manager, who is responsible to the administrators for producing program attainments that are consistent with previously chosen objectives at a performance standard judged appropriate for the instructional program. The careful specification of mutually shared responsibilities in which certain educational personnel play a relatively more important role than others could lead to improvements in educational programs provided that communication is kept open and provided that in light of changing resources and changing needs reasonable adjustments can be made in the objectives and levels of outcomes anticipated. Failure to provide for renegotiation and modifications in contracts could lead to a serious deterioration in the morale of teachers and administrators, many of whom already feel that they are the victims of mistrust and political manipulation.

Educational accountability can also be viewed within the framework of the CIPP model. Whereas evaluation represents a proactive or future orientation toward the CIPP model aimed at improving educational programs through decision-making activities, accountability is a retroactive view of the CIPP model in which records of past actions in relation to educational decision making that initiated the actions are examined for the adequacy of their implementation and the value of their effects. Stufflebeam (1971) pointed out that those responsible for a program are faced with answering questions pertaining to both *ends* (planning and recycling decisions) and *means* (structuring and implementing decisions). Answers may need to be defended in terms of technological and scientific knowledge; explicit statements of moral, societal, individual, and group values; and relevant performance data. Illustrative questions pertaining to *ends* would include: Which objectives were selected? Why were they chosen? How effectively did program personnel achieve these objectives? Sample questions relating to means would be as follows: Which designs or strategies were chosen? For what reasons were they selected? How effectively or appropriately were they implemented?

An important distinction arises between a proactive application of the CIPP model of providing current information for future decision making and a retroactive function of providing information for accountability. Proactive evaluation is *formative* or *developmental*, as decisions are used for modifying and improving programs. On the other hand, retroactive application of the CIPP model to examine prior decisions as they related to past attainments or outcomes is *summative evaluation*, which is directed toward determining the overall effectiveness of an educational program. Whereas formative evaluation is carried out typically by *internal* evaluators who are employed by a school district, summative evaluation is often conducted by *outside* evaluators. These auditlike evaluators provide information to decision makers on school boards or in legislatures, supposedly in the public interest. Use of outside evaluators, who need many of the data best obtained by internal evaluators and who can verify the adequacy of internal evaluation data, can often enhance the credibility of the contributions of internal evaluators. The interdependent nature of both internal and external evaluation points to the need for the educational institution to implement the complementary findings through improved decision making.

## EVALUATION IN BEHAVIOR MODIFICATION

When behavior is atypical or sufficiently bizarre, as in autism or hyperactivity involving extreme classroom disruption, improvements in behavior patterns can become apparent— almost dramatically at times. In the judgment of many clinically oriented educational psychologists, who working as school psychologists aid children with learning disabilities or with affective or emotional disturbances, the changes in the children's behavior brought about by behavior modification appear to be so substantial that the need for statistical support to substantiate that positive behavioral alterations did not occur by chance is considered to be relatively slight, though scientifically desirable. Often research in behavior modification has involved one, two, or three children as the experimental group. A base line of behavior is established through careful record keeping and systematic observation. This base line often serves as a substitute for a control group in that it establishes a point of reference against which changes in behavior supposedly brought about by the treatment can be evaluated. For instance, a hyperactive child will be observed during the first minute of a ten-minute period. He will be scored, for example, for the number of times that he is out of his seat, is

attending to a task, is talking to his neighbor, or is poking another pupil. A similar record is made of the autistic child. What words, if any does he use? In what self-stimulatory exercises does he engage? How much time is spent in these activities?

Once these records have been established, treatment is started that is designed explicitly to remove certain activities and to replace them through shaping with other activities judged to be socially beneficial. Records are kept of the changes or improvements in terms of the reduction in frequency of undesirable behavior or an increase in the incidence of desirable behavior. If after each application of treatment the incidence of undesirable behavior continues to decrease and the corresponding presence of desired behavior continues to increase, then sufficient evidence is thought to exist to permit an inference that the treatment has been beneficial. (See Figure 17-3.)

### Treatment, Extinction, Re-treatment

Some investigators believe that a departure from the design described is necessary to strengthen the inference that can be made regarding a change in behavior as a result of the treatment. One such approach is a sequence of treatment, extinction, retreatment. In many cases when improvement has been shown in terms of the reduction in the frequency of undesired behavior, the reinforcements on which the treatments are usually

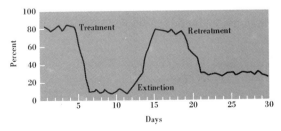

**Figure 17-3** Extinction of undesirable behavior under treatment, extinction, and re-treatment.

based are stopped, and extinction is allowed to reestablish the former undesirable behavior which is later remedied by further treatment. In some cases the second treatment (or series of treatments) is less successful than the first, as evidenced by a less marked reduction in undesirable behavior or a smaller increment of desired behavior. (See Figure 17-3.)

A serious question of ethics arises when a pupil is permitted to return to a former pattern of behavior that could be at least temporarily harmful and possibly risky of generating a conflict situation regarding how much trust he can place in adults. Usually the justification for this approach is that the second series of treatments does reestablish the desirable behavior and that scientific support of the efficacy of the treatment series for many children warrants some degree of risk with a few to establish the worth of the treatment approach.

## Multiple Base-line Treatment

A second approach for strengthening the inference that treatment has been successful is the use of multiple base-line treatment or instruction. The effect of specific instructional strategies can be assessed by using as few as three subjects if the base-line for each subject is established over time periods of different durations (e.g., one week, two weeks, or three weeks) to allow for differential levels of maturation and if the changes in performance are large enough to be beyond a reasonable probability of occurring by chance. Such a procedure may be employed either for children who are considered to fall within the norm of being representative of the general population or for the atypical hyperactive or withdrawn child.

The multiple base-line evaluation of instructional strategies avoids some problems associated with the training, extinction, retreatment method. Individual children are less likely to be confused about the kinds of responses that may be rewarding when all the treatment procedures are positive than when part of the treatment is deliberately designed to obtain a negative result. (See Figure 17-4.)

Whereas traditional experimentation involving the experimental group and the control group customarily assumes within each group that the experience will have a constant effect across all subjects over the same time period from pretest to posttest, the multiple base-line technique involving numerous monitoring observations over an extended period of time can be used when different pupils need different treatments. In such a situation levels of performance are observed at frequent intervals on more than one activity in that each child studied is exposed to a different form of activity or experience. What is the treatment activity for one child is a control activity for each of the other two. Hence the control activities for two of the children furnish base lines against which the treatment activity for the third child can be compared. For instance,

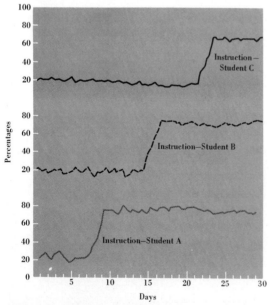

**Figure 17-4** Multiple base-line treatment of different students with similar beginning levels of competence. Instruction changes the level of functioning. The mere passage of time has little effect on level of functioning, indicating that the instruction was probably the factor contributing to the difference.

John might be needing help in the use of space in art, whereas Bill and Karl, respectively, need assistance in handling color and form. In the instance of John, who receives special instruction in the use of space, performance improves by a certain amount in the use of space. This amount is compared with the performances of Bill and Karl on the same task in space after each of several equivalent lapses of time. If the amount of change for Bill and Karl has been nonexistent or only slight, then there is a fairly strong basis to infer that the treatment in handling space has been effective for John. In turn, John can serve as a control on each of the other two tasks on which Bill and Karl will be receiving treatment. Thus each child acts as a control for the others and is a subject in a treatment procedure. By using more than one subject, the possibility that the changes are an artifact of time or of other chance factors or outcomes associated with maturation is greatly reduced, and the change in performance is very possibly directly attributable to the instruction.

## TESTS AND OBSERVATIONS IN RELATION TO THE EVALUATION PROCESS

To obtain data for carrying out evaluations, some form of measurement is essential to determine the degree to which changes in valued behaviors have occurred. There is a virtually infinite number of potential items or questions, the responses to which are behaviors reflecting different kinds of instructional outcomes. Through use of test items or observation scales, the evaluator samples a large range of behaviors to obtain measures that can be interpreted in a consistent and meaningful way relative to certain specific objectives judged to be important and relevant to the school program. Such measurement data frequently arise as a result of observation (embodying use of charts, checklists, rating forms, recording devices, motion pictures, and teacher reports) or the use of tests such as teacher-made examinations or standardized scales in reading, achievement, or special abilities. Supposedly, the responses to the items in these scales constitute a representative set or sample of behaviors from the large domain, or population, of behaviors under consideration.

On the basis of such samples of behaviors gained from testing or observation, a teacher or professional staff member endeavors to formulate inferences about the students' behaviors on the characteristic sampled and to formulate judgments regarding the extent to which the behaviors manifested meet one or more valued standards.

### Assumptions Underlying Measurement

As mentioned previously, it is assumed that the process of measurement constitutes a representative sampling of behaviors that are contained in the domain or class of behaviors, which is often referred to as the *population of behaviors*, and that each person being evaluated has been afforded sufficient exposure to whatever is necessary to bring about the behavioral changes associated with the specific behaviors that are considered important or desirable. Although these assumptions have been repeatedly stated, it is essential that they be fulfilled if evaluation is to be meaningful (valid).

### Test Defined

What then is a test? A test may be viewed as a collection of tasks, better known as items or questions, each of which is a sample of some domain or population of items or questions (stimuli). Corresponding to each item is a response or an observable behavior. Hence a test, as described previously, is a sample of behaviors. A test is a contrived task that is often, but not always, administered under more or less controlled conditions at a given place for a certain period of time. A scoring system is worked out for each of these items, and a total number of points is obtained for the performance that has been sampled. Usually a total score involving the addition of points or partial credits earned on each of several items is arrived at by means of the simple summation of points over the sampling of items. (Sometimes, in criterion-referenced tests, the frequencies of right and wrong answers to each item, which supposedly represents a behavioral objective, are examined, and a total score is not calculated. Interest centers on the proportion of examinees who attained the objective and thus on whether the criterion of performance previously set was met.) In the instance of the achievement test covering a unit of work, this rather formal definition of a test may be viewed as a collection or sample of items, each of which represents a certain specific instructional objective within a large population of objectives. Thus there well might be 500 or 1,000 objectives for a given year course in basic mathematics; however, in a testing experience only a limited number of these objectives—perhaps 40 to 50—can be sampled. If the sampling has been adequate and if the items can be considered a fair representation of what has been emphasized in a course, then the test would be viewed as a valid indicator of the achievement of the examinees required to take it. As will be discussed later, such a test would be said to possess content validity.

## Observation Defined

Observation differs from testing as a measurement procedure in that customarily the teacher or another professional person such as a psychologist focuses his attention upon certain segments of student behavior and systematically records his perceptions or impressions. There are also instances in which a person carries out self-observations and reports perceptions about himself by responding to questions or items on a test or scale.

Sometimes the observation is largely impressionistic, but quite frequently categories have been prearranged and even ordered for their degree of intensity, as in the steps of a rating scale for a given trait or collection of traits. In some instances, motion pictures or sound recordings are made so that a permanent record of behavior can be studied and subsequently categorized at the observer's convenience. Although in observations frequency data are often derived such as the number of times a child is present, is tardy, turns in his assignment, raises his hand to answer a question, or talks to his neighbor, often the judgment is quite subjective, as when a teacher reports his impression of a student's demeanor or checks a statement in a rating scale without having sufficient information to make an accurate judgment. Some of the major difficulties in the use of observation as a method of measurement include the following, which may, however, be minimized by careful selection and training of observers:

**1** The behaviors selected for observation are often isolated, unrelated segments of doubtful importance in the learning situation.

**2** Teachers frequently confuse the inferences they draw from the overt behavior they observe with the behavior itself. For example, a student in the back row who is talking to his neighbor might be judged by the teacher to be inattentive or bored, but actually the student may be highly attentive if his talking represents an attempt to find out from his neighbor, who has superior hearing, what the soft-spoken teacher was saying a moment ago when a noisy lawnmower passed by the window next to his seat.

**3** Observations are often based on a limited sample of behavior that may not be too representative of a student's long-range behavior patterns. Frequently samples of behavior must be obtained in a systematic manner over a substantial period of time in order to improve the representativeness (reliability and content validity) of the observation and to allow dependable inferences to be drawn. Teachers frequently note and remember the unusual or dramatic incident of behavior—especially that of a disruptive nature—and thus may not report a true picture of a child's typical behavior.

**4** Observations of behaviors are often recorded after a substantial amount of time has elapsed. Sources of bias involving selective perception (remembering the striking event and forgetting the commonplace) as well as personal values or preferences arise when observations have been unsystematic and haphazard, when their recording has been delayed, and when the observer does not attend conscientiously to his task.

**5** The behaviors to be observed are often inappropriately or ambiguously defined. Unless activities are described in operational form, confusing and inexact inferences are likely to be drawn. When teachers are asked to report behavior as being selfish, intelligent, hostile, or cooperative, they often make judgments within quite different frames of reference. Rather than describe a student as "hostile," the teacher might make a statement such as "pushes or strikes at fellow students on an average of two or more times a day," which is more specific and relatively easy to interpret.

Although observational procedures typically lack the degree of control and thus the freedom from error to be found in procedures associated with achievement and aptitude testing, they can often be improved by (1) selecting significant behaviors and defining them in operational terms, (2) following a systematic schedule for observations, (3) sampling over an extended period of time, (4) instructing the observer to distinguish between fact and inference, and (5) making records of the perceptions of behavior as close to the time of observation as possible.

## ESSENTIAL CHARACTERISTICS OF MEASUREMENT PROCEDURES

Measurement procedures are tools that furnish a more or less accurate basis for drawing inferences about the status of behaviors at a given moment in time or about changes that have occurred over a period of time. A certain amount of error is present in all measurement procedures—even when the finest instruments are employed, as in the physical science laboratories. To the extent that errors are present in educational and psychological measurement, corresponding errors will be associated with the inferences drawn about human behaviors. The accuracy of inferences formulated from educational measurement depends upon (1) the properties of the scale, including the absence of a true zero point or the presence of unequal units; (2) the reliability of the measurement operation; and (3) the validity of the measurement procedure.

## Scale Properties

It is obvious that an instrument designed to measure an individual's height contains both a true zero point and equal units, such as feet and inches. It is quite permissible to say that a person who measures 72 inches is twice as tall as a person who measures only 36 inches and that the difference between 50 and 60 inches is equivalent to the difference between 20 and 30 inches. In the instance of educational measurement, however, one cannot justifiably say that a person with a score of 40 on a 50-item arithmetic test knows twice as much arithmetic as a person whose score is 20. The test may not be uniformly difficult. Nor can it necessarily be concluded that the person who misses every item has no knowledge of arithmetic. The test simply may not have been sensitive enough to sample whatever knowledge he has of numerical or computational skills. Thus the zero point is meaningless in any absolute sense. (A similar statement can be made about an individual who earns a score of zero on an intelligence test; he is not necessarily completely without intelligence, for he may be able to do routine tasks about the yard and to feed himself.)

The equality of units may also be challenged in the instance of the arithmetic test. It is often customary to arrange items in order of difficulty. Thus in the case of the person who has 40 items correct, the demand upon his arithmetic ability to complete the four most difficult items he attempted might be equivalent to that required in his accurately responding to the first 36 items he finished. Thus in terms of the customary accuracy realized in educational measurement, individuals can probably be placed in a rank order of their performance—one individual in relation to another. It is highly doubtful that the difference between the scores of 45 and 35 items correct is equivalent to the difference between the scores of 15 and 5, as items differ substantially in difficulty. Even less probable would be a statement that a score of 45 represents a level of performance three times as great as that represented by a score of 15. If one could magically determine a true score or absolute zero and then proceed to construct an appropriate scale, it might be that the scores would be somewhat on the order of 245 and 215, rather than 45 and 15. In short, all measurement is *relative*, and customarily one can place individuals in a rank order along a scale in the full realization that distances between pairs of adjacent rank orders are not equivalent over the scale.

### Reliability of a Measurement Operation

*Reliability of measurement* refers to the degree of consistency or stability of performance. If individuals in a group tend to maintain the same rank orders on each of two administrations of the same test or on each of two comparable forms of a test, that instrument is said to be reliable. Reliability may also be looked at as being inversely related to the size of errors of measurement. If it were possible to hypothesize that a true score exists for a given individual, he would be expected to fluctuate a certain number of points in his obtained score from one administration of a test to another. For example, in the case of intelligence tests which have been carefully designed and standardized, it is often estimated that in about two administrations out of every three a person's score will fluctuate by about as much as 5 IQ points above or below his true score. The greater the amount of fluctuation in a person's score, the lower the degree of reliability of the test.

Many factors affect the reliability of the measurement operation. First a sufficient sampling of behaviors must be taken so that there will be an adequate basis for arriving at an accurate statement of an individual's standing. For example, a child's position, relative to other children, would be expected to fluctuate much less on a 100-item test than on a 10-item test and less on a 10-item test than on one made up of 3 items. The operation of chance factors in the selection of items is much greater when there are 10 items than when 100 questions are asked. Thus the longer a test, the higher the reliability of the measurement procedure.

Other sources of error in measurement that can influence the reliability of tests are the following: (1) failure of the child to understand or follow directions, (2) fluctuations of attention, (3) emotional disturbance or illness, (4) the threatening presence of the examiner or teacher, (5) careless mistakes in scoring operation, and (6) environmental distractions such as a fire drill, a loud noise outside the school building, a joke overheard from the next room, poor ventilation, unusual changes in temperature or humidity, or any other unexpected event that will detract from a student's attentive set.

### Validity of a Measurement Procedure

The *validity of a test* is represented by the degree of correspondence which that test shows to the behaviors it is supposed to represent. Does the test actually measure what it is intended to measure? Does the test afford a basis for drawing accurate inferences regarding the behaviors in which the examiner is interested? Three types of validity are described in *Standards for Educational and Psychological Tests and Manuals* (French & Michael, 1966): (1) *content validity*, which is particularly suited for achievement tests; (2) *criterion-related validity*, which pertains to how accurately a test predicts performance on a criterion variable such as grade point average in college or the amount of insurance sold by field representatives; and (3) *construct validity*, which refers to how well a test represents or duplicates a psychological process or activity such as anxiety, self-concept, verbal ability, or ego strength—a form of validity typically established by using the test in an experiment that is carefully designed to test certain hypotheses deduced from a theoretical framework about certain domains of human behavior.

### Content Validity

Frequently to achieve the content—or, in the educational context, curricular validity—of a test, a teacher constructs what is known as a *two-way grid* of process and content objectives prior to preparing the test items. This grid consists of two dimensions. The first dimension represents the basic topics or content coverage which the teacher deems important or to which the curriculum or the manual being followed ascribes importance; the second dimension comprises the sorts of psychological processes that are considered important, much like those described in the *Taxonomy* (Bloom, Engelhart, Furst, Hill, & Krathwohl, 1956). As the reader will recall, the lowest level in the *Taxonomy* is knowledge (Chapter 3). Succeeding levels are comprehension, application, analysis, synthesis, and finally—the highest of all—evaluation, a level embodying critical judgment.

Frequently a teacher will set up a two-way grid and decide in advance the proportionate amounts of emphasis that should be given both to the topics covered and to the learning experience that will require utilization of desired types of psychological processes or thinking activities. Figure 17-5 illustrates a two-way grid for a given course unit, which may help the reader see how careful plans can be made to develop a test that will be truly representative of the types of emphases that a teacher intends. To the extent a test fulfills on the basis of a *logical* or *rational* analysis the objectives of instruction, it will be judged as having content validity.

Content validity may also be viewed outside the context of curricular validity. For example, in testing personnel for positions in industry and business or in civil service agencies, the items typically represent characteristics that have been shown by an analysis of the elements of a job to be related to its successful performance. In addition to representing content requirements of the job, employment tests often possess what is termed *face validity*, in that on the surface they seem to have something to do with the expectations that the examinee holds regarding the demands of the job.

### Criterion-related Validity

The term "criterion-related validity" (sometimes called "predictive validity") refers to the use of a test for the purpose of predicting subsequent performance on a criterion variable. Examples of criterion variables are success in college as measured by grade point average; success on a job in terms of amount of production; or any other index of interest to management such as low termination rate, low absenteeism, number of novel contributions or patents, or effectiveness ratings. Typically, the criterion-related validity of a test is expressed in terms of its degree of relationship or correlation with measures representing criterion performance (criterion measures).

| Objective | I. Foods, 35% | II. Digestion, 15% | III. Assimilation, 10% |
|---|---|---|---|
| Knowledge of terminology, 25% | Carbohydrates<br>Protein<br>Starch<br>Vitamin<br>Acid<br>Scurvy, etc.<br>(4 or 5 items) | Salivary glands<br>Alimentary canal<br>Esophagus<br>Enzyme<br>Digestion<br>Pancreas, etc.<br>(6 or 7 items) | Assimilation<br>Absorption<br>Oxidation<br>Energy<br>Etc.<br>(1 or 2 items) |
| Knowledge of specific facts, 25% | Sources of foods<br>Uses by the body<br>(4 or 5 items) | Functions of mouth, stomach, small intestine, liver, etc.<br>(6 or 7 items) | Processes involved in energy production and storage of foods<br>(1 or 2 items) |
| Knowledge of trends and sequences, 10% | (No items) | Path of food through alimentary canal<br>Sequences involved in digestion<br>(3 or 4 items) | Sequence of assimilation processes<br>(1 item) |
| Knowledge of methods, 10% | Methods for testing foods to determine content<br>(2 or 3 items) | (No items) | (No items) |
| Understanding, 15% | Explanation of purposes and logic of classification of foods<br>(2 or 3 items) | Explanation of digestive process as applied to each class of food<br>(4 or 5 items) | Explanation of processes involved in assimilation of various classes of foods<br>(1 item) |
| Application, 15% | Analysis of foods for content<br>Development of balanced diet<br>(2 or 3 items) | Description of digestive processes for specific foods<br>(4 or 5 items) | Description of processes of assimilation applied to specific foods<br>(1 item) |
| Total (based on a test of 50 items) | 17 items | 27 items | 6 items |

**Figure 17-5** Test plan for a ninth-grade unit on foods and their uses by the human body. [*From R. C. Lindemann, Educational Measurement. Copyright 1967 by Scott, Foresman and Company. With permission of the publisher.*]

Sometimes expectancy tables are used to show what the probability of success is for individuals who have placed at different levels in test performance. For example, a person who falls in the top quarter of a scholastic aptitude examination might have a probability of .85 (an 85 percent chance) of earning a grade point average of 2.00 or higher during his freshman year of college, whereas a person in the bottom quarter might have a probability of only .31 (a 31 percent chance) of earning a grade point average of 2.00 or higher. Such expectancies are derived by taking large groups of students who have previously completed the test and by following them through a program for a given period of time—one year in the instance of college freshmen. On the basis of the examinees' criterion performance, data are collected to show what percentages of individuals who placed within different intervals of the test-score distribution (e.g., top quarter, second highest quarter, next-to-bottom quarter, or lowest quarter) earned a grade point average at or above a certain grade point level, such as 2.00. On the assumption that future groups of students will be like this trial group, predictions are made of the future success of new student bodies at the particular college.

### Construct Validity

The term "construct" refers to a hypothesized psychological process such as a trait or habit that manifests itself in a variety of situations. As mentioned previously, a construct is a psychological concept such as anxiety, creativity, flexibility, numerical ability, self-concept, or verbal ability. These terms are useful in communicating inferences that have been made about human behavior on the basis of test performance. Frequently inferences are formulated regarding unobservable psychological activities that intervene or mediate between the stimulus situation (test items) and observable behaviors (responses to test items). The validity of a construct is concerned with how well the construct fits within the framework of a psychological or educational theory of which it is thought to be a part.

The abilities that make up Guilford's structure of intellect, discussed in Chapter 15, are constructs. This model represents a theory of intelligence in terms of interrelationships between several hypothesized processes (constructs) that can be empirically verified by building several tests to represent each of the constructs. The tests are scored, intercorrelations between them are determined, and by statistical methods factors are found to be correlated with certain groups of tests that were intended to represent the construct, but not with other groups of tests that were devised to represent other constructs. The psychological interpretation of the factor, or dimension isolated, constitutes the meaning of the construct. This interpretation is formulated by examining the content of the items in the tests that were correlated with the factor—content that was placed into the tests on

the basis of the hypothesized processes underlying the construct. The content of tests *not* highly correlated with the factor in question is also studied to exclude certain possible alternative interpretations and thus sometimes, in the absence of contradictory evidence, to give relatively greater support to the hypothesis set forth.

The typical validation of the construct is quite indirect and often somewhat circular in logic, as illustrated by the factor-analysis procedures employed in verifying the constructs of the structure of intellect model. Inferences have to be made from results of experiments that are designed to test hypotheses derived from the theory of behavior.

The typical steps in construct validation are as follows:

**1** The meaning of the construct needs to be defined clearly, usually in the form of a set of postulates, propositions, or theoretical statements regarding the nature of the construct.

**2** The construct as postulated is translated into measurable operations by the construction of tests intended to duplicate the construct. Essentially, the items of the test represent hypotheses that have been derived from the theoretical statements.

**3** From these theoretical statements or postulates regarding the construct, deductions or predictions (*new* hypotheses) are formulated concerning how high-scoring and low-scoring groups of individuals on the test of the construct would react in a variety of new situations not directly covered by items in the test. These new situations, which should differ from those represented by items in the test in order to avoid circularity in thinking, may be other tests or substantial segments of experience in another activity for which logical considerations would suggest the expectation of differences in the average performance of the high-scoring group and the low-scoring group of individuals.

**4** If the two groups do indeed differ in average performance in the predicted direction for each of the new situations, then there is support for the construct. If the groups do not differ in the predicted direction for the performances investigated, the construct, as formulated, lacks support. The construct, the theory, or both may need to be revised.

**Illustrative Example of Construct Validity**   A specific example of the validation of a construct may help to clarify the steps just described. Suppose that a psychologist wishes to devise a test of achievement motivation for high school students:

I First he makes two postulates (there would be many more in a theory of achievement motivation, but for simplicity only two are cited):
  A Students with high achievement motivation identify with those parents, peers, and teachers who value intellectual activities.
  B These students are frequently reinforced or rewarded for their participation in academic pursuits.
II From these two theoretical statements he formulates several hypotheses, only three of which are presented for each postulate (six hypotheses in all):
  A Hypotheses for Postulate 1A: Compared with students of the same ability level with low achievement motivation, students with high achievement motivation:
    1 Have parents whose average number of years of higher education is greater.
    2 Tend more frequently to join their peers in literary, science, mathematics, or other academically oriented clubs on campus.
    3 Volunteer more frequently in class when the teacher poses questions.
  B Hypotheses for Postulate IB: Compared with students of the same ability level with low achievement motivation, students with high achievement motivation:
    4 More frequently indicate that they strive for an A in every course they take, irrespective of its interest value or level of difficulty.
    5 More often consult with teachers to

determine what is expected on a given paper or assignment.
    6 Spend greater numbers of hours each week talking about classroom assignments or receiving help from parents with assignments.

These hypotheses are then translated into test items—several items per hypothesis in many instances—for which a scoring system is developed in terms of logical expectations and is subsequently checked by item analysis—a procedure to be explained later. Some examples of items that correspond to each of the hypotheses stated would be:

1 The number of years of college work that your father completed was:
  a One or less
  b Two
  c Three
  d Four
  e Five
  f Six or more
2 The faculty sponsors several clubs that are related to subjects you are studying (e.g., a mathematics club or a literary club). The number of such clubs to which you belong is:
  a None
  b One
  c Two
  d Three or more
3 When the teacher asks the class as a whole a question (not just one person), how often do you volunteer to answer?
  a Never or almost never
  b Only when I feel like it
  c Usually
  d Always or almost always
4 In which of your courses do you strive for A's?
  a No course in particular
  b Only ones that interest me
  c Those in which I like the teacher
  d All courses no matter how difficult or boring
5 When you are uncertain about what is expected on an assignment such as a library or

term paper, how frequently do you seek help from the teacher?

**a** Never obtain help

**b** Ask for help only as a last resort

**c** Sometimes try to find help if convenient

**d** Usually find help

**e** Seek out the teacher as many times as or for as long a time as is necessary to understand the requirements

**6** How many hours on the average do you spend each week with your parents in talking about your schoolwork or in seeking their advice or help on assignments or homework?

**a** None

**b** Less than one hour

**c** Two to four hours

**d** Five or more hours

Once a scoring key has been worked out to allow specific weights (points) to be assigned to each possible answer, the examination is scored, and the individuals are ranked in order from high to low with repect to the examination of achievement motivation. For purposes of research and validation, a high-scoring group (e.g., those in the top quarter) and a low-scoring group (e.g., those in the bottom quarter) are formed.

**III** With reference to the two postulates set forth, several possible predictions, deductions, or *new* hypotheses can be formulated and tested with reference to the high- and low-scoring groups. A few examples may be suggested:

    **A** Compared with the group of low-scoring students of the same ability level, students in the high-scoring group show:

        **1** A higher proportion entering college the following fall.

        **2** A greater proportion earning a B average or above during the last three years of high school.

        **3** A higher proportion taking advantage of extra time allowed to check over their answers on an examination for a scholarship or an award.

        **4** A smaller proportion receiving two or more traffic citations during the school year (the rationale being that high achieving students have less time to drive and a greater desire to please their parents).

        **5** The average number of items attempted per minute on a test which they were told was a measure of their intelligence being higher.

        **6** A higher proportion indicating a desire to enter careers of teaching or research.

**IV** Positive evidence for these hypotheses would give support to the construct of achievement motivation as formulated in the postulates as well as to the hypotheses derived from them and incorporated as questions within the test of the construct. Lack of positive evidence would suggest that the postulates may be in need of modification or that other hypotheses might be more fruitful as a basis for choosing items to represent the construct. Positive evidence would need to reflect the anticipated direction of the differences observed between the high- and low-scoring groups.

Additional information about construct validation may be found in Adams (1964), Cronbach and Meehl (1955), *Standards for Educational and Psychological Tests and Manuals* (French & Michael, 1966), and Thorndike and Hagen (1961).

## SUMMARY

The procedure of measurement is concerned with obtaining scores on a test or scale that will place people in a position from high to low along the scale of the characteristic being measured, whereas evaluation consists of a judgment or interpretation regarding the appropriateness of the behaviors observed in terms of specific objectives (desired behavioral changes).

The criteria for formulating evaluative judgments need to be explicitly defined in terms of (1) clearly described dimensions of behavior; (2) a specified level of performance that is judged to be appropriate behavior; (3) indication of levels or intervals of performance that are associated with such qualitative statements of performance as "excellent," "good," or "poor"; (4) consistent application of the standards employed in formulating interpretations; (5) broad and representative sampling of behaviors in all domains that are judged relevant to learning; and (6) recognition of the major factors of child development as they influence expectations of appropriate behaviors.

Briefly stated, the key steps in the evaluation procedure, which also apply to the evaluation of school programs, include (1) developing broad goals that are related to the philosophic position of the teacher, administrator, school board, and community; (2) formulating specific behavioral objectives that are harmoniously related to the basic philosophy or values of the school and community concerning what is important to learn; (3) planning instructional strategies, designing curricula, and assembling instructional materials to effect the attainment of the specific behavioral objectives; (4) preparing a variety of measuring instruments and scales as well as observational procedures to furnish data (multiple criterion measures) so that inferences can be drawn concerning the degree to which specific objectives have been realized; (5) carrying out periodic observations in the administration of tests and scales to determine base-line data against which changes in behavior can be compared and judged as to their appropriateness relative to the specific objectives; (6) carrying out statistical analyses of the data so that comparisons and interpretations can be formulated with relatively great precision; (7) making careful interpretations of the data obtained from the several measures that reflect the specific behavioral objectives to determine how closely many of the

outcome (or criterion) measures correspond to previously valued judgmental standards regarding what would be appropriate levels of changes in performance or standing (status); and (8) formulating recommendations that lead to implementation of, or modifications in, instructional procedures and curricula as well as alterations in the specific behavioral objectives to be employed in future evaluations.

Based on the work of the Phi Delta Kappa National Study Committee on Evaluation, a comprehensive decision-making evaluation model (called the CIPP model, standing for context-input-process-product evaluation) incorporating four kinds of evaluation that serve four types of decisions was proposed. For the CIPP model, evaluation was defined as "the process of delineating, obtaining, and providing useful information for judging decision alternatives." *Context* evaluation furnishes information about needs, difficulties, and opportunities to facilitate *planning decisions* that determine goals and objectives. *Input* evaluation provides information about the relative merits of alternative procedures for aiding *structuring decisions*, which involve selection of procedural designs and strategies for achieving objectives arising from planning decisions. *Process* evaluation yields monitoring or quality-control information regarding strengths and weaknesses of ongoing program activities to support *implementing decisions*, which involve a choice of alternative ways for carrying out and improving upon the execution of previously selected procedures. *Product* evaluation affords information to determine how effectively objectives are being realized and aids *recycling decisions* concerning whether the procedures being implemented should be continued, modified, or terminated. Opportunities for feedback and dynamic interaction among the four types of decisions and the four supporting kinds of evaluation are amply provided for in the CIPP model.

Closely related to evaluation is accountability, which involves the designation of responsibilities to educational personnel for achieving mutually agreed upon instructional or other educationally related objectives. In accountability studies, evaluation is employed in judging how adequately the standards set for various educational outcomes have been met by educational personnel. In terms of the CIPP model, evaluation represents a proactive or future orientation to improving educational programs through decision-making actions, whereas accountability is a retroactive view of the CIPP model that examines how adequately procedures and strategies have been implemented and how effectively outcomes have been realized in terms of certain standards or criteria.

In representing a sampling of behaviors, most measurement procedures involve the employment of tests or observations, which in order to be useful must be reliable and valid. Such measurements or observations customarily place individuals in a rank order that is relative, not absolute. Whereas reliability is concerned with how consistent and stable measures are, validity requires that the behaviors sampled correspond to the objectives set forth by the person responsible for the evaluation process. These objectives may pertain to a sampling of the content and processes involved in school learning experiences (content validity); to a sampling of activities, as in an aptitude test, that will be predictive of subsequent performance on a job or an extended task, such as college work (criterion-related validity); or to a sampling of behaviors that represent manifestations of a hypothesized psychological process, or construct, such as achievement motivation, creativity, numerical ability, or verbal ability (construct validity). The more reliable and valid tests and observations are, the more confidence teachers and other school personnel may have in the inferences they draw from them regarding the effectivenss of the school program and concerning the kinds and amounts of learning that each student is achieving.

## SELF-DIRECTING ACTIVITIES

1 Apply one of the two evaluation models presented in this chapter to a given unit of instruction. Make sure to state the objectives, to explicate the instructional strategies and materials used, and to indicate what kinds of measures one might employ to furnish evidence that the objectives have been met.

2 Explain how an educational evaluation model can be employed to implement an accountability system in a public school setting.

3 After choosing a relatively small curricular unit, set up a grid for a test plan that encompasses both process and content objectives.

4 Select a psychological construct of interest and then describe in a step-by-step fashion how a valid measure of this construct could be developed.

5 Give examples illustrating how context, input, process, and product evaluation interact in the evaluation of school programs or in the evaluation of an innovative study in school learning.

# Chapter 18

A test situation in Ecuador. (*Courtesy of the United Nations*)

# TEACHER-MADE AND STANDARDIZED TESTS AND SCALES

In this chapter, both teacher-made and standardized tests and scales are described and illustrated. After studying this chapter, you should be able to:

❧ Cite the advantages and disadvantages of four basic types of objective achievement test items—simple completion, true-false, multiple-choice, and matching

❧ Demonstrate skill in writing achievement test items from the principles presented for their construction

❧ Identify comparative strong points and weak points of essay versus achievement examinations

❧ Show familiarity with purposes and uses of rating scales, checklists, and anecdotal records as instruments of observation

❧ Differentiate the formal characteristics and varied uses of standardized aptitude, intelligence, achievement, and personality tests, including measures of interest, temperament, adjustment, and attitudes

❧ Initiate appropriate practical steps in designing, administering, and scoring achievement tests; in using test results for improving instruction and evaluation of school programs; and in helping future students met during practice teaching or later instructional experiences to participate in evaluation procedures to facilitate their attainment of course objectives

❧ Identify and use correctly the many terms cited in the previously stated objectives as well as such other terms as the following:

scoring formula
correction for guessing
intelligence quotient
mental age
self-report inventories
observation scales

In the previous chapter, several basic principles of measurement and evaluation were described. To carry out these evaluation procedures, a teacher needs to develop skills in (1) the construction of tests and scales and (2) the selection and use of standardized tests and scales. A standardized test differs from an informal teacher-made examination in that the standardized instrument has been previously administered to one or more groups, the scores have been subjected to rather rigorous statistical analysis to establish their reliability and validity, and, in particular, norms have been derived and furnished so that comparisons of the performance of any group of students may be made with that of the norm group. Frequently use of a standardized test involves an examiner's adhering to a carefully prepared set of instructions for administration, including a specific time limit, and his employing a manual to interpret the scores.

It is the primary purpose of this chapter to set forth certain principles of test construction that may be helpful to the teacher both in choosing the form in which a question of his own design is to appear and in actually writing items of various formats. A secondary purpose is to consider briefly several principles involved in the selection and administration of standardized tests and in the interpretation of their scores relative to available reliability, validity, and normative data. Finally a number of practical considerations involving the administration, design, interpretation, and uses of measures will be set forth in terms of answers to specific questions that teachers often ask.

Tests serve a variety of purposes in evaluation. They are employed (1) to determine whether students are ready to learn new materials; (2) to identify or diagnose difficulties in the learning process and deficiencies in what supposedly has been learned; (3) to ascertain at the end of a course, at the conclusion of a unit of instruction, or at any meaningfully specified point of time in a planned learning experience what has been achieved; and (4) to predict the most likely levels of performance in new learning situations. Implied in these purposes is the obtaining of information that may be used in the evaluation of the current status of, or changes in, behaviors. Different procedures of measurement furnish evidence with varying degrees of success in the evaluation of behaviors that pertain to one or more of the four purposes just enumerated.

Once the specific objectives have been determined for a particular learning experience, a decision can be made regarding what kinds of test items will most effectively measure the content and process objectives that are judged to be important and significant. Thus, different forms of test items may be employed to bring about the expression of different kinds of behaviors that are consistent with the specific behavioral objectives sought. For example, variations in the design of test items furnish opportunities for different levels of an examinee's response to emerge, such as those levels suggested by the hierarchy of process-oriented categories that are found in *A Taxonomy of Educational Objectives: The Cognitive Domain* (Bloom, Engelhart, Furst, Hill, & Krathwohl, 1956).

## TEACHER-MADE TESTS AND SCALES

Although teacher-devised tests sometimes involve samples of behaviors in terms of products such as typing, cabinetmaking, sewing, ceramics, or handwriting that can be compared against some sort of standard specimen, or model of the task, most teachers are concerned to a relatively greater extent with the construction of pencil-and-paper achievement tests. That is, they make use of tests, the questions to which are printed or reproduced on paper (or sometimes on the blackboard) and the answers to which are written or recorded in pencil on an answer sheet.

Broadly speaking, pencil-and-paper tests are of two types: *essay* and *objective*. The essay examination typically involves a written response of usually several sentences to a specific question or to parts of a specific question. The term "objective test" refers to an examination in which the marking process is highly uniform and thus highly reliable because of an agreed-upon key that has been prepared in advance of scoring. With the possible exception of a simple completion test, in which some degree of latitude may be allowed for the appropriateness of an answer, the student will receive the same score on an objective test no matter who marks the examination. Only minor sources of error such as those due to a momentary fluctuation of attention on the part of the person doing the scoring would be expected to arise. Therefore, since there would be no, or at most very little, variation between the scores arrived at by two or more readers of the same examination, the measurement procedure is said to be objective.

In their most frequent use, there are four major formats of objective tests, although Gerberich (1956) has presented a definitive taxonomy for classifying objective test items in terms of a number of formats and operational categories. For purposes of our discussion, items will be classified as follows:

**1** Simple completion items, short-answer items, and fill-in-the-blank items. These items require students to supply answers that usually run from one to about eight or ten words. These items suggest responses that typically involve the process objective of knowledge at a recall level, although in the instance of mathematics and science, a complete problem solution or creative response is often sought.

**2** True-false items. Such items consist of statements that students are to judge as being more nearly true than false or more nearly false than true. This type of item is usually best oriented to factual material involving knowledge at a recognition level.

**3** Multiple-choice items. These items consist of a stem or a lead phrase, or some kind of question, followed by two or more alternatives in parallel structure such as nouns or verbs, prepositional phrases, or complete sentences, the most nearly correct one of which the examinee is to select as the right answer. Thus the examinee is required to discriminate among several alternatives. Multiple-choice questions are by far the most common type of objective items. They can be constructed to tap process objectives involving knowledge, comprehension, application, and even higher-level processes of synthesis and analysis that embody complex thinking and conceptualization.

**4** Matching exercises. In a matching test, each of the items of a given list (stimuli) is to be placed in correspondence with one of several possible responses within a set. The frequency of response alternatives may be smaller than, the same as, or greater than the number of elements appearing in the stimulus set. These items possess many of the same response potentialities as those to be found in multiple-choice questions.

### Essay versus Objective Examinations

Teachers customarily employ both objective and essay tests. Each approach affords certain advantages relative to the types of characteristics being measured, the potential breadth of coverage, efforts required in item writing, ease of scoring, and incentive value for students.

With respect to abilities measured, the essay examination, when appropriately designed by the test maker, affords the student an opportunity to analyze and synthesize information in his own words, on the basis of his own background and formal learning experiences. The essay task allows him to make use of problem-solving skills and higher-level psychological processes of reasoning in (1) organizing or reorganizing given facts, (2) comparing and contrasting arguments with respect to the requirements of the question posed, (3) illustrating rules or principles, (4) making new applications of principles to unique problem situations, (5) drawing inferences from data or information given, (6) explaining or hypothesizing relationships for a set of data, (7) criticizing certain statements relative to given criteria, and (8) devising new approaches to solving long-standing problems. On the other hand, the objective test, which lends itself much more effectively to a survey of the retention of factual information than the essay examination does, imposes upon the student the task of selecting one or more correct answers from among two or more options or of furnishing a word, a phrase, or possibly a sentence to complete the answer sought by the instructor. Although the essay test is particularly well suited to the evaluation of higher-level psychological processes, the objective test can also be designed to tap such psychological activities.

Whereas the essay examination is usually restricted to a limited segment of knowledge, the objective examination customarily constitutes a broad survey of a given field of knowledge. This difference in scope arises from the fact that an extensive period of time is typically required for the formulation of answers to essay items, while the objective items can be answered relatively quickly. The student who is particularly fluent is at a definite advantage in writing essay questions, as he can stress those points which he knows and omit those of which he is uncertain; in short, he can sometimes bluff his way through certain parts of an examination by creating an unusually favorable impression on other parts about which he has a great deal of information. Such

a golden opportunity is lacking in the objective test.

Students often have definite preferences for either essay or objective examinations. One may hypothesize that the student who likes considerable latitude in his expression—the one who is a divergent thinker and who thus wishes minimal restriction on what he can say—will probably prefer the essay examination, as it affords him an opportunity to organize and to express his own ideas in an effective manner. On the other hand, the convergent thinker will probably prefer the objective examination. Such a student enjoys building up an immense background of knowledge and facts and finds it comfortable and easy to pick out the answers expected of him from among a number of options, as in a multiple-choice item or a completion exercise that is highly structured.

It is probably important that a teacher give adequate notice to students concerning which type of examination will be given so that they can guide their preparation accordingly. Learning incentives can be adversely affected if a teacher gives the impression that one form of examination will be employed rather than the other and then unexpectedly reverses the student's expectations by giving a form of examination different from that for which he prepared.

From the standpoint of scoring, the objective examination affords the advantages of speed and accuracy in that answers are customarily scored right or wrong on the basis of a predetermined key. This consistency of response suggests that the reliability of objective examinations for the same amount of time in testing will probably be higher than that of essay tests. The essay examination usually requires a great deal of time to score and usually results in different amounts of credit being assigned by different teachers or by the very same teacher at different times during the scoring. However, the reliability of essay tests can be considerably improved if a list of points on which credit will be allowed can be prepared in advance and then applied in a consistent manner. Preferably all students' answers to one essay question should be read at a time before going on to the next. In contrast to the scoring of the objective test, the teacher in scoring the essay test has the opportunity to make comments and to put forth observations on the ways in which individual pupils arrive at given answers.

An essay examination is generally easier to prepare than an objective test since it requires the writing of only a few items. However, each question should be clearly stated with sufficient specificity so that comparable responses will be obtained. Each question needs to be general enough to afford the creatively oriented student an opportunity to generate new information in an insightful and original manner. The preparation of objective items requires a tremendous amount of effort if the wording is to be precise, if the answer is not to seem obvious, and if, in the instance of multiple-choice items, the student is to have a reasonable amount of difficulty in choosing among the various alternatives. The writing of objective examination items improves with experience.

The choice between using an objective or an essay examination, of course, rests upon what the teacher considers to be the important outcomes or educational objectives of the curriculum. If he can assume that the objectives can be measured with equal effectiveness by either approach, he must weigh the amount of time that will be required for scoring against the amount of time required for preparation of the questions. The authors have found in their own teaching experiences that for a class of 25 students or fewer, the time advantage probably favors the essay examination, whereas for a class of more than 25 students, the objective examination becomes advantageous—especially if it can be used three or four times without a breach in its security and without too hard a freeze of the curriculum or of instructional strategies.

The writing of essay examination items may be more demanding than many teachers think. An item such as "Tell all that you have learned about the English novel" will lead to such a diversity of interpretation and response—to say nothing of consternation on the part of the students, who will not know what is expected of them—that the reliability and validity of the responses may be in serious jeopardy.

This item might well be improved by rewording it as follows: "Compare and contrast one of Hardy's well-known novels with one of those by Thackeray from the standpoints of (1) development of plot, (2) portrayal of characters, (3) social message, (4) use of local color, and (5) employment of imagery." Before scoring the answer to this question, the teacher would need to make a list of possible answers to each part and to work out a scoring system so that the reliability of his marking would be as high as possible.

Table 18-1 presents a summary of the major characteristics of essay and objective tests. The table originally appeared in a pamphlet prepared by Stodola (1959) for the Evaluation and Advisory Service Series of the Educational Testing Service.

## CONSTRUCTING OBJECTIVE TEST ITEMS

As indicated previously, there are four major types of objective test items: (1) simple completion items, short-answer items, and fill-in-the-blank items, all of which are answered in from one to about eight or ten words; (2)

**Table 18-1   Summary of Major Differences between Essay and Objective Tests**

|  | Essay | Objective |
|---|---|---|
| Abilities measured | Requires the student to express himself in his own words, using information from his own background and knowledge | Requires the student to select correct answers from given options, or to supply an answer limited to one word or phrase |
|  | Can tap high levels of reasoning such as required in inference, organization of ideas, comparison and contrast | Can *also* tap high levels of reasoning such as required in inference, organization of ideas, comparison and contrast |
|  | Does *not* measure purely factual information efficiently | Measures knowledge of facts efficiently |
| Scope | Covers only a limited field of knowledge in any one test. Essay questions take so long to answer that relatively few can be answered in a given period of time. Also, the student who is especially fluent can often avoid discussing points of which he is unsure | Covers a broad field of knowledge in one test. Since objective questions may be answered quickly, one test may contain many questions. A broad coverage helps provide reliable measurement |
| Incentive to pupils | Encourages pupils to learn how to organize their own ideas and express them effectively | Encourages pupils to build up a broad background of knowledge and abilities |
| Ease of preparation | Requires writing only a few questions for a test. Tasks must be clearly defined, general enough to offer some leeway, specific enough to set limits | Requires writing many questions for a test. Wording must avoid ambiguities and "giveaways." Distractors should embody most likely misconceptions |
| Scoring | Usually very time-consuming to score | Can be scored quickly |
|  | Permits teachers to comment directly on the reasoning processes of individual pupils. However, an answer may be scored differendly by different teachers or by the same teacher at different times | Answer generally scored only right or wrong, but scoring is very accurate and consistent |

From *Making the classroom test: A guide for teachers*, Educational Testing Service Evaluation and Advisory Series, No. 4. © First Edition Copyright 1959 by Educational Testing Service, Second Edition 1961. Reprinted by permission of Educational Testing Service.

true-false items, which are really multiple-choice questions consisting of two alternatives; (3) multiple-choice items, which involve two or more alternatives, one of which fulfills the requirements set forth by the statement or question appearing in the stem of the item; and (4) matching exercises, which require the examinee to select one member from a list of response alternatives and place it in correspondence with a member in a second list of stimulus alternatives. (Actually the stems of all objective items can be regarded as stimuli.) The advantages and disadvantages of each of these four types of items will be briefly considered. Principles for constructing each type of item will be briefly enumerated, and illustrations will be presented in limited numbers to show how such items can be constructed. In any of these tests, as well as in essay examinations, it is important that students be given explicit instructions concerning how they are to answer items and record their responses. It may be helpful, especially in the instance of objective items, to include at least one sample question and, perhaps in the case of young children, to furnish some practice exercises. A second important principle is that items of one type be placed together so that there will not be any unnecessary confusion in mental set. Mixing up true-false, multiple-choice, and matching items in a haphazard fashion, along with a few completion items, is not considered a desirable practice. Separate sections for each type of item should be planned. A third general recommendation is that items be arranged in order of difficulty, within each section of a given type, in order to offer encouragement to the less able student and so that no examinee will spend or lose too much time on a difficult item placed near the start of a test. It may be important to have young pupils record their responses on the test paper by circling the right answer or by drawing an arrow from one element to another, in the case of matching items. Children at or above the third-grade level will probably be able to use separate sheets on which to mark their answers, provided they have been given adequate instructions. The latter arrangement affords a marked gain in the speed of scoring.

### Completion, or Free-Response, Items

Completion items consist of statements in which blanks are inserted so that examinees may fill in missing words. It is usually considered desirable to place the blank at the end of a sentence so that the idea of the sentence will not be chopped up by a number of blanks, which may lead to considerable confusion. Two examples of such an item would be:

**1** The author of *The Return of the Native* was _____.

**2** Three important causes of World War I were cited by the author of your history text to be:

   **a** _____,

   **b** _____,

   **c** _____.

The major advantages of completion items are that they are relatively easy to construct, they afford a moderately economical means of rapid coverage of content objectives, they offer an opportunity for the creative or unusual response to appear, and they allow for usually faster and probably more reliable scoring than the essay examination. On the other hand, they have certain disadvantages. Among the most noteworthy are (1) a tendency for teachers to take verbatim materials from the textbook; (2) the risk that the teacher may misinterpret or discount the value of an answer that is possibly relevant or quite clever (creative), especially if the student has been doing outside reading or independent thinking about a question in the social studies or humanities; (3) the tendency for many completion items to represent trivial or inconsequential bits of information; (4) the likelihood that some teachers will erroneously evaluate the answer to a completion item because of inaccuracies in spelling or a lack of legibility in the handwriting; and (5) the relatively greater amount of time required for scoring free-response questions, as compared with the amount required for scoring true-false or multiple-choice items.

In writing such questions, it may be important that there be great specificity so that the desired answer is the only one possible, provided that the item is one in which recall of specific information is desired. If, on the other hand, the teacher is looking for creative responses, the wording can be somewhat more general or less restrictive. It is also well to avoid the use of statements taken directly from a textbook or study guide, since such items can be answered on the basis of memory alone rather than in terms of comprehension of the material being sampled. Completion items usually place greater intellectual demands on the examinee, as it is more difficult to recall or retrieve information than it is to recognize an appropriate answer in the context of two or more alternatives.

## True-False Items

Although publishers of standardized tests, as well as testing specialists in civil service and military agencies, tend to make major use of multiple-choice items, teachers frequently employ true-false questions. Typically a true-false item is a statement or proposition expressed in sentence form; the examinee must determine whether it is correct or incorrect. An example would be:

> In the radio and television series "The Green Hornet," the central motif is that good triumphs over evil.                 T  F

**Advantages of True-False Items**  True-false items afford several advantages in test construction:

**1** They furnish a simple, direct, and basic test of a student's knowledge of factually oriented subject matter.

**2** They afford an efficient means of covering a great deal of material in a relatively short period of testing time.

**3** Although considerable skill is required in writing true-false items, most teachers can generate a large number of them in a relatively short period of time. A teacher can probably write at least ten true-false items in the time it would take him to write one multiple-choice question involving four or five alternatives.

**Disadvantages of True-False Items**
The major disadvantages of true-false items as used by many teachers are:

**1** In subject-matter areas in social studies, the humanities, and the arts, where there may be marked differences in points of view, such items may be highly ambiguous unless there is careful specification of who endorsed the particular proposition presented.

**2** True-false items often tend to sample highly trivial and inconsequential material which relies heavily upon rote memory and which penalizes the individual who is particularly proficient in problem-solving tasks and in creative endeavor.

**3** There is often a tendency simply to take material almost verbatim from a textbook, with the result that the student who merely memorizes the words in his book without understanding their import can make a high score.

**4** There is a high probability that a student can make a high score on a true-false test simply by guessing. Thus in a 100-item test, a student having no information would be anticipated, on the average, to earn a score of 50 by blind guessing.

**5** Unlike multiple-choice questions, which provide several alternatives against which any one alternative can be judged as to its relative truth or falsity, the true-false test item frequently forces a decision in a highly limited context of information, which can be exceedingly frustrating to the student who has a great deal of information of a qualifying nature.

**6** There is the risk that certain students may learn a great deal of incorrect information from test items that are false.

**Suggestions for Writing True-False Items**
In writing true-false items, the teacher may find the following suggestions helpful, all of which are illustrated with examples:

**1** Use definite and precise words so that the true-false item will be as simple and clear as possible.

### Example

> *Poor:* Demands for increased spending on highways, recreational facilities, public

welfare, penal institutions, public utilities, and other state and local services have greatly reduced the probabilities of gaining approval of school bonds.　　　　　T F

*Improved:* Rising local and state taxes have made the passing of school bond issues increasingly difficult.　　　　T F

**2** Devise statements for true-false items that express one central thought or idea. In other words, double-barreled questions should be avoided.

### Example

*Poor:* For exceptional children, special schools and special programs should be provided.　　　　　　　　　　　T F

*Improved:* Special classes should be provided for exceptional children.　　　T F

(In its original form, this item could have two answers. According to the textbook used or the viewpoint of the teacher, the essential philosophy might be that there should be special classes but not special schools or that there should be special schools, in which instance special classes might not be necessary.)

**3** Avoid the use of words known as specific determiners or cues, such as "always," "all," "never," "none," "impossible," or "without doubt," for such expressions are usually associated with items that are probably false. On the other hand, qualifying expressions such as "usually," "frequently," "sometimes," or "seldom" can create difficulties, as they are usually associated with items keyed as true.

### Example

*Poor:* Grand opera is always associated with Italian composers.　　　　　T F

*Improved:* Italian composers have made major contributions to grand opera.　　T F

**4** Whenever possible, try to prepare items that are either completely true or completely false; that is, phrase the items so that there would be unanimous agreement among experts regarding whether the answer is true or false.

### Example

*Poor:* The longest day of the year is in June.　　　　　　　　　　　　T F

*Improved:* In the Northern Hemisphere, the longest day of the year is in June.　　T F

(The very bright student would anticipate that the longest day of the year in the Northern Hemisphere is associated with the shortest day of the year in the Southern Hemisphere. The qualifying phrase appears necessary.)

**5** Prepare statements that are grammatically correct so that the conscientious student does not mark it false because of an inaccuracy in expression, rather than because of an intentional inaccuracy.

### Example

*Poor:* Reinforcement is more important in rote learning than problem solving.　　T F

*Improved:* Reinforcement is more important in rote learning than in problem solving.　　　　　　　　　　　　T F

(The omission of the word "in" might suggest that in rote learning, problem solving is less important than reinforcement.)

**6** Write statements that stress main points or ideas rather than trivial details, glittering generalities, or empty phrases.

### Example

*Poor:* At the beginning of the third movement of John Robinson's *Seventh Symphony,* an oboe solo in E flat major is played for five bars, followed by two flutes for ten bars, and then by a clarinet solo in syncopated rhythm for six bars.　　　T F

*Improved:* In his *Seventh Symphony,* John Robinson makes effective use of woodwinds to develop the principal themes.　　　　　　　　　　　　T F

**7** Avoid, wherever possible, the use of negative expressions involving the insertion of the word "not" when otherwise the expression would have precisely the opposite answer. In particular, avoid the use of double negatives, which are highly confusing and distracting.

### Examples

*Poor:* The first secretary of the United States Treasury was not Alexander Hamilton.                                                T F

*Improved:* Alexander Hamilton was the first person to become secretary of the United States Treasury.                              T F

*Poor:* In a state university, an assistant professor cannot be promoted in rank if he does not publish research articles.           T F

*Improved:* In a state university, an assistant professor is expected to publish research articles before he can be promoted in rank.  T F

**8** Whenever an item deals with a controversial matter, the person, institution, or group that subscribes to the point of view should be named.

### Example

*Poor:* There are 120 different intellectual abilities.                                             T F

*Improved:* Guilford's structure of intellect postulates 120 different intellectual abilities.                                          T F

**9** Endeavor to write statements that encourage students to apply whatever knowledge they have.

### Example

*Poor:* The area of a rectangle is given by the formula $A = lw$.                                   T F

*Improved:* The number of square feet on a stage 30 feet long and 20 feet wide is 600.   T F

*Improved:* If linoleum cost $2 per square foot, the expense of the material for a kitchen floor 19 feet by 10 feet would be $380.                                                                  T F

**10** Include enough specific material so that the examinee does not have to depend upon his own opinions to determine what the intended meaning of the item might be.

### Example

*Poor:* Objective test items are superior to essay questions.                                   T F

*Improved:* For the same amount of testing time, objective items furnish greater breadth of coverage than essay questions.  T F

*Improved:* The reliability of scores of carefully constructed objective examinations is higher than that of well-devised essay tests.                                                             T F

**11** Avoid taking material verbatim from the text and inserting it within an item; each item should be completely reworded to express the intended point or objective to be covered.

### Example

*Poor:* The brightness of a light varies inversely as the square of the distance one is from its source.                           T F

*Improved:* The amount of light on a sheet of paper 6 feet from a lamp will be one-ninth that on a sheet only 2 feet from the lamp.                                                                  T F

It may be informative to indicate the level of process objective represented by the improved version of each of the preceding test items, which illustrated the eleven principles of item construction. With a possible exception of the question illustrating the fourth principle (intended to represent the level of comprehension), the first eight items correspond to the knowledge level, as does the item illustrating the tenth principle. Only the two items demonstrating the ninth and the eleventh principles could be viewed as representing application of knowledge.

**Scoring True-False Items** Two approaches are frequently employed in marking true-false items. The first procedure is to assign one point to each correct answer and no points to any omitted or wrong answers and then to count the number of items correctly marked either on the answer sheet or on a sheet on which the test items are reproduced.

The other frequently used approach is to count up the number of items correctly answered $R$ and then to substract from it the number of items wrongly answered $W$. The scoring formula is thus $R - W$. The omitted items are not counted in the scoring process except as a check on one's arithmetic. Thus in a 60-item true-false test, an individual who answers 48 items correctly, misses 8 items and omits 4 items, would obtain a score of $48 - 8$, or 40.

The reasoning behind the use of such a scoring formula is that theoretically a student with *no knowledge* would, by blind guessing, obtain 30 correct answers and 30 incorrect answers on a 60-item test. Many test makers would argue that such a person should receive a score of zero—a score that can be found by taking the expected number of right answers (30) and subtracting the expected number of wrong answers (30). Actually, if the student has omitted no items, the score that is furnished by the formula $R - W$ would place him in precisely the same rank order as scores derived from the number correct $R$. Thus if examinees are given substantial time to take a test and are encouraged to respond to every item, there is no need to "penalize" them for so-called guessing by using the scoring formula $R - W$. Except for certain high-speed tests in which the rate of work is considered im-

portant (e.g., a clerical aptitude test), many test specialists, as do the authors, recommend against the use of scoring formulas involving a penalty for wrong answers.

The use of a scoring formula embodying a penalty frequently introduces into the scores sources of variability that the examiner does not intend or desire—sources of systematic variation known as *response sets*, which may work against the validity of the achievement tests. For example, if students suspect that a scoring formula may be used that penalizes for so-called guessing, personality characteristics may be reflected in the resulting scores. Individual differences exist among examinees concerning the risks they are willing to take in answering items about which they may have varying degrees of confidence regarding their information. (In multiple-choice tests, the complexity of the problem is undoubtedly greater, as the various alternatives have different degrees of attractiveness to the examinee, depending on his sophistication.) Thus the highly conscientious, serious student who actually has a high probability of answering an item correctly may not respond unless he is almost absolutely sure, whereas the less well-prepared and happy-go-lucky student would not hesitate to gamble in selecting an answer. Hence the well-informed but cautious student might be expected to lose a number of points, and the less adequately prepared student who makes well-educated or calculated guesses based on partial knowledge of the material covered by the items might pick up several additional points. For further information on this intriguing problem of risk taking, the reader is referred to Ebel's (1965, pp. 130–35) extensive discussion of the use of confidence weighting of answers. His approach offers a partial solution to the difficulties encountered in controlling risk-taking behavior of examinees who have various predispositions to gamble or to guess.

## Multiple-Choice Items

The preferred format for an objective test item is that of multiple choice. A multiple-choice item consists of an introductory statement (proposition) or question, referred to as the *stem*. Then follow three, four, five, or more alternatives—usually four or five—one of which ordinarily constitutes the best or preferred answer. Each of the incorrect alternatives, which should be written so as to appear plausible or reasonable to the examinee, is called a *distractor*. Four varied examples of multiple-choice items, the first one of which is at a cognitive level of comprehension and the others at the level of knowledge, are as follows:

1 If the diameter of the earth were increased by 6 feet, its circumference at the equator would be augmented by approximately:
   a 9 feet
   b 16 feet
   c 19 feet
   d 30 feet

2 A word that modifies a noun is called a(n):
   a Adjective
   b Adverb
   c Conjunction
   d Preposition

3 With respect to governmental expenditures and taxes, President Eisenhower's declared policy in 1953 was to:
   a Increase taxes and increase expenditures.
   b Decrease taxes and increase expenditures.
   c Decrease taxes and decrease expenditures.
   d Reduce expenditures but not change taxes.
   e Leave both taxes and expenditures unchanged.

4 What is a noteworthy similarity between Thoreau and Emerson?
   a Both believed that a conservative political philosophy was essential to a man's survival.

   b Both showed a great preoccupation with the sex drives as a means of stimulating creative thought.
   c Both relied heavily upon the teachings of ancient Greeks to develop their respective philosophic positions.
   d Both emphasized the importance of nature in determining man's potentialities for intellectual and spiritual growth.

## Advantages of Multiple-Choice Items

Several of the advantages of multiple-choice items are as follows:

1 Students are required to make finer discriminations and judgments in their responses to each of the several alternatives. The absolute nature of true-false items is overcome in that the student has several alternatives as a frame of reference against which he can evaluate the relative truth or correctness of each one—a situation that allows him to select what he considers to be the best answer and to eliminate several less preferable responses.

2 The possibility of making chance errors as a result of blind guessing is considerably reduced. In a 100-item test consisting of questions with five alternatives, the chance score would be 20 rather than 50, as in the case of a 100-item true-false examination, since the expectation is that, granted the presence of equally attractive alternatives, a student without knowledge will answer correctly one out of every five items. (However, many multiple-choice items become two-choice situations when poor distractors have been written.)

3 The substantial number of alternatives in the multiple-choice item in combination with the stem of the item affords the teacher an opportunity to test for various levels of complexity in the process objectives more readily than in the instance of true-false items. Thus students have a substantially increased opportunity to display their level of comprehension of the material and their ability to apply principles. Specifically, the format of the mul-

tiple-choice item permits the teacher a versatility in preparing questions that relate to a number of possible uses, several of which are:

The determination of cause-and-effect relationships

The identification and recognition of errors

The association of one outcome or observation with another

The definitions of terms

The purposes served by, or the reasons for, certain actions

The identification of differences or similarities among two or more stimulus objects

The determination of a common principle, or concept, underlying several stimulus objects

The determination of the proper order or arrangement among the number of given stimuli

The consideration of controversial issues and differing points of view

### Disadvantages of Multiple-Choice Items

Although the advantages of using multiple-choice items are numerous, certain drawbacks need to be mentioned:

**1** Multiple-choice items demand a tremendous amount of skill in question writing on the part of the teacher.

**2** The multiple-choice item may pose alternatives that the creative person, who may have a far better answer or solution, finds unsatisfactory or frustrating.

**3** Despite their superiority over true-false items, multiple-choice questions run the risk of measuring superficial information, trivial objectives, and a limited sample of instructional outcomes, as they are a poor substitute for the sorts of critical judgments and ingenious problem-solving capabilities that a well-devised essay test may reveal.

### Suggestions for Writing Multiple-Choice Items

Virtually every one of the suggestions given for the preparation of true-false items is appropriate to the writing not only of the stem but also of each of the alternatives for multiple-choice items. One additional suggestion pertains to the special attention that must be directed to making the alternatives parallel in structure. Inspection of the four previously cited illustrative multiple-choice items reveals that the alternatives for each are cast in the same form—they are all nouns, all verbs followed by direct objects, or all complete sentences. If the multiple-choice item is to fulfill its intended function, it is essential that each of the alternatives appears to be equally plausible and equally attractive to the examinee.

Some additional concerns involved in the writing of multiple-choice items are (1) the selection of vocabulary that is at a level appropriate to the examinees, (2) the submission of items to colleagues for review and criticism, (3) the eventual attainment of approximately equal numbers of individuals responding to the various distractions, (4) the intended correct answer being the alternative that receives the maximum number of answers, and (5) the avoidance of unintentional cues such as a too generally expressed alternative, an overly qualified alternative, or a grammatical slip. With reference to the last point, the reader should note that the stem of the second illustrative multiple-choice item ends with the articles "a" or "an," which is written as "a(n)." This is necessary so that all four alternatives can be considered. Use of either "a" or "an" alone would lead the examinee to eliminate two of the four alternatives because of the inappropriate form of the article.

Detailed information concerning the preparation of multiple-choice test items can be found in a chapter prepared by Ebel (1965, pp. 149–200), in which he offers 48 specific illustrations of desirable, permissible, and undesirable characteristics of multiple-choice items. Other helpful sources on item writing include the presentations by Adams (1964), Schwartz and Tiedeman (1957), and Thorndike and Hagen (1969).

**Scoring Multiple-Choice Items**   Although the authors advise against correcting for so-called chance success with multiple-choice items, the formula that is customarily employed is given by the expression $R - W / (k - 1)$, where $R$ is the number of items correctly answered, $W$ is the number of items wrongly answered, and $k$ is the number of alternatives for the multiple-choice questions. Thus in a 60-item multiple-choice examination in which there are 5 alternatives for each item, a person having 43 correct answers and 12 incorrect answers (and 5 omitted items) would have a score of $43 - 12/4$, or 40.

The rationale for this formula is that by blind guessing, a person would answer one-fifth of 60 items, or 12, correctly and would miss 48 items. By dividing 48 by the number of alternatives minus 1, the value of 12 is obtained. When this number is subtracted from the expected chance number of 12 items correct, the resulting score is zero.

**Some Illustrative Examples of Other Multiple-Choice Items**   The versatility of multiple-choice items is perhaps nowhere better illustrated than in the instance in which a reading passage or set of data is presented about which several items can be developed. Figure 18-1 shows two illustrative sets of items taken from *A Folio of Illustrative Exercises from Chicago City Junior College, English and General Course Final Examinations*, which was assembled by Engelhart and Moughamian (1966).

### Matching Items

The fourth most commonly used format for objective test items is that of matching items.

Each of several response components in a set, which may consist of words, phrases, or sentences, is placed in correspondence with a member in a second set of stimulus components, which may also be in the form of words, phrases, or sentences. Elementary school and junior high school children, in particular, often enjoy matching exercises, especially when the number of stimulus components is equal to the number of response components. If each of the response elements is used only once, children may find it somewhat satisfying, if not exciting, as they near the end of the matching exercise. Teachers who are concerned about the differential degree to which chance operates as alternative responses are successively eliminated may prefer to use different numbers of stimulus and response elements. Furthermore, students are often told that a given response element may be paired with several stimulus components.

**Suggestions for Writing Matching Items**   Most of the suggestions given for writing true-false and multiple-choice items also apply in the instance of preparing matching items. In fact, the illustrative examples shown in Figure 18-2 are so close to the multiple-choice format that virtually all the previously enunciated principles of item construction would be applicable. In many instances, as many as 10 or 15 stimulus statements will be matched against 5 possible response alternatives. In essence, the repeated use of the same alternatives allows for the generation of 10 or 15 multiple choice items, the stems of which are the stimulus components of the matching exercise.

**Some Illustrative Examples of Matching Items**   Three illustrative examples of the format of matching exercises will be given. The first example consists of a group of 20 cities in the United States (stimulus components) and a set of 14 states (response components), with the instruction that each city is to be matched with the state in which it is located. Whereas the first example represents a cognitive process involving recall and recognition at the knowledge level, the second and third examples (Figure 18-2) embody higher-level processes of comprehension (interpretation). The third exercise also requires reasoning and thus may reflect application, analysis, and possibly evaluation.

***Illustrative Example 1*** *Directions* For each of the cities in the United States presented in the first column, find the name of the state given in the second column in which the city is located. Take the letter corresponding to the state and insert that letter in the space in front of the city named. A given state may be used more than once.

| Cities | States |
|--------|--------|
| _____ 1 Amarillo | A California |
| _____ 2 Atlanta | B Colorado |
| _____ 3 Austin | C Florida |
| _____ 4 Boston | D Georgia |
| _____ 5 Chicago | E Illinois |
| _____ 6 Cleveland | F Louisiana |
| _____ 7 Dallas | G Massachusetts |
| _____ 8 Denver | H Michigan |
| _____ 9 Detroit | I New York |
| _____10 Los Angeles | J Ohio |
| _____11 Miami | K Oklahoma |
| _____12 New Orleans | L Oregon |
| _____13 Philadelphia | M Pennsylvania |
| _____14 Pittsburgh | N Texas |

| | |
|--|--|
| _____15 Portland | O Utah |
| _____16 Sacramento | |
| _____17 Saginaw | |
| _____18 Salt Lake City | |
| _____19 San Francisco | |
| _____20 Tulsa | |

The two illustrative examples in Figure 18-2 show matching items set up in multiple-choice form. Such a format permits the more rapid writing of test items and the use of answer sheets especially devised for recording responses to multiple-choice items.

## Other Teacher-made Devices and Scales

**Teacher-made Devices** Over the years teachers have come up with rather ingenious devices for the evaluation of student behaviors. Frequently they devise rating scales consisting of statements of student behaviors that are judged within a continuum from high to low—much as in the instance of a rating scale for the evaluation of teacher-training candidates on personal and professional characteristics. A useful illustration of the rating scale for classroom speech is given in Figure 18-3.

In the use of a rating scale, one particularly important source of bias is the "halo effect," which is the tendency for the rater to place a person high (or low) on several items of the scale because he placed him unusually high (or low) on one characteristic—often one dimension of behavior that the observer values to a great extent. Another source of error is that of "generosity" or "leniency," in which the rater tends to place most persons high on the characteristics being judged. It is usually recommended that the rater record his observations on one behavior dimension at a time. Additional information about observation proce-

## BIOLOGY

On a cold winter day, a Chicagoan, Mrs. Dorothy Mae Stevens, was found unconscious in a passageway after a night of exposure to 11 degree subzero weather, "she was literally frozen stiff." Her temperature had dropped to an unprecedented 64 degrees (Fahrenheit). Twenty hours after her arrival at Michael Reese Hospital, her temperature had risen to 98.2 degrees. Early Friday it was 101 and later 100. On Saturday it was also 100. When she was first found, her breathing had slowed to 3 times a minute. By Saturday it was up to 24 a minute. Her blood pressure was zero on Thursday. By Saturday it was 132 over 80. On Thursday her pulse rate was 12 a minute; on Saturday it was 100. Cortisone was administered early.

66. On Thursday Mrs. Stevens' temperature was
    A. approximately 14 degrees lower than normal.
    B. approximately 24 degrees lower than normal.
    C. considered low but not unusual because the temperature of man fluctuates as much as 40-50 degrees depending upon the external temperature.
    *D. approximately 34 degrees lower than normal.
    E. approximately 44 degrees lower than normal.

67. At a body temperature of 64 degrees
    A. the blood and lymph are frozen.
    B. the blood carries more oxygen to the cells than normally, because more gases dissolve in fluids at low temperature rather than at high temperatures.
    C. the blood vessels of the skin are dilated, because the vasoconstrictor muscles are relaxed.
    D. the heart beats more rapidly, because the cold stimulates the heart center in the medulla.
    *E. most activities slow down, because all chemical activities decrease as the temperature falls.

68. Under normal conditions a sharp rise in external temperature would result in
    A. no bodily change.
    *B. dilation of blood vessels in the skin and an increase in secretion of sweat.
    C. constriction of blood vessels in the skin and an increase in secretion of sweat.
    D. dilation of blood vessels in the skin and a decrease in secretion of sweat.
    E. constriction of blood vessels in the skin and a decrease in secretion of sweat.

69. Most of the heat lost from Mrs. Stevens' body by radiation, conduction, or convection was brought directly to the skin by the
    A. heat receptors.
    *B. blood.
    C. muscles.
    D. oxidation of foods.
    E. sweat.

70. The *immediate* cause of Mrs. Stevens' unconsciousness was probably due to the
    *A. lack of a sufficient amount of oxygen to the brain cells.
    B. lowering of the external temperature.
    C. slow pulse rate.
    D. decrease in muscle tone.
    E. low breathing rate.

71. At the temperature of 64 degrees the enzymes in the body
    A. are totally ineffective, but not destroyed.
    B. are more active than at higher temperatures.
    C. are destroyed.
    D. are not affected in any way; they cause as rapid chemical changes as at higher temperatures.
    *E. act more slowly than at higher temperatures.

72. Under normal conditions most of the heat lost from Mrs. Stevens' body would be lost by
    A. elimination of urine and feces.
    B. warming of foods and fluids passing along the digestive tract.
    C. elimination of warmed air from the lungs.
    D. warming of cold air entering the lungs.
    *E. evaporation of sweat and radiation and conduction of heat from the skin.

73. The immediate source of most of the heat normally needed for maintaining Mrs. Stevens' body temperature is the
    *A. contraction of muscles.
    B. exchange of gases between atmosphere and lung tissue.
    C. exchange of gases between blood and cells of the body.
    D. heat regulating center in the brain.
    E. secretion by glands.

For each of the following items, referring to the poetic excerpt below, blacken one lettered space to indicate the best answer.

1　Shall I compare thee to a summer's day?
　　Thou art more lovely and more temperate:
3　Rough winds do shake the darling buds of May,
　　And summer's lease hath all too short a date:
5　Sometime too hot the eyes of heaven shines,
　　And often is his gold complexion dimm'd;
7　And every fair from fair sometime declines,
　　By chance or nature's changing course untrimm'd:
9　But thy eternal summer shall not fade
　　Nor lose possession of that fair thou ow'st;
11　Nor shall Death brag thou wander'st in his shade,
　　When in eternal lines to time thou grow'st:
13　So long as men can breathe, or eyes can see,
　　So long lives this, and this gives life to thee.

122.　This poem is properly described by which of the following terms?
　　A. Dramatic monologue.　　C. Elegy.
　　B. Ballad.　　　　　　　　D. Ode.
　　　　　　　*E. Sonnet.

123.　Why should it be described in this way?
　　A. It is told by a first-person narrator.
　　B. It tells a simple story.
　　C. It concerns death.
　　D. It celebrates love in an exalted manner.
　*E. It expresses lyrical matters in a certain formal pattern.

124.　Line 6 is most clearly an example of
　　A. alliteration.　　　　C. onomatopoeia.
　　B. assonance.　　　　 *D. personification.
　　　　　　　E. simile.

125.　The prevailing rhythm and meter (particularly as illustrated by the last two lines) are
　　A. trochaic trimeter.
　　B. anapestic pentameter.
　　C. dactylic free verse.
　*D. iambic pentameter.
　　E. iambic tetrameter and pentameter.

126.　The poem is like *Dover Beach* in that
　　A. both are elegies.
　*B. both oppose something unchanging in the sadness of change or loss.
　　C. both use a highly original rhyme scheme.
　　D. the narrators of both, although deeply in love, are beset by a feeling of hopelessness.
　　E. both concern mainly summer, love, youth, and happiness.

(5 of 12 items)

**Figure 18-1** Note the versatility of multiple-choice test items as shown on this and the facing page. (*Reproduced from "A folio of illustrative exercises from Chicago City Junior College, English and General Course Final Examinations," Division of Institutional Research and Education, "Chicago City Junior College English and General Course Final Examiniation," Division of Institutional Research and Education, Chicago City Junior College, with permission of Max D. Englehart and Henry Moughamian.*)

dures and rating scales may be found in Adams (1964), Guilford (1954), and Thorndike and Hagen (1969).

Another device that teachers often use is a checklist for evaluating a variety of behaviors. For example, a physical education teacher can list the successive steps involved in hitting or putting a golf ball. Once the teacher has enumerated the activities, he can check those which the student performs adequately, or he can actually assign a numerical value or a grade that indicates the degree to which he judges the student's performance in a particular activity to be adequate. Such checklists are particularly useful in evaluating products that are completed in shop courses, in commercial subjects such as typing, and in home economics classes. Figure 18-4 shows a checklist enumerating the steps to be followed in setting up a machine so that it is ready to sew.

**Anecdotal Record**　Although not widely used because of their time-consuming requirements, anecdotal records consist of accurate descriptions of specific events; teachers describe the events in behavioristic terms and in sufficient detail so that the behavior can be appropriately interpreted within the school setting in which it occurs. In the preparation of anecdotal records, a distinction is made between the factual statements of the behavior in objective terms and the interpretation or evaluation of it. Typically the event described is concerned with the child's personal adjustment, development, or social interaction with other children and/or with the teacher. In order for the anecdotal records to be meaningful, the teacher must make frequent observations and maintain a continuity in reporting. Extensive samplings of behavior need to be taken, especially if a description of a pattern of typical behavior is desired.

Some behaviors of a highly striking or un-

Imagine that you are listening to a symposium on "The Nature of Social Change." Identify the remarks made by each of the following participants:

A   Millikan
B   Mead
C   Freud
D   Dewey
E   Banfield

203.   Before the discussion gets under way, I think we should remind ourselves that no matter what changes are made in society, we will still be dealing with the same basic personality structures and drives. Social change is not the most important factor in understanding man and society.

204.   I cannot agree. As the social environment changes, the forces impelling man to act also change, giving rise to a new pattern of habits and therefore to different behavior.

205.   The basic nature of man is not the issue here. Social change is a necessary accompaniment of modern life. The real question is how to utilize the research of social scientists who have studied change in a way that will deepen the insight of the people responsible for effecting change.

206.   One answer to that problem is to study examples of societies that have made significant social changes. From such studies, principles may emerge which can help man make deliberate changes in his society.

207.   I wonder if that is enough. More than the desire to change is needed. A society can be so crippled by social and economic weaknesses that change is unlikely even if the best intentions and efforts exist.

208.   I am afraid this discussion is becoming trapped in mechanical hypotheses. Change is a constant feature of society. The essential problem is developing a society in which change contributes to the heightening of man's awareness of his actions and the fullest development of his potentialities.

(6 of 10 items)


For each of the following items, blacken *one* lettered space to indicate that the item would be true *if the*
A   orbit of the earth were a circle rather than an ellipse
B   orbit of the moon were exactly in the same plane as the orbit of the earth
C   axis of the earth were not inclined
D   distance to the moon from the earth were twice as great
E   earth was a perfect sphere

(Assume that only one of the above imaginary conditions occurs at a time.)

159.   We would know much less about the corona of the sun. (D)

160.   A mass weighing one pound at the equator would also have the same weight at either pole. (E)

161.   An eclipse of the sun would occur each month. (B)

162.   The earth would have no seasons. (C)

163.   The orbital speed of the earth would not vary during the year. (A)

164.   Night and day would be of equal length in all latitudes all year long. (C)

**Figure 18-2**   Matching items in multiple-choice form. (*Reproduced from "A folio of illustrative exercises from Chicago City Junior College, English and General Course Final Examinations," Division of Institutional Research and Education, "Chicago City Junior College English and General Course Final Examination," Division of Institutional Research and Education, Chicago City Junior College, with permission of Max D. Engelhart and Henry Moughamian.*)

usual nature are often reported in considerable detail as a basis for generating behavioral categories that can be used in other contexts. Such striking examples of behavior are often called *critical incidents* or *significant incidents*, as they point up, in terms of certain value criteria, what are judged to be highly effective or appropriate behaviors or highly ineffective or inappropriate behaviors.

In preparing anecdotal records, it is important that the teacher record the observation as soon as possible to avoid blurring his recollections of the experience. It is well to have appropriate form sheets and pencils readily available so that both striking and less dramatic incidences of behavior can be quickly noted. After a collection of such records has been made over a period of several weeks, the teacher can study them to note changes in characteristic patterns of behavior. The following is an example of an anecdotal record:

*Behavior Observed*
I [the teacher] saw Dick talking to Mary, who sits at the desk in front of him, and overheard him say, "Mary, I want the answers to the last three problems of our arithmetic assignment. I couldn't work these problems last night, and the teacher wants our papers in a few minutes." Mary turned around and said, "I did these problems, and you shouldn't have the answers." At that moment Dick pulled Mary's ponytail and muttered, "Go to hell, you little bitch!" At that point Mary turned around and stuck her tongue

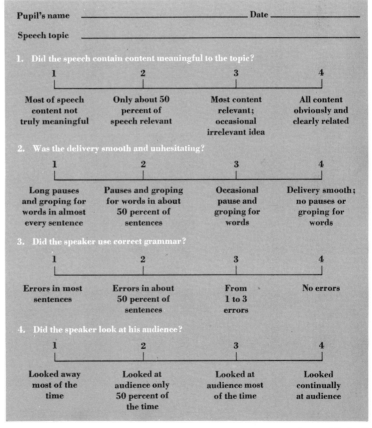

**Figure 18-3** Rating scale for classroom speech. (*From C. M. Lindvall, Measuring pupil achievement and aptitude, © 1967, by Harcourt Brace Jovanovich, Inc., p. 170, and reproduced with their permission.*)

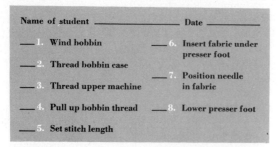

**Figure 18-4** Checklist for steps in preparing a machine to sew. (*From C. M. Lindvall, Measuring pupil achievement and aptitude, © 1967, by Harcourt Brace Jovanovich, Inc., p. 172, and reproduced with their permission.*)

out at Dick. Then Dick yanked her ponytail so hard that her head jerked back and she let out a cry. He looked over toward me and saw that I was walking quickly toward him. Then he slumped down into his seat and looked the other way as I asked him what the trouble was.

*Interpretation*

This behavior has been typical of Dick in the past few weeks. I have observed him looking at other students' papers when he takes examinations. One composition he turned in very closely resembled that of another student. When frustrated, he has shown a great deal of aggressiveness and hostility. His father's having filed recently for divorce would suggest that he is having a difficult time in adjusting both at home and at school. He lives with his mother, who works the late afternoon and evening shift at a nearby factory and thus sees very little of her son.

## STANDARDIZED TESTS

Standardized tests were defined at the beginning of this chapter. Typically, they are available to the authorized personnel in school systems, in local and state departments of education, colleges and universities, and business and industry. A multimillion dollar enterprise, standardized testing is highly competitive, and until recent years, numerous

companies tended to make rather extravagant claims concerning what their tests were capable of doing, and a few companies still make such claims. In 1954 three professional organizations—the American Psychological Association, the American Educational Research Association, and the National Council on Measurement in Education—published documents containing recommendations for the use of standardized tests. Subsequently, a joint committee of these three professional groups under the editorship of French and Michael (1966) prepared a single revision of the early documents, which has been entitled *Standards for Educational and Psychological Tests and Manuals.* In this publication, the committee has set forth what they believe to be *essential* standards, *very desirable* standards, and *desirable* standards that test publishers should meet in developing and statistically analyzing their tests and in reporting information about tests in the manuals that accompany them. In particular, attention is given to standards that relate to (1) the dissemination of information (usually in a manual) to help the potential user select the test most appropriate for his purpose; (2) the presentation of necessary information in the manual, record forms, and other accompanying material to aid the user in making correct interpretations of test results; (3) the inclusion of adequate validity information to reveal the extent to which a test can meet certain aims or objectives; (4) the citation of evidence about reliability that will allow the potential user to decide whether the scores will be sufficiently dependable (consistent and stable) for his intended applications of the test; (5) the reporting in adequate and clear detail of directions for test administration and procedures for scoring the test; and (6) an extensive description of the scales and norms used in reporting scores so that the likelihood of accurate interpretation will be enhanced.

Any school district that is seriously considering inauguration of a large-scale testing program should make use of its highly trained specialists to study the tests and manuals that might be used. In consultation with administrators, curriculum coordinators, and particularly teachers, these specialists are well-advised to consider carefully the criteria set forth in *Standards for Educational and Psychological Tests and Manuals.* If such specialists are not available, consultants from universities or state departments of education should be called in to help in test selection. These individuals may also be able to set up in-service training courses so that school personnel may gain the types of skills and understandings necessary for the selection and use of tests in evaluation programs.

Helpful information concerning the merits of various standardized tests may be found in *The Seventh Mental Measurements Yearbook* (Buros, 1972) which furnishes critical reviews of most commercially available standardized tests. Abbreviated but useful information about a variety of different published tests is given in appendix III of *Measurement and Evaluation in Psychology and Education* (Thorndike & Hagen, 1969). In addition to giving the addresses of the commercial test publishers involved, this volume also presents a short evaluation of each of the several well-known tests. These standardized measures have been classified in terms of general intelligence scales, aptitude test batteries, reading tests, elementary school achievement batteries, interest inventories, and adjustment and temperament inventories.

For the purposes of our discussion, standardized tests will be classified as follows:

**1** Achievement tests, which are employed to measure the degree to which specific objectives of learning experiences have been attained.

**2** Intelligence tests and tests of special aptitudes, which are oriented primarily toward showing students' potential for learning.

**3** Personality tests, which are aimed at pointing up students' affective or noncognitive characteristics that may be related to success in learning in essentially a social setting.

It is apparent that the second and third categories correspond to student characteristics related to school learning, whereas the first category represents the extent to which a test reflects the attainment of objectives of learning experiences. All these tests need to be reliable, valid, and interpretable if they are to be used meaningfully in the school situation.

**Achievement Tests**

The teacher is probably more directly concerned than anyone else with the use of achievement tests in the classroom, as these tests pertain directly to behaviors that supposedly correspond to the instructional objectives of the curriculum. On the other hand, intelligence and personality tests are essentially the responsibility of the school psychologist or counselor. It is important that standardized achievement tests correspond to the objectives of the curriculum if they are to be logically valid for the school. They need to sample the typical content and process objectives of school subjects. Such tests frequently require the development of local norms—i.e., norms for a given school district—since the sequence of instruction, the specific objectives of a given school, the general socioeconomic status of the community, and the ability levels of the students may vary somewhat from those represented by a national sample. Norms presented in the test manual are usually based on nationally obtained samples, which may or may not be representative of the population of students in the district in which the test is being used. Although age norms and grade norms furnish useful information regarding average performance at a given age or at a given grade level, and although percentile norms furnish an indication of how a student stands in relation to those in the standardization sample, local conditions may render such norms meaningless. For example, during the mid-1950s in a large city school system in California, it was customary to delay the teaching of algebra until the tenth grade and the teaching of geometry until the eleventh grade because it was thought that perhaps additional maturation would result in a more advanced state of readiness and greater ease in learning. It would have been grossly unfair to the California children to compare their performance in mathematics with that of children, represented in a national norm, attending schools in which these subjects were begun one year earlier.

Several cautions should be cited regarding the use of standardized achievement tests. First, the teachers and administrators responsible for the adoption of a test should study it carefully to make sure that it is appropriate in terms of content, difficulty level, and technical specifications before it is adopted. There is no point in using a test simply because other districts are using it; it must also be curricularly valid and appropriate for the particular classes involved. Second, teachers must exercise care not to teach *to* the test by drilling students on specific items contained within it. Third, teachers should not be fooled by the title of a test, which does not necessarily correspond to the objectives of instruction that it measures. Fourth, information in test manuals concerning how reliable a test may be or how valid it is in predicting future achievement should be considered cautiously, as large differences may exist in the amount of practice students have had in taking tests and in

the objectives associated with the curricula at different grade levels.

## Intelligence Tests

In Chapters 15 and 16, considerable attention was given to the nature of intelligence and to Guilford's structure of intellect, which suggests the existence of numerous relatively independent abilities. Since the use of measures of intelligence and special aptitudes is primarily the domain of the school psychologist and the school counselor, only limited consideration will be given to such tests. In the American culture, most intelligence tests are actually tests of scholastic aptitude, as they furnish general measures of learning potential in the school setting. Most intelligence tests yield measures of language function (verbal ability), general reasoning (typically involved in mathematics and science learning), and numerical, or computational, facility (arising primarily in mathematics and science learning and in business and commercial subjects).

With respect to general intelligence tests, one of the most common types of scores is the intelligent quotient, or IQ, which is an index of relative brightness or general capacity to learn. It is typically assumed that although there is some interaction between heredity and environment, the IQ will remain *relatively* constant, especially if the environment does not change substantially. Thus, if his environment is assumed to be constant, the child with a high IQ will supposedly learn more in a given unit of time than a child whose IQ is lower, and thus he will give an indication of being able to learn more in the school setting.

A person's IQ is determined by dividing his mental age (MA) by his chronological age (CA) and multiplying by 100. The MA for a given raw score represents the performance of an average person of a given CA. A 10-year-old child of average intelligence would have an MA of 10. His IQ would thus be 100, as the result of dividing his MA by his CA is unity (or 1). Multiplication by 100 is carried out to eliminate decimal points.

Similarly, a child with a CA of 10 might be shown on an intelligence test to have an MA of 13. His IQ would thus be given by the expression

$$IQ = \frac{13}{10} \times 100 = 130$$

This IQ would place him in approximately the upper 4 percent of the general population. It is apparent that the greater the advancement in a child's MA relative to his CA, the higher his IQ will be. Such an IQ determination is called a *ratio IQ*.

During the past few years, the ratio IQ has been replaced by the deviation IQ, since use of the ratio IQ involves assumptions about the linear nature of mental growth that are not justified, especially past the age of 13 or 14. The *deviation IQ*, which involves expressing an IQ for each age group in terms of what is called a *normalized standard score* (to be explained in Chapter 19), is illustrated in Figure 19-7. In essence what is done is to find for each obtained, or raw, score on an IQ test the percentage of individuals in a given group who fall below (or exceed) that score. These percentages are related to the number of standard deviations in a normal distribution (to be explained in Chapter 19) that would be required to yield the percentages of cases observed above or below that score. For example, if 92 percent of scores fall below a certain person's obtained score, reference to appropriate tables of the normal curve would show that the standard deviation required is 1.40. If 1 standard deviation is worth 15 IQ

points, this individual's IQ score must be 100 + 1.40(15), or 100 + 21, or 121. An application of this procedure is shown in Table 18-2. The sections in the next chapter on percentile and percentile rank and on standard scores, along with the chart shown in Figure 19-7, will provide some of the background necessary for understanding the rationale behind determination of the deviation IQ score. For additional information, the reader is referred to the detailed and lucid explanation by Adams (1964, pp. 215–216).

It may be helpful to interpret performance on intelligence tests in terms of the percentages of cases that fall in given intervals of IQ and below certain IQ points. These percentages are furnished in Table 18-2. Additional information regarding the interpretation of test scores in terms of IQ, percentiles, and other types of score units will be given in Chapter 19.

**Table 18-2  Distribution Percentages of Revised Stanford-Binet IQs**

| IQ range | Percent of cases | Cumulative percent |
|---|---|---|
| 140 and over | 1.3 | 99.9 |
| 130–139 | 3.1 | 98.6 |
| 120–129 | 8.2 | 95.5 |
| 110–119 | 18.1 | 87.3 |
| 100–109 | 23.5 | 69.2 |
| 90–99 | 23.0 | 45.7 |
| 80–89 | 14.5 | 22.7 |
| 70–79 | 5.6 | 8.2 |
| 60–69 | 2.0 | 2.6 |
| Below 60 | 0.6 | 0.6 |

Adapted from L. M. Terman and M. A. Merrill, *Stanford-Binet Intelligence Scale*, Boston, Houghton Mifflin Co., 1960.

Certain cautions should be exercised in the interpretation of intelligence test scores. Most of these tests have been geared to the American middle-class culture, which is highly oriented toward college preparatory work involving a heavy emphasis on language function and a moderate emphasis on mathematical reasoning.

If an IQ test is being used as an indicator of future academic success in college, it is important to recognize that substantial differences exist among colleges in terms of both the average and the range of intelligence of student bodies, grading standards, and kinds and levels of intellectual ability required for various majors. Many of these abilities are not measured by typical tests of scholastic aptitude. Thus individual predictions of future college success from IQ tests are likely to be open to marked degrees of error.

For certain disadvantaged groups, for very young children, and for individuals who place high in aptitudes other than those which the typical intelligence test measures, the IQ scores obtained may not be too meaningful. Thus, in the instance of the so-called culturally disadvantaged groups, low test scores may well reflect inequities in society rather than in the test itself. Living in an enriched environment, having extensive experience in test taking (known as "test wiseness"), possessing a high level of motivation, experiencing favorable conditions during a test administration, and enjoying superior health can individually and collectively be expected to yield somewhat higher IQ scores, whereas deficiencies in one or more of these factors could be associated with somewhat lower IQ scores.

In any event, scores on IQ tests, whether individually administered by a trained school psychologist or given as pencil-and-paper tests to groups of students by counselors or teachers, are highly reliable on both an ab-

solute and a relative basis. The reliability indexes of most standardized IQ tests are about as high as can be found (usually well above .90, where 1.00 would represent perfect reliability), and errors of measurement are minimal.

## Measures of Personality Characteristics

On the basis of their informal, day-to-day observations as well as in terms of their limited use of systematic observations, as in the accumulation of anecdotal records, teachers endeavor to draw inferences about the emotional characteristics, motivational patterns, and personal and social adjustment of their students. Teachers may also find it necessary to formulate judgments regarding their students' future vocational capabilities and interests, in response to frequent questions along these lines from the students themselves and from their parents. Not uncommonly, the teacher may be almost forced to make certain inferences or to suggest certain courses of action regarding a student's career plans or a course of study that might be advantageously followed in his preparation for professional work or for another career.

Thus the teacher may need to examine prior and current scholastic achievement information as well as intelligence and aptitude test data in relation to interest and temperament measures to determine alternative courses of action that a student might wish to consider. In short, the teacher is serving as a counselor, and unless he has had advanced training in the problems concerned with individual appraisal and in the principles and technology of measurement and evaluation, he runs a substantial risk of making erroneous inferences of a serious magnitude. Thus in the use and interpretation of measures of interest, values, and temperament, the teacher is usually well-advised to work closely with a trained specialist, generally the school counselor or school psychologist.

Personality characteristics serve as indicators of how an individual may react to environmental stresses and strains in a social setting. R. L. Thorndike and Hagen (1961, p. 25) have cited and succinctly described five personality variables as follows:

A *Character*, certain qualities defined by society as estimable or the reverse.

B *Adjustment*, degree of ability to fit into and live happily in the culture in which one is placed.

C *Temperament*, qualities relating to energy level, mood, and style of life.

D *Interest*, activities that are sought or avoided.

E *Attitudes*, reactions for or against the people, the phenomena, and the concepts that make up society.

Measurement of these aspects has not been so reliably or validly realized as that of achievement, intelligence, and certain special aptitudes. Motivationally related behaviors are exceedingly difficult to measure, as the social context in which they occur is in a highly dynamic state at all times. Moreover, the individual is highly variable from day to day in his own feeling states and in his level of tolerance of frustration and anxiety.

**Interest Tests** On the assumption that a teacher has the necessary competencies, the data furnished by interest tests can offer useful evidence for informal guidance within the classroom. Interest tests are made up of questions that require the examinee to express his preferences for various activities or to indicate his likes or dislikes for these activities. As previously mentioned, interest tests tend to be considerably less reliable and probably less valid than most standardized intelligence, aptitude, or achievement tests. The interests of children, and even those of adults, fluctuate considerably. Elementary and high school students are quite impressionable regarding vocational aspirations—especially in view of their almost continual exposure to the portrayal of the glamorous side of various careers through the media of television and motion pictures.

Probably most interest tests cannot furnish information of any reasonable degree of stability until a student is well advanced in his high school program. Their most frequent use in the school setting is to motivate students to think about and to investigate the advantages and disadvantages of various types of careers.

The two most widely used inventories are the Kuder Preference Record and the Strong Vocational Interest Blank. On these tests the individual is required to check his preferences or his likes and dislikes in answer to a number of questions. The Kuder instrument reports the extent to which students prefer one kind of activity, such as scientific, literary, or artistic, to others, such as mechanical, business, or social service. Although a student may show a high level of interest in one of these broad categories, his test standing does not guarantee that he has either the ability or the necessary perseverance to be successful in an occupation that would be in keeping with his interest patterns.

The Strong Vocational Interest Blank has been subjected to substantial validation efforts. The item responses of examinees who have been highly successful in a given occupation have been compared with those of individuals in the general population. Those items which have been shown to be highly valid for the prediction of success in that occupation are given weights, and the weights associated with responses to particular item alternatives are totaled to yield a score for an examinee. Thus if a student checks item alternatives in essentially the same manner that successful participants in the occupation do, there is an indication that he might find this occupation greatly satisfying, provided he has the necessary ability, training, and temperament to succeed in it.

**Temperament and Adjustment Inventories** The two measures just described constitute what are called *self-report inventories*. They simply represent a means of self-observation—they are devices that permit an examinee to present information about himself. The school psychologist often uses standardized self-inventories to gain some indication of the student's adjustment level and patterns of temperament. Such measures tend to be susceptible to faking and, in light of their relatively low reliability, to offer interpretations of questionable significance. Frequently the respondent endeavors to answer the items in a way that will be socially acceptable or desirable.

Such inventories probably yield fairly reliable and valid measures for students who, on their own, initiate requests to obtain information about themselves. Such scales typically furnish several dimensions, or constructs, of behavior, for which profiles showing relative strengths and weaknesses can be drawn and interpreted subjectively. It is recommended that only the highly trained counselor or school psychologist make use of such measures in school settings and that he obtain prior permission from students' families in order to avoid a charge of invasion of privacy.

**Measures of Attitudes** Psychologists and sociologists have devised many kinds of attitude scales. In the educational setting, two of the most important and useful types of attitudinal measures are those involving (a) how highly one regards or displays confidence in himself (self-concept or self-esteem) and (b) how one feels about schoolwork and about related learning activities involving interaction with peers and school personnel. An example

of a standardized measure that was designed not only to identify students who might experience difficulties in their academic work because of certain attitudes or poor study methods but also to diagnose for counseling purposes those attitudes that might contribute to learning difficulties is the Study Attitudes and Methods Survey (SAMS) (Michael, Michael, & Zimmerman, 1972). The SAMS affords scores on six affective dimensions, including among others alienation toward authority and political manipulation.

**Projective Measures** Since individuals' responses on self-inventories may not furnish scores that can be validly interpreted in light of conscious or unconscious falsification of responses, another kind of measure, known as the *projective test*, is sometimes employed. The Rorschach Ink Blot Test is a well-known example It furnishes ambiguous pictorial stimuli to which the individual responds in terms of his momentary impressions or perceptions. Similarly, the Thematic Apperception Test consists of pictures to which a person responds by writing or telling a short story regarding what is taking place in the picture. In responding to such ambiguous stimulus situations, the person supposedly attributes to them his own feelings, needs, and frustrations. without being aware that he is doing so and thus without feeling threatened with social disapproval. The use of such measures requires a great deal of specialized training, which even the school psychologist may not possess. In general, teachers should rarely make use of such tests unless they have had extensive training in their administration and interpretation or have had the opportunity to consult with highly trained specialists.

## SOME PRACTICAL CONSIDERATIONS

Teachers frequently pose questions about testing and evaluation procedures. In their experience, the authors have found the following twelve questions among those most frequently asked:

## Question 1: How frequently should teachers give tests?

How often a teacher should give a test, of course, depends on the purposes that the results will serve. Although there is no one answer to this question, it is essential to recognize that the frequency of testing varies with the kinds and levels of student behaviors involved.

If long-term gains are to be measured, students need to have enough time and an adequate range of experience to assimilate facts that have been presented, to develop the necessary concepts and problem-solving skills in certain kinds of tasks, and to integrate their learning experiences.

Thus in the high school and college setting, a test over each substantial unit of work is common. Such a test can be a valuable learning experience for the student, and if feedback is almost immediate, it can help him both in his studying and in the tying together of many loose ends.

In certain skill areas such as arithmetic and spelling, it may be advantageous to give tests several times a week or at the completion of any small unit of instruction. Administering a test or short exercise almost every day to spot student difficulties and to monitor the state and level of instruction is not unusual. Some teachers believe that daily tests motivate students to do their daily homework assignments. However, the conscientious student who has a high level of aspiration may find daily tests extremely threatening and anxiety-producing, especially if he feels that he needs time to consolidate his position with new material. Frequent tests may not be an optimal investment of such a student's time.

It may also be advisable for a teacher to give a test whenever he believes that there is a need to gain some indication of how effective the instruction has been over a period of time. Of course there is the risk that short tests may be highly unreliable and thus of quite limited value for drawing inferences about behavioral changes. Obviously, the greater the sampling of items on one or more tests, the more reliable the measurement.

## Question 2: What directions should be given to students in helping them prepare for examinations?

Prior to any formal examination that may cover a unit of work amounting to two or three weeks of concerted effort on the part of the class, the thoughtful teacher is well-advised to submit to the class, especially at the high school or college level, a list of objectives that will spell out in considerable detail what is considered to be important for the course. As a matter of fact, these objectives should be made available at the beginning of the unit of work, and at the close of the unit attention may be directed to a review of them and to an enumeration of about how many items on the examination will be concerned with each one. Such consideration on the part of the teacher will do much to improve the quality of the learning experience that students will have in preparing for an examination. It gives the students an opportunity to see what is judged to be important and what is judged to be relatively unimportant. The teacher should also use such a list of objectives in the preparation of his lesson plans, as an aid in organizing and guiding his instruction.

## Question 3: How difficult should the items of an examination be?

It is customary to develop achievement test items with a range of difficulty levels from relatively easy to relatively hard. (Difficulty level is indicated by the proportion or percentage of individuals answering the item correctly—the smaller the proportion of examinees responding correctly, the more difficult the item.) Although some specialists in educational measurement have argued that items should be of approximately 50 percent level of difficulty (i.e., that one-half of the examinee group should be able to answer a given item correctly), a slight loss in certain technological specifications such as reliability can be tolerated by varying difficulty level in order to realize somewhat greater gains in student motivation.

Frequently, teachers arrange items in an examination in order of difficulty so that, especially in objective tests, almost every student will be able to answer the first three, four, or five items correctly and only the better students will be able to respond correctly to the most difficult and thought-provoking items. Customarily, the experience a teacher gains over a period of two or three years will indicate for groups of known ability levels approximately how difficult items should be to attain a meaningful range of scores. Often there is considerable merit in giving a few difficult problem-oriented essay questions as a challenge to the most able students, with the full realization that even they may not be able to answer an item at a level of sophistication that would be completely satisfactory to the teacher with demanding expectations.

### Question 4: How much time should be allowed for an examination?

The teacher, of course, is better acquainted with the material he has been teaching than is almost anyone else. Whenever a teacher makes out a test, he tends to run the risk of underestimating how long it will take even the average student in his class to complete it. During his first year of college teaching experience, one of the authors received some excellent advice from an experienced mathematics instructor. He said, "It would be well for you to take the examination and simply treble the time it took you to complete it; after all, you have had a chance to think through the questions, since you prepared them, and you know almost in advance what the answers will be." It is advisable for a teacher to take a test that covers a major unit of work so that he can be fair in allowing time for its administration; at the same time, this will enable him to spot and correct possible ambiguities in the wording of the items.

### Question 5: What should be included in the examination that the classroom teacher makes up?

Actually, any sort of item that the teacher deems to be important in terms of fulfilling the objectives of the course should be included in a classroom examination. Items may be based upon lecture material, class discussion, assigned readings, outside projects on which students have worked, or any other activity that the teacher thinks is important. However, it seems that greater learning will take place and additional motivation for further learning will be realized if students are consulted in advance concerning what they would like to see incorporated within a test. At any rate, whenever a test covers a major unit of work or an entire course, students may advantageously be given an outline, as suggested previously, concerning what the objectives will be, and they may be advised concerning what material in the course they are required to know.

### Question 6: Should teachers give surprise tests or unannounced examinations?

The teacher who gives surprise tests or who gives examinations whose content is quite different from that which the students have been led to expect not only is obtaining non-valid scores but also is doing much to lower motivation. He is running the risk of developing negative attitudes toward learning. Such arbitrary and often punitive activities on the part of teachers build ill will and frequently create resentment among capable students who are desirous of learning. It seems that fair play on the part of the teacher is one of the essential elements in the testing and evaluation process, just as it is in teaching itself.

Students have every right, in the opinion of the authors, to know in advance what they will be held responsible for on examinations and what they may be expected to produce during the examination experience. Knowing in advance what they are likely to be asked will encourage students to study those areas which are most important for a course and encourage them to devote their attention to learning the necessary sorts of problem-solving skills and to applying their newly acquired knowledge to new situations. Thus it is the authors' position that a constructive orientation to testing is to be preferred to the generation of hostility or anxiety in students.

### Question 7: What kinds of roles may students themselves assume in contributing to examination procedures?

In his experience as a graduate student, one of the authors noted a useful procedure followed by his professor in experimental psychology and has since incorporated it into his own teaching. On each essay examination, students are given an opportunity to make up one question of their own and to answer it. This makes students feel that they are being dealt with fairly in a course and also permits them to demonstrate to the instructor one area in which they believe they have a very high level of competence. Such an opportunity also affords each student a partial chance to compensate for what he may have felt to be any degree of unfairness in the other items included in the examination. It is possible in an essay test, as in an objective test, for the sampling of the items to be somewhat different from what the student had expected, even though he may have been given an outline or list of objectives.

Devising his own question affords a student an opportunity not only to select an area in which he feels confident of his performance but also to show what his creative potentiali-

ties are. One of the authors has often noticed that students about whom he has had some reservations concerning their level of mastery were unusually brilliant in certain areas when given the opportunity to demonstrate the high-level specialization they possessed.

There are also advantages to giving students a periodic opportunity to submit items or questions for an examination, accompanied by a justification or rationale for their inclusion. Such a procedure will probably induce students to think about the objectives of the course, to become personally involved in the evaluation procedures, and to become highly proficient in the area represented by the question.

### Question 8: In what kind of format or in what form of communication should items be presented?

For elementary school children who may have a language difficulty or who may not read too well, oral presentation of true-false items or short completion items may be feasible. At higher levels of the educational ladder, many items become so complex that reading them to students becomes an imposition upon their perceptual capabilities. In such instances items should be presented in written form—preferably mimeographed, printed, or otherwise reproduced in a highly legible manner. If items are read orally, they may need to be presented several times so that students who fail to hear or comprehend key words on the first or second reading can be sure to pick them up before the teacher goes on to the next item.

### Question 9: What are the advantages, if any, to using open-book tests?

The teacher who is secure and comfortable in the classroom and who at the same time has respect for the development of the problem-solving and original capabilities of his fellow beings in the classroom will give serious consideration to the frequent use of open-book tests. Admittedly, if a teacher is interested primarily in ascertaining how many facts, names, dates, and isolated bits of information a student can remember, the closed-book test is definitely more appropriate. Many psychologists, however, including the authors of this book, challenge the use of tests that put a heavy reliance upon the memory of facts and details. Such tests tend to work against the development of understanding, skills, applications, and higher-level processes such as those of analysis, synthesis, and evaluation.

The teacher who is truly interested in determining how well students can think for themselves will find that open-book tests, whether in the essay, multiple-choice, true-false, or simple completion form, are highly useful. Such tests tend not only to reduce anxiety on the part of the students but also to give them an opportunity to apply information they have learned, to use notes and references in a meaningful way, and to do the sorts of things which in later life they are much more likely to be experiencing. Furthermore, there is the advantage of eliminating or minimizing cheating, since the use of books does away with cheating almost entirely.

This open-book approach is also adaptable to the measurement of some noncognitive objectives such as students' attitudes toward, and opinions of, various matters. Such open-book tests, as pointed out before, give the student an opportunity to show his divergent thinking capabilities, to demonstrate what his creative potentialities are, and to give expression in some detail to problems of considerable interest to him. The effective use of open-book tests should also include the opportunity, previously suggested, for students to generate certain questions on their own. Such freedom in the classroom would seem to the authors to give students a maximum opportunity to develop intrinsic motivation, to explore new fields of interest to them, and to loosen some of the shackles that have been placed for so many years upon creative learning potentialities.

In all seriousness, one may ask the question: How often in life does one as an engineer, a scientist, a doctor, a lawyer, a skilled mechanic, or a tradesman find that he is denied access to a book or a reference manual when he comes across a point he wishes to check? How artificial tests in the classroom have become when students are required simply to store vast amounts of knowledge—much of it unrelated and inconsequential—so that it can be regurgitated on an examination with no purpose other than to provide the teacher with a certain score so that he can assign a mark! Despite the importance of having a base of factual information on which to build problem-solving capabilities, this primitive way of looking at the evaluation process is truly unfortunate and regrettable in that it discourages many students from seeking advanced learning or from pursuing the study of more challenging problems.

**Question 10: What kinds of standards should teachers employ in assigning course marks to students or grades to their tests?**

The most serious concerns in assigning marks arise from (1) ambiguities and inconsistencies in the criteria for grading or the definitions of what grades mean and (2) the absence of sufficient relevant and objective information for determination of grades. Variability in the philosophy of instructors and of institutions as well as fluctuations in the judgment of the same teacher from one time to another (lack of reliability) tends to have an adverse influence on the validity of marks. In the final analysis, the evaluation of performance is a subjective decision that rests on the philosophy of the teacher and the school, the criteria employed, and the purposes to which marks will be put.

Some of the difficulties might be avoided by assigning multiple marks to different aspects of school performance such as attendance, attitude, effort and interest, homework, participation in class activities, and test scores. What is being suggested, in essence, is a specification of the weights to be assigned to each of the measurable objectives so as to improve the validity of grades, just as the delineation of objectives for a test can improve its validity. If a school system is seriously interested in having a grade represent achievement per se, it may be advantageous to employ a currically valid standardized achievement test in determining marks. Such a test furnishes an objective indication of performance that is not influenced by personality characteristics such as a student's deportment, the level of his conformity to the teacher's expectations, or the teacher's marked like or dislike of him.

Many teachers seem to feel obligated to use absolute standards in arriving at some sort of decision concerning the excellence of educational achievement. They frequently exhibit the naive belief that on any test they construct and administer, a score of 90 or above is without question an A. They fail to realize that the ability levels of students differ from one class to another during the same or in successive semesters and, too, that as a result of using different forms of a test or of building new tests, the test itself may be harder or easier one semester than another. A related problem concerns the belief of far too many teachers that there is some sort of magic attached to grading on the curve—that is, the use of normal probability distribution, which will be considered later, in assigning fixed proportions of As, Bs, Cs, Ds, and Fs to be given. Many teachers allow some sort of abstract mathematical model, or mathematical device, to serve as a tool for judgment and decision making when actually circumstances of the real world make its application ridiculous. In the instance of a class of honor students, for example, use of the normal-curve model would be absurd because most honor students who are members of an unselected sample would be expected to earn As and Bs on the examinations and in course standings.

**Question 11: What are some of the essential requirements for teachers to be successful in testing practices?**

First, the teacher must be a master of the subject matter in his own right—a scholar who is thoroughly familiar with the field he is teaching. A high level of knowledge and comprehension of the basic principles of his subject or subjects is necessary if he is to ask significant, meaningful, novel, and challenging questions of students on examinations. This thorough knowledge is also necessary (but not sufficient) to his communicating basic concepts in a precise and clear way so that acceptable and scorable answers can be presented to his questions. A thorough knowledge of his field and the comprehension of its many intricacies also put him in a position to define the objectives of each unit of the curriculum and to state them in a form of observable behaviors that can be readily translated into test items.

The skillful teacher can relate the instructional procedures, class discussion, and assigned activities in a classroom situation to the objectives of the curriculum. His own experiences in having learned the material contained in a unit of the curriculum make him sensitive to, and empathic with, the students concerning their problems in learning. This empathy enables him to understand the psychological processes and thinking skills that are required for an understanding and comprehension of the principal objectives of the unit of instruction, and it also enables him to incorporate these features into his test items.

The teacher can also apply information from his broad background to new situations in both instruction and evaluation practices, which will not only challenge and interest students in their learning experiences in the classroom but also stimulate further inquiry on their part into unexplored areas of the curriculum for the enrichment of all.

Second, to be skillful and effective in his testing practices, the instructor himself must be able to write effectively. In preparing items, he needs to be able to communicate precisely and concisely the information and the instructions that the students need in order to respond to the questions, whether they are in the essay form or the objective form.

In writing items, the teacher should be capable of expressing the basic concepts involved in his own words rather than in the wording of a textbook or manual with which the students may have had to work. Writing items has been said by many to be an art. However, experience in writing items over an extended period of time is very likely, if the teacher gives conscious attention to his efforts, to result in substantial improvements in those item-writing skills required in good test construction.

Third, the teacher who is effective in testing practices is also one who will take great pains in returning the papers as early as possible following the testing. This feedback to the students is essential for guiding their learning and for enhancing and maintaining their motivation. The teacher who wishes to maximize the positive outcomes of testing will entertain questions from students regarding the items and will feel comfortable discussing different points of view concerning what the appropriate answers should be, especially in the areas of the social sciences in high school and college and in the more subjective areas of the college curriculum.

Fourth, the teacher who desires to be successful in the testing and evaluation program of his class is one who is highly empathic and sympathetic to the needs and the learning difficulties of the students. He will at all times attempt to be fair in the questions that he asks; to be diligent and as objective as possible in the way in which he scores the questions; to be impartial in arriving at some sort of evaluation concerning what are excellent, good, average, passing, and failing levels of performance; and to be positive in his attitude when making suggestions to students concerning ways in which they could improve. Such a positive approach may be expected to enhance the degree of the students' proficiency in a given skill as well as their level of understanding and conceptualization of subject matter.

Fifth, the teacher who is successful in using classroom tests will learn from previous experiences. He will look at test items to determine the typical difficulties that students have had in responding to them—difficulties associated not only with the students' learning processes but also with ambiguities and inaccuracies in the wording of items.

Sixth, as will be seen in the next chapter, the skillful teacher will also make certain simple statistical analyses of the responses to the test items. He may, for example, separate the papers in terms of those students who have placed in the upper half in total performance on the instrument and those who have placed in the bottom half. Then he determines what proportion of students in the top half of the group answered items correctly and what proportion of students in the bottom half responded correctly. This procedure, known as *item analysis*, serves to point up whether an item is differentiating between those who, as a group, are successful on the test and those who tend to be less successful. Customarily on objective test items, such analysis leads to the retention of those items which are more effective in differentiating between students who have learned a unit rather well and those who have been relatively unsuccessful in their learning.

As mentioned previously, the proportion of

individuals in the examinee group who answer an item correctly can be taken as an index of the difficulty level of the item. After studying the range of difficulty levels of items, a teacher is able to judge whether, on the whole, the test has been about right in terms of difficulty, too hard, or too easy. Such information will enable the teacher to make improvements in the test if he should have occasion to teach the unit again to a new group. Other sorts of statistical guides such as the determination of reliability coefficient, the calculation of the mean or median, and the computation of the standard deviation (a measure of spread or variability of scores) will also be of considerable aid to the teacher. These special topics will be considered in the next chapter.

### Question 12: What are some of the common errors or mistakes that teachers make in the testing practices they employ in the classroom?

First of all, one might say that failing to follow some of the practices suggested in the previous sections could be viewed to some extent as representing misjudged courses of action in the evaluation process. However, there are several additional shortcomings in teacher practice that could be listed. Perhaps one of the most serious errors that teachers make is failing to allow sufficient time for the preparation of test questions. Test writing cannot be done effectively if it is put off until the evening before the examination is to be given. Students deserve a fair test and one that has been constructed carefully, especially if it covers a major unit of work.

A second mistake that many teachers make is failing to build the test carefully around the objectives of the course, if indeed the objectives have ever been adequately defined. The result is either inadequate emphasis on certain topics that have been covered or undue stress on topics to which relatively little attention has been given.

Third, many teachers who set out to prepare an objective test fail to include a sufficient number of items so that a reliable measure can be obtained. As indicated previously, the reliability of a test is highly dependent upon the number of questions included, since the number of questions represents how adequately a set of behaviors in a given domain of knowledge has been sampled. Obviously, if only a few items are included, the chance factor operating in one's obtaining a high or a low score can be great. For example, in a 10-item true-false test, it can be shown that there is a high probability that one may obtain as many as eight items correct purely on a chance basis.

Fourth, as has been implied in Question 9, teachers frequently tend to write items that cover trivial details or isolated bits of subject matter of little or no practical or meaningful consequence. For example, basing items upon material covered in footnotes in history books, for example, seems to be both a punitive and a misdirected practice on the part of many high school teachers. An occasional item on an important footnote might well be justified, but the teacher who takes a sadistic delight in basing perhaps as many as 30 to 40 percent of the items on isolated tabular entries or obscure footnotes is completely overlooking the important body of knowledge contained in the textbook as a whole.

Fifth, especially in the instance of the essay test or the simple completion test, the scoring problem is one that poses many difficulties for the classroom teacher. Although suggestions for improving the scoring of essay tests have been made previously, it may be well to state again that the preparation of some sort of outline concerning what would be an acceptable answer or group of answers is helpful in increasing the objectivity of the scoring (minimizing bias in giving credit) and in enhancing the reliability of the scores. The scoring of essay tests requires careful planning and a systematic approach so that students will be fairly treated.

In the case of essay tests, teachers frequently find it advantageous to score one question at a time and occasionally to interrupt the scoring process with a coffee break, for example, so that their attention set will be as nearly uniform as possible throughout the extended chore of grading the essay questions. A teacher who has many essays to score frequently tends to vary in his tolerance of the answers, to become impatient, and to be lenient in his marking at times and more difficult at other times. Thus the spacing of the scoring effort may be important in minimizing fluctuations in values assigned to a question. To ensure consistency in marking, the scoring of one question at a time is usually advisable. The scorer's reaction to a given question may be influenced by the student's responses to other items.

Occasionally a student who is well known to the teacher as being either an excellent or a poor student may perform on one item of an essay test in such a manner as to create either a positive or very negative carryover effect to the responses he makes to the other items. This tendency for the scorer to rate an individual very high or very low on several items because of a very high or a very low performance on one or two questions is identified as the halo effect.

Sixth, perhaps one of the most serious errors that teachers make is exhibiting an almost naive belief in the accuracy of the measures or instruments they use. In many instances, a teacher will judge a 1- or 2-point difference on a 50-item test as being truly significant. Errors of measurement are quite substantial even in achievement and scholastic aptitude tests, which are very carefully built and which are found, on a relative basis, to be highly reliable. One of the authors will never forget an experience he had in a college course in freshman German in which he earned a score of 92.5 on the midterm examination. A grade of A was supposed to run from 93 to 100, a B from 85 to 92. In the distribution of scores, the two highest marks were 96 and 94, followed by the score of 92.5 The next highest score was an 87. The teacher, believing in the absolute sanctity of this test, gave the author a B+ on the examination, to his great consternation. At least a 3- or 4-point difference in the examination scores was probably required to indicate any reliable difference in standing.

## SUMMARY

In carrying out evaluation procedures, teachers devise their own tests and scales and also make use of standardized measures. To evaluate achievement, teachers rely heavily upon the essay and objective tests that they devise. Assuming a fill-in-the-blank, true-false, multiple-choice, or matching format, the objective test offers several advantages: great breadth of coverage, especially of factual material; ease and accuracy of scoring; a relatively high degree of reliability; and, if carefully constructed, the potential of measuring higher-level cognitive processes. The essay test, which poses difficulties in scoring and has a somewhat limited scope in terms of coverage, has the advantages of being easy to prepare and of affording the opportunity to tap the higher-level intellectual processes of reasoning, application, analysis, synthesis, and evaluation.

Irrespective of the format of the questions, the skillful teacher endeavors to prepare a test that will evoke the sorts of student behaviors that correspond most closely to the specific content and process objectives sought. The construction of essay and objective tests requires clarity of expression, emphasis on main points rather than trivialities, and sufficient specificity and qualifications in wording to reduce ambiguity and to allow the examinee to interpret the questions correctly and make the appropriate response. In the instance of the multiple-choice item, it is essential that the alternative responses be plausible, reasonable, and attractive if the item is to serve its intended function. For most achievement tests in the multiple-choice or true-false format, the authors have recommended against the use of scoring formulas that offer a penalty for so-called guessing.

In classroom evaluation, teachers may also find rating scales, checklists, and anecdotal records to be useful indicators of student behaviors. In using these measures, as well as others, it is important that a clear distinction be made between the factual information obtained and the inferences or interpretations that may be made on the basis of the information.

Standardized tests have been conveniently classified as falling into the categories of (1) achievement, (2) intelligence and aptitude, and (3) personality. In evaluating scores on these tests, the teacher very frequently needs to rely upon the special competencies of school psychologists and counselors. It is essential that manuals accompanying standardized tests furnish adequate information regarding (1) purposes and objectives, (2) administration and scoring, (3) reliability, 4) validity, (5) norms and scales used in reporting scores, and (6) interpretability.

Answers to 12 practical questions that teachers often ask were set forth. The 12 general topics considered were related to (1) frequency of test administration, (2) directions to help students prepare for an examination, (3) appropriate difficulty levels for items in examinations, (4) appropriate time allowances for taking tests, (5) the nature of examination content, (6) the disadvantages of giving unan- nounced tests, (7) the nature of student participation in contributing items to examinations, (8) various formats for communicating test items, (9) the advantages of giving open-book tests, (10) the relative nature of standards for assigning course marks and grades to examination scores. (11) essential requirements for teachers to be successful in testing practices, and (12) typical errors that teachers make in classroom testing activities.

## SELF-DIRECTING ACTIVITIES

1 After setting up a two-dimensional grid containing process and product objectives for a unit of instruction, write objective-type test items that correspond to the objectives. Try also to point out an instructional strategy that could be used to facilitate attainment of each objective being measured.

2 Devise a checklist or rating scale appropriate to a given curricular experience that would permit observation of behaviors of students in a systematic way.

3 Take a set of items in a standardized achievement test and classify them according to the hierarchy of process objectives in Bloom's *Taxonomy*. Check the classifications chosen for the items with those of a friend who has independently undertaken the same task.

4 After doing an error analysis of a sequence of responses in problem solving tasks in mathematics assignments or after analyzing errors in grammar and language mechanics in a set of English compositions, devise multiple-choice items, the incorrect alternatives of which represent the most frequently committed errors observed. Make sure that each item corresponds to a clearly stated objective of a desired outcome of learning either in mathematics or in English composition.

5 After obtaining appropriate permission, spend an afternoon or morning observing a school psychologist administering, scoring, and interpreting individual tests—one or more intelligence or personality tests.

# Chapter 19

One of the authors, Professor William Michael, at the blackboard.

# STATISTICAL METHODS

After studying the chapter and working through the illustrative problems presented, you should be able to:

❡ Tabulate data and portray them in graphical form

❡ Differentiate among and calculate measures of central tendency (mean, median, and mode) and variability (range and standard deviation) in frequency distributions of scores

❡ Distinguish between percentiles and percentile ranks and exhibit competence in computing and interpreting these statistics in the context of test scores

❡ Calculate various types of standard scores and use them in the interpretation of test score data

❡ Explain interrelationships of correlation and prediction relative to two variables and carry out computational procedures associated with correlation and prediction

❡ Describe basic principles underlying probability sampling in educational studies

❡ Outline essential principles of statistical inference in hypothesis testing with both continuous data or measures (e.g., significance of difference between means of two groups exposed to two different treatments) and discrete or enumerative data (e.g., significance of difference in frequency or proportion of individuals in two groups responding to a given question or treatment)

❡ Illustrate the similarities and differences between test reliability and the standard error of measurement

❡ Define terms cited in the first eight objectives as well as such additional terms as:

    normal frequency distribution
    skewness
    variance
    $T$ score
    $z$ score
    stanine
    test profile
    product-moment correlation
    regression line
    rank-difference correlation
    predictor variable
    criterion variable
    research hypothesis
    null hypothesis
    probability
    level of significance (.05 and .01 level)
    Type I error
    Type II error
    sampling error
    sampling distribution
    chi-square
    item analysis
    contingency table
    observed frequency
    expected frequency
    statistic
    parameter

In the two previous chapters, as well as in some of the others, it was apparent that the use of tests and scales is quite common in the study and description of human behavior. In the research activities of educational psychology, investigators find it both necessary and desirable to describe the behaviors that they have observed in the form of relatively precise measures derived from scales that supposedly represent valid indicators of these behaviors. If individual differences did not exist, there would be no need for tests or scales. Such devices permit the placement of individuals along points of a continuum. The measures corresponding to these points permit an expression of how much of the characteristic or trait being measured a person possesses.

The process of quantifying psychological variables has perhaps constituted one of the major contributions to the furthering of psychology as a science. As implied in the previous paragraph, this process involves finding numerical values to describe the standing of an individual on a scale, test, or other device that is assumed to define the psychological variable under consideration. It is customary to refer to the procedures for manipulating the data obtained from tests or scales as *statistical methods*. Such methods involve the use of specific mathematical techniques and mathematical models to describe the behaviors observed.

Frequently students have difficulty in understanding and carrying out the mathematical operations involved in statistical methods and in using formulas embodying symbolic representation of certain operations or procedures. Actually statistical methods constitute a highly convenient and precise way of describing observations of human behavior.

Although the beginning student may have certain anxieties concerning his ability to handle statistics, he will soon appreciate the many advantages that statistical methods afford in psychological research, some of which are as follows: (1) They afford a relatively exact description of observed phenomena; (2) they can be readily communicated to others who are carrying out research; (3) they force the investigator to be precise and definite in the experimental operations that he employs—in other words, they tend to make the investigator use operational definitions of key psychological variables or processes so that they can be treated in a quantitative manner and thus can be replicated by others who are doing research; (4) they enable the investigator to summarize his results in a meaningful and convenient form in that he can take masses of data and reduce them to a simply communicated form; (5) they afford the investigator an opportunity to make certain inferences or generalizations from data that he has gathered from small samples, provided that the samples have been randomly selected, to much larger groups of individuals, known as *populations*; (6) they give the investigator the opportunity to make predictions concerning the extent to which measures on a dependent variable (an outcome event) may be related to an antecedent or independent variable (an input event) that has been subjected to manipulation (e.g., relating the number of trials required to learn a list of English-German words to prior amounts of reinforcement that have been given to each of several previous experiences); and (7) they allow the investigator to make inferences regarding some possible causal factors underlying highly complex events, provided that the experimental design employed affords a high degree of control over extraneous or unwanted sources of variation in the observed measures. As can be seen, a knowledge of statistics is actually essential if one is to read professional literature that reports research in education and psychology. Thus it will be the authors' purpose to introduce the reader to a simple over-view of some of the key statistical methods that are used in educational psychology. Necessarily the emphasis on illustrative material will be directed primarily toward how statistics are employed in analyzing data gathered from experiments and especially from the use of tests and other evaluative instruments.

Readers who have taken courses in elementary educational or psychological statistics will probably benefit simply from scanning or briefly reviewing the material presented in this chapter. On the other hand, readers who have done relatively little work in statistics may find it necessary to read the chapter carefully and to check their work on several of the calculation aids provided. It is not necessary to understand the derivations of the formulas presented in order to grasp how they are applied in the analysis of data. It is hoped, however, that through his study of the following pages, the reader will develop some understanding of the basic uses of statistics, largely at a consumer level, and will become familiar with the vocabulary that is often employed in the educational and psychological literature.

The following topics will be considered: (1) the tabulation and graphical representation of data; (2) the use of measures of central tendency—the mean, median, and mode; (3) the application of the percentile and the percentile rank (a) to determine an individual's standing relative to that of several other individuals in a group or (b) to find scores that allow the separation of a distribution into certain segments such as quarters or fifths; (4) the expression of the amount of variation, dispersion, or scatter in a distribution of scores in terms of such statistics as the standard deviation or the range; (5) the determination and application of standard scores, especially in the interpretation of test results; (6) the use of various indexes of relationship, such as the product-moment correlation and the rank-difference correlation—indexes that permit the establishment of a degree of correspondence between two sets of measures usually derived for one sample of individuals, as in reporting the extent to which test scores are predictive of criterion measures (criterion-related validity); (7) the consideration of sampling procedures as applied to the selection of groups for experiments or in the choice of individuals to be interviewed or sent questionnaires in a field study; (8) a consideration of elementary principles of statistical inference, with particular attention directed toward the testing of hypotheses, as in determining whether the differences observed in the average scores of two groups or the differences in the proportions of two groups of individuals who respond in a designated manner to a question could be due to errors of random sampling or chance; and (9) special topics including item analysis, test reliability, and the standard error of measurement. Most of the examples to be presented will pertain to the analysis of test data or to the analysis of measures that are derived from tests, as teachers and other school personnel are frequently involved in the evaluation of test results.

## TABULATION AND GRAPHICAL REPRESENTATION OF DATA

Data assume either a continuous or a discrete form. Whenever a test or scale is employed, the measurement operation yields numbers from high to low that supposedly represent points along a continuum. Only the lack of perfect reliability and the absence of a high degree of precision prevent the differentiation of the measured performance of individuals into a virtually infinite number of graded steps along the continuum. Whenever measurement exists, the resulting data are approximate. Thus a score of 87 implies that an individual falls between 86.5 and 87.5. In the illustrative examples to be presented, calculations are carried out for a sequence of scores that are treated as continuous measures.

Whenever a counting operation is involved, as in determining how many individuals fall into certain categories or classifications, *discrete data* are said to result. Thus the numbers of boys and girls in a sixth-grade class constitute enumerative or discrete data, just as an enumeration of objects such as chairs, desks, automobiles, or shoes would. Such objects cannot be fractionated—that is, divided into fractional parts. The numbers of discrete units in a given classification are referred to as *frequencies.*

Table 19-1 presents the scores of 40 students on an achievement examination. As an initial basis for their simplification, the scores have been arranged from high to low—an ordering that permits the description of each score in relation to the others as well as the determination of the range. The symbol customarily used for the total number of individuals in a sample is *N*.

Even this frequency distribution of scores does not achieve a degree of simplification that would be afforded by placing data into a

**Table 19-2   Frequency Distribution of Integral Scores**

| Scores | Frequency (*f*) | Scores | Frequency (*f*) |
|--------|-----------------|--------|-----------------|
| 99 | 1 | 81 | 3 |
| 96 | 1 | 80 | 2 |
| 94 | 1 | 78 | 1 |
| 92 | 1 | 77 | 1 |
| 91 | 1 | 76 | 3 |
| 90 | 1 | 75 | 3 |
| 89 | 1 | 74 | 1 |
| 88 | 3 | 72 | 1 |
| 87 | 1 | 71 | 2 |
| 86 | 2 | 70 | 1 |
| 84 | 1 | 68 | 1 |
| 83 | 4 | 66 | 1 |
| 82 | 1 | 65 | 1 |

set of mutually exclusive categories of the same width or size, known as *class intervals.* The most elementary type of interval is that of unit width; in other words, each score is treated as its own interval. In Table 19-2, each score is listed separately, and the number of times that the score appears is indicated in an adjacent column headed "frequency (*f*)." Thus one person earned a score of 99, one person earned a score of 96, two persons earned a score of 86, three persons earned a score of 88, four persons earned a score of 83, and so forth. Each score represents an interval of one unit distance. For example, a score of 88 goes from 87.5 to 88.5.

In Table 19-3, an interval of size of five units has been chosen for generation of the frequency distribution of the 40 scores presented in Table 19-1. The first two columns of Table 19-3 give the class interval and the frequency with which cases fall in that interval. For example, it will be noted in Table 19-1 that four individuals earned scores of 90, 91, 92,

**Table 19-1   Forty Test Scores Ranked in Order from High to Low (Data Fictitious)**

| | | | |
|----|----|----|----|
| 99 | 87 | 81 | 75 |
| 96 | 86 | 81 | 75 |
| 94 | 86 | 80 | 74 |
| 92 | 84 | 80 | 72 |
| 91 | 83 | 78 | 71 |
| 90 | 83 | 77 | 71 |
| 89 | 83 | 76 | 70 |
| 88 | 83 | 76 | 68 |
| 88 | 82 | 76 | 66 |
| 88 | 81 | 75 | 65 |

and 94. In Table 19-3, these four scores have been lumped together and placed in a class interval from 90 to 94. Similarly, seven people earned scores between 85 and 89, which make up a class interval from 85 to 89. It will be noted in Table 19-3 that the last two columns furnish the precise limits for each class interval and the midpoint (halfway value) for each interval. (The third to fifth columns will be explained subsequently.)

Examination of the 40 scores in Table 19-1 reveals that their range is from 99 to 65, or between 99.5 and 64.5—a spread of 35 points. Division of this value by a class-interval width of 5 would yield 7 intervals. Conversely, if one desired 7 intervals, division of 35 by 7 would suggest that a width of 5 would be appropriate. If one preferred that the intervals have a width of 4, the estimated number required would be about 9.

There is a certain advantage in having the width of an interval an odd number such as 5 or 3, for the midpoint of such an interval, as can be seen in Table 19-3, is a whole number—a definite computational advantage for subsequent statistical operations. It should be noted that if the size of an interval is an even number, the midpoint will not be a whole number. The value will contain a one-half. For example, the midpoint of an interval of a width of 4 units, such as 68 to 71 (the precise limits being 67.5 and 71.5), would be 69.5, one-half the distance from 68 to 71 and also one-half the distance from 67.5 to 71.5. Of incidental interest is the fact that for aesthetic reasons, some statisticians prefer that the lower limit, when expressed as an approximate number, be exactly divisible by the width of the interval. For example, in Table 19-3 the approximate lower limits of 65, 70, 75, 80, 85, 90, and 95 are all divisible by 5.

The third column of Table 19-3 indicates how many cases have been accumulated to the upper limit of each interval. This information is obtained by adding up the number of cases

in each interval, including the interval that contains the upper limits specified. For example, if the number of cases up to 79.5 is desired, that would be given by the sum of 3 + 5 + 8, which is 16. The fourth and fifth columns represent these cumulative frequencies after they have been changed to proportions and percentages, respectively, of the total sample size. Thus up to 84.5, the *cumulative frequency* (cum *f*) of 27 constitutes a cumulative proportion of .675 of the total frequency of 40, or a cumulative percentage of 67.5 (the cumulative proportion multiplied by 100). Cumulative data are necessary for calculation of other statistics such as percentiles, or centiles, which will be considered a little later.

### Histogram

A pictorial representation of a frequency distribution is helpful in communicating statistical information, especially to school-board members, who take particular delight in reading charts and diagrams. The histogram, which resembles a bar graph, is commonly used. In Figure 19-1, the data of Table 19-3 are shown in graphical form. On the vertical axis are the frequencies that begin at zero. The exact limits of the class intervals fall along the

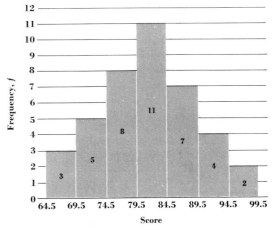

**Figure 19-1** Histogram of test scores.

**Table 19-3  Frequency Distribution of Grouped Test Scores and Related Information**

| Class interval | Frequency (f) | Cumulative frequency (cum f) | Cumulative proportion (cum p) | Cumulative percentage (cum 100p) | Exact interval limits | Midpoint (X) |
|---|---|---|---|---|---|---|
| 95–99 | 2 | 40 | 1.000 | 100.0 | 94.5–99.5 | 97.0 |
| 90–94 | 4 | 38 | .950 | 95.0 | 89.5–94.5 | 92.0 |
| 85–89 | 7 | 34 | .850 | 85.0 | 84.5–89.5 | 87.0 |
| 80–84 | 11 | 27 | .675 | 67.5 | 79.5–84.5 | 82.0 |
| 75–79 | 8 | 16 | .400 | 40.0 | 74.5–79.5 | 77.0 |
| 70–74 | 5 | 8 | .200 | 20.0 | 69.5–74.5 | 72.0 |
| 65–69 | 3 | 3 | .075 | 7.5 | 64.5–69.5 | 67.0 |
|  | N = 40 |  |  |  |  |  |

horizontal axis. Customarily, this axis does not begin at zero unless the lowest score for an interval is near zero.

The histogram constitutes an area representation of the frequencies—the larger the frequency for a given interval, the higher the block of the histogram and the greater the area. Each individual could be thought of as constituting a small rectangle of a given unit of area. For the 40 people in the total sample, there would be 40 units of area.

### Frequency Polygon

Some statisticians prefer using a broken-line graph that connects the midpoints of each class interval at a height that corresponds to the frequency appearing in that interval. Such a graph is called a *frequency polygon*. The frequency distribution in Table 19-3 is portrayed as a frequency polygon in Figure 19-2. One advantage of the frequency polygon over the histogram is that when two or more frequency distributions are being compared, it is often somewhat easier to draw two overlapping polygons than to present two overlapping histograms.

### Cumulative-Percentage Curve, or Ogive

The cumulative percentages in the fifth column of Table 19-3 may also be represented graphically. The cumulative percentages are placed on the vertical axis, and the upper exact limits of each interval are marked along the horizontal axis as shown in Figure 19-3. This curve, which is sometimes called an *ogive*, can be quite useful in estimating percentiles (or centiles).

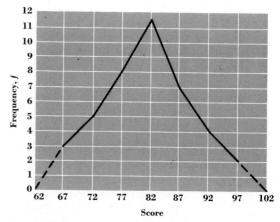

**Figure 19-2**  Frequency polygon of test scores.

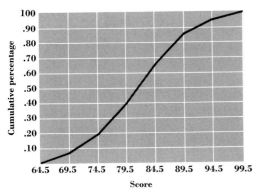

**Figure 19-3**  Cumulative proportions of test scores.

## MEASURES OF CENTRAL TENDENCY

In educational and psychological research, it is customary to describe groups in terms of some measure of average or typical performance. The mean, the median, and the mode are the three measures of central tendency employed—especially the mean and the median, in the instance of the treatment of test scores.

### The Mean

The *mean*, which is commonly called an *arithmetic average*, is found by adding all the scores of a group and by dividing the resulting sum by the total number of scores. For the data in Table 19-1, the sum of scores is 3,240, which when divided by 40 yields a mean of 81.0. Thus a score of 81.0 is the arithmetic average of 40 individuals. This average then describes the group.

Such operations as the calculation of the mean are often more easily explained and communicated through the use of a combination of symbols that represent a shorthand way of explaining the basic arithmetic operations involved. An expression consisting of several symbols to explain a mathematical operation is called a *formula.* The formula for

---

**Calculation Aid 19-1   Calculating the Mean of Ungrouped Data**

**Problem**
　Find the mean of the 40 ungrouped test scores in Table 19–1

**Symbols defined**
　$X$ = any obtained score (raw score)
　$N$ = number of cases (total frequency)
　$\Sigma$ = sum, usually read "sigma"
　$M$ = mean (sometimes written $\overline{X}$)

**Formula**
$$M = \frac{\Sigma X}{N}$$

**Computational steps**
　1. Sum the 40 scores ($N = 40$); find that $\Sigma X = 3,240$.
　2. Place the numbers in the formula and carry out the necessary arithmetic:
$$M = \frac{\Sigma X}{N} = \frac{3,240}{40}$$
$$= 81.0$$

---

the calculation of the mean is shown in Calculation Aid 19-1, in which the steps for the computation of the mean are explained for the ungrouped data of Table 19-1.

In Table 19-3, the scores have been grouped by steps of five. This grouping procedure can be expected to introduce a slight amount of error in the calculation of the mean, as all cases within an interval are assumed to fall at the midpoint of that interval. The midpoint of each interval is multiplied by the frequency in that interval, and the resulting (weighted) sum is divided by the number of cases to determine the mean.

The computation in Calculation Aid 19-2 reveals that the mean is estimated to be 81.25. This value of 81.25 is the point about which the histogram shown in Figure 19-1 could be balanced if one were to pretend that each block of the histogram were a weight proportional to its height. The discrepancy of .25 between the value of 81.25 and 81.00 for

---

### Calculation Aid 19-2  Calculating the Mean of Grouped Data

**Problem**

Find the mean of the 40 test scores that have been grouped in Table 19-3 Computations are shown in the work-layout form below.

**Symbols defined**

$M$ = mean
$\Sigma$ = sum
$f$ = frequency, or number of cases, in each interval
$X_c$ = midpoint of each interval
$N$ = total number of cases

**Formula**

$$M = \frac{\Sigma f X_c}{N}$$

**Computational steps**

1. Multiply the frequency of each interval by the value for the midpoint of the interval.
2. Sum the products determined in step 1; find that $\Sigma f X_c = 3{,}250$.
3. Place the numbers in the formula and carry out the required calculation:

$$M = \frac{3{,}250}{40} = 81.25$$

**Work-layout form**

| Class Interval | $f$ | $X_c$ | $fX_c$ |
|---|---|---|---|
| 95–99 | 2 | 97 | 194 |
| 90–94 | 4 | 92 | 368 |
| 85–89 | 7 | 87 | 609 |
| 80–84 | 11 | 82 | 902 |
| 75–79 | 8 | 77 | 616 |
| 70–74 | 5 | 72 | 360 |
| 65–69 | 3 | 67 | 201 |
| | $N = 40$ | | $\Sigma f X_c = 3{,}250$ |

---

### Calculation Aid 19-3    Calculating the Median of Ungrouped Data

---

**Problem**

Determine the median of the 40 ungrouped test scores in Table 19-1.

**Symbols defined and formula**

To avoid unnecessary complexity, symbols and formulas will be omitted.

**Computational steps**

1. Take one-half the number of cases $N$ or simply multiply $N$ by .50 to find how many cases lie above or below the median: $.50\ N = .50\ (40) = 20$.

2. Determine where the 20th case falls. By counting up from the bottom score, it is seen that the median falls between 80.5 and 81.5—somewhere amid the three 81s. Assume that the three cases constitute equal amounts of score distance to the unit interval from 80.5 to 81.5.

3. Add to the lower limit of 80.5 an increment given by the distance that two cases would have to cover—namely, a distance of $2/3$.

This step may be summarized to yield the median:

$$\text{Median} = 80.5 + \tfrac{2}{3} = 80.5 + .67 = 81.17$$

---

grouped and ungrouped data is due to grouping error. Such a discrepancy would not be considered serious, especially in view of the expected amounts of error that arise in the process of measurement involving use of tests and scales.

### The Median

The *median* is a point on the scale of continuous measures that separates the upper half of cases from the lower half. For example, in the set of scores 21, 17, 15, 12, and 6, the median is 15, since two cases lie above 15 and two cases lie below it. If there is an odd number of frequencies, the median is the middle score, provided that there are no tied scores in the vicinity of the median. In the instance of an even number of scores, such as 28, 26, 21, 17, 16, and 15, the median would be estimated as

the average of 21 and 17, which is 19 (although theoretically there is an infinite number of points that fall between 20.5 and 17.5, which are the lower and upper limits, respectively, of 21 and 17).

In the instance of tied scores near the median, the determination is somewhat more difficult, as shown in Calculation Aid 19-3. The median is calculated for the situation in which the scores are ungrouped. Formulas have been omitted, as the arbitrarily defined symbols constituting such formulas would be quite complex. Instead, the logic of the procedure is emphasized.

If the frequency distribution is quite nearly symmetrical in shape, the mean and the median are nearly identical, and one measure is about as useful as the other. On the other hand, if there is a marked piling up of cases at one end of the distribution and a gradual tapering off of cases over a substantial portion of the continuum, the mean and the median will differ considerably. Such frequency distributions are said to be *skewed.* In such a distribution the median will furnish a more nearly accurate picture of what the typical person receives. For example, in the distribution of scores 2, 5, 8, 9, 10, 12, 13, 14, 17, and 96, the median is 11, but the mean is 18.6. Obviously the median comes closer to describing what is typical of the group. Whenever there is a small number of extreme scores, the mean will differ somewhat from the median.

Figure 19-4 is a graphical illustration of a symmetrical distribution that is frequently encountered in educational and psychological measurement—a bell-shaped frequency distribution, often called the *normal curve.* In addition, the figure shows a pictorial representation of a negatively skewed distribution, in which the tail of the curve is at the left, and a positively skewed distribution, in which the elongated tail is at the right. These curves represent smoothed frequency polygons for large samples. Differences in the positions of the mean and the median in the two skewed distributions are clearly apparent, whereas in the symmetrical distribution their identity in value is readily evident.

## The Mode

In a distribution of scores, the one that occurs most often is called the *mode.* In Table 19-1 the mode is 83, as that score occurs more often than any other score. When data have been grouped as in Table 19-3, the midpoint of

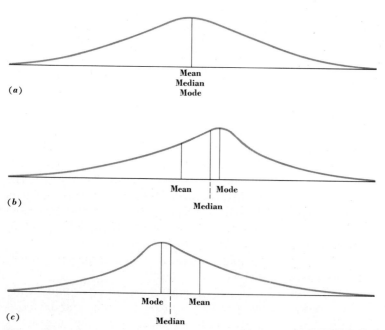

**Figure 19-4** Normal frequency distribution (a), negatively skewed frequency distribution (b), and positively skewed frequency distribution (c). Note the influence that extreme cases have in displacing the mean toward the skewed end of distributions b and c.

the interval containing the greatest number of cases is taken as an estimate of the mode. In some frequency distributions, there may be two or three modes if there is a marked piling up of cases at two or three points or small intervals of the score continuum. Such distributions are called *bimodal* or *trimodal*.

## FRACTIONATION OF SCORE DISTRIBUTIONS: PERCENTILE AND PERCENTILE RANK

An obtained test score, known as a *raw score*, that stands by itself furnishes little meaning concerning an individual's level of performance. A fairly obvious and reasonably easy and direct approach to interpreting an individual's score is to compare his rank or position with that of others in the group who have taken the test or with respect to the scores in a sample on whom the test has been standardized. An initial approach is simply to place individuals who are within a sample in rank order. Since this procedure fails to take into account how large or small a group is, it is helpful to relate the score earned to the percentage or fraction of individuals falling below (or above) that score. Thus to say that a person has placed in the top quarter or the bottom tenth or that he has exceeded the performance of 60 percent of the individuals in his own group, or in a standardized sample, conveys useful information.

Two common statistics that involve percentages of individuals who fall below a point on the score scale are the percentile (centile) rank and the percentile (centile). The *percentile rank* is a number between 0 and 100 that tells what percentage of individuals within a norm group earned scores below a certain specified score. Simply expressed, one is asking the question: Given a specific score, what percentage of individuals falls below that score? On the other hand, the *percentile* represents a point on the score scale below which an indicated number of cases falls. Essentially the converse of the question just cited with respect to percentile rank is involved: Given a specified percentage of individuals who are to fall below a certain point on the score scale, what is the required value of the point?

For the data presented in Table 19-1 one might be interested in determining the percentile rank of score 83, which four different individuals earned. A simple formula in which $N$ is the total number of individuals within the group is

$$\text{Percentile rank} = 100 \times \frac{\begin{array}{c}\text{number of individuals below score}\\ + \text{ } \frac{1}{2}\text{ individuals at score}\end{array}}{N}$$

As can be seen from Calculation Aid 19-4, the percentile rank is 60. The significance of the second term in the numerator involving the addition of one-half the number of individuals at the score is that of the individuals receiving a score of 83, one-half would be assumed to fall between 82.5 and 83.0 (and the other half between 83.0 and 83.5). If one counts the two 83s and the remaining scores below 83, it is seen that there are exactly 24 scores, a number that is 60 percent of the total frequency of 40. Similarly, the percentile rank of the single score 74 is seen to be 100 (7 + .5/40), or 18.75, as 7.5 individuals are assumed to fall below the score 74.0—seven persons below 73.5 and one-half person between 73.5 and 74.0

The calculation of the 50th percentile is the same in principle as that of the median, which by definition is the 50th percentile—the score point separating the upper half of the cases from the lower half. In Calculation Aid 19-5 it is seen that for the data in Table 19-1 the 60th percentile, designated as $P_{60}$, is exactly 83.0, which checks with the fact that the percentile

## Calculation Aid 19-4   Calculating Percentile (Centile) Rank for Ungrouped Data

### Problem 1

Determine the percentile rank for the score of 83 in the data of Table 19-1.

### Symbols defined

To avoid unnecessary complexity, symbols will be omitted except for $N$.

### Formula

$$\text{Percentile rank} = 100 \times \frac{\text{number of individuals below score} + \frac{1}{2} \text{ individuals at score}}{N}$$

### Computational steps

1. Count the number of individuals below the score of 83 (not including 83). This number is found to be 22.
2. After counting the number of individuals who received a score of 83, take one-half that number. Then $\frac{1}{2}(4) = 2$.
3. Add the numbers found in steps 1 and 2 and then divide this resulting frequency by the total number $N$.
4. Multiply the values in step 3 by 100 to convert it from a proportion to a percentage.

These steps may be incorporated into the formula as follows:

$$\text{Percentile rank} = 100 \, \frac{22 + \frac{1}{2}(4)}{40}$$

$$= 100\left(\tfrac{24}{40}\right)$$

$$= 100(.6) = 60$$

### Problem 2

Determine the percentile rank for the score of 74 in the data of Table 19-1. By steps similar to those for Problem 1 it is seen that

$$\text{Percentile rank} = 100 \, \frac{7 + \frac{1}{2}(1)}{40}$$

$$= 100 \, \frac{7.5}{40}$$

$$= 18.75$$

rank for the score of 83 is also 60. Both the 25th and the 75th percentiles ($P_{25}$ and $P_{75}$) are shown in Calculation Aid 19-5 for ungrouped data. The $P_{25}$ value separates the bottom one-fourth of the individuals in the frequency distribution from the top three-fourths, and $P_{75}$ differentiates the top one-fourth from the bottom three-fourths. The $P_{25}$ and $P_{75}$ values are often called *quartiles*—$Q_1$ and $Q_3$—and the median ($P_{50}$) is designated as $Q_2$. These three score points form bases of separation of a group into quarters. (Many teachers and counselors erroneously refer to these quarters as quartiles; the quartiles are points on the scale, not segments of the score distribution.)

---

### Calculation Aid 19-5 Calculating Percentiles (Centiles) for Ungrouped Data

**Problem**

Find the 60th percentile ($P_{60}$) for the 40 scores in Table 19-1.

**Symbols defined and formula**

To avoid unnecessary complexity, symbols and formulas will be omitted.

**Computational steps**

1. Take .60 times $N$; $.60(40) = 24$, the number of cases below the 60th percentile—the point on the scale separating the upper 40 percent of cases from the bottom 60 percent.

2. Count 24 cases up from the bottom score. This process carries one to the score 83. However, there are four 83s. The 22nd score includes 82; the 23rd and 24th scores include 83. Assume that the four 83s are equally spread over the interval from 82.5 to 83.5.

3. Add to the lower limit of 82.5 the increment of distance determined by taking $^2/_4$ of the distance of the interval of one-unit width, the 2 coming from $24 - 22$.

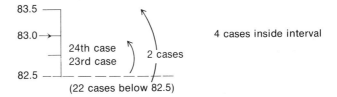

This third step may be summarized as follows:

$$P_{60} = 82.5 + \frac{24 - 22}{4}(1)$$

$$= 82.5 + 0.50 = 83.0$$

**Similarly for other examples**

$$P_{25} = Q_1 = 74.5 + \frac{10 - 8}{3}(1)$$

$$= 74.5 + 0.67$$

$$= 75.17$$

$$P_{50} = \text{median} = 80.5 + \frac{20 - 18}{3}(1)$$

$$= 80.5 + 0.67$$

$$= 81.17 \text{ (previous calculation)}$$

$$P_{75} = Q_3 = 87.5 + \frac{30 - 30}{3}(1)$$

$$= 87.5 + 0.00$$

$$= 87.5 \text{ (upper limit of the 30th score)}$$

## MEASURES OF DISPERSION OR VARIABILITY

Although it is helpful to know the central tendency of a group of scores, the extent to which scores are spread about the mean or the median is of particular interest to the educational psychologist or research worker who is curious about individual differences. There are several bases for studying the variability of measures, including the use of the range, the employment of two or more percentiles, and the calculation of the variance and standard deviation.

### Range

As stated previously, the range represents the distance along the continuum of scores from the lowest score to the highest score. For the data in Table 19-1, the high score is 99 and the lowest is 65. Since each score covers a whole unit, the range would be given by 99.5 – 64.5, or 35.0. This same value could also be arrived at by subtracting 65 from 99 and adding 1. Many research workers who are involved with small samples often report the mean or the median as the statistic of central tendency and the range as the statistic of variability. (A *statistic* is defined as a descriptive measure of a sample or group.)

### Percentile

Although a single percentile does not yield a direct indication of variability, the use of two percentiles—such as $P_1$ and $P_{99}$, $P_{10}$ and $P_{90}$, or $P_{25}$ ($Q_1$) and $P_{75}$ ($Q_3$)—furnishes the investigator with information regarding the score points between which the middle 98, 80, or 50 percent, respectively, of the cases lies. If a distribution of scores is *nearly symmetrical* about the mean or the median, as in the instance of the normal curve, one often-employed statistic of variability is the *quartile deviation*, which is given by the formula

$$Q = \frac{Q_3 - Q_1}{2}$$

For the data of Table 19-1 and for values presented in Calculation Aid 19-5 for $Q_1$ and $Q_3$, the value for $Q$ is given by (87.50 – 75.17) /2, which is equal to 6.16. This figure would be interpreted to indicate that if one goes 6.16 units above or below the median of 81.17, approximately the middle 50 percent of the cases (i.e., 20 cases) would be expected to fall. Thus for the data of Table 19-1, an actual count of cases between 81.17 + 6.16 and 81.17 – 6.16 —that is, between 87.33 and 75.01—is very nearly 20. [Use of interpolation would give .49 (3) + 18 + .83 (1), which is equal to 20.3 cases falling between 75.01 and 87.33.] If, however, the frequency distribution is even moderately skewed, use of $Q$ can give quite a misleading impression about where the middle 50 percent of the cases lies.

### Variance and Standard Deviation

By far the most widely used statistics for describing dispersion are variance and standard deviation. Defined as the mean of the squares of the deviations of each of the scores from the mean of a distribution, *variance* is widely used in describing numerous findings and relationships in the more advanced topics of statistics. Of greater use to the consumer of statistical data and to the teacher, who is often concerned with interpreting the variability of test scores, is the *standard deviation*, which is the square root of the variance. The formulas for these two statistics are given for ungrouped data in Calculation Aid 19-6.

For the ungrouped data, two sets of procedures are furnished: (1) one for processing of

---

### Calculation Aid 19-6   Calculating the Standard Deviation from Ungrouped Data

---

**Problem**

Calculate the variance and standard deviation for ungrouped data in Table 19-1 by using (1) raw or obtained scores and (2) deviation scores.

**Symbols defined**

$N$ = total number of cases

$X$ = raw or obtained score

$X^2$ = raw score squared (multiplied by itself)

$M$ = mean of distribution of scores

$x = X - M$, deviation score defined as difference between raw score and mean

$x^2$ = deviation score squared

$\Sigma$ = sum

$\sigma^2$ = variance of distribution of scores

$\sigma$ = standard deviation

**Formulas**

1. Raw score:

   **a.** Variance:

   $$\sigma^2 = \frac{1}{N}\left[\Sigma X^2 - \frac{(\Sigma X)^2}{N}\right]$$

   **b.** Standard deviation:

   $$\sigma = \sqrt{\frac{1}{N}\left[\Sigma X^2 - \frac{(\Sigma X)^2}{N}\right]}$$

2. Deviation score:

   **a.** Variance:

   $$\sigma^2 = \frac{\Sigma x^2}{N}$$

   **b.** Standard deviation:

   $$\sigma = \sqrt{\frac{\Sigma x^2}{N}}$$

**Raw-score approach**

1. To simplify the computational effort, subtract the smallest raw score, which is 65, from each of the raw scores and enter the new scores in a column headed $X$ (as has been done in the work-layout form below). Such a procedure will not change the variability of scores, but will reduce the mean by 65 from 81 to 16. Note that the range is still 35.0 units.
2. Sum the raw scores in the first column ($\Sigma X = 640$).
3. Square each score and enter the values in a second column.
4. Find the sum of the squares scores in the second column ($\Sigma X^2 = 12,894$).
5. Also square the sum $\Sigma X$; that is $(\Sigma X)^2 = (640)^2 = 409,600$.
6. Substitute the values obtained into formula for variance:

$$\sigma^2 = \frac{1}{N}\left[\Sigma X^2 - \frac{(\Sigma X)^2}{N}\right]$$

$$= \frac{1}{40}\left[12,894 - \frac{(640)^2}{40}\right] = \frac{1}{40}(12,894 - 10,240)$$

$$= \frac{1}{40}(2,654) = 66.35$$

7. Take the square root of the variance to obtain the standard deviation:

$$\sigma = \sqrt{66.35} = 8.15^-$$

---

## Calculation Aid 19-6 *(Continued)*

### Work-layout form (abbreviated)

(*Note:* Each raw score in Table 19-1 has had 65 points subtracted from it.*
The new mean is 16.)

| $X$ | $X^2$ | $X - M = x$ | $x^2$ |
|---|---|---|---|
| 34 | 1,156 | $34 - 16 =$ 18 | 324 |
| 31 | 961 | $31 - 16 =$ 15 | 225 |
| 29 | 841 | $29 - 16 =$ 13 | 169 |
| 27 | 729 | $27 - 16 =$ 11 | 121 |
| 26 | 676 | $26 - 16 =$ 10 | 100 |
| 25 | 625 | $25 - 16 =$ 9 | 81 |
| 24 | 576 | $24 - 16 =$ 8 | 64 |
| 23 | 529 | $23 - 16 =$ 7 | 49 |
| 23 | 529 | $23 - 16 =$ 7 | 49 |
| 23 | 529 | $23 - 16 =$ 7 | 49 |

(The next 28 entries in each column have been omitted to conserve space.)

| | | | |
|---|---|---|---|
| 1 | 1 | $1 - 16 = -15$ | 225 |
| 0 | 0 | $0 - 16 = -16$ | 256 |
| $\Sigma X = 640$ | $\Sigma X^2 = 12,894$ | $\Sigma x = 0$ | $\Sigma x^2 = 2,654$ |

$(\Sigma X)^2 = 409,600$

### Deviation-score approach

1. Form the difference between each raw score $X$ and the mean $M$, the difference being designated a deviation score $x$. These deviation scores constitute a separate column of entries.
2. As a check on the accuracy of the work, the sum of the deviation scores should equal zero; that is, $\Sigma x = 0$.
3. Square each deviation score and enter the value in a separate column.
4. Find the sum of these squared deviation scores ($\Sigma x^2 = 2,654$).
5. Substitute this value into the formula for variance:

$$\sigma^2 = \frac{\Sigma x^2}{N}$$
$$= \frac{2,654}{40} = 66.35$$

6. Take the square root of the variance to obtain the standard deviation:

$$\sigma = \sqrt{66.35} = 8.15^-$$

*Subtracting 65 from each score simplifies the arithmetic involved. The range of the scores is still 35—from −0.5 to 34.5—and the standard deviation remains unchanged.

---

raw scores through use of desk calculators or electronic computers and (2) another requiring use of deviation scores (differences between raw scores and the mean of a group), which is actually the theoretical basis for the determination of both the variance and the standard deviation. The variance is found to be 66.35; and the standard deviation, 8.15.

If a distribution of scores is nearly symmetrical with a tendency for a proportionately large number of cases to be concentrated near the mean or the median—a distribution that could be considered approximately normal or bell-shaped in form—the standard deviation affords a conveniently and readily grasped interpretation of the variability of scores. Mathematical statisticians have shown that for the normal frequency distribution, approximately 34 percent of individual scores will fall between the mean and a distance along the continuum of scores of either 1 standard deviation above or 1 standard deviation below the mean. In other words, approximately 68 percent of the scores will fall between the mean minus 1 standard deviation and the mean plus 1 standard deviation. Thus for the ungrouped data in Table 19-1, approximately 68 percent of the cases—or about 27—would be expected to place between $81.0 - 8.15$ and $81.0 + 8.15$, or between 72.85 and 89.15. Actual counting of scores beginning with 74 and terminating with 88 yields 26 cases. If that portion of the score 89 between 88.5 and 89.15 is counted, then .65 cases could be added to the 26, to yield a count of 26.65 cases.

When there are approximately 400 to 500 cases in a group, a distance of 6 standard deviations will just about cover the entire range of scores. As can be seen from Table 19-4, a sample of 40 cases could be expected to cover a range of about 4.3 standard deviations—2.15 standard deviations above the mean and 2.15 standard deviations below the mean, provided that the distribution is symmetrical. If the obtained standard deviation of 8.15 for the 40 scores reported in Table 19-1 is multiplied by 4.3, the result is 35.04—a number that is amazingly close to the obtained range of 35.0 points between 64.5 and 99.5.

## STANDARD SCORES

Closely related to the standard deviation is the *standard score*, which permits one to determine how many standard deviations a raw score is above or below the mean. Standard scores may assume several forms. If the score distribution is approximately normal in form, standard scores permit comparisons of the relative standings of examinees on several tests with various numbers of items, with markedly different means, and with unlike standard deviations. If the scores are normally distributed, percentile equivalents or standard scores can be readily estimated from statisti-

cal methods (e.g., Guilford, 1965, tables B and C, pp. 568–579).

The basic formulas for a standard score is given by

$$z = \frac{X - M}{\sigma}$$

where $z$ = standard score
$X$ = obtained or raw score
$M$ = mean of distribution of scores
$\sigma$ = standard deviation of scores

Typically most $z$ scores range between about $-3$ and $+3$, since for samples of 400 or 500 cases, 6 standard deviations will cover virtually the entire range. The mean of standard scores is 0, and their standard deviation is 1 (unity). For the data presented in Table 19-1, the standard scores that correspond to the raw scores are shown in Calculation Aid 19-7. Thus it is seen that standard scores for raw scores of 90, 81, and 65 are, respectively, 1.10, 0.00, and $-1.96$. In other words, the raw score of 90 is 1.10 standard deviations above the mean, the obtained score of 81 is 0 standard deviations above or below the mean because it is at the mean, and the raw score of 65 is 1.96 standard deviations below the mean.

Another form of the standard score is the $T$ score, which for any normal distribution as-

**Table 19-4   Ratio of the Total Range of Scores to the Standard Deviation ($\sigma$) in a Distribution for Samples of Different Sizes ($N$)**

| N | Range/$\sigma$ | N | Range/$\sigma$ | N | Range/$\sigma$ |
|---|---|---|---|---|---|
| 5 | 2.3 | 40 | 4.3 | 400 | 5.9 |
| 10 | 3.1 | 50 | 4.5 | 500 | 6.1 |
| 15 | 3.5 | 100 | 5.0 | 700 | 6.3 |
| 20 | 3.7 | 200 | 5.5 | 1,000 | 6.5 |

Adapted by permission from *Statistical methods*, 3rd ed., by George W. Snedecor, © 1940 by the Iowa State University Press, Ames, Iowa.

sumes a mean of 50 and a standard deviation of 10 instead of a mean of 0 and a standard deviation of 1, as in the instance of $z$ scores. The advantages of the $T$ score over the $z$ score are that negative numbers are avoided and two-digit scores ranging from 20 to 80 are easy to handle. To convert from $z$ scores to $T$ scores, the following transformation formula may be used:

$$T = 50 + z(10)$$

From the worked-out examples in Calculation Aid 19-7, it is apparent that the $T$ scores

---

### Calculation Aid 19-7   Calculating Standard Scores

**Problem**

For the data in Table 19-1, find $z$ scores and $T$ scores for the raw scores of 90, 81, and 65.

**Symbols defined**

$X$ = raw or obtained score

$\sigma$ = standard deviation of obtained scores ($\sigma = 8.15$)

$M$ = mean of distribution of raw scores ($M = 81.0$)

$z$ = standard score for normal distribution with mean of zero and standard deviation of 1

$T$ = standard score for normal distribution with mean of 50 and standard deviation of 10

**Formulas**

$$z = \frac{Z - M}{\sigma}$$

$$T = 50 + z(10)$$

**Computational steps**

1. To obtain $z$ scores:
   a. Find the difference between the raw score and the mean (a deviation score).
   b. Divide this deviation score by the standard deviation.
2. To obtain $T$ scores:
   a. Multiply $z$ score by 10.
   b. Add this product to 50.
3. The computational procedures for $z$ scores may be illustrated as follows:

$$z = \frac{90 - 81}{8.15} = 1.10$$

$$z = \frac{81 - 81}{8.15} = 0.00$$

$$z = \frac{65 - 81}{8.15} = -1.96$$

4. The computational procedures tor $T$ scores may be illustrated as follows:

$$T = 50 + 1.10(10) = 61.0$$
$$T = 50 + 0.00(10) = 50.0$$
$$T = 50 + (-1.96)(10) = 30.4$$

corresponding to raw scores of 90, 81, and 65 (and to the previously cited z scores of 1.10, 0.00, and −1.96) are 61, 50, and 30.4.

A slight modification of the *T* score is one employed by the Educational Testing Service in reporting scores on tests of the College Entrance Examination Board series and of the Graduate Record Examination. A mean of 500 and a standard deviation of 100 are taken. This procedure not only eliminates negative scores but also allows three digits to be reported without the presence of a decimal point.

Figure 19-5 shows a normal curve illustrating the interrelationships of z scores, T scores, and percentiles at steps of one-half standard deviation. In addition, the percentages of cases expected in each of the segments of the normal curve are indicated. These percentages have been derived from statistical tables, such as those given by Guilford (1965, pp. 568–579), that present proportions of area of the normal probability distribution.

Still another type of standard score that has received considerable attention in recent years is the stanine. The *stanine* is a nine-step standard score scale that assumes a normal distribution of raw scores. A graph of its major properties, presented in Figure 19-6, will help to clarify the meaning of the stanine. As can be seen, there are nine major seg-

ments of area. Each of these, with the exception of the upper and lower tail segments, covers a range of one-half standard deviation. From high to low, the nine segments of area are numbered from nine to one. The numerical designation of the stanine and the percentage of the cases associated with it are as follows: nine, 4 percent; eight, 7 percent; seven, 12 percent; six, 17 percent; five, 20 percent; four, 17 percent; three, 12 percent; two, 7 percent; and one, 4 percent. These percentages are approximate.

The advantages of the stanine scale are many. It permits the reporting of scores in one digit and thus is a compact means for using only one column of an IBM card to record a test measure. Statistical calculations of one-digit numbers, especially in the instance of correlation coefficients (which are described in the next section), are very much simplified. The use of stanines can also be justified on the grounds that the degree of precision in educational and psychological measurement is such that a description of performances at nine levels is about as accurate a differentiation as can be made by most teachers or observers in evaluating essay examinations, term papers, and other measures of behaviors.

Even when scores may not be normally distributed, a process of normalizing that

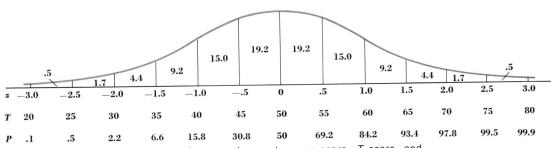

**Figure 19-5** Representation of various scoring systems: z score, T score, and percentile.

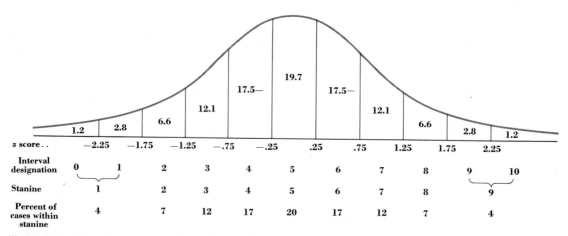

| | | | | | | | | | | | |
|---|---|---|---|---|---|---|---|---|---|---|---|
| | | 1.2 | 2.8 | 6.6 | 12.1 | 17.5— | 19.7 | 17.5— | 12.1 | 6.6 | 2.8 | 1.2 |

**z score..**    −2.25    −1.75    −1.25    −.75    −.25    .25    .75    1.25    1.75    2.25

| Interval designation | 0 | 1 | 2 | 3 | 4 | 5 | 6 | 7 | 8 | 9 | 10 |
|---|---|---|---|---|---|---|---|---|---|---|---|
| Stanine | 1 | | 2 | 3 | 4 | 5 | 6 | 7 | 8 | 9 | |
| Percent of cases within stanine | 4 | | 7 | 12 | 17 | 20 | 17 | 12 | 7 | 4 | |

**Figure 19-6** Graphical representation of normal frequency distribution showing the formation of stanines from z-score values and the percentage of cases within each stanine.

forces data into normal form can be used rather easily with the stanine. The scores are placed in rank order from high to low. The top 4 percent are given a stanine of 9; the next highest 7 percent, a stanine of 8; the next highest 12 percent, a stanine of 7; and so forth. In the event of the appearance of ties near the breaking points, between two stanine groups, the whole set of tied scores will need to be assigned to one stanine or the other. The decision rests upon looking at the distribution as a whole and finding, by a process of trial and error, that distribution of percentages which will come closest to the theoretically expected set of percentages. This procedure permits, in effect, a description of various ranges of scores between specified percentiles in terms of stanines—for example, the individuals placing between the 89th and 96th percentiles would be placed in stanine 8.

Figure 19-7 shows a chart prepared by the Psychological Corporation illustrating the interrelationships of several systems for reporting scores. Percentiles, z scores, T scores, stanines, IQs, and other types of scores are represented. Percentiles and standard scores are often referred to as *derived scores*, since

they are obtained from information that is furnished by raw scores. These derived scores offer the important advantage of furnishing a comparable basis for the interpretation of distributions of test scores with different numbers of items and with different means and standard deviations.

## Test Profiles Based on Derived Scores

A graphical portrayal of an individual's relative standing on each of several different measures of performance is called a *profile* or *profile chart*. To allow comparisons of an individual's relative strengths and weaknesses on each of several tests or scales or to compare one individual's standing with that of another individual on each of several different measures, it is essential that all scores be expressed in common units, or anchored to a common base. Typically, the raw scores of each individual on each of several tests or scales are converted to standard scores or percentile scores.

Calculation Aid 19-8 presents an illustrative example of the conversion of raw scores to standard scores (both z scores and T scores) of three individuals on four tests. These derived scores have been plotted on a grid to form three sets of profiles, which appear in Figure 19-8. These profiles may be interpreted in terms of both standard scores, which are placed on the left vertical axis, and percentile scores, which are placed on the right vertical axis. Even though the various tests contain different numbers of items and show marked differences in their means and standard deviations, the profile demonstrates that the derived scores, when expressed in standard form,

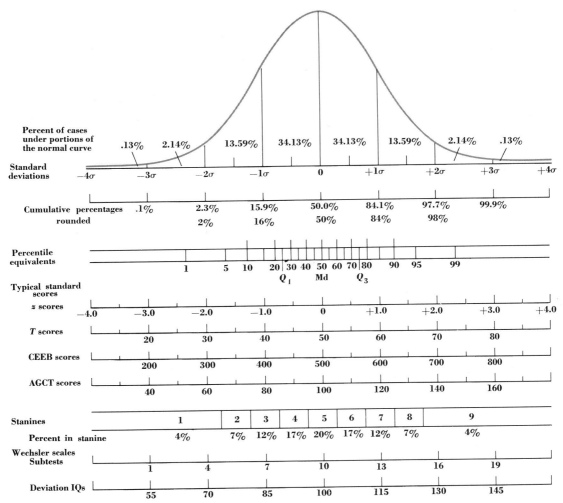

**Figure 19-7** Interpretation of various score systems anchored to the normal probability function. *Note:* This chart cannot be used to equate scores on one test to scores on another test. For example, both 600 on the CEEB and 120 on the AGCT are 1 standard deviation above their respective means, but they do not represent "equal" standings because the scores were obtained from different groups. (*Reproduced from Test Service Bulletin, No. 48, 1955. The Psychological Corporation, New York, New York.*)

---

### Calculation Aid 19-8   Converting Raw Scores on Several Tests to Standard Scores to Allow Comparison of Performance of Different Examinees

---

#### Problem

Determine the standard scores of different examinees on four tests so that profiles can be drawn that allow a comparison of the high and low levels of performance for each examinee as well as among the examinees.

#### Symbols and formulas

The symbols used have been defined previously, and the formulas have been illustrated (see Calculation Aid 19-7).

#### Computational steps

1. Take the raw score of each examinee and convert it to a $z$ score as illustrated in Calculation Aid 19-7. These computations are shown in the work-layout section.
2. Convert each $z$ score thus obtained to a $T$ score as shown in Calculation Aid 19-7.
3. Prepare a grid as shown in Figure 19-8. This consists of bounding vertical lines at the extreme left and the extreme right to designate standard scores and corresponding percentile scores that were taken from Figure 19-5. Additional vertical lines are inserted between the two bounding lines to stand for each of the test variables. The horizontal lines show different levels of standard scores and their corresponding percentiles for each examinee on each of the tests.
4. Plot the point on each vertical line representing the standard test score of each examinee. Connect the points to form the profile of each examinee.
5. By inspection, make comparisons of the relative strengths and weaknesses of each examinee on each of the tests.
6. By inspection, carry out comparisons of the performance of all examinees on each test in turn.
7. If a comparison is desired of the total performance of three examinees, an unweighted average of the $T$ scores (or $z$ scores) of each examinee on the four tests is found by adding the $T$ scores ($z$ scores) over the four tests for each examinee and then dividing by the number of tests (4).

**Descriptive statistics**
**for four different tests**

| | Vocabulary (110 Items) | Reading (70 Items) | Mathematical Reasoning (40 Items) | Spatial Relations (90 Items) |
|---|---|---|---|---|
| | $M = 60.0$ | $M = 40.0$ | $M = 21.0$ | $M = 36.0$ |
| | $\sigma = 16.0$ | $\sigma = 8.0$ | $\sigma = 6.0$ | $\sigma = 12.0$ |
| Raw Scores of Examinees ($X$) | | | | |
| John | 92 | 60 | 27 | 42 |
| Paul | 44 | 30 | 30 | 66 |
| Mary | 84 | 52 | 39 | 60 |

$z$ Standard Scores $\left( z = \dfrac{X - M}{\sigma} \right)$

| | Vocabulary | Reading | Mathematical Reasoning | Spatial Relations |
|---|---|---|---|---|
| John | $\dfrac{92 - 60}{16} = 2.0$ | $\dfrac{60 - 40}{8} = 2.5$ | $\dfrac{27 - 21}{6} = 1.0$ | $\dfrac{42 - 36}{12} = 0.5$ |
| Paul | $\dfrac{44 - 60}{16} = -1.0$ | $\dfrac{30 - 40}{8} = -1.25$ | $\dfrac{30 - 21}{6} = 1.5$ | $\dfrac{66 - 36}{12} = 2.5$ |
| Mary | $\dfrac{84 - 60}{16} = 1.5$ | $\dfrac{52 - 40}{8} = 1.5$ | $\dfrac{39 - 21}{6} = 3.0$ | $\dfrac{60 - 36}{12} = 2.0$ |

$T$ Standard Scores $[T = 50 + z(10)]$

| | Vocabulary | Reading | Mathematical Reasoning | Spatial Relations |
|---|---|---|---|---|
| John | $50 + 2(10) = 70$ | $50 + 2.5(10) = 75$ | $50 + (1.0)(10) = 60$ | $50 + (.5)(10) = 55$ |
| Paul | $50 + (-1.0)(10) = 40$ | $50 + (-1.25)(10) = 37.5$ | $50 + (1.5)(10) = 65$ | $50 + (2.5)(10) = 75$ |
| Mary | $50 + (1.5)(10) = 65$ | $50 + (1.5)(10) = 65$ | $50 + (3.0)(10) = 80$ | $50 + (2.0)(10) = 70$ |

Average *T* Score (*T*) for Four Tests

John $\dfrac{70 + 75 + 60 + 55}{4} = 65$

Paul $\dfrac{40 + 37.5 + 65 + 75}{4} = 54.4$

Mary $\dfrac{65 + 65 + 80 + 70}{4} = 70$

possess the same means, standard deviations, and ranges and also comparable percentile equivalents for each of the four tests. It is interesting to note that for the reading test, a raw score of 30 represents a standard *T* score of 37.5 and that for the test involving mathematical reasoning, the raw score of 30 represents a standard score of 65; in other words, when these standard scores are referred to the percentile equivalents, the *T* score of 37.5 places a person at about the 10th percentile, whereas the *T* score of 65 puts the individual at the 93rd percentile.

## CORRELATION AND PREDICTION

The determination of relationships among variables is an essential task for the research worker in educational psychology. In fact, both the psychologist and the layman frequently want to know the relationships between scholastic aptitude and achievement, between interests and success in school, between interests and success out of school, or between any number of measurable dimensions of human behavior. In addition to determining the degree of relationship between two variables, psychologists are often concerned with predicting standing on one variable from knowledge of an individual's placement on a second variable, especially when measures on the second variable represent a relatively small expenditure of time and money compared with that required for the second vari-

able. For example, a $10 or $15 investment in a scholastic aptitude test can give a high school senior some indication of his probability of success in a four-year college program, which may cost him and his family from $15,000 to $20,000.

A *correlation coefficient* is an index number that expresses the degree of relationship be-

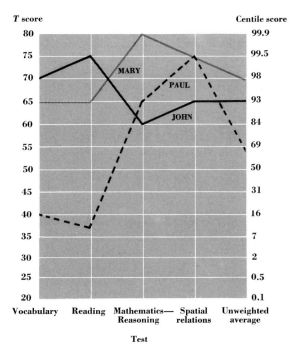

**Figure 19-8** Profiles of three examinees—John, Paul, and Mary—on four tests and an unweighted composite.

tween two or more variables such as aptitude test scores, grade point averages, height, weight, or reaction-time measures. Typically, the determination of the correlation coefficient involves taking two sets of scores for one group of individuals—one set of scores on one variable and a second set of scores on the second variable—and, by a mathematical procedure, calculating an index number that expresses the strength of the association. Although there are many indexes of correlation, as well as numerous special applications of correlational methods, the discussion will be limited to the product-moment and rank-difference coefficients of correlation. The symbols for these two coefficients are, respectively, $r$ and $\rho$ (rho). These indexes vary from 1.00, which indicates a perfect positive relationship; through 0, for no apparent relationship; to $-1.00$, which reveals a perfect inverse relationship.

Care must be taken not to interpret a relatively large coefficient as indicating that one variable is necessarily a cause of the other. In some cases, a third variable with which each one correlates may be influential. For example, since a high positive correlation has been shown between amount of cigarette smoking and the incidence of coronary disease, many investigators have concluded that smoking causes heart disease. Although this conclusion may be correct, another possible alternative may be that psychological stress contributes to cigarette smoking as well as to the occurrence of coronary difficulties. Perhaps there is a whole host of interrelated causes—known as *multiple causation*—of heart disease.

Another source of difficulty in the interpretation of a correlation coefficient is that it does not indicate the percentage of relationship. Thus, a correlation coefficient of .40 does not mean a 40 percent degree of association. Nor is a coefficient of .40 indicative of twice as much relationship as that concomitant with a coefficient of .20. One possible interpretation of a percentage relationship is in terms of the squared value of the correlation coefficient, $r^2$, known as the *coefficient of determination*. The logic behind this coefficient is that if one postulates the presence of 100 elements in one variable and 100 elements in a second variable, $r^2$ tells the proportion of elements that are common to the two variables. In the instance of a correlation of .40, the value for $r^2$ is .16. This means that a proportion of .16, or equivalently 16 percent, of the factors in one variable are associated with, or are determined by, elements of the second variable. Since for an $r$ of .20, the proportion of overlap is $(.20)^2$, or .04, and since for an $r$ of .40 the square is .16, it is apparent that a coefficient of .40 represents four times—not twice—the amount of relationship that is afforded by a coefficient of .20.

## Product-Moment Correlation

Perhaps one of the most satisfactory ways to interpret a product-moment coefficient of correlation is to make use of graphical methods. Thus, for the two sets of fictitious scores involving 10 persons and 2 tests—vocabulary scores represented by variable $X$ and reading scores by variable $Y$—in Table 19-5, a scatter diagram, or scatterplot, can be constructed as shown in Figure 19-9. (Admittedly, for reasons of simplicity and computational ease, this sample is quite small; ordinarily samples involving a much larger number of cases are required in correlational research efforts.) In this scatter diagram each point represents, as the reader may recall from high school algebra or geometry, the simultaneous values in $X$ and $Y$ that have occurred. In other words, each point stands for the scores that each of the 10 individuals in turn—A, B, . . . , J—received on the two tests. For example, Mike (person B) earned a score of 20 in the vocabulary test

**Table 19-5 Raw Scores of Ten Examinees on Two Tests—Vocabulary (Variable *X*) and Reading Comprehension (Variable *Y*) (Data Fictitious)**

| Persons | Vocabulary test (*X*) | Reading comprehension test (*Y*) |
|---|---|---|
| **A.** John | 23 | 20 |
| **B.** Mike | 20 | 14 |
| **C.** Bill | 16 | 7 |
| **D.** Sam | 14 | 15 |
| **E.** Joe | 12 | 13 |
| **F.** Bob | 9 | 4 |
| **G.** Paul | 7 | 16 |
| **H.** Art | 5 | 3 |
| **I.** Wayne | 3 | 7 |
| **J.** Ralph | 1 | 1 |

(variable *X*) and a score of 14 on the reading comprehension test (variable *Y*). The *X* values are plotted along the *X* axis and the *Y* values along the *Y* axis. When a perpendicular to the *X* axis is erected at *X* = 20 and another perpendicular to the *Y* axis at *Y* = 14, the intersection of the two perpendiculars constitutes the point that represents graphically the

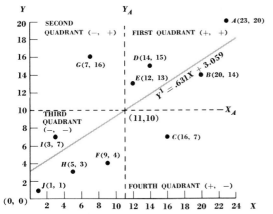

**Figure 19-9** Correlation scatter diagram of scores on two achievement tests for 10 persons—along with two auxiliary axes forming the origin at the means of the *X* and *Y* variables and with a regression line for the prediction of the most probable scores in *Y* from knowledge of the scores in *X*.

standing of person B on each of the two test measures simultaneously. As the reader will recall from algebra, a point is identified by inserting two numbers within parentheses (20,14) —the first number indicating the horizontal (abscissa) distance and the second number designating the vertical (ordinate) distance with respect to the origin (0,0).

The 10 points plotted in Figure 19-9 seem to fall within an ellipse, or oval, and their pattern suggests that in general those individuals who score high in vocabulary also tend to score high in reading. To facilitate the understanding of the coefficient, two auxiliary axes $X_A$ and $Y_A$ have been drawn through the means of the *X* and *Y* variables ($M_x = 11$ and $M_y = 10$), and four quadrants have been found with respect to the new origin at (11,10). In these quadrants, which are numbered in the figure, the points may be interpreted as follows: first quadrant—individuals who are above (+) the mean in *X* and also above (+) the mean in *Y*; second quadrant—persons who place below (−) average in *X* but above (+) average in *Y*; third quadrant—examinees who fall below (−) the mean in *X* as well as below (−) the mean in *Y*; and fourth quadrant—individuals who stand above (+) the mean in *X* but below (−)

the mean in $Y$. Points that fall in the first and third quadrants are consistent with the existence of a positive correlation, as they indicate that persons who are above (or below) average in one variable are also above (or below) average in the second variable. As can be seen, 8 of the 10 points fall in the first and the third quadrants, and only 2 points fall in the second and fourth quadrants. Placement in the second and fourth quadrants reveals that persons high in one variable tend to be low in the other—a fact working against obtaining a high correlation.

These quadrants also serve useful purposes in the calculation of the product-moment correlation from deviation scores—a procedure that is described in detail in Calculation Aid 19-9. The $x$ and $y$ deviation scores for each individual represent horizontal and vertical distances, respectively, of his point from the origin—distances that are found by subtracting the $X$ and $Y$ means from the $X$ and $Y$ *raw scores*. These deviation scores are often called *moments*. Thus the deviation scores $x$ and $y$ of person B are $20 - 11$ and $14 - 10$, or 9 and 4, respectively. The corresponding deviation scores of person C would be $16 - 11$ and $7 - 10$, or 5 and $-3$. As can be seen in Calculation Aid 19-9, the heart of the correlation comes from the products of the deviation scores (moments) for each individual. Obviously, if a high proportion of individuals falls into the first and third quadrants, the sum of the product moments and thus the sign of the correlation coefficient will be positive; on the other hand, if the majority of points falls into the second and fourth quadrants, the sum of the product moments and hence the sign of the correlation coefficient will be negative.

From the computations in Calculation Aid 19-9, which illustrates the use of two different deviation-score formulas and one raw-score formula (the latter being handy for use with desk calculators), the correlation coefficient turns out to be .719. A coefficient of this magnitude suggests that in terms of the coefficient of determination, slightly more than 50 percent of the elements in reading scores are accounted for or held in common with those making up vocabulary scores. In statistical language it would be said that more than 50 percent of the variance in the distribution of reading scores is associated with the variance in vocabulary scores. Again caution needs to be exercised not to conclude that the possession of a high vocabulary level is necessarily causally related to high performance in reading. Furthermore, the presence of only 10 cases would seriously restrict the extent to which one generalizes these findings.

**Rank-Difference Coefficient**

In classroom practice teachers frequently place children in rank order, not only in test performance but also on several characteristics being observed such as creativity, sociability, or extent of participation in class discussion. Often a teacher may be interested in ascertaining whether those individuals who rank high or low in one dimension, such as spelling, correspondingly rank high or low in a second characteristic, such as arithmetic. Use of rank-order data affords a relatively quick and simple way of estimating the correlation between two sets of measures. In Calculation Aid 19-10 computations are shown for the determination of a rank-difference coefficient of correlation known as $\rho$ (rho). The coefficient was calculated for the data of Table 19-5 after they had been converted to ranks—the same data for which the product moment $r$ was found. The value of .676 for $\rho$ is slightly less than that of .719, found for the product-moment coefficient. Since no distinction is made of the magnitude of the differences between scores in a set when ranks are used, the smaller coefficient is not surprising as it is

## Calculation Aid 19-9 Calculating the Product-Moment Coefficient of Correlation between Two Variables

### Problem

Calculate the product-moment coefficient of correlation for ungrouped data presented in the work-layout form of this calculation aid and portrayed in Figure 19-9 by using (1) deviation scores and (2) raw or obtained scores.

### Symbols defined

$N$ = total number of cases
$X$ = raw or obtained score on first variable (i.e., vocabulary test)
$Y$ = raw or obtained score on second variable (i.e., reading test)
$M_x$ = mean of distribution of $X$ scores
$M_y$ = mean of distribution of $Y$ scores
$x = X - M_x$, deviation score in $X$
$y = Y - M_y$, deviation score in $Y$
$x^2$ = deviation score in $X$ squared
$y^2$ = deviation score in $Y$ squared
$xy$ = product of two deviation scores for same individual (known as *product moment*)
$\sigma_x$ = standard deviation of scores in $X$
$\sigma_y$ = standard deviation of scores in $Y$
$\Sigma$ = sum
$X^2$ = raw score in $X$ squared
$Y^2$ = raw score in $Y$ squared
$r$ = Pearson product-moment coefficient of correlation

### Formulas

1. Deviation score:

    a. Basic formula: $\quad r = \dfrac{\Sigma xy}{N\sigma_x\sigma_y}$

    b. Alternative formula: $\quad r = \dfrac{\Sigma xy}{\sqrt{(\Sigma x^2)(\Sigma y^2)}}$

2. Raw score: $\quad r = \dfrac{N\Sigma XY - (\Sigma X)(\Sigma Y)}{\sqrt{[N\Sigma X^2 - (\Sigma X)^2][N\Sigma Y^2 - (\Sigma Y)^2]}}$

### Computational steps for use of deviation scores

1. Calculate the means of the $X$ and $Y$ distributions of raw scores so that deviation scores can be found. (See the work-layout form for deviation scores.)
2. Determine the deviation scores $x$ and $y$ of each person. These entries appear in the fourth and fifth columns in the work-layout form.
3. Next find the product moments $xy$, the entries for which are in the sixth column of the work-layout form. (This column includes two types of entries: positive products and negative products.)
4. Then calculate the squares of the deviation scores for $X$ and $Y$ and enter these values in the seventh and eighth columns of the work-layout form.
5. The entries in each of the columns are summed for further utilization (thus $\Sigma xy = 303$; $\Sigma x^2 = 480$; and $\Sigma y^2 = 370$).
6. Calculate both $\sigma_x$ and $\sigma_y$ (as shown in the work-layout form).
7. Substitute the numerical information into the basic formula for correlation coefficient $r$ as follows:

$$r = \frac{\Sigma xy}{N\sigma_x\sigma_y}$$

$$= \frac{303}{10(6.928)(6.083)}$$

**Calculation Aid 19-9** *(Continued)*

$$= \frac{303}{421.43} = .719$$

8. The entries obtained for $\Sigma xy$, $\Sigma x^2$, and $\Sigma y^2$ may be substituted directly into an alternative formula that yields a faster solution:

$$r = \frac{\Sigma xy}{\sqrt{(\Sigma x^2)(\Sigma y^2)}}$$

$$= \frac{303}{\sqrt{(480)(370)}} = .719$$

**Computational steps for use of raw scores**

1. Square each $X$ and each $Y$ and enter these values into the fourth and fifth columns (see the work-layout form for raw scores).
2. Next find the products of $X$ and $Y$ and place the resulting values in the sixth column of the work-layout form (for raw scores).
3. Find the sum of the entries in the second to sixth columns (thus $\Sigma X = 110$, $\Sigma Y = 100$, $\Sigma X^2 = 1,690$, $\Sigma Y^2 = 1,370$, and $\Sigma XY = 1,403$).
4. Calculate $(\Sigma X)^2$, $(\Sigma Y)^2$, $N(\Sigma X)^2$, $N(\Sigma Y)^2$, $(\Sigma X)(\Sigma Y)$, and $N(\Sigma XY)$ as shown on the work-layout form.
5. Substitute the values obtained in steps 3 and 4 into the formula for $r$ as follows:

$$r = \frac{N\Sigma XY - (\Sigma X)(\Sigma Y)}{\sqrt{[N\Sigma X^2 - (\Sigma X)^2][N\Sigma Y^2 - (\Sigma Y)^2]}}$$

$$= \frac{10(1,403) - (110)(100)}{\sqrt{[10(1,690) - (12,100)][10(1,370) - 10,000]}}$$

$$= \frac{3,030}{\sqrt{(4,800)(3,700)}} = \frac{3,030}{4,214.3} = .719$$

**Work-layout form (raw scores)**

| Persons | X | Y | $X^2$ | $Y^2$ | XY |
|---------|-----|-----|-----|-----|-----|
| A | 23 | 20 | 529 | 400 | 460 |
| B | 20 | 14 | 400 | 196 | 280 |
| C | 16 | 7 | 256 | 49 | 112 |
| D | 14 | 15 | 196 | 225 | 210 |
| E | 12 | 13 | 144 | 169 | 156 |
| F | 9 | 4 | 81 | 16 | 36 |
| G | 7 | 16 | 49 | 256 | 112 |
| H | 5 | 3 | 25 | 9 | 15 |
| I | 3 | 7 | 9 | 49 | 21 |
| J | 1 | 1 | 1 | 1 | 1 |
| | $\Sigma X = 110$ | $\Sigma Y = 100$ | $\Sigma X^2 = 1,690$ | $\Sigma Y^2 = 1,370$ | $\Sigma XY = 1,403$ |

$$(\Sigma X)^2 = (110)^2 = 12,100$$
$$(\Sigma Y)^2 = (100)^2 = 10,000$$
$$N(\Sigma X)^2 = 10(12,100) = 121,000$$
$$N(\Sigma Y)^2 = 10(10,000) = 100,000$$
$$(\Sigma X)(\Sigma Y) = (110)(100) = 11,000$$
$$N(\Sigma X)(\Sigma Y) = 10(110)(100) = 110,000$$

**Work-layout form (deviation scores)**

| Persons | Vocabulary Test X | Reading Test Y | $X - M_x = x$ | | $Y - M_y = y$ | | $xy$ | $x^2$ | $y^2$ |
|---|---|---|---|---|---|---|---|---|---|
| A | 23 | 20 | $23 - 11 =$ | 12 | $20 - 10 =$ | 10 | 120 | 144 | 100 |
| B | 20 | 14 | $20 - 11 =$ | 9 | $14 - 10 =$ | 4 | 36 | 81 | 16 |
| C | 16 | 7 | $16 - 11 =$ | 5 | $7 - 10 = -3$ | | $-15$ | 25 | 9 |
| D | 14 | 15 | $14 - 11 =$ | 3 | $15 - 10 =$ | 5 | 15 | 9 | 25 |
| E | 12 | 13 | $12 - 11 =$ | 1 | $13 - 10 =$ | 3 | 3 | 1 | 9 |
| F | 9 | 4 | $9 - 11 = -2$ | | $4 - 10 = -6$ | | 12 | 4 | 36 |
| G | 7 | 16 | $7 - 11 = -4$ | | $16 - 10 =$ | 6 | $-24$ | 16 | 36 |
| H | 5 | 3 | $5 - 11 = -6$ | | $3 - 10 = -7$ | | 42 | 36 | 49 |
| I | 3 | 7 | $3 - 11 = -8$ | | $7 - 10 = -3$ | | 24 | 64 | 9 |
| J | 1 | 1 | $1 - 11 = -10$ | | $1 - 10 = -9$ | | 90 | 100 | 81 |
| | $\Sigma X = 110$ | $\Sigma Y = 100$ | $\Sigma x = 0$ | | $\Sigma y = 0$ | | $\Sigma xy = 303$ | $\Sigma x^2 = 480$ | $\Sigma y^2 = 370$ |
| | | | $(\Sigma xy = 342$ | | $\Sigma xy = -39)$ | | | | |
| | | | $+$ | | $-$ | | | | |

**Statistics derived from sums of entries in the columns**

$$M_x = \frac{\Sigma X}{N} = \frac{110}{10} = 11.0$$

$$M_y = \frac{\Sigma Y}{N} = \frac{100}{10} = 10.0$$

$$\sigma_x = \sqrt{\frac{\Sigma x^2}{N}} = \sqrt{\frac{480}{10}} = 6.928$$

$$\sigma_y = \sqrt{\frac{\Sigma y^2}{N}} = \sqrt{\frac{370}{10}} = 6.083$$

based on the use of relatively more crude information.

**Prediction**

As indicated previously, the determination of the degree of association between two sets of measures suggests that it should be possible to predict one measure from the other. Whenever cognitive measures are employed, there is a fairly high probability that the trend of the relationship between them will follow a straight line—a property known as *linearity*— although there are situations in which a curve may describe the nature of the relationship somewhat more accurately (especially in the instance of physiological and motivational variables). Thus in Figure 19-9 a line has been drawn for the prediction of the most probable scores in a reading test from knowledge of scores in a vocabulary test. The predicted scores are represented by points that fall along the line that describes the trend of the data. Based on the least-squares principle of calculus, the equation for this line affords a means for prediction of standing in $Y$ for a given value in $X$ with a minimum degree of error— the error of prediction being defined as the difference between the obtained score $Y$ and the predicted score $Y'$. In educational measurement, the amount of error for individual prediction is relatively great, as inspection of Figure 19-9 will reveal.

One may ask why it is necessary or even

## Calculation Aid 19-10   Completion of Rank-Difference Coefficient of Correlation between Two Variables

### Problem
Calculate the rank-difference coefficient of correlation for the data presented in Calculation Aid 19-9 and Figure 19-9.

### Symbols defined
$\rho$ = rho, rank-difference coefficient of correlation
$N$ = number of cases
$d$ = difference between rank orders of person's standing on each pair of scores
$d^2$ = square of difference in rank
$R_x$ = ranks for variable $X$
$R_y$ = ranks for variable $Y$
$\Sigma$ = sum

### Formula
$$\rho = 1 - \frac{6 \Sigma d^2}{N(N^2 - 1)}$$

### Computational steps
1. Rank each of the two sets of scores by assigning 1 to the highest score, 2 to the second highest score, and so forth. (In the event of tied scores within a set, take the mean of the rank and assign that value to each of the raw scores of the same value.)
2. For each person, find the difference $d$ between the ranks $R_x$ and $R_y$ and enter the difference in a separate column (the sixth column in the work-layout form below). The algebraic sum of the $d$ values should equal zero (a check on one's work).
3. Square each of the $d$s and then add (the sum being 53.50 on the work-layout form).
4. Substitute the value obtained for $\Sigma d^2$ and 10 for $N$ in the formula as follows:

$$\rho = 1 - \frac{6(53.50)}{10(100 - 1)} = 1 - \frac{321.00}{990}$$
$$= 1 - .324$$
$$= .676$$

### Work-layout form

| Persons | X | Y | $R_x$ | $R_y$ | d | $d^2$ |
|---|---|---|---|---|---|---|
| A | 23 | 20 | 1 | 1 | 0 | 0.00 |
| B | 20 | 14 | 2 | 4 | −2 | 4.00 |
| C | 16 | 7 | 3 | 6.5 | −3.5 | 12.25 |
| D | 14 | 15 | 4 | 3 | 1 | 1.00 |
| E | 12 | 13 | 5 | 5 | 0 | 0.00 |
| F | 9 | 4 | 6 | 8 | −2 | 4.00 |
| G | 7 | 16 | 7 | 2 | 5 | 25.00 |
| H | 5 | 3 | 8 | 9 | −1 | 1.00 |
| I | 3 | 7 | 9 | 6.5 | 2.5 | 6.25 |
| J | 1 | 1 | 10 | 10 | 0 | 0.00 |
| | | | | | | $\Sigma d^2 = \overline{53.50}$ |

desirable to predict standing in $Y$, given $X$, when both the $X$ and $Y$ scores for each person are already known. The answer is that initially one group is employed as a pilot or trial sample so that predictions can be made for future samples of individuals from similar populations (a populaton being defined as a very large group of individuals with many characteristics in common). Customarily one would wish to take a sample of 200 or more cases in order to achieve relatively stable prediction equations that would not be expected to fluctuate substantially from sample to sample.

In Calculation Aid 19-11 the equation of the prediction line ($Y$ from $X$) has been calculated along with an estimate of errors of prediction. It is assumed that the measures are continuous and that a score such as 21 covers the interval from 20.5 to 21.5. Errors of prediction arise because the correlation between the two variables is not perfect—the lower the correlation, the greater the errors of prediction. (As discussed earlier, discrepancies between observed or obtained scores in $Y$ and the predicted values of $Y'$ constitute errors of prediction.)

An example may be helpful in illustrating the use of the prediction equation. Person B (Mike) earned a score of 14 on $X$ and obtained a score of 15 on $Y$. According to the equation for the prediction line (often called the *regression line*) given in Calculation Aid 19-11, the predicted score in $Y$ that lies on the line is given by

$$Y' = .631 (14) + 3.059$$
$$= 8.834 + 3.059$$
$$= 11.89$$

The error in prediciton is thus $Y - Y'$, or $15.00 - 11.89$, which is 3.11 score points.

An overall estimate of errors of prediction for a group is furnished by the standard error of estimate. This indicator of error is based on a pooling of all the data and on the assumption that errors in predicting $Y$ from $X$ are nearly uniform over the entire range of $X$ values (a circumstance known as the assumption of *homoscedasticity*). The standard error of estimate, which is the standard deviation of all observed values about their corresponding predicted values on the regression line, turns out to be 4.23 for the data in Table 19-5 (see Calculation Aid 19-11). The interpretation would be that for every 100 people who receive a particular score in $X$, 68 of them—that is, 68 percent—would fall between the predicted score plus or minus 1 standard error of estimate. Thus, for every 100 individuals who received a score of 14 in the vocabulary test ($X$), about 68 would be expected to earn reading scores ($Y$) between $11.89 + 4.23$ and $11.89 - 4.23$, or between 16.12 and 7.66—a range indicating a substantial amount of error in the instance of individual prediction.

It is informative to note that if one draws two lines parallel to the prediction line in Figure 19-9—one line 4.23 units above and the other 4.23 units below—seven out of ten cases by actual count fall between the two lines (that is, within 1 standard error of estimate above or below the corresponding predicted values on the regression line). For small samples such a close degree of correspondence between what is expected and what is found by actual count, or verification, will often not result because of sampling errors.

It would also be possible to predict scores in the vocabulary test ($X$) from those in the reading measure ($Y$). In two variable correlations there are always two regression lines—one for predicting $Y$ from $X$ and the other for predicting $X$ from $Y$. The second line will not be shown or discussed. The second line, however, can be determined by using the same

## Calculation Aid 19-11  Determination of Equation of a Regression Line for Prediction of Y from X and of the Standard Error of Estimate

### Problem

Determine the equation of the regression line for prediction of Y from X and obtain an estimate of errors of prediction (standard error of estimate).

### Symbols defined

$Y'$ = predicted score in Y (dependent variable)

$X$ = score in predictor variable X (independent variable)

$\sigma_x, \sigma_y$ = respective standard deviations of scores in variables X and Y

$r_{yx}$ = product-moment coefficient of correlation between Y and X

$b_{yx}$ = slope or direction of prediction line—indicator of how much gain can be expected in $Y'$ for each unit of increase in X

$a_{yx}$ = intercept of regression line on Y axis, distance from origin (0.0) along Y axis to where line intercepts or cuts Y axis

$\sigma_{yx}$ = standard error of estimate, which is 1 standard deviation of observed scores in Y around predicted scores on regression line— distance above or below prediction line that forms two parallel lines between which about 68 percent of observed cases fall

### Formula

**1.** $Y' = b_{yx} X + a_{yx}$, the equation of the regression or prediction line, where

$$b_{yx} = r_{yx} \left( \frac{\sigma_y}{\sigma_x} \right)$$

$$a_{yx} = M_y - b_{yx}(M_x)$$

**2.** $\sigma_{yx} = \sigma_y \sqrt{1 - r_{yx}^2}$

### Computational steps

**1.** From data previously obtained, find $b_{yx}$ and $a_{yx}$. Thus

$$b_{yx} = .719 \left( \frac{6.083}{6.928} \right) = .631$$

$$a_{yx} = 10.00 - 11.00(.631)$$
$$= 10.00 - 6.941$$
$$= 3.059$$

**2.** Substitute the values of $b_{yx}$ and $a_{yx}$ into formula (1):

$Y' = .631 X + 3.059$

**3.** Substitute values for $\sigma_y$ and $r_{yx}$ into formula (2) to obtain the standard error of estimate:

$$\sigma_{yx} = (6.083) \sqrt{1 - (.719)^2}$$
$$= (6.083) \sqrt{1 - .516961}$$
$$= (6.083)(.695^+)$$
$$= 4.23$$

### Example of application

What is the most probable (predicted) score in Y for a person with a score in X of 15?

$Y' = .631(15) + 3.059$
$= 9.465 + 3.059 = 12.52$

Note that for every 100 persons who earned a score of 15 in X, 68 would be expected actually to fall between $12.52 + 4.23$ and $12.52 - 4.23$, or between 16.75 and 8.29.

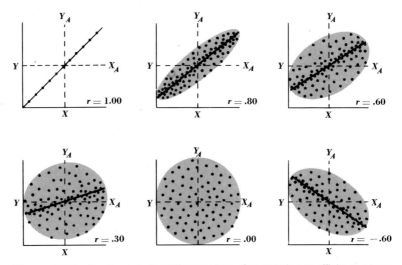

**Figure 19-10** Scatterplots for different sizes of correlation coefficients, along with regression lines for prediction. Note that as the correlation increases, the slope of the regression line increases and the dispersion of the scatter of points about the prediction line decreases (the less the dispersion, the higher the accuracy of prediction).

formulas, provided that a $Y$ is substituted for every $X$ and an $X$ is substituted for every $Y$.

### Interrelationships between Correlation and Regression Lines

Figure 19-10 affords an opportunity to study what the shape of the scatterplot is when standard scores are used for various sizes of correlation coefficients, how steep the prediction line is as a function of correlation size, and how much dispersion of observed values in $Y$ (portrayed as points) around the line (the locus of predicted scores) is present relative to the magnitude of the correlation. In general, the higher the correlation coefficient, the steeper the prediction line and the less the dispersion of points (the smaller the errors of prediction) about the prediction line. For the case in which the correlation is $-.60$, the errors of prediction are of the same size as those with the correlation of $.60$; only the direction of the line is different.

### Prediction When Data Have Been Grouped into Intervals

Although no calculation aid will be presented showing how to determine a product-moment coefficient of correlation or the equations of the regression line from grouped data (see Guilford, 1965, pp. 366–374), a scatter diagram is shown in Figure 19-11 that describes the correlation and shows the prediction characteristics of grouped data. The horizontal divisions show by intervals of width 4 the $X$ variable, a composite aptitude score, and the vertical axis designates by intervals of width .3 the $Y$ variable, grade point average, which is a criterion measure of academic success. The scatter diagram reveals the pattern of relationship between scores on the scholastic aptitude test (the predictor) and achievement level as indicated by grade point average (the criterion variable). As expected for a correlation coefficient of .665, there is a decided trend for those who receive higher test scores to earn higher grade point averages, as is evident from

| | X (composite aptitude score) | | | | | | | | | |
|---|---|---|---|---|---|---|---|---|---|---|
| Y (grade point average) | 2–5 | 6–9 | 10–13 | 14–17 | 18–21 | 22–25 | 26–29 | 30–33 | 34–37 | $f_y$ |
| 3.6–3.8 | | | | | | 1 | 2 | 2 | 3 | 8 |
| 3.3–3.5 | | | | | | | 1 | 4 | 3 | 8 |
| 3.0–3.2 | | | | | 1 | 4 | 3 | 5 | 3 | 16 |
| 2.7–2.9 | | | 1 | 2 | 4 | 5 | 5 | 5 | 2 | 24 |
| 2.4–2.6 | | 5 | 6 | 3 | 8 | 10 | 2 | 1 | | 35 |
| 2.1–2.3 | | 7 | 8 | 8 | 10 | 9 | 7 | 5 | | 54 |
| 1.8–2.0 | 2 | 7 | 3 | 12 | 11 | 7 | 3 | 1 | | 46 |
| 1.5–1.7 | 1 | 9 | 7 | 6 | 1 | 1 | | | | 25 |
| 1.2–1.4 | 1 | 2 | | 4 | 1 | | | | | 8 |
| .9–1.1 | | 3 | | 1 | | | | | | 4 |
| $f_x$ | 4 | 28 | 24 | 39 | 31 | 35 | 31 | 24 | 12 | 228 = N |
| $M_c$ | 1.62 | 1.74 | 2.08 | 1.97 | 2.18 | 2.42 | 2.58 | 2.85 | 3.22 | |
| $\sigma_c$ | .24 | .37 | .37 | .43 | .39 | .46 | .46 | .51 | .45 | |

$M_x = 20.03 \qquad M_y = 1.29 \qquad r_{yx} = .665$

$\sigma_x = 8.44 \qquad \sigma_y = .585 \qquad \sigma_{yx} = .437 \qquad Y' = .037X + 1.046$

**Figure 19-11** Scatter diagram showing the relation of grade point average to scholastic aptitude test (data grouped into class intervals). (*Adapted with permission from J. P. Guilford, W. B. Michael, & S. W. Brown, Exercises to Accompany Fundamental Statistics, 4th ed., New York: McGraw-Hill, 1966.*)

the rise (with one exception) in the mean grade point averages $M_c$ in the columns that show the frequencies with which certain intervals of grade point average are obtained for a single specified interval of scores in scholastic aptitude. It is also apparent that the standard deviations of the columns, which represent a measure of errors of prediction, are roughly comparable—an average value for which would be approximated by the standard error of estimate $\sigma_{yx}$ of .437.

The equation of the trend line for prediction of grade point average from composite aptitude test scores is also given in Figure 19-11. Thus, the predicted grade point average of an individual who has an aptitude test score of 32 would be

$$Y' = .037 (32) + 1.046, \text{ or } 2.23$$

It would be anticipated that 68 out of every 100 individuals who received an aptitude score of 32 would fall in grade point averages roughly between 2.23 − .44 and 2.23 + .44, or between 1.79 and 2.67.

**Criterion-related Validity** As may be recalled from Chapter 17, the coefficient of correlation involved in predicting standing on a criterion variable from scores on a test is referred to as the *criterion-related validity coefficient* for that test. Some writers prefer the term *predictive validity coefficient*. Thus, the index number of .665 for the data presented represents the criterion-related or the predictive validity coefficient for the composite aptitude test. Incidentally, if two forms of a test were correlated or if the same test were given on two occasions, the resulting correlation could be referred to as an estimate of the reliability of the test.

**Expectancies** Another way of interpreting a correlation coefficient, especially when it is a validity coefficient, is in terms of probability (likelihood) or expectation that an individual who falls within a certain score interval on the $X$ variable (e.g., aptitude test) will place at or above (or below) a certain point on the second variable—usually the criterion variable (e.g., grade point average). Thus for the data presented in Figure 19-11, one could ascertain by actually counting (empirically) the probability that students within each of the score intervals on the composite aptitude test would have of earning grade point averages at or above a certain level. For example, an admissions officer could estimate the probability of a student's obtaining a grade point average of 2.05 or higher (falling in the class intervals of 2.1 to 2.3 and in higher intervals) for each of several intervals of aptitude test scores by taking the ratio of the number of individuals within that test-score interval who fall at or above 2.05 in grade point average to the total number of individuals within that test-score interval. Thus the probability $P$ of a student's earning 2.05 or higher in the criterion variable $Y$ for each of the test-score intervals would be

$$P = \frac{0}{4} = .00 \text{ for score interval 2 to 5}$$

$$P = \frac{7}{28} = .25 \text{ for score interval 6 to 9}$$

$$P = \frac{14}{24} = .58 \text{ for score interval 10 to 13}$$

$$P = \frac{16}{39} = .41 \text{ for score interval 14 to 17}$$

$$P = \frac{18}{31} = .58 \text{ for score interval 18 to 21}$$

$$P = \frac{27}{35} = .77 \text{ for score interval 22 to 25}$$

$$P = \frac{28}{31} = .90 \text{ for score interval 26 to 29}$$

$$P = \frac{23}{24} = .96 \text{ for score interval 30 to 33}$$

$$P = \frac{12}{12} = 1.00$$

An admissions officer needs to realize that the probability estimates are approximate and that, in view of the relatively small number of cases in each of the columns of data, there would be considerable fluctuation in the probability values if different samples of students were taken. Greater stability could be expected if three- or four-score intervals were combined or if samples of 1,000 or more cases were taken. In the next section, brief attention will be directed to problems of sampling.

## SAMPLING PROCEDURES

The educational psychologist, for reasons of economy in time, money, and effort, usually finds it advantageous to carry out his research work with relatively small groups of individuals. It is desirable, however, for his results to be broadly generalizable and applicable to much larger numbers of people than those whom he has studied. The educational psychologist also recognizes that when he selects subjects to participate in his studies, the data he obtains can fluctuate in value from one group to another even though his several groups have been chosen in a systematic way from a very large group of individuals.

## Sample

A sample is a relatively small group—a subgroup or subset—of individuals who have been chosen from a total or entire group, referred to as a *population.* Descriptive data obtained from a sample, such as the mean of a distribution of test scores or the proportion of individuals who respond in a particular manner to an item in a questionnaire, are called *statistics.* Corresponding descriptive properties of a population are termed *parameters.* Statistics furnish relatively inexpensive and efficient estimates of the values of parameters. Even when samples have been taken from a relatively homogeneous and carefully defined population, it is important to obtain some measure of the amount of fluctuation in the value of a statistic that can be expected from one sample to another, as well as some indication of the range of discrepancies between the values for a statistic and the fixed value of the parameter. (The parameter is fixed because the population represents the total group of individuals.) This discrepancy between the magnitude of a statistic and that of the parameter is called a *sampling error.*

Statisticians have been able to show that if samples are chosen in a prescribed manner, it is possible to estimate quite accurately the variability in error that would occur in repeated selections of samples. For example, if an observer employs a *probability sample*—that is, a sample in which each individual belonging to the population is guaranteed a known chance of being chosen—quite accurate estimates of sampling error are possible. This sort of procedure is used during the evening of a national election, when research personnel of television networks, making use of giant computers, have been able to forecast within one or two percentage points what the popular vote will be for each of the major candidates in a given state or other geographical area. Thus probability sampling has been used actually to construct a miniature population—a model or replica of the total voting population.

Two kinds of probability sampling will be described briefly, although several different types exist.

**Random Sampling** A simple *random sample* is said to exist when each person in the population has an equal chance of being chosen and when every possible combination of individuals within the population has the same probability of being selected. It is not uncommon to assign numbers to each of the members of the population and to use some physical means of selection—for example, having a blindfolded person choose one numbered slip of paper at a time from a bin containing several thousand such slips of uniform size and texture. Simpler procedures include use of specially prepared tables of random numbers.

**Stratified Random Sampling** The amount of error in sampling can often be reduced if an attempt is made initially to describe and categorize a population in terms of essential characteristics or dimensions, known as *strata,* that may be logically related to the outcomes or observations of a study—for example, chronological age, sex, IQ level, ethnic background, and socioeconomic status. Attitudes of parents in a given city toward the school program, for instance, may be expected to differ depending upon whether they are middle-aged and well-to-do or young and relatively nonaffluent. In other words if demographic characteristics are correlated with the behavior observed, it may be helpful to divide the population into several subpopulations, each of which is formed by a permutation of the demographic factors. From each resulting stratum a random sample is chosen.

As a second example, a college administrator might be interested in asking questions of members of the student body that pertain to attitudes they hold toward social privileges and the quality of special campus services, such as housing, parking, counseling, and cultural activities. Since a student's membership in the freshman, sophomore, junior, or senior class might be related to his responses, and since the sex of the student might be associated with markedly different answers to certain questions, the investigators would be well-advised to subdivide the entire college population into eight subpopulations (derived from four classes and the two sexes) and to select students on a random basis from each of these eight strata. Thus the investigator might take 5 percent of the student body from each of the eight strata, and in so doing he would obtain a sample that was highly representative of the total college population. This procedure would probably lead to a higher degree of representativeness of the population than simple random sampling would. If the total population is sampled randomly, it is quite likely that certain strata will be disproportionately represented.

## Sampling Distributions

When successive random samples are taken from a population, it is not uncommon to find considerable variability within the frequency distribution of the values for a statistic. The frequency distribution of the means of several fairly large randomly chosen samples will form approximately a normal distribution around the true mean of the population. Likewise, the frequency distribution of the per-

centages or proportions of responses to a single item in a questionnaire will approximate a normal curve (actually a smoothed binomial probability distribution) for a series of randomly selected samples. The frequency distribution of a statistic derived from random sampling procedures is called a *sampling distribution*, and the standard deviation of this sampling distribution, which is employed as an indicator of the amount of sampling error, is called the *standard error* of the statistic.

In general, the size of the sampling error is *inversely proportional to the square root of the number of individuals in the sample.* For example, the standard error of the mean of a sample $\sigma_M$ (the standard deviation of the distribution of an infinite number of sample means about the population mean) is given by the formula

$$\sigma_M = \frac{\sigma_{pop}}{\sqrt{N}}$$

where $\sigma_{pop}$ is the standard deviation of all scores in the population and $N$ is the number of individual scores in the sample. If the standard deviation of a population were 10, the standard errors for samples of sizes 25, 100, and 400 would be, respectively,

$$\sigma_M = \frac{10}{\sqrt{25}} = 2.00 \qquad \sigma_M = \frac{10}{\sqrt{100}} = 1.00$$

$$\text{and} \qquad \sigma_M = \frac{10}{\sqrt{400}} = .50$$

If the mean of the population were 50, one would expect that approximately 68 percent of the means of randomly drawn samples of sizes 25, 100, and 400, respectively, would vary between 48 and 52, between 49 and 51, and between 49.5 and 50.5. Thus the larger the sample, the smaller the degree of sampling error.

Information about the size of sampling error is helpful in determining the amount of error that is likely to be present in estimating a population value (parameter) from a statistic. Since detailed consideration of this problem is highly complex and considerably beyond the scope of this book, the reader is referred to basic texts in statistics by Guilford (1965) and A. L. Edwards (1967).

An understanding about the size of sampling error is also very important in testing the reasonableness of research hypotheses regarding experimental effects. In the next section, considerable attention will be given to tests of significance that are essential in ascertaining whether the magnitudes of differences in observations are sufficiently large to be considered dependable, or reliable, and whether support therefore exists for experimental hypotheses with respect to which data have been obtained.

## SIGNIFICANCE OF DIFFERENCES

In carrying out an experimental study involving two or more groups that receive different treatments, an investigator is interested in determining whether differences observed in average scores (if the data are continuous) or in frequencies, or proportions, of individuals responding in a designated manner (if data are discrete) are large enough so that he can be fairly confident that they are not chance events or sampling accidents. In other words, he is trying to ascertain whether an observed difference is statistically significant or reliable. If the difference is large enough to be significant and if the investigator has been able to control or account for other factors that could contribute to the generation of the difference, he may be able to infer that there is a difference in the average effectiveness of the two or more treatments that he has used. On the basis of statistics obtained from two or more sam-

ples, the investigator endeavors to generalize his findings to much larger groups (populations) and to conclude that the treatments would lead to the realization of differences in the parameters of the two or more corresponding populations from which the samples were drawn.

Subsequent to setting up a research or experimental hypothesis that there is a difference in average scores or in frequencies (proportions) of individuals responding in a certain way, he usually recasts the experimental hypothesis, which may be derived from a theory, in what is called *null form*—that is, he hypothesizes that there is no difference in the parameters of the two or more populations from which the two or more samples were taken. (Many investigators state the null hypothesis, which is actually a statistical hypothesis, in the form that the two or more samples all come from the same population. If differences in sample data appear to be so large that it is unreasonable to believe that all the samples could arise from a common population, the null hypothesis is considered untenable and is rejected.) In essence, what the investigator is saying is that any difference observed between two or more groups simply arises by errors of random sampling, or, in the layman's language, by chance. If he is able to show that there is quite a low probability of obtaining by random sampling an observed difference in sample values as large as, or larger than, the one or ones found, he has a high level of confidence in questioning the truth of the null hypothesis. Thus he may reject the null hypothesis, for he believes that it is probably false. Since the null hypothesis appears to be untenable, he feels that he has support for his research hypothesis that there is probably a difference in two or more of the population values (parameters). Thus he concludes that the obtained difference(s) in the sample values (statistics) is (are) statistically significant, although he does run a small risk of being incorrect.

## Significance of Difference between Two Means

One of the most common situations for testing the tenability of the null hypothesis arises in connection with determining the significance of the difference between the means of two groups of subjects that have been exposed to different treatments. Thus two randomly assigned groups of fourth-grade pupils might have been given experience with large steps (treatment A) and with small steps (treatment B), respectively, in programmed instruction in mathematics. After the investigator has administered an achievement test to the two groups at the conclusion of the study, he wants to know whether the observed differences between the two sample means on the posttest are large enough to suggest that the null hypothesis of no difference is probably false and that the treatments are differentially effective.

In experimental work as well as in field studies, it is not possible to be absolutely certain that the null hypothesis is false irrespective of how large the observed difference may be. There exists the probability, however small, that the null hypothesis might be correct and that the obtained difference is actually an error of sampling. Hence, any decision to reject or to fail to reject the null hypothesis is a probabilistic or relative one involving certain risks. The customary levels of risk employed by a research worker for rejection of the null hypothesis are .05 and .01. In other words, if a difference as large as, or larger than, the one found can occur by chance in 5 observations (or 1 observation) out of every 100, there is a probability of 5/100 or .05 (1/100 or .01) of his being wrong in rejecting the null hypothesis. By convention,

if an observed difference is large enough for one to reject the null hypothesis at the .05 level, it is said to be significant at this level. Although an investigator would conclude that an observed difference probably reflects a true difference, there is, as was just said, a risk that for every 100 times he repeated the same experiment under virtually identical conditions, on 5 occasions he would obtain a difference by sampling error as large as the one found or larger, even when there was truly no difference.

Two kinds of errors are possible in testing the null hypothesis. The type just discussed occurs when a decision is made to reject the null hypothesis when in reality it is correct. This kind of error is called the *Type I*, or $\alpha$, *error* where $\alpha$ represents the probability level, or risk, that the investigator has chosen for rejection of the null hypothesis. Therefore, the level of risk is customarily .05 or .01 when efforts are directed toward ascertaining whether a given difference is statistically reliable. In addition to the risk of rejecting the null hypothesis when it is actually true, there is the *Type II*, or $\beta$, *error* of failing to reject the null hypothesis of no difference when in actuality it is false (there really is a difference). In other words, one may fail to reject the null hypothesis and conclude that the observed difference is probably due to chance when in reality a genuine difference in the population values (parameters) does exist. Hence, even if differences exist in the effectiveness of two treatments, the experimenter may erroneously conclude from his statistical analysis that the treatments do not differ differentially in their impact upon the subjects. An analogy may serve to summarize the previous arguments: On the basis of circumstantial evidence, the decision of a jury to convict a man who is really innocent is a Type I error, whereas the decision to acquit a man who is actually guilty constitutes a Type II error.

Although many investigators believe it to be more nearly precise and elegant to say that one either "rejects" or "fails to reject" the null hypothesis, it is somewhat simpler to employ the expression "to reject" or "to accept" the null hypothesis. Thus, in this terminology, a Type I error would be made when one rejects the null hypothesis when actually it should be accepted and a Type II error takes place when one accepts the null hypothesis when in reality it should be rejected. Determining the probability of a Type II error is a highly complex process involving the use of power functions—a topic that is considerably beyond the scope of this text.

Calculation Aid 19-12 involves the determination of the significance of the difference between the means of two randomly chosen samples that have received two treatments, A and B. Based on fictitious data, the difference of 6.1 found between the means of 36.2 and 30.1 of groups 1 and 2 is being examined to ascertain whether it is large enough to be considered reliable. The direction of subtraction is assumed to be immaterial, as the differences could be either positive or negative by sampling error. In other words, is the positive or negative difference of 6.1 great enough to suggest that in a well-controlled study the two treatments do differ in their average effectiveness as measured by a posttest? In essence, the investigator who tentatively assumes that the null hypothesis is true pretends that the experiment is being repeated several hundred times under comparable conditions and that in this imaginary situation a frequency distribution of virtually an infinite number of differences between pairs of sample means is being generated. All these differences are assumed to arise because of errors of sampling—half the errors on the average being positive, and half of them being negative. This frequency distribution is called a *sampling distribution*, or *error curve*, and in the instance of differ-

ences between means, statisticians have found that for samples of about 30 or more cases the shape of this distribution will approximate that of a normal curve. If the null hypothesis is assumed to be true, the mean of the differences between pairs of sample means will be zero (0)—the same value as that found for the hypothesized difference between the means for the two populations from which the respective sets of samples receiving treatment A and treatment B were drawn.

The standard deviation of this sampling distribution is defined as the *standard error of the difference between means* and is written $\sigma_{M1-M2}$. This standard error is required so that the observer can determine how many standard errors (that is, how many standard deviations in the sampling distribution) his observed difference between means is removed from the mean difference of zero. Such information will permit a means for estimating the probability of obtaining by random sampling a difference between means—either positive or negative—as large as the one found or larger. The determination of the probability depends upon one's consulting a special table that furnishes amounts of area under the normal curve relative to different standard score values from the mean of that curve. A difference between two sample means that tends to fall near the left-hand or right-hand extremity of the normal curve (which is assumed to describe the sampling distribution of differences between means) represents a relatively rare event if the null hypothesis is actually true. Thus such a large observed difference suggests to the investigator that he has reason to doubt whether the null hypothesis of a zero difference could actually be correct and indicates that his alternative research hypothesis is probably supported.

One may follow through in a step-by-step fashion the computation of the critical ratio, or $\bar{z}$ score, in Calculation Aid 19-12. The

## Calculation Aid 19-12   Calculating Critical Ratio, or $\bar{z}$ Test, for Determining the Significance of Difference between Two Means (Large-Sample Approach)

### Problem
Calculate the critical ratio, $CR$ or $\bar{z}$ test, for ascertaining the significance of the difference between two sample means.

### Symbols defined
$N_1, N_2$ = numbers of individuals in sample 1 and sample 2, respectively

$M_1, \sigma_1$ = mean and standard deviation of first sample receiving treatment A

$M_2, \sigma_2$ = mean and standard deviation of second sample receiving treatment B

$\sigma_{M_1} = \dfrac{\sigma_1}{\sqrt{N_1 - 1}}$, estimate of standard error of mean of first sample, standard deviation of first sampling distribution—i.e., standard deviation of frequency distribution of means of an infinite number of samples randomly drawn from first population

$\sigma_{M_2} = \dfrac{\sigma_2}{\sqrt{N_2 - 1}}$, estimate of standard error of mean of second sample, standard deviation of second sampling distribution

$\sigma_{M_1 - M_2} = \sqrt{\sigma_{M_1}^2 + \sigma_{M_2}^2}$, estimate of standard error of differences between means, standard deviation of sampling distribution made up of differences between means of infinite number of pairs of random samples

$CR \equiv \bar{z}$ = critical ratio, standard score of sampling distribution of differences between pairs of sample means

### Formula
$$z = \frac{M_1 - M_2}{\sigma_{M_1 - M_2}}$$
$$= \frac{M_1 - M_2}{\sqrt{\sigma_{M_1}^2 + \sigma_{M_2}^2}}$$

### Data (posttest scores)

Group 1 Receiving
Treatment A ($N_1 = 65$)
$M_1 = 36.2$
$\sigma_1 = 12.0$

Group 2 Receiving
Treatment B ($N_2 = 50$)
$M_2 = 30.1$
$\sigma_2 = 14.0$

### Computational steps
1. Find the difference between the two sample means, which is $M_1 - M_2 = 36.2 - 30.1$, or 6.1, and place that difference in the numerator of the expression for the critical ratio.
2. Next calculate $\sigma_{M_1}$ and $\sigma_{M_2}$ as follows:

$$\sigma_{M_1} = \frac{\sigma_1}{\sqrt{N_1 - 1}} = \frac{12.0}{\sqrt{65 - 1}} = \frac{12.0}{8} = 1.50$$

$$\sigma_{M_2} = \frac{\sigma_2}{\sqrt{N_2 - 1}} = \frac{14.0}{\sqrt{50 - 1}} = \frac{14.0}{7} = 2.00$$

3. Square the values of $\sigma_{M_1}$ and $\sigma_{M_2}$ and add them to obtain $\sigma_{M_1}^2 + \sigma_{M_2}^2$. Thus
$$\sigma_{M_1}^2 + \sigma_{M_2}^2 = (1.50)^2 + (2.00)^2 = 2.25 + 4.00$$
$$= 6.25$$

4. Then take the square root of the sum of squares to find $\sigma_{M_1 - M_2}$ as follows:
$$\sigma_{M_1 - M_2} = \sqrt{2.25 + 4.00} = \sqrt{6.25}$$
$$= 2.50$$

## Calculation Aid 19-12 *(Continued)*

(This value of 2.50 for the standard error of the difference between means is interpreted as indicating that by sampling error alone 68 percent of the differences between pairs of sample means would be expected to fall between −2.50 and +2.50 around the hypothesized difference of zero between the two population means— the same zero value as that for the mean of all differences between pairs of sample means if the null hypothesis is true.)

5. Next calculate the $\bar{z}$ ratio (or critical ratio) as follows:

$$\bar{z} \equiv CR = \frac{36.2 - 30.1}{2.50} = \frac{6.1}{2.50}$$
$$= 2.44$$

### Interpretation of results

The value of $\bar{z}$ of 2.44 (irrespective of sign), which is greater than 1.96, indicates that the probability of a difference as large as 6.1, or larger, between means could occur by sampling accident with a probability $P$ less than .05 ($\bar{z} > 1.96$, $P < .05$). Hence, the difference between the two means is statistically significant between the .05 and .01 levels (but not at the .01 level); the null hypothesis is rejected at the .05 level (but still not rejected at the .01 level); the research hypothesis of a difference between means is supported; and the inference is made that the treatments are differentially effective.

---

determination of the proportion of area in the two tails of the normal curve formed by the erection of perpendiculars at the calculated $\bar{z}$-score values is shown graphically in Figure 19-12. The $\bar{z}$ value of 2.44 tells the experimenter that his observed difference of 6.1 is 2.44 standard deviations removed from the mean difference of zero and thus allows him an analytic basis for estimating the probability of obtaining a difference either as large as, or larger than, his observed difference from use of appropriate area tables for the normal curve. As indicated in Figure 19-12, these proportions of area in the two tails combined are equivalent to the probability with which a difference between means—either positive or negative—as large as the ones found, or larger, could arise as a result of errors of random sampling when the true difference is actually zero.

Fortunately, when one is working at the .05 and .01 levels, it is not necessary to look up the probability values in a table. It has been determined that if a value for the critical ratio, or $\bar{z}$, is ±1.96 or larger numerically, the probability associated with $\bar{z}$ is equal to or less than

.05. If the value for the critical ratio, or $\bar{z}$, is numerically equal to or greater than ±2.58, the probability is equal to or less than .01. (It is conventional not to state the exact probability levels, but simply to form an upper bound. Thus the expressions $P \leqq .05$ and $P \leqq .01$ mean, respectively, that the probability is less than or equal to .05 and that it is less than or equal to .01.) In other words, if a $\bar{z}$ of 1.96 or more numerically is obtained, the observer rejects the null hypothesis at or beyond the .05 level, states that the difference between means is statistically significant at or beyond the .05 level, declares that there is support for his research hypothesis, and infers that the treatments are probably differentially effective. If $\bar{z}$ is equal to or exceeds 2.58 numerically, he can formulate similar statements with a higher level of confidence of occurrence. Although certain purists among mathematical statisticians could object to the statement about to be made, it is intuitively helpful to say that if an obtained difference is significant at the .05 (.01) level, the observer can be 95 (99) percent confident or sure that a genuine difference exists between the two population means and that in an adequately controlled experiment a difference in the effectiveness of the two methods or treatments has been demonstrated.

To return now to the data presented in Calculation Aid 19-12, it is noted that the value 2.44 for $\bar{z}$ is larger than 1.96 but smaller than 2.58. Thus one may conclude that (1) the observed difference of 6.1 is statistically significant at or beyond the .05 level and thus is not likely to be a sampling error, (2) the null

hypothesis is untenable (would be rejected) beyond the .05 level, (3) the two samples probably come from two populations with different means, (4) the research hypothesis is supported, and (5) a difference probably exists in the average effectiveness of the two methods. Since $\bar{z}$ failed to reach a value of 2.58, one would proceed to state that relative to the .01 level, (1) the observed difference of 6.1 is statistically not significant and possibly reflects a sampling error, (2) the null hypothesis

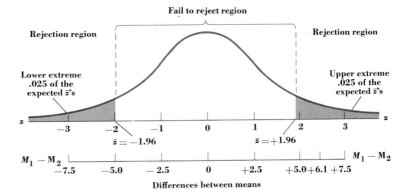

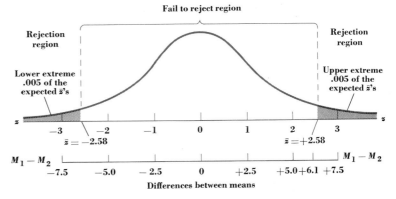

**Figure 19-12** Two sampling distributions of differences between means $M_1 - M_2$ or of $\bar{z}$, where $\bar{z}$ represents the number of standardized errors $M_1 - M_2$ is from a hypothesized zero difference. The shaded areas in the tails constitute a critical region for $M_1 - M_2$ or $\bar{z}$ that permits rejection of the null hypothesis at the .05 and .01 levels in the first and second distributions, respectively. Note that the obtained difference of 6.1, which corresponds to a $\bar{z}$ of 2.44, from data in Calculation Aid 19-12, permits rejection of the null hypothesis at the .05 level, but not at the .01 level.

is tenable or plausible, (3) the two samples do not necessarily come from two populations with different means, (4) the research hypothesis is not supported, and (5) the difference in the average effectiveness of the two methods of instruction or treatment has not been demonstrated.

Although the difference between means is statistically significant at the .05 level, it is important to note that there is considerable overlap in the two distributions of scores. Whether the difference is large enough to suggest practical significance in the sense that one method might be used in preference to the other is a judgmental matter that would depend upon a host of factors such as the relative costs, teacher or pupil preference, and the relative acceptability of each method to the school community. It is important to note that if large-enough samples are taken, almost any difference between means will be statistically significant. For example, a significant difference of .20 inches in mean heights for samples of 10,000 men in Iowa and of 12,000 men in Missouri would not lead a clothing manufacturer to ship suits of different sizes to the two states.

In summary, the essential steps involved in the testing of a null hypothesis are set forth in the following outline, which shows the conceptual steps in the statement of the null hypothesis in the instance of two-tailed tests of the significance of a difference between means (large-sample approach):

I Research hypothesis (operationally stated): There is a difference in the mean level of performance in the two populations from which the two samples were selected.

 A Example: On the Smith verbal aptitude test, there is a difference in the average level of performance of two populations of boys and girls as reflected by a difference between the means in the two samples (one sample of boys and one sample of girls, each with its own mean).

II Null hypothesis (statistically oriented):

 A There is no difference between the means of the two populations from which the two samples were chosen, although the variances of the two populations may differ.

 B The two means in the two populations are equal even though the variances may differ.

 C The mean of the sampling distribution of differences between an infinite number of pairs of means corresponding to an infinite number of pairs of randomly selected samples is zero.

 D Any difference between two sample means may be readily attributed to random sampling error or chance. (*Note:* The difference between the two population means may be any hypothesized amount, but in most problems a difference of zero is hypothesized; actually the null hypothesis is not necessarily one of a zero difference, but one set up for possible rejection.)

III Probability statement: If the null hypothesis is true (that there is no difference), how probable is it in random sampling that a difference numerically or absolutely as large as the one found or larger (either positive or negative) could arise by errors of random sampling? The determination of the probability of occurrence of an observed event such as a difference as large as, or larger than, the one found constitutes the major amount of computational work, or "busy work," in carrying out a significance test. The following steps are involved:

 A Selection, in advance, of a probability level for rejection of the null hypothesis ($\alpha = .05$, $\alpha = .01$, or other level).

**B** Selection of a statistical model to be employed such as the normal probability distribution, $t$ distribution, $\chi^2$, $F$ ratio, and the like. (Note that the normal curve will be employed in this discussion.)

**C** Actual calculation of the significance statistic such as $\bar{z}$, $t$, $\chi^2$, and $F$ or direct reference to a tabular entry as in the determination of whether a sample correlation coefficient is large enough to be significant.

**D** Determination from the value obtained in C as to the magnitude of the probability $P$ of the observed event such as a difference between two sample means numerically as large as the one found or larger arising by chance or random error—the magnitude of $P$ often being expressed as $P > .05$, $.01 < P \leq .05$, or $P \leq .01$. (See Table 19-6 for explanations of the inequality signs.)

**IV** Acceptance or rejection of the null hypothesis: In terms of whether the value obtained for the probability in IIID is greater than or less than or equal to the specified magnitude of $\alpha$ in IIIA, the null hypothesis is either accepted or rejected. Thus:

**A** If the observed event is likely (probability $P > \alpha$), the null hypothesis is accepted.

  **1** Example for acceptance: If, say, $\bar{z} = 1.10$, $P > .05$, the null hypothesis is accepted—is considered tenable or likely.

**B** If the observed event is unlikely (probablity $P \leq \alpha$), the null hypothesis is rejected.

  **1** Example for rejection: If, say $\bar{z} = 2.25$, $P < .05$, the null hypothesis is rejected—is considered untenable or unlikely.

**V** Conclusion regarding the null hypothesis: In statistical terms the conclusion concerning the null hypothesis can be conceived relative to acceptance or rejection of the null hypothesis in two ways: An inference can be made regarding the nature of the population with respect to the parameter under consideration, and a statement regarding statistical significance can be formulated.

**A** If the null hypothesis is accepted:

  **1** It is not unreasonable to believe (or it is likely) that the two samples came from two populations with the *same* or equal means (i.e., that the parameters under consideration can reasonably be expected to be equal), or

  **2** The observed difference between the two sample means is *not* statistically significant.

**B** If the null hypothesis is rejected:

  **1** It is reasonable to believe (or it is likely) that the two samples came from two populations with *different* means (i.e., that the parameters under consideration probably do differ), or

  **2** The observed difference between the two sample means is statistically significant.

**VI** Conclusion regarding the research hypothesis when it has been stated in positive terms: In light of the results appearing in VA and VB, the following statements, respectively, may be formulated:

**A** The research hypothesis is not supported.

**B** The research hypothesis is supported.

**VII** Practical inferences or implications: The practical inference or implication refers to the sort of conclusion that is meaningful to the layman in terms of administrative action or decision making.

**A** Example: For the Smith verbal aptitude test given as an example earlier, the following statements might be made depending upon whether the null hypothesis was (1) accepted or (2) rejected. (The greatest hazards in statis-

**Table 19-6  Mnemonic Table for Null Hypothesis: Two-tailed Test of Significance of Differences between Means for Large-sample Approach**

| z-Value (Critical Ratio) | Associated Probability Value (P) | Acceptance or Rejection of Null Hypothesis | Conclusion regarding Null Hypothesis (NH) | Conclusion regarding Statistical Significance | Conclusion regarding Research Hypothesis (RH)* | Tail-area Picture relative to z Value |
|---|---|---|---|---|---|---|
| $z < 1.96$ ($z$ less than 1.96) | $P > .05$ ($P$ greater than .05) | Accepted (tenable) | The NH is supported. It is not unreasonable to believe that the two samples come from two populations with equal means. | Not significant (NS). The difference between the two means is statistically not significant. | RH not supported | Less than 95%. Large tail area (relatively low confidence level—less than 95%) |
| $1.96 \leq z < 2.576$ ($z$ greater than, or at least equal to, 1.96, but less than 2.576) | $.01 < P \leq .05$ ($P$ less than, or at most equal to .05, but greater than .01) | Rejected at .05 level, but accepted at .01 level (untenable at .05 level but tenable at .01 level) | The NH is probably not supported. It is reasonable to believe that the two samples come from two populations with different means. | Significant at .05 level, but not at .01 level (S). The difference between the two means is statistically significant at .05 level (but not at .01 level) | RH supported | Between 95 and 99%. Small tail area (relatively high confidence level—between 95 and 99%) |
| $z \geq 2.576$ ($z$ greater than, or at least equal to, 2.576) | $P \leq .01$ ($P$ less than, or at most equal to, .01) | Rejected at .01 level as well as at .05 level (untenable at both .05 and .01 levels) | The NH is very probably not supported. It is very reasonable to believe that the two samples come from two populations with different means. | Very significant at or beyond .01 level (as well as at .05 level) (VS). The difference between the two means is statistically significant at or beyond .01 level—very significant. | RH very strongly supported | At least 99%. Very small tail area (relatively very high confidence level—at least 99%) |

* If research hypothesis is positively stated.

tical inference arise at this step in terms of overstatement or misapplication of the findings. Statistical significance, though present, may be inconsequential relative to the degree of practical significance involved.)

1 There is no reliable evidence of a differential between boys and girls in verbal ability. Segregation of the groups for learning, planning of special learning materials for either sex, or development of differential norms (unless there were marked differences in variability of scores) would not be justified.

2 There is reliable evidence of a differential between boys and girls in verbal ability. Consideration could be given to the possible segregation of the sexes (probably impractical), to the development of separate types of learning material, or to the establishment of two sets of score norms for boys and girls (a likely action).

To show the interrelationships between essential features of testing the null hypothesis, a summary chart is presented in Table 19-6. Throughout the discussion on the null hypothesis, it has been assumed that the direction of the sampling errors could be either positive or negative and that the difference between means correspondingly could be positive or negative. In somewhat more advanced treatments of the null hypothesis, it is not uncommon to find that an investigator prefers a given direction in the statement of his null hypothesis, for the logic of his experiment may dictate an interest in the direction of the difference. If the experimenter had been interested in ascertaining whether treatment A was superior to treatment B rather than in the question of whether there was a difference in the average effectiveness of the two methods irrespective of the direction of the difference, then a one-tailed test rather than a two-tailed test would be required. Such a test involves the placement of 5 percent of the area in one tail of the sampling distribution rather than $2^{1}/_{2}$ percent of the area in each of the two tails. Had one been testing the research hypothesis that treatment A was superior to treatment B (and the corresponding null hypothesis that the mean of the population receiving treatment A was lower than, or at most equal to, the mean of the population receiving treatment B), the values in $\bar{z}$ required for rejection of the null hypothesis at the .05 and .01 levels would have been +1.65 and +2.33 instead of ±1.96 and ±2.58. For the problem presented in Calculation Aid 19-12, the difference would have been significant at both the .05 and the .01 levels. Additional consideration of one-tailed tests is beyond the scope of this text, although the interested reader can find helpful discussions in both Guilford (1965) and A. L. Edwards (1967).

### Other Significance Tests

For continuous data, many other types of significance tests exist. A somewhat more sophisticated test for ascertaining the difference between means than that afforded by the critical ratio is the $t$ test, which is commonly used for testing the significance of the difference between means for samples of any size, although its use is almost mandatory when samples are smaller than 30. When three or more samples are employed or when different levels of two or more treatments are being simultaneously applied to different groups, a useful significance test for ascertaining whether there are reliable differences among the several means is the $F$ test, which is employed in analysis-of-variance studies. Actually these topics are beyond the scope of this text. The interested reader may wish to consult references by Guilford (1965) or A. L. Edwards (1960, 1967).

## Significance of Differences between Frequencies, or Proportions

When data are discrete rather than continuous, as in the instance of the frequencies of individuals in two groups who respond to a question in a designated manner, an appropriate statistical test for determining the significance of the differences in the frequencies, or proportions, of responses among two or more groups is chi square, which is designated by the symbol $X^2$. As shown in Calculation Aid 19-13, the $X^2$ significance is aimed at showing whether discrepancies between observed frequencies and those which would be theoretically required to guarantee the truth of the null hypothesis are sufficiently great to lead the investigator to doubt whether they could reasonably be due to errors of random sampling.

In research involving use of questionnaires and interviews, it is customary to ascertain whether significant differences in the frequencies of the responses to given items exist for two groups. For example, suppose that two randomly chosen samples of 300 teachers and 200 administrators are asked, "Do you believe that teachers should be excused from noon yard duty?" If 240 teachers say "yes" and if only 50 administrators give an affirmative reply, is the difference in frequency of "yes" responses statistically significant? Put another way, is the difference between the proportions of "yes" answers—.80 for teachers and .25 for administrators—large enough to suggest that it is not a random sampling error? If the difference is statistically reliable, support is obtained for the research hypothesis that the populations of teachers and administrators do differ in their responses and apparently (by inference) in their attitudes.

The data given have been arranged in what is called a *fourfold contingency table*, as shown in the work-layout section in Calculation Aid 19-13. A null hypothesis is set up that there is no relationship between occupational status and mode of response, or equivalently that there is no difference in the proportions of "yes" responses in the two populations from which the two samples were supposedly chosen randomly. The corresponding research hypothesis would be that there is a relationship—the higher the relationship, the greater the difference in the proportions of "yes" answers in the two groups. Calculation of $X^2$ yields a value of 149.02. When compared with the tabular entry of 10.827 from the $X^2$ sampling distribution, which is reproduced in Calculation Aid 19-13, a value as large as 149.02, or larger, would arise by errors of random sampling not even once in 1,000 samples. Thus the null hypothesis is soundly rejected, and support is obtained for the research hypothesis that these two populations probably do differ in their respective frequencies of affirmative responses. It may be helpful to note that if the difference in proportions of teachers and administrators answering "yes" had been only .02 or .03, the value of $X^2$ would have been quite small and would be considerably less than the value of 3.841 required for significance at the .05 level. In the event of a small $X^2$ value, the investigator would fail to reject the null hypothesis, and he would infer that the difference observed in the two proportions, or frequencies, was a reasonable sampling error.

## APPLICATION OF $X^2$ APPROACH TO ITEM ANALYSIS

$X^2$ tests are highly useful in carrying out item analyses required in test development in that a method is afforded for ascertaining whether responses to an achievement or aptitude test item, or to an item in a questionnaire or self-inventory form, differentiate between two groups of respondents. For example, in aptitude and achievement tests, it is customary

---

**Calculation Aid 19-13   Calculation of $\chi^2$ for Determination of Significance of Difference between Frequencies or Proportions for Two Samples When Data Have Been Arranged in a Fourfold Contingency Table (Data Fictitious)**

---

**Problem**

Calculate the $\chi^2$ test for a fourfold table to ascertain whether there is a significant difference in proportions of teachers and administrators who answer "yes" (or "no") to a question, or, equivalently, determine whether there is a significant relationship between occupational membership (being a teacher or an administrator) and mode of response (answering "yes" or "no").

**Symbols defined**

$N$ = total number of subjects

$N_1$ = number of individuals in first group (teachers)

$N_2$ = number of individuals in second group (administrators)

$p_1$ = proportion of individuals in first group who answer "yes"

$p_2$ = proportion of individuals in second group who answer "yes"

$q_1 = 1 - p_1$, proportion of individuals in first group who answer "no"

$q_2 = 1 - p_2$, proportion of individuals in second group who answer "no"

$f_o$ = observed frequency within cell of fourfold table

$f_e$ = theoretically expected frequency within cell of fourfold table (expected frequencies being those required to to guarantee null hypothesis of no relationship)

$k$ = number of cells in contingency table ($k = 4$ in fourfold table for this problem)

$\sum\limits_{1}^{k}$ = sum of certain quantities to be specified over $k$ cells of contingency table

**Formula**

$$\chi^2 = \sum_{1}^{k} \frac{(f_o - f_e)^2}{f_e}$$

which states that $\chi^2$ is equal to the sum over $k$ cells ($k = 4$) of the squared difference between the observed frequency and the expected frequency divided by the expected frequency within each cell.

**Computational steps**

1. After arranging the observed frequencies $f_o$ of "yes" and "no" answers into a fourfold table as shown in the work-layout form below, sum the frequencies along each row and each column to obtain the marginal totals as well as the grand total of cases.

2. Next, obtain for each of the four cells the expected frequencies $f_e$ by first multiplying the total frequency in the row containing the cell by the total frequency in the column containing the cell, and then by dividing this product by the total frequency. (These theoretically expected frequencies guarantee the independence, or lack of correlation, of the two variables—mode of response and occupational membership—and hence the set of frequencies for the null hypothesis of no relationship. It will be noted that if the expected frequencies are used, the proportions of "yes" answers for the two groups are the same—namely, $^{174}/_{300}$ and $^{116}/_{200}$, or .58 and .58—a fact that yields a difference of zero between the two theoretically expected proportions of "yes" answers. Thus, the null hypothesis of no relationship is the equivalent of the null hypothesis of no difference in the theoretically expected proportions of "yes" answers.)

3. Next, obtain for each cell the difference or discrepancy between $f_o$ and $f_e$—the value for which is the same numerically (66) for all cells. (Such an occurrence of equal values will always take place in fourfold tables with specified marginal frequencies, but ordinarily will not occur in contingency tables with greater numbers of rows or columns. Note that the algebraic sum of the discrepancies is zero—a check on one's work. In essence, these discrepancies represent sampling errors of the observed frequencies relative to the theoretically expected frequencies if the null hypothesis is assumed to be true.)

4. For each cell the discrepancy $f_o - f_e$ is squared and divided by the expected frequency, and all the resulting entries are added together to give the value for $\chi^2$.

## Calculation Aid 19-13 *(Continued)*

5. If in a fourfold table allowing what statisticians call "one degree of freedom" the discrepancies are great enough to yield $\chi^2$ values as large as, or larger than, 3.841, 6.635, and 10.827 (values appearing in $\chi^2$ tables for one degree of freedom), the null hypothesis is rejected at the .05, .01, or .001 level, respectively. Since $\chi^2$ equals 149.02, as seen in the work-layout form, the null hypothesis is rejected beyond the .001 level, and a very significant difference in the proportions of the "yes" answers (or "no" answers) for the two groups is said to exist. In other words, the discrepancies are too great to permit the investigator to believe that they are likely to be sampling errors. The probability $P$ of such extreme or more extreme departures by chance is less than .001 ($P < .001$). Hence, the null hypothesis is considered highly untenable, and strong support is obtained for the research hypothesis of a relationship between the two variables or for the existence of a difference between the proportions of individuals in the two populations who would answer "yes" or equivalently who would answer "no."

**Work-layout form**

*Question:* Do you believe that teachers should be excused from noon yard duty?

| | No | Yes | Row totals | Proportions reporting |
|---|---|---|---|---|
| Teachers | $f_0 = 60$ $f_e = \dfrac{300 \times 210}{500} = 126$ $f_0 - f_e = -66$ | $f_0 = 240$ $f_e = \dfrac{300 \times 290}{500} = 174$ $f_0 - f_e = 66$ | $300 = N_1$ | $p_1 = \dfrac{240}{300} = .80$ $(q_1 = .20)$ |
| Administrators | $f_0 = 150$ $f_e = \dfrac{200 \times 210}{500} = 84$ $f_0 - f_e = 66$ | $f_0 = 50$ $f_e = \dfrac{200 \times 290}{500} = 116$ $f_0 - f_e = -66$ | $200 = N_2$ | $p_2 = \dfrac{50}{200} = .25$ $(q_2 = .75)$ |
| Column totals | 210 | 290 | $500 = N$ | |

$$\chi^2 = \frac{(240 - 174)^2}{174} + \frac{(60 - 126)^2}{126} + \frac{(150 - 84)^2}{84} + \frac{(50 - 116)^2}{116}$$

$$= \frac{4{,}356}{174} + \frac{4{,}356}{126} + \frac{4{,}356}{84} + \frac{4{,}356}{116}$$

$$= 25.04 + 34.57 + 51.86 + 37.55$$

$$= 149.02 \ (P < .001)$$

prior to doing an item analysis to rank-order scores from high to low. Two contrasting groups, such as those individuals placing in the upper half and those in the lower half of the score distribution or those in the upper quarter and those in the bottom quarter, are formed. In a true-false test or in a multiple-choice examination, in which the right answer is pitted against a category of all the wrong answers for the various distractors, a fourfold table can be set up to include the frequencies of the right and wrong answers for the high-scoring and low-scoring groups. For computa-

tional convenience, equal numbers are usually taken for the two groups being contrasted. In such an arrangement the calculation of $\chi^2$ would be carried out in the same manner as in the example shown in Calculation Aid 19-13. A significant value for $\chi^2$ (the same values being used for significance as those reported in Calculation Aid 19-13) would suggest that a dependable difference exists in the proportion of high-scoring and low-scoring examinees who gave correct answers. Such an item would ordinarily be retained within an examination, as it discriminates significantly between individuals in the high-scoring and low-scoring groups. In other words, an item is said to have discriminating power when there is a positive relationship between whether individuals place in the high- or low-scoring group and whether they answer the test question correctly or incorrectly.

## APPLICATION OF $X^2$ APPROACH TO ANALYSIS OF ITEMS WITH MULTIPLE-ANSWER OPTIONS

The $X^2$ approach is also useful not only in determining whether an item involving two or more choices such as "yes," "?," or "no" differentiates between high-scoring and low-scoring samples but also in showing whether responses to an item differentiate members of two occupational groups, individuals in two different psychiatric classifications such as psychotic or neurotic, or samples of persons classified in other ways.

Thus it is not uncommon in the validation of occupational interest inventories to compare the responses of one group of successful people in a given occupation, such as engineering, with those of individuals taken at random from a general population. For example, the respondents in each of these two groups might be asked to reply "agree"(A), "uncertain or undecided" (U), or "disagree" (D) to the item "enjoy making repairs on defective or malfunctioning household appliances." If a significant difference in patterns of response is obtained, then certain of the alternatives can be assigned scoring weights. If several items serve to differentiate between a sample of engineers and a sample of members of a general population, a scale consisting of a collection of items related to the interests of successful engineers can be formed. From this scale predictions can be made of probable interests in engineering-related activities—predictions that are useful in counseling students. Suppose that for two samples of engineers and nonengineers, the

frequencies of the responses to the alternatives of the item just cited were as follows:

|               | D  | U  | A  | Total |
|---------------|----|----|----|-------|
| Engineers     | 12 | 18 | 70 | 100   |
| General sample | 58 | 32 | 10 | 100   |
| Total         | 70 | 50 | 80 | 200   |

The $X^2$ value of 79.14, which has been computed in Calculation Aid 19-14, is statistically significant beyond the .001 level, and thus the pattern of responses very probably differentiates engineers from the general population. In short, there is a relationship between whether an individual is an engineer or a member of the general population and the degree to which he expresses a preference for making repairs on appliances. Thus a person developing a set of questions for identifying interest patterns of engineers would probably give a substantial positive weight of 1 or 2 points to alternative A, a weight of possibly zero to alternative U, and perhaps a weight of −1 or −2 to alternative D.

## TEST RELIABILITY AND ERROR OF MEASUREMENT

In Chapter 17 mention was made of test reliability—the consistency or stability of test scores—which can be estimated by correlating scores on the same test form on two occasions or by correlating scores on two carefully constructed parallel forms that are administered either during one testing period or at two different points within an extended time interval. A third approach involves use of internal-consistency methods, which in essence furnish an estimate of the extent to which the items in one available form of a test that can be administered on only one occasion are intercorrelated with one another. A detailed description of internal consistency and other approaches to estimation of test reliability is

## Calculation Aid 19-14  Calculation of $\chi^2$ for Ascertaining Whether a Pattern of Responses to a Three-Choice Interest Inventory Item for a Group of 100 Engineers Differs Significantly from That of a Sample of 100 Individuals in a General Population (Data Fictitious)

### Problem

Calculate the value of $\chi^2$ for a $3 \times 2$ table to determine whether a significant difference exists in frequencies of responses to a three-choice test item for two groups, or, equivalently, ascertain whether a relationship is present between group membership and mode of response.

### Symbols defined

The principal symbols involved have been previously defined with the exception of the numerical designation of $k$, which is 6 instead of 4.

### Formula

Same as in Calculation Aid 19-13.

### Computational steps

**1 to 4.** Same steps as in Calculation Aid 19-13 (see work-layout form for details).

**5.** For a $3 \times 2$ contingency table (involving two degrees of freedom given by the number of rows minus 1, times the number of columns minus 1), the tabled $\chi^2$ values required for significance at the .05, .01, and .001 levels are, respectively, 5.991, 9.210, and 13.815. Since the obtained value of 79.14 for $\chi^2$ exceeds 13.815, the null hypothesis is rejected beyond the .001 level, and the pattern of frequencies of responses for the engineers and that for the general sample are said to differ very significantly. Thus the item significantly differentiates between the two groups.

### Work-layout form

*Item:* Enjoy making repairs on defective or malfunctioning household appliances.

| | Disagree (D) | Uncertain or Undecided (U) | Agree (A) | Totals |
|---|---|---|---|---|
| Engineers | $f_o = 12$ <br> $f_e = \dfrac{100 \times 70}{200} = 35$ <br> $f_o - f_e = -23$ | $f_o = 18$ <br> $f_e = \dfrac{100 \times 50}{200} = 25$ <br> $f_o - f_e = -7$ | $f_o = 70$ <br> $f_e = \dfrac{100 \times 80}{200} = 40$ <br> $f_o - f_e = +30$ | 100 |
| General Sample | $f_o = 58$ <br> $f_e = \dfrac{100 \times 70}{200} = 35$ <br> $f_o - f_e = +23$ | $f_o = 32$ <br> $f_e = \dfrac{100 \times 50}{200} = 25$ <br> $f_o - f_e = +7$ | $f_o = 10$ <br> $f_e = \dfrac{100 \times 80}{200} = 40$ <br> $f_o - f_e = -30$ | 100 |
| Totals | 70 | 50 | 80 | 200 = Grand total |

$$\chi^2 = \frac{(12 - 35)^2}{35} + \frac{(58 - 35)^2}{35} + \frac{(18 - 25)^2}{25} + \frac{(32 - 25)^2}{25} + \frac{(70 - 40)^2}{40} + \frac{(10 - 40)^2}{40}$$

$$= \frac{529}{35} + \frac{529}{35} + \frac{49}{25} + \frac{49}{25} + \frac{900}{40} + \frac{900}{40}$$

$$= 15.11 + 15.11 + 1.96 + 1.96 + 22.50 + 22.50$$

$$= 79.14 \ (P < .001)$$

furnished by Guilford (1965, pp. 438–467) and Magnusson (1967, pp. 59–122, 187–189).

The *standard error of measurement*, which is defined theoretically as the standard deviation of an infinite number of obtained (observed) scores for an individual on an infinite number of parallel or equivalent test forms about his true score (the mean score on the infinite number of forms), gives some indication of the extent of fluctuation one can expect in the distribution of obtained scores that a person receives around his true score. Although theoretically the standard error of measurement differs somewhat from one person to another and sometimes varies from one point of the score scale to another, it is often necessary for reasons of practicality and economy to assume that the standard error of measurement is relatively constant for each person over the continuum of test scores. Whereas the standard deviation of a group of individuals furnishes an indication of *interindividual* variability, the standard error of measurement affords a basis for describing *intraindividual* variability. The standard error of measurement is given by the formula $\sigma_e = \sigma\sqrt{1 - r_{tt}}$, where $\sigma$ is equal to the standard deviation of the obtained test scores and $r_{tt}$ is an estimate of the reliability (self-correlation) of the test. For example, if in an IQ test the standard deviation is 16 and its reliability is .91, the standard error of measurement would be given as follows:

$$\sigma_e = 16\sqrt{1 - .91}$$
$$= 16(.3)$$
$$= 4.8$$

Thus, if a person's true IQ happened to be 120, in about two out of three test administrations his obtained IQ score would be expected to fluctuate between roughly 115 and 125.

It is informative to note briefly that the problems of test reliability that involve the sampling of items (behaviors) from a large pool of items (population of behaviors) are somewhat analogous to those involved in the sampling of individuals from populations. It will be remembered that the standard error of a statistic is inversely related to the size of the sample of individuals. The size of the reliability coefficient increases directly as a function of the number of test items (assuming that they are relatively homogeneous in content and function, in difficulty level, and in discrimination power), and the size of the standard error of measurement is inversely proportional to the number of items. Actually, a test may be viewed as a sampling situation in which the items constitute a sample drawn from a population of items, which themselves may have been stratified by certain content or process dimensions. The standard error of measurement is a standard deviation of a frequency distribution of a person's scores obtained from a sampling of several parallel test forms about a "parameter"—namely, his true score.

In review, it will be remembered that three kinds of standard errors have been considered: (1) the standard error of estimate, which allows an indication of the amount of error involved in the prediction of one measure from another; (2) the standard error of a statistic, which furnishes a basis for estimating the amount of fluctuation of a statistic derived from successive random samples of individuals about the parameter of the population; and (3) the standard error of measurement, which permits an estimate of the amount of fluctuation that can be expected for a set of obtained scores for an individual on repeated administrations of equivalent forms of a test about his true score. In educational psychology, research workers have an obligation to give some indication of the amount of error to be expected in their various forms of observations. These three types of standard errors serve a useful function for the interpretation of errors of observation in different contexts of educational and psychological research.

## SUMMARY

This chapter has discussed ways in which the data of research in educational psychology can be reported and interpreted. Consideration was given to ways in which scores can be described through (1) the formation of frequency distributions; (2) the reporting of measures of central tendency such as the mean, the median, and the mode; (3) the employment of indicators of variability such as the range and standard deviation; (4) the identification of the relative position of an individual's score as expressed in percentiles and percentile ranks; (5) the use of standard scores that allow a comparable base for interpreting the relative standing of individuals on several different measures of unrelated function and content; and (6) the demonstration of the relationship between the sets of measures in terms of the computation of two different correlation coefficients and the calculation of a regression equation for predicting standing on one variable from knowledge of placement on the other. A great deal of attention was devoted to errors of observation in relation to prediction and to problems of sampling and statistical inference—the estimation of parameters from statistics and especially hypothesis testing. Systematic procedures for testing the significance of the differences between means of two samples (critical ratio) and between frequencies, or proportions, of responses for two samples ($X^2$) were developed and illustrated, and applications to item analysis were set forth. The relationship of sampling principles to test reliability and errors of measurement was also discussed.

## SELF-DIRECTING ACTIVITIES

1 Volunteer to assist a school psychologist or school counselor to draw a set of test profiles and then endeavor to interpret several of them. Check this interpretation with that of the counselor or school psychologist.

2 Find a teacher or school administrator who would like to see what the nature and degree of relationship is between scores on a scholastic aptitude test and grades earned by his students in a given course or in a given set of courses. Draw a scatterplot, calculate the Pearson product-moment correlation coefficient, and plot the best fitting line for prediction of the criterion from the test scores. Make at least three or four predictions for students who registered quite different aptitude test scores, and check the discrepancy between the observed grade (or grade point average) and the predicted grade (or grade point average).

3 After choosing a college professor who is emotionally secure and not easily threatened psychologically by creative students, volunteer to do an item analysis of one of his recent examinations.

4 Try to find a school official who has recently administered a questionnaire to two different groups of individuals such as parents and teachers. By applying the chi-square technique described in the text, determine on which questions a significant difference exists in the type or pattern of responses given.

5 From five or six classes of students enrolled in the same subject, select two random samples of boys and girls and determine their scores on a recent examination. Carry out a critical ratio ($\bar{z}$ test) to determine whether there is a statistically significant difference in mean test scores associated with sex.

6 Take a standardized interest test or temperament scale, a "good" score on which is hypothetically a requirement for employment in two extremely different kinds of jobs: one requiring a person to work in isolation at highly intellectual tasks and the other a position requiring a team membership in a small group of workers whose job is to develop a public relations program in relation to merchandising a product. Take the test twice— once for each job—and check to see how many items were answered differently for the two job opportunities which pay exceedingly well.

7 Cite 10 or 15 cautions that teachers should exercise in the construction, administration, scoring, and interpretation of either essay or objective tests at either the elementary or secondary level of instruction.

# BIBLIOGRAPHY

Adams, G. S. *Measurement and evaluation in education, psychology, and guidance.* New York: Holt, 1964.

Adler, A. *Essays in individual psychology.* New York: Grove Press, 1959.

Adler, M. J. *The difference of man and the difference it makes.* New York: Holt, 1968.

Albert, D. J. The effect of spreading depression on the consolidation of learning. *Neuropsychologia,* 1966(a), 4, 49–64.

Albert, D. J. The effects of polarizing currents on the consolidation of learning. *Neuropsychologia,* 1966(b), 4, 65–77.

Albert, D. J. Memory in mammals: Evidence for a system involving nuclear ribonucleic acid. *Neuropsychologia,* 1966(c), 4, 79–92.

Alkin, M. C. Accountability defined. *Evaluation Comment,* 1972, 3, 1–5 (Publication from the Center for the Study of Evaluation, UCLA).

Allport, G. W. Attitudes. In C. Marchison (Ed.), *A handbook of social psychology.* Worcester, Mass.: Clark University Press, 1935, pp. 798–844.

Allport, G. W. *Pattern and growth in personality.* New York: Holt, 1961.

Allport, G. W., Vernon, P. E., and Lindzey, G. *Study of values.* (Rev. ed.) Boston: Houghton Mifflin, 1951.

America: 24 Million Illiterates; U.S. Office of Education Reports. 121: 137 0.25, 1969.

American Association for the Advancement of Science. *Science—a process approach. Competency measures.* Washington, D.C.; AAAS, 1966.

American Association for the Advancement of Science. Formulating hypothesis 3—the effect of temperature on dissolving time. *Science—A process approach,* Part F. (Rev. ed.) Xerox Corp., 1970.

Ames, L. B. The sequential patterning of prone progression in the human infant. *Genetic Psychological Monographs,* 1937, 19, 409–460.

Ames, L. B. The constancy of psychological motor tempo in individual infants. *Journal of Genetic Psychology*, 1940, 57, 445–450.

Anastasi, Anne. *Psychological testing.* New York: Macmillan, 1954.

Anastasi, Anne. Age changes in adult test performance. *Psychological Reports*, 1956, 2, 509.

Andersson, B. The effect of injections of hypertonic NaCl solution into the different parts of the hypothalamus of goats. *Acta Physiologica Scand.*, 1953, 28: 188–201.

Asch, S. E. Studies of independence and submission in group pressure. *Psychological Monographs*, 1956, 70. No. 416.

Asher, E. J. The inadequacy of current intelligence tests for testing Kentucky mountain children. *Journal of Genetic Psychology*, 1935, 46, 480–486.

Atkinson, R. C. An experiment in computer assisted instruction. Paper presented at the University of California, Santa Barbara, 1968.

Ausubel, D. P. The use of advance organizers in the learning and retention of meaningful verbal material. *Journal of Educational Psychology*, 1960, 51, 267–272.

Ausubel, D. P. Stages of intellectual development and their implications for early childhood education. In P. B. Neubauer (Ed.), *Concept of development in early childhood education.* Springfield, Ill.: Charles C Thomas, 1965, 8–51.

Ausubel, D. P. *Readings in school learning.* New York: Holt, 1969.

Ayers, A. Jean. Reading: A product of sensory integrative process. In Helen K. Smith (Ed.), *Perception and reading.* Newark, Del.: International Reading Assn., 1968.

Babich, F. R., Jacobson, A. L., Bubash, Suzanne, and Jacobson, Anne. Transfer of a response to naive rats by injection of ribonucleic acid extracted from trained rats. *Science*, 1965, 49, 656–657.

Baldwin, A. L., Kalhorn, J., and Breese, F. H. Patterns of parent behavior. *Psychological Monographs*, 1945, 58, No. 268.

Baldwin, B. T. The relation between mental and physical growth. *Journal of Educational Psychology*, 1922, 13, 193–203.

Barbe, W. B. Helping gifted children. *Gifted Child Quarterly*, 1959, 3, 4–9, 16.

Baruch, Dorothy. *New ways in discipline: You and your child today.* New York: McGraw-Hill, 1949.

Baumeister, A. A. Effects of dietary control on intelligence in phenylketonuric children. *American Journal of Mental Deficiency*, 1967, 71, 840–847.

Bayley, Nancy. *Studies in the development of young children.* Berkeley: University of California Press, 1940.

Bayley, Nancy. On growth of intelligence. *American Psychologist*, 1955, 10, 805–818.

Baylow, I. H. Lateral dominance characteristics and reading achievement in the first grade. *Journal of Psychology*, 1963, 55, 323–328.

Bechterev, V. M. von. *La psychologie objective.* (Translated by N. Kostyleff) Paris: Alcan, 1913.

Beck, Joan. *How to raise a brighter child.* New York: Trident Press, 1967.

Becker, W. C., Madsen, C. H., Jr., Arnold, Carole R., and Thomas, D. R. The contingent use of teacher attention and praise in reducing classroom behavior problems. *Journal of Special Education*, 1967, 1, 287–307.

Beilin, H., and Franklin, I. Logical operations in length and area measurement: Age and training effects. Paper presented at the meeting of the Society for Research on Child Development, Pennsylvania State University, University Park, 1961.

Békésy, G. von. The ear. *Scientific American*, 1957, 197, 68.

Bereiter, C., and Engelmann, S. *Teaching disadvantaged children in the preschool.* Englewood Cliffs, N.J.: Prentice-Hall, 1966.

Bereiter, C., and Engelmann, S. An academically oriented preschool for disadvantaged children: Results from the initial experimental group. In D. W. Brian and J. Hill (Eds.). *Psychology and early childhood education.* Toronto: Ontario Institute for Studies in Education, 1968, Monograph Series No. 4.

Berenda, Ruth W. *The influence of the group on the judgments of children.* New York: King's Crown, 1950.

Bergson, H. L. Introduction à la metaphysique. *Revue de Metaphysique et de Morale*, January 1903, 1–25.

Bernstein, B. Social structure, language and learning. *Educational Research*, June 1961(a), 3, 163–176.

Bernstein, B. Social class and linguistic development: A theory of social learning. In A. H. Halsey, Jean Floud, and C. A. Anderson (Eds.), *Education, economy, and society.* New York: Free Press, 1961(b), pp. 288–314.

Bessell, H. Human development in the elementary school classroom. In L. N. Solomon and Betty Berzon (Eds.). *New perspectives on encounter groups.* San Francisco: Jossey-Bass, 1972, pp. 349–367.

Bexton, W. H., Heron, W., and Scott, T. H. Effects of decreased variation in the sensory environment. *Canadian Journal of Psychology*, 1954, 8, 70–76.

Binet, A. *The development of intelligence in children.* (Translated by E. S. Kite) Baltimore: Williams & Wilkins, 1916.

*Biological Sciences Curriculum Study BSCS.* Processes of Science. Boulder: University of Colorado, 1965.

Bischof, L. J. *Intelligence: Statistical concepts of its nature.* Garden City, N.Y.: Doubleday, 1954.

Bjonerud, C. E. Arithmetic concepts possessed by the preschool child. *The Arithmetic Teacher*, 1960, 7, 347–350.

Blatt, B., and Garfunkel, F. Educating intelligence: Determinants of school behavior of disadvantaged children. *Exceptional Children*, 1967, 33, 601–608.

Block, J. Mastery learning speech given to Kappa Delta Pi. Santa Barbara, Calif., May 1972.

Bloom, B. S., Engelhart, M. D., Furst, E. J., Hill, W. H., and Krathwohl, D. R. *Taxonomy of educational objectives: The cognitive domain.* Handbook I. New York: Longmans, 1956.

Bloom, B. S., Hastings, J. T., amd Madaus, G. P. *Handbook on formative and summative evaluation of student learning.* New York: McGraw-Hill, 1971.

Bond, H. M. Wasted talent. In E. Ginsberg (Ed.), *The nation's children: Development and education.* New York: Columbia University Press, 1960.

Bradway, K. P., and Robinson, N. M. Significant IQ changes in 25 years: A follow-up. *Journal of Educational Psychology*, 1961, 52, 701–709.

Brady, J. V. Ulcers in executive monkeys. *Scientific American*, October 1958, 95–100.

Brand, H. (Ed.). *The study of personality.* New York: Wiley, 1954.

Broderick, Mary. Creativity in children: Some case studies. *The National Elementary Principal*, 1966, 46(2), 18–24.

Brogden, W. J., Lipman, E. A., and Culler, E. The role of incentive in conditioning and extinction. *American Journal of Psychology*, 1938, 51, 110.

Bronfenbrenner, U. Some familial antecedents of responsibility and leadership in adolescents. In L. Petrullo and B. M. Bass (Eds.), *Leadership and interpersonal behavior.* New York: Holt, 1961, pp. 239–271.

Bronfenbrenner, U. The changing American child—A speculative analysis. In U. Bronfenbrenner (Ed.), *Influences on humand development.* Hinsdale, Ill.: The Dryden Press, 1972.

Brown, R. *Words and things.* New York: Free Press, 1958.

Brownell, W. A. *Arithmetic abstractions.* Berkeley: University of California Press, 1967.

Bruner, J. S. *The process of education.* Cambridge, Mass.: Harvard University Press, 1966.

Buchwald, A. M., and Young, R. D. Some comments on the foundations of behavior therapy. In C. M. Franks (Ed.), *Behavior therapy appraisal and status.* New York: McGraw-Hill, 1969.

Buros, O. K. (Ed.). *The sixth mental measurements yearbook.* Highland Park, N.J.: Gryphon Press, 1965.

Buros, O. K. (Ed.). *The seventh mental measurements yearbook.* Highland Park, N.J.: Gryphon Press, 1972, 2 vols.

Burt, C. The latest revision of the Binet intelligence tests. *Eugenics Review*, 1939, 30, 255–260.

Burton, A. Encounter existence and psychotherapy. In A. Burton (Ed.), *Encounter: The theory and practice of encounter groups.* San Francisco, Calif.: Jossey-Bass, 1969, pp. 7–26.

Campbell, D. T. Social attitudes and other acquired behavioral dispositions. In S. Koch (Ed.), *Psychology: A study of a science.* Vol. 5. New York: McGraw-Hill, 1963, pp. 94–172.

Carmichael, L. The onset and early development of behavior. In P. H. Mussen (Ed.), *Carmichael's manual of child psychology.* New York: Wiley, 1970, 447–564.

Carroll, J. A. A model for school learning. *Teachers College Record*, 1963, 64, 723–733.

Caspari, E. Genetic endowment and environment in the determination of human behavior: Biological viewpoint. *American Educational Research Journal*, 1968, 5(1), 43–55.

Chall, Jeanne. *Learning to read: The great debate.* New York: McGraw-Hill, 1967.

Chall, Jeanne, Roswell, Florence G., and Blumenthal, Susan Hahn. Auditory blending ability: A factor in success in beginning reading. *The Reading Teacher*, 1963, 17(2), 113–120.

Chamberlin, C. D., Chamberlin, E., Drought, H. E., and Scott, W. E. *Adventure in American education.* Vol. 4. *Did they succeed in college?* New York: Harper & Row, 1942.

Chein, I. The image of man. *Journal of Social Issues*, 1962, 18, 1–35.

Chemical Education Material Study (CHEMS). *Chemistry: An experimental science.* San Francisco: Freeman, 1963.

Chomsky, Noam. *Aspects of the theory of syntax.* Cambridge, Mass.: M. I. T. Press, 1965.

Child, I. L., The relation of somatotype to self-ratings on Sheldon's temperament traits. *Journal of Personality*, 1950, 18, 440–453.

Child, I. L., and Whiting, J. W. M. *Child training and personality.* New Haven, Conn.: Yale University Press, 1953.

Churchman, C. W., and Ackoff, R. L. Toward an experimental measure of personality. *Psychological Review*, 1947, 54, 41–52.

Clark, M. Experiences at the Easlin Institute, Big Sur, California. Private communication to J. A. R. Wilson, Spring 1972.

Clemmens, R. L. Minimal brain damage in children. *Children*, 1961, 8(5), 179–184.

Cline, V. B., Richards, J. M., Jr., and Needham, W. E. Creativity tests and achievement in high school science. *Journal of Applied Psychology*, 1963, 47, 184–189.

Coffield, W. H., and Blommers, P. Effects of non-promotion on educational achievement in the elementary school. *Journal of Educational Psychology*, 1956, 47, 235–250.

Cohen, J. Factorial structure of the WISC at ages

7–6, 10–6, and 13–6. *Journal of Consulting Psychology*, 1959, 23, 285–299.

Cole, L., and Hall, I. H. *Psychology of adolescence.* (5th ed.) New York: Holt, 1964.

Cole, L. E. *Human behavior: Psychology as a biosocial science.* New York: World, 1953.

Cole, M. and Maltzman, I. *A handbook of contemporary Soviet psychology.* New York: Basic Books, 1969.

Coleman, J. S., Campbell, E. Q., Hobson, C. J., McPartland, J., Mood, A. M., Wienfield, F. D., and York, R. L. *Equality of educational opportunity.* Washington, D.C.: Government printing office, 1966.

Coles, R. *Erik H. Erikson: The growth of his work.* Boston: Little, Brown, 1970.

Commins, W. D. More about sex differences. *School and Society*, 1928, 28, 599–600.

Cook. W. M. Ability of children in color discriminations. *Child Development*, 1931, 2, 303–320.

Côté, Dominique G., Levy, S. H., and O'Conner, P. *Le Francais: Ecouter et parler.* New York: Holt, 1962.

Coulson, W. R., and Rogers, C. R. (Eds.). *Man and the science of man.* Columbus, Ohio: Merrill, 1968.

Cronbach, L. J. *Educational psychology.* New York: Harcourt, Brace & World, 1963.

Cronback, L. J. Heredity, environment, and educational policy. *Harvard Educational Review*, 1969, 39, 338–347.

Cronbach, L. J., and Meehl, P. Construct validity in psychological tests. *Psychological Bulletin*, 1955, 52, 281–302.

Crow, L. D., and Crow, Alice. *Human development and learning.* New York: American Book, 1956.

Crowder, N. A. *The arithmetic of computers: An introduction to binary and octal mathematics.* Vol. 1. Santa Barbara, Calif.: Western Design Division, U.S. Industries, 1960(a).

Crowder, N. A. Automatic tutoring by intrinsic programming. In A. A. Lumsdaine and R. Glaser (Eds.), *Teaching machines and programmed learning.* Washington, D.C.: National Education Association, 1960(b), 286–298.

Deans, Edwina. *Arithmetic: Children use it.* Washington, D.C.: Association for Early Childhood Education (International), 1954.

Dennis, W. Infant reactions to resistance: An evaluation of Watson's theory. *Transactions of N.Y. Academy of Science*, 1940, 2, 202–218.

Dennis, W. Infant development under conditions of restricted practice and minimum social stimulation. *Genetic Psychological Monographs*, 1941, 23, 143–189.

De Robertis, E. D. P. *Histophysiology of synapses and neurosecretion.* New York: Macmillan, 1964.

Deutsch, M. Facilitating development in the preschool child: Social and psychological perspective. *Merrill-Palmer Quarterly of Behavior and Development*, 1964, 10, 249–263.

Devereux, E. C., Jr., Bronfenbrenner, U., and Suci, G. J. Patterns of parent behavior in the United States of America and the Federal Republic of Germany: A cross-national comparison. *International Social Science Journal*, 1962, 14, 488–506.

Dodwell, P. C. Children's understanding of number and related concepts. *Canadian Journal of Psychology*, 1960, 14, 191–205.

Dodwell, P. C. Children's understanding of number concepts: Characteristics of an individual and of a group test. *Canadian Journal of Psychology*, 1961, 15, 29–36.

Doll, E. A. *The measurement of social competence.* Minneapolis: Minneapolis Educational Publishers, 1953.

Dollard, J., and Miller, N. E. *Personality and psychotherapy: An analysis in terms of learning, thinking, and culture.* New York: McGraw-Hill, 1950.

Doman, G. J. *How to teach your baby to read.* New York: Random House, 1964.

Doman, G. J. Little children can learn to read. *P.T.A. Magazine*, 1965, 59(5), 30–32.

Doty, R. W., and Giurgea, C. Conditioned reflexes established by coupling electrical excitations of two cortical areas. In A. Fessar, R. W. Gerard, J. Kononski, and J. F. Delafresnaye (Eds.), *Brain mechanisms and learning.* Springfield, Ill.: Charles C Thomas, 1961, pp. 133–152.

Dowling, J. ITA (initial teaching alphabet) reading experiment. *Reading Teacher*, 1964, 18, 105–110.

Dreger, R. M., and Miller, K. S. Comparative psychological studies of Negroes and whites in the United States. *Psychological Bulletin*, 1960, 57, 361–402.

Durkin, Dolores. *Children who read early.* New York: Teachers College, 1966.

Durkin, Dolores. When should children begin to read? In H. M. Robinson (Ed.), *Innovation and change in reading instruction.* Sixty-seventh Yearbook of the National Society for the Study of Education. Chicago: University of Chicago Press, 1968.

Durkin, Dolores. *Teaching young children to read.* Boston: Allyn & Bacon, 1972.

Durrell, D. D., and Murphy, Helen A. The auditory discrimination factor in reading readiness and reading disability. *Education*, 1963, 73, 556–560.

Dutton, W. H. *Evaluating pupils' understanding of arithmetic.* Englewood Cliffs, N.J.: Prentice-Hall, 1964.

Dykstra, R. Summary of the second grade phase of the Cooperative Research Program in Primary Reading Instruction. *Reading Research Quarterly*, 1968, 4(1), 49–70.

Eastburn, L. A. Relative efficiency of instruction in large and small classes on three ability levels. *Journal of Experimental Education*, 1936, 5, 17–22.

Eaton, M. T. A survey of the achievement in social studies of 10,110 sixth grade pupils in 464 schools in Indiana. *Bulletin of the School of Education, Indiana University*, 20, 1944.

Ebel, R. L. *Measuring educational achievement.* Engelwood Cliffs, N.J.: Prentice-Hall, 1965.

Eccles, J. C., and Jaeger, J. C. The relationship between the mode of operation and the dimensions of the junctional regions at synapses and motor end organs. *Proceedings of the Royal Society*, 1958, 148, 38–57.

Educational Testing Service. *Making the classroom test: A guide for teachers*, Educational Testing Service Evaluation and Advisory Series, No. 4. Princeton, N.J.: Educational Testing Service, 1961.

Educational Testing Service. *Let's look at first graders: A guide to understanding and fostering intellectual development in young children.* New York: Board of Education, 1965.

Edwards, A. L. *Experimental design in psychological research.* (2nd ed.) New York: Holt, 1960.

Edwards, A. L. *Statistical methods.* (2nd. ed.) New York: Holt, 1967.

Edwards, A. S., and Jones, L. An experimental field study of north Georgia mountaineers. *Journal of Social Psychology*, 1938, 9, 317–333.

Ehrenfels, C. von. Uber gestaaltqualitaten. *Vierteljahrsschrift fur Wissenschaftliche Philosophie*, 1890, 14, 249–292.

Ehrenfels, C. von *The Austrian philosophy of values.* Norman: University of Oklahoma Press, 1930.

Eichorn, Dorothy H. Biological correlates of behavior. In H. W. Stevenson (Ed.), *Child psychology.* Sixty-second Yearbook of the National Society for the Study of Education. Chicago: University of Chicago Press, 1963, pp. 4–61.

Elkind, D. The development of quantitative thinking: A systematic replication of Piaget's studies. *Journal of Genetic Psychology*, 1961(a), 98, 37–46.

Elkind, D. Children's discovery of the conservation of mass, weight, and volume: Piaget replication study II. *Journal of Genetic Psychology*, 1961(b), 98, 219–227.

Elkind, D. Quantity conceptions in junior and senior high school students. *Child Development*, 1961(c), 32, 551–560.

Emery, J. R., and Krumboltz, J. D. Standard versus individualized hierarchies in desensitization to reduce test anxiety. *Journal of Counseling Psychology*, 1967, 14, 294–209.

Engelhart, M. D., and Moughamian, H. *A folio of illustrative exercises from Chicago City Junior College, English and general course final examinations.* Chicago: Chicago City Junior College, Division of Institutional Research and Evaluation, 1966.

Engelmann, S. *Preventing failure in the primary grades.* Chicago: Science Research Associates, 1969(a).

Engelmann, S. *Teaching in the primary grades.* Chicago: Science Research Associates, 1969(b).

Epstein, A., Giolas, T. G., and Owens, E. Familiarity and intelligibility of monsosyllabic word lists. *Journal of Speech and Hearing Research*, 1968, 11 (2), 435–438.

Erikson, E. H. *Childhood and society.* New York: Norton, 1963.

Ertl, J. Evoked potentials, neural efficiency and IQ. Paper presented at International Symposium for Biocybernetics, Washington, D.C., Feb. 8, 1968.

Ertl, John. Good-bye IQ, hello EI (Ertl Index). Phi Delta Kappan interview. *Phi Delta Kappan*, October, 1972, 89–94.

Eson, M. E. *Psychological foundations of education.* New York: Holt, 1964.

Estes, W. K. An experimental study of punishment. *Psychological Monographs*, 1944, 47 (Whole No. 263).

Everett, Evalyn G. Behavioral characteristics of early and late maturing girls. Unpublished master's thesis, University of California, 1943.

Eysenck, H. J. Learning theory and behavior therapy. *Journal of Mental Science*, 1959, 105, 61–75.

Fantz, R. L. A method for studying depth perception in infants under six months of age. *Psychological Record*, 1961(1), 11, 27–32.

Fantz, R. L. The origin of form perception. *Scientific American*, 1961(b), 204, 66–72.

Fantz, R. L. Pattern vision in newborn infants. *Science*, 1963, 140, 296–297.

Fantz, R. L. Visual experience in infants: Decreased attention to familiar patterns relative to novel ones. *Science*, 1964, 146, 668–670.

Fantz, R. L. Pattern discrimination and selective attention as determinants of perceptual development from birth. In Aline H. Kidd and Jeanne L. Rivoire (Eds.), *Perceptual development in children.* New York: International Universities Press, 1966, pp. 143–173.

Faust, Margaret S. Developmental maturity as a determinant in prestige of adolescent girls. *Child Development*, 1960, 31, 173–184.

Feigenberg, I. M. Probabilistic prognosis and its significance in normal and pathological subjects. In M. Cole and I. Maltzman (Eds.), *A handbook of contemporary Soviet psychology.* New York: Basic Books, 1969, pp. 354–369.

Feldman, M. P., and MacCulloch, M. J. Aversion therapy for sexual deviations as reported in S. Rachman and J. Teasdale (Eds.), *Aversion therapy and behavior disorders: An analysis.* Coral Gables, Fla.: University of Miami Press, 1969.

Ferguson, G. A. Psychology of the Negro: An experimental study. *Archives of Psychology*, 1916, 5(36), 1–138.

Ferster, C. B. Perspectives in Psychology XXV.

Transition from animal laboratory to clinic. *Psychological Record*, 1967, 17, 147–150.

Festinger, L. Behavioral support for opinion change. *Public Opinion Quarterly*, 1964, 18, 404–418.

Festinger, L., and Carlsmith, J. M. Cognitive consequences of forced compliance. *Journal of Abnormal and Social Psychology*, 1959, 58, 203–210.

Fey, W. F. Correlates of certain subjective attitudes toward self and others. *Journal of Clinical Psychology*, 1958, 13, 44–49.

Fine, R. *Freud: A critical re-evaluation of his theories*. New York: McKay, 1962.

Fjerdingstad, E. J., Nissen, T., and Røgaard-Peterson, H. H. Effect of RNA extracted from the brain of trained animals on learning in rats. *Scandinavian Journal of Psychology*, 1965, 6, 1–6.

Flanders, H. A. Using interaction analysis in the in-service training of teachers. *Journal of Experimental Education*, 1962, 30, 313–316.

Flavell, J. H. *The developmental psychology of Jean Piaget*. Princeton, N.J.: Van Nostrand, 1963.

Flory, C. D. Osseous development in the hand as an index of skeletal development. *Monographs of the Society for Research in Child Development*. Washington, D.C.: National Research Council, 1936.

Forgus, R. H. *Perception: The basic process in cognitive development*. New York: McGraw-Hill, 1966.

Foulke, E. Listening comprehension as a function of word rate. *Journal of Communication*, September 1968, 18, 198–206.

Franks, C. M. Reflections upon the treatment of sexual disorders by the behavioral clinician: An historical comparison with the treatment of the alcoholic. *Journal of Sex Research*, 1967, 3, 212–223.

Franks, C. M. Behavior modification and its pavlovian origins: Review and perspectives. In C. M. Franks (Ed.), *Behavior therapy: Appraisal and status*. New York, McGraw Hill, 1969(a).

Franks, C. M. Implications of behavior therapy for the future of clinical psychology. Paper read at Symposium, Training Behavior Therapists, A. M. Graziano, Chairman. American Psychological Association, Washington, D.C., 1969(b).

French, J. W., and Michael, W. B. (Eds.) *Standards for educational and psychological tests and manuals*. Washington, D.C.: American Psychological Association, 1966.

Freud, Anna. Emotional and social development of young children. In *Feelings and learning*. Washington, D.C.: Association for Childhood Education (International), 1965.

Freud, S. *An outline of psychoanalysis.* (Translated by J. Strachey) New York: Norton, 1949.

Freud, S. *The standard edition of the complete works of Sigmund Freud.* London: Hogarth, 1953.

Friedlander, B. F. A psychologist's second thought on concepts, curiosity and discovery in teaching and learning. *Harvard Educational Review*, 1965, 35, 18–38.

Fuller, J. L. Experiential deprivation and later behavior. *Science*, 1967, 158, 1645–1653.

Furth, H. G. *Piaget and knowledge: Theoretical foundations.* Englewood Cliffs, N.J.: Prentice-Hall, Inc., 1969.

Gagné, R. M. Military training and principles of learning. *American Psychologist*, 1962, 17, 83–91.

Gagné, R. M. *The conditions of learning.* New York: Holt, 1965.

Gagne, R. M. *The conditions of learning.* 2nd ed. New York: Holt, 1970.

Gardner, R. A., and Gardner, B. T. Teaching sign language to a chimpanzee. *Science*, 1969, 165, 664–672.

Garrett, H. E. *How classroom desegregation will work.* Richmond, Va.: Patrick Henry Press, 1967.

Gastaut, H., and Rogers, A. Les méchanismes de l'activité nerveuse supérieure au niveau des grandes structures fonctionelles du cerveau. In H. H. Jasper and G. D. Smirnov (Eds.), Moscow Colloquium on electroencephalogy of higher nervous activities, *EEG Clinical Neurophysiology*, Suppl 13, 1960.

Gerberich, J. R. *Specimen objective test items.* New York: Longmans, 1956.

Geschwind, N., and Levitsky, W. Human brain: Left-right asymmetrics in temporal speech region. *Science*, 1968, 161, 186–187.

Gesell, A. *The first five years of life.* New York: Harper & Row, 1940.

Gesell, A. The developmental aspect of child vision. *Journal of Pediatrics*, 1949, 35, 310–317.

Gesell, A. The ontogenesis of infant behavior. In L. Carmichael (Ed.), *Manual of child psychology.* (2nd ed.) New York: Wiley, 1954, pp. 335–373.

Getzels, J. W., and Jackson, P. W. *Creativity and intelligence.* New York: Wiley, 1962.

Gibson, Eleanor J. A systematic application of the concepts of generalization and differentiation to verbal learning. *Psychological Review*, 1940, 47, 196–229.

Gilbert, H. W. Response to decline and fall of group intelligence testing. *Teachers College Record*, 1966, 67, 282–285.

Gilgash, C. A. Glutamic acid: Its effect on the mental functioning of adult male mental retardates. *Science Education*, 1967, 51, 324–327.

Glasser, W. *Reality therapy: A new approach to psychiatry.* New York: Harper & Row, 1965.

Glasser, W. *Schools without failure.* New York: Harper & Row, 1969.

Goertzel, V., and Goertzel, Mildred G. *Cradles of eminence.* Boston: Little, Brown, 1962.

Gordon, H. *Mental and scholastic tests among retarded children: An inquiry into the effects of schooling on various tests.* London: Board of Education, Educational Pamphlet, 1923, No. 44.

Gray, B. B., and Ryan, B. P. *A language program for the non-language child.* Champaign, Ill.: Research Press, 1973.

Guilford, J. P. *Psychometric methods.* (2nd ed.) New York: McGraw-Hill, 1954.

Guilford, J. P. Les dimensions de l'intellect. In H. Laugier (Ed.), *L'analyse factorielle et ses applications.* Paris: Centre National de la Reserche Scientifique, 1956, pp. 53–74.

Guilford, J. P. *A revised structure of intellect.* Los Angeles: University of Southern California Psychological Laboratory, 1957(a).

Guilford, J. P. Creative abilities in the arts. *Psychological Review*, 1957(b), 64, 110–118.

Guilford, J. P. Models for human problem solving. Paper presented to the staff of Project Talent, Los Angeles, September 1964.

Guilford, J. P. *Fundamental statistics in psychology and education.* (4th ed.) New York: McGraw-Hill, 1965.

Guilford, J. P. Basic problems in teaching for creativity. In C. W. Taylor and F. E. Williams (Eds.), *Instructional media and creativity.* New York: Wiley, 1966, pp. 71–103.

Guilford, J. P. *The nature of human intelligence.* New York: McGraw-Hill, 1967.

Guilford, J. P., Michael, W. B., and Brown, S. W. *Exercises to accompany fundamental statistics.* (4th ed.) New York: McGraw-Hill, 1966.

Guthrie, E. R. *The psychology of learning.* (Rev. ed.) New York: Harper & Row, 1952.

Guttman, N. The pigeon and the spectrum and other perplexities. *Psychological Reports*, 1956, 2, 449–460.

Guttman, N., and Kalish, H. I. Experiments in discrimination. *Scientific American*, 1958, 198(1), 77–82.

Halverson, H. M. An experimental study of prehension in infants by means of systematic cinema records. *Genetic Psychological Monographs*, 1931, 10, 107–286.

Halverson, H. M. Genital and sphincter behavior of the male infant. *Journal of Genetic Psychology*, 1940, 56, 95–136.

Halverson, H. M. Variations in pulse and respiration during different phases of infant behavior. *Journal of Genetic Psychology*, 1941, 59, 259–330.

Hamachek, D. E. *Encounters with the self.* New York: Holt, 1971.

Hamilton, N. T. and Landin, J. *Set theory: The structure of arithmetic.* Boston: Allyn and Bacon, 1961.

Handler, P. *Biology and the future of man.* New York: Oxford University Press, 1970.

Hansen, J. T. Use of standardized tests in evaluating a method of teaching reading. Paper presented at the meeting of the National Council on Measurement in Education, New York, February 1967.

Hardin, G. J. *Biology.* San Francisco: Freeman, 1961.

Harlow, H. F. The formation of learning sets. *Psychological Review*, 1949, 56, 51–65.

Harris, A. J. Lateral dominance, directional confusion, and reading disability. *Journal of Psychology*, 1957, 44, 283–294.

Harris, A. J. Diagnosis and remedial instruction in reading. In H. M. Robinson (Ed.), *Innovation and change in reading instruction.* Sixty-seventh Yearbook of the National Society for the Study of Education. Chicago: University of Chicago Press, 1968, pp. 159–194.

Harris, D. B. Child psychology and the concept of

development. In D. S. Palermo and L. P. Lipsitt (Eds.), *Research readings in child psychology.* New York: Holt, 1963, pp. 21–31.

Harris, J. A. *The measurement of man.* Minneapolis: University of Minneapolis Press, 1930.

Harrison, M. Lucille. The nature and development of concepts of time among young children. *Elementary School Journal,* March 1934, 34, 507–514.

Havighurst, R. J. *Adolescent character and personality.* New York: Wiley, 1949.

Havighurst, R. J. *Human development and education.* New York: Longmans, 1953.

Hawthorne, N. *The scarlet letter* (1850). New York: Random House, 1928.

Heath, R. G. Electrical self-stimulation of the brain in man. *The American Journal of Psychiatry,* 1963, 120(6), 571–577.

Hebb, D. O. *The organization of behavior.* New York: Wiley, 1949.

Hebb, D. O. Drives and the C.N.S. (conceptual nervous system). *Psychological Review,* 1955, 62, 243–254.

Hebb, D. O. Sensory deprivation: Facts in search of a theory. *Journal of Nervous and Mental Disease,* 1961, 123, 40–43.

Hebb, D. O. *A textbook of psychology.* (2nd ed.) Philadelphia: Saunders, 1966.

Held, R., and Bauer, J. A., Jr. Visually guided reaching in infant monkeys after restricted rearing. *Science,* 1967, 155, 718–720.

Henmon, V. A. C., and Nelson, M. S. *The Henmon-Nelson tests of mental ability.* Boston: Houghton Mifflin, 1931.

Herskovits, M. J. On the relation between Negro-white mixture and standing in intelligence tests. *Pedagogical Seminary and Journal of Genetic Psychology,* 1926, 33, 30–42.

Hess, E. H. Imprinting in animals. *Scientific American,* March 1958, 81–90.

Hess, E. H. Imprinting in birds. *Science,* 1964, 146, 1128–1139.

Hess, W. R. Causality, consciousness, and cerebral organization. *Science,* 1967, 158, 1279–1283.

Hewett, F. M. Teaching speech to an autistic boy through operant conditioning. *American Journal of Orthopsychiatry,* October 1965, 35, 927–936.

Hilbert, D. *Foundations of geometry.* La Salle, Ill.: Open Court, 1938.

Hilgard, E. R. Human motives and the concept of self. *American Psychologist,* 1949, 4, 374–382.

Hilgard, E. R., and Bower, G. H. *Theories of learning.* New York: Appleton-Century-Crofts, 1966.

Hirsch, H. D. M. An experimental study of east Kentucky mountaineers. *Genetic Psychological Monographs,* 1928, 3, 183–244.

Hochberg, J. E., and Brooks, V. The psychophysics of form: Reversible perspective drawing of spatial objects. *American Journal of Psychology,* 1960, 73, 337–354.

Hofstaetter, P. R. The changing composition of "intelligence": A study in T-technique. *Journal of Genetic Psychology,* 1954, 85, 159–164.

Holland, J. G., and Skinner, B. F. *The analysis of behavior: Program for self-instruction.* New York: McGraw-Hill, 1961.

Hollis, Florence. *Casework: A psychosocial therapy.* New York: Random House, 1964.

Holmes, J. A., and Hyman, W. Spelling disability and asyntaxia in a case involving injury to the language formation area of the brain. *Journal of Educational Psychology,* 1957, 48, 542–550.

Homme, L. E., de Baca, C. P., Cottingham, L., and Homme, Angela. What behavioral engineering is. In A. M. Graziano, *Behavior therapy with children.* New York: Aldine, Atherton, 1971, pp. 44–55.

Horney, Karen. *Our inner conflicts: A constructive theory of neurosis.* New York: Norton, 1945.

Horney, Karen. Finding the real self. *American Journal of Psychoanalysis,* 1949, 9, 3–7.

Hudgins, C. V. Conditioning and the voluntary control of the pupillary light reflex. *Journal of Genetic Psychology,* 1933, 8, 3–51.

Hudson, W. Pictorial depth perception in subcultural groups in Africa. *Journal of Social Psychology,* 1960, 52, 183.

Hull, C. L. *Principles of behavior.* New York: Appleton-Century-Crofts, 1943.

Hunt, J. McV. An instance of the social origin of conflict resulting in psychosis. *American Journal of Orthopsychiatry,* 1938, 8, 158–164.

Hunt, J. McV. *Intelligence and experience.* New York: Ronald, 1961.

Hunt, J. McV. Has compensatory education failed? Has it been attempted? *Harvard Educational Review,* 1969, 39, 278–300.

Hurlock, Elizabeth B. An evaluation of certain incentives used in school work. *Journal of Educational Psychology*, 1925, 16, 145–159.

Hurlock, Elizabeth B. *Child development.* (2nd ed.) New York: McGraw-Hill, 1950.

Hurlock, Elizabeth B. *Child development.* (3rd ed.) New York: McGraw-Hill, 1956.

Hurlock, Elizabeth B. *Child development.* (4th ed.) New York: McGraw-Hill, 1964.

Huston, J. P. Reinforcement reduction. A method of training ratio behavior. *Science*, 1968, 159, 444.

Hyden, H. Biochemical aspects of learning and memory. In K. H. Pribram (Ed.), *On the biology of learning.* New York: Harcourt, Brace, Jovanovich, 1969.

Ibsen, H. *A doll's house* (1879). Boston: W. H. Baker, 1928.

Ilg, Frances L., and Ames, Louise B. *School readiness.* New York: Harper & Row, 1965.

Inhelder, B. Intelligence and memory. Lecture at meeting of *American Educational Research Association*, Los Angeles, March 1969.

Inhelder, B., and Piaget J. *The growth of logical thinking from childhood to adolescence.* New York: Basic Books, 1958.

Irwin, O. C. The amount and nature of activities of newborn infants. *Genetic Psychological Monographs*, 1930, 8, 1–192.

Isaac, S., and Michael, W. B. *Handbook in research and evaluation.* San Diego, Calif.: Robert R. Knapp.

Jackson, P. W., and Messick, S. The person, the product and the response: Conceptual problems in the assessment of creativity. *Journal of Personality*, 1965, 33, 309–329.

Jackson, P. W., and Messick, S. *Characteristics of creative production and products.* New York: McGraw-Hill, 1967.

Jacobsen, C. F., Wolfe, J. B., and Jackson, J. A. An experimental analysis of the functions of frontal association areas in primates. *Journal of Nervous and Mental Diseases 1, 1935, 82, 1–14.*

Jacobson, A. L., Babich, F. R., Bubash, Suzanne, and Jacobson, Ann. Differential approach tendencies produced by injections of RNA from trained rats. *Science*, 1965, 150, 636–637.

Jacobson, E. *Progressive relaxation.* Chicago: University of Chicago Press, 1938.

Jenkins, J. R. Effects of incidental cues and encoding strategies on paired associate learning. *Journal of Educational Psychology*, 1968, 59, 410–413.

Jenkins, M. D. Intellectually superior Negro youth: Problems and needs. *Journal of Negro Education*, 1950, 19, 322–332.

Jensen, A. R. Social class, race, and genetics: Implications for education. *American Educational Research Journal*, 1968, 51, 1–42.

Jensen, A. R. How much can we boost IQ and scholastic achievement? *Harvard Educational Review*, Winter 1969, 39 (1).

Jersild, A. T. *Child psychology.* Englewood Cliffs, N.J.: Prentice-Hall, 1954.

Joffe, J. M. *Prenatal determinants of behavior.* Oxford: Pergamon Press, 1969.

Johntz, W. Teaching and testing the disadvantaged. *Proceedings of the Western Regional Conference on Testing Problems.* Berkeley, Calif.: Educational Testing Service, 1966.

Jonçich, Geraldine. *The sane positivist: A biography of Edward L. Thorndike.* Middletown, Conn.: Wesleyan University Press, 1968.

Jones, Mary C. The development of early behavior patterns in young children. *Journal of Genetic Psychology*, 1926, 33, 537–585.

Jones, Mary C. The later careers of boys who were early or late maturing. *Child Development*, 1957, 28, 113–128.

Jones, Mary C. A study of socialization patterns at the high school level. *Journal of Genetic Psychology*, 1958, 40, 87–111.

Jones, Mary C., and Bayley, Nancy. Physical maturing among boys as related to behavior. *Journal of Educational Psychology*, 1950, 41, 129–148.

Jones, Mary C., and Mussen, P. H. Self-conceptions, motivations, and interpersonal attitudes of early and late maturing girls. *Child Development*, 1958, 29, 491–501.

Jost, H., and Sontag, L. W. The genetic factor in autonomic nervous system function. *Psychosomatic Medicine*, 1944, 6, 308–310.

Jung , C. G. *The collected works of . . .* (Edited by H. Read, M. Fordham, and A. Adler) New York: Pantheon, 1957.

Kagan, J., and Lewis, M. Studies of attention in the human infant. *Merrill-Palmer Quarterly of Behavior and Development*, 1965, 11, 95–127.

Kagan, J., and Moss, H. A. The stability of passive and dependent behavior from childhood through adulthood. *Child Development*, 1960, 31, 577–591.

Karraker, R. J. Token reinforcement systems in regular public school classrooms. In Carl E. Petts, (Ed.), *Operant conditioning in the classroom.* New York: Thomas Y. Crowell, 1971.

Katona, G. *Organizing and memorizing: Studies in the psychology of learning and teaching.* New York: Columbia University Press, 1940.

Katz, Phyllis A., and Deutsch, M. *Visual and auditory efficiency and its relationship to reading in children.* New York Medical College, Institute for Developmental Studies, 1963.

Keats, J. A. *Formal and concrete thought processes.* Princeton, N. J.: Princeton University, Department of Psychology, 1955.

Kelley, T. L. *Essential traits of mental life.* Cambridge, Mass.: Harvard University Press, 1935.

Kellogg, Rhoda, and O'Dell, Scott. *Psychology of children's art.* New York: Random House, 1967.

Kellogg, W. N., and Kellogg, L. A. *The ape and the child: A study of environmental influence upon early behavior.* New York: McGraw-Hill, 1933.

Kendler, H. H. *Basic psychology.* New York: Appleton-Century-Crofts, 1963.

Kendler, H. H., and Kendler, Tracy S. Vertical and horizontal processes in problem solving. *Psychological Review*, 1962, 69, 1–16.

Kennedy, W. A., Van de Riet, V., and White, J. A normative sample of intelligence and achievement of Negro elementary school children in the southeastern United States. *Monographs of the Society for Research in Child Development*, 1963, 28, No. 6.

Kibler, R. J., Barker, L. L., and Miles, D. T. *Behavioral objectives and instruction.* Boston: Allyn and Bacon, 1970.

Kidd, Aline H., and Rivoire, Jeanne (Eds.). *Perceptual development in children.* New York. International Universities Press, 1966.

Kimmel, Mary E. Antabuse in a clinic program. *American Journal of Nursing*, 1971, 7(6), 1173–1175.

Kinsey, A. C. *Sexual behavior in the human female.* Philadelphia: Saunders, 1953.

Kinsey, A. C., Pomeroy, W. B., and Martin, C. E. *Sexual behavior in the human male.* Philadelphia: Saunders, 1948.

Klein, G. S., and Krech, D. The problem of personality and its theory. *Journal of Personality*, 1951, 20, 2–24.

Koch, R. The dilemma of the clinician in the diagnosis of mental retardation. Paper presented at the meeting of the California State Psychological Association, Santa Barbara, Jan. 26, 1968.

Koegel, R. L., and Covert, Andrea. Self-stimulation-induced interference with learning in autistic children. Santa Barbara, California Institute of Applied Behavioral Science, University of California, Santa Barbara, 1972, 17 pp. (Mimeographed)

Kohler, W. *The mentality of apes.* (Translated by E. Winter) New York: Harcourt, Brace & World, 1925.

Korr, I. M., Wilkinson, P. N., and Chornock, F. W. Axonal delivery of neuroplasmic components to muscle cells. *Science*, 1967, 155, 342–345.

Krathwohl, D. R., and Payne, D. A. Defining and assessing educational objectives. In Robert L. Thorndike (Ed.), *Educational measurement*, Washington, D. C.: American Council on Education, 1970, pp. 17–45.

Krathwohl, D. R., Bloom, B. S., and Masia, B. B. *Taxonomy of educational objectives: The affective domain.* Handbook II. New York: McKay, 1964.

Krech, D., Rosenzweig, M. R., and Bennett, D. Effect of learning on ability to learn. Paper presented at the meeting of the California Educational Research Association, San Francisco, March 1958.

Krech, D., Rosenzweig, M. R., and Bennett, E. L. Effects of environmental complexity and training on brain chemistry. *Journal of Comparative and Physiological Psychology*, 1960, 53, 509–519.

Kretschmer, E. *Physique and character.* (Translated by W. J. H. Sprott) New York: Harcourt, Brace & World, 1925.

Kretschmer, E. *Physique and character.* (2nd ed.) London: Kegan Paul, Trench, Trubner & Co., Ltd., 1945.

Kuznets, G. M., and McNemar, O. Sex differences in intelligence test scores. In G. M. Whipple (Ed.), *Intelligence: Its nature and nurture.*

Thirty-ninth Yearbook of the National Society for the Study of Education. Bloomington, Ill.: Public School, 1940, pp. 211–220.

Lambert, W. W., Solomon, R. L., and Watson, P. D. Reinforcement and extinction as factors in size estimation. In D. S. Palermo and L. P. Lipsitt (Eds.), *Research readings in child psychology.* New York: Holt, 1963.

Lazarus, A. A. Group therapy of phobic disorders by systematic desensitization. *Journal of Abnormal and Social Psychology*, 1961, 63, 504–510.

Lazarus, A. A. The results of behavior therapy in 126 cases of severe neurosis. *Behavior Research and Therapy*, 1963, 1, 69–79.

Lazarus, A. A. Behavior therapy in groups. In G. M. Gazda (Ed.), *Basic approaches to group psychotherapy and counseling.* Springfield, Ill.: Charles C Thomas, 1968, pp. 149–175.

Lazovick, A. D., and Lang, P. J. A laboratory demonstration of systematic desensitization psychotherapy. *Journal of Psychological Studies*, 1960, 11, 238–247.

Lee, J. M., and Lee, Dorris May. *The child and his curriculum.* New York: Appleton-Century-Crofts, 1950.

Lesser, G. S., Fifer, G., and Clark, D. H. Mental abilities of children from different social class and cultural groups. *Monographs of the Society for Research in Child Development*, 1965, 30, No. 4.

Lessing, L. Getting the whole picture from holography. *Fortune*, September 1971, 84 (3), 110–114, 144, 146.

Lewin, K. *A dynamic theory of personality.* (Translated by K. E. Zener and D. K. Adams) New York: McGraw-Hill, 1935.

Li, Choh Hao, and Dixon, J. S. Retention of the biological potency of human pituitary growth hormone after reduction and carbonidomethylation. *Science*, 1966, 154, 785–786.

Lichtenstein, F. E. Studies in anxiety: I. The production of a feeding inhibition in dogs. *Journal of Comparative and Physiological Psychology*, 1950, 43, 16–29.

Lieberman, M. A. Behavior and impact of leaders. In L. N. Solomon and Betty Berzon (Eds.), *New perspectives in encounter groups.* San Francisco: Jossey-Bass, 1972, pp. 135–170.

Lieberman, M. A., Yalom, I. D., Miles, M. B. Impact on participants. In L. N. Solomon and Betty Berzon (Eds.), *New perspectives in encounter groups.* San Francisco: Jossey-Bass, 1972, pp. 119–134.

Lindeman, R. H. *Educational measurement.* Chicago: Scott, Foresman, 1967.

Lindvall, C. M. *Measuring pupil achievement and aptitude.* New York: Harcourt, Brace & World, 1967.

Lorenz, K. Innate bases of learning. In K. H. Pribram, *On the Biology of Learning.* New York. Harcourt Brace Jovanovich, 1969.

Loretan, J. G. Decline and fall of group intelligence testing. *Teachers College Record*, 1965, 65, 10–17.

Loretan, J. G., and Umans, S. *Teaching the disadvantaged.* New York: Teachers College, 1966.

Lovaas, O. I., Freitas, L., Nelson, K., and Whalen, C. The establishment of imitation and its use for the development of complex behavior in schizophrenic children. *Behavior Research and Therapy*, 1967, 5, 171–181.

Lovaas, O. I., and Schreibman, Laura. Stimulus overselectivity of autistic children in a two-stimulus situation. *Behavior Research and Therapy*, 1971, 9, 305–310.

Lovell, K. and Gorton, A. A study of some differences between backward and normal readers of average intelligence. *British Journal of Educational Psychology*, November 1968, 38 (3), 240–248.

Lowenfield, V. *Creative and mental growth.* New York: Macmillan, 1957.

MacKinnon, D. W. The structure of personality. In J. McV. Hunt (Ed.), *Personality and the behavior disorders.* New York: Ronald, 1944, 3–48.

MacKinnon, D. W. Personality and the realization of creative potential. *American Psychologist*, 1965, 20, 273–281.

Mace, G. A. Psychology and aesthetics. *British Journal of Aesthetics*, 1962, 2, 3–16.

Maddi, S. R. Motivational aspects of creativity. *Journal of Personality*, 1965, 33, 330–347.

Madsen, C. H., Becker, W. C., and Thomas, D. R. Rules, praise and ignoring: Elements of elementary classroom control. *Journal of Applied Behavior Analysis*, Summer 1968, 139–150.

Madsen, C. H., Becker, W. C., and Thomas, D. R. Rules, praise and ignoring: Elements of elementary classroom control. In Carl E. Pitts (Ed.), *Operant conditioning in the classroom.* New York: Thomas Y. Crowell, 1971, pp. 194–212.

Mager, R. F. *Preparing instructional objectives.* Palo Alto, Calif.: Fearon, 1962.

Magnusson, D. *Test theory.* Reading, Mass.: Addison-Wesley, 1967.

Mahl, G. F., Rothenberg, A. Jr., Delgado, M. R., and Hamlin, H. Psychological responses in the human to intracerebral electrical stimulation. *Psychosomatic Medicine,* 1964, 26, 337–368.

Maier, H. W. *Three theories of child development.* New York: Harper & Row, 1965.

Mandler, G. Transfer of training as a function of degree of response overlearning. *Journal of Experimental Psychology,* 1954, 47, 411–417.

Marshall, Sybil. *Experiment in education.* London: Cambridge University Press, 1963.

Maslow, A. H. A theory of human motivation. *Psychological Review,* 1943, 50, 370–396.

Maslow, A. H. *Toward a psychology of being.* (2nd ed.) Princeton, N. J.: Van Nostrand, 1968.

Maslow, A. H. *The farther reaches of human nature.* New York: Viking, 1971.

Mathis, B. C., Cotton, J. W., and Sechrest, L. *Psychological foundations of education: Learning and teaching.* New York: Academic, 1970.

McAulay, J. D. What's wrong with social studies? *Social Education,* 1952, 16, 377–378.

McClelland, D. C. *Personality.* New York: Sloane, 1951.

McConnell, J. V., Jacobson, A. L., and Kimbel, D. P. Flatworm reaction to shock. In S. A. Mednick (Ed.), *Learning.* Englewood Cliffs, N. J.: Prentice-Hall, 1964.

McDonald, F. J. *Educational psychology.* San Francisco: Wadsworth, 1959.

Mehler, J., and Bever, T. G. Cognitive capacity of very young children. *Science,* 1967, 158, 141–142.

Menzies, R. Further studies on conditioned vasomotor responses in human subjects. *Journal of Experimental Psychology,* 1941, 29, 457–482.

Merrill, M. A. The significance of the I.Q.'s on the revised Stanford-Binet scale. *Journal of Educational Psychology,* 1938, 29, 641–651.

Merry, Frieda K., and Merry, R. V. *The first two decades of life.* New York: Harper & Row, 1950.

Merry, Frieda K., and Merry, R. V. *The first two decades of life.* (2nd ed.) New York: Harper & Row, 1958.

Metfessel, N. S., and Michael, W. B. A paradigm involving multiple criterion measures for the evaluation of the effectiveness of school programs. *Educational and Psychological Measurement,* 1967, 27, 931–943.

Metfessel, N. S., Michael, W. B., and Kirsner, D. A. Instrumentation of Bloom's and Krathwohl's taxonomies for the writing of educational objectives. *Psychology in the Schools,* 1969, 6(3), 227–231.

Metropolitan Life Assurance. How old are you? In P. H. Mussen and J. J. Conger, *Child development and personality.* New York: Harper & Row, 1956, p. 317.

Michael, W. B., and Metfessel, N. S. A paradigm for developing valid measurable objectives in the evaluation of educational programs in colleges and universities. *Educational and Psychological Measurement,* 1967, 27, 373–383.

Michael, W. B., Michael, J. J., and Zimmerman, W. S. *Study attitudes and methods survey.* San Diego: Educational and Industrial Testing Service, 1972.

Miller, N. E. Learnable drives and rewards. In S. S. Stevens (Ed.), *Handbook of experimental psychology.* New York: Wiley, 1951, 435–472.

Mink, W. D., Best, P. J., and Olds, J. Neurons in paradoxial sleep and motivated behavior. *Science,* 1967, 148, 1335–1337.

Money, J., and Ehrenhardt, A. A. Preservation of I.Q. in hyperthyroidism of childhood. *American Journal of Mental Deficiency,* 1966, 71, 237–243.

Monroe, Marion. *Reading aptitude test manual.* Boston: Houghton Mifflin, 1935.

Montessori, Maria. *The Montessori method* (1909). New York: Schocken Books, 1964.

Montgomery J., and McBurney, R. Orientation talk to relatives of residents. In C. E. Pitts (Ed.) *Operant conditioning in the classroom.* New York: Thomas Y. Crowell, 1971, pp. 105–112.

Moore, Gladys B. To buy or not to buy. *Journal of Reading,* March 1970, 13 (6), 437–440.

Moore, O. K., and Anderson, A. R. The responsive

environments project. In R. D. Hess and Roberta M. Bear (Eds.), *Early education: Current theory, research and practice.* Chicago: Aldine, 1968, pp. 171–189.

More, D. M. Developmental concordance and discordance during puberty and early adolescence. *Monographs of the Society for Research of Child Development*, 1953, 18, No. 1.

Moss, H. A. Sex, age, and state as determinants of mother-infant interaction. *Merrill-Palmer Quarterly*, 1967, 13, No. 1, 19–36.

Mowrer, O. H. *Learning theory and personality dynamics.* New York: Ronald, 1950.

Mowrer, O. H. The psychologist looks at language. *American Psychologist*, 1954, 9, 660–694.

Mowrer, O. H. Integrity group principles and procedures. *The Counseling Psychologist*, 1972, 3(2), 7–33.

Mussen, P. H. *The psychological development of the child.* Englewood Cliffs, N. J.: Prentice-Hall, 1963.

Mussen, P. H., and Conger, J. J. *Child development and personality.* New York: Harper & Row, 1956.

Mussen, P. H., and Jones, Mary C. The behavior-inferred motivations of late and early maturing boys. *Child Development*, 1958, 29, 61–67.

Newberry, H. The measurement of three types of fetal activity. *Journal of Comparative Psychology*, 1941, 32, 521–530.

Newman, H. H., Freeman, F. N., and Holzinger, K. J. *Twins: A study of heredity and environment.* Chicago: University of Chicago Press, 1937.

Nilsson, L. Drama of life before birth. *Life*, Apr. 30, 1965, 54–72.

Nimnicht, G., Meier, J., McAfee, O., and Rogers, B. Progress report on research at the new nursery school. Greeley: Colorado State College, 1967. (Mimeographed)

Olds, J. *The growth and structure of motives.* New York: Free Press, 1956.

Olds, J. Differentiation of reward systems in the brain by self-stimulation techniques. In E. R. Ramey and D. S. O'Doherty (Eds.), *Electrical studies of the unanesthetized brain.* New York: Harper & Row, 1960, pp. 17–51.

Olmstead, R. W., and Jackson, E. B. Self-demand feeding in the first week of life. *Pediatrics*, 1950, 6, 396–401.

Olsson, P. A., and Myers, I. L. Non-verbal techniques in an adolescent group. *International Journal of Group Psychotherapy*, 1972, 22(2), 186–191.

Otis, A. S. *The Otis group intelligence scale manual of directions.* (Rev. ed.) New York: Harcourt, Brace & World, 1921.

Palermo, D. S., and Lipsitt, L. P. (Eds.). *Research readings in child psychology.* New York: Holt, 1963.

Pasamanick, B., and Knoblock, H. The contributions of some organic factors to school retardation in Negro children. In S. W. Webster (Ed.), *The disadvantaged learner.* San Francisco: Chandler, 1966.

Patterson, G. R. Responsiveness to social stimuli. In L. Krasner and L. P. Ullman (Eds.), *Research in behavior modification.* New York: Holt, 1965(a), pp. 157–178.

Patterson, G. R. An application of conditioning techniques to the control of a hyperactive child. In L. P. Ullman and L. Krasner (Eds.), *Case studies in behavior modification.* New York: Holt, 1965(b), pp. 370–375.

Paul, G. L. Outcome of systematic desensitization. I. Background procedures, and uncontrolled reports of individual treatment. In C. M. Franks (Ed.), *Behavior therapy appraisal and status.* New York: McGraw-Hill, 1969(a).

Paul, G. L. Outcome of systematic desensitization. II. Controlled investigations of individual treatment technique variations, and current status. In C. M. Franks (Ed.), *Behavior therapy appraisal and status.* New York: McGraw-Hill, 1969(b).

Paul, G. L. Inhibition of physiological response to stressful imagery by relaxation training and hypnotically suggested relaxation. *Behavior Research and Therapy*, 1969(c), 7, 249–256. Oxford: Pergamon Press.

Pavlov, I. P. L'excitation psychique des glandes salivaires. *Journal de psychologie*, 1910, 7, 107–114.

Pavlov, I. P. *Conditional reflexes.* London: Oxford University Press, 1927.

Peller, L. E. Language and development. In P. B. Neubauer (Ed.), *Concepts of development in early childhood education.* Springfield, Ill.: C. C. Thomas, 1965.

Penfield, W. The cerebral cortex in man. I. The

cerebral cortex and consciousness. *Archives of Neurology and Psychiatry*, 1938, 40, 417–442.

Penfield, W. Consciousness memory, and man's conditional reflexes. In K. H. Pribram (Ed.), *On the biology of learning.* New York: Harcourt Brace Jovanovich, 1969.

Penfield, W., and Jasper, H. H. *Epilepsy and the functional anatomy of the human brain.* Boston: Little, Brown, 1954.

Penfield, W., and Roberts, L. *Speech and brain mechanisms.* Princeton, N. J.: Princeton University Press, 1959.

Perls, F. S. *Gestalt therapy verbatim.* Lafayette, Calif.: Real People Press,1969.

Peterson, D. R., and London, P. A role for cognition in the behavioral treatment of a child's eliminative disturbance. In L. P. Ullman and L. Krasner (Eds.), *Case studies in behavior modification.* New York: Holt, 1965, pp. 289–295.

Phillips, E. L. Achievement place: Token reinforcement procedures in a home style rehabilitation setting for "pre-delinquent" boys. In C. E. Pitts (Ed.), *Operant conditioning in the classroom.* New York: Thomas Y. Crowell, 1971, pp. 120–136.

Phillips, Laura W. Mediated verbal similarity as a determinant of the generalization of a conditioned GSR. *Journal of Experimental Psychology*, 1958, 55, 56–62.

Piaget, J. *The language and thought of the child.* New York: Harcourt, Brace & World, 1926.

Piaget, J. *Judgment and reasoning in the child.* New York: Harcourt, Brace & World, 1928.

Piaget, J. *The child's conception of the world.* New York: Harcourt, Brace & World, 1929.

Piaget, J. *The child's conception of physical causality.* London: Routledge, 1930.

Piaget, J. *Play dreams and imitation in childhood.* New York: Norton, 1951.

Piaget, J. *The origins of intelligence in children.* New York: International Universities Press, 1952.

Piaget, J. *The construction of reality in the child.* New York: Basic Books, 1954.

Piaget, J. Les relations entre la perception et l'intelligence dans le dévelopment de l'enfant. *Bulletin de Psychologie*, 1956, 10, 376–381.

Piaget, J. In J. Tanner and B. Inhelder (Eds.), *Discussions on child development.* Vol. 3. New York: International Universities Press, 1958, p. 114.

Piaget, Jean. *The theory of stages in cognitive development.* Monterey, Calif.: CTB/McGraw-Hill, 1969.

Piaget, J. *Structuralism.* New York: Basic Books, 1970.

Piaget, J., and Inhelder, B. *The growth of logical thinking from childhood to adolescence.* New York: Basic Books, 1956.

Pines, Maya, *Revolution in learning.: The child from one to six.* New York: Harper & Row, 1967.

Pitman, I. J. Learning to read. *Journal of the Royal Society of Arts*, 1961, 109, 149–180.

Platt, J. R. *Excitement of science.* Boston: Houghton Mifflin, 1962.

Popham, W. J. Simplified designs for school research. In R. E. Schutz and R. L. Baker, *Instructional product research.* New York: American Book, 1972, pp. 137–160.

Popham, W. J., and Baker, E. *Establishing instructional goals.* Englewood Cliffs, N. J. Prentice-Hall, 1969.

Pratt, K. C. The neonate. In L. Carmichael (Ed.), *Manual of child psychology.* New York: Wiley, 1954, pp. 190–254.

Premack, D. The education of Sarah: A chimp learns the language. *Psychology Today*, 1970, 4, 55–58.

Pressy, L. W. Sex differences shown by 2544 children on a group scale of intelligence, with special reference to variability. *Journal of Applied Psychology*, 1918. 2, 323–340.

Preston, R. C. *Teaching social studies in elementary schools.* New York: Holt, 1957.

Pribram, K. H. (Ed.) *Brain and behavior adaptation.* Baltimore: Penguin, 1969.

Pribram, K. H. *Languages of the brain.* Englewood Cliffs, N. J.: Prentice-Hall, 1971.

Psychological Corporation. *Test Service Bulletin No. 48* New York: Psychological Corporation, 1955.

Rank, O. *The trauma of birth.* New York: Harcourt, Brace & World, 1929.

Raven, J. C. The comparative assessment of personality. *British Journal of Psychology*, 1950, 60, 115–124.

Razran, G. H. S. A simple technique for controlling

subjective attitudes in salivary conditioning of adult human subjects. *Science*, 1939, 89, 160–161.

Reynolds, J. H. Cognitive transfer in verbal learning. *Journal of Educational Psychology*, 1966, 57, 382–388.

Reynolds, J. H. Cognitive transfer in verbal learning: II. *Journal of Educational Psychology*, 1968, 59, 133–138.

Rheingold, H. L., Gewirtz, J. L., and Ross, H. W. Social conditioning of vocalizations in the infant. *Journal of Comparative and Physiological Psychology*, 1959, 52, 68–73,

Rich, J. M. *Humanistic foundations of education.* Belmont, Calif.: Wadsworth, 1971.

Risley, T., and Wolf, M. M. Establishing functional speech in echolalic children. *Behavior Research and Therapy*, 1967, 5, 73–88.

Robeck, M. J. A study of the revision process in program instruction. Unpublished master's thesis, University of California, Los Angeles, 1965.

Robeck, Mildred C. Subtest patterning of problem readers on the WISC. *California Journal of Educational Research*, 1960, 11, 110–115.

Robeck, Mildred C. Children who show unusual tension when reading: A group diagnosis. In J. A. Figurel (Ed.), *Challenge and experiment in reading: International Reading Association Conference.* New York: Scholastics Magazine, 1962, pp. 7, 133–138.

Robeck, Mildred C. Effects of prolonged reading disability: A preliminary study. *Perceptual and Motor Skills*, 1964, 19, 7–12.

Robeck, Mildred C. *How the anthropologist studies man.* Sacramento: California Project Talent, California State Department of Education, 1965.

Robeck, Mildred C. *Acceleration programs for intellectually gifted students.* Sacramento: California State Department of Education, 1968(a).

Robeck, Mildred C. *Special class programs for intellectually gifted students.* Sacramento: California State Department of Education, 1968(b).

Robeck, Mildred C. Identifying and preventing reading disabilities. In J. A. R. Wilson (Ed.), *Diagnosis of learning difficulties.* New York: McGraw-Hill, 1971, p. 157–188.

Robeck, Mildred C., and Wilson, J. A. R. *KELP summary test booklet.* New York: McGraw-Hill, 1967.

Robeck, Mildred C. and Wilson, J. A. R. *Psychology of reading: Foundations of instruction.* New York: Wiley, 1974.

Rock, Irvin. *The nature of perceptual adaptation.* New York: Basic Books, 1966.

Roe, Anne. *Early differentiation of interests: A report to the Second (1957) Research Conference on the Identification of Scientific Talent.* Salt Lake City: University of Utah Press, 1958.

Rogers, C. R. *Counseling and psychotherapy: Newer concepts in practice.* Boston: Houghton Mifflin, 1942.

Rogers, C. R. *Client-centered therapy.* Boston: Houghton Mifflin, 1951.

Rogers, C. R. The characteristics of a helping relationship. *Personnel and Guidance Journal*, 1958, 37, 6–16.

Rogers, C.R. Some thoughts regarding the current presuppositions of the behavioral sciences. In W. R. Coulson and C. R. Rogers, (Eds.), *Man and the science of man.* Columbus, Ohio: Merrill, 1968, pp. 55–83.

Rogers, C. R. Foreword, In L. N. Solomon and Betty Berzon (Eds.), *New perspectives in encounter groups.* San Francisco: Jossey-Bass, 1972.

Romer, A. S. Major steps in vertebrate evolution. *Science*, 1967, 158, 1629–1638.

Rosen, B. C. and D'Andrade, R. The psycho-social origins of achievement motivation. *Sociometry*, 1959, 22, 185–195; 215–217.

Rosenberg, M. J. Cognitive reorganization in response to the hypnotic reversal of attitudinal affect. *Journal of Personality*, 1960, 28, 39–63.

Rosenthal, R., and Jacobson, Lenore. *Pygmalion in the classroom.* New York: Holt, 1968.

Rosenzweig, M. R., Krech, D., and Bennett, E. L. Brain chemistry and adaptive behavior. In H. F. Harlow and C. H. Woolsey (Eds.), *Biological and biochemical bases of behavior.* Madison: University of Wisconsin Press, 1958, pp. 367–400.

Rosenzweig, M. R., Krech, D., and Bennett, E. L. Heredity, environment, brain biochemistry, and learning. In W. Dennis (Ed.), *Current trends in psychological theory.* Pittsburgh: University of Pittsburgh Press, 1961, pp. 87–110.

Rothbart, Mary K. Birth order and mother-child interaction in an achievement situation. *Journal of Personality and Social Psychology*, 1971, 17, No. 2, 113–120.

Rusk, R. R. The intelligence of Scottish children. In G. M. Whipple (Ed.), *Intelligence: Its nature and nurture.* Thirty-ninth Yearbook of the National Society for the Study of Education. Bloomington, Ill.: Public School, 1940.

Ryans, D. G. *Characteristics of teachers.* Washington, D.C.: American Council on Education, 1960.

Sakulina, N. P. The significance of drawing in the sensory training of the pre-school child. *Sensory Training of Pre-School Children*, Moscow: Izd Akad., Pedag. Nauk RSFSR, 1963.

Salzinger, Suzanne, Salzinger, K., Portnoy, Stephanie, Eckman, P. M., Deutsch, M., and Zubin, J. Operant conditioning of continuous speech in young children. *Child Development*, 1962, 33, 683–695.

Sandiford, P. *Educational psychology.* New York: Longmans, 1928.

Sarkisov, S. A. *The structure and functions of the brain.* Naomi Raskin, translation editor. Bloomington, Ind.: University Press, 1966.

Schmidt, G. W., and Ulrich, R. F. Effects of group contingent events upon classroom noise. *Journal of Applied Behavior Analysis*, 1969, 2, 171–179.

Schmidt, G. W., and Ulrich, R. E. Effects of group contingent events upon classroom noise. In C. E. Pitts (ed.), *Operant conditioning in the classroom.* New York: Thomas Y. Crowell, 1971, pp. 252–266.

Schopenhauer, A. *The world as will and idea* (1819). (Translated by R. B. Haldane and J. Kemp) London: Routledge, 1948.

Schultz, W. C., and Seashore, C. Promoting growth with non-verbal exercises. In L. N. Solomon and Betty Berzon (Eds.), *New perspectives on encounter groups.* San Francisco: Jossey-Bass, 1972, pp. 188–194.

Schwartz, A., and Tiedeman, S. C. *Evaluating student progress in the secondary school.* New York: Longmans, 1957.

Scott, W. A. Attitude change through reward of verbal behavior. *Journal of Abnormal and Social Psychology*, 1957, 55, 72–75.

Searle, L. V. The organization of hereditary brightness and maze-dullness. *Genetic Psychological Monographs*, 1949, 39, 279–325.

Sears, P. S. Levels of aspiration in academically successful and unsuccessful children. *Journal of Abnormal and Social Psychology*, 1940, 335, 498–536.

Sears, R. R., Rau, Lucy, and Alpert, R. *Identification and child rearing.* Stanford, Calif.: Stanford University Press, 1965.

Segundo, J. P., Galeano, C., Sommer-Smith, J. A., and Roig, J. A. Behavioral and E.E.G. effects of tones reinforced by cessation of painful stimuli. In A. Fessar, R. W. Gerard, J. Konorski, and J. F. Delafresnaye (Eds.), *Brain mechanisms and learning.* Springfield, Ill.: Charles C Thomas, 1961, pp. 265–292.

Selye, H. *The stress of life.* New York: McGraw-Hill, 1956.

Semler, I. T., and Iscoe, I. Structure of intelligence in Negro and white children. *Journal of Educational Psychology*, 1966, 57, 326–336.

Shapiro, S. B. Tradition innovation. In A. Burton, *Encounter: The theory and practice of encounter groups.* San Francisco, Calif.: Jossey-Bass, 1969.

Sheldon, W. H. *The varieties of human physique.* New York: Harper & Row, 1940.

Sheldon, W. H., Dupertius, C. W., and McDermott, E. *Atlas of man: A guide for somato typing the adult male at all ages.* New York: Harper & Row, 1954.

Sherfey, Mary Jane. *The nature and nurture of female sexuality.* New York: Random House, 1972.

Sherif, M. *The psychology of social norms.* New York: Harper & Row, 1936.

Sherman, J. A., and Baer, D. M. Appraisal of operant therapy techniques with children and adults. In C. M. Franks (Ed.), *Behavior therapy: Appraisal and status.* New York: McGraw-Hill, 1969.

Sherman, M., and Key, C. B. The intelligence of isolated mountain children. *Child Development*, 1932, 3, 279–290.

Shirley, Mary M. *The first two years: A study of twenty-five babies.* Vol. 2. Minneapolis: University of Minnesota Press, 1933, Child Welfare Monograph, No. 7.

Shirley, Mary M. A behavior syndrome characterizing prematurely born children. *Child Development*, 1939, 10, 115–128.

Shuey, A. M. *The testing of Negro intelligence.* Lynchburg, Va.: J. P. Bell, 1958.

Shultz, G. Uninsulted child. *Ladies Home Journal*, June 1956, 73, 60–63.

Silberman, C. E. Let's give slum children the chance they need. *SRA Insight*, 1964, 4, 1–2.

Simpson, G. G. The crisis in biology. *American Scholar*, 1967, 36, 363–377.

Skinner, B. F. *Science and human behavior*. New York: Macmillan, 1953.

Skinner, B. F. The science of learning and the art of teaching. *Harvard Educational Review*, 1954, 24, 86–97.

Skinner, B. F. The experimental analysis of behavior. *American Scientist*, 1957, 45, 347–371.

Skinner, B. F. Teaching machines. *Science*, 1958, 128, 969–977.

Skinner, B. F. *Cumulative record*. New York: Appleton-Century-Crofts, 1961.

Skinner, B. F. Learning and behavior. New York: Carousel Films, 1962.

Skinner, B. F. Teaching science in high school: What is wrong? *Science*, 1968, 159, 704–710.

Skinner, B. F. *Beyond freedom and dignity*. New York: Alfred A. Knopf, 1971.

Slobodian, June. Girls not superior after all? *Phi Delta Kappan*, 1966, 48, 180–181.

Sluckin, W. *Imprinting and early learning.* Chicago, Ill.: Aldine, 1965.

Smedslund, J. The acquisition of conservation of substance and weight in children. II. External reinforcement of conservation of weight and of the operations of addition and subtraction. *Scandinavian Journal of Psychology*, 1961(a), 2, 71–84.

Smedslund, J. The acquisition of conservation of substance and weight in children. III. Extinction of conservation of weight acquired "normally" and by means of empirical controls on a balance scale. *Scandinavian Journal of Psychology*, 1961(b), 2, 85–87.

Smedslund, J. The acquisition of conservation of substance and weight in children. V. Practice in conflict situations without external reinforcement. *Scandinavian Journal of Psychology*, 1961(c), 2, 156–160.

Smedslund, J. The acquisition of conservation of substance and weight in children. VI. Practice on continuous vs. discontinuous material in conflict situations without external reinforcement. *Scandinavian Journal of Psychology*, 1961(d), 2, 203–210.

Smith, H. C. Psychometric checks on hypotheses derived from Sheldon's work on physique and temperament. *Journal of Personality*, 1949, 17, 310–320.

Snedecor, G. W. *Statistical methods*. Ames, Iowa: Iowa State University Press, 1940.

Snygg, D. The relative difficulty of mechanically equivalent tasks. I. Human learning. *Pedagogical Seminary and Journal of Genetic Psychology*, December 1935, 47(2), 299–320.

Spache, G. D. Personality patterns of retarded readers. *Journal of Educational Research*, 1957, 30, 461–469.

Spache, G. D. Is this a breakthrough in reading? *Reading Teacher*, January 1962, 14–15, 258–263.

Spalding, Romalda Bishop, and Spalding, W. T. *Writing road to reading*. New York: Morrow, 1969.

Spearman, C. General intelligence objectively determined and measured. *American Journal of Psychology*, 1904, 15, 201–293.

Spearman, C. *The abilities of man*. New York: Macmillan, 1927.

Spearman, C., and Jones, L. W. *Human ability*. London: Macmillan, 1950.

Sperry, R. W. Cerebral organization and behavior. *Science*, 1961, 133, 1749–1757.

Stephens, J. M. *Educational psychology*. New York: Holt, 1952.

Stoddard, G. D. *The meaning of intelligence*. New York: Macmillan, 1943.

Stodola, Q. *Making the classroom test: A guide for teachers*. Evaluation and Advisory Service Series, No. 4. Princeton, N. J.: Educational Testing Service, 1959.

Stone, I. *The passions of the mind: A novel of Sigmund Freud*. London: Cassell, 1971.

Strong, A. C. Three hundred fifty white and colored children measured by the Binet Simon measuring scale of intelligence: A comparative study. *Pedagogical Seminary and Journal of Genetic Psychology*, 1913, 20, 485–515.

Stott, R. H. *Child development, an individual longitudinal approach*. New York: Holt, Rinehart and Winston, 1967.

Stufflebeam, D. L. The relevance of the CIPP Evaluation Model for educational accountability. *Journal of Research and Development in Education*, 1971, 5, 19–25.

Stufflebeam, D. L., Foley, W. J., Gephart, W. J., Guba, E. G., Hammond, R. L., Merriam, H. O., and Provus, M. M. *Educational evaluation and design making.* PDK National Study Committee on Evaluation. Itasca, Ill.: Peacock, 1971.

Suchman, J. R. The child and the inquiry process. Paper presented at the Eighth ASCD Curriculum Research Institute, Western Section, Anaheim Calif., Dec. 3, 1962.

Sullivan, H. S. The illusion of personal individuality. *Psychiatry*, 1950, 13, 317–332.

Sullivan, W. *Sullivan associates readers.* New York: McGraw-Hill, 1965.

Suppes, P., and Hill, S. *First course in mathematical logic.* Boston: Ginn, 1965.

Sussman, D. Number readiness of kindergarten children. Unpublished doctoral dissertation, University of California, Los Angeles, 1962.

Swanson, J. R., Freedman, S. A., and Knight, M. R. *Florida Department of Education Planning Model.* Tallahassee, Fla.: Bureau of Research, Florida Department of Education.

Taba, Hilda, and Elkins, Deborah. *Teaching strategies for the culturally disadvantaged.* Chicago: Rand McNally, 1966.

Tanner, J. M. Earlier maturation in man. *Scientific American*, 1968, 218, 21–27.

Tanner, W. P. As reported in E. R. Hilgard and G. H. Bower, *Theories of learning.* New York: Appleton-Century-Crofts, 1966.

Taylor, S. E. *An evaluation of forty-one trainees who had recently completed the "reading dynamics" program.* Eleventh Yearbook of the National Reading Conference. Milwaukee, Wis., 1962.

Taylor, W. F. Close readability scores as indices of individual differences in comprehension and aptitude. *Journal of Applied Psychology*, February 1957, 41, 19–26.

Terman, L. M. *Measurement of intelligence.* Boston: Houghton Mifflin, 1916.

Terman, L. M. *Genetic studies of genius.* Stanford, Calif.: Stanford University Press, 1925, 1926, 1930, 1947, 1959, 5 vols.

Terman, L. M., amd Merrill, M. *Measuring intelligence.* Boston: Houghton Mifflin, 1937.

Terman, L. M., and Merrill, M. *Stanford-Binet intelligence scale.* Boston: Houghton Mifflin, 1960.

Terman, L. M., and Oden, M. H. *The gifted child grows up.* Stanford, Calif.: Stanford University Press, 1947.

Terman, L. M., and Oden, M. H. *The gifted group at mid life.* Stanford, Calif.: Stanford University Press, 1959.

Thomas, A., Chess, S., and Birch, H. G. *Temperament and behavior disorders in children.* New York: New York University Press, 1968.

Thomas, D. R., Becker, W. C., and Armstrong, Marianne. Production and elimination of disruptive classroom behavior by systematically varying teacher's behavior. In C. E. Pitts (Ed.), *Operant conditioning in the classroom.* New York: Thomas Y. Crowell, 1971, pp. 166–183.

Thompson, B. Longitudinal study of auditory discrimination. *Journal of Educational Research*, 1963, 56, 376–378.

Thompson, G. G. The effect of chronogical age on aesthetic preferences for rectangles of different proportions. *Journal of Experimental Psychology*, 1946, 36, 50–58.

Thompson, G. G., and Hunnicutt, C. W. The effect of repeated praise or blame on the work achievement of "introverts" and "extroverts." *Journal of Educational Psychology*, 1944, 35, 257–266.

Thompson, R. F., Mayers, Kathleen S., Robertson, R. T. and Patterson, Charlotte J. Number coding in association cortex of the cat. *Science*, April 10, 1970, 168: 271–273.

Thorndike, E. L. *Educational psychology.* Vol. 2. New York: Teachers College, 1913.

Thorndike, E. L. Mental discipline in high school studies. *Journal of Educational Psychology*, 1924, 15, 1–22, 83–98.

Thorndike, E. L. Sex differences in status and gain in intelligence scores from thirteen to eighteen. *Pedagogical Seminary and Journal of Genetic Psychology*, 1926, 33, 107–161.

Thorndike, R. L. Book Review: Rosenthal, R., and Jacobson, L. Pygmalion in the classroom. *American Educational Research Journal*, November 1968, 5(4), 708–711.

Thorndike, R. L., and Hagen, E. *Measurement and evaluation in psychology and education.* (2nd ed.) New York: Wiley, 1961.

Thorndike, R. L., and Hagen, E. *Measurement and evaluation in psychology and education.* (3rd ed.) New York: Wiley, 1969.

Thune, L. E. Warm up effect as a function of level of practice in verbal learning. *American Psychologist*, 1950, 5, 251.

Thurstone, L. L. *Multiple-factor analysis.* Chicago: University of Chicago Press, 1947.

Thurstone, L. L. *The differential growth of mental abilities.* Chapel Hill: University of North Carolina Psychometric Laboratory, Bulletin No. 14, 1955.

Tinker, M. A. *Bases for effective reading.* Minneapolis: University of Minnesota Press, 1965.

Todd, R. Notes on corporate man. *The Atlantic Monthly*, 1971, 228(4), 83–86.

Tolman, E. C. *Purposive behavior in animals and men.* New York: Appleton-Century-Crofts, 1932.

Tolman, E. C. *Purposive behavior in animals and men.* Berkeley: University of California Press, 1949.

Torrance, E. P. *Guiding creative talent.* Englewood Cliffs, N. J.: Prentice-Hall, 1963.

Torrance, E. P. *Gifted children in the classroom.* New York: Macmillan, 1965.

Torrance, E. P. Prediction of adult creative achievement among high school seniors. *Gifted Child Quarterly*, 1969, 13 (H), 223–229.

Tower, D. B. The neurochemical substrates of cerebral function and activity. In H. F. Harlow and C. H. Woolsey (Eds.), *Biological and biochemical bases of behavior.* Madison: University of Wisconsin Press, 1958, 285–366.

Tryon, R. C. Genetic differences in maze-learning ability in rats. In G. M. Whipple (Ed.), *Intelligence: Its nature and nurture.* Thirty-ninth Yearbook of the National Society for the Study of Education. Bloomington, Ill.: Public School, 1940.

Tuddenham, R. D. Jean Piaget and the world of the child. *American Psychologist*, March 1966, 21, 201–217.

Tumin, M. M. Obstacles to creativity. *ETC: A review of general semantics*, 1954, 11, 261–271.

Tyler, R. W. *Basic principles of curriculum and instruction.* Chicago: University of Chicago Press, 1950.

Ullman, L. P. Behavior therapy as social movement. In C. M. Franks (Ed.), *Behavior therapy: appraisal and status.* New York: McGraw-Hill, 1969.

Ullman, L. P., and Krasner, L. (Eds.). *Case studies in behavior modification.* New York: Holt, 1965.

Vanuxem, M. Education of feeble-minded women. *Teachers College Contribution to Education*, 1925.

Venger, L. A. On the modes of visual perception of object shape in early and pre-school age. *The development of cognitive and volitional processes in pre-school children.* Moscow: Izd Prosvesh Chenil. 1965.

Wallace, J. G. *Concept growth and the education of the child: A survey of research on conceptualization.* New York: New York University Press, 1967.

Wallach, M. A., and Kogan, N. A new look at the creativity-intelligence distinction. *Journal of Personality*, 1965, 33, 348–369.

Wallas, G. *The art of thought.* (Rev. and abr. ed.) London: Watts, 1945.

Walter, W. J. Slow potential waves in the human brain associated with expectancy, attention, and decision. *Arch. für Psychiat. und Zeitschrift. für die ges Neurologie*, 1964, 206, 309–322.

Watson, J. B. Psychology as the behaviorist views it. *Psychological Review*, 1913, 20, 158–177.

Watson, J. B., and Morgan, J. J. B. Emotional reactions and psychological experimentation. *American Journal of Psychology*, 1917, 28, 163–174.

Watson, J. B., and Rayner, R. Conditioned emotional reactions. *Journal of Experimental Psychology*, 1920, 3, 1–14.

Webster, S. W. *The disadvantaged learner.* San Francisco: Chandler, 1966.

Wechsler, D. *The measurement of adult intelligence.* Baltimore: Williams & Wilkins, 1944.

Wechsler, D. *Wechsler adult intelligence scale manual.* New York: Psychological Corporation, 1955.

Welsh, R. S. The use of stimulus satiation in the elimination of juvenile fire setting behavior. In A. M. Graziano (Ed.), *Behavior therapy with children.* New York: Aldine, Atherton, 1971.

Wender, Paul H. *Minimal brain dysfunction in children.* New York: Wiley-Interscience, 1971.

Wepman, J. M. Auditory discrimination, speech, and reading. *Elementary School Journal*, 1960, 60, 325–333.

Wertheimer, M. Untersuchungen zur lehre von der gestalt. II. *Psychologie Forschung*, 1923, 4, 301–335.

Wertheimer, M. *Productive thinking.* New York: Harper & Row, 1945.

Wertheimer, M. *Productive thinking.* (Enlarged ed.) New York: Harper & Row, 1959.

Wheeler, L. R. A comparative study of the intelligence of east Tennessee mountain children. *Journal of Educational Psychology*, 1942, 33, 321–334.

Whipple, G. M. Sex differences in intelligence test scores in the elementary school. *Journal of Educational Research*, 1927, 15, 111–117.

White, B. L. *Human infants: Experience and psychological development.* Englewood Cliffs, N.J.: Prentice-Hall, 1971.

Whitmire, E. D. A study of sex differences in 1349 unrelated children. Unpublished master's thesis, Stanford University, 1920.

Whitney, L. R., and Barnard, K. E. Implications of operant learning theory for nursing care of the retarded child. *Mental Retardation*, 1966, 4(3), 26–29.

Williams, W. C. *Patterson III.* Norfolk, Conn.: New Directions, 1949.

Williams, W. C. *Collected earlier poems.* Norfolk, Conn.: New Directions, 1951.

Wilson, J. A. R. Relation of vocational choice to test grades. Unpublished paper, New Westminster, B. C.: T. J. Trapp Technical High School, 1949.

Wilson, J. A. R. A study of the effect of special work for gifted non-motivated students at the eighth grade level. *California Journal of Educational Research*, 1959, 10(3), 123.

Wilson, J. A. R. Exploratory study of the effects of individual work on the functioning of maladjusted pre-school children. Paper presented at the California Educational Research Association Conference, Santa Rosa, Calif., Mar. 13, 1965.

Wilson, J. A. R. *Evaluation report Title One projects.* Santa Barbara, Calif.: Santa Barbara School District, 1967, (Mimeographed)

Wilson, J. A. R., and Hayward, Jean. Linear programmed materials in subject A instruction. *California Journal of Educational Research*, 1964, 15, 6–11.

Wilson, J. A. R., and Robeck, M. C. Teaching machines and spelling. *AV Communications Review*, 1961, 9, No. 6.

Wilson, J. A. R., and Robeck, Mildred C. *Kindergarten evaluation of learning potential.* New York: McGraw-Hill, 1967.

Wilson, J. A. R., and Robeck, M. C. Creativity in the very young. In W. B. Michael (Ed.), *Teaching for creative endeavor.* Bloomington: Indiana University Press, 1968.

Wilson, J. A. R., and Stier, L. D. Instability of subscores on forms of SRA primary mental ability tests: Significance for guidance. *Personnel and Guidance Journal,* 1962, 40, 708–711.

Wilson, Nora M. The relationship of achievement in spelling to varied modes of instruction. Unpublished master's thesis, University of California, Santa Barbara, 1965.

Wingfield, A. H. *Twins and orphans: The inheritance of intelligence.* London: Dent, 1928.

Witkin, Belle Ruth. Auditory perception—implications for language development. *Journal of Research and Development in Education,* Fall 1969, 53–71.

Witty, P. A. Studies of the intelligence of Negroes and Negro-white mixtures. In G. M. Whipple (Ed.), *Intelligence: Its nature and nurture.* Thirty-ninth Yearbook of the National Society for the Study of Education. Bloomington, Ill.: Public School, 1940.

Witty, P. A. Introduction. In N. B. Henry (Ed.), *Mental health in modern education.* Fifty-fourth Yearbook of the National Society for the Study of Education. Part II. Chicago: University of Chicago Press, 1955.

Wohlwill, J. F., and Lowe, R. C. An experimental analysis of the development of the conservation of number. *Child Development*, 1962, 33, 153–167.

Wolpe, J. Experimental neurosis as learned behavior. *British Journal of Psychology,* 1952, 43, 243–268.

Wolpe, J. The systematic desensitization treatment of neuroses. *Journal of Nervous and Mental Disease,* 1961, 123, 189–203.

Woodcock, R. W., and Clark, Charlotte R. Comprehension of a narrative passage by elementary school children as a function of listening rate, retention period, and IQ. *Journal of Communication*, September 1968, 18, 259–271.

Wooldridge, D. E. *The machinery of the brain.* New York: McGraw-Hill, 1963.

Wundt, W. M. *Principles of physiological psychology.* Leipzig: W. Engelmann, 1874.

Wundt, W. M. *Grundzuge der physiologischen psychologie.* Vols. 1 and 2. Leipzig: W. Engelmann, 1893.

Yerkes, R. M. The mind of a gorilla. *Genetic Psychology Monographs*, 1927, 2, 1–92.

Yerkes, R. M. *The mind of a gorilla.* Baltimore: Johns Hopkins Press, 1928.

Young, J. Z. *A model of the brain.* Oxford: Clarendon Press, 1964.

Young, P. C. Intelligence and suggestibility in whites and Negroes. *Journal of Comparative Psychology*, 1929, 9, 339–359.

Zaporozhets, A. V. Some of the psychological problems of sensory training in early childhood and the preschool period. In M. Cole and I. Maltzman (Eds.), *A Handbook of Contemporary Soviet Psychology.* New York: Basic Books, 1969, pp. 86–120.

Zoepfel, M. Auditory discrimination in the learning difficulties of children with neurological disabilities. *The Reading Teacher*, November 1964, 15, 114–118.

Zuckerman, M. Hallucinations, reported sensations and images. In J. P. Zubeck (Ed.), *Sensory deprivation: Fifteen years of research.* New York: Appleton-Century-Crofts, 1969.

# INDEX

**575**